W9-AEP-746

Yours truly,

William Jay

Drawn by Chas. Martin

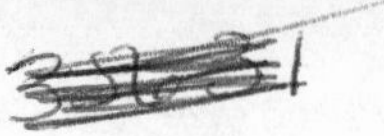

MISCELLANEOUS WRITINGS

ON

SLAVERY.

BY WILLIAM JAY.

NEGRO UNIVERSITIES PRESS
NEW YORK

Originally published in 1853 by John P. Jewett & Co.

Reprinted in 1968
by Negro Universities Press
A DIVISION OF GREENWOOD PUBLISHING CORP.
New York

Library of Congress Catalogue Card Number: 68-55896

Reprinted from a copy in the collections of
The New York Public Library
Astor, Lenox and Tilden Foundations;

Printed in the United States of America

CONTENTS.

INQUIRY

INTO THE

CHARACTER AND TENDENCY

OF THE

AMERICAN COLONIZATION,

AND

AMERICAN ANTI-SLAVERY

SOCIETIES.

"Give me the liberty to know, to utter, and to argue freely, according to my conscience, above all liberties."—MILTON.

PREFACE.

No allusion has been made in the following pages to certain popular objections to the Colonization Society; nor have any cases of individual cruelty been cited, to illustrate the evils of slavery. It is proper that the reasons for this departure from the ordinary mode of discussing these two subjects should be given, that they may not be misunderstood.

The objections I have omitted to notice, are, the mortality to which the emigrants are exposed in consequence of the climate of Liberia; the demoralizing traffic which the colonists have carried on with the natives, in rum and military stores; and the improvident application of the funds of the Society, which has rendered it bankrupt.

These objections, serious as they are in themselves, are not inseparable from the system of Colonization. Another, and more salubrious site, may be selected; the traffic complained of, may be discontinued; and the fiscal affairs of the Society may be managed with prudence and economy. But there are inherent evils in the system, and it is important that the public attention should not be diverted from these evils, by the contemplation of others which are only accidental.

So, also, it is important, that the sinfulness of slavery should not be merged in that of its unauthorized abuses. Many contend for the lawfulness of slavery who readily admit the sinfulness of insulated cases of cruelty. It has, therefore, been my object to show that, admitting the slaves to be treated as a prudent farmer treats his cattle, — that they have enough to eat, are sheltered from the inclemency of the weather, and are not subjected to a greater degree of severity than is necessary to extort from them a due amount of labor, — American slavery is, nevertheless, a heinous sin, and, like every other sin, ought to be immediately abandoned.

February, 1835

PART I.

AMERICAN COLONIZATION SOCIETY.

INTRODUCTION.

On the 1st of January, 1835, there were in the United States, 2,245,144 slaves.* This number about equals the population of Holland, and exceeds that of Scotland, of the Danish Dominions, of the Swiss Confederation, and of various Republics in South America. These millions of human beings are held as chattels by a people professing to acknowledge, that "all men are created equal, and endowed with certain unalienable rights, among which are life, liberty, and the pursuit of happiness:" they are, moreover, kept in ignorance, and compelled to live without God, and to die without hope, by a people professing to reverence the obligations of Christianity.

But slavery has ceased in other countries, where it formerly prevailed; and may we not hope that it is gradually expiring in this? Such a hope is, alas, forbidden by the following statement of our slave population, at different periods:

United States,	1790,	697,697	1835,	2,245,144
Kentucky,	"	12,430	1830,	165,350
Mississippi and Alabama,	1800,	3,489	"	182,953
Louisiana,	1810,	34,660	"	109,631
Missouri,	"	3,011	"	24,990

Perhaps, however, the *political* evils of slavery may be gradually mitigated, and finally removed, by an increasing preponderance in the white population. Unfortunately, we are compelled by facts to anticipate a very different result. A comparison of the census of 1830, with

* According to the ratio of increase between 1820 and 1830.

that of 1820, affords us the following ratio of increase in the free and slave population, for the intermediate ten years:

	Free.	Slave.
North Carolina,	13.4 per ct.	20.2 per ct.
South Carolina,	8.7	22.1
Alabama,	124	180.4
Mississippi,	66.8	100.1
Missouri,	104.3	144.7
Louisiana,	25.6	58.7
Tennessee,	59.5	77.7
Kentucky,	19.6	30.4
Arkansas Territory,	104.3	180

It is obvious, from these details, that, if the present system be continued, the time cannot be far distant, when the slaves will possess a frightful numerical superiority over their masters. Already do they bear to the whites, in the slave States and Territories, the proportion of 1 to 2.79. In South Carolina and Louisiana, they are now a majority.

But in our contemplation of slavery, the sufferings of the slaves claim our consideration, no less than the dangers to which the whites are exposed. The ordinary evils of slavery, are, in this country, greatly aggravated by a cruel and extensive slave-trade. Various circumstances have, of late years, combined to lessen the demand for slave-labor in the more northern, and to increase it in the more southern and western portions of the slave-region; while the enlarged consumption of sugar and cotton is enhancing the market value of slaves. The most profitable employment of this species of labor, is unfortunately found in those States, which, from their recent settlement, possess immense tracts which are still to be brought into cultivation, and in which, consequently, there now is, and will long continue to be, an urgent demand for slaves. Hence has arisen a prodigious and annually increasing transportation of slaves to the south and west.

There are no official data from which the amount of this transportation can be ascertained; but from facts that have transpired, and from estimates made at the *South*, there is reason to believe that it exceeds thirty thousand a year. One of the peculiar abominations of this trade, is, that its victims are almost exclusively children and youths. Instead of removing whole families and gangs of negroes, the dealers for the most part, according to their own advertisements, select individuals, "of both sexes, from twelve to twenty-five years."

He surely can have little claim to the character of a patriot or a Christian, who does not desire that his country may be delivered from the sin and curse of slavery; or who refuses even to consider the means proposed for effecting this great object.

A powerful institution is now in operation, which professes to be, not merely a remedy for slavery, but the ONLY remedy that can be devised. It appeals to religion and patriotism, for those pecuniary aids, which, it contends, are alone wanting, to enable it to transport our whole colored population to Africa, there to enjoy the freedom denied to them here; and there to become the dispensers of religion, and the arts and sciences, to that benighted continent.

If the claims of the American Colonization Society are founded in truth, they cannot be resisted without guilt. Very many, however, who are alike distinguished for piety and talents, instead of allowing these claims, strenuously maintain, that the *practical tendency* of the Society, is to perpetuate the evils it professes to remove; and to extend to Africa, the vices, but not the blessings of civilization. These conflicting opinions, on a subject so momentous, demand a calm and patient investigation; since he who either supports or opposes the Colonization Society, without first ascertaining its true character, the results it has produced, and the influence it exerts, incurs the hazard, as far as his example and efforts extend, of increasing the wretchedness he would relieve, and of fastening upon his country, the burden under which she is struggling.

If, in a question involving the temporal and eternal happiness of unborn millions, we could satisfy our consciences by bowing to the authority of great names, we should still be painfully embarrassed in selecting those, to whose decision we should surrender our own judgments. The excellent of the earth are to be found among the friends and enemies of this association; and if various ecclesiastical bodies in our own country, have recommended it to the patronage of their churches, it is regarded with abhorrence by almost the whole religious community of Great Britain; and the last effort made by WILBERFORCE in the great cause of negro liberty, was, to address to the people of Great Britain his solemn protest against the doctrines and conduct of the American Colonization Society.

This Institution may have been formed by good men, and from the purest motives, yet it is possible that its operation may not have been such as they anticipated. "So many unforseen, concealed, and inappreciable causes," says a very eminent writer, "have an influence on human institutions, that it is impossible to judge *a priori* of their effects. Nothing but a long series of experiments can unfold these effects, and point out the means of counteracting those that are hurtful."

The following inquiry has been commenced, and pursued under a deep sense of the importance of the subject, and with a solemn recollection, that no deviation from truth can escape the notice and displeasure of HIM, unto whom all hearts are open, and from whom no secrets are hid.

CHAPTER I.

ORIGIN, CONSTITUTION, AND CHARACTER OF THE AMERICAN COLONIZATION SOCIETY.

On the 23d of December, 1816, the Legislature of Virginia passed a resolution requesting the Governor to correspond with the President of the United States, "for the purpose of obtaining a territory on the coast of Africa, or at some other place not within any of the States, or territorial governments of the United States, to serve as an asylum for such persons of color as are now free, and may desire the same, and for those who may hereafter be emancipated within this Commonwealth."

Within a few days of the date of this resolution, a meeting was held at Washington to take this very subject into consideration. It was composed almost entirely of southern gentlemen. Judge Washington presided: Mr. Clay, Mr. Randolph, and others, took part in the discussions which ensued, and which resulted in the organization of the American Colonization Society. Judge Washington was chosen President, and of the seventeen Vice Presidents, only five were selected from the free States, while the twelve managers were, it is believed, without one exception, slave-holders.

The first two articles of the constitution are the only ones relating to the object of the Society. They are as follows:

Art. I. This Society shall be called the American Society for colonizing the free people of color of the United States.

Art. II. The object to which its attention is to be *exclusively* directed, is to promote and execute a plan for colonizing (with their consent) the free people of color residing in our country, in Africa, or such other place as Congress shall deem most expedient. And the Society shall act to effect this object in coöperation with the general government and such of the States as may adopt regulations on the subject.

It is worthy of remark, that this constitution has no preamble setting forth the motives which led to its adoption, and the sentiments entertained by its authors. There is no one single principle of duty or policy recognized in it, and the members may, without inconsistency, be Christians or infidels; they may be the friends or enemies of slavery, and may be actuated by kindness or by hatred towards "the free people of color."

The omission of all avowal of *motives* was, probably, not without design, and has not been without effect. It has secured the coöperation of three distinct classes. First, such as sincerely desire to afford the free blacks an asylum from the oppression they suffer here, and by their means to extend to Africa the blessings of Christianity and civilization, and who at the same time flatter themselves that colonization will have a salutary influence in accelerating the abolition of slavery: secondly, such as expect to enhance the value and security of slave property, by removing the free blacks: and, thirdly, such as seek relief from a bad population, without the trouble and expense of improving it.

The doors of the Society being thrown open to all, a heterogeneous multitude has entered, and within its portals men are brought into contact, who in the ordinary walks of life, are separated by a common repulsion. The devoted missionary, ready to pour out his life on the sands of Africa, is jostled by the trafficker in human flesh; the humble, self-denying Christian, listens to the praises of the Society from the unblushing profligate; and the friend of human rights and human happiness greets as his fellow-laborer the man whose very contribution to the cause is extorted from the unrequited labor of his fellow-men. This anomalous amalgamation of characters and motives, has necessarily led to a lamentable compromise of principle. Whatever may be the object each member proposes to himself, he is conscious it can be effected only by the harmonious coöperation of all the other members. Hence it is all important to avoid giving and taking offence; and never was the maxim, "bear and forbear," more scrupulously obeyed. Certain irreconcilable opinions, but regarded by their holders as fundamental, are, by common consent, wholly suppressed; while in matters of less importance, the expression of opposite sentiments is freely allowed, and borne with commendable patience.

The advocates of slavery forbear shocking its opponents by justifying it in the *abstract*, and in return for this complaisance, those opponents forbear condemning it in *particulars*. Each party consents to make certain concessions to conciliate the other. The Southron admits slavery to be a *political* evil; the northern member courteously replies, that under *present circumstances*, it is unavoidable, and therefore justifiable. The actual condition of the slave, his mental bondage, his bodily sufferings, are understood to be forbidden topics.

The oppressor of the free negro dwells on his depravity and degradation; the friend of the free negro admits, and often aggravates the charges against him, but carefully abstains from all allusion to the true causes of that depravity and degradation, unless to excuse them as being inevitable. Both parties unite in depicting in glowing colors, the effects of the oppression of the free negro, in order to prove the *humanity* of banishing him from the country; while both refrain from all attempts to remove or lessen the oppression.

The simplicity of the object of the Society as stated in its constitution, tends in a powerful degree to encourage and enforce this compromise of principle. The constitution, in fact, vests a discretionary veto in every member on the expression of unpalatable opinions. The attention of the Society is to be "exclusively" directed to the colonization of persons of color, and the constitution contains no allusion to slavery. Hence any denunciation of slavery as sinful,* any arguments addressed to slave

* Candor requires the admission that there is at least one exception to this remark. At the annual meeting of the Society in 1834, the Rev. Mr. Breckenridge, in his speech, insisted on the sinfulness of slavery. A distinguished lay member of the Society, who was present, complained to the author of Mr. B.'s unconstitutional conduct, and declared that he was strongly tempted publicly to call him to order.

holders to induce them to manumit their slaves, would be unconstitutional, and are therefore carefully avoided. But the free blacks cannot be transported without money, and much money cannot be had, without the aid of the enemies of slavery. It is therefore permitted to represent the Society as an antidote to slavery, as tending to effect its abolition, anything in the constitution to the contrary notwithstanding. But then this abolition is to be brought about at some future indefinite period. True it is, that the constitution is as silent, with respect to manumission, as it is to slavery; but by common consent, this silence is not permitted to interpose the slightest obstacle to a unanimous, vigorous, and persevering opposition to present manumission. Were the American Bible Society to deprecate the emancipation of slaves, and to censure all who proposed it, the outrage would excite the indignation of the whole community. But what would be a perversion of its avowed object in a Bible Society, is perfectly lawful in a Colonization Society, not because it is authorized by the constitution, but because it is *expedient* to conciliate the slave-holders.

Many of the supporters of the Society are interested in the *American* slave-trade* — a trade replete with cruelty and injustice. To condemn *this* trade, or to labor for its suppression, would be unconstitutional. The *African* slave-trade rather interferes with, than promotes the interests of the slave-owners, and the Society deems it unnecessary to seek for any constitutional warrant to justify the most violent denunciation of the *foreign* traffic; or an application to foreign powers to declare it piratical.†

To hold up the free blacks to the detestation of the community, is unconstitutional; to recommend them to the sympathy of Christians, to propose schools for their instruction, plans for encouraging their industry, and efforts for their moral and religious improvement, would be such a flagrant departure from the "exclusive" object of the Society, that no member has

* The first President of the Society, was, as we shall see hereafter, no inconsiderable dealer.

† See proceedings of Am. Col. Society of 20th January, 1827.

hitherto been rash enough to make the attempt. At the same time it is quite constitutional to vindicate the cruel laws which are crushing these people in the dust, and to show that the oppression they suffer is "an ordination of Providence."

The constitution indeed forbids the transportation of the free blacks without "their consent;" but it is very constitutional to justify and encourage such oppression of them, as shall compel them to seek in the wilds of Africa, a refuge from American cruelty.

The natural result of this compromise of principle, this suppression of truth, this sacrifice to unanimity, has been the adoption of *expediency* as the standard of right and wrong, in the place of the revealed will of God. Unmindful of the poet's precept,

> Be virtuous ends pursued by virtuous means,
> Nor think the intention sanctifies the deed,

good men and good Christians have been tempted by their zeal for the Society, to countenance opinions and practices inconsistent with justice and humanity. Confident that their motives were good and their object important, they have been too little scrupulous of the means they employed; and hence the Society has actually exerted a demoralizing influence over its own members, by leading them occasionally to advance in its behalf opinions at variance with truth and Christianity. Unhappily the evil influence of the Society has not been confined to its own members. It has, to a lamentable extent, vitiated the moral sense of the community, by reconciling public opinion to the continuance of slavery, and by aggravating those sinful prejudices against the free blacks, which are subjecting them to insult and persecution, and denying them the blessings of education and religious instruction.

We are sensible that these are grave assertions, and that many will deem them very extraordinary ones. The reader's belief is not solicited for them *at present*, nor will it be for any assertion hereafter made, till supported by unquestionable evidence. The remarks in this chapter are intended only as a general statement of the case against the Society, and as an explanation of the process by which many excellent men belonging to it, have insensibly been seduced into conduct of at least doubtful morality. The charges now made will in due time be substantiated by authentic facts, and by quotations from the language, both official and private, of members of the Society.

True it is, that colonizationists protest most earnestly against being judged by any but the official language of the Board of Managers. To the justice of this protest it is impossible to assent. The Society is arraigned at the bar of the public, not *for the object avowed in the constitution*, but for the influence it exerts in vindicating and prolonging slavery, and in augmenting the oppression of the free blacks. This influence, if exerted at all, must be exerted by individuals in the capacity of members, agents, and officers of the Society, and the only means they possess of exerting this influence, is by the expression of their sentiments. To insist, therefore, that these sentiments may not be quoted, to show what influence the Society does exert, is to contradict the plainest suggestions of common sense. Certainly the whole Society is not necessarily responsible for the sentiments of a single member; but the question is not, whether one or two or more members have said improper things, but whether the influence *generally* exerted by the Society, is what it is alleged to be; and this is a question of fact, to be decided by evidence, and that evidence necessarily consists of the opinions expressed by its officers, agents, and distinguished members, and auxiliary associations.

This protest, moreover, comes with an ill grace from a Society that has appealed to the *letters* and the *speeches* of its members, to repel the objection urged against it in certain quarters, of a desire to interfere with the rights of slave-holders.* Should the members and officers of an Anti-Slavery Society, continually, at its public meetings, deliver addresses in favor of intermarriages between whites and blacks — should auxiliaries pass resolutions approving of such marriages — should these addresses

* See Afr. Rep., VI, 198.

and resolutions be published and circulated at the expense of the Society, and should its official magazine recommend such marriages,—would it not be the excess of disingenuousness for the Society to attempt to repel the charge that its influence was exerted to bring about an amalgamation of the two races, by denying that it was responsible for the language of its members, and by appealing to its constitution and official reports, in which no allusion was made to the subject? All that can fairly be demanded, is that the quotations be honestly made, and that they sufficiently numerous and explicit to establish the facts they are brought to prove. It must not, however, be supposed, that we intend to prove our charges against the Society, *only* by the declarations of individual members. On the contrary, we shall summon as witnesses, the MANAGERS of the parent Society, and its auxiliaries; and shall exhibit in evidence their *official* reports and addresses. In the following pages will be found numerous extracts from colonization documents; and it is right to observe, that they are for the most part merely *selections*, and bearing generally but a small proportion to the whole number of extracts to the same point, that might have been adduced. Some few of the extracts have been made by other writers; but the great mass of them have been selected by the author, and in no instance has he given a quotation which he does not believe is fairly and honestly made. To prevent mistakes, it may be well to mention, that the African Repository is a monthly magazine, and is, as appears from the title-page, "published by order of the Managers of the American Colonization Society." The Editor is understood to be the Secretary of the Society. This periodical, together with the annual reports, and occasional official addresses, is the *only* publication for which the managers of the Society are responsible; when *colonization* newspapers are mentioned, nothing more is intended by the expression, than that they are papers which espouse the cause of the Society.

CHAPTER II.

INFLUENCE OF THE SOCIETY ON THE CONDITION OF FREE PERSONS OF COLOR.

THE object of the Society is declared by the constitution, to be *exclusively* the colonization of free persons of color, with their own consent. Now there is nothing in this object necessarily benevolent. A colony may be established for commercial purposes, or as a military station, or as a receptacle for convicts, or to aid the diffusion of Christianity. The absence in the constitution of all avowed motive for the proposed colony, invites the coöperation of all who advocate the scheme from any motive whatever. For the purpose of raising money, it is the policy of the Society to appeal to all the various and discordant motives that can be incited in behalf of the colony. A strong and very general prejudice exists against the free blacks. It is unfortunately the policy of the Society to aggravate this prejudice, since the more we abominate these people, the more willing we shall be to pay money for the purpose of getting rid of them. The influence of the doctrine of *expediency* on good men, will be seen in the unchristian language they have used in regard to this unhappy and oppressed portion of their fellow-men.

"Free blacks are a greater NUISANCE than even slaves themselves." *Address of C. C. Harper, Afr. Rep.*, II, 189.

"A horde of miserable people — the objects of universal suspicion — subsisting by plunder." *Speech of Gen. Mercer, Vice President.*

"Of all classes of our population, the *most vicious* is that of the free colored — contaminated themselves, they extend their vices to all around them." *Speech of Mr. Clay, Vice President, 12th Report,* p. 21.

"Averse to labor, with no incentives to industry, or motives to respect, they maintain a precarious existence by petty thefts and plunder." *African Rep.*, VI, 135.

"They are alike injurious by their conduct and example to all other classes of society." *Memorial of Manchester Col. Soc. to Virginia Legislature.*

"A large mass of human beings who hang as a *vile excrescence* upon society." *Address of C. L. Mosby, before a Col. Soc. in Virginia.*

"This class of persons a CURSE AND CONTAGION wherever they reside." *African Rep.*, III, 203.

"Of all the descriptions of our population, and of *either* portion of the African race, the free persons of color are by far, as a class, the *most corrupt, depraved and abandoned.*" *Speech of Mr. Clay, African Rep.*, VI, 12.

"An anomalous race of beings, the *most depraved upon earth.*" *African Rep.*, VII, 230.

"They are a mildew upon our fields, a scourge to our backs, and a stain upon our escutcheon." *Memorial of Kentucky Col. Soc. to Congress.*

"I will look no farther when I seek for the most degraded, the *most abandoned race on the earth*, but rest my eye on this people." *Address before the Lynchburg Col. Society.*

"There is a class (free blacks) among us, introduced by violence, notoriously ignorant, degraded and miserable, *mentally diseased*, broken-spirited, acted upon by no motives to honorable exertions, scarcely reached in their debasement by the heavenly light." *Editorial Article, Afr. Rep.*, I, 68.

We may here remark, that the tone of these extracts is very different from that used when the speaker desires to excite sympathy for the wretched. We are told that these people are vicious and debased, but no hint is given that their vice and debasement are the result of sinful prejudices and cruel laws. No appeal is made to the spirit of Christianity to pour oil and wine into the wound of suffering humanity. We are not reminded that these wretches are our brethren, for whom Christ died. Nothing is omitted to impress us with a sense of the depth of the misery into which they are plunged; but for what object are these frightful pictures presented to us? Is it to urge us to feed the hungry, to clothe the naked, to instruct the ignorant, and to reform the wicked? No, but to transport them to Africa!

To an unsophisticated Christian it would seem that the true way of relieving the wretchedness and vice of these people would be, first to protest against their unrighteous oppression, and to procure the repeal of those laws which forbid their instruction; and then to make them partakers of the blessings of education and religion. But far from the Colonization Society are all such old-fashioned ways of doing good. Instead of protesting against the causes of all this misery, THE SOCIETY EXCUSES AND JUSTIFIES THE OPPRESSION OF THE FREE NEGROES, AND THE PREJUDICES AGAINST THEM.

"SEVERE NECESSITY places them (free negroes) in a class of degraded beings." *Address of Mr. Rives to Lynchburg Col. Soc., Afr. Rep.*, V, 238.

"The severe legislation,—*I will not say that under all circumstances it is too severe*,—the severe legislation of the slave States, which drives their emancipated blacks to the free States, and scatters the NUISANCE there, attests that we have a share in this evil." *Speech of G. Smith, Esq., Vice President, 14th Report*, p. xiii.

"This law," (a law by which a manumitted negro becomes again a slave if he remains twelve months in the State,) "odious and unjust as it may at first view appear, and hard as it may seem to bear upon the liberated negro, was doubtless dictated by *sound policy*, and its repeal would be regarded by none with more unfeigned regret than by *the friends of African Colonization. It has restrained many masters from giving freedom to their slaves,* and has thereby contributed to check the growth of an evil already too great and formidable." *Memorial from Powhatan Col. Soc. to Virginia Legislature.*

"I am clear, that whether we consider it with reference to the welfare of the State, or the happiness of the blacks, it were better to have them left in CHAINS, than to have liberated them to receive such freedom as they enjoy, and greater freedom we *cannot, must not* allow them." *Afr. Rep.*, III, 197.

"The habits, the feelings, all the prejudices of society, prejudices which neither refinement, nor argument, nor education, NOR RELIGION ITSELF can subdue, mark the people of color, whether bond or free, as the subjects of a degradation *inevitable and incurable.*" *Address of the Connecticut Col. Soc.*

"The managers consider it clear that causes exist and are now operating to prevent their improvement and elevation to any considerable extent as a class in this country, which are fixed not only beyond the control of the friends of humanity, but of any human power; CHRISTIANITY can not do for them here what it will do for them in Africa. This is not the fault of the colored man, nor of the white man, but AN ORDINATION OF PROVIDENCE, *and no more to be changed than the laws of nature.*" *15th Rep.*, p. 47.

"We do not ask that the provisions of our constitution and statute book should be so modified as to relieve and exalt the condition of the colored people *whilst they remain with us.* Let these provisions stand in ALL THEIR RIGOR to work out the ultimate and unbounded good of these people." *Memorial of the New York State Col. Soc. to the Legislature.*

"If we were constrained to admire so uncommon a being," (a pious, highly cultivated, scientific negro,) "our very admiration would be mingled with disgust, because in the physical organization of his frame we meet an insurmountable barrier even to approach to social intercourse, and in the Egyptian color which nature has stamped on his features, a principle of repulsion so strong as to forbid the idea of a communion, either of interest, or of feeling, as utterly abhorrent." *Afr. Rep.*, VII, p. 331.

We find from the foregoing extracts that the Board of Managers of the American Colonization Society officially declare, that no human power can counteract the causes which prevent the elevation and improvement of the free black in this country. That not even the religion of Christ can in this land of light, of Bibles, and of temples, do for him what it can amid the darkness and paganism of Africa. And we find a powerful State Society recommending to the Legislature to do evil that good may come. Now if it be true, that the degradation of the free blacks is *inevitable*, and cannot even be removed by Christianity, then, indeed, as the Society affirms, it is not the "fault" of the white man, and he not being in fault, there is no reason why he should change his conduct towards them or repeal those laws which Mr Smith will not say are under all circumstances "too severe." Let us see what are these laws, which a most worthy colonizationist and a distinguished officer of the Society intimates are not too severe; and what are those causes of degradation which we are assured by the Board of Managers are an ordination of Providence, and no more to be changed than the laws of nature.

In some of the States, if a free man of color is accused of crime, he is denied the benefit of those forms of trial which the Common Law has established for the protection of innocence. Thus in South Carolina it is thought quite unnecessary to give a Grand and Petit Jury the trouble of inquiring into his case; he can be hung without so much ceremony. But who is a *colored* man? We answer, the *fairest* man in Carolina, if it can be proved that a drop of negro blood flowed in the veins of his mother. The following extract from a late Charleston paper gives us a curious instance of the administration of criminal justice in a Christian country in the nineteenth century:

"Trial for Murder.—William Tann, a free *colored* man, was tried on Friday last, at John's Island, for the *murder* of Moses, the slave of Jos. D. Jenkins, Esq., of that place. The *Court* consisted of William H. Inglesby and Alexander H. Brown, Esqrs., Judicial Magistrates," (Justices of the Peace,) "of this city, together with *five freeholders.* The murder was committed at John's Island on the 4th *July*, 1832, Tann shooting down Moses with a musket loaded with buckshot. Tann was at that time *overseer* of a Mr. Murray, and from the *fairness of his complexion was thought to be and passed for a* WHITE MAN. He was *accordingly* bound over to answer for this offence to the COURT OF SESSIONS, but it having been decided on an *issue* ordered and tried at Walterborough, for the purpose of ascertaining his *caste*, that he was of MIXED BLOOD, he was *turned over* by the Court, to the jurisdiction of *Magistrates and Freeholders.* The Court found him guilty, and sentenced him to be hung on Friday, the 24th April, next," 1835.—*Charleston Courier.*

In South Carolina, if a free negro "entertains" a runaway slave, he forfeits ten pounds, and if unable to pay the fine, which must be the case ninety-nine times in a hundred, he is to be sold as a slave for life. In 1827, a *free woman and her three children* were thus sold, for harboring two slave children.

In Mississippi, every negro or mulatto, not being able to *prove* himself free, may be sold as a slave. Should the certificate of his manumission, or the evidence of his parent's freedom, be lost or stolen, he is reduced to hopeless bondage. This provision extends to most of the slave States, and is in full operation in the District of Columbia.

In South Carolina, any assembly of free negroes, even in the presence of white persons, "in a confined or secret place, for the purpose of *mental instruction*," is an unlawful assembly, and may be dispersed by a magistrate, who is authorized to inflict twenty lashes on each free negro attending the meeting.

In the city of Savannah, *any person* who teaches a free negro to read or write, incurs a penalty of thirty dollars. Of course, a father may not instruct his own children.

In Maryland, a Justice of the Peace may order a free negro's ears to be cut off for striking a *white* man. In Kentucky, for the same offence, he is to receive thirty lashes, "well laid on." The law of Louisiana declares, "Free people of color ought never to insult or strike *white* people, nor presume to conceive themselves equal to the whites; but, on the contrary, *they ought to yield to them on every occasion*, and never speak or answer them but with respect, under the penalty of imprisonment, according to the nature of the case."

The corporation of Georgetown, in the District of Columbia, passed an ordinance, making it penal for any free negro *to receive from the post-office, have in his possession*, or circulate, any publication or writing whatsoever of a *seditious* character.

In North Carolina, the law prohibits a free colored man, whatever may be his attainments or ecclesiastical authority, to preach the gospel.

In Georgia, a white man is liable to a fine of *five hundred dollars* for teaching a free negro to read or write. If one free negro teach another, he is to be *fined* and *whipped* at the discretion of the court! Should a free negro presume to preach to, or exhort his companions, he may be seized without warrant, and whipped thirty-nine lashes, and the same number of lashes may be applied to each one of his congregation.

In Virginia, should free negroes or their children assemble at a school to learn reading and writing, any Justice of the Peace may dismiss the school with twenty stripes on the back of each pupil.

In some States, free negroes may not assemble together for any purpose, to a greater number than *seven*. In North Carolina, free negroes may not trade, buy, or sell, out of the cities or towns in which they reside, under the penalty of forfeiting their goods, and receiving, in lieu thereof, thirty-nine lashes.

The laws of Ohio against the free blacks are peculiarly detestable, because not originating from the fears and prejudices of slave-holders. Not only are the blacks excluded in that State from the benefit of public schools, but with a refinement of cruelty unparelleled, they are doomed to idleness and poverty, by a law which renders a white man who employs a colored one to labor for him one hour, liable for his support through life!

By a late law of Maryland, a free negro coming into the State is liable to a fine of fifty dollars for every week he remains in it. If he cannot pay the fine, he is SOLD.

In Louisiana, the penalty for instructing a free black in a *Sunday School*, is, for the first offence, five hundred dollars; for the second offence, DEATH!

Such, in a greater or less degree, is the situation of three hundred thousand of our fellow-citizens; and the only comfort, the only consolation, the only mitigation of their sufferings, which a Society, said to be "full of benevolence and the hallowed impulses of Heaven's own mercy," proposes, or even *wishes* for them, is their transportation to Africa!

Is this a harsh assertion? Let us attend to the proofs that THE SOCIETY DISCOURAGES ALL ATTEMPTS TO IMPROVE THE CONDITION OF THE FREE BLACKS.

We have already seen that the managers of the American Colonization Society officially declare, that, in their opinion, no human power can remove the causes which prevent the improvement and elevation of the free negroes to any considerable extent in this country; and that the New York Society, in addressing the Legislature, expresses their desire, that the provisions in the constitution and statute book of that State, relative to the blacks, may "*stand in all their rigor.*" The provision in the constitution here alluded to, is that recent one, which, by requiring a freehold qualification, virtually deprived the blacks of the elective franchise, which the fathers of the Revolution had given them. In the Convention by which the new constitution was formed, many of the most distinguished citizens and able lawyers, including Rufus King and Chancellor Kent, had protested against this proscription as unjust and anti-republican; but the Colonization Society declare to the Legislature, without whose consent this provision cannot be changed, that *they* wish it to stand in all its rigor. Not contented with giving their sanction to past acts of injustice, the Society use their influence with the Legislature to prevent its benevolent operation in future. Their Memorial proceeds:—"Persuaded that their condition here is *not susceptible* of a radical and permanent improvement, *we would deprecate* any legislation that should encourage the vain and injurious hope of it."

The Connecticut Colonization Society, in its address already quoted, denies that even "*religion itself*" can subdue the prejudices existing against these people. The same address authoritatively decides, that the free blacks "constitute a class by themselves, a class out of which no individual *can be elevated.*"

The Kentucky State Colonization Society, in its official address, says :

"It is *against* this increase of colored persons, who take but a nominal freedom, *and cannot rise from their degraded condition*, that this Society attempts to provide." *Afr. Rep.*, VI, 82.

"The people of color must, in this country, remain for ages, probably forever, a separate and distinct caste, weighed down by causes powerful, universal, *invincible*, which neither legislation NOR CHRISTIANITY can remove." *Afr. Rep., Edit. Art.*, VII, 196.

"We have endeavored, but in vain, to restore them (the free negroes) either to self-respect, or to the respect of others. It is *not our fault* that we have failed. It is not theirs. It has resulted from a cause over which neither we nor they *can ever have control.*" *Speech of Rev. Dr. Nott before N. York Col. Soc.*

This last extract claims attention from the extraordinary assertions which it contains, and from the high character of the author. No explanations are given of the *vain* endeavors which have been made to restore the blacks either to self-respect, or to the respect of others. When, where, by whom, and how were these efforts made? Dr. Nott is addressing the State Society, and speaks in the plural number. We confess we see nothing like such efforts in the Memorial of that Society to the Legislature. It is moreover to be recollected, that the American Society, in its address to its auxiliaries, warns them against such efforts.

"The moral, intellectual, and political improvement of people of color within the United States, are objects foreign to the powers of this Society." *Address of the Am. Col. Soc. to its auxiliaries. Afr. Rep.*, VII, 291.

Let us see also what two *religious* colonization papers say on this subject.

"If the *free* people of color were generally taught to read, it might be an inducement to them to *remain* in this country; we would offer them no such inducements." *Southern Religious Telegraph, February*, 19, 1831.

"It must appear evident to all, that *every endeavor* to divert the attention of the community, or even a portion of the means which the present crisis so imperatively calls for, from the Colonization Society, to measures calculated to bind the colored population to this country, and seeking to raise them to a level with the whites, whether by founding colleges, *or in any other way*, tends directly in the proportion that it succeeds, *to counteract and thwart the whole plan of colonization.*" *New Haven Religious Intelligencer, July*, 1831.

We perceive from these extracts, that the improvement of the free blacks is represented by colonizationists as impossible, and of course it is folly to attempt what is impracticable. The very attempt, moreover, is calculated to counteract and thwart the whole plan of colonization, as far as it succeeds. But this is not all. Some might think the obligations of Christianity required us to instruct the ignorant, and to succor the oppressed. To remove this prejudice, we are assured that even Christianity cannot help the negro in America! When before, has the power of our blessed religion in changing the heart, subduing evil affections, and removing unholy prejudices, been questioned by professing Christians?

The influence of the gospel of Christ, has led thousands and tens of thousands to offer themselves as willing victims at the stake or in the amphitheatre — it has prostrated the temples, the altars, and the gods of paganism — it has triumphed over ancient and endeared superstitions — it has delivered the Hindoo from the fetters of caste, and tamed the North American savage; and yet according to colonizationists, it is utterly impotent, when brought into collision with the prejudices of *American* Christians, towards an unhappy portion of their fellow countrymen!

And what unsuccessful experiments justify this depreciation of the gospel of Jesus Christ? When have those who thus speak of the inefficacy of religion in subduing these sinful prejudices, tried its power? When have colonizationists warned Christians that the negro is created by the same Almighty Being, descended from the same parent, redeemed by the same Saviour, and made an heir of the same immortality with themselves? When have we been reminded by them of that heart-searching declaration which will be uttered by the Judge at the last day, "inasmuch as ye did it not to one of the least of these my brethren, ye did it not to me?"

Admitting that the blacks who have gone to Africa have improved their condition, what is the total amount of good thus effected? Of the 319,467 free negroes in the United States, 2,122 have in the last eighteen years been sent to Liberia. Supposing them to be happy in their new abode, at what a deplorable sacrifice of the happiness of their brethren here, has their own been purchased! To raise funds for their transportation, our churches and halls, in all parts of the United States, have rung with reproaches and accusations against the free people of color. Orators, preachers, legislators, have denounced them as nuisances, vile excrescences on the body politic — ignorant, depraved, debased, and utterly incapable of improvement and elevation. The laws oppressing them have been vindicated, and all legislation deprecated, that would even encourage the hope of their permanent improvement.

And is it possible that this general and united effort to prevent these people from rising, and to render them odious to the community, should have no practical effect on public opinion and conduct? Already do we hear their forcible expulsion from the country, urged in petitions, and advocated in our State Legislatures. He must be wilfully blind to passing events, who does not perceive that the persecution of these people is increasing in extent and malignity. La Fayette remarked in his last visit with astonishment, the aggravation of the prejudices against the blacks, and stated that in the revolutionary war, the black and white soldiers messed together without hesitation.

In no instance, perhaps, has colonization had so direct and obvious an influence in augmenting the injuries and oppression of this unhappy race, as in Connecticut. To that State have good men long rejoiced to look as to a bright pattern of a Christian republic. There they beheld political liberty in its highest perfection, and so divested, by the influence of religion, of those irregularities of conduct which too often attend it, that the State was proverbially distinguished as "the land of steady habits." In no part of the world were the blessings of education more highly valued, or more generally diffused. The Colonization Society had there taken a strong hold on the affections of the people, and had found in Connecticut divines and politicians, and in the religious periodicals of New Haven, zealous and able champions.

The city of New Haven had been long, alike distinguished

for its literary institutions, and for the sobriety and piety of its inhabitants. It is not, therefore, surprising that some of the most intelligent and influential of our colored citizens were led to believe that New Haven would be a proper site for a school for their children, and that *such* a school would *there* find generous patrons. In 1831, a convention was held in Philadelphia, of delegates from the free colored people in other States, and it was determined that an effort should be made to raise funds for "a collegiate school, on the manual labor system." A committee was appointed to carry the plan into execution. This committee published in Philadelphia, "An appeal to the benevolent," in which they stated the necessity of the proposed school, on account of the difficulty which colored children experienced in gaining admission into ordinary seminaries, or mechanical establishments; and that the proposed seminary would be located at New Haven, and "established on the self-supporting system, so that the student may cultivate habits of industry, and obtain a useful *mechanical* or *agricultural* profession, while pursuing classical studies."

Bishops White and Onderdonk, and the Rev. Doctors McAuley, Bedell, and Ely, of Philadelphia, gave the committee written certificates of their approbation of the education of colored youth. Little, alas, did these gentlemen anticipate the feeling this effort would excite among the Christians of New Haven. No sooner had intelligence of the intended school reached that city, than the mayor summoned a town meeting, "to take into consideration a scheme, said to be in progress, for the establishment in this city of a college for the education of colored youth." The meeting was held on the 8th of September, 1831, and it was "Resolved by the Mayor, Aldermen, Common Council, and free men of the city of New Haven, in city meeting assembled, that we will *resist* the establishment of the proposed college in this place by every lawful means." This resolution was preceded by a preamble, stating that "in connection with this establishment, the immediate abolition of slavery in the United States is not only recommended and encouraged by the advocates of the proposed college, but demanded as a right," and "that the propagation of sentiments, favorable to the immediate emancipation of slaves, *in disregard* of the civil institutions of the States to which they belong, and as auxiliary thereto, the contemporaneous founding of colleges for educating colored people, is an unwarrantable and dangerous interference with the internal concerns of other States, and ought to be discouraged."

That the education of colored citizens in Connecticut is an unwarrantable interference with the internal concerns of other States, and that the friends of the proposed college ever recommended the immediate emancipation of slaves *in disregard* of the civil institutions of the States to which they belong, are assertions which the Mayor, Aldermen, Common Council, and free men of the city of New Haven prudently permitted to rest on their own authority, without adducing any other evidence of their truth.

But surely, the pious and excellent colonizationists of New Haven, who are so anxious to civilize the natives of Africa, must have been indignant at this attempt to keep Americans in ignorance. Alas, in that crowded assembly, there was but one voice raised against its unholy resolution, and that was the voice of a decided anti-colonizationist, the Rev. S. S. Jocelyn, while one of the public advocates of the resolution was the Secretary of the New Haven Committee of Correspondence of the American Colonization Society.

The Colonization party in New Haven could have prevented this high-handed oppression, but their influence was exerted not for, but *against* the improvement and elevation of their colored brethren.

Unhappily for the character of Connecticut, for that of our common country, and even of Christianity itself, the proceedings in New Haven were but the commencement of a series of outrages on justice, humanity, and the rights of freemen.

There are occasions on which it is treason to truth and honor, if not to religion, to suppress our indignation; and while we shall scrupulously adhere to truth in relating the measures pursued in Connecticut, to prevent the education of a certain class of colored persons, we shall not shrink from a free expression of our opinions of those measures, and of their authors.

Miss Crandall, a communicant in the Baptist church, and, as we believe, a lady of irreproachable character, had for some time been at the head of a female boarding school, in the town of Canterbury, Connecticut, when in the autumn of 1832, a pious colored female applied to her for admission into her school, stating that she wanted "to get a little more learning — enough, if possible, to teach colored children." After some hesitation, Miss Crandall consented to admit her, but was soon informed that this intruder must be dismissed, or that the shool would be greatly injured. This threat turned her attention to the cruel prejudices and disadvantages under which the blacks are suffering, and she resolved to open a shool *exclusively* for colored girls. It has been thought expedient to doubt the philanthropy of this resolution, and to attribute it to pecuniary motives. Whatever may have been her motives, and pecuniary ones would not have been unlawful, she had a perfect right to open a school for pupils of any color whatever; and had not the moral sense of the community been perverted, this attempt to instruct the poor, the friendless, and the ignorant, would have met with applause instead of contumely. She discontinued her school, and in February, 1833, gave public notice of her intention to open one for colored girls. This notice excited prodigious commotion in the town of Canterbury. That *black* girls should presume to learn reading, and writing, and music, and geography, was past all bearing. Committee after committee waited on Miss Crandall, to remonstrate against the intended school, but to no purpose. More efficient means were found necessary to avert the impending calamity, and a legal town meeting was summoned to consider the awful crisis. At this meeting resolutions were passed, expressing the strongest disapprobation of the proposed school, and the preamble declared that "the obvious tendency of this school would be to collect within the town of Canterbury, large numbers of persons from other States, whose characters and habits might be various and unknown to us, thereby rendering insecure the *persons, property, and reputations* of our citizens."

Had this extreme nervous apprehension of danger been excited in the good people of Canterbury by the introduction of some hundreds of Irish laborers into their village to construct a railroad or canal, we should still have thought their temperament very peculiar; but when we find them thus affecting to tremble, not merely for their property, but for their *persons* and *reputations*, at the approach of fifteen or twenty "young ladies and little misses of color," we confess we are astonished that the collected wisdom of these people was not able to frame an argument against the school, less disgraceful to themselves.

Andrew T. Judson, Esq., acted as clerk to this meeting, and supported the resolutions in a speech, in which he is reported to have said, "that should the school go into operation, their sons and daughters would be forever ruined, and property no longer safe." For his part, he was not willing, for the honor and welfare of the town, that even *one corner* of it should be appropriated to such a purpose. After the example which New Haven had set, he continued, "shall it be said that *we* cannot, that we dare not resist?" Mr. Judson further stated, that they had "A LAW which should prevent that school from going into operation."

The resolutions of the town meeting, as became so grave a matter, were communicated to Miss Crandall by the "civil authority and selectmen," but strange as it may seem, that lady stood less in dread of them, than they did of the "young ladies of color," for she refused to retreat from the ground she had taken.

The example of New Haven, we have seen, was held up to the people of Canterbury by Mr. Judson, for their encouragement, and as an earnest of their ultimate success. Still the cases were not exactly similar. "The civil authority and selectmen" of Canterbury, had not the imposing array of power and influence displayed by "the Mayor, Aldermen, Common Council, and free men of the city of New Haven." The latter, by the mere expression of their opinion, had prevented the establishment of a college for colored youth; the former were set at naught by an unprotected female. Some means more efficacious than the fulminations of a town meeting were, therefore, next to be tried. Mr. Judson had indeed a certain LAW in reserve, but it was necessary that *certain influences* should be previously brought into action, before a civilized and Christian people could be induced to tolerate the application of that law. Colonization, as already remarked, had taken a deep hold on the affections of the people of Connecticut. Their most eminent men had enrolled themselves in the ranks of the Society. To this powerful association recourse was now had. On the 22d of March, 1833, the "civil authority and selectmen" of Canterbury made their "APPEAL TO THE AMERICAN COLONIZATION SOCIETY." In this most extraordinary paper, they expatiate on the *benevolence* of the Society towards the colored population, and deplore the opposition it encounters from certain individuals who have formed "the Anti-Slavery Society." These men, they assert, wish to admit the blacks "into the bosom of our society," and would "justify intermarriages with the white people." They then recite their own grievances, detail the proceedings of their town meeting, dwell on Miss Crandall's pertinacity in pursuing her own plans, express their horror of abolition principles, and state that Mr. Garrison had said that the excitement in Canterbury "is one of the genuine flowers of the colonization garden;" and they add, "Be it so; we APPEAL *to the American Colonization Society*, to which our statement is addressed — we appeal to every philanthropist, and to every Christian!" Mr. Judson's name appears at the head of the signers to the appeal.

Had Miss Crandall appealed to the Society in behalf of her school, she would probably, and very properly, have been told that the subject of her school was not embraced in the constitutional objects of the Society; and may we not ask, if the Society has no right to encourage, has it any right to discourage the establishment of schools of any description whatever? In the singleness of its object it has often been compared to the Bible Society; what would have been thought of *such* an appeal to the American Bible Society? How the appeal was answered we shall presently see.

Having thus identified their cause with that of the Colonization Society, and secured the sympathy of its numerous and powerful friends in Connecticut, Mr. Judson and his associates proceeded to further operations. Foiled in their attempts to persuade or intimidate, they now resolved on coercion. On the 1st of April, another town meeting was convened, at which it was "Voted that a petition in behalf of the town of Canterbury, to the next General Assembly, be drawn up, in suitable language, deprecating the evil consequences of bringing from *other towns* and other States people of color for *any* purpose, and more especially for the purpose of disseminating the principles and doctrines opposed to THE BENEVOLENT COLONIZATION SYSTEM, praying said Assembly to pass and enact such laws as in their wisdom will prevent *the evil*." Mr. Judson, with others, was apppointed a committee to prepare the petition, and to request other towns to forward similar petitions. The malignity of this vote is equalled only by its absurdity. The desired law is to prevent the evil of blacks passing not only from other States, but *other towns*. Every black citizen of Connecticut is to be imprisoned in the town in which the law happens to find him, and he may not travel into the adjoining town for "any purpose," and all this especially to prevent interference with "the *benevolent* colonization system."

Did the Colonization Society protest against such an outrage being committed in its behalf? did it indignantly disclaim all connection, all sympathy with men who in its name were striving to perpetuate such abominable tyranny? It is not known, that in any way whatever, it has ever expressed its disapprobation of these proceedings. Certain it is, that the effect of the "appeal," and of this vote, was not such as to induce the Canterbury gentlemen to falter in their career; we have seen that Mr. Judson had a LAW, which was to arrest the school. When the "appeal" had been before the public just one month, the selectmen resolved to avail themselves of this law.

Among the pupils of Miss Crandall, was a colored girl about seventeen years of age, who had come from Rhode Island to enjoy the advantages of the school. The pursuit of knowledge under discouraging difficulties has rarely failed to excite applause; and the virtuous struggles of the poor and obscure to improve and elevate themselves, claim the sympathy of Christian benevolence. In the present instance we behold a youthful female, of a despised and depressed race, attempting to emerge from the ignorance and degradation into which she had been cast by birth; and abandoning her home and friends, and travelling to another State, applying for instruction to the only seminary in the whole country open to receive her. And now let us see what sympathy this poor and defenceless, but innocent and praiseworthy girl, experienced from the admirers of "the benevolent colonization system." On the day after her arrival, she was ordered by the selectmen to leave the town. This order, as illegal as it was inhumane, was disregarded; and on the 22d of April, Mr. Judson and his fellow functionaries instituted, on behalf of the town, a suit against her under an old vagrant act of Connecticut, and a writ was issued to the sheriff, to require her appearance before a Justice of the Peace. The writ recited, that according to the statute, she had forfeited to the town $1.62 for each day she had remained in it, since she was ordered to depart; and that in default of payment, she was TO BE WHIPPED ON THE NAKED BODY NOT EXCEEDING TEN STRIPES, unless she departed within ten days after conviction. The barbarous and obsolete law under which this suit was brought, was intended to protect towns from the intrusion of paupers who might become chargeable. The friends of the school had offered to give the selectmen bonds to any amount, to secure the town from all cost on account of the pupils; and of course this suit was a wicked perversion of the law, and the plaintiffs ought to have been indicted for a malicious prosecution under color of office. With equal propriety might the civil authority of New Haven warn a student in Yale College, from New York, to leave the city, and on his refusal, order him to be whipped on the naked body as a vagrant pauper.

About the time of the return of this writ, the Legislature of Connecticut assembled, and so successfully had the Canterbury persecution been identified with colonization, that a law was passed to suppress the school, and all others of a similar character. Its preamble declared that "attempts have been made to establish literary institutions in this State, for the instruction of colored persons belonging to other States and countries, which would tend to the *great increase* of the colored population of this State, and thereby to the *injury* of the people." The act provides, that every person who shall set up, or establish any school, academy, or literary institution, for the instruction or education of colored persons who are not inhabitants of Connecticut; or who shall teach in such school, or who shall board any colored pupil of such school, not an inhabitant of the State, shall forfeit one hundred dollars for the first offence, two hundred dollars for the second, and so on, doubling for each succeeding offence, unless the consent of the civil authority and selectmen of the town, be previously obtained.

Mr. Judson's late attempt to enforce the whipping law, reminded the Legislature of the propriety of abolishing that relic of barbarism, and it was accordingly repealed, and thus were the backs of Miss Crandall's pupils saved from the threatened laceration.

It is painful and mortifying to reflect on the law obtained by Mr. Judson and his associates, for the suppression of the school, and which has very generally received the title of "the Connecticut Black Act." It is an act alien to the habits, the character, the religion of Connecticut. It is an act which neither policy nor duty can vindicate. It is an act which will afford its authors no consolation in the prospect of their final account, and which their children will blush to remember.

It is not surprising that a *Connecticut* Legislature, about to pass a law for the *discouragement* of learning, should wish for an excuse; nor that they should find themselves constrained to *invent* one. Miss Crandall had fifteen or twenty girls in her school, and it does not appear that the Legislature had ascertained how many of them had come from other States, nor that they had inquired into the amount of injury sustained by the citizens of Canterbury, in their "persons, property, and reputations," from these "misses of color;" and yet they unhesitatingly assert, that the "increase" of the colored population in the State, occasioned by such schools, would be "great;" and that such increase would tend to the "injury of the people." To test the truth of these two assertions, let it be recollected, first, that no evidence existed that any other seminary for blacks was at this time contemplated in Connecticut; and that the free colored people are, as a class, sunk in abject poverty, and that very few of them have the means of sending their children from other States into Connecticut, and there maintaining them at school; and, secondly, that no portion of this population would be so little likely to occasion "injury to the people," as those who were placed at a religious school, and instructed in morals and literature. As to the sincerity of the apprehensions felt by the Legislature, let it be further recollected, that the law is intended to prevent the ingress of such blacks *only*, as might come for the honorable and virtuous purpose of education, while not the slightest impediment is opposed to the introduction of cooks, waiters, scullions, shoeblacks, &c., in any number. The *best* are excluded, the *worst* freely admitted.

We have seen that colonizationists regard all attempts to elevate the free blacks, as an interference with their system, and the Black Act is admirably calculated to prevent such attempts. Connecticut closes her schools to blacks from New York and elsewhere. If this is right, — and what State more religious than Connecticut? — other States may be expected to follow *her example*. Hence no seminary, in any one State, for the instruction of the blacks, can be founded by their joint contributions; from the academies, boarding schools, and colleges of the whites, they are already excluded; of course, they are — doomed to perpetual ignorance. Let each State, it is said, instruct its own youth. It is well for Yale College that this doctrine is applied only to *black* aspirants for knowledge.

In 1828, an African Mission School was established at Hartford, for the purpose of educating colored youth, "to be selected from our numerous African population," and, of course, from other States besides Connecticut. It was under the patronage of the Bishops of the Protestant Episcopal Church in the

United States. No outcry was excited against this school; no citizen of Hartford trembled for his property, person, or reputation. Why not? Because the school was auxiliary to colonization, and those instructed in it were to be sent *out* of the country.

No sooner was the passage of the Black Act known in Canterbury, than this triumph over justice, humanity, and constitutional liberty, was celebrated by a *feu de joie*, and the ringing of bells. Nor was the act permitted to remain a dead letter. Miss Crandall was prosecuted under it, and being unable to procure bail, was committed to PRISON. The next day bail was obtained, and she returned to her school. Well, indeed, might the public press, with some memorable exceptions, execrate the Black Act; and well, indeed, might Mr. Judson feel impatient, under the obloquy that was falling upon him, as the chief instigator and manager of the prosecution. "A friend in need, is a friend indeed." And *now* was the time when he needed and received that countenance, for which he had appealed to the Colonization Society. It was not probably expected that the managers of the parent Society would officially notice the appeal, but a mode was devised, on the part of Connecticut colonizationists, of publicly expressing their approbation of Mr. Judson's conduct. On the anniversary of the declaration that "all men are created equal," and a few days after Miss Crandall's imprisonment, the Windham County* Colonization Society convened, and appointed Mr. Judson their *orator* and *agent*, thus proclaiming that HE was the man they delighted to honor. Another response to the appeal was in a few days heard from New York. The chairman of the executive committee of the New York City Colonization Society, is the editor of the New York Commercial Advertiser, and its columns were loaded with criminations of Miss Crandall, and vindications of the Black Act. "The inhabitants of Canterbury" were declared to be "as quiet, peaceable, humane, and inoffensive people, as can be named in the United States." The constitutionality of the

* The County in which Canterbury is situated.

Black Act was broadly maintained, and it was averred to be "just such a law in its spirit, if not in its provisions, as we are in the constant practice of enforcing in this city, to prevent our charitable institutions from being filled to overflowing with black paupers from the South, and white paupers from Europe." Of the gentleman who drafted the Black Act, the public were assured, "a warmer heart than his throbs in few bosoms, and the *African race* has no firmer friend than him."*

On the 23d of August, Miss Crandall was brought to trial. The *crime* with which she was charged, was fully proved. One of the witnesses testified: "The school is usually opened and closed with prayer; the Scriptures are read and explained in the school daily; portions are committed to memory by the pupils, and considered part of their education."

The orator and agent of the Windham Colonization Society, opened the case on the part of the prosecution, and to this gentleman, it is believed, belongs the distinction of having been the first man in New England to propound publicly the doctrine, that free *colored* persons are not citizens. This doctrine was essential to the validity of the Black Act, since by the federal Constitution, citizens of one State are entitled to all the privileges of citizenship in every other State; and the Act prohibited colored persons from other States from going to school in Connecticut, a prohibition palpably unconstitutional, if free blacks are citizens. The presiding judge submitted the cause to the jury without comment; and some of them having scruples about Mr. Judson's new doctrine, refused to agree in a verdict of guilty, and a new trial was consequently ordered. In the ensuing October, Miss Crandall was again placed at the bar, while the vice president of the New Haven Colonization Society, Judge Daggett, took his seat on the bench. The cause against the defendant was again argued by the Windham Colonization orator and agent; and Judge Daggett, warned by the result of the preceding trial, of the necessity of enlightening the consciences of the jury, delivered an elaborate charge. Rarely

Commercial Advertiser, July 16 and 29, 1833.

has any judge enjoyed such an opportunity of defending the poor and fatherless, of doing justice to the afflicted and needy, of delivering the spoiled out of the hand of the oppressor. The merits of the cause turned on the simple question whether free blacks are citizens or not. We might have presumed that a judge, aware of his solemn responsibility, would have prepared himself for the decision of this momentous question, by the most patient and thorough research. On the opinion he might pronounce, would perhaps rest the future education, comfort, freedom, and not unlikely, everlasting happiness of multitudes of his fellow-men. Under such circumstances, the public had a right to expect that he would resort to every source of information; that he would consult the opinions of eminent statesmen and jurists; investigate the constitutional history of the rights of these people; study the proceedings of Congress in relation to them, and bring together such a mass of facts, such an array of arguments, as would prove that his decision, whatever it might be, was the result of conscientious inquiry, and that the bench was elevated far above the prejudices and passions, which had brought to the bar an innocent and benevolent female.

The judge, in his charge, expresses himself in the following words: * "Are the free people of color citizens? I answer, No." The grounds on which this answer is given, appear to be the following:

> 1st. "They are not so styled in the Constitution of the United States. In that clause of the Constitution which fixes the basis of representation, there was an opportunity to have called them citizens, if they were so considered. But that makes free *persons* (adding three-fifths of all other persons) the basis of representation and taxation."

The words of the Constitution referred to by the Judge, are, (Art. 1. Sec. 3,) "Representatives and direct taxes shall be apportioned among the several States which may be included within this Union, according to their respective numbers, which shall be determined by adding to the whole number of free per-

* We quote from a newspaper report of the charge, and have no knowledge that the accuracy of the report has ever been denied.

sons, including those bound to service for a term of years, and excluding Indians not taxed, three-fifths of all other persons."

Now, it seems, free *colored* persons cannot be citizens, because they are not in this section so called; but unfortunately free *white* persons are not called citizens, and they also must therefore be disfranchised! Apprentices ("those bound to service for a term of years,") are likewise included among free *persons*, and they also cannot be citizens!

Had free *white* persons been spoken of as *citizens*, and free *black* persons only as "persons," then indeed there would have been some force in the judge's first reason; but as there is not the slightest reference in the Constitution to the complexion of the "free persons," we cannot understand the argument, and proceed, therefore, to his

2d reason. "They (free negroes) are not so styled, (citizens,) so far as I am aware, in the laws of Congress, or of any of the States."

It would thus seem that men with *black* skins cannot be citizens, unless the laws expressly declare them to be so. So far as we are aware, men with *red* hair are not styled citizens in the laws of Congress, or of any of the States.

3d reason. "His Honor then read from Kent's Commentary, Vol. II, p. 210, a note in which the commentator speaks of the degraded condition of the blacks, and the disabilities under which they labor, and thence *inferred* that, in Kent's opinion, they were not citizens."

Had the judge found it convenient to consult the *text* of this learned and independent jurist, the following passage would have saved him the trouble of drawing an inference.

"The article in the Constitution of the United States, declaring that citizens of each State were entitled to all the privileges and immunities of citizens in the several States, applies to natural born or duly naturalized citizens, and if *they* remove from one State to another, they are entitled to the privileges that persons of the *same description* are entitled to in the State to which the removal is made, and to none other. If, therefore, for instance, free persons of color are not entitled to vote in Carolina, free persons of color emigrating there from a Northern State would not be entitled to vote."

Here is an express admission of the citizenship of free colored persons, and their case is cited to illustrate the rights of *citizens* under the federal Constitution. If a free black, according to the commentary, moving from one State to another, is, under the federal Constitution, entitled only to such privileges as the free blacks in the latter State enjoy, it follows irresistibly that he *is entitled* to such privileges as the free blacks do there enjoy. Now, the free blacks of Connecticut enjoy a legal right to go to school, and to *any* school that will receive them; hence, according to Chancellor Kent, a free black removing from another State into Connecticut, has the same right, and hence the Black Act is plainly and palpably unconstitutional.

4th. "Another reason for believing that people of color are not considered citizens, is found in the fact, *that when the United States Constitution was adopted, every State except Massachusetts tolerated slavery.*"

Why a *free* black man cannot be a citizen, because another black man is a slave, is a problem we confess ourselves unable to solve.

Such are the arguments, and the only ones adduced by the judge, to support his portentous decision; a decision which tends to strip the free negro of his property and rights; renders him an alien in the land of his birth; exposes him to contumely and oppression, and prepares the way for his forcible deportation to the shores of Africa.

In order to do full justice to Judge Daggett, it may be proper to notice his answers to objections, since these answers may, perhaps, be regarded as negative arguments. To the assertion, that free blacks own vessels which participate in the peculiar privileges of American shipping, and that they sue in the United States courts, he simply replied, that these claims have never been settled by judicial decisions. To the argument that free blacks may be guilty of high treason, he replied, "So may any person who resides under the government, and enjoys its protection, if he rises up against it."

Having thus fairly stated the judge's arguments, we will now take the liberty of presenting a few *facts* having an important bearing on this question; facts, be it remembered, that were accessible to the Judge, had he thought it worth while to look for them.

By the fourth of the "Articles of Confederation," it was provided, that "the *free inhabitants* of these States shall be entitled to all the privileges and immunities of free citizens in the several States." While these articles were under consideration in Congress, it appears from the journals, that on the 25th of June, 1778, "the delegates from South Carolina moved the following amendment *in behalf of their State:*—'In Article Fourth, between the words free inhabitants, insert WHITE.' Passed in the negative—Ayes, 2 States, Nays 8 States—1 State divided." Here then was a solemn decision of the Revolutionary Congress, that free negroes should be entitled to all the privileges and immunities of free citizens in the several States. Judge Daggett thinks that the Constitution of the United States did not regard free blacks as citizens, because in 1788 all the States, with one exception, tolerated slavery; yet, in 1778, Congress decided that free blacks were citizens, although all the States, *without one exception,* tolerated slavery. Ten years after this decision, the new Constitution was formed, and the clause respecting citizenship in the several States was transferred to it from the Articles of Confederation, with slight verbal alterations. That the clause embraced free negroes at the time it was transferred, was settled by the vote we have quoted; no words were added to exclude them; no intimation was given that the new Constitution was disfranchising thousands, and tens of thousands, who Congress had declared were invested with all the rights and immunities of free citizens. No desire was expressed to disfranchise these people, and in the debates on the Constitution, this disfranchisement was never alluded to either in the language of praise or of censure; and for more than forty years after the adoption of the Constitution, no suspicion existed that it had divested the free blacks of the citizenship they enjoyed under the Confederation, till the discovery was made by the agent and orator of the Windham Colonization Society, and juridically announced by the Vice President of the New Haven Colonization Society.

Judge Daggett "*is not aware that free blacks are styled citizens in the laws of Congress or of any of the States!*" How laborious has been his search for such laws, we shall now see. Probably the judge will admit that when the law speaks of *male* citizens, they recognize the existence of *female* citizens; and most judges would admit, that where the law speaks of *white* citizens, they recognize the existence of citizens who are *not white.*

The act of Congress of 1792, for organizing the militia, provides for the enrolment of "free *white male* citizens."

The act of Congress of 1803, "to prevent the importation of certain persons into certain States, when by the laws thereof their admission is prohibited," enacts that masters and captains of vessels shall not "import or bring, or cause to be imported or brought, *any negro, mulatto, or other person of color,* not being a native, a CITIZEN, or registered seaman of the United States," &c.

The constitution of Judge Daggett's own State, limits the right of suffrage to "free *white male* citizens." Why *male* citizens, if there are no *female* citizens? and why *white* citizens, if there can be no *colored* ones? Seven or eight State constitutions, in the same manner, recognize the existence of *colored* citizens. Had the judge extended his inquiries into State laws, to those of Massachusetts, he would have found one prohibiting any negro "other than a CITIZEN of the United States," or a subject of the Emperor of Morocco, from tarrying in the Commonwealth longer than two months. Had he taken the trouble to consult the statute book of New York, he would have found the following clause in the act relative to elections, viz.: "If the person so offering to vote be a *colored* man, the following oath shall be tendered to him: 'You do swear (or affirm) that you are of the age of twenty-one years, that for three years you have been *a* CITIZEN OF THIS STATE,'" &c. *Revised Statutes,* I, 134.

Had the judge condescended to look into the debates of the New York Convention of 1821, on the question of admitting the free blacks to the right of suffrage, he would have discovered to his astonishment, that the New York lawyers and judges had no hesitation in admitting these people to be citizens, whatever might be their objections to permitting them to vote. He would have found Chancellor Kent earnestly contending for their rights to citizenship in other States under the federal Constitution. He would have found Rufus King, (no mean authority,) concluding an argument in their behalf, with these words: "As certainly as the children of any white man are citizens, so certainly the children of the black man are citizens."

Had the judge opened the constitution of the State of New York, he would have met with a clause in the article respecting the elective franchise, declaring, "No man of color, unless he shall have been three years a CITIZEN OF THIS STATE," &c.

On the 4th of September, 1826, Governor Clinton, of New York, addressed a letter to the President of the United States, demanding the immediate liberation of Gilbert Horton, a colored man, as "A CITIZEN of this State," he having been imprisoned in Washington as a fugitive slave.

In every State in the Union, we believe, without one exception a native free born negro may legally take, hold, and convey real estate. Will Judge Daggett deny this to be an attribute of citizenship?* Will he maintain that any but citizens may exercise the right of suffrage? But in eight or ten States, free negroes may legally vote. True it is, that in others, this privilege is denied to them, but it is not true that none are citizens who cannot vote. The act of Congress respecting naturalization, provides, that in a certain case, the *widow* and *children* of a deceased alien "shall be citizens of the United States."

Impressed colored sailors have been claimed by the national government, as "citizens of the United States;" and colored men going to Europe, have received passports from the department of State, certifying that they were citizens of the United States.

The proposed constitution of the new State of Missouri re-

* Real estate in the city of New York to the value of fifty thousand dollars was lately devised to a free colored man in that city, but according to the judge, he is not a citizen, and of course cannot take by devise. If so, the property must go to the heir at law, or escheat to the State.

quired the Legislature to pass such laws as might be necessary "to prevent free negroes and mulattoes from coming to settle in the State, under any pretext whatever." The Legislature ot New York, in reference to this provision, on the 15th November, 1820, "Resolved, if the provisions contained in any proposed constitution of a new State deny to any CITIZENS of the existing States the privileges and immunities of citizens of such new State, that such proposed constitution should not be accepted or confirmed, the same, in the opinion of this Legislature, being void by the Constitution of the United States." This resolution was adopted in high party times, by an almost unanimous vote.

The constitution being submitted to Congress, the article excluding colored citizens, was deemed by the House of Representatives a violation of the national compact, and that body refused to receive Missouri into the Union. A compromise was at last agreed to, and Congress admitted Missouri on the express condition that the offensive clause in her constitution should never authorize any law by which *any citizen* of any of the States should be excluded from the enjoyment of any of the privileges and immunities to which such citizen is entitled by the Constitution of the United States; and that the Legislature of Missouri should by a solemn act declare their assent to this condition. The Legislature passed the act required, and *thereupon* the State became a member of the Union. Yet Judge Daggett is not aware of any act of Congress recognizing free blacks as citizens!

Admit free negroes to be *men*, and to be *born* free in the United States, and it is impossible to frame even a plausible argument against their citizenship. The only argument on this point we have ever met with, in which the conclusion is legitimately deduced from the premises, is by a late writer,* who maintains that the negroes are a distinct race of animals. Now it must be conceded, that the negro, if not *a human* being, is not

* The author of "Evidences against the Views of the Abolitionists, consisting of physical and moral proofs of the natural inferiority of the negroes." New York, 1833.

a citizen. We recommend the following reasoning to the future judicial apologists of the Black Act.

> "His (the negro's) lips are thick, his zygomatic muscles large and full, his jaws large and projecting, his chin retreating, his forehead low, flat, and slanting, and as a consequence of this latter character, his eyeballs are very prominent, apparently larger than those of the white men; all of these peculiarities at the same time contributing to reduce his *facial* angle almost to a level with the BRUTE. If then it is consistent with science to believe that the mind will be greater in proportion to the *size and figure of the brain*, it is equally reasonable to suppose that the acknowledged meanness of the negro's intellect only coincides with the *shape of his head;* or in other words, that his want of capability to receive a complicated education, renders it improper and impolitic that he should be allowed the privileges of CITIZENSHIP in an enlightened country." P. 25, 26.

The author is an ultra colonizationist, and the conclusion to which he arrives is, "let the blacks be removed, *nolens volens*, from among us."

We have dwelt the longer on the Connecticut decision, on account of its immense importance to a numerous class of our fellow countrymen. The victims of a cruel prejudice, and of wicked laws, they especially claimed the aid and sympathy of the humane, when striving to elevate themselves by the acquisition of useful knowledge. But Judge Daggett's doctrine crushes them to the earth. Denounced by a powerful society, extending its influence over every part of our country, as "NUISANCES," and judicially declared not to be citizens, they are delivered over to the tormentors, bound hand and foot. If not *citizens*, they may be dispossessed of their dwellings, for they cannot legally hold real estate — they may be denied the means of a livelihood, and forbidden to buy and sell, or to practise any trade, for they are no longer protected by the Constitution of the United States. Nay, they may be expelled from town to town, and from State to State, till finding no resting place for the soles of their feet, they "CONSENT" to embark for Africa.

However inconclusive we are disposed to regard Judge Daggett's arguments, they were satisfactory to the jury, and a verdict was given against Miss Crandall. The cause was removed to the Connecticut Court of Errors, where all the proceedings were set aside on technical grounds. Certain of the "quiet, peaceable, humane, and inoffensive people of Canterbury," tired with the law's delay, determined on ejecting the school by a summary process, and accordingly mobbed the house by night, and smashed in the windows. It was now discovered, that it was the "persons" of inoffensive females, and not of Mr. Judson and his associates, that were endangered, and the school was abandoned; thus were the efforts of the admirers of "the benevolent system of colonization" crowned with entire success.

Soon after Judge Daggett's decision, a most inflammatory petition to the Connecticut Legislature, was circulated in New Haven. We quote from a printed copy.

"If they (the negroes) have rights, we humbly hope it is not yet too late to presume that the *white* man also, the only legal native American *citizen* whom we shall ever consent to acknowledge, may be permitted to suggest that he has *some* rights. If he (the white man) purchases a piece of land, the negro who locates near him, deteriorates its value from 20 to 50 per cent.; for who will have a negro neighborhood, or live in unceasing fear of theft and trespass? The white man cannot labor upon equal terms with the negro; he is compelled to yield the market to the African, and with his family ultimately becomes the tenant of an alms-house, or is driven from the State to seek a better lot in the western wilds. THUS HAVE THOUSANDS of our most valuable citizens been *banished* from home and kindred, for the accommodation of the most debased race that the civilized world has ever seen."

The petitioners, as might be supposed, are colonizationists. "If the negro cannot consistently with our interest or our *feelings* be admitted to the same rights that we enjoy, let him seek a *country* where he will find those who are his equals; *let us unite in aiding him to reach that country*."

It has never been denied that good men belong to the Colonization Society; and it ought not to be denied that even good men are fallible, and subject to erroneous opinions and unwarrantable prejudices. To us it appears unquestionable, that the facts developed in the preceding pages, prove a tendency in the Society to excite in the community, a persecuting spirit towards the free blacks. That the pious, and respectable members of the Society, detest the horrible outrages recently committed upon these people in New York, Philadelphia, and elsewhere, it would be both foolish and wicked to doubt; and yet no one who candidly and patiently investigates the whole subject, can fail to be convinced that these outrages never would have happened, had the Society never existed. The assertion is not hazardous, that of the multitudes composing the negro mobs, there was not an individual less disposed than the Canterbury town meeting, to laud the "benevolent colonization system." Every wretch who participated in beating and plundering free negroes, would rejoice in their expulsion from their country, and in the Society he beholds an instrument for the accomplishment of his wishes. But how is it possible that the best and the worst of men can unite in supporting the same institution? In the first place, these good men, as is abundantly evident from their own confessions, are actuated by motives of supposed public policy, as well as benevolence, in promoting the colonization of people whom they regard as nuisances; and in the second place, there are in the constitution, three talismanic words, which through the influence of existing prejudices have blinded the eyes of these good men to the *practical* operation of the Society on the colored people. The words are "WITH THEIR CONSENT." It is speciously argued, if the free blacks *consent* to go to Africa, why not send them? if they do not wish to go, they are at liberty to remain. This argument seems for the most part to have benumbed the consciences and understandings of colonizationists, as to the cruel persecution which their Society necessarily encourages. They would be horrified at the idea of their agents scouring the country, and seizing men, women and children, placing them on the rack, till as joint after joint was dislocated, the suffering wretches *consented* to go to Africa; and yet the Society feels no compunction in countenancing legal oppression having the same ultimate object in view, and in transporting negroes whose *consent* they well know has been extorted by the most abominable persecution. Many will feel disposed to deny the truth of these assertions; but not, we trust, after seeing the proof of them, which we will now proceed to offer.

We have already adverted to the cruel laws by which these

people are oppressed, and kept, purposely kept, in ignorance and degradation. Now let it be recollected, that with but few exceptions, these laws have been either enacted, or are kept in force by legislatures which have formally and in their legislative capacity, passed resolutions in favor of the Society. Fourteen States have thus avowed their attachment to colonization. Now had these States, including *Connecticut*, *Ohio*, and several of the slave States, repealed their laws against the free blacks, and forborne to enact new ones, their sincerity in approving a plan for the removal of these people *with their consent* would have been less questionable than it is now, when they persist in a course of policy well calculated to *coerce* that consent. The Society appears to be a particular favorite with the slave States, with the exception of South Carolina, where its true character seems to have been misunderstood.

Now hear the acknowledgment of a Southern writer. We have before us the fourth edition, 1834, of "A Treatise on the Patriarchal System of Society:" by a Florida slave-holder. It is a treatise, in sober earnestness, on the means of perpetuating slavery, and increasing its profits. The author says, p. 12—"Colonization in Africa has been proposed to the free colored people: *to forward which*, a general system of persecution against them, upheld from the pulpit, has been *legalized* throughout the Southern States." The writer does not explain his allusion to the Southern pulpit; but we may judge of its influence on the condition of the free blacks, from the avowal already quoted from the Southern *Religious* Telegraph, of its repugnance to these people being taught to *read*, because such an acquirement would be an inducement with them to remain in this country; or, in other words, that the better they were treated here, the less likely would they be to consent to go to Africa.

The Legislatures of Maryland and Virginia, it is well known, have made large appropriations for colonization, and yet these Legislatures are among the most malignant persecutors of the free blacks. The original bill making the Virginia appropriation, contained a clause for the *compulsory* transportation of free blacks. Let it be recollected that the Colonization Society has ever been the peculiar favorite of Virginia, and that her most distinguished citizens have been enrolled among its officers; and let us now see *how* colonization has been promoted in that State. On a motion to strike out the compulsory clause, Mr. Brodnax thus expressed himself *against* the motion:

IT IS IDLE TO TALK ABOUT NOT RESORTING TO FORCE. *Every body must look to the introduction of force of some kind or other.* If the free negroes are willing to go, they will go; if not willing, THEY MUST BE COMPELLED TO GO. Some gentlemen think it politic not *now* to insert this feature in the bill, though they *proclaim their readiness to resort to it when it becomes necessary;* they think, that for a year or two, a sufficient number will consent to go, and THEN THE REST CAN BE COMPELLED. For my part, I deem it better to approach the question and settle it at once, and avow it openly. The intelligent portion of the free negroes know very well what is going on. Will they not see your debates? Will they not see that COERCION IS ULTIMATELY TO BE RESORTED TO? I have already expressed it as my opinion, that few, *very few*, will *voluntarily* consent to emigrate, if no *compulsory measures be adopted.* Without it, you will still, no doubt, have applicants for removal equal to your means. Yes, sir, people who will not only consent, but beg you to deport them. But what *sort of consent?*—a consent extorted by a species of oppression, calculated to render their situation among us insupportable! Many of those who have been already sent off, went with their avowed consent, but under the influence of a more decided compulsion than any which this bill holds out. I will not express in its fullest extent, the idea I entertain of *what has been done, or what enormities will be perpetrated to induce this class of persons to leave the State.* Who does not know that when a free negro, by crime or otherwise, has rendered himself obnoxious to a neighborhood, how easy it is for a party to visit him one night, take him from his bed and family, and apply to him the gentle admonition of a severe flagellation, to induce him to go away? In a few nights the dose can be repeated, perhaps increased, until, in the language of the physicians, *quantum suff.* has been administered to produce the desired operation, and the fellow becomes perfectly willing to move away. I have certainly heard, (if incorrectly, the gentleman from Southampton will put me right,) that *all the large cargo of emigrants, lately transported from that country to Liberia, all of whom professed to be willing to go, were rendered so by some such ministration as I have described.* Indeed, sir, *all of us* look to FORCE of some kind or other, direct or indirect, moral or physical, legal or illegal."

Another member, Mr. Fisher, in opposing the motion, said:

"If we wait till the free negroes *consent* to leave the State, we shall wait until time is no more. They never will give their consent. He believed if the compulsory principle were stricken out, this class would *be forced to leave by the harsh treatment of the whites.*"

The compulsory clause was stricken out, but we have the assurance of Mr. Brodnax, that they who objected to it at *present*, were ready to resort to force whenever it should become necessary; and he tells us, that *all* look to *force* of some kind or other; and he might have added, "all of us look to the Colonization Society as the instrument by which the forcible expulsion of the free negroes is to be effected." Nor do they look in vain. At the very time that the negroes of Southampton were suffering the barbarities he describes, the managers of the Society addressed their auxiliaries, urging them to increased efforts in raising funds, and, alluding to the excitement occasioned by the insurrection at Southampton, remarked, "the free people of color have awakened from their slumber, to a *keen* sense of their situation, and *are ready* in large numbers to emigrate to the Colony of Liberia." *Address, 17th Nov.* 1831.

A large number of these miserable people did indeed *consent* to go to Africa, and the managers well knew *how* their consent was obtained. "I *warned* the managers against this Virginia business," said Mr. Breckenridge in his speech before the Society, "and *yet* they sent out two shiploads of vagabonds, not fit to go to such a place, and that were *coerced* away as truly as if it had been done with a cartwhip."

Hear the confession of Mr. Gurley, the Secretary of the Society, on this subject:

> "Our friends at Norfolk appealed to us, and said the people were persecuted, and that it was a matter of *humanity* to take them. Our agent said they were *driven* from the county, and had appealed to him, and begged to go to Liberia." *Speech before the Society.*

Hear the testimony of Thomas C. Brown, from Liberia, given in May, 1834:

> "I am acquainted with several from Southampton County, Virginia, who informed me that they received several hundred lashes from the patrols to make them willing to go. In one instance, a man was several times compelled to witness the lashes inflicted on his wife, and then to be severely flogged himself. In another instance, a family received information from their white neighbors, that unless they went to Liberia, they should be whipped. Having no means of redress, they were obliged to go."

Hear the New York Colonization Society, when addressing the public:

"We say to them (the free blacks), we think you may improve your condition by going thither, but if you prefer remaining here, you will be *protected* and *treated with kindness.*" *Proceedings of New York Col. Soc.*, 1831.

Hear the same Society, when addressing the *Legislature:*

"We do not ask that the provisions of our constitution and statute book should be so modified as to *relieve* and exalt the condition of the colored people while they remain with us. Let these provisions stand in ALL THEIR RIGOR, to work out the ultimate and unbounded *good* of this people." In plain English, to coerce their consent to go to Africa. *Memorial to New York Legislature*, 1832.

We have seen what are the Connecticut and Virginia plans for promoting colonization: now for the Pennsylvania plan. At a public meeting held in the borough of Columbia, (Penn.) at the Town Hall, 23d August, 1834, the following, among other resolutions, were unanimously passed.

"Resolved, that we will not purchase any articles that can be procured elsewhere, or give our VOTE for any office whatever, to any one who employs negroes to do that species of labor white men have been accustomed to perform.

"*Resolved, that the Colonization Society ought to be supported by all the citizens favorable to the removal of the blacks from this country.*"

Here we find the support of the Society avowedly coupled with a most detestable plan of persecution. And now for the practical operation of this meeting of the friends of the "benevolent colonization system." It appears from a Columbia paper, that one or two nights after the meeting, a mob collected, and partly tore down the dwelling of a black man; they then proceeded to the office of another black man, who had had the presumption to *deal in lumber*, "a species of labor *white* men had been accustomed to perform," broke open the windows and door, rifled the desk, scattered the papers in the street, and attempted to overturn the building. Surely the Society may reasonably anticipate the consent of the blacks to emigrate, when in Connecticut, Pennsylvania, and Virginia, such cogent arguments are used to obtain it. Were the Society governed, as it ought to be, by Christian principles, it would shrink from encouraging persecution by accomplishing its object, the exportation of its victims. It would say explicitly to the authors of these atrocities, "You shall gain nothing by your cruelty, through our instrumentality. We will not encourage your farther persecutions, by removing those whose consent you have obtained by such unjustifiable means; we will not, to please you,

> 'Keep the word of promise to the ear,
> And break it to the hope.'"

But alas, it has virtually given official notice that it will transport all whose consent can be obtained, no matter by what barbarity. Hear the declaration of Mr. Gurley, the Secretary of the Society:

> "Should they (free blacks) BE URGED BY ANY STRESS OF CIRCUMSTANCES to seek an asylum beyond the limits of the United States, humanity and religion will alike dictate that they should be assisted to remove and establish themselves in freedom and prosperity in the land of their CHOICE." *Letter to gentlemen in New York.*

True it is the free blacks have been rendered by prejudice and persecution an ignorant and degraded class; but they are still competent to appreciate the practical character of colonization philanthropy.

The following resolutions, passed by a meeting of free blacks in New Bedford, in 1832, express the unanimous opinion of all their brethren who have intelligence to form, or courage to express an opinion on the subject.

> "Resolved, That in whatever light we view the Colonization Society, we discover nothing in it but terror, prejudice, and oppression. The warm and beneficent hand of philanthropy is not apparent in the system, but the influence of the Society on public opinion is more prejudicial to the interests and welfare of the people of color in the United States, than slavery itself.
>
> "Resolved, That the Society, to effect its purpose, the removal of free people of color (not the slaves) through its agents, teaches the public to believe that it is patriotic and benevolent to withhold from us knowledge, and the means of acquiring subsistence; and to look upon us as unnatural and illegal residents in this country, and thus by the force of prejudice, if not by law, endeavor to compel us to embark for Africa, and that too apparently by our own free will and consent."

And now let us ask what purpose is to be answered by persecuting this people, and keeping them ignorant and degraded? Does any one believe that they will ever be removed from the country? They now amount to 362,000. In 16 years, 2,162 have been sent away, some at first voluntarily, but many of them through coercion. But can cruelty, be it ever so extreme, furnish the Society with funds and ships sufficient to transport such a multitude? They must, in spite of Connecticut and Virginia persecution, remain with us. And if they are to remain with us, what conduct towards them do policy and religion prescribe? Conduct precisely opposite to that pursued by the Society. We must instruct and elevate them, if we would not be incumbered by an ignorant and depraved population; we must treat them with justice and kindness, if we would avoid the displeasure of HIM who has declared, "Ye shall not oppress one another."

CHAPTER III.

INFLUENCE OF THE COLONIZATION SOCIETY ON AFRICA — SUPPRESSION OF THE SLAVE-TRADE.

VERY many who now despair of extirpating slavery by means of the Society, continue to support it from a belief that it will confer rich blessings on Africa. These anticipated blessings are the suppression of the slave-trade, and the diffusion of religion and civilization. Let us at present inquire how far the first may reasonably be expected.

In the declarations of the Society and its members on this subject, we shall find an astonishing medley of ignorance, rash assertion, and honest confession.

"Sierra Leone has repaid Africa with still greater blessings; her example, her influence and efforts, *have given peace and security* to the neighboring coast; and who can estimate the extent of misery prevented, and of happiness conferred, to a population *delivered* from all the horrors of the slave-trade?" *Fifth Rep.* p. 18.

"The line of coast from Sierra Leone to Cape Mount, is now under British protection; and from Cape Mount to Trade Town, a distance of one hundred and twenty miles, the slave-trade *cannot be* prosecuted with the *least hope of success*. *Afr. Rep.*, II, p. 125—*Editorial*.

"Every colony of civilized inhabitants, established on that coast, and resolved to stop this trade to the extent of its means, will, at all events, put an end to it for a considerable distance. The colonies of *Sierra Leone*, and of Liberia, both *produce* this effect within their respective vicinities." *Judge Blackford's Address to the Indiana Colonization Society*. *Afr. Rep.*, VI, p. 66.

Of these compliments to Sierra Leone, it must be observed, one is paid officially by the Board of Managers, and the other by the Editor of the Repository. We beg the reader to keep them in mind, as we shall hereafter inquire into their *truth*. We will now proceed to notice some assertions relative to the agency of the Liberia colony in suppressing the slave-trade.

"In fact, the Colonization Society proposes the ONLY means by which this accursed trade can ever be effectually stopped; and, indeed, the Colony of Liberia, which this Society has planted, *has already freed about two hundred and fifty miles of that coast from the ravages of these enemies of the human race*." *Address of J. A. McKinney*, 4*th July*, 1830. *Afr. Rep.*, VI, p. 231.

"The flag that waves on Cape Montserado, proclaims to the slave trader that there is one spot, even in Africa, consecrated to freedom, *one spot which his polluted foot shall not tread*." *Speech of G. Smith, V. Pres.* 13*th Jan.* 1831. 14*th Rep.*

"Did we desire to put an end to these outrages upon humanity, (the slave-trade,) the Colonization Society offers itself as the ONLY efficient means. The slaver has dared to show herself *but once* within the limits of Liberia, and then she received the rewards of her temerity." *Proceedings of N. Y. Col. Soc.* 1832.

"No slaver now dares come *within one hundred miles of the settlement*." *Rev. Dr. Hawkes's Speech at Col. Meeting in New York, October*, 1833.

"In less than thirteen years since its foundation, Liberia contains about 3000 free and happy citizens, who have removed from oppression and bondage to the enjoyment of liberal institutions. The *slave-trade* has been UTTERLY DESTROYED along its ENTIRE COAST, formerly the most frequented mart of human flesh." *Report of Philadelphia Young Men's Col. Soc. made* 24*th Feb.* 1835, *U. S. Gazette*, 4*th March*, 1835.

The above are specimens of the assertions which have been rashly made and credulously received. Let us now attend to the honest confession on this subject, and let the reader compare them with the foregoing assertions. That these confessions may be better understood, it may be well to mention, that in the remarks accompanying a map of Liberia, published in the 6th vol. of the African Repository, it is stated, "The colony of Liberia extends from the Gallinas River to the territory of Kroo Settra, a distance of about 280 miles along the coast. The territory at present, (1830,) under the *actual* jurisdiction of the colony, extends from Grand Cape Mount, to Trade Town, a distance of about 150 miles." It appears, from the map, that the *last* limits embrace Cape Mount, Cape Montserado, on which is built the town of Monrovia, Bushrod Island, Bassa Cove, and Trade Town.

"The records of the colony afford abundant and unequivocal testimony of the *undiminished* extent and atrocity of the slave-trade. From eight to ten, and even fifteen vessels have engaged at the same time in this odious traffic, *almost within reach of the guns of Liberia*, and as late as July, 1825, there were existing contracts for eight hundred slaves to be furnished in the short space of four months, WITHIN EIGHT MILES OF MONROVIA." *Rep.* X, p. 44, 1827.

"From all I can learn, I am induced to believe, that the slave-trade is now carried on at the Gallinas, between Cape Mount and Sierra Leone, and to the leeward of this place, to a *greater extent* than it has been for many years." *Letter from R. Randall, Agent at Liberia*, 28*th Dec.* 1828. *Afr. Rep.*, V, p. 4.

"*Frequently within sight of the colonial factories*, the slave-traders carry on their operations. The slave-trade never has been carried on with more activity, than it is at this time. There is established at Gallinas, a regular slave-agent, who furnishes slaves to the slave-vessels. He receives his goods from trading vessels, and it is said principally from an American vessel. He purchases large numbers of slaves, and furnishes the slave-vessels, which principally bring out specie. These vessels run up and down the coast until a convenient opportunity offers, when they run in and get their cargoes of slaves. Some of them are captured, and I have been informed, they have been bought afterwards by their *original owners*, and that the same vessel has frequently been bought and sold several times." *Letter from R. Randall, Agent at Liberia, Feb.* 1829, *Afr. Rep.*, V, p. 148. The same letter states the astounding fact, that "Mamma, the proprietress of Bushrod Island, just in front of Monrovia, whose town is not more than a *quarter of a mile* from our settlements on that island," was engaged in the slave-trade, and had sold several hundred—p. 150.

"It is painful to state, that the managers have reason to believe that the slave-trade is still prosecuted to a great extent, and with circumstances of *undiminished* atrocity. The fact that much was done by Mr. Ashmun to banish it from the territory, under the colonial jurisdiction, is unquestionably true, but it *now exists even on the territory;* and a little to the north and south of Liberia, it is seen in its true characters of fraud, and rapine, and blood." *Rep.*, XIII, p. 13.—1830

Now, be it recollected, that it was *after* this official annunciation by the Board of Managers, that the slave-trade existed even on the territory of Liberia, that the African Repository published without contradiction the vaunt of Mr. McKinney already quoted, that the colony had freed about two hundred and fifty miles of the coast from the slave-trade!

"I hope the Board will adopt some more effectual measures for suppressing the slave-trade *within the territory of Liberia.* Since the death of Don Miguel of Bassa, Peter Blanco, a Spanish slave-trader, for some years a resident in the Gallinas, has opened a slave factory at GRAND CAPE MOUNT. Such a thing ought not to be, as it is only forty-five miles from here. I am sorry to remark, that this abominable traffic is carried on with the utmost activity, all along the coast. Capt. Parker, during his trading at the Gallinas of about three weeks, saw no less than nine hundred shipped." *Letter from A. D. Williams, Agent of the Society at Liberia,—10th Sept.* 1830. *Afr. Rep.*, VI, p. 275.

"With *undiminished* atrocity and activity is this odious traffic now carried on all along the African coast; slave factories are established in *the immediate vicinity of the colony*," &c. *Rep.*, XIV, p. 11—1831.

"The cursed practice of slave-trading, I regret to say, is still carried on *between this and Sierra Leone.*" *Letter of Rev. Mr. Cox; Monrovia, 8th of April,* 1833. *Afr. Rep.*, IX, p. 252.

"Bassa Cove was purchased* by Governor Pinney from King Joe Harris, the native sovereign of that fine harbor. It was bought at a moderate price, and without a drop of spirits. The negotiation was effected in November last, 1834, and affords peculiar satisfaction to the friends of humanity, inasmuch as no less than 500 SLAVES had been shipped from there in *October.*" *N. Y. Commercial Advertiser, 17th March,* 1835. The same fact is stated in the "*Colonization Herald,*" *4th April,* 1835.

Such are the refutations furnished by the Society itself, of all its boasts about suppressing the slave-trade; and yet we are told that the Society is the ONLY means of putting an end to the traffic! It seems never to occur to these gentlemen, that the abolition of slavery would, as a matter of course, put an immediate and total stop to the trade.†

* Bassa Cove is situated *between* Monrovia and Trade Town, and has therefore been for years under the jurisdiction of the colony; of course the purchase alluded to, must have been of the *possession* of the native occupants.

† To what extent the importation of slaves in the United States is now carried, we are ignorant. In 1819, Mr. Middleton of South Carolina, stated on the floor of Congress, that, in his opinion, 13,000 Africans were annually smuggled into the Southern States. Mr. Wright of Virginia, estimated the number at 15,000.

But in what way does the Society expect to destroy this commerce? By planting colonies of ignorant and depraved negroes on the African coast. Every slave factory is of itself a colony, and for the most part, of intelligent *white* men; and yet it is supposed, that negro colonists, who, when in America, were "the most depraved of the human race," will be too virtuous to yield to the temptations of a lucrative commerce. Why should the free negroes of America, who Mr. Clay assures us, are "of all descriptions of our population, the most corrupt, depraved, and abandoned," have, when removed to Liberia, a greater abhorrence for the iniquity of the slave-trade, than their brethren of Sierra Leone? If the trade has been *actually promoted* by the latter colony, why will it be suppressed by the former?

"The acting Attorney General at Sierra Leone declared, 1812, on the trial of certain persons for the infraction of the British abolition laws, that the town of Sierra Leone was 'the heart from which all the arteries and veins of the slave-trading system, had for years been animated and supplied.'" *Dr. Thorpe's Views of the present Increase of the Slave-trade*, p. 71.

The following facts are gathered from documents published by the British Parliament in 1832. Chief Justice Jeffcott, of Sierra Leone, in 1830, delivered a charge to the Grand Jury, in which he declared that he had received credible information, that persons in the colony were engaged in aiding and abetting the slave-trade, and fitting out ships for the trade. He asserted, that the colony "established for the *express purpose* of suppressing this vile traffic, was made a *mart for carrying it on*." He also stated, that within the last ten years, twenty-two thousand Africans had been located in the colony by the British Government, at an expense of nearly seven millions sterling, and that now there are not to be found in the colony above seventeen or eighteen thousand men! These extraordinary and appalling declarations attracted the attention of the British Government, who appointed a Commission to inquire into their truth. The Commissioners, in their report dated the 26th of October of the same year, state that, from the testimony taken before them, "they cannot but conclude that the nefarious system of *kidnapping* has prevailed in this colony to *a much greater extent* than was even alluded to in the charge of the Chief Justice." From the testimony published with the report, it appears that the slave-vessels are in the habit of bringing out specie, for the purchase of supplies on the coast; and that "Mr. Hilary Teague, who resides at the *American settlement at Liberia*, at Cape Mesurado, near the Gallinas, and who trades between *that* place (Gallinas, a slave-factory) and Sierra Leone, purchasing some goods from a Mr. Lake, a merchant in the colony, produced a bag containing about one thousand dollars, on which was marked the name of the Spanish schooner Manzanares. This vessel took in her cargo at the Gallinas, and was subsequently condemned as a slave-ship."

Here we find a colonist of Liberia trading at a slave-factory, and afterwards exhibiting 1000 dollars in specie, received in all human probability from a slave-ship. It is surely unreasonable to suppose that petty colonial merchants will refuse to sell supplies to slave-ships for specie. Indeed, every new colony on the coast, will, while slavery continues, give new facilities to this accursed commerce; nor can the government at home prevent avaricious and unprincipled colonists from participating in it. No one can question the desire of Great Britain to purge Sierra Leone of this enormity, and yet we find the following statement in the English Monthly Review, for May, 1833. "One of the schoolmasters in Sierra Leone has been tried for *selling* some of his scholars. There were lately upwards of one hundred liberated Africans, who were kidnapped from Sierra Leone, and were conveyed to a place near the banks of the river Pongos. Here they were detained, till an opportunity occurred of re-shipping them as slaves."

CHAPTER IV.

INFLUENCE OF THE COLONIZATION SOCIETY ON AFRICA—DIFFUSION OF CIVILIZATION AND CHRISTIANITY.

Although the Society is not a missionary institution, builds no churches, employs no ministers, and distributes no Bibles or tracts, yet it has persuaded the public that Liberia is a missionary establishment, and the radiating point from which a flood of light and holiness is to spread over Africa. So confidently and constantly has the *missionary* influence of the Society been asserted, that many of the members unfeignedly believe it, and their contributions are lavished, and their prayers are offered for the regeneration of Africa by emigrants, who, when in the United States, were denounced as "a curse and contagion wherever they reside." Let us attend to the stupendous objects the Society proposes to accomplish.

"It would illuminate a CONTINENT. It would publish the name of Christ on the dark mountains of Africa, and the burning sands of the desert. It would kindle up holiness and hope among uncounted tribes, whose souls are as black with crime and misery, as are the forms of matter that veil them." *Afr. Rep.*, I, 164 — *Editorial.*

"The little band at Liberia, who are spreading over the wilderness around them a strange aspect of life and beauty, are in *every sense a missionary station.* Every ship freighted from our shores with their suffering kindred, will be freighted also with the *heralds of the cross.* You will see the light breaking in upon one and another dark habitation of cruelty. The night of heathenism will depart. One tribe after another will come to the light of Zion, and the brightness of her rising. Ethiopia will awake and rise from the dust, and look abroad on the day and stretch forth her hand to God. The light will spread and kindle and brighten till ALL THE FIFTY MILLIONS of Africa are brought to the glorious liberty of the sons of God." *Address to the Kentucky Col. Society by Mr. Breckenridge.*

"They (the emigrants) go to unchain MILLIONS of slaves fettered in the bondage of death." *Afr. Rep.*, IX, 198.

"Like the star in the East, which announced the Saviour to the astonished Magi, it (the Society) points to the advent of the same Redeemer, coming in the power of his Spirit to roll away the darkness of a thousand generations." *Speech of Mr. Frelinghuysen, Vice President.*

"This Society proposes to add another regenerated CONTINENT to our globe, and ONE HUNDRED AND FIFTY MILLIONS to the family of civilized man." *Speech of Elliot Cresson before the Society. African Rep.*, IX, 360.

The number of agents to be employed, are proportioned to the mighty work to be achieved.

"The Society proposes to send out not *one* or *two* pious members of Christianity into a foreign land, but to transport annually, for an indefinite number of years in one view of its scheme, 6,000, in another 56,000 missionaries of the descendants of Africa itself, to communicate the benefits of our religion and the arts." *Mr. Clay's Speech before Kentucky Col. Society. Afr. Rep.*, VI, 24.

It will be observed that these missionaries are to communicate the benefits of both *religion* and the *arts*, and they are to be taken from two classes. The 6,000 are to be the annual increase of the free negroes; the 56,000 are to be manumitted slaves. The character of the first class is thus given by Mr. Clay, in the *same* speech in which he proposes their employment:

"Of all descriptions of our population, and *of either* portion of the African race, the free people of color are by far, as a class, the most corrupt, depraved, and abandoned."

As this seems rather an unpromising character for teachers of religion, we presume this portion are to be confined to instruction in the *arts;* and that the explanation of religious mysteries, and the inculcation of moral duties, are to be entrusted to the 56,000 just released from bondage. Of the peculiar opportunities afforded them by the laws of the slave States, for fitting themselves for their new vocation, we may speak hereafter. Of this "great company of preachers," about three thousand have already set up their tabernacle at Liberia. We might naturally suppose, that a colony of *missionaries* would be "a holy city," a sort of New Jerusalem, and such we are assured it is. We have heard of "the *poetry* of philanthropy," as applied to the sympathy expressed by abolitionists for the sufferings of the slaves; the following extracts prove that there is a poetry of colonization which

"Can give to airy nothing
A local habitation and a name."

"It (the colony) is already to the African tribes like a city set upon a hill, which cannot be hid. *A thousand barbarians*, who have long made merchandise of their brethren, and been regarded themselves as the objects of a bloody and accursed traffic, come within its gates, *and are taught the doctrine of immortality,—the religion of the Son of God.*" 8*th Report*, p. 14.—1825.

Here we have a solemn and official annunciation by the Board of Managers, of one of the most extraordinary facts ever recorded in the annals of missionary exertions. It appears from official documents, that at the date of this report, the whole number of emigrants *could not* have been more than 242, and had probably been reduced by death below that number; and of this number, a large portion were, of course, women and children. Yet this little band of Christian missionaries, just escaped from the ignorance and vice in which they had been enveloped in America, and still struggling for existence in a sickly climate, and amid all the hardships and privations of a recent settlement in a savage land; casting aside the fear of man, and with a faith almost miraculous in divine protection, admit within their gates an army of barbarians, four times the number of the whole of their little community,—barbarians too, who had long been engaged in a bloody and accursed traffic, making merchandise of their brethren; and these barbarians, suddenly divested of their savage character, sit humbly at the feet of the newly-arrived messengers of Heaven, and the natives of *Africa* receive instruction in the doctrine of immortality and the religion of the Son of God, from lips that had never uttered any other language than broken English! It is singular that in the subsequent documents of the Society, we hear nothing farther of these thousand barbarians. How many became converts to the religion in which they were instructed; how long their attendance on the missionaries were continued, and why it was afterwards totally suspended, are points on which no information has been vouchsafed to us.

It is natural we should wish to know more of these wonderful teachers, and fortunately we are presented with the following picture of them by an eye-witness.

"The holy Author of our religion and salvation has made the hearts of a large proportion of these people, the temples of the Divine Spirit. I have seen the proudest and profanest foreigners that ever visited the colony, trembling with amazement and conviction, almost literally in the descriptive phraseology of St. Paul, find the secrets of their hearts made manifest, and falling down upon their faces, worship God, and report that God is in the midst of these people of a truth." *Ashmun's letter*, 31*st December*, 1825. *Afr. Rep.*, II, 90.

We should certainly conclude from these accounts, that these holy men were blessed with

> "Composed desires, affections ever even,
> Tears that delight, and sighs that waft to Heaven."

Yet strange to tell, we are presented with the following perplexing statement, by the same eye-witness:

"About twelve months since it (the colony) had entirely given way, as the committee are but too well apprised, to a blind and furious excitement of the worst passions, caused by a somewhat unfortunate policy operating on *ignorance and invincible prejudice.* During my absence for health, the people were obliged to taste some of the bitter fruits of *anarchy*, and by the singular mercy of God, only escaped those *tragedies of blood*, which can find no modern parallel but in the history of the civil murders and devastations of St. Domingo." *Ashmun's letter*, 15*th January*, 1825. *Afr. Rep.*, I, 23.

The excitement here alluded to, and its unhappy consequences, occurred, it will be seen by a comparison of dates, in 1824; and that wonderful moral change, which rendered the hearts of a large proportion of these people the temples of the Divine Spirit, must have been effected in 1825. Yet it was in the *beginning* of 1825, that the managers announced at their annual meeting at Washington, the marvellous fact of the instruction of the thousand barbarians within the gates of the colony, a fact which of course must have happened several months previous to the date of the report, and consequently during or about the time of the "furious excitement!"

In March, 1825, the editor of the African Repository gives us the following delightful intelligence:

"The eye of the stranger is struck with the religious aspect of the settlement. He beholds on Cape Montserado, standing in lonely beauty, a Christian village. There flourish the virtues of the gospel, defended by the Almighty from the influences of paganism, cherished and refreshed by the dews of his grace." *Afr. Rep.*, I, 5.

The secret of this surprising exhibition of Christian loveliness and purity, is thus explained:

"It is well known that this little community is made up of SELECTED INDIVIDUALS, and that the Board have *ever* required of those seeking their patronage, satisfactory evidence that their *morals were pure and their habits industrious. Hence* this settlement has from its origin exhibited great decency and sobriety, respect for the Sabbath, and the other peculiar duties and ordinances of our religion. It has thus shed a benign and sacred light upon the heathen, and the feelings of the profane and lawless stranger as he treads upon Cape Montserado, are subdued into unwonted seriousness." *Afr. Rep.*, IX, p. 19, 1826.

But again we are perplexed by the assertion of the Governor of the colony.

"For at least two years to come, *a much more discriminating selection of settlers must be made than* EVER HAS BEEN—even in the first and second expeditions by the Elizabeth and Nautilus in 1820 and 1822—or the prosperity of the colony will inevitably and rapidly decline." *Ashmun's Letter, 3d of March*, 1828. *Afr. Rep.*, IV, 86.

In the 11th Report the managers assure us:

"No village perhaps, in our own land, exhibits less which is offensive, and more that is gratifying to the eye of the Christian, than the village of Monrovia. Crimes are almost unknown, and the universal respect manifested for the Sabbath, and the various institutions and duties of Christianity, have *struck the natives with surprise*, and excited the admiration of foreigners." *Afr. Rep.*, XI, p. 14, 1828.

But how are we to reconcile this with the following statements?

"Permit me to say, sir, there must be *a great revolution* in this colony, before it can have a salutary influence on the surrounding natives; that is, before it can have a *moral* influence over them." *Letter from Rev. G. M. Erskine, 3d of April*, 1830. *Afr. Rep.*, VI, 121.

"We stand in much need of a work-house and some acres of land enclosed, for confining licentious females, and other disorderly and lazy persons." *Letter from A. D. Williams, Agent, 10th of Sept.*, 1830. *Afr. Rep.*, VI, 275.

"There are several enterprising merchants here. It is not, however, a favorable spot for small storekeepers and wandering pedlars, who, I am told, generally become stripped of what they may have got, and in wandering about in the interior for small traffic, *disgust the natives by their immoralities.*" *Letter from Lieut. Page to Sec. of Navy, 9th of April*, 1832. *Afr. Rep.*, VIII, 141.

"With respect tc the character of the people composing this expedition, I regret to be compelled to state, that they are, with the exception of the Pages from Virginia, and a few others, the *lowest and most abandoned of their class.* Our respectable colonists themselves are becoming alarmed at the *great number* of ignorant and *abandoned* characters that have arrived here within the last twelve months." *Letter from Dr. Mechlin, Agent, Sept.*, 1832. *Afr. Rep.*, VIII, 298.

"Let them (the friends of the Society in America) know, that to extend knowledge and promote sound piety, a quire of paper is at the present moment of more worth than a Bible. Bibles and tracts have been sent here, and either *used as waste paper*, or made food for worms. Why? Not because the people despise either, but because we have not a *reading* population. Until this is secured, *Bibles would be of more value in China.*" *Letter from J. B. Pinney, Agent, 7th of March*, 1834.

On the 17th of June, 1833, Mr. Gurley, Secretary of the Society, in a speech at a colonization meeting in New York, hazarded the following most extraordinary assertion,—"TEN THOUSAND NATIVES had placed themselves under the protection of the colony, *receiving from it instruction in civilization.*"

The Society, at its annual meeting on the 20th of January, 1834, unanimously

"Resolved, that this Society *is* cheered in its enterprise by the beneficent effects which its operations *have* upon the natives of Africa itself." *Afr. Rep.*, IX, 360.

On the 20th of February, 1834, the Rev. Mr. Pinney, Agent at Liberia, thus writes from the colony:

"The colonists are very ignorant of everything about the *interior.* Except the tribes along the coast, nothing at all is known, and *of them*, little but their manner of traffic. *Nothing has been done for the natives* hitherto *by the colonists*, except to educate a few who were in their families in the capacity of *servants.*"

Mr. Pinney appears not to have been acquainted with the fact, that "a thousand barbarians" had been taught the doctrine of immortality within the gates of the colony, or that "ten thousand natives" had received instruction in civilization!

Had any missionary society been guilty of such extravagant anticipations and such gross and palpable contradictions, the whole community would have joined in loading it with ridicule and odium.

It is deeply to be regretted that some distinguished colonizationists have of late attempted to lead the public to hope that in *future* no emigrants but such as are of good *moral character* will be permitted to go to Liberia. It is difficult to reconcile such an attempt with moràl rectitude, unless it be accompanied with a total and avowed abandonment of colonization as a means of relieving the country from the nuisance of a free colored population, and from the guilt and curse of slavery. Of the gross inconsistency, (not to use a harsher term,) of colonizationists on this subject, the proceedings of a colonization meeting in Cincinnati, October 31st, 1834, afford a striking example. On motion of the Rev. Dr. Beecher, the following resolution was unanimously adopted:

"Resolved, that the establishment of colonies in Africa by the *selection* of colored persons who are *moral*, *industrious*, and *temperate*, is eminently calculated of itself to advance the cause of civilization and religion among the benighted native population of that continent; as well as to afford facilities to the various missionary societies for the prosecution of their pious designs."

This resolution would be utterly without point or meaning, were it not laudatory of the plans of the Colonization Society; and no person of common intelligence would conjecture from the resolution, that the "selection" mentioned in it was utterly at variance with, and directly opposed to, the avowed *objects* of the Society. Slavery in our country cannot be abolished by colonization, without removing more than two millions of slaves; and how is it possible to remove this number, and yet select for colonists only "the moral, industrious, and temperate?" Nevertheless, the meeting

"Resolved, that the friends of humanity and the friends of God should cherish the Colonization Society, because of its influence TO ABOLISH SLAVERY, and advance the best interests of the African race."

Pages might be quoted to show that the professed ultimate object of the Society, is to remove the *whole* colored population to Africa, without any *selection* whatever. In 1824, a Committee of the Board, in an official report, declared that the national interest

"Required that the *whole mass* of free persons of color, and those who may become such with the consent of their owners, should be progressively removed from us as fast as their own consent can be obtained, and as the means can be found for their removal and for their proper establishment in Africa." *Afr. Rep.*, VII, p. 113.

"But the Colonization Society hopes for, and aims at much more—the abolition of slavery, and the removal of ALL the black people from the United States." *Proceedings of New York Col. Soc.*, 2*d Anniversary.*

We have remarked that EXPEDIENCY is unhappily the governing principle of the Society, and to this principle must be attributed the recent *talk* about *select* emigrants.

Funds are low, and temperance is popular, and all at once we hear that the colonies in Liberia are to be temperance colonies; and that the emigrants are to be "moral, industrious, and temperate." And so we are to send the good negroes away, and keep the bad at home. And yet, by transporting the few moral, industrious and temperate individuals that can be selected in a vicious and ignorant population of between two or three millions, we are to abolish slavery! Surely colonizationists, by holding such language, pay but a poor compliment to their own candor, or the common sense of the community. The truth is, there never has been, and never will be, a selection made.* The two *last* cargoes sent by the Society, were, by the public confession of Mr. Breckenridge, "two cargoes of vagabonds."

* Since the first edition of this work, a public meeting has been held, (17th March,) in New Orleans, preparatory to the departure of some manumitted slaves to Africa. At this meeting, the intended emigrants were arrayed before the audience, and the agent of the American Colonization Society informed them that the Society was "unalterably determined to send to the colony none but such as are willing to pledge themselves to total abstinence from ardent spirits." He also announced that one negro had been rejected as an emigrant "on account of his habits of intoxication." A pledge was then read to the negroes, and they were ordered to signify their assent by rising, which they accordingly did. See *New York Journal of Commerce*, 1*st of April*, 1835.

This New Orleans *scene* will afford no gratification to the friends of temperance; nor will it permanently advance the cause of colonization. In a population universally addicted to intoxication, ONE is selected as a public example of the abhorrence of the Society to drunkenness, and is shut out from the promised land, not for refusing to take the pledge, but on account of his intemperate habits; while his companions are required to promise total abstinence, under the penalty of spending *their lives in bondage.*

If the Society wishes to promote temperance, instead of extorting pledges from miserable slaves, let them exercise the power they possess of excluding all intoxicating liquors from their colony.

Will it be pretended that all the coercion exerted to induce the blacks to emigrate, operates only on the good? or that it is the drunken and profligate who find favor in the eyes of colonizationists, and are permitted to remain in peace and quietness at home?

The Society itself has borne abundant testimony to the depravity of the free blacks, and its friends, with scarcely an exception, zealously maintain that the slaves are unfit for freedom; and yet, as we have seen, it is proposed to transport them all to Africa. And now we would ask, on what principle of common sense, on what record of experience does the Society expect that a population, which, in a land of Bibles and churches, is sunk in vice and ignorance, will, when landed on the shores of Africa, and immersed in all the darkness of paganism, become on a sudden a Christian society, and employed in teaching thousands of barbarians "the doctrine of immortality, the religion of the Son of God!"

Pious colonizationists would themselves be shocked at the proposal of disgorging on the islands of the Pacific the tenants of our prisons, under the pretext of instructing the natives in "religion and the arts;" and yet they flatter themselves that emigrants, who, by their own showing, are less intelligent, and scarcely less guilty than our prisoners, will, by undergoing a salt water baptism, land in Africa wholly regenerated, and qualified, as heralds of the cross, to convert millions and millions to the faith of the Gospel. So monstrous an absurdity can be the offspring only of a deep and sinful prejudice. Hatred to the blacks can alone delude us into the belief that in banishing them from our soil, we are doing God service. Were it not for this hatred, we should feel and acknowledge, that Christianity must be propagated in Africa, as elsewhere, by faithful and enlightened missionaries. If the climate or other circumstances require that such missionaries be of African descent, it is our duty to educate them before we send them. But, alas, instead of educating negroes, we wish to keep them in ignorance, and yet pretend that our *nuisances* will, in Africa, be converted into blessings. But if colonizationists are so perverse as to believe that a bitter fountain will send forth sweet waters, let them contemplate the following picture of Sierra Leone, drawn by a devoted friend to the Society:

"Including the suburbs of the town, (Free Town,) there are some six or eight thousand inhabitants, about eighty of whom are white. The morals of Free Town are *fearfully bad.* As in colonies, too generally where the restraints of home, of friends, of those we love, and those we fear, are broken off, licentiousness prevails to a most lamentable degree. The abomination is not committed under the cover of midnight, nor am I speaking of the natives whose early habits might plead some apology for them; it is done at noonday, and to use a figure, the throne as well the footstool has participated in the evil; and the evil, I am told, is increasing. Sanctioned as it is by those who take the lead in the Society, and who ought to form the morals of the colony, avarice has been added to lust, and those who otherwise might have been virtuous, have sold themselves to work wickedness. Humanity and philanthropy, which have struggled so hard and so long to help this degraded country, must weep and cover itself with sackcloth, to see its best interests so wickedly perverted." *Letter from Rev. M. B. Cox, Methodist Missionary in Liberia. Afr. Rep.*, IX, p. 209.

There is still an important consideration which does not seem to have engaged the attention of colonizationists. It is proposed to transport to Africa, our whole colored population, and of course to found a mighty nation in Liberia. But how long will this nation remain dependent on the Board of Managers at Washington? Instead of millions, suppose the colony to be only ten thousand strong. Who is to govern it, who defend it, and fight its battles? Were the colony now to declare independence, how would the Society reduce it to subjection; and if not subjected, what becomes of the mighty plan of making it the receptacle of our slaves and free negroes? Suppose the colonists, like their brethren of Sierra Leone, engage in the slave-trade, who is to punish or control them? Suppose in time they find the influx of emigrants inconvenient, and refuse to admit them, who shall coerce them?

On the whole, the system of African colonization is full of absurdities, and contradictions, and evils, which are not seen because they are concealed by a veil of prejudice. It is a system which strikingly exposes the folly of human wisdom, when opposed to the precepts of the Gospel of Christ. Had America possessed that fear of the Lord which is the beginning of true wisdom, slavery would long since have ceased from among us, and our colored brethren, treated with Christian kindness, instead of being ignorant and degraded, would have been valued and useful citizens; and our churches, instead of uniting to send "cargoes of vagabonds" to Africa, under the guise of Christian missionaries, would have aided the descendants of her sons, furnished by us with all the stores of human learning, and selected for their piety and zeal, in proclaiming the glad tidings of salvation throughout that benighted continent.

CHAPTER V.

INFLUENCE OF THE SOCIETY ON SLAVERY.

In 1822, a committee was appointed by a public meeting in Boston, to report on the character and tendency of the American Colonization Society. The committee, in their report, remark:

> "It is only from the belief which the committee very cordially entertain that the active members of the American Colonization Society are perfectly disposed to frame their measures with reference to the entire suppression of the slave-trade, and to a gradual and prudent, but COMPLETE EMANCIPATION of those now held in slavery, that we can regard the Society as having any claim upon the sympathy or assistance of the people of New England."

Such were the expectations by which Northern philanthropists were at first induced to countenance the Society. There is scarcely to be found a colonization article or speech that does not warrant these expectations, that does not promise the exertion by the Society of a mighty MORAL INFLUENCE in abolishing slavery.

Now it is obvious that such an influence must operate in one or more of the following ways, viz.:

1. On the *conscience* of the slave-holder, convincing him that slave-holding is sinful, and that his Maker requires him to liberate his slaves.

2. On the *reputation* of the slave-holder, making him feel that his standing in the community is lowered by keeping his fellow-men in bondage, and enjoying, without compensation, the fruits of their labor.

3. On the *interests* of the slave-holder, persuading him that emancipation would enhance his property.

4. On the *fears* of the slave-holder, alarming him for the safety of himself and family.

5. By the power of *example*, showing the slave-holder, by the conduct of others whom he esteems, what his own ought to be.

We flatter ourselves that we shall prove that the influence of the Society is in no *degree* exerted in any one of these ways, except the last. Of the *extent* of this last mode, we shall speak hereafter.

It will not be pretended that the Society addresses itself to the *conscience* of the slave-holder. Such addresses are not authorized by the constitution, and have been repeatedly disclaimed by the Society. But when the Society disclaims appeals to the conscience, it disclaims the most powerful of all means for the removal of slavery.

"We never made any headway," says a British writer, "in the abolition of the slave-trade, and of slavery, till it was taken up by the religious men, prosecuted as a concern of the soul, with reference to eternity, and by motives drawn from the cross of Christ."

Mr. G. Smith, a most estimable officer of the Society, remarked, in a temperance address: "I never heard that temperance had any success any where, unless the appeals in its favor were made directly to the *consciences* of the rum-dealers. Strike out these, and it is in vain that you seek for other means to propel the triumphant car of temperance. Hitch to that car, health, economy, expediency, the public good, what you please, if you leave out the appeal to men's consciences, you have, as we say at the North, a *weak team*." And surely a more weak, broken-winded, good-for-nothing team, than colonization, was never hitched to the car of abolition. How, and in *what direction*, does this team draw? It is amusing to observe how wary colonizationists are of approaching this question. They dwell on the political evils of slavery, and call on religion and patriotism for aid in removing them; and when, in breathless attention, we are waiting to learn by *what process* the moral influence of the Society is to deliver us from the curse of slavery, in a moment the scene shifts to Africa, and we are entertained with visions of its future bliss and glory. It may be safely asserted, that not one colonization writer or orator in a hundred, ever attempts to explain how the Society is to induce masters to liberate their slaves. Occasionally, however, the effort is made. Mr. Knapp, in a speech before the Society, thus explains the matter:

> "In my opinion, it (slavery) may be cured in *less* time than it has been growing up. Open once the facilities of emigration — show an object for it, and, like any other business, it will increase to any extent we may wish. The natural world has yielded her impossibilities, as they were thought, to the efforts of enlightened men; why should we not be as successful in the moral? A fair and permanent road is now built over the Alps, the passage of which was once considered as sufficient to give immortality to the successful adventurer." 10*th Rep.*, p. 6.

So, it seems, that if we open once the facilities of emigration, that is, provide ships, &c., the planters will at once call in their slaves from their cotton and sugar fields, and ship them to Africa; but *why* they will do so, is a problem, which, after all, Mr. Knapp omits to solve.

> "This work, (colonization,) as it advances, tends to improve the character, and elevate the condition of the free people of color, and thus to take away one standing and very influential argument against both individual and general abolition. This, to an unprejudiced mind, is one of the most obvious tendencies of African colonization. Elevate the character of the free people of color; let it be seen that they are men indeed; let the degrading associations which follow them be broken up by the actual improvement of their character as a people, and negro slavery must wither and die." *New Haven Christian Spectator for March*, 1833.

As the Society utterly disclaims all attempts to elevate the free blacks *here*, the meaning of the above is, that when the slave-holder in America learns that black men in Liberia are intelligent and respectable, he will release his slaves from their fetters. We wonder if similar intelligence from the West Indies will produce the same effect; if so, it may be obtained at far less expense of time and money, than from Africa.

Let us now attend to the process by which an excellent vice president of the Society supposes slavery is to be abolished.

"Let Africa *begin* to enter upon the redemption of her character, which guilty Christian nations have for centuries combined to keep down to the lowest point of degradation, and she will begin to be respected, and the condition of her outcast children on our shores, will awaken a livelier sympathy. And when Africa shall have put on the garment of civilization, and the influence of her regeneration shall be *felt throughout this land*, our most tenacious and obstinate slave-holder will shrink from the relation he bears to her children. The poor creature whom he formerly regarded as a few removes above the brute, will now present himself before the new associations of his master's mind, as his fellow-man and his equal, and the slave will be permitted to go free." *Speech of G. Smith, Esq.*, 14*th Rep.*, p. 11.

It would seem, that at the close of the fourteenth year of the Society's labors, Africa had not yet, in the opinion of Mr. Smith, *begun* to enter upon the redemption of her character. How soon a *beginning* is to be made, and in how many years, or centuries, the Society expects to complete the work of dressing Africa in the garment of civilization, we are not informed. But when this work shall have been finished, and when it shall have produced a general sensation (how strong and of what kind we know not) throughout America, THEN the motions of the sugar-mill and cotton-gin are to be arrested, and the fetters are to fall from the slave. Why? Because the commands of God, and the interests and safety of the master, require it? No; but because the master will *then* make the discovery, that his poor slave, but little removed as he is from the brute, is still his fellow-man and his equal! This is certainly a most marvellous process for teaching the Southern planters a plain, simple truth; a truth, too, which was proclaimed by their own representatives, so long ago as 1776, in the Declaration of Independence, but which unfortunately seems not to have had the influence which Mr. Smith supposes it will exert, when taught by the regeneration of

We may now judge a little of the elements of that moral influence which a Christian Society exerts against slavery. Conscience and the word of God, death, judgment, and eternity, enter not into its composition.

"The Society," declares one of its vice presidents, "tends, and may powerfully tend, to rid us *gradually* and entirely in the United States, of slaves and slavery." *R. G. Harper.* See 14*th Rep.*, p. 23.

Let us now see *how gradually* this riddance is to be effected.

"We have never supposed that the Society's plan could be accomplished in a few years; but, on the contrary, have *boasted* that it will demand a CENTURY for its fulfilment." *Mr. Fitzhugh, Vice President. Afr. Rep.*, IV, p. 344.

It may seem singular that philanthropists should exult in the conviction that their plan for doing good would require a century for its fulfilment; but the benevolence of the "colonization system" is peculiar.

"There are those, sir, who ask, 'And could not a quarter of a century cease and determine these two great evils,' (free blacks and slaves?) You and I, my dear sir, on whom the frost of time has fallen rather perceptibly, would say a CENTURY." *Speech of Mr. Custiss.* 13*th Rep.*, p. viii.

"The sudden abolition of slavery in a community where it existed to any considerable extent, would be *pernicious.* But this is danger which can occasion *no alarm*, admitting that the colonization scheme contemplates the ultimate abolition of slavery, yet that result could *only* be produced by the slow and gradual operation of CENTURIES." *Afr. Rep.*, I, p. 217.

"It is not expected to remove so great an evil as two millions of slaves suddenly: *if* it can be accomplished in a CENTURY, it will be as much as the most sanguine of our friends ought to expect." *Judge Best's Address to the Indiana Col. Soc. Afr. Rep.*, IX, p. 71.

"It is not the work of a day, nor a year; it is not the work of one time, nor of two; but it is one which will now commence, and may continue for AGES." *View of Slavery, by Humanitas, a Colonization advocate. Baltimore*, 1822.

Thus we see that the continuance of slavery, with all its licentiousness, ignorance, and suffering, for at least a century to come, is calmly contemplated by zealous and distinguished colonizationists. But still the Society expects ultimately to abolish slavery. Let us therefore inquire what it must effect to fulfil this expectation.

The increase of our slave population, from the census of 1820 to that of 1830, was 472,568. Estimating the future increase at the same ratio, it will be for the ten years ending in 1840, 617,263; and for the ten years ending in 1850, 806,762. The *annual* increase is *now* upwards of 54,000, and the *daily* excess of births over deaths, 147. In 1850, it will be 80,676 annually, and 221 daily!

From this statement it will be perceived what must be the power of the "moral influence" of the Society to remove to Africa merely the *annual increase* of our slave population; and hence we may judge of its ability to deliver the country from slavery. In forming an opinion on this subject, we shall be further aided by inquiring what advantages the Society has enjoyed, and what have been the results of its labors.

Never has any voluntary association received in an equal degree the applause and patronage of both state and church. Men of all parties, and of all religions, and of no religion, have zealously espoused its cause. On the roll of its officers, are emblazoned the names of the most popular leaders of rival political parties. The Legislatures of fourteen States have passed resolutions in its favor. The highest ecclesiastical judicatories, of almost every religious denomination, have recommended it to the patronage of their churches. Politicians have declaimed, ministers have preached, and Christians have prayed in its behalf. To promote its objects, liberal contributions have been made from the coffers of the nation, and the pockets of individuals. Under color of providing for the removal to Africa, of about three hundred recaptured negroes, the general government appropriated 130,000 dollars, which were "applied to an object affiliated to our design, and essentially, though collaterally, contributing to its advancement; the sending out of agents of the United States to the African coast, and the transportation of persons in the public ships. By these means *we* have obtained, in fact, *all* we could have expected to gain, had Congress decided to aid our enterprise." *Speech of Gen. Harper, 7th Rep.*, p. 12.

Since 1820, $220,449 have been poured into the treasury. If to this be added $45,645, the debt due by the Society at the beginning of 1834, we have a total of $266,094 expended, independent of the $130,000 paid by government. Such have been the pecuniary means of the Society; and now let us see how far its "moral influence" has progressed in freeing the country of its millions of slaves. Since December, 1816, when the Society was organized, to the present time (1st of January, 1835,) it has transported *eight hundred and nine* manumitted slaves to Africa — equal to the increase of the slave population for *five and a half days!* But it will be said that some years elapsed before the Society was in a capacity to transport emigrants. Be it so; let us inquire, then, how many manumitted slaves have been sent out the last *five* years. In 1830–'33, six hundred and sixty-six were transported; in 1834, *none*,* making a removal on an average, *of less than the increase of one day in each year!* In the eighteenth year of the Society's existence, it finds itself compelled to pause and rest, after the mighty effort of arresting the increase of the slave population for FIVE DAYS AND A HALF.

Such are the results of the *moral influence* about which we have heard so much. And upon *whom* has this influence operated? Surely upon those who were most within its sphere, the presidents, vice presidents, and managers of the Society. Unfortunately, facts do not confirm this very natural supposition. Judge Washington was President of the Society, from its first organization, till his death in 1829. In a letter to the Society, he observed: "We may fairly hope it will lead to the sure but gradual abolition of slavery." *Afr. Rep.*, VII, p. 20.

Whatever were the *hopes* of this gentleman, he was personally beyond the reach of the Society's moral influence. In a published letter in 1821, after stating that his slaves had got the idea that as nephew to General Washington, or President of the Colonization Society, he could not hold them in bondage, he adds, "I called the negroes together in March last, and after stating to them what I had heard, I assured them that I had no intention to give freedom to any of them."

* In 1834, the Philadelphia Society sent out one hundred and ten slaves, manumitted by the will of their master, who also left two thousand two hundred dollars for their transportation. The Society, at the same time, gave a passage to fourteen emigrants for the Parent Institution, free of expense.

The judge was as good as his word. He did indeed shortly after part with *fifty-four* of his slaves, but it was not to the agent of the Society, to be transported to Liberia, but to a slave-dealer, to be shipped to New Orleans. Mr. Carroll, a large slave-holder, succeeded to the presidential chair, but for aught that appears to the contrary, neither he nor Mr. Madison, the present incumbent, ever liberated a single slave. Mr. Clay, a vice president, publicly intimated that *he* did not intend to send his slaves to Africa. Mr. Fitzhugh, another vice president, the proprietor of "numerous slaves," speaking of slavery, remarked: "No plea can be urged in justification of its continuance but the *plea of necessity.*" *Afr. Rep.*, V, p. 354.

The will of this gentleman, who died in 1830, is a singular comment on this plea of necessity. The following extract is given in the African Repository under the head of

PHILANTHROPIC EXAMPLE.

"After the year 1850, I leave all my negroes unconditionally free, with the privilege of having the expenses of their removal to whatever places of residence they may select, defrayed. If they consent to go to the Colony, (Liberia,) they are to be paid fifty dollars each on their arrival." *Afr. Rep.*, VI, 247.

It will be perceived that the testator believed in the "necessity" of requiring his slaves to toil for *twenty years* for his heirs, after he himself was in the grave, before they could be permitted to labor for themselves; and also the necessity of leaving the children who might be born of these slaves in the *twenty years*, in interminable bondage, for it will be observed that the prospective manumission is confined to Mr. Fitzhugh's "negroes," and not to the children to be hereafter born. Should this *philanthropic example* be universally followed, in how many centuries would slavery cease?

Mr. Custiss, well known as a zealous advocate of the Society, in a speech before it thus exclaims:

"Lend us your aid to strike the fetters from the slave, and to spread the enjoyment of unfettered freedom over the whole of our favored and happy land." *7th Report*, p. 13.

Had Mr. Custiss applied to the Board for a passage for his slaves to Liberia, the boon would unquestionably have been granted. But such a boon was not the aid *he* desired. In the New York Commercial Advertiser of January 31, 1829, it is stated that Philip Lee, the son of General Washington's favorite servant, is the slave of Mr. Custiss, the adopted son of Washington: that Philip is a pious, faithful, and in all respects an exemplary man, and has a wife and children, to whom he is tenderly attached; and that $1,000 are required to deliver Philip and his family from slavery. "Much interest has been excited in the District of Columbia, where it is supposed one half of the sum required will be raised." The paper farther states, that $121 had been subscribed in New York.

In the appendix at the 15th Report, p. 41, is a list of persons who have manumitted slaves to be sent to Liberia. The list does not profess to give all, but contains fifteen names, and it is remarkable that the name of any one present or former officer of the American Colonization Society is not to be found among them, with the exception of Mr. Fitzhugh, who is included, on account of his testamentary devise.

We will not assert that no officer of the Society has ever parted with a slave that he might go to the Colony: but we do say, that although our acquaintance with colonization documents is not superficial, we have met with no record of such a "philanthropic example."

If such be the impotency of the moral influence of the Society upon its officers, its orators and advocates, what will be its power on slave-holders generally?

But let us suppose, what we all know to be untrue, that *every* slave-holder in our country is in very deed anxious to get rid of his slaves, and that the whole slave population is now and will continue to be at the disposal of the Society, and we ask, *can* this population be transported to Africa, and there maintained? We have seen that before *any* impression can be made on its present amount, its *increase*, rising to more than fifty-four thousand annually, must be removed. But it is surely not to be removed, merely to perish by famine in the wilderness. In the ordinary calculations of the expense of carrying these people to Africa, they seem to be considered only as articles of freight, which are to be delivered at Liberia at so much per piece. Thirty dollars are usually assumed as the cost of a passage; but let it be recollected that after they arrive, houses, implements of husbandry, food and clothing for at least one *year* must be provided for them. It is with difficulty a new colony can provide for its own maintenance, and it is folly to suppose that it can also provide for an annual influx of fifty thousand emigrants, emigrants too, sunk in brutal ignorance, unaccustomed to supply their own wants, and bringing with them nothing but the rags on their backs. Place fifty thousand such persons in the wilds of Africa, and they would be far more likely to starve before the end of a year, than they would be at that time to furnish the necessaries of life to fifty thousand more emigrants. The Colony is now poor, and has only about three thousand inhabitants, and it is admitted (see 15th Rep., p. 10,) that an addition of one thousand emigrants in any one year since its establishment would have been fatal to it. How many years then must elapse, before it can receive fifty-four thousand *every year?* and when that period arrives, *what* will *then* be the annual increase? Admitting the whole marine and the whole treasury of the United States to be surrendered to the Society, does any sane man believe that Liberia can be brought to such a state of cultivation as to maintain an *annual* accession to her population of fifty-four thousand in less than twenty-five years? But in the year 1860 the annual *increase* of slaves, instead of fifty-four thousand, will be one hundred and four thousand; and unless the Society will then be able to transport *more* than this mighty multitude, each year, it will not even diminish the present amount of the slave population!

In supposing the slave-holders ready to colonize their slaves, we have given full effect to the reiterated assertions of colonizationists on this subject. These gentlemen are fond of representing the Southern masters as unfortunately burthened with a grievous load, which they are impatient to shake off; and from which no other human agency than the Society can possibly relieve them. Granting the premises, we see what sort of relief the Society is capable of affording. We have intentionally removed one difficulty, that we might consider another. Let us now reverse the supposition, and admitting the ability of the Society *immediately* to transport to Africa, and there maintain all the slaves in the United States, let us inquire *how* the consent of the masters is to be obtained.

Let it be remembered that the Society has studiously avoided every measure to obtain such consent, and boasts that it *addresses arguments to no master*. But if we are to believe colonizationists, no arguments are necessary to induce the masters to liberate their slaves. Our sympathy is perpetually demanded, not for the slave, but his *unfortunate* master, who is imploring the Society to deliver him from the curse entailed upon him by his ancestors! So far from slave-holders wishing to abolish slavery, they are endeavoring to transmit it as a precious inheritance to their latest posterity. As we have already observed, we do not solicit the reader's belief, in *any* assertion we may make, until we have demonstrated its truth; and we assert that there is a *general* disposition among slave-holders, to perpetuate slavery. We know, and cheerfully acknowledge, that there are exceptions, but we believe they are exceedingly rare. The whole tendency of slave legislation is to rivet the chains of its victims. Hence the cruel obstacles it raises to manumission, and the wicked efforts it makes to brutalize the human mind. But not contented with holding their own slaves with an iron grasp, they have striven, and with woful success, to extend the curse beyond their own borders. When Missouri was to be admitted into the Union, every slave representative in Congress, without one solitary exception, colonizationist or not, voted to render it a *slave State*. So anxious was Virginia to strengthen the slave interest, that rebellion and civil war were the price she was willing to pay for another mart in human flesh. Her House of Delegates

"Resolved, that the General Assembly of Virginia will support the good people of Missouri in their just rights, and admission into the Union, and will coöperate with them in RESISTING WITH MANLY

FORTITUDE any attempt which Congress may make to impose restraints or restrictions on the price of their admission, not authorized by the great principles of the Constitution, and in violation of their rights, liberty, and HAPPINESS!"

General Charles C. Pinckney, of South Carolina, in a public address, delivered in 1824, maintained that slavery, as it exists in that State, is

"No greater or more unusual evil than befalls the poor in general; that its extinction would be attended with calamity to the country, and to the people connected with it, in every character and relation; that no necessity exists for *such extinction;* that slavery is sanctioned by the Mosaic dispensation; that it is a fulfilment of the denunciation pronounced against the second son of Noah; that it is not inconsistent with the genius and spirit of Christianity, nor considered by St. Paul as a moral evil." *Address before the Agricultural Society of South Carolina.*

Governor Miller, of South Carolina, in his message to the Legislature in 1829, remarks:

"Slavery is not a national evil; on the contrary, it is a NATIONAL BENEFIT. Slavery exists in some form every where, and it is not of much consequence, in a *philosophical* point of view, whether it be voluntary or involuntary. In a *political* point of view, involuntary slavery has the advantage, since all who enjoy political liberty are then in fact free."

It gives us pleasure to state, that the African Repository pronounces the doctrines of Messrs. Pinckney and Miller "abominable." We have explained in our introduction the tacit compact by which colonizationists are never to defend slavery in the *abstract*, nor condemn it in *particulars.* A scrupulous observance of this compact enabled the Repository to exclaim, with great truth, when accused of hostility to slave-holders,

"Have we sought to render the owners of slaves odious, by retailing anecdotes of their cruelty? Every honorable man will do us the justice to answer no." *Afr. Rep.*, IV, p. 59.

But the question is, not what Mr. Gurley thinks of these doctrines, but how they are regarded by slave-holders. Now there is no evidence that General Pinckney's rank in Carolina society was affected by his "abominable" doctrines; on the contrary, judging from the eulogium pronounced at his decease, he was regarded as one of the most distinguished and *pious* members of the slave-holding community. And so far were the people of Carolina from being offended by the "abominable" doctrines of their governor, that after his term of service expired, they elected him to the Senate of the United States.

Governor Hayne, of the same State, in his message to the Legislature (1833,) labors to prove that slavery adds to the military strength of a nation, and concludes with declaring that

> "The existence of slavery in the South is not only to be regarded as an evil not to be deplored, but that it brings along corresponding advantages, in elevating the character, contributing to the wealth, enlarging the resources, and adding to the strength of the State in which it exists."

It must be confessed, these are strange sentiments to be advanced by the chief magistrates of a people who regard slavery as a curse, and are anxious to colonize their slaves. Let us now attend to the official declarations of the present Governor of South Carolina, and see what comment they afford on the supposed desire of the slave-holders to get rid of their slaves, a supposition on which *the whole theory of abolition by colonization is founded.*

> "It is demonstrable that cotton could not be produced by the labor of *hired* freemen, for *double* the average price it has commanded for ten years past. It is obvious that the *abolition* of that kind of labor which is the *basis of our wealth and prosperity*, would annihilate, at a single blow, that entire branch of foreign commerce which brings the industry of the exporting States into competition with that of the manufacturing States. I am thoroughly convinced that the institution of domestic slavery, paradoxical as it may seem, is *an indispensable element in an unmixed representative republic.* HOW SACRED IS OUR OBLIGATION to provide for our POSTERITY all the necessary means of *defending* and *preserving* an institution as essential to their existence and to their liberty, as it is obnoxious to the *prejudices* of those who have the greatest possible facilities for assailing it." *Inaugural Speech, Dec.*, 1834.

In December last, a lecture on "Domestic Slavery," was delivered before "the Law Class of William and Mary College," and published in the Southern Literary Messenger, for January, 1835. The following introductory passage will help to show the feeling that is cherished at the South:

"This subject, (slavery,) is too interesting to be passed in silence. The time too is rife with proofs, that unless we mean *tamely to surrender* a most important interest, we must hold ourselves always on the alert to DEFEND it with tongue and pen."

A few years since, the State of Louisiana passed a law, prohibiting the importation of slaves from other States, but the extension of the sugar cultivation demanding more labor, the law was repealed in 1833, and this State is now importing multitudes of slaves from Maryland and Virginia. Soon after the repeal of the law, two thousand were offered for sale in New Orleans, in the course of a single week.

We may judge how anxious the people of Louisiana are to send their slaves to Africa, from the following notice of a late sale in New Orleans:

Willis,	18	years old,	brought	$1400
Jack,	29	"	"	1200
Adam,	20	"	"	1300
Tom,	16	"	"	1175
Dick,	30	"	"	1000
Bill,	14	"	"	660
Malinda,	29	"	"	500

A letter from an intelligent gentleman, personally acquainted with the state of slavery at Natchez, says:

"The prospects of the blacks in the South-west, are gloomy in the extreme. Cotton can be afforded at 6 cents per pound; last year, (1832,) it was worth from 9 to 13 cents; this year it is worth from 14 to 18 cents. Last year about 1000 negroes were sold in Natchez, and I am confident 1500 will be disposed of in that market this year. In my opinion, the slaves, if ever free, will owe their liberty to their own strength and the blessing of Heaven; for their masters, as a Methodist minister once expressed it, think only of making more cotton, to buy more negroes, to make more cotton to buy more negroes."

So far are masters from wishing to send their negroes to Africa, that they are continually increasing their stock, and hence slaves are rising in value. A late Georgia paper announces, that at a sale of seventy-one negroes, *of all ages and kinds*, the average price was $438.

A convention has recently been held in Tennessee, for amending the State Constitution, and one *amendment* is, a prohibition to the Legislature to abolish slavery.

The Augusta Chronicle, (Geo.) of Oct., 1833, says:

"We firmly believe, that if the Southern States do not quickly unite and declare to the North, if the question of slavery be longer *discussed* in any shape, they will instantly secede from the Union; that the question must be settled, and very soon, by the SWORD, as the only possible means of self-preservation."

The Richmond Inquirer and the Washington Globe are both mightily indignant at the proposition that Congress should abolish slavery in the District of Columbia.

So far is it from being true, as stated by colonizationists, that the South is ready to surrender its slaves, that every day affords new proofs that the public sentiment both at the North and the South, is now more tolerant to slavery than at any other period during the last thirty years. Who believes that even ten years ago any Connecticut Legislature would have ventured to pass the Black Act? or that Judge Daggett himself would have pronounced his portentous and extraordinary opinion? At what time, before the influence of the Colonization Society was felt throughout our land, did the citizens of the North merit or receive such commendations from the slave press as the following?

"Public sentiment at the North, in reference to *Southern interests*, was never in a *sounder state* than it is now. The language of the Northern press is cheering in the extreme; the feeling in favor of the South, *and against the abolitionists*, is deep and almost universal. *Charleston Courier*, 21*st July*, 1834.

When, until late years, have the Governors of even slave States, dared to promulgate such "abominable" doctrines as those we have quoted?

Unless we greatly deceive ourselves, have now shown that

no desire exists at the South to get rid of slavery, at least to such an extent as to render colonization in the remotest degree instrumental in abolishing it; and it is an unquestioned fact, that in eighteen years only about 900 manumitted slaves have been sent to Africa. But certain laws have been recently passed by Virginia and Maryland, which are triumphantly cited by colonizationists as proofs of the growing desire at the South to abolish slavery,—a desire which is attributed to the influence of the Society.

The law of Virginia appropriates $18,000 a year for five years, for the transportation of colored persons to Africa. Now it is evident that the effect of this law upon slavery in Virginia, must depend on the *class* of colored persons to be transported. Will it be believed that this law, received with such joy and triumph by colonizationists, *confines the application of its appropriation to the removal of such blacks as were free at the date of its passage?* In other words, it declares to the slave-holders, "We will not assist you in manumitting your slaves." By a previous law, any manumitted slave, who does not leave the State in twelve months, becomes again a slave: this *new* law provides that such a manumitted slave shall *not* be sent to Africa,—of course it affords no possible inducement or facility whatever to manumission; and its whole operation is confined to the removal *of nuisances*,—and we have already seen, from the avowal of members of the Legislature, that this removal is virtually to be compulsory. The philanthropy that rejoices in *such* a law, is indeed of a peculiar cast, but it is the philanthropy of "the benevolent colonization system."*

The Maryland law of 1832 appropriates $200,000 to be applied through the agency of the Maryland Colonization Society, to the removal to Africa, of "the people of color now free, and such as shall hereafter become so."

*A party writer, in a late number of the Richmond Enquirer, says: "An opposition man, who stated in the spring, that he considered the removal of the deposits as affecting the value of his property thirty per cent., admits now, that he never saw a more WHOLESOME STATE OF THINGS; negro boys and men will fetch from $600 to $700." Is Virginia sick of this wholesome state of things?

On the 20th of January, 1833, the American Colonization Society

"Resolved, that the Society view with the highest gratification, the continued efforts of the State of Maryland to accomplish her patriotic and BENEVOLENT SYSTEM in regard to her colored population; and that the last appropriation by that State of $200,000 in aid of African Colonization, is hailed by the friends of the system as a BRIGHT EXAMPLE to other States."

Let us now examine this "benevolent system," this "bright example," and see how it accords with *Christian* love and sincerity.

In forming our opinion of the true character of this scheme, it will not be improper to take into consideration the *avowed* motives which gave it birth. The Legislature, in their session of 1831, adopted the following resolutions:

"Resolved, that the increased proportion of the free people of color, in this State, to the white population—the *evils growing out of their connection and unrestrained association with the slaves, their habits and manner of obtaining a subsistence, and their withdrawing* A LARGE PORTION *of employment from the laboring class of the white population*, are subjects of momentous and grave consideration to the good people of this State.

"Resolved, that as philanthropists and lovers of freedom, we deplore the existence of slavery among us, and would use our utmost exertions to ameliorate its condition: yet we consider the unrestricted power of manumission as fraught with ultimate evils, of a more dangerous tendency than the circumstance of slavery alone; and that any act, having for its object the mitigation of these joint evils, not inconsistent with other paramount considerations, would be worthy the attention and deliberation of the representatives of a free, liberal-minded and enlightened people."

Another resolution followed, declaring that, by the colonization of free people of color in Africa, "these evils may be measurably diminished, and a committee was appointed to frame a bill upon "the principles" of these resolutions.

Such, then, are the principles of the Maryland benevolent system; and which of them is derived from the gospel of Christ? So far as the system relates to the free blacks, it proposes their removal, not out of kindness to them, but because they are supposed to be injurious to *slave property;* because *their habits and manner of obtaining a subsistence*, the necessary results of wicked laws, are vicious; and because they enter into competition with *white laborers*. This last accusation against the free blacks, is a most extraordinary one, when made by a people who keep in their employment more than ONE HUNDRED THOUSAND BLACK LABORERS, who toil without wages, and subsist on the scantiest fare; and yet the interference of *these* laborers with "the laboring class of the white population," occasions no uneasiness, and leads to no plan for their removal. And what are the principles of this system with regard to slaves? Why, that it is worse to give a slave his liberty here, than to keep him in bondage; but at the same time, that "the utmost exertions" ought to be made to "ameliorate his condition." Let us now proceed to the practical application of these principles. At the next session, a report was presented, in which calculations are entered into, to show that "the WHOLE of this population (of free blacks) can be removed in the course of one generation alone." But the legislators are philanthropists and lovers of freedom, and deplore the existence of slavery. Let us see how the committee propose to remove this deplored evil. The report says of the slaves, "they are property, and must be so regarded, and without *their owners' consent*, none of them can be touched."

Here we have a principle which secures to Maryland the blessings of slavery *forever*. In no country in the world, in ancient or modern times, has slavery been abolished by the unanimous consent of slave-holders. *Never* has it been peaceably abolished but by law. The Northern and Eastern States could abolish slavery without the consent of the owners: the Republican States of South America could do the same: the Legislature of Maryland can rule fifty thousand of their free colored citizens with a rod of iron, can deny them the most common and inestimable rights of humanity; but it cannot rescue a human being from unmerited and involuntary bondage!

Let us now turn to the famous appropriation act. By this act, masters are allowed to manumit their slaves, but then the manumitted slaves are to be transported beyond the limits of the State; and should a parent or a child, a husband or a wife shudder at parting forever from a near and dear relative, the separation may be avoided by a renunciation, in open court, of the newly acquired liberty, and a public consent to *continue a slave!* Such is the bearing of this benevolent system on *slavery*. Let us now contemplate its effects on the free blacks. The appropriation bill authorizes no compulsion, and imposes no penalties on a refusal to go to Africa. It was not expedient that *this* bill should contain such provisions, and therefore they were inserted in *another* bill passed by the same Legislature, and within two days of the other, entitled, "An act, relating to free negroes and slaves." This act, like the Connecticut Black Act, is a bold and flagrant violation of the constitutional rights of free citizens. A citizen of New York, if his complexion be colored, may not visit a dying child or parent in Maryland, without incurring a penalty of fifty dollars for every week he remains, and if he is unable to pay the fine, why then he is to be *sold by the sheriff at public sale for such time as may be necessary to cover the aforesaid penalty.* But if a free negro is sold for a limited time, he is, in fact, SOLD FOR LIFE. During the term for which he is sold, he is a chattel, and may be transported at the pleasure of his master; and when the expiration of his term finds him in a cotton field in Missouri, or a sugar mill in Louisiana, who is to rescue him from interminable bondage? Should a colored citizen of Maryland cross its boundary on business, ever so urgent to himself and family, on returning to his home, more than a month after, he also is liable to be seized and SOLD, unless previous to his departure he had complied with certain vexatious, legal formalities; and which, from ignorance, he would be extremely likely to neglect, or perform imperfectly.

A striking illustration of this "benevolent system," lately occurred. A free colored man, living near the line of the District of Columbia, petitioned the Maryland House of Delegates for leave to bring his grandchild from the City of Washington. The child had probably been left an orphan, and he naturally wished to take it into his own house. The petition was rejected!

A brisk slave-trade is carried on between Maryland and the

Southern States, and it is well known that free negroes are often the victims of this trade; instances occurring of whole families being kidnapped. Under such circumstances, many would wish to have the means of protecting, if necessary, the freedom of themselves and children; but the new bill forbids them to keep any military weapon, without a special license from a county court, or city corporation; a condition amounting virtually to a total prohibition. No free negro may attend a religious meeting not conducted by a white person.

As the law thus discourages, and in a great measure prohibits religious instruction, exhortation, and social prayer, among fifty thousand of the population of Maryland, no wonder it *presumes* every one of that fifty thousand to be a *thief*. Hence no person may, under the penalty of five dollars, buy of a free negro "any bacon, pork, beef, mutton, corn, wheat, tobacco, rye, or oats," unless he shall at the time exhibit a certificate from a Justice of the Peace, or three respectable persons, that he or they believe the said negro came honestly by the identical article offered for sale.

Such are some of the features of the law, and they are well calculated to induce the free negroes to avail themselves of the benevolent and munificent provision made by the *other* law for their transportation to Africa. The concluding section, however, is the most operative of the whole, and promises to afford ample employment for the two hundred thousand dollars, and to furnish Liberia with an abundant population. It is as follows:

> "Sect. 12. And be it enacted, that if any *free* negro or mulatto shall be convicted of ANY crime, committed after the passage of this act, which may not, under the laws of this State, be punished by hanging by the neck, such free negro or mulatto may, in the discretion of the court, be sentenced to the penalties and punishments now provided by law, or be banished from this State, OR BE TRANSPORTED INTO SOME FOREIGN COUNTRY."

Hence, if a free negro steals a pound of tobacco, he may be shipped off to Liberia. In civilized countries, it has been the aim of the Legislature, to apportion punishments to crimes, but Maryland has set "a bright example" of a simplification of the criminal code, without a parallel in the history of jurisprudence. She tells her judges, "in the case of free black offenders, you need give yourselves no trouble in comparing the different shades of guilt, and weighing those circumstances which aggravate or mitigate the offence. In certain cases, you must hang them; in all others, without exception, you may send them to Africa."

This is the "benevolent system," the "bright example" lauded by the American Colonization Society. This is the system which is cited as a proof that Maryland desires to abolish slavery. A symptom of this desire occurred in the Maryland House of Delegates, in 1834. Mr. Mann moved an inquiry into the expediency of abolishing slavery, *after a certain period.* So great was the excitement produced by this motion, that the mover withdrew it, *and the minute of the motion was expunged from the journal.*

The $200,000, it seems, are entrusted to the Maryland Colonization Society; and that Society, wishing still farther to increase its funds, has appealed to the benevolence of the North. The appeal is founded on two solemn official declarations: first, that it aims at the extirpation of slavery in Maryland, by colonization; and secondly, that it contemplates "founding a nation on the principle of temperance."

We have seen that a committee of the Maryland Legislature insisted on the possibility of the removal of the *whole* free black population in one generation. The Society in their address, repeatedly declare their object to be the extirpation of slavery by colonization; and the Legislature forbids, as we have also seen, manumission at home. Of course, slavery can only be extirpated by the removal, not of a select portion, but of *all* the slaves.

In what terms ought we then to speak of the following resolution of the Maryland Society, published to conciliate the friends of temperance at the North?

"Whereas it is desired that the settlement about to be made by this Society, should, as far as practicable, become a *moral* and temperate community; and as this is to be effected, in a great degree, by the *character* of the emigrants, who leave America for a new home in

Africa: and whereas, the sad experience of this country has shown the demoralizing effects of the use of ardent spirits,

Be it resolved, that no emigrant shall be *permitted* to go from Maryland to a settlement from this Society in Africa, who will not first bind himself, or herself, to abstain therefrom."

So the Society is to carry to Africa 100,000 slaves, and thus exterminate slavery in their State; and yet they will positively refuse to carry one of them until he has taken the temperance pledge. But what if a portion of them will not consent to take the pledge? must slavery continue, or must means be taken to coerce their consent?

None but those wilfully blind, can examine this subject without seeing that the measures adopted by Virginia and Maryland are mere contrivances to get rid of the free blacks; and far more disgraceful in the latter, than in the former case, because more disguised by insincere professions.

The New York Journal of Commerce, a colonization paper, had the candor in speaking on the subject, to remark, "It is true these States do not propose to resort, in the *first instance*, to compulsory measures; but does any one doubt that they will resort to such measures, if the number of volunteer emigrants should not be sufficient to exhaust the appropriations made for their removal?" And a Baltimore paper, (the Chronicle,) alluding to the Maryland acts, avows, "The INTENTION of those laws was, and their effect must be, to EXPEL the free people of color from the State."

Yet do these cruel and perfidious measures receive the support and approbation of the Colonization Society.

There is still a powerful objection to the whole colonization scheme, as a means of removing slavery, to which we have not yet adverted. No principle of political economy is more obvious than that prices depend on supply and demand. If the first is diminished, while the latter is increased, or even remains stationary, prices necessarily rise. We can all understand, that should half the sheep in the United States be suddenly destroyed, or carried out of the country, the value of the remaining half would instantly be enhanced. So also, we have no difficulty in seeing, that should the cholera sweep off from the Southern plantations, two or three hundred thousand slaves, there would be an increased activity in the man-market, and human flesh would rise many per cent. in price. Yet it seems never to occur to colonizationists, that were it possible for them to produce any sensible diminution of the slaves by transportation, the same consequences would follow. The Society proposes reducing the number of laborers, but without diminishing the demand for them. Let us suppose every free negro safely landed at Liberia — of course all the laborers remaining in the cotton and sugar-fields of the South, are slaves. Now the Society is gradually sending away these slaves, not by freeing at once any town or county from them, but by picking them up throughout the whole slave-region, as it can meet with conscientious masters; taking a few in one place, and a few in another; now stripping a plantation of its slaves in Virginia, and now in Missouri. This indiscriminate mode of obtaining emigrants, necessarily and absolutely prevents the substitution of white for black labor. The plantations thus divested of laborers, must remain barren till new slaves are procured. But the proprietor is too conscientious to buy any, and is hence compelled to sell his estate. The purchaser immediately goes into the market to re-stock the farm. Others do the same, and hence arises a new demand for slaves, and of course an increase of their value. But as slaves grow more and more valuable, the disposition to make presents of them to the Colonization Society will decline. Thus does the inevitable mercantile operation of the Society, independent of all moral considerations, necessarily tend to defeat its object. The idea of abolishing slavery, by increasing the demand for slaves, is about as wise, as would be a plan for lessening the circulation of infidel books, by raising a fund for their purchase.

We have now examined the means by which the Society proposes to effect the removal of slavery, and trust we have shown their utter worthlessness. Were the impracticability of this scheme its *only* objection, the friends of humanity and religion would not be called on, as they now are, to meet it with unrelenting hostility — to labor without rest, and without weariness, for its entire prostration. Alas, though powerless for good, it is mighty for evil; and its baneful influence is leading multitudes of good and well-intentioned men, unconsciously to countenance doctrines and measures, necessarily tending to perpetuate slavery and all its abominations in our land. This is an assertion that ought not rashly to be made nor hastily believed. We appeal to common sense and undisputed facts.

Admitting that colonization could, in the course of ages, extirpate slavery, ought we, therefore, to reject every means of shortening the sufferings of the slave, by hastening his liberation? But colonizationists, not content with insisting on the efficiency of their own plan, discourage and oppose every other. Now should their plan prove delusive, after the lapse of centuries, their influence in preventing the adoption of any other, will have been fatal, as far as it may have gone, to the freedom of millions.

"It (colonization) is the ONLY possible mode of emancipation at once safe, and rational, that human ingenuity can devise." *Speech of Mr. Custiss. 13th Report*, p. 8.

"Colonization is the ONLY expedient by which these evils can be mitigated." *Speech of J. A. Dix. Afr. Rep.*, IV, 168.

"To this country it offers the ONLY possible means of gradually ridding ourselves of a mighty evil." *1st Rep., N. Y. Colonization Society.*

"The colonizing scheme, leading as it does to voluntary manumission, is the ONLY one which true wisdom can dictate." *Speech of Mr. Key, Vice President. Afr. Rep.*, IV, p. 299.

"I would urge this system of colonization upon your notice, as the ONLY rational plan which has yet been suggested for relieving our Southern brethren from the curse of slavery." *Speech of Chancellor Walworth of N. Y.*

"The only rational and practical plan ever devised for the emancipation of the slaves of independent States." *N. Y. Courier and Enquirer, 12th May*, 1834, *a colonization paper.*

"This great end (abolition) is to be attained in NO OTHER way than by a plan of extensive colonization." *Letter of R. G. Harper, Vice President. 2d Rep.*, p. 3.

"In our opinion, the Colonization Society presents the ONLY safe and feasible plan for the liberation of our slaves from bondage." *Report of Wilmington Col. Society. Afr. Rep.*, IX, 319.

We have seen the nature and extent of the moral influence of this *only* rational plan in favor of abolition; let us now examine that which it exerts in *behalf of slavery.*

In the first place, we ask, what must be the natural effect on public opinion of such disclaimers as the following?

"It is no Abolition Society; it addresses, as yet, arguments to no master. It denies the design of attempting emancipation, *partial* or *general.*" *Address of J. B. Harrison to Lynchburgh Col. Society. Afr. Rep.*, III, 197.

"Into their (the Society's) accounts, the subject of emancipation does not *enter at all.*" *Afr. Rep.*, IV, p. 306.

"The friends of colonization wish to be distinctly understood on this point. From the beginning, they have disavowed, and they do yet disavow, that their object is the emancipation of slaves." *Speech of J. S. Green, before the New Jersey Society.*

"From its origin, and throughout the whole period of its existence, it has constantly disclaimed all intention whatever of interfering in the smallest degree with the rights of property, or the object of emancipation, *gradual* or *immediate.*" *Speech of Mr. Clay, Vice President. Afr. Rep.*, VI, p. 13.

"Recognizing the constitutional and legitimate existence of slavery, it seeks not to interfere, *directly* or *indirectly*, with the rights it creates." *Afr. Rep.*, III, p. 16.

"He considered himself publicly pledged, so long as he had any thing to do with the Society, to resist every attempt to connect it with emancipation, either in *theory* or *practice.*" *Speech of Gen. Jones, a Manager of the Am. Col. Soc.*, 23*d Jan.*, 1834.

"The *emancipation of slaves*, or the amelioration of their condition, with the moral, intellectual, and political improvement of the people of color within the United States, are objects *foreign* to the powers of this Society." *Address of the Board of Managers to its Auxiliaries. Afr. Rep.*, VII, p. 291.

Thus we see the friends of the Society utterly deny that emancipation, partial or general, gradual or immediate, direct or indirect, in theory or in practice, is included among its objects; and yet the Society "is the ONLY possible mode of emancipation at once safe and rational, that human ingenuity can devise!"

A worthy vice president of the Society, Mr. G. Smith, remarked:

"They who denounce us for not favoring or promoting the emancipation of slaves, might just as well denounce the Bible or Temperance Society, because they do not step out of their respective spheres, to favor or promote the emancipation of slaves." *Afr. Rep.*, IX, p. 358.

But what if a Bible or a Temperance Society should announce itself to the world, as about to abolish slavery; should declare itself to be the ONLY possible instrument by which slavery could be abolished; and should oppose and ridicule the employment of any other instrument, and should then falsify all its professions, and exert its influence to justify and perpetuate slavery?

Instead of denouncing the Society for *not* stepping out of its sphere to favor or promote the emancipation of slaves, we denounce it for *leaving that sphere,* and for favoring and promoting continued slavery. The *professed* constitutional object of the Society, is the colonization of free blacks and manumitted slaves. *We fully admit, it has no more right to meddle with emancipation or slavery, than a Bible Society;* and we condemn it, because disregarding its professed object, and in utter contempt of its own constitution, it has lent itself to support and perpetuate a system of cruelty and wickedness. It is painful to make these assertions, but duty requires them, and facts justify them. We will now proceed to show that the Society (and by the term we intend colonizationists generally) has stepped out of its sphere to acknowledge that man may have property in man; to justify him for holding this property; and to vilify all who would persuade him instantly to surrender it.

"We hold their slaves, as we hold their other property, SACRED." *Speech of J. S. Green, before New Jersey Colonization Society. Afr. Rep.*, I, p. 283.

"To the slave-holder, they (the Society) address themselves in a tone of conciliation and *sympathy.* We know your RIGHTS, say they, and we RESPECT them." *Afr. Rep.*, VII, p. 100.

"The rights of the masters are to remain SACRED in the eyes of the Society." *Address of Rockbridge Col. Soc. Afr. Rep.*, IV, p. 274.

"We decline assenting to the opinion of some abolitionists, that though the master's right over his living slaves should be conceded, yet he has no claim of property in the unborn, for the reason that there can be no property in a thing not *in esse.* This position is wholly untenable, under any jurisprudence." *Am. Quar. Review, transferred to Afr. Rep.*, IX, p. 35.

The right of property in human flesh, cannot surely be more sacred than that in RUM; and yet it would sound strange, to hear a religious society addressing the rum-seller in a tone of conciliation and sympathy, and assuring him that they regarded his property in rum as *sacred*, and respected his right to traffic in it.

If it be a question whether man can lawfully have property in man, who authorized the Society to settle it? That it is a question, is evident from the following exclamation of Lord Chancellor Brougham, in one of his speeches: "Talk not of the property of the planter in his slaves. I deny the right—I acknowledge not the property." And yet the right of the West Indian and the Virginia planter, rested on precisely the same basis, the sanction of *human* laws.

Not only does the Society acknowledge slaves to be property, but it excuses and justifies those who hold this property.

No motive can operate so powerfully in inducing a master to liberate his slaves, as the conviction that, by retaining them, he is acting contrary to the will of his Maker, and exposing himself to his displeasure.

In a manual of devotion, lately published by the excellent Bishop Meade, of Virginia, himself a zealous colonizationist, there is a prayer to be used by the head of a family. This prayer, intended expressly for the slave-region, has this affecting petition: "O heavenly Master, hear me while I lift up my heart in prayer, for those unfortunate beings who *call me master*. O God, make known unto me my whole duty towards them and their oppressed race, and give me courage and zeal to do it at all events. *Convince me of sin, if I be wrong in retaining them another moment in bondage.*"

It is observable, that in this prayer, the slave-holder, when in communion with his Maker, far from claiming a sacred right of property in his fellow immortals, dares not make any claim to them whatever, but alludes to them as those "who *call* me master." It is also obvious, that the question of immediate emancipation is pressing on his conscience, and fearful lest he is committing sin in holding slaves "another moment," he implores the Divine guidance. He will, of course, seek for light wherever it may be found, and will naturally turn to the Colonization Society, to learn the opinion of the eminent men who belong to it, on this momentous subject. Now let us see what opiates that Society administers to quiet his uneasy conscience, and to lull it in profound repose.

First, he is assured, that by freeing his slaves, he would be guilty of great inhumanity towards *them.*

"The very commencing act of freedom to the slave, is to place him in a condition still worse, if possible, both for his moral habits, his outward provision, and for the community that embosoms him, than even that, deplorable as it was, from which he has been removed." *Address to Col. Soc. N. Carolina. Afr. Rep.*, III, p. 66.

"What but sorrow can we feel at the *misguided piety* which has set so many of them free by death-bed devise, or sudden conviction of injustice?" *Address to Lynchburgh Col. Soc. Afr. Rep.*, III, p. 193.

"There are in the United States 238,000 blacks denominated free, but whose freedom confers on them, we might say, no privilege but the privilege of being more *vicious and miserable* than slaves *can be.*" *Rev. Mr. Bacon, of New Haaen. 7th Rep.*, p. 99.

"Policy, and even the *voice of humanity*, forbade the progress of manumission." *Afr. Rep.*, IV, p. 268.

"It would be as humane to throw them from *the decks in the middle passage*, as to set them free in our country." *Afr. Rep.*, IV, p. 226.

Was Washington wanting in humanity, when he liberated all his slaves? and was he surpassed in benevolence by his nephew, the President of the Society, who avowed his intention of never giving freedom to any of his? Was it "misguided piety" that induced Jefferson to set his free by his last will? Was it an act of perfidious cruelty in the State of Georgia to purchase the freedom of a slave, who had disclosed an intended conspiracy,—thus under the pretence of rewarding him, perpetrating an act as inhuman as throwing a fellow being from the decks in the middle passage? Is the recent act of North Carolina, in paying $1800 for the freedom of a slave, who had, with singnlar intrepidity, preserved a public building from fire, of the same character?

Much as we respect Mr. Bacon's character, we cannot but believe, that could his sincerity be tested by his being compelled to choose between being a slave in Louisiana, or a free black even in Canterbury, he would prefer the latter alternative. It is the more remarkable, that Mr. Bacon should have been led to make such unadvised assertions, when New Haven itself afforded full proof of their incorrectness. Hear the testimony of his estimable and distinguished fellow townsman, Professor Silliman.

"We need not look far from home to see the pleasing effects of the benevolent and disinterested exertions of an eminent friend* of the Africans, aided by a kindred spirit. It is delightful to the benevolent mind, to see so many of our colored people living in neat and comfortable dwellings, furnished in decent taste, and in sufficient fulness, thus indicating sobriety, industry, and self-respect; to see their children in clean attire, hastening on a Sabbath morning to the Sunday school, and on other days, with cheerful and intelligent faces, seeking the common school." *Silliman's 4th of July Oration*, 1832.

The slave-holder is farther instructed by the Society, that the continuance of slavery here, is at present, and under existing circumstances, unavoidable, and that he is perfectly excusable and innocent in keeping his fellow-men in bondage; and that all the cruel laws relative to slavery are right and proper. Is all this calumny? Attend to the testimony.

"Slavery is an evil entailed upon the present generation of slave-holders, which they *must* suffer, whether they will or not." *African Rep.*, V, p. 179.

"The existence of slavery among us, though not *at all* to be objected to our Southern brethren, *is a fault.*" *Address of N. Y. Colonization Society. Afr. Rep.*, VII, p. 136.

May we ask, how came the States of Missouri, Alabama, and Mississippi, which within thirty years were nearly in a state of nature, to be now thronged with slaves?

"It (the Society) condemns no man because he is a slave-holder." *Editorial Article — Afr. Rep.*, VII, p. 200.

"Acknowledging the *necessity* by which its (slavery) present continuance, and rigorous provisions for its maintenance, are *justified.*" *Afr. Rep.*, III, p. 16.

"It is the business of the free, *their safety requires it*, to keep the slaves in ignorance." *Proceedings of New York Col. Soc.*, 2d *Ann.*

"The laws of Virginia now discourage, and *very wisely*, perhaps, the emancipation of slaves." *Speech of Mr. Mercer, V. President*, I *Rep.*

* The Rev. S. S. Jocelyn, an active and public opponent of the Colonization Society.

"They (the abolitionists) confound the *misfortunes* of one generation with the crimes of another." *Afr. Rep.*, VII, p. 202.

"We all know, from a variety of considerations which it is unnecessary to name, and in consequence of the policy which is obliged to be pursued in the Southern States, that it is extremely difficult to free a slave; and hence the enactment of those laws, which a *fatal necessity* seems to demand." *Afr. Rep.*, II, p. 12.

"I am not complaining of the owners of slaves: they *cannot* get rid of them." *Address before Hampden Col. Soc. Afr. Rep.*, IV, p. 226.

"There are men in the Southern States who long to do something effectual for the benefit of their slaves, and would gladly emancipate them, did not *prudence* and compassion *forbid* such a measure." I *Rep.*, p. 100, *App.*

"Suppose the slaves of the South to have the knowledge of freemen, — they would be free, or exterminated by the whites. This renders it *necessary* to prevent their instruction, and to keep them from *Sunday Schools*, or the means of gaining knowledge." *Proceedings of New York Col. Soc.*, 2d *Ann Rep.*

"The treatment of the slaves is in general *as good* as circumstances and the *cruel necessity* of the case will permit." *Proceedings of New York Col. Soc.*, 2d *Ann.*

"We believe that there is not the slightest moral turpitude in holding slaves, under existing circumstances, in the South." *Afr. Rep.*, IX, p. 4.

Thus do we find the whole system of American slavery justified on the tyrant's plea, necessity. But this is not all. The scriptures themselves are wrested to confound those who recommend abolition.

The President of the Geneva Colonization Society, S. M. Hopkins, Esq., in an address delivered 5th of August, 1834, and published by *request* of the Society, after citing various texts to prove slavery warranted by the Bible, thus goes on:

"Here are then five places in the New Testament, where the duty of servants (slaves) is expressly and formally treated by way of *precept*, and one case of *example*, making six in all. In every one, the duty of obedience is insisted on, and in one or more, where the duty of masters is treated, there is not the least reference nor hint of the idea, that *Christian* masters should manumit their slaves; much less that other Christians should *preach manumission*. But I go farther; as I understand the Epistle to Timothy, and as it is understood by such commentators as I have consulted, there is an express injunction, applicable to those times and circumstances, NOT TO PREACH MANUMISSION."*

* Mr. Hopkins professes to be opposed to slavery, all this Scripture to the contrary notwithstanding.

We will not trouble ourselves at present with Mr. Hopkins's theology; but we may surely be permitted to inquire, how it comes that the Constitution forbids colonizationists to recommend and promote abolition, but gives them full liberty to oppose it? Why is the Constitution sacred, only when it guards the interests and soothes the conscience of the slave-holder? and why is it a thing of nought, when colonizationists would empty the vials of their wrath upon the heads of those who proclaim the sinfulness of slavery, and the dutyand policy of immediate emancipation? *

Let us now scrutinize a little this plea of necessity, which is urged by colonizationists with so much confidence in behalf of slavery. Does a Christian society, do ministers of the gospel of Christ, maintain that it is *ever* necessary to violate the command of Jehovah? necessary to keep millions in ignorance of the revealed will of God? necessary to trample upon human rights, and to outrage the plainest principles of justice and humanity? Do Protestants insist that it is necessary to deny the Bible to more than one-third of the inhabitants of the Southern States? What necessity required that Missouri should be a slave State? What necessity multiplied the slaves in Alabama, and Mississippi from three thousand to one hundred and eighty-two thousand, since the year 1800? What necessity prevented Kentucky from liberating her twelve thousand slaves in 1790, when New York could liberate ten thousand in one day in 1827? What necessity will render Florida and Arkansas slave States? Why did not necessity prevent the abolition of slavery in South America, Mexico, and the West Indies?

The Society, whose moral influence is to free us from slavery, not only quiets the conscience of the slave-holder, by showing the lawfulness of slavery, but it promises to enhance the value of slave-labor, and to divest it of a portion of that danger which

* It is due to candor to state, that *all* the principles imputed in this work to colonizationists, are not held by them indiscriminately. A few individuals have honorably and publicly disclaimed one or more of them. These disclaimers have however been made, we believe, without an exception, *since* the discussions excited by abolitionists. No doubt many members would indignantly reject the doctrines on which we have commented. The pious and well-intentioned supporters of the Society, are just beginning to understand its true character, and hence the numerous converts from colonization within the last twelve months.

usually attends it. Let us see how colonization promotes the interests of slave-holders; and let us attend, in the first instance, to Mr. Archer, of Virginia.

"He was not one of those (however desirable it might be, and was in abstract speculation) who looked to the complete removal of slavery among us. If that consummation were to be considered feasible at all, *it was at a period too remote to warrant the expenditure of any resources of contemplation or contribution now.* The progress of slavery was subjected to the action of a law of the utmost regularity of action. Where this progress was neither stayed nor modified by causes of collateral operation, it hastened with a frightful rapidity, disproportioned entirely to the ordinary law of the advancement of population, to its catastrophe, which was *repletion.*

"If none were *drained* away, slaves became, except under peculiar circumstances of climate and production, inevitably and speedily redundant, first to the occasions of *profitable employment,* and as a consequence, to the facility of comfortable provision for them. No matter what the humanity of the owners, fixed restriction on their resources must transfer itself to the comfort and subsistence of the slave. At this last stage, the evil in this form had to stop. When this stage had been reached, what course or remedy remained? Was open butchery to be resorted to, as among the Spartans with the Helots? or general emancipation and incorporation, as in South America? or abandonment of the country by the masters, as must come to be the case in the West Indies?

"Either of these was a deplorable catastrophe. Could all of them be avoided, and if they could, how? There was but one way, but that might be made effectual, fortunately. *It was to provide and keep open a drain for the excess of increase beyond the occasions of profitable employment. This might be done effectually by extension of the plan of the Society.* * * * * *After* the present class of *free* blacks had been exhausted by the operation of the plan he was recommending, others would be supplied for its action, in the proportion *of the excess* of the colored population it would be *necessary* to throw off, by the process of voluntary manumission or sale. This effect must result from the depreciating value of the slaves, ensuing their disproportionate multiplication. This depreciation would be *relieved* and retarded at the same time by the process. It was on grounds of interest, therefore, the most indispensable PECUNIARY INTEREST, that he addressed himself to the PEOPLE AND LEGISLATURES OF THE SLAVE-HOLDING STATES." 15*th Report*, p. 22.

However we may be surprised at the indiscretion of the managers in printing and circulating this speech with their annual report, we cannot but admire its honest frankness. Here is no colonization poetry, but plain, common-sense prose; no pictures of the African Elysium, — no anticipations of the conversion of millions and millions of Pagans, but intelligent remarks on the true means of perpetuating slavery, and keeping up the price of slaves. Knowing the utter futility of abolishing slavery by colonization, Mr. Archer will not expend on that topic even his "contemplation." But the time will come when negroes will be so plenty, that it will be difficult to find either work or food for them; and this state of things, if not prevented, will lead to the abolition of slavery. But the Society may prevent such a result by sending off the free blacks, and *after* they are gone, by sending off such slaves as may be manumitted; and by keeping open this drain, the undue multiplication of slavery will be prevented, and their depreciation in the market arrested.

Let us now attend to the managers themselves. In the 2d Report, p. 9, they declare that they confidently believe that the

"Colonization of the *free* people of color, will render the slave who *remains* in America, more obedient, more faithful, more honest, and consequently more *useful* to his master."

"By removing the most fruitful sources of discontent (free blacks) from among our slaves, we should render them more industrious and attentive *to our commands.*" *Address of Putnam (Georgia) Col. Society.*

"What greater pledge can we give for the moderation and safety of our measures, than our *own interests* as slave-holders, and the ties that bind us to the slave-holding community to which we belong?" *Speech of Mr. Key, Vice Pres. 11th Report*, p. 14.

"The *injury* they (the free blacks) do to the slave-holder's *property*, by their influence upon his servants, would, if valued, amount to more than sufficient to convey them from us." *Address of Rev. J. C. Young to Col. Society. Afr. Rep.*, IX, 59.

"To remove these persons from among us, will *increase the usefulness*, and improve the moral character of those who remain in servitude, *and with whose labors the country is unable to dispense.*" *Address to a N. Carolina Col. Soc. Afr. Rep.*, III, 67.

"None are obliged to follow our example, and those who do not, will find the *value of their negroes increased*, by the departure of ours." *Kentucky Luminary.*

"The free negroes corrupt our slaves. From what has been adduced, the expediency of removing this NUISANCE from the community is clearly inferable, both in relation to their interests and *ours;* and this can only be attained by means of the Colonization Society." *Internal Improvements of South Carolina, by Robert Mills*, p. 15.

So much for the moral influence of the Society in abolishing slavery, by rendering it *profitable*. Now for its agency in rendering it *safe*.

"The tendency of the scheme, and one of its *objects*, is to SECURE slave-holders, and the whole Southern country, against certain evil consequences growing out of the present three-fold mixture of our population." *Address of a Virginian Col. Soc. Afr. Rep.*, IV, 274.

"By removing these people, (free blacks,) we rid ourselves of a large party who will always be ready to assist our slaves in any mischievous design they may conceive." *Address to a Col. Soc. in Virginia. Afr. Rep.*, I, 176.

"Are they (the free blacks) VIPERS sucking our blood? We will HURL them from us." *Address to Lynchburg Col. Society. Afr. Rep.*, III, 201.

"By thus repressing the rapid increase of blacks, the white population would be enabled to reach, and soon overtop them; the consequence would be SECURITY." *Afr. Rep.*, IV, 344.

"The removal of *every single free black* in America, would be productive of nothing but SAFETY to the slave-holder." *Afr. Rep.*, III, 202.

"So far from having a dangerous tendency, when properly considered, it will be viewed as an additional *guard* to our peculiar species of property." *New Orleans Argus.*

"They (the objects of the American Colonization Society) are in the *first* place to aid *ourselves*, by relieving us from a species of population (free blacks) *pregnant with future danger*." *Speech of Gen. Harper, Vice President. 7th Report*, p. 7.

"I am a Virginian. I dread for her the corroding evil of this numerous caste, (free blacks.) I tremble for the danger of a disaffection spreading, through their seduction, among *our servants*." *Address of I. B. Harrison. Afr. Rep.*, III, 197.

Thus does the Society aim at abolishing slavery, by declaring it lawful, increasing its profits, and lessening its dangers; and as we shall presently see, covering with obloquy, and denouncing as fanatics, all who dissent from its assertion, that this is "the only possible mode" of relieving the country from slavery.

And why is it the only possible mode? Because the laws of most of the slave States prohibit manumission at home, and therefore no master in those States could liberate his slaves, did not the Society enable him to evade the law, by sending his slaves to Africa? But who made these laws? Slave-holders. Who alone can repeal these laws? Slave-holders. Then slave-holders prevent themselves from liberating their slaves; and hence it is optional with them to grant manumission or not. Of course colonization is *not* the only possible mode of effecting abolition, since the slave-holders, if they pleased, might easily discover "a more excellent way."

It will not probably be denied, that he who recommends a wicked act, or applauds it after it is committed, participates in the guilt of it; and as by the confession of colonizationists, the laws in question prevent abolition, those who advise or approve those laws, partake of the guilt of continuing slavery. Let us now inquire in what relation the Colonization Society stands to these laws.

In the first place, let it be recollected that several of the Legislatures by whom these laws have been enacted, or by whom they are kept in force, have decidedly approved of the Society. Now listen to the official declaration of the Board of Managers.

> "The managers could with no propriety depart from their original and avowed purpose, and make emancipation their object. And they would further say, that if they were not thus restrained by the terms of their association, they would still consider *any* attempts to promote the increase of the free colored population by manumission, *unnecessary, premature, and dangerous.*" *Memorial of the American Col. Soc. to the several State Legislatures. Afr. Rep.*, II, 60.

We find here an illustration of the remarks in our introduction, on the *convenient* restraints of the Constitution. The managers are *restrained* from promoting *emancipation* by the Constitution, but they are at perfect liberty to promote the *permanency of slavery*, by denouncing manumission. And to whom is this denunciation made? To the very Legislatures who are striving to effect the same object by the laws we have mentioned. And yet colonizationists mourn over the *misfortune* of the master who is prevented by *law* from liberating his slaves? But perhaps the language we have quoted was used inadvertently, and does not represent the sentiments of colonizationists generally. Let us see.

> "This law, (a law of Virginia, by which a manumitted negro becomes again a slave if he remains twelve months in the State,) odious and unjust as it may at first view appear, and hard as it may seem to bear

upon the liberated negro, was doubtless dictated by *sound policy*, and its repeal would be regarded by none with *more unfeigned regret than the friends of African Colonization. It has restrained many masters from giving freedom to their slaves*, and has thereby contributed to check the growth of an evil already too great and formidable." *Memorial from Powhattan Col. Soc. to Virginia Legislature.*

"To set them (the slaves) loose among us, would be an evil more intolerable than slavery itself." *Report of Kentucky Col. Society Afr. Rep.*, VI, 81.

"As long as our present feelings and PREJUDICES exist, the abolition of slavery cannot be accomplished without the removal of the blacks." *2d Report N. York Soc.*

"If the question were submitted, whether there should be either immediate *or gradual* emancipation of all the slaves in the United States, without their removal, painful as it is to express the opinion, I have no doubt that it would be unwise to emancipate them." *Speech of Mr. Clay, Vice President, to Kentucky Soc. Afr. Rep.*, VI, 5.

Here we find a vice president of the Parent Society advocating perpetual slavery in preference to even *gradual* emancipation.

"They (colonizationists) entertain the opinion generally, that if universal emancipation were practicable, neither the interest of the master, the happiness of the slave, nor the welfare of the colony which they have at heart, would make it desirable." *Mr. Barton's Address to a Col. Soc. in Virginia. Afr. Rep.*, VI, 291.

"Resolved, That we superadd our decided opinion that colonization ought to keep *equal* pace with manumission of people of color throughout the United States." *Proceedings of Col. Meeting at Plattsburgh, N. York, 4th July*, 1833.

"*Any* scheme of emancipation, without colonization, they know to be productive of nothing but evil." *Speech of Mr. Key, a Vice President. Afr. Rep.*, IV, 300.

"We would say, liberate them ONLY on condition of their going to Africa or Hayti." *Afr. Rep.*, III, 26.

"I am strongly opposed to emancipation in EVERY SHAPE AND DEGREE, unless accompanied by colonization." *Letter from R. G. Harper, Vice President, to Secretary of the Society, 20th August*, 1817.

"It is a well-established point, that the public safety forbids *either* the emancipation or the general instruction of the slaves." *7th Report*, p. 94.

"So long as we can hold a pen, we will employ it heart and hand, against the advocates of immediate emancipation, or ANY emancipation that does not contemplate *expatriation.*" *N. Y. Courier and Enquirer, a Col. paper, 10th July*, 1834.

"Emancipation, with liberty to remain on this side of the Atlantic, is but an act of dreamy madness." *Speech of Mr. Custiss*, 13*th Report*, p. 8.

"What right, I demand, have the children of Africa to a homestead in the white man's country?" *Speech of Mr. Custiss*, 14*th Report*, p. 21.

It is a pity Mr. Custiss does not ask his conscience what right *he* has to confine a child of Africa to a homestead on his own plantation; and why money was raised by public subscription to purchase permission for Philip Lee to leave a homestead to which he had no right.

What abundant cause for gratitude to Almighty God, have the Northern States, that the colonization scheme was not devised some forty years sooner. Had the doctrines taught by the Society been then held by our statesmen and divines, the dark cloud of slavery would now be brooding over our whole land.

We have seen that the whole influence of the Society and of the colonizing Legislatures, is to vindicate and preserve and enforce the laws against manumission. And now, after defending and strengthening this barrier against human freedom, the Society glorifies itself for its benèvolence in having opened a little crevice through which, in sixteen years, a few hundred captives, out of millions, have escaped! Had the Society and its friends opposed these laws, they would long since have been swept away, and thousands and tens of thousands would have been free, who are now pining in bondage. In 1782, Virginia repealed her restraining law, and in nine years, 10,000 slaves ware manumitted. The slave-holders became alarmed,—their vocation was in danger of becoming disreputable, and the law was reënacted.

We have all heard much of the evils resulting from the traffic in ardent spirits, and we know that multitudes are endeavoring to suppress it, by insisting that it is sinful, and that Christian duty requires its immediate abolition. Now let us suppose a society for abolishing it, to be formed on the model of the Colonization Society, and ask ourselves how it would proceed, and what would be the prospect of its success. Such a society would begin by informing the venders, that it held their *property in rum* SACRED, and *respected* their *right* to sell it; that as yet, it addressed arguments to no vender to induce him to abandon the traffic; that it was, indeed, a political evil, but it was one they had unfortunately engaged in, and which the necessities of themselves and families *compelled* them to continue for the present; that the society *condemned no man* for being a rumseller; *that it had no connection* with the fanatics and incendiaries who denounced the business as sinful, and demanded its immediate abolition, — but, inasmuch as the society knew that the venders were anxious to get rid of the rum they unfortunately possessed, it had appointed agents who would gratuitously afford their aid in removing and emptying rum-casks, and it trusted the *moral influence* of this proffered aid would, in a century or more, effect the total abolition of the traffic.

The absurdity of the conclusion, in the supposed case, is obvious; and did not prejudice impair our vision, we should see an equal absurdity in the professed expectations of colonizationists. But is our illustration a parallel case? No: for our ideal society does not profess to regard any other evil as greater than the indefinite continuance of the traffic, while the real one boldly and unequivocally declares for perpetual slavery in preference to emancipation, either immediate or gradual, without expatriation. Now if the expatriation of the whole body of slaves be both physically and morally impossible; if the slaves could not be transported and maintained in Africa, were the masters willing to surrender them; and if the masters would not surrender them, even if they could instantly be transported and maintained, then it follows irresistibly, that the moral influence of the American Colonization Society is to perpetuate slavery in the United States.

We can scarcely persuade ourselves, that any honest colonizationists can, in view of all the facts which have been developed, seriously believe that slavery will ever be removed by colonization. Still there may be some who are indulging the hope that this scheme is promoting emancipation. We entreat the attention of such to the proofs we will now offer, that the Society is in fact

AN ANTI-ABOLITION ASSOCIATION.

On the 9th of January, 1828, Mr. Harrison, of Virginia, in addressing the Society at its annual meeting, used the following language:

"The Society having declared that it is in no wise allied to any *Abolition* Society in America or elsewhere, is ready when there is need, TO PASS A CENSURE upon such societies in America." 11*th Report*, p. 14.

The pledge thus given in behalf, and in the presence of the Society, was published and circulated by the Board of Managers. It was a gross violation of the constitution, and an unblushing outrage on the multiplied professions of the Society, that its *only* object was the colonization of free blacks. But we cannot understand the full meaning and unholy nature of this pledge, without adverting to the Abolition Societies to which it related. This pledge, be it remembered, had no reference to the associations *now* known as *Anti-Slavery Societies*, and which are accused of a design to destroy the Union — to drench the land in human gore, and to produce by marriage an amalgamation of color. Such societies were unknown, such charges unheard of, when this pledge was given. The Abolition Societies which were to be censured, were societies founded by JAY and FRANKLIN, and which advocated *gradual* emancipation.

The first society ever formed, it is believed, for the abolition of slavery, was organized in the city of New York, January, 1785, under the presidency of JOHN JAY. The principles maintained by this society, may be gathered from the preamble to its constitution.

"The benevolent Creator and Father of all men, having given them all an *equal* right to life, liberty, and property, no sovereign power on earth can justly deprive them of either, but in conformity to impartial government, and laws, to which they have expressly or tacitly consented. It is our duty, therefore, as free citizens and Christians, not only to regard with compassion the injustice done to those among us, who are held as slaves, but to endeavor, by lawful means, to enable them to *share equally with us in the civil and religious liberty* with which an indulgent Providence has blessed these States, and to which these our brethren *are by nature as much entitled as ourselves.*"

The next Abolition Society was that of Pennsylvania, founded in 1787, under the presidency of FRANKLIN. Slave-holders were expressly excluded. The constitution declares, that it has pleased

"The Creator of the world to make of one flesh all the children of men," and that it is the special duty of those who acknowledge the obligations of Christianity, to use such means as are in their power to extend the blessings of freedom "to every part of our race."

Abolition Societies gradually multiplied, and exercised a salutary influence in promoting emancipation at the North. But they were not confined to the North; they soon sprang up in the slave States, and scattered and feeble rays of light began to pierce the dense cloud which brooded over the southern country. Unity of action and of purpose was secured by triennial conventions of delegates from the several societies. No organized opposition had ever been offered to these associations. The moral sense of the community, unperverted by colonization, would not *then* have tolerated the scenes we have since witnessed. The respect in which Abolition Societies were held, is evinced by the following extract from the journals of Congress:

"*House of Representatives*, 18*th Feb.* 1809.

"Resolved, That the Speaker be requested to acknowledge the receipt and *acceptance* of Clarkson's History of Slavery, presented by the American Convention, for promoting the abolition of slavery, and improving the condition of the Africans, and that the said work be deposited in the library."

The Speaker accordingly returned an official letter of thanks to the convention.

Only *three months* before Mr. Harrison, as herald of the Colonization Society, proclaimed war against Abolition Societies, the convention met at Baltimore, the capital of a slave State.

To this convention delegates or communications were sent from the following Abolition Societies, viz.:

New York,
Rhode Island,
Pennsylvania,
Western Pennsylvania,
Maryland, with 5 branches,
Tennessee,
West Tennessee,
Munro Co., Ohio,
Andover, Mass.,
Williams College, Mass.,
Loudon Co., Virginia,
N. Carolina, with 40 branches,
Delaware,
Centreville, Penn.,
Brownsville, do.

This convention, among other measures, petitioned Congress for the abolition of slavery in the District of Columbia, and exhorted the friends of abolition to use their efforts to procure "the removal of all existing legal impediments in the way of educating the people of color." Such was the promising state of public feeling, at the very moment when the Colonization Society announced its crusade against Abolition. The vigor and constancy with which it has been carried on to the present time, are known to all who have watched its progress. The Abolition Societies and their conventions have withered under the "CENSURE" of their powerful enemy, and have shrunk from public notice. Within the last two years, they have been partially succeeded by more sturdy associations, named Anti-Slavery Societies, which, instead of quailing beneath the frowns of their foe, have dared to grapple with him in mortal conflict, and to stake the hopes of freedom on the issue. If, in this struggle, abolitionists have not always distinguished themselves by their courteous bearing, let it be recollected, that they believe the happiness of millions depends on their efforts; and, also, that by their haughty adversary, they have been treated as wretches who deserve punishment; not as the generous and disinterested champions of the oppressed and friendless. Let us observe the manner in which they are assailed by members of a *religious* society.

"It (the Society) is nowise mingled or confounded with the broad-sweeping views of a *few fanatics* in America, who would urge us on to the sudden and total abolition of slavery." *Afr. Rep.*, III, 197.

"Come, ye abolitionists, away with your *wild enthusiasm*, your mis guided philanthropy." *Afr. Rep.*, VII, 100.

"Resolved, that we view all attempts to prejudice the public mind, or excite the popular feeling, on the subject of slavery, as unwise and injurious, and adapted to perpetuate the evil which it is proposed to eradicate." *Col. Meeting at Northampton, Mass.* *Afr. Rep.*, VIII, 283.

After a public discussion of the colonization scheme in Utica, the Common Council came to the rescue of the Society, by discharging resolutions against the abolitionists. For example:

"Whereas, certain individuals now in our city, are *disturbing the peace* of the good citizens thereof, by inculcating sentiments which we deem *demoralizing* in themselves, and little short of TREASON towards the government of our country," &c.,

"Resolved, that, in the opinion of this meeting, it is the solemn duty of every patriot and philanthropist, to discountenance and OPPOSE the efforts of Anti-Slavery Societies." *Col. Soc. of Middletown, Conn. 6th March*, 1834.

It would have been, of course, unconstitutional to *aid* these efforts; but it seems the Society had full authority to oppose them. In short, with colonization societies, every thing is constitutional that is expedient, and nothing that is not.

"The emancipation, to which this resolution directs your attention, is not that *unconstitutional* and dangerous emancipation, contemplated by a few visionary enthusiasts, and a still fewer number of *reckless incendiaries* among us." *Speech of Chancellor Walworth, at Col. Meeting in New York, 9th Oct.*, 1833.

"I avail myself of this opportunity, to enter my solemn protest against the attempts which are making by a *few fanatics*. Let us talk no more of nullification; the doctrine of immediate emancipation is a direct and palpable nullification of that Constitution which we have SWORN to support." *Speech of D. B. Ogden at New York Colonization Meeting.*

"We owe it to ourselves not to remain silent spectators while this WILD FIRE is running its course. We owe it to those *misguided men*, (the abolitionists,) to interpose and save them and their country from the fatal effects of their *mad* speculations." *Speech of Hon. T. Frelinghuysen, V. President, before Am. Col. Society, 21st Jan.*, 1834.

We are not informed which article of the constitution of the Society imposes on its members the onerous duty mentioned by the honorable gentleman.

The abolitionists in New York gave notice of a meeting for

forming a City Anti-Slavery Society. In reference to this notice, the chairman of the Executive Committee of the New York Colonization Society, Mr. Stone, published in his paper, 2d of Oct., 1833, the following from a correspondent:

"Is it possible that our citizens can look quietly on, while the flames of discord are rising, — while even our pulpits are sought to be used for the base PURPOSE of encouraging scenes of *bloodshed* in our land? If we do, can we look our Southern brethren in the face and say, we are opposed to interfering with their rights? No, we cannot." *

The hint thus kindly given, was readily taken, and a mob of five thousand scattered the abolitionists. After another mob, in July, had assaulted the dwellings and temples of abolitionists, this officer of a Christian benevolent society, thus stated the CONDITION on which abolitionists might be permitted to enjoy the common rights of American citizens, security of person and freedom of speech, the press, and religious worship.

"While, then, our civil authorities should receive the aid of every good citizen, in their efforts to put down the mobs *now* nightly engaged in deeds of violence, yet there should be *a distinct understanding*, that the protection of *law*, and the aid of the military, can *only* be enjoyed or expected, ON CONDITION that the causes of these mischiefs shall be abated, and the outrages upon public feeling, from the FORUM, the PULPIT, and the PRESS, shall no more be repeated by these reckless incendiaries." *Commercial Advertiser*, 11*th July*, 1834.

Another colonization editor† published the same day, and while the mob were committing their grossest outrages, the following article:

"Now we tell them, (the abolitionists,) that when they openly and publicly promulgate doctrines which outrage public feeling, they have no right to demand protection of the people they insult. Ought not, we ask, our city authorities to make them understand this — to tell them that they prosecute their TREASONABLE and BEASTLY plans at their own peril?" *N. Y. Courier and Enquirer*, 11*th July*, 1834.

* This communication was accompanied by an editorial admission of the civil rights of abolitionists. It is to be regretted, that the editor, as will be seen by the next quotation, afterwards proposed a *condition* on which alone, in his opinion, those rights should be protected.

† Mr. James Watson Webb.

On conditions similar to those proposed by these gentlemen, the Roman emperors were ever ready to afford protection to the Christian martyrs; nor did the Spanish Inquisition require more, than that none should "promulgate doctrines" it disapproved.

Far be it from us to insinuate, that the conduct of these two editors was in conformity with the advice or wishes of any respectable colonizationists; and candor requires the acknowledgment, that we have never heard it justified; but it is unfortunately true, that the insults they have poured upon abolitionists, have been countenanced by the example of gentlemen from whom better things were expected. All this violence and obloquy are not without an object; and that object is INTIMIDATION. Utterly vain is the hope of maintaining the cause of colonization, or of suppressing that of abolition, by *discussion.* In *every instance* in which colonizationists have ventured to meet their opponents in public disputation, they have invariably retired with diminished strength. Hence great efforts have been made by colonizationists, and by the advocates of slavery, to prevent the public from ever listening to the facts and arguments adduced by the abolitionists. After a mob of five thousand had assembled to prevent the formation of the New York Anti-Slavery Society — after the most unfounded calumnies had been spread through the community against its members, the Society published an address, explaining their real sentiments and objects. One would have thought it an act of common justice, to give this address a candid perusal; but such an act would not have been *expedient,* and accordingly the zealous editor of the Commercial Advertiser thus endeavored to prevent it:

"We are quite sure that a discerning public will consign it to oblivion, by abstaining from a purchase of the *pestilent* document. Their curiosity, we *hope,* will not overstep their discretion, in furthering the purposes of the authors by its dissemination. Let this flagitious address descend to the tomb of the Capulets. The address in extenso, *we* have not read."

The abolitionists, on the contrary, are so far from *fearing* the effects of discussion, that they are ever anxious to promote it;

and when an acrimonious colonization pamphlet* appeared against them, they provokingly advertised it for sale, and urged the public to read it.†

In the war now waging between the abolitionists and colonizationists, a third party has come to the aid of the latter. Those who maintain the sinfulness of slavery, and the safety and duty of immediate emancipation, plant themselves on scriptural ground, and urge the promises, and threats, and commands of the word of God. They professedly act as Christians, and only as Christians; and it cannot be supposed that the infidel portion of the community view with indifference an opportunity of wounding Christianity through its zealous disciples. At the same time, the absence of Christian motive as a principle of the colonization scheme, and the countenance given by that scheme to most unchristian prejudices, naturally invite antichristian support. Certain it is, that many infidel newspapers are zealous advocates of colonization, and that the mobs of our cities are always ready to espouse its cause.

There is no evidence that, with the exception of certain editors, the mobs which disgraced the city of New York the last summer were instigated by members of the Society; yet these mobs were its avowed champions. The first mob assembled on the 9th of July, at the Chatham street chapel, the place in which some anti-slavery meetings had recently been held; and *breaking* open the doors, took possession of the building. They then organized, and appointing a chairman, *passed resolutions approving of the Colonization Society;* and by a formal vote, adjourned till the *next meeting* of the Anti-Slavery Society, — a very significant hint. The following guarded notice of this transaction, appeared the next day in one of the journals.

"From the non-assemblage of the persons who had designed to occupy the chapel, it was evident that the objects of the meeting had been abandoned, and the *friends of colonization* thereupon entered, organized a meeting, passed resolutions in favor of their own opinions, and peaceably dispersed." *New York Daily Advertiser.*

* Reese's Review.

† See the New York Emancipator.

The mob did indeed adjourn *as a colonization meeting*, but they had too much business on their hands to *disperse*. They *immediately* proceeded to vindicate the honor of the American name, by mobbing the Bowery Theatre, in revenge for some insulting expressions said to have been used by an Engiish actor.

"After finishing their work at the Bowery Theatre, the mob, (says the New York Journal of Commerce,) in a very excited state, repaired to the residence of Lewis Tappan, (a prominent abolitionist,) and attacked it with bricks and stones. The door, window-blinds, shutters, &c., were soon demolished, after which the mob entered, broke up the furniture, and made a bonfire of it in the street." Such was the commencement of four days of riot and outrage, by the admirers of "the benevolent colonization system." The managers of the city Colonization Society, mortified at the character and conduct of their new allies, published a card declaring that the "*tumultuous meetings*" at which certain resolutions had been passed, approving the objects of the New York Colonization Society, "had been held without any previous knowledge of the Board," and recommending to every *friend* of the cause of colonization to abstain "from all participation in proceedings *subversive of the rights of individuals, or in violation of the public peace.*" When before have the friends of a *religious* and *benevolent* cause needed *such* a recommendation?

The Journal of Commerce, a colonization paper, assigns *infidelity* as one of the causes of the riots.

"It was noticed, (it observes,) as a fact full of instruction, that last Sunday night, when many of the churches and lecture rooms were closed for fear of the mob, Tammany Hall was brilliantly lighted up for the meeting of infidels, who carried on their mummery without the slightest apprehension of danger. The buildings which have been attacked, are six churches, (belonging to four different denominations,) one school-house, occupied as a church, three houses of clergymen, a house and store occupied by elders of churches, and a number of houses occupied by colored families. Thus, with the exception of some colored persons, the vengeance of the mob has been exclusively directed against churches, ministers and elders. At the sacking of Mr. Tappan's house, a fellow was heard to say, that every rascal of a church member ought to be thrown off the dock, or to that effect. We think, therefore, we see inscribed on the banner of this guilty throng, ENMITY TO THE CROSS OF CHRIST."

Yet this guilty throng commenced its operations with lauding the Colonization Society.

In Utica, after a public discussion on Colonization, a mob assembled and burned in effigy a clergyman who had taken part against the Society; and also a layman who had become distinguished for his zeal in the temperance cause; and a bundle of Temperance Recorders was committed to the flames.

The following is from the New York Courier and Enquirer, 12th of May, 1834, and is part of an article in defence of the Colonization Society, and in vituperation of the abolitionists.

"Colleges and institutions are every year founded, not for the purposes of general education, but to initiate a new *race of monks and fanatics in the arts and mysteries of clerical ambition*, to teach them how best to subjugate the human mind, and render female weakness subservient to well-disciplined Jesuitism. One half of our colleges are nothing more than seminaries for educating uncompromising bigots," &c., &c.

In this very same article, we are assured "the Colonization Society holds out the ONLY rational and practicable mode of bringing about the emancipation of the blacks;" and we are warned against the "*accursed*, and disorganizing, and incendiary devices," of the abolitionists.

Soon after the mobs, a poem was published, entitled, "Fanaticism Unveiled." The author, in his advertisement, declaims against the "crusade which is now waged by a few wretched fanatics against the Colonization Society." Of the religious character of this poetical champion of the Society, some estimate may be made from the following lines:

"And do not dunces spend their cash on
Such things as we have brought in fashion?
Fictitious tales in aid of piety,
Invented for the Tract Society.
Sectarian Seminaries made
To teach the true fanatic trade;
And schools where infancy is told,
That while one world is paved with gold,
Another lying somewhat lower,
With children's skulls is sprinkled o'er."

The Society unquestionably comprises a vast number of as pure and devoted Christians as can be found in this or any other country; and we are fully persuaded, that they verily believe, that in supporting colonization, they are doing God service. The zealous coöperation they are now receiving from persons of very opposite character from themselves, should lead them to inquire whether they may not be mistaken.

It certainly does not follow that a system must be bad, because bad men support it; but it does follow, that when mobs and infidels espouse a particular object, it is because that object is recommended to them by other than religious considerations. Yet colonizationists are fond of representing their Society as a *religious* institution; and the ministers of the Gospel are earnestly urged to preach annual sermons in its behalf.

That multitudes of religious men belong to the Society is not denied, but the participation of such men in an object, does not necessarily render it a religious object: otherwise the slave trade was a Christian commerce, because John Newton was a slave-trader; and Free-Masonry must be a holy fraternity, since it can boast the names of more good men than were ever enrolled in the ranks of colonization. But in what sense can the Society be termed a religious one? It is not professedly founded on any one principle of the Gospel of Christ. It exercises no one act of benevolence towards the free blacks in this country; and in transporting them to Africa, it is by its own confession removing nuisances. It takes no measures to Christianize Africa, but landing on its shores an ignorant and vicious population. It employs no missionary, it sends no Bible, and it cannot point to a single native, converted to the faith of Jesus through its instrumentality. On the contrary, may we not, in reference to the facts disclosed in the preceding pages, affirm, without the imputation of bigotry or prejudice, that the general influence of the Society is decidedly anti-christian? We have seen that it practically tends to the debasement and persecution of the free blacks; to the hardening of the consciences of the slave-holders, and to the indefinite continuance of slavery.

The objects of the Society, as stated in the declarations of its orators, are of such vast importance, and such god-like benevolence, that it is no wonder good men have been so dazzled by the gorgeous visions presented to their imaginations, as to have omitted to scrutinize the machinery by which these visions are to be realized.

No one surely needs an apology for having believed in colonization, when WILBERFORCE could thus express himself:

"You have gladdened my heart by convincing me, that sanguine as had been my hopes of the happy effects to be produced by your institution, all my anticipations are scanty and cold compared with the reality." *Letter to Mr. Cresson.* 15*th Rep.*, p. 15.

No one surely needs to blush at acknowledging that he has been deceived in the Society since WILBERFORCE placed his name at the head of a protest against it. The following extract from this protest will show how truly the Society is *now* estimated by British philanthropists.

"Our objections to it are briefly these: while we believe its pretexts to be delusive, we are convinced that its *real* effects are of the most dangerous nature. It takes its root from a cruel prejudice and alienation in the whites of America, against the colored people, slave or free. This being its source, the effects are what might be expected — that it fosters and increases the spirit of caste, already so unhappily predominant — that it widens the breach between the two races — exposes the colored people to great practical persecution, in order to *force* them to emigrate: and finally is calculated to swallow up and divert that feeling which America, as a Christian and a free country, connot but entertain, that slavery is alike incompatible with the law of God, and the well being of man, whether of the enslaver or the enslaved. We must be understood *utterly to repudiate the principles of the American Colonization Society.*"

The opponents of slavery in England, as well as here, at first hailed the Society as an auxiliary, and the anti-slavery societies there, in the warmth of their zeal, began to remit contributions to its funds: by these same people the Society is now regarded with detestation. Probably no religious periodical possesses in an equal degree the confidence of the religious community here, as the London Christian Observer. The Observer formerly commended the Society. Hear the present sentiments of its late editor, the distinguished Z. Macauley, Esq., M. P.

> "The unchristian prejudice of color, which alone has given birth to the Colonization Society, though varnished over with other more plausible pretences, and veiled under a profession of Christian regard for the temporal and spiritual interests of the negro, which is belied by the whole course of its reasonings, and the spirit of its measures, is so detestable in itself, that I think it ought not to be tolerated; but on the contrary, ought to be denounced and opposed by all humane, and especially all pious persons in this country." *Letter*, 14*th July*, 1833, *to Mr. Garrison*.

For a quarter of a century, William Allen, a London Quaker, has been prominent in every good work, and his name is familiar to all acquainted with the great catholic institutions of England. This eminent and zealous philanthropist thus writes:

> "Having heard thy exposition of the origin and main object of the American Colonization Society, at the meeting on the 13th inst., at Exeter Hall, and *having read their own printed documents*, I scarcely know how adequately to express my surprise and indignation, that my correspondents in North America should not have informed me of the real principles of the said Society; and also, that Elliott Cresson, knowing as he must have known the abominable sentiments it has printed and published, should have condescended to become its agent." *Letter*, 15*th of* 7*th Month*, 1833.

Mr. Buxton, the successor of Mr. Wilberforce as the parliamentary leader in the cause of abolition, thus expresses himself:

> "My views of the Colonization Society you are aware of. They do not fall far short of those expressed by my friend Mr. Cropper, when he termed its objects *diabolical*." *Letter of July* 12*th*, 1833.

But is it only in Britain that good men have found themselves disappointed in the Society? Who compose our present anti-slavery societies? Pious, conscientious men, who, with scarcely an exception, were formerly advocates of colonization. A clergyman of Massachusetts, in the following passage, expresses the sentiments of a numerous and increasing body.

> "I have been constrained to withdraw my confidence and coöperation from this scheme. It is a scheme in which I was once deeply interested. I have spoken and preached, and written and taken contributions in its behalf. I did not then understand the real nature and tendency of the scheme. I meant well in espousing it, but I now see my error and my sin; and though it was a sin of ignorance, I desire to repent of it."

Almost daily do we hear of colonizationists awaking as from a dream, and expressing their astonishment and regret at the delusion into which they had fallen.

To the Christian members of the Society, we would now address ourselves, and ask, Have we not *proved* enough to induce you to pause, to examine, and to pray, before you longer lend your names, and contribute your funds to the purposes of colonization? Do no secret misgivings of conscience now trouble you? and are you perfectly sure that in supporting the Society, you are influenced by the precepts of the Gospel, and not by prejudice against an unhappy portion of the human family? If on a full investigation of the subject, you discover that colonization is not what you believed and hoped it was, remember that it is your duty to obviate, as far as possible, by a frank and open declaration of your opinion, the evil your example has done. Be not ashamed, be not slow to follow Wilberforce in entering your protest against the Society. If that Society leads to the degradation and oppression of the poor colored man — if it resists every effort to free the slave — if it misleads the conscience of the slave-holder, you are bound, your God requires you to oppose it, not in secret, but before the world. Soon will you stand at the judgment seat of Christ; there will you meet the free negro, the slave, and the master, — take care lest they all appear as witnesses against you.

PART II

AMERICAN ANTI-SLAVERY SOCIETY.

CHAPTER I.

PRINCIPLES OF THE AMERICAN ANTI-SLAVERY SOCIETY—CHARACTER OF AMERICAN SLAVERY.

THE principles professed by the American Anti-Slavery Society, are set forth in the following articles of its Constitution, viz.:

ARTICLE 2. The object of this Society is the entire abolition of slavery in the United States. While it admits that each State, in which slavery exists, has by the Constitution of the United States, the exclusive right to legislate in regard to its abolition in that State, it shall aim to convince all our fellow-citizens, by arguments addressed to their understandings and consciences, that slave-holding is a heinous crime in the sight of God; and that the duty, safety, and best interests of all concerned, require its immediate abandonment, without expatriation. The Society will also endeavor in a constitutional way to influence Congress to put an end to the domestic slave-trade, and to abolish slavery in all those portions of our common country which come under its control, especially in the District of Columbia, and likewise to prevent the extension of it to any State that may hereafter be admitted to the Union.

ARTICLE 3. This Society shall aim to elevate the character and condition of the people of color, by encouraging their intellectual, moral and religious improvement, and by removing public prejudice; that thus they may, according to their intellectual and moral worth, share an equality with the whites, of civil and religious privileges; but the Society will never in any way, countenance the oppressed in vindicating their rights, by resorting to physical force.

ARTICLE 4. Any person *who consents to the principles of* this Constitution, who contributes to the funds of this Society, and is not a slave-holder, may be a member of this Society, and shall be entitled to vote at its meetings.

Here we have great moral principles frankly and unequivocally avowed; the objects to be pursued are distinctly stated; and none are permitted to join in the pursuit of these objects without assenting to the principles which avowedly render their attainment desirable. The whole structure of the Society, therefore, is totally different from the Colonization Society; this being founded on principle, that on expediency; this availing itself only of certain professed motives, that inviting the coöperation of motives of all sorts, however contradictory.

In order to judge of the fitness of the *objects* contemplated by the Society, we must first inquire into the soundness of the *principles* by which they are recommended.

The first great principle of the Society, and indeed the one from which all the others are deduced, is the *sinfulness of slavery.* To determine whether slavery as it exists in the United States is sinful, we must know what it is. Where an institution is *unavoidably* liable to great abuses, those abuses may fairly be taken in account in estimating its true character; but in order to avoid all captious objections, we will now inquire, what are the lawful, or rather legal features of American slavery, and we will leave wholly out of view, all acts of oppression and cruelty not expressly sanctioned by law. The following definitions of American slavery, are, it will be perceived, from high authority:

"A slave is one who is in the power of a master to whom he belongs. The master may sell him, dispose of his person, his industry, his labor; he can do nothing, possess nothing, nor acquire anything but which must belong to his master." *Louisiana Code, Art.* 3.

"Slaves shall be deemed, taken, reputed and adjudged to be chattels personal in the hands of their masters and possessors, to all intents and purposes whatsoever." *Laws of South Carolina—Brevard's Digest,* 229.

It will be observed that these definitions apply to slaves, without distinction of sex or age.

But not only are those now in servitude, but their children after them, the subjects of these definitions.

The law of South Carolina says of slaves, "all their issue and offspring born or to be born, shall be, and they are hereby declared to be and remain FOREVER HEREAFTER absolute slaves, and shall follow the condition of the mother."

Slavery is not confined to *color*. Mr. Paxton, a Virginia writer, declares that "the best blood in Virginia flows in the veins of the slaves." In the description lately given of a fugitive slave in the public papers, it was stated, "He has sometimes been mistaken for a white man." The following from a Missouri paper proves that a white man may without a *mistake* be adjudged a slave.

"A case of a slave suing for his freedom, was tried a few days since in Lincoln county, of which the following is a brief statement of the particulars. A youth of about ten years of age sued for his freedom on the ground that he was a free white person. The court granted his petition to sue as a pauper upon inspection of his person. Upon his trial before the jury he was examined by the jury and by two learned physicians, all of whom concurred in the opinion that very little if any trace of negro blood could be discovered by any of the external appearances. All the physiological marks of distinction which characterize the African descent had disappeared.

"His skin was fair, his hair soft, straight, fine and white, his eyes blue, but rather disposed to the hazle-nut color; nose prominent, the lips small and completely covering the teeth, his head round and well formed, forehead high and prominent, the ears large, the tibia of the leg straight, the feet hollow. Notwithstanding these evidences of his claims, he was proven to be a descendant of a mulatto woman, and that his progenitors on his mother's side had been and still were slaves; consequently, he was found to be a SLAVE."

The laws of South Carolina and Virginia expressly recognize *Indian* slaves.

Not only do the laws acknowledge and protect existing slavery, but they provide for reducing free persons to *hereditary* bondage. In South Carolina, *fines* are imposed on free negroes for certain offences, and in default of payment, they are made slaves. If a colored citizen of any other State enters Georgia, he is fined, and if he cannot raise the money, he is sentenced to perpetual slavery, and his children after him. In Maryland, if a free negro marries a white, the negro becomes a slave. In almost every slave State, if a free negro cannot *prove* that he is free, he is by law sold at public auction as a slave for life. This is both law and practice in the District of Columbia, and with the sanction of the Congress of the United States. In no civilized country but the slave States, are children punished for the crimes of their parents; but in these, *the children of free blacks, to the latest posterity*, are condemned to servitude for the trivial offences, and often for the most innocent act of their ancestors.

It necessarily follows from the legal definitions we have given of a slave, that he is subjected to an *absolute and irresponsible despotism.*

The master has in point of *fact* the same power over his slave that he has over his horse. Some few laws there may be, forbidding the master to treat his slave with cruelty, and so the common law everywhere forbids cruelty to beasts; but it is far easier to enforce the latter than the former. Any spectator of cruelty to a beast, may ordinarily be a witness against the offender; but a slave may be mutilated or murdered with impunity in the presence of hundreds, provided their complexions are colored; and even should the crime be proved by competent testimony, the master is to be tried by a court and jury who are all interested in maintaining the supreme authority of slave-holders. But although no laws can in fact restrain the power of the master, yet laws to a certain degree indicate what kind of treatment is tolerated by public opinion. Thus when we find the laws of South Carolina *limiting* the time which slaves may be compelled to labor, to fifteen hours a day, we may form some opinion of the amount of toil which Southern masters think it right to inflict upon the slaves; and when we recollect that the laws of Maryland, Virginia and Georgia, forbid that the criminals in their penitentiaries shall be made to labor more than ten hours a day, we discover the relative place which white felons and unoffending slaves occupy in the sympathies of slave-holders.

The slave is, at all times, liable to be punished at the pleasure of his master; and although the law does not warrant him in *murdering* the slave, it expressly justifies him in *killing* him, if he dares to resist; that is, if the slave does not submit to any chastisement which a brutal master may of his sovereign pleasure choose to inflict, he may legally be shot through the head.

In South Carolina, if a slave be killed "on a sudden heat or passion, or by *undue correction*," the murderer is to pay a fine and be imprisoned six months. What would be thought of such a punishment for the murder of a white apprentice?

In Missouri, a master is by law expressly authorized to imprison his slave during pleasure, and thus may a human being be legally incarcerated for life without trial, or even the allegation of a crime.

The despotism of the slave-holder, be it remembered, is a negotiable despotism; it is daily and hourly bought and sold, and may at any moment be delegated to the most brutal of the species.

The slave, being himself property, can own no property. He may labor fifteen hours a day, but he acquires nothing by his labor. In South Carolina, a slave is not *permitted* to keep a boat, or to raise and breed for his own benefit, any horses, cattle, sheep, or hogs, under pain of forfeiture, and any person may take such articles from him.

In Georgia, the master is fined thirty dollars for *suffering* his slave to hire himself to another for his own benefit. In Maryland, the master forfeits thirteen dollars for each month that his slave is permitted to receive wages on his own account.

In Virginia, every master is finable who *permits* a slave to work for himself at wages. In North Carolina, "all horses, cattle, hogs, or sheep, that shall belong to any slave, or be of any slave's mark in this State, shall be seized and sold by the county wardens."

In Mississippi, the master is forbidden, under the penalty of fifty dollars, to let a slave raise cotton for himself, "or to keep stock of any description."

Such is the anxiety of the slave laws to repress every benevolent desire of the master to promote in the slightest degree the independence of the slave.

Slaves, being property, are like cattle liable to be leased and mortgaged by their owners, or sold on execution for debt.

A slave having no rights, cannot appear in a court of justice to ask for redress of injuries. So far as he is the subject of injury, the law regards him only as a brute, and redress can only be demanded and received by the owner. The slave may be beaten, (robbed he cannot be,) his wife and children may be insulted and abused in his presence, and he can no more institute an action for damages, than his master's horse. But cannot he be protected by his master's right of action? No: The master must prove *special* injury to his property, to recover damages. Any man may with perfect impunity whip another's slave, unless he so injure him as to occasion "a loss of service, or at least a diminution of the faculty of the slave for bodily labor." Such is the decision of the Supreme Court of Maryland. In Louisiana, if a third person maim a slave, so that he is "forever rendered unable to work," the offender pays to the owner the value of the slave, and is also to be at the expense of his maintenance; but the unfortunate slave, mutilated or crippled for life, receives not the slightest compensation. The master's right of action is a protection to his *property*, not of the comfort or security of the slave; indeed, it tends to degrade the latter to the level of the other live stock on his master's farm.

A necessary consequence of slavery, is the absence of the marriage relation. No slave can commit bigamy, because the law knows no more of the marriage of slaves, than it does of the marriage of brutes. A slave may, indeed, be formally married, but so far as legal rights and obligations are concerned, it is an idle ceremony. His wife may, at any moment, be legally taken from him, and sold in the market. The slave laws utterly *nullify* the injunction of the Supreme Lawgiver, "What God hath joined, let not man put asunder."

Of course, these laws do not recognize the parental relation as belonging to slaves. A slave has no more legal authority over his child, than a cow over her calf.

The Legislature of the slave States, when legislating respecting slaves, seem regardless alike of the claims and the affections of our common nature. No right is more sacred, or more universally admitted, than that of self-preservation; but the wretched slave, whether male or female, is denied the right of self-defence against the brutality of any person whomsoever having a white skin. Thus the law of Georgia declares, "if any slave shall presume to strike any *white* person, upon trial or conviction before the justice or justices, according to the directions of this act, he shall, for the first offence, suffer such punishment as the said justice or justices shall in their discretion think fit, not extending to life or limb; and for the second offence, suffer DEATH."

The same law prevails in South Carolina, except that death is the penalty for the third offence.

In Maryland, the justice may order the offender's ears to be cropped. In Kentucky, "any negro, mulatto, or *Indian*, bond or *free*," who "shall at any time *lift his hand* in opposition to *any* white person, shall receive thirty lashes on his or her bare back, well laid on, by order of the justice."

In South Carolina, "if any slave, who shall be out of the house or plantation where such slaves shall live or shall be usually employed, or without some white person in company with such slaves, shall *refuse to submit* to undergo the examination of *any* white person, it shall be lawful for *any* white person to pursue, apprehend, and *moderately correct* such slave; and if such slave shall assault and strike such white person, such slave may be LAWFULLY KILLED."

We have seen that the slave laws regard the slave, so far as human rights and enjoyments and social relations are concerned, as a mere brute; we are now to see, that so far as he can be made to *suffer* for his acts, he is regarded as an intelligent and responsible being.

Divine equity has established the rule, that the servant which knew not his master's will, and did commit things worthy of stripes, shall be beaten with *few* stripes. If there was ever a case to which this rule was applicable, it is to the unlettered, ignorant, brutalized slave, intentionally deprived of the ability to read the laws of God or man. A code of laws prepared for the government of such beings, one would suppose would be distinguished for its lenity; and in the mildness of its penalties, would form a striking contrast to a code for the government of the enlightened and instructed part of the community, whose offences would, of course, be aggravated by the opportunities they had enjoyed of learning their duty. Alas, the slave code punishes acts not *mala in se* with a rigor which public opinion would not tolerate for a moment, if exercised towards *white* felons, and it visits *crimes* with penalties far heavier, when committed by the poor ignorant slave, than it does when they are perpetrated by the enlightened citizen.

Thus in Georgia, *any* person may inflict twenty lashes on the bare back of a slave found without license off the plantation, or without the limits of the town to which he belongs. So also in Mississippi, Virginia, and Kentucky, at the discretion of a justice.

In South Carolina and Georgia, *any* person finding more than seven slaves together in the highway without a white person, may give each one twenty lashes.

In Kentucky, Virginia, and Missouri, a slave, for keeping a gun, powder, shot, a *club*, or other weapon whatsoever, offensive or defensive, may be whipped thirty-nine lashes by order of a justice.

In North Carolina and Tennessee, a slave travelling without a pass, or being found in another person's negro quarters, or *kitchen*, may be whipped forty lashes, and *every* slave, in whose company the visitor is found, twenty lashes.

In Louisiana, a slave, for being on *horseback* without the written permission of his master, incurs twenty-five lashes; *for keeping a dog*, the like punishment.

By the law of Maryland, for "rambling, riding, or going abroad in the night, or riding horses in the day-time, without leave," a slave may be whipt, *cropt*, or *branded* on the cheek with the letter R, or otherwise punished, not extending to life, or "so *as to render him unfit for labor*."

Such are a *few* specimens only of the punishments inflicted on slaves, for acts not criminal, and which it is utterly impossible they should generally know are forbidden by law.

Let us now view the laws of the slave States in relation to

crimes, and we shall find that their severity towards blacks and whites, is in inverse ratio to the moral guilt of the offenders.

In Virginia, the laws have recently been revised, and by the revised code, there are seventy-one offences for which the penalty is DEATH, when committed by slaves, and *imprisonment* when by whites.*

In Mississippi, the number of these offences is thirty-eight, or rather many of them are not punishable at all, when committed by whites: as, for instance, *attempting* to burn out-buildings, to commit forgery, to steal a horse, &c., &c.

Imprisonment of a slave as a punishment for crime, except in Louisiana, is utterly unknown in the slave States. To shut him up in prison, would be depriving his master of his labor, and burthening the public with his maintenance; it is, therefore, more economical to flog him for trifles, and to hang him for serious offences.

Where human life is held so cheap, and human suffering so little regarded, it is not to be expected that the dispensers of slave justice will submit to be troubled with all those forms and ceremonies which the common law has devised for the protection of innocence. We have seen that, in many instances, any *white person* may instanter discharge the functions of judge, jury, and executioner. In innumerable instances, all these functions are united in a single justice of the peace; and in South Carolina, Virginia, and Louisiana, LIFE may be taken, according to law, without intervention of grand or petit jurors. In other States, a trial by jury is granted in *capital* cases; but in no one State, it is believed, is it thought worth while to trouble a *grand jury* with presenting a slave. In most of the slave States, the ordinary tribunal for the trial of slaves charged with offences not capital, is composed of justices and freeholders, or of justices only. A white man cannot be convicted of misdemeanor, except by the unanimous verdict of twelve of his peers. In Louisiana, if the court is *equally divided* as to the guilt of a slave, judgment is rendered *against him.*

* An enumeration of these offences, together with references to the statutes alluded to in this work, may be found in "Stroud's Sketch of the Slave Laws."

In 1832, *thirty-five* slaves were executed at Charleston, in pursuance of the sentence of a court, consisting of two justices and five freeholders, on a charge of intended insurrection. No indictments, no summoning of jurors, no challenges for cause or favor, no seclusion of the triers from intercourse with those who might bias their judgment, preceded this unparalleled legal destruction of human life.

However much we may pride ourselves, as a nation, on the general diffusion of the blessings of education, it ought to be recollected that these blessings are forcibly withheld from two millions of our inhabitants; or that one-sixth of our whole population are doomed by law to the grossest ignorance.

A law of South Carolina, passed in 1800, authorizes the infliction of twenty lashes on every slave found in an assembly convened for the purpose of "mental instruction," held in a confined or secret place, although in the presence of a white. Another law imposes a fine of £100 on any person who may teach a slave to write. An act of Virginia, of 1829, declares every meeting of slaves at any school, by day or night, for instruction in reading or writing, an unlawful assembly, and any justice may inflict twenty lashes on each slave found in such school.

In North Carolina, to teach a slave to read or write, or to sell or give him *any* book (Bible not excepted) or pamphlet, is punished with thirty-nine lashes, or imprisonment, if the offender be a free negro, but if a white, then with a fine of $200. The reason for this law, assigned in its preamble is, that "teaching slaves to read and write, tends to excite dissatisfaction in their minds, and to produce insurrection and rebellion."

In Georgia, if a white teach a free negro or slave to read or write, he is fined $500, and imprisoned at the discretion of the court; if the offender be a colored man, bond or free, he is to be fined or whipped at the discretion of the court. Of course a father may be flogged for teaching his own child. This barbarous law was enacted in 1829.

In Louisiana, the penalty for teaching slaves to read or write, is one year's imprisonment.

These are specimens of the efforts made by slave legislatures, to enslave the *minds* of their victims; and we have surely no reason to hope that their *souls* are regarded with more compassion.

In vain has the Redeemer of the world given the command to preach the gospel to every creature; his professed disciples in the slave States have issued a counter order; and as we have already seen, have by their laws, incapacitated 2,000,000 of their fellow-men from complying with the injunction, "search the Scriptures." Not only are the slaves debarred from reading the wonderful things of God — they are practically prevented, with a few exceptions, from even *hearing* of them.

In Georgia, any justice of the peace may, at his discretion, break up any religious assembly of slaves, and may order *each slave present* to be "corrected without trial, by receiving on the bare back twenty-five stripes with a whip, switch or cow-skin."

In South Carolina, slaves may not meet together for the purpose of "religious worship" before sunrise or after sunset, unless the *majority* of the meeting be composed of white persons, under the penalty of twenty lashes well laid on. As it will be rather difficult for the slave to divine before he goes to the meeting, how many blacks and how many whites will be present, and of course which color will have the "majority," a due regard for his back will keep him from the meeting.

In Virginia, all evening meetings of slaves at any meeting-house are unequivocally forbidden.

In Mississippi, the law *permits* the master to suffer his slave to attend the preaching of a *white* minister.

It is very evident that when public opinion tolerates such laws, it will not tolerate the general religious instruction of the slaves. True it is, a master may carry or send his slaves to the parish church, and true it is that some do attend, and receive benefit from their attendance.

On this, as well as on every other subject relating to slavery, we would rather fall short of, than exceed the truth. We will not assert there are no Christians among the slaves, for we trust there are some. When, however, we recollect, that they are denied the Scriptures, and all the usual advantages of the Sunday school, and are forbidden to unite among themselves in acts of social worship and instruction, and that almost all the sermons they hear are such as are addressed to educated whites, and of course above their own comprehension, we may form some idea of the obstacles opposed to their spiritual improvement. Let it be also recollected that every master possesses the *tremendous* power of keeping his slaves in utter ignorance of their Maker's will, and of their own immortal destinies. And now with all these facts and their consequences and tendencies in remembrance, we ask if we do not make a most abundant and charitable allowance when we suppose that 245,000 slaves possess a saving knowledge of the religion of Christ? And yet after this admission, one which probably no candid person will think too limited, there will remain in the bosom of our country, TWO MILLIONS of human beings, who, in consequence of our laws, are in a state of heathenism! But probably many will refuse their assent to this conclusion without further and more satisfactory evidence of its correctness. To such persons we submit the following testimony, furnished by slave-holders themselves. In 1831, the Rev. Charles C. Jones preached a sermon before two associations of planters in Georgia, one of Liberty County, and the other of McIntosh County. This sermon is before us, and we quote from it.

> "Generally speaking, they (the slaves) appear to us to be without God and without hope in the world, a NATION OF HEATHEN in our very midst. We cannot cry out against the Papists for withholding the Scriptures from the common people, and keeping them in ignorance of the way of life; for we *withhold* the Bible from our servants, and *keep* them in ignorance of it, while we *will* not use the means to have it read and explained to them. The cry of our perishing servants comes up to us from the sultry plains as they bend at their toil — it comes up to us from their humble cottages when they return at evening to rest their weary limbs — it comes up to us from the midst of their ignorance and superstition, and adultery and lewdness. We have manifested no emotions of horror at abandoning the souls of our servants to the adversary, the roaring lion that walketh about seeking whom he may devour."

On the 5th of December, 1833, a committee of the Synod of South Carolina and Georgia, to whom was referred the subject of the religious instruction of the colored population, made a report which has been published, and in which this language is used :

"Who would credit it, that in these years of revival and benevolent effort, in this Christian republic, there are over TWO MILLIONS of human beings in the condition of HEATHEN, and in some respects in a worse condition? From long-continued and close observation, we believe that their moral and religious condition is such that they may justly be considered the HEATHEN of this Christian country, and will bear comparison with heathen in any country in the world. The negroes are destitute of the Gospel, and *ever will be under the present state of things.* In the vast field extending from an entire State beyond the Potomac to the Sabine river, and from the Atlantic to the Ohio, there are to the best of our knowledge not *twelve* men exclusively devoted to the religious instruction of the negroes. In the present state of feeling in the South, a ministry of their own color could neither be obtained NOR TOLERATED.

"But do not the negroes have access to the Gospel through the stated ministry of the whites? We answer, No ; the negroes have no regular and efficient ministry ; as a matter of course, no churches; neither is there sufficient room in white churches for their accommodation. We know of but *five* churches in the slave-holding States built expressly for their use ; these are all in the State of Georgia. We may now inquire if they enjoy the privileges of the Gospel in their own houses, and on our plantations. Again we return a negative answer. They have no Bibles to read by their own firesides — they have no family altars; and when in affliction, sickness, or death, they have no minister to address to them the consolations of the Gospel, nor to bury them with solemn and appropriate services."

In a late number of the Charleston (S. C.) Observer, a correspondent remarked:

"Let us establish missionaries among our own negroes, who in view of religious knowledge, are as debasingly ignorant as any one on the coast of Africa ; for I hazard the assertion, that throughout the bounds of our synod, there are at least one hundred thousand slaves, speaking the same language as ourselves, who never *heard* of the plan of salvation by a Redeemer."

The editor, instead of contradicting this broad assertion, adds: "We fully concur with what our correspondent has said respecting the benighted heathen among ourselves."

Such is American slavery, — a system which classes with the beasts of the field, over whom dominion has been given to man, an intelligent and accountable being, the instant his Creator has breathed into his nostrils the breath of life. Over this infant heir of immortality, no mother has a right to watch, no father may guide his feeble steps, check his wayward appetites and train him for future usefulness, happiness and glory. Torn from his parents, and sold in the market, he soon finds himself laboring among strangers under the whip of a driver, and his task augmenting with his ripening strength. Day after day and year afer year is he driven to the cotton or sugar-field, as the ox to the furrow. No hope of reward lightens his toil; the subject of insult, the victim of brutality, the laws of his country afford him no redress; his wife, such only in name, may at any moment be dragged from his side; his children, heirs only of his misery and degradation, are but articles of merchandise; his mind, stupified by his oppressors, is wrapped in darkness; his soul, no man careth for it; his body, worn with stripes and toil, is at length committed to the earth, like the brute that perisheth.

This is the system which the American Anti-Slavery Society declares to be sinful, and ought therefore to be immediatly abolished; and this is the system which the American Colonization Society excuses, and which, it contends, ought to be perpetual, rather than its victims should enjoy their rights in "the white man's land."

To one whose moral sense has not been perverted, it would seem a temerity bordering on blasphemy, to contend that *such a system* can be approved by a just and holy God, or sanctioned by the precepts of his blessed Gospel. Slavery, we are told, is not forbidden in the Bible; but who will dare to say that cruelty and injustice and compulsory heathenism are not?

We are often reminded, that St. Paul exhorts slaves to be obedient to their masters; but so he does subjects to their rulers. If, in the one instance, he justified slavery, so did he despotism in the other. The founder of Christianity and his apostles, interfered not with political institutions, but laid down rules for the conduct of individuals; and St. Paul, in requiring masters to give their servants that which is *just and equal*, virtually condemned the whole system of slavery, since he who receives what is just and equal cannot be a slave. If it was right in the time of St. Paul to hold *white* men as slaves, would it be wrong to do so now? If slavery is lawful *now*, it must have been lawful in its commencement, since perseverance in wrong can never constitute right. Let it be explained how free men with their posterity, to the latest generation, can now be lawfully reduced to slavery, and forever kept in ignorance of the duties and consolations of Christianity, and we will unite with those who justify American slavery.

CHAPTER II

PROPOSED OBJECTS AND MEASURES OF THE AMERICAN ANTI-SLAVERY SOCIETY — CENSURE OF ABOLITIONISTS.

THE next great principle maintained by the Society is, that slavery being sinful, it ought immediately to cease. Admitting the premises, the conclusion seems irresistible. Sin is opposition to the will of our Creator and Supreme Lawgiver. His wisdom and goodness are alike infinite, and if slavery be inconsistent with his will, it must necessarily be inconsistent with the welfare of his creatures. Reason and revelation, moreover, assure us that God will punish sin; and therefore to contend that it is necessary or expedient to continue in sin, is to impeach every attribute of the Deity, and to brave the vengeance of Omnipotence.

These principles lead the Society to aim at effecting the following objects, viz.:

1st. The immediate abolition of slavery throughout the United States.

2d. As a necessary consequence, the suppression of the Amercan slave-trade.

3d. The ultimate elevation of the black population to an equality with the white, in civil and religious privileges.

But principles may be sound, and objects may be good, and yet the measures adopted to enforce those principles, and to attain those objects, may be unlawful. Let us then inquire what are the measures contemplated by the Society.

Slavery exists under the authority of the State Legislatures, in the several States; and under the authority of Congress in the District of Columbia, and in the United States' Territories.

The members of the Society are all represented in Congress, and the Constitution guarantees to them the right of petition. They will therefore petition Congress to exercise the power it possesses, to abolish slavery in the District of Columbia and the Territories. But the Society is not represented in the State Legislatures, and therefore petitions to them might be deemed officious, and would not probably lead to any advantageous result. The Society will therefore use the right possessed by every member of the community, the right of speech and of the press. They will address arguments to the understandings and the consciences of their fellow-citizens, and endeavor to convince them of the duty and policy of immediate emancipation. Legislatures are with us but the mere creatures of the people, and when the people of the slave States demand the abolition of slavery, their Legislatures will give effect to their will by passing the necessary laws.

The means by which the Society will endeavor to secure to the blacks an equality of civil and religious privileges, are frankly avowed to be the encouragement of their intellectual, moral, and religious improvement, and the removal of existing prejudices against them. To prevent any misapprehensions of the real design of the Society, the constitution expressly declares that the Society will never "*in any way countenance the oppressed in vindicating their rights by resorting to physical force.*"

Such are the principles and designs of those who are now designated as abolitionists; and never since the settlement of the country, has any body of citizens been subjected in a equal degree, to unmerited and unmeasured reproach.

We have seen with what kind of temper colonizationists speak of free negroes, and we may well question, when we call to mind the obloquy they have heaped upon abolitionists, whether the latter are not in their opinion the greater *nuisances*. Much as the free negroes have suffered from the charges of the Society, still there have been limits to the invectives hurled against them. No chancellor has adjudged *them* to be "reckless incendiaries."* No counsellor, learned in the law, has charged *them* with being guilty of "a palpable nullification of that Constitution which they had *sworn* to support." † No honorable senator has denounced *them* as "fanatics, increasing injury and sealing oppression." ‡ The chairman of the Executive Committee of the New York Colonization Society never asserted that *their* DESIGN was "beyond a doubt to foment a servile war in the South." § Nor did even the New York Courier and Enquirer ever propose that the city authorities should inform *them*, that they must prosecute "their treasonable and BEASTLY plans at their own peril;" in other words, that they should not be protected from mobs. ‖ Nor, finally, has any city corporation accused *them* of holding sentiments "demoralizing in themselves, and little short of *treason* towards the government of our country." ¶

But abolitionists are neither astonished nor dismayed at the torrent of insult and calumny that has been poured upon them, as though some strange thing had happened unto them. They remember that Wilberforce and his companions experienced similar treatment, while laboring for the abolition of the slave-

* Speech of Chancellor Walworth of New York.

† Speech of D. B. Ogden, Esq., of New York.

‡ Hon. Mr. Frelinghuysen, of the Senate of the United States.

§ Commercial Advertiser, 9th June, 1834.

‖ Courier and Enquirer, 11th July, 1834. The same paper of the 27th Dec., 1834, contains the following: — "We do say, and say in all *the earnestness of conviction, that no meeting of abolitionists should ever be suffered to go on with its proceedings in the United States*. Whenever these wretched disturbers of the public peace, and plotters of MURDER, RAPINE, AND A DISSOLUTION OF THE UNION, have the impudence to hold a meeting, it is the duty of the rational citizens, — always a vast majority in every place, — to go to that meeting, and there, by exercising the right of every American citizen, make the expression of their disapprobation and disgust loud enough, and emphatic enough, to render it impossible for treason to go on with its machinations. Let sedition be driven from its den, as often as its minions congregate."

¶ Resolutions of the Corporation of the City of Utica.

trade; and they remember also the glorious triumphs they achieved, and the full though tardy justice that has been done to their motives. A few brief reminiscences may be both interesting and useful.

In 1776, the British House of Commons rejected a resolution, that the slave-trade "was contrary to the laws of God and the rights of man." Yet that trade is now piracy by act of Parliament.

In 1788, on a bill being introduced into the House of Lords, to mitigate the horrors of the trade, Lord Chancellor Thurlow ridiculed "the sudden fit of philanthropy that had given it birth," and Lord Chandos predicted "the insurrection of the slaves, and the massacre of their masters, from the *agitation* of the subject."

In 1789, on a motion of Mr. Wilberforce, that the House would take the trade into consideration, a member pronounced the attempt to abolish it "hypocritical, *fanatic*, and methodistical," and contended that abolition must lead to "insurrections, massacre and ruin."

In 1791, Col. Tarleton, in the House of Commons, speaking of the proposed abolition of the slave-trade, declared that "the measure was fit only for the bigotry and superstition of the twelfth century." Lord John Russell asserted that abolition was "visionary and delusive, a feeble attempt, without the power to serve the cause of humanity."

Lord Sheffield could "trace in the arguments for abolition nothing like reason, but on the contrary, downright frenzy."

In 1792, the abolitionists were denounced in Parliament, as "a junto of sectaries, sophists, enthusiasts, and fanatics."

In 1793, the Duke of Clarence, now William IV, in his place in the House of Lords, declared the abolitionists to be "fanatics and hypocrites," and so far violated parliamentary decorum, as to apply these epithets to Mr. Wilberforce by name. Yet has he lived to crown the labors and fulfil the hopes of Wilberforce, by giving his assent to the bill abolishing slavery throughout the British dominions.

In 1804, Lord Temple declared in Parliament, that to abolish the slave-trade, would be "*the death-warrant of every white inhabitant in the islands.*"

Ten times did Mr. Wilberforce bring the subject of the abolition of the traffic before Parliament, and ten times was he doomed to witness the failure of his efforts; nor was this detestable commerce suppressed till *thirty* years after the first motion against it had been made in the House of Commons. Now, it is prohibited by the whole Christian world.

When the abolitionists of the present day think of these facts, and recollect the reproaches heaped on Wilberforce and his colleagues by a chancellor and dignified senators, well may they thank God and take courage. And who are these men, we would ask, whom colonizationists are honoring with epithets similar to those which the advocates of the slave-trade so liberally applied to the philanthropists who opposed it? We will suffer an authority justly respected by the religious community to answer the question.

Abbott's Religious Magazine, in an article on the mobs against the *New York* Abolitionists, says:

"The men against whom their fury was directed, were in general ministers of the Gospel, and other distinguished members of Christian churches. The *more prominent* ones, were the very persons who have been most honored in times past, on account of their personal exertions and pecuniary contributions for every benevolent purpose. Let the whole land be searched, and we believe that no men will be found to have done so much for the promotion of temperance, purity, and every benevolent and religious object."

CHAPTER III.

FANATICISM OF ABOLITIONISTS.

One of the most usual terms by which abolitionists are designated by their opponents is, "the fanatics." It seems they are fanatics, because they believe slavery to be sinful. The grounds for this belief have been already stated. But is the sinfulness of slavery a *new* doctrine? or has it been held only by weak and misguided men? Is Wilberforce to be denounced as a "wretched fanatic," because he declared, "slavery is the full measure of pure unsophisticated wickedness, and scorning all competition or comparison, it stands alone without a rival, in the secure, undisputed possession of its detestable preëminence?"

Was Jonathan Edwards a poor "misguided" man, for thus addressing slave-holders? "While you hold your negroes in slavery, you do wrong, exceedingly wrong—you do not as you would that men should do to you; you commit sin in the sight of God; you daily violate the plain rights of mankind, and that in a higher degree than if you committed theft or robbery." Were Porteus, Horseley, Fox, Johnson, Burke, Jefferson, and Bolivar, "miserable enthusiasts?" Yet hear their testimonies.

"The Christian religion is opposed to slavery in its spirit and in its principles; it classes men-stealers among murderers of fathers and of mothers, and the most profane criminals upon earth." *Porteus.*

"Slavery is injustice which no consideration of policy can extenuate." *Horseley.*

"Personal freedom is the right of every human being. It is a right of which he who deprives a fellow creature, was absolutely criminal in so depriving him; and which he who withheld, was no less criminal in withholding." *Fox.*

"No man is by nature the property of another. The rights of nature must be some way forfeited, before they can be justly taken away." *Johnson.*

"Slavery is a state so improper, so degrading, and so ruinous to the feelings and capacities of human nature, that it ought not to be suffered to exist." *Burke.*

"The Almighty has no attribute which can take sides with *us* in such a contest," — (a contest with insurgent slaves.) *Jefferson.*

"Slavery is the infringement of all laws; a law having a tendency to preserve slavery, would be the grossest sacrilege." *Bolivar.*

We would take the liberty of recommending to the consideration of certain Methodist colonizationists, the following language of John Wesley.

"Men-buyers are exactly on a level with men-stealers. Indeed, you say, I pay honestly for my goods, and am not concerned to know how they are come by. Nay, but you are — you are deeply concerned to know that they are honestly come by. Otherwise, you are a partaker with a thief, and are not a jot honester than him. But you know they are not honestly come by; you know they are procured by means nothing so innocent as picking of pockets, or robbery on the highway. Perhaps you will say, I do not buy my negroes, I only use those left me by my father. So far is well, but is it enough to satisfy your conscience? Had your father, have you, has any man living a right to use another as a slave? It cannot be, even setting revelation aside."

But abolitionists are fanatics, not merely because they believe slavery sinful, but also because they contend it ought *immediately* to be abolished. In their fanaticism on this point, as well as on the other, they are kept in countenance by a host of divines and statesmen, and by the unanimous opinion of thousands and tens of thousands of Christians. Men of all ranks and characters, from John Wesley or Daniel O'Connell have exhibited this fanaticism; it has been borne by the republicans of France, the Catholics of South America, the people of England, Scotland, and Ireland.

So long ago as 1774, John Wesley declared: "It cannot be that either war or contract can give any man such a property in another, as he has in his sheep and oxen. Much less is it possible that any child of man should ever be *born a slave.* If, therefore, you have any regard to justice, (to say nothing of mercy, nor the revealed will of God,) render unto all their due. Give liberty to whom liberty is due, that is, to every child of man, to every partaker of human nature."

Jonathan Edwards was fanatic enough to assert: — "Every man, who cannot show that his negro hath, by his voluntary conduct, forfeited his liberty, is obligated *immediately* to manumit him."

One million five hundred thousand persons petitioned the British Parliament for the total and immediate abolition of slavery. Indeed, Mr. O'Connell expressed the nearly unanimous sentiment of the whole nation, when he exclaimed, — "I am for speedy, immediate abolition. I care not what creed or color slavery may assume, I am for its total, its *instant* abolition.

We have not yet exhausted the proofs of the alleged fanaticism of abolitionists. It seems they are fanatics for wishing to elevate the blacks to a civil and religious equality with the whites. Certain colonization editors deny to abolitionists, as we have seen, the constitutional right of freedom of speech, the press, and pulpit, and even of peaceably assembling together; and multitudes seem to think, that they have forfeited the protection of the ninth commandment. Men of all ranks have united in charging upon them designs which they indignantly disclaim, and in support of which, not a particle of evidence has been or can be adduced. One of the designs falsely imputed to them, is that of bringing about an amalgamation of colors by intermarriages. In vain have they again and again denied any such design; in vain have their writings been searched for any recommendation of such amalgamation. No abolitionist is known to have married a negro, or to have given his child to a negro; yet has the charge of amalgamation been repeated, and repeated, till many have, no doubt, honestly believed it.

During the very height of the New York riots, and as if to excite the mob to still greater atrocities, the editor of the Commercial Advertiser asserted that the abolitionists had "*sought* to degrade" the identity of their fellow citizens, as a "nation of white men, by reducing it to the condition of MONGRELS." *Com. Adv. 11th July*, 1834.

No one in the possession of his reasoning faculties can believe it to be the duty of white men to select black wives; and abolitionists have given every proof the nature of the case will admit, that they countenance no such absurdity.

But most true it is, that the Anti-Slavery Society avows its intention to labor for the civil and religious equality of the blacks. It has been found *expedient* to accuse it of aiming also at their *social* equality. He must be deeply imbued with fanaticism, or rather with insanity, who contends, that *because* a man has a dark skin, he is, *therefore*, entitled to a reception in our families and a place at our tables.

We all know white men whose characters and habits render them repulsive to us, and whom no consideration would induce us to admit into our social circles; and can it be believed that abolitionists are willing to extend to negroes, merely on account of their color, courtesies and indulgences which, in innumerable instances, they withhold, and properly withhold, from their white fellow citizens? But who pretends that, because a man is so disagreeable in his manners and person that we refuse to associate with him, *therefore* he ought to be denied the right of suffrage, the privilege of choosing his trade and profession, the opportunities of acquiring knowledge, and the liberty of pursuing his own happiness? Yet such is our conduct towards the free blacks, and it is this conduct which the Society aims at reforming. The Society does contend, that no man ought to be punished for the complexion God has given him. And are not black men *punished* for the color of their skin? Read the laws of the slave States relative to free negroes; alas! read the laws of Ohio and Connecticut; read the decision of Judge Daggett; behold them deprived of the means of education, and excluded from almost every trade and profession; see them *compelled* to wander in poverty and ignorance. Now, all this, abolitionists contend is *wrong*, and their opposition to this system of persecution and oppression is fanaticism! Be it so; but it is only *modern* fanaticism, and it was not so regarded when in 1785, JOHN JAY declared:

> "I wish to see all unjust and unnecessary discriminations every where abolished, and that the time may soon come, when all our inhabitants, of every COLOR and denomination, shall be free and EQUAL PARTAKERS OF OUR POLITICAL LIBERTY."

It requires no great exercise of candor to admit that the prejudices existing against the blacks are sinful, whenever they lead us to treat those unhappy people with injustice and inhumanity. They have their rights as well as ourselves. They have no right to associate with us against our will, but they have a right to acquire property by lawful industry; they have a right to participate in the blessings of education and political liberty. When, therefore, our prejudices lead us to *keep* the blacks in poverty, by restricting their industry,* to *keep* them in ignorance, by excluding them from our seminaries, and preventing them from having seminaries of their own; to *keep* them in a state of vassalage by denying them any choice in their rulers; our prejudices are so far sinful, and so far only does the Anti-Slavery Society aim at removing them.

CHAPTER IV.

INCENDIARISM AND TREASON OF ABOLITIONISTS.

It is not enough that abolitionists should be represented as fanatics; it has been deemed expedient to hold them up to the community as incendiaries and traitors. The chairman of the Executive Committee of the New York Colonization Society, thus speaks of the Anti-Slavery Society, in his paper of the 9th June, 1834:

> "The *design* of this Society is, beyond a doubt, to foment a servile war in the South; they have been heard to say, blood must be shed, and the sooner the better; this Society owes its existence not to the love of liberty, or any particular affection for the slaves, but to cruel and bitter hatred, and malignity."

In an earlier paper, he inserted an article accusing abolitionists of seeking to use the pulpits "for the base *purpose* of encouraging scenes of bloodshed."

Here we find the most atrocious *designs* imputed to men well known in the community for active benevolence and private

* As one instance among the innumerable restrictions on the industry of these people, we may mention that no free black, however moral and intelligent, can obtain a license in the city of New York to drive a cart!

worth; and yet not a scintilla of evidence is offered in support of the extraordinary fact, that such men should harbor such designs. In this case the accused can of course offer only negative proof of their innocence. That proof is to be found, first, in their individual characters; secondly, in the fact that many of the abolitionists are emphatically *peace* men, that is, they hold the Quaker doctrine of the unlawfulness of war, and maintain that it would be sinful in the slaves to attempt effecting their freedom by force of arms; * thirdly, in the fundamental principle of the Society that they will "never in any way countenance the oppressed in vindicating their rights by resorting to physical force;" and, fourthly, in the fact that abolitionists as such, have in no instance recommended or committed an act of unlawful violence.

But by declaiming against slavery, abolitionists are exciting odium against slave-holders. If he who labors to render any particular sin, and those who are guilty of it odious, is of course a "reckless incendiary," few are more justly and honorably entitled to this epithet, than the excellent Chancellor of New York. Few have shown more intrepidity in denouncing the venders of ardent spirits than this gentleman; and abolitionists in their warfare against slavery, may well take a lesson from the example he has set them of an honest and fearless discharge of duty. Had the President of the New York Temperance Society and his associates exercised the same tenderness and gentleness towards drunkards and venders, that he now shows towards slave-holders, Temperance Societies would have checked the progress of drunkenness as little as colonization promises to do that of slavery.

THOMAS JEFFERSON was not denounced as a reckless incendiary, when in the midst of a slave population, he declared that the Almighty had no attribute that could take side with the masters in a contest with their slaves; nor did JOHN JAY forfeit the confidence of his countrymen, when during the Revolutionary war, he asserted, "till America comes into this measure,

* This sentiment is held and avowed by the much calumniated Mr. Garrison.

(abolition of slavery) her prayers to heaven for liberty will be IMPIOUS;" nor when addressing the Legislature of New York, then a slave State, he told them that persons "free by the laws of God, are held in slavery by the laws of man."

Nor were FRANKLIN and his associates regarded as incendiaries for uniting in 1787, "to extend the blessings of freedom to every part of our race," or for refusing to permit slave-holders to participate with them in this glorious effort.

It was not sufficient to ridicule abolitionists as fanatics, or to stigmatize them as incendiaries; they must be branded as traitors and nullifiers. On the 9th of October, 1833, a few days after a mob had assembled to deprive American citizens of one of their dearest constitutional rights, that of peaceably expressing their opinions, a numerous colonization meeting was convened in New York for the purpose of taking advantage of the recent excitement to raise the sum of $20,000. Gentlemen of high rank and influence addressed the meeting. Not a word of disapprobation of the late outrage escaped them; on the contrary, the violence offered to the abolitionists seemed to be extenuated, if not justified, by the grievous charges now brought against them.

The Hon. Mr. Frelinghuysen of New Jersey, justly distinguished for his piety, his talents, and his station as a Senator of the United States, addressed the meeting. "In the course of his address," says the N. Y. Commercial Advertiser, 10th of October, "he dwelt with emphasis, and just discrimination upon the proceedings of both *cis* and *trans*-Atlantic abolitionists, who are *seeking to destroy* our happy Union."

Chancellor Walworth, one of the most estimable citizens, and the highest judicial officer of the State of New York, alluding to the emancipation to be effected by colonization, remarked:

"The emancipation, however, to which this resolution directs your attention, is not that *unconstitutional* and dangerous emancipation contemplated by a few visionary enthusiasts, and a still fewer reckless incendiaries among us, which cannot be effected without violating the rights of property secured by that constitution which we have *sworn* to support—that emancipation which *would arm one part of the Union against another*, and light up the flame of civil war in this now happy land." *N. Y. Journal of Commerce.*

David B. Ogden, Esq., a gentleman whose legal eminence and whose purity of character justly give to his opinions peculiar weight, used the following language:

"I avail myself of this opportunity, to enter my solemn protest against the attempts which are making by a few FANATICS, who, without looking to the fearful consequences involved in such an issue, are advocating the immediate emancipation of slaves, in the Southern District. As citizens of the United States, we have no right to interfere with the claims of our Southern brethren to the property of their slaves. The Constitution of the United States recognizes their right to it, and they have not only a sure and undeniable right to that property, but they are entitled to the full protection of the constituted authorities, in enforcing the enjoyment of it. Let us not talk any more of nullification; *the doctrine of immediate emancipation is a direct and palpable nullification of that Constitution we have sworn to support.*" *N. Y. Journal of Commerce.*

We might have selected many similar charges from other sources, but we have taken *these* on account of the high character of the accusers, and because the authors are all of the legal profession, and, of course, aware of the importance of precision in all charges of a criminal nature. Not one of these gentlemen sitting as a criminal judge, would permit the merest vagabond to be put on his defence on a vague charge of stealing, but would quash any indictment that did not specify the time and place of the offence, and the property alleged to be stolen; yet they did not scruple to hold up their fellow-citizens and fellow Christians to the indignation of the public, on charges destitute of all specification, and unsupported by a particle of testimony.

Abolitionists are here accused of seeking to destroy our happy Union; of contemplating a violation of property, secured by the Constitution they had sworn to support; of pursuing measures which would lead to a civil war; and of being guilty of direct and palpable nullification. When — where — how were these crimes attempted? What proof is offered? Nothing, absolutely nothing, is offered but naked assertion. Is this equitable? Is it doing to others as these gentlemen would wish others to do to them?

But it is not enough that abolitionists should be denounced at home; they must also be defamed abroad. Mr. Gurley, Secretary of the American Colonization Society, writes a letter (1833) to Henry Ibbotson, Esq., England, and to give it greater weight, dates it, "Office of the Colonization Society, Washington." In this letter, he undertakes to enlighten his foreign correspondent on some of the "*fundamental* errors" of the abolitionists, and ranks among them the opinion, "that, in present circumstances, slavery ought to be abolished, by means not acting solely through, but, *in a great degree against, and in defiance of the will of the South.*" Not a tittle of evidence is given, that such an opinion is held by a single individual in the United States.

Mr. Jeremiah Hubbard, clerk of the Yearly Meeting of *Friends,* in North Carolina, in a letter to a friend in England, (Afr. Rep., X, p. 37,) declares that "the primary object" of the abolitionists "appears to be, that of producing such a revolution in public sentiment as to cause the *national legislation* to bear *directly* upon the slave-holders, and to *compel* them to emancipate their slaves."

Now, to all these charges, and to each and every one of them, the members of the Anti-Slavery Society plead NOT GUILTY, and desire to be tried by God and their country. But, alas, no trial is vouchsafed to them: judgment has already been given, and execution awarded against them, without trial and without evidence, solely on the finding of a voluntary and irresponsible inquest. All they can now do, is to ask for a reversal of the judgment as false and illegal, cruel and oppressive.

It is, of course, difficult to disprove charges, where the counts of the indictment are utterly void of certainty, and where, from the nature of the case, none but negative testimony can be offered by the accused. We have a right to presume that the treason and nullification charged on abolitionists, have reference to their efforts to procure the abolition of slavery in the United States. Now slavery exists under the authority of Congress, and also under the authority of State Legislatures. We will proceed in the first place to exhibit some facts relative to slavery in the former instance, and inquire how far the conduct of abolitionists in respect to it is treasonable and unconstitutional; and we will then make the same inquiry as to their conduct in regard to slavery in the several States.

CHAPTER V.

SLAVERY UNDER THE THE AUTHORITY OF CONGRESS.

At the last census, there were in the territories of Arkansas, Florida, and the District of Columbia, twenty-six thousand one hundred and thirty-eight slaves. We will confine our remarks at present to slavery as it is exhibited at the seat of the federal government, and in a portion of territory over which the Constitution of the United States has given to Congress "exclusive jurisdiction." In this District of ten miles square, there are six thousand slaves; and the laws under which they are held in bondage, are among the most cruel and wicked of all the slave laws in the United States. This District, moreover, placed as it is under the immediate and absolute control of the national government, is the great slave mart of the North American continent.

In 1829, Mr. Miner, a member of the House of Representatives, from Pennsylvania, introduced a resolution for the gradual abolition of slavery in the District. In his speech in support of this resolution, many appalling facts were disclosed. It appeared that in the last five years, seven hundred and forty-two colored persons had been committed to the public prison of the city of Washington. And were these persons accused or convicted of crime? NOT ONE. Four hundred and fifty-two were lodged in the UNITED STATES PRISON by slave-traders, for safe-keeping prior to exportation. The residue were imprisoned on suspicion, real or affected, of being fugitive slaves; and if not claimed as such, were by *authority of Congress*, to be SOLD AS SLAVES FOR LIFE, to raise money to pay their JAIL FEES!

Such are the facts in regard to the prison in the Capital of our confederate Republic; and let it be recollected that there are other prisons besides this in the District of Columbia.

Of the practical operation of a system sanctioned by the laws of Congress, takes the following sample:

"Visiting the prison," says Mr. Miner, "and passing through the avenues that lead to the cells, I was struck with the appearance of a woman, having three or four children with her, one at the breast. She presented such an aspect of woe, that I could not help inquiring her story. It was simply this: she was a slave, but had married a man who was free. By him she had eight or nine children. Moved by natural affection, the father labored to support the children; but as they attained an age to be valuable in the MARKET, perhaps ten or twelve, the master sold them. One after another was taken away and sold to the slave-dealers. She had now come to an age to be no longer profitable as a breeder, and her master had separated her from her husband and all the associations of life, and sent her and her children to YOUR prison for sale."

The law of the District, virtually the law of Congress, by which any colored person, without the allegation of a crime, may be seized and thrown into a cell, and unless he can *there* prove his freedom, or is claimed by another, is sold for life as a slave to pay his jail fees, is for unblushing injustice and atrocity utterly unrivalled by any enactment of the despots of the old world. Mr. Miner states, that in 1826–7 no less than FIVE persons were thus sold into perpetual bondage, for jail fees. In one case, the UNITED STATES MARSHAL lost his fees. Hear Mr. Miner.

"In August, 1821, a black man was taken up and imprisoned as a runaway. He was kept confined until October, 1822,—four hundred and five days. In this time, vermin, disease, and misery had deprived him of the use of his limbs. He was rendered a cripple for life, and finally discharged, *as no one would buy him.* Turned out upon the world a miserable pauper, disabled by OUR means from gaining subsistence, he is sometimes supported from the Poor-house, sometimes receives alms in your streets."

Mr. Miner thus speaks of the AMERICAN SLAVE-TRADE, as carried on in the District:

"The slave-trade, as it exists and is carried on here, is marked by instances of injustice and cruelty scarcely exceeded on the coast of Africa. It is a mistake to suppose it is a mere purchase and sale of *acknowledged* slaves. The District is full of complaints on the subject, and the evil is increasing. So long ago as 1802, the extent and cruelty of the traffic, produced from a grand jury, at Alexandria, a presentment so clear, so strong, and so feelingly drawn, that I shall make no apology for reading it to the House."

Mr. Miner then read the following:

"*January Term*, 1802.

"We the grand jury for the body of the County of Alexandria, in the District of Columbia, present as a grievance the practice of persons coming from distant parts of the United States into this District, for the purpose of purchasing slaves, where they exhibit to our view a scene of wretchedness and human degradation, disgraceful to our characters as citizens of a free government. True it is that these dealers, in the persons of our fellow-men, collect within this District from various parts, numbers of those victims of slavery, and lodge them in some place of confinement until they have completed their numbers. They are then turned out in our streets and exposed to view, loaded with chains as though they had committed some heinous offence against our laws. We consider it a grievance that citizens from distant parts of the United States should be permitted to come within this District, and pursue a traffic fraught with so much misery to a class of beings entitled to our protection by the laws of justice and humanity; and that the interposition of civil authority cannot be had to prevent parents being wrested from their offspring, and children from their parents, without respect to the ties of nature. We consider these grievances demanding *legislative* redress," — that is, redress by Congress.

As illustrative of the horrors and iniquities of the traffic, Mr. Miner informed the House of an incident that had occurred during the previous session of Congress. A free colored man had married a slave; with the avails of his industry, he had, in the course of some years, purchased the freedom of his wife and children. He left home on business, and on his return found his house tenantless. His wife and children were missing. It was soon ascertained that they had been kidnapped by slave-dealers, and confined in a private slave-prison, in Alexandria; from whence they had afterwards been sent to a distant market, and were forever lost to the husband and the father.

"There is a man now in this District," continued Mr. Miner, "who was in the hands of the slave-dealers, about to be sent off to the South, when he laid his hand on a block, and with an axe severed it from his arm. Can the slave-trade on the coast of Africa be more horrible, more dreaded, or more prolific of scenes of misery? To me all this is dreadful, and I think it should not be tolerated here."

In 1828, a petition for the suppression of this trade, and for the gradual abolition of slavery, and signed by more than ONE

THOUSAND of the inhabitants of the District, was presented to Congress. From this document we extract the following:

"While the laws of the United States denounce the *foreign* slave-trade as piracy, and punish with death those who are found engaged in its perpetration, there exists in this District, the seat of the national government, a DOMESTIC SLAVE-TRADE scarcely less disgraceful in its character, and even more demoralizing in its influence. These people are without their consent torn from their homes; husband and wife are frequently separated and sold into distant parts; children are taken from their parents without regard to the ties of nature, and the most endearing bonds of affection are broken forever.

"Nor is this traffic confined to those who are legally slaves for life. Some who are entitled to freedom, and many who have a limited time to serve, are sold into *unconditional slavery*, and owing to the defectiveness of our laws, they are generally carried out of the District before the necessary steps can be taken for their release.

"We behold these scenes continually taking place among us, and lament our inability to prevent them. The people of this District have within themselves *no means of legislative redress*, and we therefore appeal to your honorable body, as the ONLY ONE vested by the American Constitution with power to relieve us."

We will now exhibit the flourishing condition of the slave-trade under the PROTECTION OF CONGRESS in 1834. The following advertisements are all taken from the same sheet, printed a few months since at the Capital of the American Republic:

"CASH FOR TWO HUNDRED NEGROES.

"We will give cash for two hundred likely young negroes of both sexes, families included. Persons wishing to dispose of their slaves, will do well to give us a call, as we will give higher prices in cash than any other purchasers who are now or may hereafter come into this MARKET. All communications will meet attention. We can at all times be found at our residence on Seventh street, immediately south of the Centre Market-house, Washington, D. C.

"*September* 13, 1834. Joseph W. Neal & Co."

"CASH FOR FOUR HUNDRED NEGROES,

Including both sexes, from twelve to twenty-five years of age. Persons having likely servants to dispose of, will find it to their interest to give us a call, as we will give higher prices in cash than any other purchaser who is now or may hereafter come into this MARKET.

"Franklin, Armfield & Co.

"*Alexandria, September* 1*st*, 1834."

"CASH FOR ONE HUNDRED NEGROES,

Including both sexes, from twelve to twenty-five years of age. Persons having likely servants to dispose of, will find it to their interest to give us a call, as we will give higher prices in cash than any other purchaser who is now in this city.

"We can at all times be found at Isaac Beer's tavern, a few doors below Lloyd's tavern, opposite Centre Market, Washington city. All communications promptly attended to.

"*September* 1*st*, 1834. Birch & Jones."

Thus we find cash offered for seven hundred slaves at one time, in the District of Columbia. Does any one inquire how these slaves are to be disposed of? We call his attention to the following advertisement in the same paper:

"ALEXANDRIA AND NEW ORLEANS PACKETS.

"Brig TRIBUNE, Captain Smith, and Brig UNCAS, Captain Boush, will resume their regular trips on the 20th of October: one of which will leave this port every thirty days throughout the shipping season. They are vessels of the first class, commanded by experienced officers, and will at all times go up the Mississippi by steam, and every exertion used to promote the interests of shippers and comfort of passengers. Apply to the Captains on board, or to

"Franklin & Armfield.

"*Alexandria, September* 1*st*."

Most grievously disappointed and astonished would any Northern gentleman be, who had taken passage in one of these Alexandria and New Orleans packets, on finding himself on board a SLAVER.

From a letter of the 23d of January, 1834, by the Rev. Mr. Leavitt, and published in New York, it appears that he visited the slave-factory of Franklin & Armfield, at Alexandria, and was "informed by one of the principals, that the number of slaves carried from the District last year was about one thousand, but it would be much greater this year. He expected *their house* alone would ship at least eleven or twelve hundred. They had *two* vessels of their own constantly employed in carrying slaves to New Orleans." One of the vessels being in port, Mr. Leavitt went on board of her.

"Her name is the TRIBUNE. The Captain very obligingly took us to all parts of the vessel. The hold is appropriated to the slaves, and is divided into two apartments. The after-hold will carry about eighty women, and the other about one hundred men. On either side were *two platforms* running the whole length; one raised a few inches, and the other half way up to the deck. They were about five or six feet deep. On these the slaves lie, as close as they can stow away."

In 1831, the Brig Comet, a slaver, belonging to this very house, and which had sailed from Alexandria with a cargo of one hundred and sixty slaves, was wrecked on Abaco, one of the Bahamas.

But this vile commerce is carried on by land, as well as by water. Slave-coffles are formed at the prisons in the District, and thence set off on their dreary journey into the interior, literally in chains. A gentleman thus describes a coffle he met on the road in Kentucky:

"I discovered about forty black men all chained together in the following manner:—each of them was hand-cuffed, and they were arranged in rank and file. A chain, perhaps forty feet long, was stretched between the two ranks, to which short chains were joined, which connected with the hand-cuffs. Behind them were, I suppose, *thirty women* in double rank; *the couples tied hand to hand.*"

These coffles pass the very Capitol in which are assembled the Legislators by whom they are authorized, and over whose heads is floating the broad banner of the Republic, too justly, alas! in such instances, described by an English satirist as

"The fustian flag that proudly waves,
In splendid mockery o'er a land of slaves."

But the tale of iniquity and infamy is not yet ended. In the Capital of our confederated Republic, and with the sanction of the Congress of the United States of America, MEN ARE LICENSED FOR FOUR HUNDRED DOLLARS TO DEAL IN HUMAN FLESH!

And now we ask, Ought these things so to be? If not, who can remedy them? There is no power on earth but Congress. No State Legislature can interfere with the District of Columbia, or suppress the accursed traffic of which it is the seat. But who shall rouse Congress to action? Do we wait for the interposition of slave-holders? It is they who foster and encourage the trade. Do we appeal to the benevolence of the Colonization Society? Alas, all their sympathy is expended on the victims of the *African* commerce; their *constitution* authorizes no interference with the *American* traffic. We have seen how far their first President himself embarked in this trade. No less than four Vice Presidents of the Society are at this moment, February, 1835, members of Congress, and three of them Senators; but not a word has fallen from their lips, relative to slavery, or the slave-trade in the District of Columbia. We are wrong; one of them has spoken.

Mr. CHARLES FENTON MERCER, one of the most devoted officers of the Society, during the present session of Congress voted to lay on the table a petition presented to the House of Representatives for the abolition of slavery in the District, thus endeavoring to stifle all inquiry into those outrages upon human rights and human happiness which are perpetrated under the authority of the national Legislature. Yet this very gentleman has distinguished himself by his zeal against the *African* slave-trade.

The American Anti-Slavery Society avows its intention to endeavor to influence Congress to refuse any longer to authorize these abominations. And is it for this avowal that its members are branded as traitors and nullifiers? If so, then they appeal for their justification to the Constitution of the United States.

By the 8th Section of the 1st Article of that instrument Congress is authorized to "*exercise exclusive legislation in all cases whatsoever*," over the District of Columbia; and by the first article of the amendments, Congress is restrained from making any law "abridging the freedom of speech or the press, or the right of the people peaceably to assemble, and to petition the government for a redress of grievances." Hence abolitionists have believed that Congress possess the right to abolish slavery in the District of Columbia, and that they themselves are authorized to petition that it may be abolished. Such a belief may, perhaps, indicate a "wild fanaticism;" it seems, however, to be a fanaticism shared by the Legislatures of Pennsylvania and New York, and even by the House of Representatives.

In 1828, the Pennsylvania Legislature, by an almost unanimous vote:

"Resolved, That the Senators of this State in the Senate of the United States, are hereby requested to procure, if practicable, the passage of a law to abolish slavery in the District of Columbia, in such a manner as they may consider consistent with the rights of individuals and the Constitution of the United States."

On the 9th of January, 1829, the House of Representatives

"Resolved, That the Committee of the District of Columbia be instructed to inquire into the *expediency*, (not the *right*,) of providing by law for the gradual abolition of slavery in the District, in such manner that no individual shall be injured thereby."

On the 28th of January, 1829, a Committee of the New York Assembly reported to the House:

"Your Committee cannot but view with astonishment that in the Capital of this free and enlightened country, laws should exist, by which the free CITIZENS of a State are liable, without trial, and even without the imputation of a crime, to be seized while prosecuting their lawful business, immured in prison, and though free, unless claimed as a slave, to be sold as such for the payment of JAIL FEES."

The Committee recommended the following resolution, which was adopted by the Assembly:

"Resolved, (if the Senate concur herein) That the Senators of this State, in the Congress of the United States, be and are hereby instructed, and the Representatives of this State are requested to *make every possible exertion*, to effect the passage of a law for the abolition of slavery in the District of Columbia."

And now again do we ask, are abolitionists fanatics and incendiaries, and nullifiers, and traitors, and all that is foolish, and all that is wicked, because they wish Congress to suppress slavery and the slave-trade in the District of Columbia? It cannot be that Messrs. Frelinghuysen, Walworth, Ogden, and other upright and intelligent colonizationists have founded their grievous charges against abolitionists on *this* ground. Let us then see how far abolitionists have merited these charges, for their endeavors to abolish slavery existing under the authority of the several States.

CHAPTER VI.

SLAVERY UNDER STATE AUTHORITY.

We have seen that the charges against the abolitionists are vague and without specifications. *Friend* Hubbard and Mr. Gurley, however, give their accusations something of a tangible shape. The one asserts that abolitionists are laboring to abolish slavery by causing the *national legislation* to bear directly on the slave-holders, and *compel* them to emancipate their slaves: the other insists that it is one of their *fundamental* principles, that slavery is to be abolished in a great degree *against and in defiance of the will of the South.* The obvious and only meaning of these assertions is, that it is the wish and object of the abolitionists to induce *Congress* to abolish slavery in the *States.* One would think that this charge, if true, might be easily proved: some petition, some recommendation might be quoted; but so far from having ever seen any proof of this charge, we have never seen even an *attempt* to prove it.

Perhaps the testimony on this point of a Vice President of the American Colonization Society, and one who is equally distinguished by his moral worth and his zeal in the cause of colonization, will be listened to with respect by many of his brethren. Gerritt Smith, Esq., of New York, in a speech at the Anniversary Meeting of the Society, 20th of January, 1834, speaking of the Anti-Slavery Society, remarked:

> "I believe that Society to be as honest as our own — as benevolent and *patriotic* as our own. Its members love their fellow-men, and love *their country, and love the union of the States,* as sincerely and as strongly as we do; and much as is said to the contrary on this point, I have never seen a *particle of evidence,* that the Anti-Slavery Society meditates *any interference* with the provisions of the laws of the slave States on the subject of slavery. It alleges, and I have no doubt, sincerely, that it is by moral influence alone, and mainly by the changes wrought by the application of truth to the conscience, that it seeks to compass its object."

It seems Mr. Smith has never seen a particle of evidence in support of the charge that abolitionists meditate interference with the laws of the slave States. They who make the charge, offer not a particle of evidence in its behalf. We will now offer a MASS of evidence in proof of its utter falsity.

Our first witness is one whose competency and credibility will not be questioned; and who, like Mr. Smith, is a Vice President of the Colonization Society. The following is extracted from a letter to John Bolton, Esq., of Savannah, written for publication by the Hon. DANIEL WEBSTER, and dated 17th May, 1833:

"In my opinion, the domestic slavery of the Southern States is a subject within the exclusive control of the States themselves; *and this, I am sure, is the opinion of the whole North.* Congress has no authority to interfere in the emancipation of slaves, or in the treatment of them in any of the States. This was so resolved in the House of Representatives in 1790, on the report of a committee consisting almost entirely of Northern members; and I do not know an instance of the expression of a different opinion in either House of Congress since. I cannot say that particular individuals might not possibly be found, who suppose that Congress may possess some power over the subject, *but I do not know any such persons*, and if there be any, I am sure they are very few. The servitude of so great a portion of the population of the South is undoubtedly regarded at the North as a great evil, moral and political, and the discussions upon it which have recently taken place in the Legislatures of several of the slave-holding States, have been read with very deep interest. But it is regarded, nevertheless, as an evil, the remedy for which *lies with those Legislatures themselves, to be provided and applied according to their own sense of policy and duty.* The imputations which you say, and say truly, are constantly made against the North, are, in my opinion, *entirely destitute of any just foundation.*"

Thus we find that Mr. Webster, living in Boston, the seat of the New England Anti-Slavery Society, a fellow-townsman of Garrison's, and surrounded by abolitionists, knows nothing of the nullifiers denounced by Mr. Ogden, nothing of the men who Mr. Gurley says are for freeing the slaves in defiance of the will of the South, nothing of those who the North Carolina Quaker tells us, are for bringing the "national legislation" to bear upon emancipation.

And has DANIEL WEBSTER, a sworn sentinel on the ramparts of the Constitution, been sleeping at his post, and is it to more faithful and more intelligent watchmen, that we owe the discovery of the meditated treason?

Mr. Webster's letter contains, as far as it goes, THE POLITI-

CAL CREED OF THE ABOLITIONISTS, and we may challenge the whole Colonization Society to name a single abolitionist who does not most heartily assent to its doctrines. The New York Emancipator transferred the letter to its columns, remarking:

"Mr. Webster's opinion on the subject of slavery in the States of this Union, so far as expressed, is just the same as has been more than once avowed in every Anti-Slavery paper in the country — that it is a subject within the *exclusive control* of the States themselves." *Emancipator, 6th July*, 1833.

Not only has Mr. Garrison declared his readiness to sign his name to every sentiment expressed in Mr. Webster's letter, but he has used in the Liberator the following language:

"Abolitionists as clearly understand, and as sacredly regard the constitutional powers of Congress, as do their traducers; and they know, and have again and again asserted, that *Congress has no more rightful authority to sit in judgment upon Southern slavery than it has to legislate for the abolition of slavery in the French colonies.*"

We will now select a few from the many official declarations of abolitionists on this subject.

"The national compact was so framed as to *guarantee* the legal possession of slaves; and *physical* interference would be a violation of Christian principles." *1st Rep. of New England Anti-Slavery Society*, p. 21.

"We do not aim at any interference with the constitutional rights of the slave-holding States; for Congress, as is well understood, has no power to abolish slavery in the several States." *Address of the N. Y. city Anti-Slavery Society*, p. 5.

"We *freely and unanimously* recognize the sovereignty of each State, to legislate *exclusively* on the subject of slavery which is tolerated within its limits; we consider that Congress has no right to interfere with any of the slave States in relation to this subject." *Declaration of Anti-Slavery Convention at Philadelphia, 4th of December*, 1833.

"While it admits that each State in which slavery exists has by the Constitution of the United States *exclusive* right to legislate in regard to its abolition, it shall aim to convince all our fellow-citizens, by arguments addressed to their *understandings* and *consciences*, that slaveholding is a heinous sin in the sight of God." *Constitution of American Anti-Slavery Society.*

In December, 1833, the managers of the New York city Anti-Slavery Society printed and circulated a petition to Congress, for the abolition of slavery in the District of Columbia. It commenced as follows:

"To the Honorable, the House of Representatives.

"Your petitioners, inhabitants of the city of New York, beg leave to represent to your Honorable Body, that whatever views they may entertain of the evils of slavery as it exists in certain States of the Federal Union, they are fully aware that these evils *are beyond the constitutional control of the federal government;* and so far from soliciting your interposition for their removal, they would *deprecate the interference of Congress on this subject, as a violation of the national compact.*"

The petition then proceeds to assert the constitutional power of Congress to abolish slavery in the District, and asks for its exercise.

And now we ask, is there anything in the extracts we have given, to justify, excuse, or palliate the heavy accusations made against abolitionists? Surely ti must now be conceded that however *unconstitutional* may be the emancipation contemplated by abolitionists, it is not to be effected by *Congress.* We lament that Chancellor Walworth did not condescend to explain *how* and *why* it was unconstitutional. He is accustomed to assign reasons for his decisions, and it may fairly be doubted whether, in withholding the reasons for the judgment he has pronounced against abolitionists, he has administered equity. He has adjudged that the emancipation contemplated by abolitionists would "violate the rights of property;" but in what way, does not appear. As physical force is disclaimed, and congressional interference deprecated, the alleged violation of property must arise from the appeals made to the holders to surrender it. But surely the President of the New York Temperance Society does not regard property in human flesh and blood so much more sacred than property in rum, that while he is laboring to induce the owners of the latter, throughout the United States, to part with their property, he looks upon every man who tells his fellow-citizens that it is their duty to manumit their slaves, as violating the rights of property! The venders of ardent spirits in New Orleans and elsewhere, have as valid and constitutional a title to their liquors as they have to their slaves. Now hear what Mr. Frelinghuysen says of a traffic expressly sanctioned by the laws of every State in the Union:

"It is mere tampering with temptation to come short of positive, decided, and uncompromising opposition. We must not only *resist*, we must *drive* it. To stand on the defensive merely, is to aid in its triumph." *7th Rep. Am. Temp. Soc.*, p. 51.

Yet they who by arguments are resisting, or driving the traffic in the souls and bodies of men, are accused of "seeking to destroy our happy Union!"

The State Legislatures have as much right to authorize lotteries, as they have to authorize slavery, yet the Pennsylvania Society for abolishing lotteries is established for the avowed purpose of abolishing, by moral influence, lotteries in *other* States, for there are none in its own. No objection is made to the constitutionality of that Society, yet epithets seem to be wanting to express the abhorrence felt for those who are aiming by the same means to rescue millions from a bondage destructive to their happiness in this world, and in that which is to come!

In the remarks we have made on the language used by Chancellor Walworth and his two associates, no unkind feelings have mingled. Not a suspicion of the goodness of their motives has crossed our mind; we admire them for their talents, and esteem them for their virtues; and sincerely do we regret, that men who possess the power of doing so much good, should ever, through want of information, so grievously misapply it.

And now it may be asked, if abolitionists intend to use only moral means, what good can they effect by using those means at the North, where slavery does not exist? But although slavery does not exist at the North, it is excused and justified at the North; and Southern Christians are countenanced in keeping their fellow-men in bondage and in ignorance, by their Northern brethren. We have already seen the baneful influence of the Colonization Society on the treatment of the free negroes at the North; the Black Act of Connecticut is still in force, and Judge Daggett's decision remains unreversed. Slavery is in full vigor under the authority of Congress, and sanctioned by a majority consisting of *Northern* members; and our whole country is disgraced, and humanity and religion outraged by an extensive and abominable slave-trade, conducted under the same sanction. If, therefore, it could be foreseen, that no slave in any of the States would ever be liberated, through the influence of Northern Anti-Slavery Societies, there would still remain great and glorious objects to stimulate their zeal, to employ all their energies, and abundantly to reward all their labors. But neither their labors nor rewards will be confined to the North. The consciences of Southern Christians, so long lulled by the opiate of colonization, are awakening to duty. Southern divines are beginning to acknowledge the sinfulness of slavery, and recent slave-holders are now proclaiming the safety and duty of immediate emancipation.

While Northern colonizationists are sounding the tocsin, and girding on their armor, and rushing to the battle, to protect the *rights* of their Southern brethren, those very brethren are beginning to listen to the friendly admonitions of abolitionists, and are inquiring what they must do to escape the mighty perils to which they are exposed. On the 19th of March, a convention of gentlemen from different parts of Kentucky assembled at Danville, and amid a slave population of 165,000, organized "THE KENTUCKY ANTI-SLAVERY SOCIETY, *Auxiliary to the American Anti-Slavery Society;* and appointed a delegate to attend the anniversary of the parent Institution at New York!

While the professors of many of our Northern colleges are laboring with trembling solicitude to stifle all discussion respecting slavery among their pupils, JAMES M. BUCHANAN, a professor of Centre College, has had the moral courage to accept the station of President of the Kentucky Society. Indeed, the whole nation has been roused from its lethargy, and in almost every circle and neighborhood, the subject of abolition is attracting attention; the violence and persecution experienced by abolitionists, instead of suppressing, has promoted discussion; and they have reason to hope, that slavery will ultimately be abolished, by the voluntary action of the South, in compliance with the dictates of policy and of duty.

CHAPTER VII.

SAFETY OF IMMEDIATE EMANCIPATION.

ALTHOUGH we may have succeeded in proving that the emancipation contemplated by abolitionists is not "unconstitutional," yet many may conscientiously doubt whether it would be safe and wise.

A few years only have elapsed since the use of ardent spirits was universally countenanced by all classes of the community; and when the few who contended that their use was sinful, and ought to be immediately abandoned, were deemed no less visionary and *fanatical* than those are now who hold the same doctrine in regard to slavery.

The whole Colonization Society, with scarcely a solitary exception,* denounce immediate emancipation as dangerous, or rather as utterly ruinous, to the whites. Their objections were thus briefly summed up by the Rev. Dr. Hawkes, in his speech at a colonization meeting in New York:

> "But if the plan of colonization be abandoned, what remains? Are the slaves fitted for freedom? No; and if they are let loose at once, they must of *necessity*, to procure a living, either beg or steal, or destroy and displace the whites." *New York Com. Adv.*, 10*th Oct.*, 1833.

Here we have broad, unqualified assertions, without a particle of proof. We find it taken for granted, that if the slaves are at once restored to liberty, they must, from *necessity*, beg or steal, or destroy and displace the whites. What causes will produce this necessity, we are uninformed; why it will be *impossible* for liberated slaves to work for wages, is unexplained. Slavery is property in human beings. Immediate emancipation is therefore nothing more than the immediate cessation of this property. But how does this cessation of property imply that those who were the subjects of it must be "let loose?" Will they not, like other persons, be subject to the control of law,

* The only exception known to the writer, is G. Smith, Esq.

and responsible for their conduct? If incapable of providing for themselves, may they not, like children, apprentices, and paupers, be compelled to labor for their own maintenance? Immediate emancipation does not necessarily contemplate any relaxation of the restraints of government or morality; any admission to political rights, or improper exemption from compulsory labor. What then does such emancipation imply? It implies, that black men, being no longer property, will be capable of entering into the marriage state, and of exercising the rights, and enjoying the blessings of the conjugal and parental relations; it implies, that they will be entitled to the fruits of their honest industry, to the protection of the laws of the land, and to the privilege of securing a happy immortality, by learning and obeying the will of their Creator.

Now it is almost universally supposed that such emancipation would, as a matter of course, lead to insurrection, robbery, and massacre. Yet this opinion will, on examination, be found utterly irreconcilable with the divine economy, the principles of human nature, and the testimony of experience.

It is a trite remark, that nations are punished and rewarded in this world, and individuals in the next; and both sacred and profane history will be searched in vain for an instance in which the Supreme Ruler has permitted a nation to suffer for doing justice and loving mercy. To believe that God would permit any community to be destroyed, merely because it had ceased to do evil, is to call in question the equity of his government, or the power of his providence. Who that acknowledges the truth of Revelation, can doubt, that if slavery be sinful, the sooner we part with it, the more confidently may we rely on the divine favor and protection? Infidelity alone will seek safety in human counsels, when opposed to the divine will.

But the opinion we are considering is no less at variance with the motives and passions of our common nature than with the dictates of Christian faith.

What is the theory on which this opinion rests? Why, that cruelty, injustice and grievous oppression, render men quiet, docile, and inoffensive subjects; and that if delivered from this cruelty, injustice, and oppression, they will rob and murder their deliverers!

This theory is happily unsupported by any facts, and rests upon the simple dogma that the slaves are not *yet* fitted for freedom. Now we would ask, What it meant by fitness for freedom? Ought a man to be a slave, unless he can read, write, and cipher? Must he be taught accounts, before he can receive wages? Should he understand law, before he enjoys its protection? Must he be instructed in morals, before he reads his Bible? If all these are pre-requisites for freedom, how and when are they to be acquired in slavery?

If one century of bondage has not produced this fitness, how many will? Are our slaves more fit now, than they were ten, twenty, fifty years ago? Let the history of slave legislation answer the inquiry. When the British government insisted that female slaves should no longer be flogged naked in the colonies, the Jamaica legislature replied, that it would be impossible to lay aside the practice "UNTIL the negro women have acquired more of the sense of shame which distinguishes European females." Slaves, while such, will become fit for freedom as soon, but not sooner, than negro women will become modest in consequence of the West Indian mode of correction. No postponement of emancipation will increase the fitness of slaves for freedom; and to wait for this fitness, resembles the conduct of the simpleton who loitered by the brook, expecting to pass dry shod after the water had run off.

The conclusion to which religion and common sense would lead us on this subject, is most abundantly confirmed by experience. Passing by the emancipation of the serfs of Europe, let us advert to various instances of the sudden abolition of negro slavery, and let us see how far the theory we are considering is supported by facts.

On the 10th of October, 1811, the Congress of Chili decreed that every child born after that day should be free.

On the 9th of April, 1812, the government of Buenos Ayres ordered that every child born after 1st January, 1813, should be free.

On the 19th of July, 1821, the Congress of Colombia passed an act, emancipating all slaves who had borne arms in favor of the Republic, and providing for the emancipation, in eighteen years, of the whole slave population of 280,000.

On the 15th of September, 1821, the government of Mexico granted instantaneous and unconditional emancipation to every slave.

On the 4th of July, 1827, ten thousand slaves were emancipated in the State of New York by act of the Legislature.

In all these various instances, *not one* case of insurrection or of bloodshed is known to have resulted from emancipation. But St. Domingo — ah, what recollections are awakened by that name! With that name are associated the most irrefragable proofs of the safety and wisdom of immediate emancipation, and of the ability of the African race to value, defend, and enjoy the blessings of freedom. The apologists of slavery are constantly reminding abolitionists of the "SCENES IN ST. DOMINGO." Were the public familiar with the origin and history of those scenes, none but abolitionists would dare to refer to them. We will endeavor in the next chapter to dispel the ignorance which so extensively prevails relative to the "scenes in St. Domingo," and we trust our efforts will furnish new confirmation of the great truth, that the path of duty is the path of safety.

CHAPTER VIII.

EMANCIPATION IN ST. DOMINGO AND GUADALOUPE, AND PRESENT STATE OF ST. DOMINGO.

In 1790, the population of the French part of St. Domingo was estimated at 686,000. Of this number, 42,000 were white, 44,000 free people of color, and 600,000 slaves. At the commencement of the French Revolution the free colored people petitioned the National Assembly to be admitted to political rights, and sent a deputation to Paris to attend to their interests. On the 8th of March, 1790, a law was passed, granting to the colonies the right of holding representative assemblies, and of exercising, to a certain extent, legislative authority. On the 28th of the same month, another law was passed, declaring that "all *free persons* in the colonies, who were proprietors, and residents of two years' standing, and who contribute to the exigencies of the State, shall exercise the right of voting."

The planters insisted that this law did not apply to free *colored* persons. They proceeded to elect a general assembly, and in this election the free blacks were, with but few exceptions, prevented from voting. The newly elected assembly issued a manifesto, declaring they would rather die, than divide their political rights with "a bastard and degenerated race." A portion of the free colored people resolved to maintain the rights given them by the mother country, and assembled in arms under one of their own number named Oge. A letter addressed by this chief to the St. Domingo assembly is fortunately extant, and explains the true origin of those awful calamities, which it is found expedient to ascribe to the abolition of slavery.

"Sirs, — A prejudice for a long time upheld, is at last about to fall. Charged with a commission honorable to myself, I call upon you to proclaim throughout the colony the decree of the National Assembly of the 28th of March, which gives, without distinction, to every *free* citizen the right of being admitted to all duties and functions whatever. My pretentions are just, and I do hope you will regard them. *I shall not have recourse to any raising of the slave gangs.* It is unnecessary, and would be unworthy of me. I wish you to appreciate duly the purity of my intentions. When I solicited of the National Assembly * the decree I obtained in favor of our American colonists, known under the hitherto injurious distinction of the mixed race, *I never comprehended in my claims the negroes in a state of slavery.* You and our adversaries have mixed this with my proceedings to destroy my estimation in the minds of all well-disposed people: but I have demanded only concessions for a class of *free men*, who have endured the yoke of your oppression for two centuries. We have *no wish* but for the execution of the decree of the 28th of March. We insist on its promulgation; and we cease not to repeat to our friends, that our adversaries are not merely unjust to us, but to themselves, for they do not seem to know *that their interests are one with ours.* Before employing the means at my command, I will see what good temper will do; but if, contrary to my object, you refuse what is asked, I will not answer for those disorders which may arise from merited revenge."

The shout of battle was the only answer returned to this letter. The free blacks were defeated, and their brave leader being taken prisoner, was, with a barbarity equalled only by its folly, broken alive on the wheel. A ferocious struggle now commenced between the two parties, and Oge's death was awfully avenged. On the 15th of May, 1791, the French Convention issued a decree declaring explicitly, that "free *colored* persons were entitled to all the rights of citizenship." The planters, however, refused to submit till after 2,000 whites and 10,000 blacks had perished. The free blacks had armed their own slaves; and many of the slaves belonging to the whites, taking advantage of the disturbed state of the island, revolted. The general assembly at length became alarmed, and on the 20th of September, 1791, issued a proclamation announcing their acquiescence in the decree of the 15th of May, admitting the free blacks to political equality with the whites. This proclamation immediately restored peace, and *the free blacks even assisted the planters in reducing to obedience their revolted slaves.* The peace, however, was of short duration. Intelligence was soon received that the French Convention had yielded to the clamors of the planters, and on the 24th of September, only four days after the Assembly's proclamation, had repealed the decree giving political rights to the free blacks. The irritation caused by this

* Oge had been one of the deputies who were sent to Paris.

measure may easily be imagined, and the feelings of the free blacks were exasperated by an act of folly and presumption on the part of the Colonial Assembly. This body passed an order for disarming the whole free colored population. That population, however, instead of surrendering their arms, challenged their proud oppressors to take them, and immediately renewed the war.

On the 4th of April, 1792, the vacillating policy of the French government led it once more to pass a decree, investing the free negroes in the colonies with political rights; and three Commissioners, with 6,000 troops, were sent to St. Domingo to enforce the decree. The Commissioners arrived on the 13th of September, and assumed the government of the island. In June, 1793, they quarrelled with the governor, and each party took arms. The Commissioners called to their aid 3,000 revolted slaves, promising pardon for the past, and freedom for the future. About this time it was estimated that no less than 10,000 of the white inhabitants had fled from the island, in consequence of its disturbed state, and this, be it remembered, before a single slave had been emancipated. The Commissioners were successful in their contest with the governor, and retained the supreme power in their own hands. But a new danger threatened them. The planters were dissatisfied with the political rights conferred on the blacks, and were in many instances hostile to the Republic which had been reared on the ruins of the French Monarchy. They therefore entered into intrigues with the British Government, inviting it to take possession of the island, hoping that thus the old order of things would be restored. The Commissioners became acquainted with the intentions of the British to invade the island. Their only defensive force consisted of the 6,000 French troops and about 15,000 militia. On the latter they were sensible but little reliance could be placed. Under these circumstances, they determined to emancipate the slaves, in order that the whole colored population might thus be induced to array itself under the Republican standard. Bryant Edwards, a well-known English writer, and a most devoted apologist for slavery, in his history of this affair, after stating as a fact within his own knowledge, the overtures made by the St. Domingo planters to Great Britain, and that the Commissioners could not muster more than 22,000 effective men, adds; "These being necessarily dispersed in detachments throughout the different provinces, became, on that account, little formidable to an invading army. Aware of this circumstance, the Commissioners, on the first intimation of an attack from the English, resorted to the desperate expedient of proclaiming all manner of slavery abolished."

The proclamation was made in September, 1793, and on the 19th of the same month, the British armament, under Colonel White, arrived at Jeremie, and took possession of the town, and afterwards entered Port au Prince. Thus we find that the abolition of slavery in St. Domingo was not, as is generally supposed, the result of an insurrection by the slaves, but an act of political expediency. Let us now see what were the consequences of this act. The whole colored population remained loyal to the Republican cause. The British were masters only of the soil covered by their troops, and at length, wearied out by the inveterate opposition they experienced, they abandoned all hopes of conquest, and in 1798 evacuated the island. In the mean time, the intercourse between the colony and the mother country became more and more interrupted. The seas were scoured by British cruisers, and the colonists were left by France to govern themselves. The whole colonial administration had been entirely subverted, the Commmissioners had returned to France, and it became necessary to adopt some political system. Under these circumstances, Toussaint, a black, who had acquired power and influence, submitted, in 1801, to a general assembly, a republican constitution, which was adopted, and the island was declared to be an independent State on the 1st of July, 1801. But during all this time, what was the conduct of the emancipated slaves? Before we answer this question, let us remind the reader that the emancipation was not only *immediate* but *unpremeditated.* No measures had been taken to *fit* about 600,000 slaves for freedom, but suddenly, unexpectedly, almost in the twinkling of an eye, they ceased to be property, and were invested with the rights of human nature. And was the theory of the Rev. Dr. Hawkes verified in St. Domingo? Did the manumitted slaves maintain themselves by begging and stealing, or did they destroy and displace the whites? Let an eye-witness answer the inquiry. Col. Malefant, then a resident on the island, says in his *Memoire historique et politique des colonies et particulierement de celle de St. Domingue,*" p. 58:—

"After this public act of emancipation, the negroes remained quiet both in the south and in the west, and they continued to work upon all the plantations. There were estates, indeed, which had neither owners nor managers resident upon them, for some of them had been put in prison by Montburn, and others, fearing the same fate, had fled to the quarter which had just been given up to the English. Yet upon these estates, though abandoned, the negroes continued their labors, where there were any, even inferior agents to guide them, and on those estates where no white men were left to direct them, they betook themselves to planting of provisions: *but upon all the plantations where the whites resided, the blacks continued to labor quietly as before.*"

In another place, (p. 125,) he says:

"How did I succeed in the plain of the Cul de Sac, and on the plantation Gouraud, more than eight months after liberty had been granted to the blacks? Let those who knew me at that time, and even the blacks themselves be asked. They will reply that not a *single* negro upon that plantation, consisting of four hundred and fifty laborers, refused to work, and yet this plantation was thought to be under the worst discipline, and the slaves the most idle of any in the plain. I myself inspired the same activity into three other plantations of which I had the management."

He goes on to assert that "the colony was flourishing under Toussaint—*the whites lived happily, and in peace upon their estates, and the negroes continued to work for them.*" Toussaint came into power under the French authority, 1796, and remained in power till 1802, or the commencement of the war with France. Thus it appears that the manumitted slaves continued quietly at work, from their emancipation in 1793, till 1802, a period of about eight years.

This was not, let it be remembered, a season of peace. During most of the time a fierce war was waged against the English invaders. In this war a portion of the planters took part with the enemy, and experienced at the hands of the blacks, those cruelties which so often distinguish a civil war. But on a careful and scrupulous examination of the history of this period, we cannot find, that from the date of the emancipation in 1793, to the French invasion in 1802, a *single white man* was injured by the liberated slaves, unless he had previously placed himself in the attitude of a political enemy by siding with the British. Immediately on the evacuation of the island by the British, profound tranquillity prevailed, and the planters who remained, and the emigrants who returned, enjoyed their estates without molestation.

Malefant is not the only witness we can cite to these facts. General Lacroix, who published his "Memoirs for a history of St. Domingo," at Paris, in 1819, speaking of the colony, in 1797, says:

"It marched as by enchantment towards its ancient splendor: cultivation prospered; every day produced perceptible proofs of its progress. The city of the Cape, and the plantations of the North, rose up again visibly to the eye." P. 311.

The author of "the History of St. Domingo," printed in London, 1818, speaking of Toussaint, says:

"When he restored many of the planters to their estates, there was no restoration of their former property in human beings. No human being was to be bought or sold. Severe tasks, flagellations, and scanty food, were no longer to be endured. The planters were obliged to employ their laborers on the footing of hired servants; and the negroes were *required* to labor for their own livelihood. The amount of remuneration was not left to individual generosity or private agreement, but it was fixed by law, that the cultivators should have for their wages a third part of the crops. While this ample encouragement was afforded for the excitement of industry, penalties were at the same time denounced for the punishment of idleness."

"The effects of these regulations were visible throughout the country. *Obliged* to work, but in a moderate manner, and for handsome wages, and at liberty for the most part to choose their own masters, the plantation negroes were in general contented, healthy and happy."*

* These representations are confirmed by the fact, that the exports from St. Domingo in 1801, seven years after emancipation, were of sugar, 18,535,-132 lbs.; coffee, 43,420,270 lbs.; cotton, 2,480,340 lbs. *McCulloch's Dict. of Commerce*, p. 926.

And now let abolitionists be reminded of the "scenes in St. Domingo;" yes, let those scenes be constantly kept before the public as an awful and affecting memento of the justice due to the free blacks, and as a glorious demonstration of the perfect safety of immediate and unconditional emancipation.

Yet men who believe it safe to do *immediate* justice, and who find from history that God never permits a nation to suffer for obeying his commands, are held up to the derision and detestation of the community as fanatics and incendiaries. Let us see what new proofs of their fanaticism are afforded by the history of the abolition of slavery in Guadaloupe.

On the 20th of April, 1794, a British armament, under Sir Charles Grey, took the French island of Guadaloupe, many of the planters, as in St. Domingo, being royalists and favoring the cause of the invaders.

On the 5th of June following, a French force, under Victor Hugo, arrived to dispute the possession of the island. The Republican general immediately proclaimed the freedom of the slaves, in pursuance of a decree of the National Assembly of the preceding February, and arming the negroes, led them against the enemy. The English were soon confined within narrow quarters, and by the 10th of December, were compelled to evacuate the island. From this time, Guadaloupe remained a dependance of France till 1810, when it was retaken by the English.

On the abolition of slavery *la police rurale* was substituted for it. The slaves were converted into free laborers, and were entitled to their food and one-fourth of the produce of their labor. They were 85,000 in number, and the whites only 13,000. So far was the cultivation of the island from being suspended by emancipation, that in 1801, an official report stated the plantations as follows, viz.: of sugar, 390; of coffee, 1355; of cotton, 328; and 25 grass farms. The peace of Amiens unhappily afforded Bonaparte an opportunity to re-establish slavery in Guadaloupe. In the summer of 1802, Richepanse landed on the island at the head of a powerful French force, and in a short time, by the indiscriminate massacre of all who opposed his purpose, fulfilled the object of his mission at the sacrifice, it is said, of nearly 20,000 negro lives.

Immediately preceding this atrocious act, all was peace and prosperity; and so late as February, 1802, the supreme council of Guadaloupe, in an official document, alluding to the tranquillity which reigned throughout the island, observed:

"We shall have the satisfaction of having given an example, which will prove that *all classes* of people may live in perfect harmony with each other, under an administration which secures JUSTICE TO ALL CLASSES."

In Guadaloupe, we see an instance of a great preponderating slave population suddenly emancipated, and yet peaceably pursuing their labors for seven years, and living in harmony with the white proprietors.

If we are to believe colonizationists, the negro character is to be exhibited in all its perfection in Liberia; but in America, the black man can never rise from his present degradation. Do we inquire the reason, we are promptly told that no equality can subsist between the white and black races, and that the latter to be great and happy must live alone. Strange it is, that instead of referring to St. Domingo as an apt illustration of their theory, they are fond of citing the *present state of that island* as a warning against abolition,—as a proof that free negroes are too indolent to work, too deficient in enterprise to attain national prosperity. If such be the fact how faithless must be their predictions of the future glory of Liberia. Let us now attend to the gloomy and disheartening account which the chairman of the Executive Committee of the New York Colonization Society gives us of St. Domingo; an account which, if true, ought to induce the Society to abandon their enterprise.

"More than thirty years have elapsed since slavery was abolished in St. Domingo. Through scenes of unparalleled devastation and blood, the blacks *expelled their white masters*, and have ever since lived under a government of their own. But from the day of their emancipation to the present, the population, for the most part, have been idle and worthless."

"St. Domingo was the garden of the new world — the richest of the Indies. But its villas has gone to ruin, and its fields run to waste. Thorns and briars have choked their gardens, and the plantations have been barren from idleness. The government has ever been despotic, and of necessity; and AT LAST its power has been called forth for the regulation of labor — the labor of freemen, to prevent the island from going entirely to ruin. The following extract from a late Haytien enactment is in point, and will serve as a practical commentary upon the mad schemes of our *well-meaning* but deluded philanthropists. We have extracted the following articles, which render the condition of the free blacks *very little different from, if not actually worse than the condition of the slaves in any part of the United States.*" * *Com. Advertiser, 24th of September*, 1834.

Then follow extracts from the rural code of Hayti, from which it appears, that all persons without land or occupation are compelled to labor, and are liable to imprisonment for idleness.

It is remarkable that the philanthropists, on whose mad schemes this code is supposed to be a commentary, are admitted on the 24th of September to be "well-meaning," whereas, on the 9th of June preceding, we were assured by this same gentleman, that the "*design*" of these philanthropists was "to foment a servile war in the South." To convince us how unfit negroes are for freedom, we are here informed that thirty years after slavery was abolished in St. Domingo, the government has *at last* exerted its power for the regulation of labor, to prevent the island from going entirely to ruin. It so happens that the regulation of labor, instead of being an expedient resolved on *at last* to save the island from ruin, was coeval with the act of emancipa-

* This last assertion is so very extraordinary, that we are constrained to believe Mr. Stone has never read the "enactment" from which he quotes. The present rural code of Hayti was adopted in 1826. It is a document filling about fifteen folio pages, and displays a strong desire to secure justice to the laborers. By this code, all "who shall not be able to show that they possess the means of subsistence, shall be bound to cultivate the earth." Such persons are required to hire themselves as farm laborers, but they are at perfect liberty to *select* their employer. The parties enter into written contracts for not less than three, nor more than nine years. The compensation to the laborers on a farm, varies according to the terms of the contract, from one-fourth to one-half of the whole produce of the farm. All disputes between the employer and his people are settled by a justice of the peace. The employer can no more flog or otherwise punish his "cultivators," than an American farmer can his hired laborers. Not even for crimes is corporal punishment allowed in Hayti. The cultivator has, by law, the whole of Saturday and Sunday to himself, and on other days he cannot be required to work *after* sunset. There is nothing to prevent him from accumulating property by industry and economy, buying a farm and hiring laborers in his turn.

tion. On the 28th of February, 1794, Etienne Polverel, "civil commissary of the Republic, delegated to the French Leeward islands in America, for the purpose of reëstablishing the public order and tranquillity," published in the name of the French people a rural code for the government of the liberated slaves in St. Domingo. It is long, and descends to minute particulars; a brief extract will show that it *regulated labor.*

"The ordinary day's labor is limited to about nine hours, viz.: from sunrise to half-past eight — from half-past nine to twelve — and from two to sunset; and in crop time, it shall be extended to eight o'clock in the evening. The laborers shall be bound to obey the overseers, and the overseers to obey each other, according to their rank; but their authority shall be confined to the cultivation and good order of the plantation. Those laborers who in these points shall refuse to obey the order of the overseers, shall be subject to *a month's imprisonment, with labor during the day on public works,*" &c., &c.

This code continued in force till August, 1798, when it was somewhat modified by Toussaint, and we have already seen, on the authority of the history of St. Domingo, that "the planters were obliged to employ their laborers on the footing of hired servants, and the negroes were *required* to labor for their livelihood." Hence it appears that the regulation of labor in St. Domingo is not, as Mr. Stone seems to suppose, a recent exertion of power on the part of the government.

But what shall we say of the ruined villas, the barren plantations, the gardens choked with thorns? Admitting Mr. Stone's melancholy picture to be correct, cannot we explain it on other principles than such as would be fatal to the freedom and happiness of millions? The zealous editor seems wholly to have forgotten the terrible war which the Haytiens were compelled to wage in defence of their liberty. In 1802, a French army landed in St. Domingo, for the purpose of again reducing its inhabitants to slavery, and a war ensued, which, for its desolating fury, is probably without a parallel. A historian of this war, thus concludes his account of it:

"At length, in the month of December, 1803, the island was finally abandoned, a mere handful of the French troops escaping the destruction which had already overtaken 60,000 of their fellows! Thus for nearly two years, with a very brief interval, had a war raged in St. Domingo, singularly ferocious and vindictive in its character, and directed latterly more to extermination than to conquest, sparing neither sex nor age, and sweeping away from the whole face of the plains of that beautiful island *every trace of cultivation.* So complete was the extinction of all sugar culture in particular, that for a time not an ounce of that article was procurable. The very roots and fruits on which subsistence depended, were cultivated only in *mornes.* Desolation, therefore, could hardly be conceived more complete, than prevailed in 1804 and 1805 over all those parts of the colony *which had formerly been covered with plantations;* and it is well known how soon the rank vegetation of a tropical climate converts the neglected plantation into jungle."

And is it a proof that slaves ought never to be emancipated that St. Domingo has not in thirty years, after such wide-spread desolation, become again in the hands of men recently delivered from bondage, and for the most part, poor and ignorant, "the garden of the new world?" And was, indeed, that an "idle and worthless" population which successfully resisted the arms of England and of France, and achieved their freedom by a heroic sacrifice of their lives and property — a sacrifice which, had their complexion been white, would have been celebrated by poets and orators in every portion of the civilized world?

Let us now inquire, whether the *present state* of the island is in truth such as is alleged.

The Rev. Simon Clough, D. D., LL. D., has lately published a pamphlet, ("Appeal to the Citizens of the United States") in which he undertakes to justify slavery from the Scriptures, and to prove that all clergymen who advocate immediate abolition, are "false teachers," and ought to be dismissed by their congregations. Now this most veracious teacher, speaking of St. Domingo, assures us, p. 16: "At the *present time,** there is not ONE sugar, coffee, or cotton plantation on the island. There is now exported about five million pounds of inferior coffee, *which grows wild, and is picked up by the inhabitants off the ground,* where it falls after it becomes ripe."

Strange it is, that this island, if in the state described by Messrs. Stone and Clough, should support a population of

* The pamphlet was published in New York, 1834.

935,050.* Still more strange is it, that when the *whole* export of coffee is only about five million pounds, it should appear from the report of the Secretary of the Treasury, that the coffee exported in 1833, from Hayti to the United States *alone*, amounted to eleven million, seven hundred eighty-four thousand, eight hundred and thirty-five pounds. Most passing strange is it, that the imports into this country, in the same year, from an island in which there is not ONE sugar, coffee, or cotton plantation; with an idle and worthless population; with its fields run to waste, and its plantations barren from idleness, should nevertheless *exceed in value* our imports in the same period, from either Prussia — Sweden and Norway — Denmark, and the Danish West Indies — Ireland and Scotland — Holland — Belgium — Dutch East Indies — British West Indies — Spain — Portugal — all Italy — Turkey and the Levant — or any one republic in South America! †

Neither Mr. Stone nor Dr. Clough professes to speak from *personal observation*. Let us then listen to an eye-witness. In 1831, was published in a London periodical, the journal of a traveller in Hayti. The following are extracts:

" *Port au Prince, Island of Hayti, June* 25, 1830.

"Being aware that this city had very recently suffered greatly by fire, I expected to see an unsightly waste of ruin and decay; but the lots are rebuilt, and many a splendid and substantial edifice, *surpassing those to be seen in the city of Kingston in Jamaica*, has arisen as the first fruits of the security which property enjoys, by the recognized independence of Hayti.

"I have made an excursion or two, just out of the town, to the little cottage settlements on the side of the mountain above the city. I am told, that in the ancient regime, (that is the phrase here for the old state of things,) the plains were a source of so abundant a return for the industry of the proprietor, that the mountains in this neighborhood were comparatively neglected, so that the 'Camp des Fourmis,' the range of hills so called, extending from Point Lamentine to the Cul de Sac, were heretofore never cultivated as they are now. At *present* they are covered with *a thousand small settlements appropriated to coffee*, and provisions, and fruits, and vegetables, in which the advantages of irrigation, presented by the frequent springs, bursting from the moun-

* Census of 1824.

† See documents accompanying Letters from Secretary of the Treasury to the Speaker of the House of Representatives, 21st April, 1834.

tain ravines, have been diligently attended to in the agricultural economy. The water is trenched over the sunny surface of each projecting irregularity of the ridge; and height above height, the cottage of the humble cultivator is seen; or the substantial country-seat of the Haytien merchant, with its baths, bowers, and terraced gardens, has been erected.

"Port au Prince, though by no means a handsome town, is at this day, in style, and one may say splendor, far superior to what it was in the colonial period of its history.

"The frequent calamities to which it had been subjected from fire, and the immense and valuable property lost by earthquakes in the years 1820 and 1822, have led the Haytiens to attempt providing against the two-fold liability, as they expressed it, of being *bouleverse et incendie*. They have commenced reërecting some of the houses destroyed by these conflagrations, with stone or brick, cased over wooden frames, at once to sustain the shock of the earthquake, and to repel the action of the fire. They cover the roofs with tiles or slates, rather than shingles; and erect their stores for merchandise with fire-proof terraces, and wrought-iron doors and windows. These buildings have galleries and arched colonnades, with heavy cornices and balustrades screening the roof; and floors of variegated marble, and tiles in the upper as well as lower stories. If continued generally, they will render this city not only one of the most elegant in the West Indies, but one in which the houses will exhibit an interior economy, the very best adapted to the necessities of the climate. The decorations are appropriate. The rich, varied mahogany of the country is manufactured into elegant furniture by the artisans here; and the French taste of gilded mirrors, or Molu clocks, and porcelain vases, filled with artificial flowers, impart to the dwellings of the simple Haytiens an air of refinement not unworthy of Europe.

"The scene presented to the view of the traveller who quits the city of Port au Prince, to journey on the highway to the mountains, through a wild waste, is not a solitary one. On the road he will meet a multitude of cultivators coming to the city market, with horses and asses loaded with provisions. He will see wagons with produce drawn by hardy and healthy cattle. If he departs from the high road, and turns to the right hand through one of the woodland paths, he will find himself entering into open grounds, covered with verdant fields; he will see traces every where visible of *renewed* cultivation; mansions *re-erected;* aqueducts *reconducting* their streams to irrigate the land; the sound of water-mills at work; cottages no longer deserted, but tenanted by laborers once more issuing from them to gather in the harvest of the teeming soil.

"The island of Jamaica does not exhibit a plantation better established than Chateau Blond; whether we consider the resources of the land, or the *mechanical* economy by which those resources are commanded, it is a splendid establishment.

"To me who have had an opportunity from the day of my birth, and long residence in a slave colony, of forming by comparison a correct estimate of this people's advancement, the general quiet conduct and respectful behavior of all classes here, publicly and privately, is a matter exciting great surprise."

All this, it may be said, is anonymous testimony. It is so, and yet it seems entitled to at least as much weight as the bare, naked assertions of Messrs. Stone and Clough. We will now offer testimony to which we presume no objection will be made. The following are extracts from "the report of the select committee on the extinction of slavery throughout the British Dominions, with minutes of evidence, ordered by the House of Commons to be printed, 11th August, 1832."

Evidence of Mr. Robert Sutherland.

"Are there many persons who work for hire in Hayti?

"Yes, the whole cultivation is carried on by free labor.

"Do these persons work with industry and vigor?

"I have no reason to think they do not. The proof that free labor in Hayti answers, is this: that after the French were expelled, *there was absolutely no sugar work;* there was no mill; there was nothing of that kind which could be put in use; it was destroyed; and since that period, various plantations have grown up in Hayti. Men have gone to the expense of thirty and forty thousand dollars, to build up those sugar works; and it stands to reason, that unless these men were repaid for their capital they would not continue that sort of work. And there is another thing to be observed, that sugar is not the staple commodity of Hayti; they only make sufficient for their own consumption. Coffee is the staple commodity of the island.

"If a man can show that he has the means of subsistence of his own, is he compelled to labor under the *code rurale?*

"Decidedly not.

"Do you believe that corporal punishment is inflicted upon any of the laborers in Hayti?

"I believe it is impossible. I have seen the peasantry in the Highlands of Scotland where I was brought up, and I declare that the negroes in St. Domingo are comparatively as much superior to them in comfort as it is possible for one man to be over another."

Evidence of the Vice Admiral, the Hon. Charles Fleming, member of Parliament.

"Was told that vagrants and deserters worked by compulsion, but he did not see any himself. Had never heard of any working under the lash. *The lash was prohibited by law.* The Haytiens appeared to him the happiest, best fed, and most comfortable negroes he had ever seen; better off even than in the Caraccas: infinitely better than in Jamaica; there was no comparison between them. He could not speak positively of the increase of the Haytien population since 1804, but believed it had *trebled* since that time. They now feed themselves, and they export provisions, which neither the French nor the Spaniards had ever done before.

"He saw a *sugar estate* near Cape Haytien, General Boulon's, extremely well cultivated, and in beautiful order. It was wrought by blacks, all free. A new plantation was forming on the opposite side of the road. Their victuals were very superior to those in Jamaica, consisting chiefly of meat, cattle being very cheap. The highest contract beef in Hayti, was 2d.; in Jamaica, it was 12d. *He saw no marks of destitution any where.* The country seemed improving, and trade increasing. The estate he visited near the Cape was large; it was calculated to make 300 hogsheads of sugar. It was beautifully laid out, and as well managed as any estate he had seen in the West Indies. His official correspondence as Admiral with the Haytien government, made him attribute much efficiency to it, and it bore strong marks of civilization. There was a better police in Hayti, than in the new South American States; the communication was more rapid; the roads much better. One had been cut from Port au Prince to Cape Haytien, that would do honor to any country. A regular post was established. The government is one quite worthy of a civilized people. The negroes of Hayti are certainly richer, and happier, and in a better condition than he had ever seen elsewhere. They were all working in the fields when he was there. He rode about very much. He did not think any acts of oppression were practised on the people of Hayti by the government."

Mr. Jeremie, late first president of the royal court of St. Lucia, informs us that in St. Domingo

"Is found a *happy, flourishing, and contented peasantry*, engaged in the cultivation of their own small freeholds; and as these persons acquire capital, they form larger establishments, and are gradually rising. This proves that the general wants of the community are supplied, and, if well governed, that community must soon acquire strength and rise to importance." *Essays on Colonial Slavery*, 1832, p. 63.

The following facts, collected from the new and valuable "Dictionary of Commerce and Commercial Navigation," by J. R. McCulloch, London edition, 1834, abundantly confirm the foregoing testimonies.

In 1786, the exportation of coffee was about 35,000 tons. In consequence of the subsequent devastation of the island, the exportation for some years almost totally ceased; but it has now risen to about 20,000 tons! p. 309.

The amount of the following articles, exported in 1832, was estimated as follows, viz.:

Coffee,	50,000,000 lbs.
Cotton,	1,500,000 lbs.
Tobacco,	500,000 lbs.
Cocoa,	500,000 lbs.
Dye wood,	5,000,000 lbs.
Tortoise shell,	12,000 lbs.
Mahogany,	6,000,000 feet
Hides,	80,000—p. 927.

The quantity of sugar exported in 1832, is not stated; but in 1826, it amounted to 32,864 lbs.; and it should be recollected, that about twenty years before, not an ounce of that article was manufactured on the island, p. 926.

The imports into France, in 1831, from Hayti, exceeded in value the imports from Sweden — Denmark, the Hanseatic Towns — Holland — Portugal — Austria — the French East Indies — or China, p. 637.

In the same year, the importation of French wines into Hayti amounted to 108,495 gallons, p. 1250.*

Cotton manufactures, to the amount of 6,828,576 yards, were exported from Great Britain to Hayti in 1831, being about one-tenth the number of yards exported the same year to the United States, p. 446.

Our readers are now competent to judge for themselves how far the assertions of Mr. Stone and the Rev. Dr. Clough are consistent with truth; and also what *is* "the practical commentary" offered by the history and present state of St. Domingo, on "the mad schemes of our well-meaning but deluded philanthropists."

CHAPTER IX.

EMANCIPATION IN THE BRITISH WEST INDIES.

The British Government, in part to conciliate the West India proprietors, and in part through apprehension of the *danger* of immediate emancipation, determined to abolish slavery in such a manner as to *fit* the slave for freedom. Instead of breaking his yoke, it was to be reduced in weight; and six years were to be occupied in filing off his manacles. On the first of last August, the slave was told and believed, that slavery was abolished; but on the morrow, he was summoned to his usual task, and required to work as before, without reward. Astonished and disap-

* The quantity of French wine imported the same year into Great Britain for home consumption, was 254,366 gallons, p. 1255.

pointed, he doubted the legality of the mandate, and hesitated to obey it. He was then informed, that, although no longer a slave, he was nevertheless *an apprentice*, and must toil on for six years longer, before he could enjoy the fruits of his labor. Had emancipation been nominally, as well as really, prospective, the slave would have regarded it as a boon; but he did not readily comprehend the distinction between slavery and apprenticeship.

There was, however, a very important distinction, which he soon discovered, and which did not promote his acquiescence in protracted wrong. The lash was, by act of Parliament, wrested from the master's hand; and while he was authorized to command his apprentices to labor, he was forbidden to punish them for idleness or insubordination. On this subject a Jamaica paper remarks:

> "It is clear, and there is no use in disguising the fact, that the apprentices can no longer be coerced in the way they formerly were; for in the first place, no magistrate can legally inflict more than twenty-nine stripes, and, in the next, it is not possible to furnish magistrates enough for the purpose. The hope, therefore, of coercing, is absurd, and must be abandoned."

The conduct of the West India negroes, under these circumstances, proves how utterly groundless are the apprehensions entertained of emancipation. Disappointed and irritated, and at the same time almost wholly released from the control of their masters, they have exhibited a meekness, patience, and forbearance, utterly without a parallel. The great mass of the apprentices continue to labor, but some have either refused to work, or accomplish less than their appointed tasks. None of the insurrections, murders and conflagrations, which were so confidently predicted by the enemies of abolition, have occurred. Not one life has yet been taken, not one dwelling fired,* throughout the British West Indies, by the emancipated slaves.

This forbearance is the more remarkable, when we consider the numerical superiority of the negroes, in the West Indies,

* Two sheds, called *trash houses*, were lately burned in Jamaica, probably, but not certainly, by an apprentice.

and particularly in Jamaica, where there are 331,000 slaves, and only 37,000 whites.

Whatever may be the result of the apprenticeship experiment, abolitionists are not responsible for it. It was adopted contrary to their advice, and is inconsistent with the doctrines they profess. The emancipation which they believe to be most consonant with the will of God, most conducive to the safety and happiness of the whites, is *immediate and unconditional.* They rejoice that their doctrines are at this moment subjected to a severe and practical test, and they await the issue with unshaken confidence.

The Legislatures of Bermuda and Antigua, have adopted the very course which the American Anti-Slavery Society recommends to the slave States. With the permission of the British government, these Legislatures dispensed with the apprenticeship altogether, and on the first of last August, granted *immediate and unqualified emancipation.* That we may judge of the fanaticism, the madness, the reckless incendiarism of these Legislatures, we must take into consideration the number of slaves they "let loose upon the community," and their relative proportion to the white population.

In Bermuda there are 5,500 whites, 4,650 slaves, and 500 free blacks. In Antigua, 2,000 whites, 30,000 slaves, and 4,500 free blacks.*

The Bermuda Gazette, of the 4th of August, thus speaks of the great change effected on the 1st.

"The day was as remarkable for quietude, exemption from labor, and solemnity, as that which marks the Sabbath in a Christian land. The only bustle perceptible was in preparation for attending public worship, which his Excellency the Governor most wisely ordered to be performed: thereby dedicating it wholly to God, the willer and doer of this great work. The churches and other places of public worship on the island were crowded to excess, every possible accommodation being afforded to the colored people. From every quarter we hear of their orderly, nay more, exemplary behavior. Four days of universal freedom have now passed, and four days of more perfect regularity and quiet have these famed peaceful islands never witnessed."

* American Almanac.

Such was the *immediate* result of turning loose 4,000 slaves. Let us now attend to the subsequent testimony. The Hon. Mr. Butterfield, Chief Justice of Bermuda, in his charge to the grand jury on the 6th of November, referring to the abolition of slaves in the island, observed:

"This measure, which was necessarily one of fearful experiment, has not, I am happy to say, disappointed the hopes of the public, whose feelings in its favor were expressed with a unanimity as unexampled as, I am proud to say, altogether honorable to the character of the country. On the contrary, it is a subject of congratulation, and certainly of commendation to the emancipated, that in *three months* during which we have been able to mark its working, *the general character and comfort of society have improved*, and the evils which some of its best friends apprehended, were *in all cases* overrated, and in some have hitherto had no existence."

But in Bermuda the whites were equal to the blacks, and the manumitted slaves were perhaps restrained from outrage by the consciousness of their own weakness. It seems as if Providence had provided *facts* to refute every argument that can be urged against abolition. Let us now turn to Antigua, where the slaves were to the whites as 15 to 1, and the free blacks as 3 to 2, and see how far in this overwhelming preponderance of the colored over the white population, immediate emancipation confirmed Dr. Hawkes's theory. Let the Antigua newspaper of 7th of August, answer.

"The great doubt is solved, *the alarming prognostications of the advocates of slavery are falsified*, the highest hopes of the negroes' friends fulfilled, and their pledge honorably redeemed. A whole people, comprising thirty thousand souls, have passed from slavery into freedom, not only without the slightest irregularity, but with the solemn and decorous tranquillity of a Sabbath. A week has nearly elapsed, and although all eyes and ears are open, and reports spread rapidly, we have not heard of a single act of insolence, insubordination or violence committed by any one of them, under false and licentious notions of freedom."

From the same paper, of the 14th of August:

"It is with the highest satisfaction we announce, that we know of and believe that there *is no gang of laborers in the island, which has not returned to its accustomed employment.*"

So that two weeks after the slaves were "let loose," instead of begging and stealing, they were all quietly at work.

We quote from the same paper of the 21st of August:

"The third week of freedom will close with this day, and again we are bound to express our gratitude and praise to the Divine goodness, for the perfect peace and tranquillity which the island enjoys. Not the least symptom of insubordination has manifested itself any where; and the daily accounts from all quarters testify to the excellent disposition and conduct of the new freemen."

In a letter from Antigua, dated August 30th, and published in a Norfolk paper, we find the following:

"The operations of commerce have experienced no interruption; public confidence remains unshaken. *Two sugar plantations have recently leased for as much as they were worth with the negroes included, prior to emancipation.*"

While the Jamaica papers are filled with complaints of the conduct of the apprentices, and predictions of the ruin of the island, one of them (10th September) says:

"In Antigua, all appears to be peaceable and quiet. Its rulers evinced more wisdom, and proved themselves to be better tacticians, than those of any other colonies, Bermuda excepted. In getting rid of the apprenticeship, they got rid of the source, and *only* source of heartburning between them and their laborers; and we maintain, as a *free* colony, will soon experience advantages not to be enjoyed by others, so long at least as the humbug continues."

About eight months have now elapsed since the thirty thousand slaves of Antigua were suddenly "let loose," and, as yet, we have not heard of a single outrage committed by them. It had been customary in this island, as an additional security against insurrection, to proclaim martial law at the Christmas holidays, during which times the slaves had peculiar opportunities for forming conspiracies. The great act of justice accomplished on the first of August, relieved the planters of all apprehension of insurrection; and not only was the usual proclamation withheld at the last Christmas, *but the militia was exempted from duty*. In a late speech by the Speaker of the

Antigua House of Assembly, he adverted to the "universal tranquillity" that prevailed, and to the "respectful demeanor of the lower classes;" and declared that "the agricultural and commercial prosperity of the colony was absolutely on the ADVANCE."

CHAPTER X.

GRADUAL AND IMMEDIATE EMANCIPATION.

If we have been successful in our endeavors to prove that the removal of slavery by colonization is both morally and physically impossible, then it necessarily follows, that the slaves must be emancipated here, or that slavery must be indefinitely continued.

Should the former alternative be adopted, the important question occurs,—Ought the emancipation to be *gradual* or *immediate?*

If this question is to be determined with reference to moral obligation, it is certainly difficult for those who regard slavery as sinful to justify its continuance even for a limited time. If, however, the question is to be decided on the ground of mere political expediency, there are many and powerful objections to *gradual* emancipation; and what may at first view appear paradoxical, the strength of these objections is proportioned to the number of slaves to be emancipated.

In New York, slavery was for the most part gradually abolished; that is, the children born after a certain day became free as they respectively reached the age of twenty-eight years; and when the whole number of slaves was reduced to ten thousand, they were liberated in a single day. In New York, the white population so greatly exceeded the black, that no jealousy was entertained of the free negroes, and no inconvenience experienced in uniting free and slave labor. But in those States in which nearly all the laborers are slaves, where every free black is regarded as a nuisance and an incendiary, and where the planter would, on no consideration, permit him to labor in company with his slaves, much difficulty would necessarily attend a *gradual* relinquishment of slave labor.

Suppose, in South Carolina for instance, ten thousand slaves should be annually manumitted by law. This would certainly be gradual emancipation, as it would require about forty years to free the whole number. Now, what would become of these ten thousand yearly discharged from the plantations? Would their late masters be willing to hire them, and turn them back into their cotton fields? The supposition is extravagant. The planter would dread their influence on his remaining slaves, and these would certainly, and with great reason, be dissatisfied at seeing their late companions working for wages, while they themselves were denied any compensation for their toil. But if the ten thousand liberated slaves were not employed, how could they obtain a livelihood, and how could the planters supply their place on the plantations? The idea that by gradual emancipation the slaves will become *fit* for freedom, is visionary in the extreme. How is it possible that the liberation of a portion of the slaves, can qualify those who remain in chains to become useful citizens? The house of bondage is not the school in which men are to be trained for liberty.

As then gradual emancipation, however desirable, if no other can be obtained, is so full of difficulty, and, in the opinion of slave-holders, so *dangerous* that they have almost universally passed laws to prevent it, the only alternative is *immediate emancipation* or *continued slavery*.

It seems scarcely possible that any conscientious man, after considering the results of immediate emancipation in St. Domingo and Guadaloupe, in New York, in Mexico, in South America, and in the West Indies, should join in the popular clamor against it, as necessarily leading to massacre and rapine. No reason can be assigned why the whites would not possess the same physical power to prevent or suppress outrage after, as before emancipation; but abundant reason may be given, why the blacks, when restored to their rights, and enjoying the protection and privileges of civil society, should be less disposed to destroy their benefactors and deliverers, than they are when smarting under cruelty and injustice, to destroy those whom they regard as their tyrants and oppressors.

Who, with the knowledge that no white man has ever been murdered in consequence of immediate emancipation, dares to declare in the presence of his Maker, that self-preservation forbids the abolition of slavery?

But we are met with the inquiry, How are the owners to be compensated for the loss of their property? This same objection was made to the suppression of the African slave-trade. British merchants had invested large capitals in the traffic, and it was contended that to prohibit the trade was to violate the rights of property. All governments possess the right to suppress practices injurious to society, and to abate nuisances.*

If a particular manufactory is found to be deleterious to the health of a city, it is not only the right, but the duty of the civil authority, to suppress it. If the national interests require an embargo, the measure is adopted, although it virtually wrests from the merchant his property, by depriving him of the use of his own ships.

The State of New York abolished slavery without compensating the slave-holders. The same has been done in Mexico, and in various instances in South America; and the compensation given by Parliament to the West India proprietors, probably arose from the consideration that the legislators who enacted the abolition law, were not *themselves* personally affected by it; and in order, therefore, to avoid the reproach of indulging their benevolence at the expense of others, granted a pecuniary compensation to the owners of the emancipated slaves.

To contend that the slaves in the Southern States ought not to be emancipated by law, except on the payment to their masters, of their market value, is to contend that slavery ought

* "How little to be respected," exclaimed Lord Mulgrave, late Governor of Jamaica, "is that rigid regard for the rights of property, which says a man shall do what he likes with his own, when his *own* is his fellow-man."

to be perpetual. Such a payment is MORALLY IMPOSSIBLE. By whom can it be made? The Federal Government have neither the will nor the constitutional power to make it. But admitting it possessed both, the appropriation of the *national* funds to this purpose would not be such a payment, because a very large proportion of those funds would be drawn from the slave-holders themselves; and it would be an insulting mockery to offer to pay them with their own money. To suppose that the free States would be willing, from motives of disinterested benevolence, to make a present to their neighbors of a THOUSAND MILLIONS OF DOLLARS * is obviously absurd: nor is it less absurd to insist that this sum ought to be paid to the masters by the Legislatures of the slave States; since the pockets of the masters are the only sources whence those Legislatures could obtain the money.

So far as the whole amount of wealth in the community is concerned, it would be enhanced, not diminished by emancipation. This may seem a strange assertion to follow the estimate we have just made of the market value of the slave population. But what is the price paid for a slave? Nothing more than the amount of his wages for *life*, paid in *advance;* paid, it is true, to another, but still paid as an equivalent for labor to be performed, and to be refunded with interest out of that labor. Now it is obvious that it is the *product* of this labor which can alone add anything to the aggregate wealth; and that no diminution of that wealth can be caused by paying for the labor as it is performed, monthly, or yearly, instead of paying for the whole of it in advance.

This argument, it may be said, applies only to the purchase and sale of slaves; but that where a planter is already in possession of them, he would certainly lose a part of his profits by being compelled to pay him wages, and this loss would be so much deducted by emancipation from the general stock. The fallacy of this opinion may be perceived by recollecting that it can in no degree affect the national wealth, whether the

* Estimating the slaves at an average value of $400, the amount would *now* nearly equal this sum, and in a few years far exceed it.

horse with which a farmer tills his corn-field was reared by himself or purchased from his neighbor. It is the corn produced, and not the money paid for the animal by one man and received by another, that augments the riches of the country.

If the slaves are worth a thousand millions of dollars, it is evidence that their *labor* must be worth *much more ;* because to their price is to be added the cost of their maintenance, and the whole is to be reimbursed with profit out of their labor. Now colonization would utterly annihilate all this labor ; it calls upon the South to surrender a commodity worth more than a thousand millions ; and upon this surrender, which would convert the whole slave region into a wilderness, it rests all its hopes of the ultimate abolition of slavery !

Emancipation, on the contrary, instead of removing millions of laborers, would stimulate their industry, improve their morals, quicken their intelligence, and convert a dangerous, idle, and vicious population into wholesome citizens. Were all the slaves in South Carolina emancipated to-morrow, every branch of industry would derive new energy, and every species of property an increased value from the additional security which such a measure would give to society. All dread of insurrection would vanish, and one-half of the population, who are now regarded as implacable foes, would be converted into useful friends.

But it is objected, that the emancipated blacks will form a bad population. One would think, from this objection, that the slaves now form a *good* population, and that they are to be rendered ignorant and immoral by freedom. Unquestionably, the liberated slaves, like all other vicious and degraded people, will, while such, form a bad population ; but if they are such while in bondage, and must ever remain such until liberated, then emancipation is the only process by which a bad can be converted into a good population. As soon as they are free, they will be accessible to education and religious instruction, and all those various motives which operate as a wholesome restraint on the evil passions of our nature. It would be most unjust to estimate the future character of the emancipated slaves, supposing slavery to be immediately abolished, by the *present* character of the free negroes. These last, in the slave States, are a hated and persecuted race. They are *kept* not only in ignorance, but in idleness. The planters will not employ them, for fear they will contaminate the slaves; and the whole legislation of the Southern States towards this people, is to degrade and brutify them. But these wicked efforts are the results of slavery, and would cease with it. Were slavery abolished, then it would be the obvious interest of the South to improve the black population, and the causes which necessarily render the free blacks vicious, would no longer operate. The same remark applies, although with less force, to the free blacks of the North. Colonization and slavery have both had their influence in keeping alive and aggravating the prejudices against color, and these prejudices have led to that system of persecution and oppression to which the free blacks here are subjected.

And now what injury or loss would the planter sustain by the emancipation of his slaves? As a trader in human flesh, his vocation would, indeed, be gone, but as the cultivator of the soil, his profits would be undiminished. The number of laborers would be as great as before; and they would still be dependent on labor for their support. They now cost their owner their food and clothing, and their maintenance in sickness, in youth, and in old age; the expense also of the idle and worthless, is as great as that of the good. Their cost as free laborers would be but little more than at present, while their characters would be improved, and the employer could select such laborers as his occasions required. The laborers, finding their wages, and of course their comforts, depending on their good conduct, would be prompted to industry and sobriety; and having nothing to gain by insurrection, and feeling no injuries to avenge, all malignant designs against their employers would be laid aside, and they would soon make such advances in intelligence and morality, as would contribute no less to the good order and peace of society, than to their own happiness.

Abolitionists are constantly called on for a plan of emancipation. They have little encouragement to respond to the call. If they propose the simple plan of proclaiming by act of the

State Legislatures, the immediate and unqualified abolition of slavery, they are denounced as reckless incendiaries. If they intimate that abolition does not necessarily inhibit all compulsory labor, and point to the rural code of St. Domingo and the apprentice system of the West Indies, they are reproached with wishing to substitute one kind of slavery for another. But, in truth, they are under no obligation of duty or policy to propose any specific plan. No Temperance Society has felt itself bound, because it pronounced the traffic in ardent spirits to be sinful, to furnish venders with plans for employing their capitals in other occupations.

The details of emancipation, and the various legal provisions proper to render it safe and convenient, are not prescribed by the great principles of justice and religion, but by considerations of local policy. It is not probable that if all the Southern Legislatures were sincerely anxious to abolish slavery, any two of them would do it in precisely the same manner, and under the same regulations. We have seen one plan pursued in St. Domingo, another in Bermuda and Antigua, a third in the other British West Indies, and still different plans in South America.

Of all these plans, that adopted in Mexico, Bermuda and Antigua, of immediate, total and unqualified emancipation, will, there is reason to believe, be found in all cases the most safe and expedient.

This plan removes from the slave all cause for discontent. He is free, and his own master, and he can ask for no more. Yet he is, in fact, for a time, absolutely dependent on his late owner. He can look to no other person for food to eat, clothes to put on, or house to shelter him. His first wish therefore is, to remain where he is, and he receives as a favor, permission to labor in the service of him whom the day before he regarded as his oppressor. But labor is no longer the badge of his servitude, and the consummation of his misery; it is the evidence of his liberty, for it is *voluntary*. For the first time in his life, he is a party to a contract. He negotiates with his late master, and returns to the scene of his former toil, and the scene of his stripes and his tears, with a joyful heart, to labor for HIMSELF. The wages he has agreed to accept, will, in fact, be little more than the value of his maintenance; for it is not to be expected, that in a treaty with his employer his diplomacy will gain for him any signal advantages; but still there will be a charm in the very name of *wages* which will make the pittance he receives appear a treasure in his eyes. Thus will the transition from slave to free labor be effected instantaneously, and with scarcely any perceptible interruption of the ordinary pursuits of life. In the course of time, the value of negro labor, like all other vendible commodities, will be regulated by the supply and demand, and justice be done both to the planter and his laborers. The very consciousness, moreover, that justice *is* done to both parties, will remove their mutual suspicions and animosities, and substitute in their place feelings of kindness and confidence. No white man in Antigua, surrounded as he is by blacks, now dreams of insurrection, or fears the midnight assassin. Can as much be said of our Southern planters?

In concluding this chapter, we beg leave to address the following questions to the reader, and we beseech him seriously to inquire what duties are prompted by the answers which his conscience and understanding may compel him to return.

Do you believe it to be agreeable to the will of God, and the welfare of our country, that slavery should be perpetual?

Is it either possible or probable that slavery can or will be removed by colonization?

If slavery be not abolished by law, is it not probable that it will, in time, be terminated by violence?

Do the precepts of Christianity and the lessons of history recommend gradual, in preference to immediate emancipation?

CHAPTER XI.

DANGER OF CONTINUED SLAVERY.

WHILE slave-holders and colonizationists delight to expatiate on the danger of immediate emancipation, and to represent its advocates as reckless incendiaries, ready to deluge the country in blood, they seem scarcely conscious that *any danger* is to be apprehended from slavery itself. Yet the whole history of slavery is a history of the struggles of the oppressed to recover their liberty. The Romans had their servile wars, in one of which forty thousand slaves were embodied in arms, Italy ravaged, and Rome herself menaced.

A European writer remarks:

> "The formidable rebellion of the Jamaica slaves, in 1762, is well known; and in almost every island in the Archipelago, have repeated insurrections broken out; sometimes the result of plans laid with the utmost secrecy, and very widely extended, always accompanied by the horrors of African warfare."

The destruction of property in Jamaica, in the insurrection of 1832, was estimated by the Legislature at £1,154,583. Any commotion of the emancipated slaves, that should cost the island one-hundredth part of this sum, would be hailed both there and here, as demonstrative of the folly and hazard of emancipation.

And have we not in our own country had melancholy, heart-rending proofs of the danger of slavery?

In 1712 and 1741, negro insurrections occurred in New York, and we may judge of the alarm they excited, by the shocking means used to prevent their recurrence. Of the leaders of the last insurrection, thirteen were burned alive, eighteen hung, and eighty transported. In the single State of South Carolina, there have been no less than seven insurrections designed or executed. In 1711, the House of Assembly complained of certain fugitive slaves, who "keep out armed, and robbing and plundering houses and plantations, and putting the inhabitants of this province in great fear and terror." In 1730, an open rebellion occurred, in which the negroes were actually armed and embodied. In 1739, there were no less than three rebellions, as appears from a petition from the Council and Assembly to the king, in which they complain of an "insurrection of our slaves, in which *many of the inhabitants were murdered in a barbarous and cruel manner;* and that was no sooner quelled, than another was projected in Charleston, and a third lately in the very heart of the settlement, but happily discovered time enough to be prevented." In 1816, there was a conspiracy of the slaves in Camden and its vicinity, "the professed design of which was to *murder all the whites and free themselves.*" The conspiracy in Charleston in 1822, and the sacrifice of human life to which it led, are well known. But in no instance has the danger of slavery been so vividly illustrated as in the tragedy of Southampton.

A fanatic slave conceived, from some supposed signs in the heavens or peculiarity in the weather, that he was called by God to destroy the whites. He communicated his commission to five other slaves, who engaged to aid him in executing it.

The conspirators agreed to meet at a certain place on the night of the 21st of August, 1831. They assembled at the appointed hour, and the leader, Nat Turner, beheld with surprise a sixth man, who had not been invited by him to join the enterprise, but who had learned from another source the cause of the meeting; and on inquiring for what purpose he had come, received the remarkable answer,—"My life is worth no more than that of others, and my liberty is dear to me." With these *six* associates, Turner commenced the work of destruction. By sunrise, the number of murderers was swelled to fourteen, and by ten o'clock the same morning, to forty!

From the testimony given on the trial of Turner, and which has been published, it appears that there was no previous concert, except between Turner and his six original associates, and that no white or free colored man was privy to their design.

The dates we have given of the various insurrections, prove conclusively that they were in no degree connected with discussions respecting abolition; and at the time of the Southampton massacre, there was no Anti-Slavery Society in the United States advocating immediate emancipation.

Abolitionists have been often charged with a desire to foment insurrections; but the charge is wholly gratuitous, and no proof whatever of such sublimated wickedness has ever been adduced against them. On the contrary, their characters, professions and conduct repel the calumny. The whole history of abolition shows that its only tendency is to insure peace and safety.

We have brought *facts* to establish the danger of slavery; let us now attend to the confessions of slave-holders to the same point. A South Carolina writer, while urging the necessity of a stricter police over the slaves, thus describes them:

"Let it never be forgotten, that our negroes are truly the Jacobins of the country; that they are the anarchists, and the domestic enemy; THE COMMON ENEMY OF CIVILIZED SOCIETY, AND THE BARBARIANS WHO WOULD IF THEY COULD BECOME THE DESTROYERS OF OUR RACE." *

The Southern Religious Telegraph says:

"Hatred to the whites, with the exception in some cases of attachment to the person and family of the master, is nearly universal among the black population. We have then a FOE cherished in our very bosoms — a foe WILLING TO DRAW OUR LIFE-BLOOD, whenever the opportunity is offered, and, in the mean time, intent on doing us all the mischief in his power."

Now, be it recollected that these "destroyers of our race," these foes, willing "to draw the life-blood" of the whites, are rapidly advancing to an immense numerical majority. And on what grounds do the whites rest their hopes of security from these Jacobins and anarchists, — on equal laws, the diffusion of education, and the influence of religion? Let Governor Haynes of South Carolina, answer the question.

"A STATE OF MILITARY PREPARATION must always be with us a state of perfect domestic security. A profound peace, and consequent apathy, may expose us to the danger of domestic insurrection." *Message to the Legislature*, 1833.

Thus, profound peace, which is a blessing to all other people, will be a curse to the slave-holders, and they are to hold all that is dear to them by the tenure of *military preparation!*

* A refutation of the calumnies inculcated against the Southern and Western States. *Charleston*, 1822.

Is it, we ask, possible, for any nation to have a worse population than that described in the preceding extracts, or to be doomed to a more deplorable fate than that of perpetual military preparation ?

We have now seen what are the religious and political principles, and what are the historical facts which lead the American Anti-Savery Society *to recommend* immediate emancipation to their Southern brethren.

But it is demanded, with an air of supercilious triumph, what have Northern men to do with slavery, and what right have they to interfere with the domestic institutions of the South? And is this question addressed to the followers of HIM who commanded his disciples to "go into all the world, and to preach the Gospel to every creature?" As well might it be asked of the Christians of America, what they have to do with the religion of Brahma, — what right they have to interfere to rescue the widow from the burning pile, or the devotee from the wheels of Juggernaut. Christians are no less bound by the injunction to "do good unto all men," to endeavor, by lawful means, to break the fetters of the slave, than to deliver the victim of Pagan superstition. The obligation is imperative, and they who duly respect its authority, will not be deterred by violence or denunciation from obeying its monitions. The same moral sense which has led abolitionists to oppose slavery, will, we trust, forever lead them to repudiate in their practice the detestable doctrine that the end sanctifies the means. The means they employ, except in relation to slavery under the authority of Congress, are wholly confined to *arguments* addressed to the conscience and understanding; and intended only to excite the *voluntary* action of the masters. With them, and with them alone, rests the power of deciding on the course they will pursue. But let them ponder well the consequences to themselves and their posterity, of their momentous decision.

By rejecting abolition, they reject all the rich and varied blessings in morals, in security, in political power and wealth which it offers to their acceptance. And what do they retain? — the licentiousness, cruelty, and injustice; the depression of enterprise, the wasting of strength, the fearful forebodings, the hourly jeopardy, the frowns of public opinion, and the reproaches of conscience, which are and must be the inseparable attendants on slavery. Before they refuse to retreat from the volcano on which they are standing, let them look into the terrific crater which yawns beneath them.

If slavery is to be perpetual, it will be well to estimate, not only the number of slaves with which our Southern country is to be peopled, but also the ratio they are to bear to their masters. It must be recollected that all those moral checks on population which arise from religion, the refinements of civilized life, and the difficulty of sustaining a family, are wanting to the slave. Hence there is always a tendency to a far more rapid multiplication in a slave than a free population. Certain circumstances may indeed check this tendency, but experience proves that in this country they exist to a very slight extent, if at all. Our slaves are increasing in a constantly accelerated ratio. In the ten years from 1840 to 1850, judging from the result of the last census, the increase will be 1,049,275, a number greater than all the slaves just liberated in the West Indies! The next ten years, a still greater number will be added, and so on indefinitely. In the mean time, new and powerful checks will be operating to retard the progress of the white population. The evils attendant on slavery will offer strong inducements to the young and indigent to forsake the land of their fathers, and to seek a safer home, and a wider field for enterprise. Virginia affords a striking illustration of this remark. The domestic slave-trade annually relieves that State of more than six thousand slaves, and yet, notwithstanding this drain, they continue to increase.

In 1830, the colored population in the counties east of the Blue Ridge, exceeded the white by 81,078, whereas, forty years before, in the same counties, the whites had a majority of 25,098.

The number of slaves must at length reach the point of profitable employment, after which, each additional one becomes an incumbrance. Soon after this point is reached, the traffic in slaves must cease, and the owners will be unable to dispose of their superfluous hands. The consequence will be the gradual impoverishment of the proprietors. As the slaves increase in number, and diminish in value, their masters will gradually become less interested in their welfare, and more apprehensive of their physical strength. Fear is a cruel passion, and especially as it silences the remonstrances of conscience by the plea of self-preservation. As the danger becomes more pressing, the precautions of the master will become more and more rigorous: every slave being regarded and treated as an enemy, will, in fact, become one; and every increase of cruelty will but hasten the final catastrophe.

In the mean time, slavery will have ceased in every other part of the civilized world. In Brazil, it will probably receive its death-blow in the first popular revolution. In the Danish Islands, it will expire in two years; and in the French and Spanish colonies, it cannot long survive.* And when this loathsome leprosy shall alone cling to the republicans of our Southern and Western States, in what light will they, must they, be regarded by the rest of the human race? This is an age in which public opinion has snatched the sceptre from kings and senates, and reigns an imperious and absolute despot. She may, indeed, be influenced, but not resisted. She called for the abolition of the African slave-trade, and the traffickers in human flesh, for centuries encouraged and protected by law, became a proscribed race. She is now calling for the freedom of the slave, and his shackles are falling from him. Emancipation will soon become the common cause of Christendom, as the abolition of the slave-trade was a few years since.

In 1822, the House of Representatives requested the President to enter into negotiations with the several maritime powers, for the effectual suppression of the slave-trade, and its ultimate denunciation as piracy; and negotiations were accordingly opened on this subject with Great Britain, Spain, Portugal, Russia, France, the Netherlands, Buenos Ayres and Colombia.

* The voluntary manumissions in the French Colonies from 1st of January, 1831, to 1st of June, 1833, were 21,962. Since the late Abolition Act of Great Britain, an Anti-Slavery Society has been organized in Paris, with the Duc de Broglie at its head. It is said to have "derived its existence in the verv bosom of the Chamber of Deputies."

In 1821, Portugal persisting in the traffic, the British House of Commons called upon the king, to endeavor, by negotiation, to prevail on the powers of Europe *to exclude from their ports the produce of the Portuguese Colonies.* Portugal yielded, and the trade has been renounced by every Christian nation in Europe and America. And may not the same, or similar means, be adopted by other nations to put an end to American slavery? It is by no means improbable, that before many years elapse,* laws will be passed, and treaties made, for excluding the products of slave-labor from Europe.

So long ago as 1806, Mr. Windham, in the House of Commons, "did not hesitate to say, that when the proper time arrived, and the consent of other powers could be obtained for its abolition, slavery ought not to be suffered to exist among the institutions of any civilized State."

The emperor of Austria has issued a decree, declaring—"Every man, by the right of nature, sanctioned by reason, must be considered a free person. Every slave becomes free from the moment he touches the Austrian soil, or an Austrian ship."

The Edinburgh Review insists, that "the existence of slavery in America is an atrocious crime, with which no means can be kept."

Mr. Buckingham, member of Parliament, lately asserted at a public meeting: "The greater proportion of the people of England demand not merely emancipation, but the immediate emancipation of the slaves, *in whatever quarter of the world they may be found.*"

Daniel O'Connell, shortly before the abolition of slavery in the British Dominions, declared in public, "The West Indies will be obliged to grant emancipation, and then *we will turn to America, and to every part of Europe, and require emancipation.*"

A society has just been formed in England, entitled, "the British and Foreign Society for the universal abolition of negro slavery and the slave-trade."

* A statement has recently been laid before the British Parliament of the amount of such produce of American slave-labor imported into Great Britain as enters into competition with the productions of the West Indies.

Our pride may revolt at the idea of foreign interference, but it will be the interference not of force, but of public opinion, against which our fleets and armies will be of no avail.

We cannot compel other countries to buy our cotton and sugar, or to admit our citizens from the South, when they visit Europe, to the usual courtesies of social intercourse. "When an American comes into society," says Daniel O'Connell, in a numerous assembly, "he will be asked, 'Are you one of the thieves, or are you an honest man? If you are an honest man, then you have given liberty to your slaves; if you are among the thieves, the sooner you take the outside of the house the better.'"

The very coarseness of this invective in the mouth of the great agitator, indicates the temper of the British population on this subject; a temper which, fostered as it is by the progress of liberal principles, will, in time, become the temper of all Europe, and, indeed, of all the world. While the slave-holders are suffering, without sympathy and without redress, from the harassing influence of this temper, their slaves will be multiplying with a fearful rapidity, and becoming each day more conscious of their own strength; and unless their fetters are loosened, they will inevitably be BURST.

Our Southern brethren are the masters of their own destiny; may a gracious God lead them to know the things which belong to their peace, before they be forever hidden from their eyes.

A VIEW OF THE ACTION

OF THE

FEDERAL GOVERNMENT;

IN

BEHALF OF SLAVERY.

"We, the People of the United States, do ordain and establish this Constitution."—*Federal Constitution.*

INTRODUCTION

TO SECOND EDITION.

THE rapid sale of the first edition of this work, and the almost immediate call for another, afford gratifying evidence of the awakening attention of the public to the action of the Federal Government in behalf of slavery. That action is so iniquitous in itself, and so dangerous in its consequences to the liberties of the country, that it needs only to be fully known, to be restrained by the patriotism and moral sense of the community, within the limits prescribed by the Constitution and the obvious principles of humanity and justice. It is not easy, however, to enlighten those who prefer darkness to light; nor to persuade men to act in opposition to their supposed pecuniary or political interests. But there can be no triumph where there is no struggle — that religion is worthless, which coöperates with human depravity; and that patriotism an empty name, which only echoes the shout of the multitude.

If the friends of human liberty have in this country much to cover them with grief and shame, they have also much to stimulate their exertions, and much to assure them of ultimate success. Their own rights — the virtue, happiness and liberty of their descendants — the honor, prosperity and freedom of their country, are all involved in the issue. Slavery is a perfidious, encroaching enemy, that must either conquer or be conquered. Let the warfare now waged against it be succeeded by a peace, and soon Texas, the Valley of the Mississippi, and in time even the Atlantic States would be added to its dominions. Every dictate, therefore, of patriotism or religion, of personal interest, of paternal affection, unites in urging us to use all lawful means to stay the progress of the destroyer, and to teach our children after us to continue the contest.

But is not the struggle hopeless, and ought we not to sit down in utter despair at the prospect of desolation, misery and disgrace with which our country is threatened? So we are advised by high authority; PUBLIC OPINION, we are told, is against us. Indeed! and is it not also against every defeated candidate for office, and every losing political party? But who hears our baffled politicians advising submission to the victors because public opinion is against the vanquished? Public opinion is a mighty agent for good or for evil; but it is as fickle as it is powerful. It strowed the path of the Redeemer with palm branches, and afterwards nailed him to the cross.

For ages it guarded and preserved all the oppressions and cruelties of the feudal system; it is now gradually, but surely destroying its every vestige. But a few years since, public opinion not merely sanctioned, but actually required the use of intoxicating liquors; it is now their potent enemy.

But perhaps the most extraordinary change this mighty agent has undergone, is in relation to slavery itself; and the friends of emancipation will find in the history of this transformation one of their most powerful inducements to perseverance.

For more than two hundred years before its abolition, had the African slave-trade been pursued by Christian nations, under the fostering protection of their rulers. No difference of religious faith, of government, or of climate, offered any check to this accursed commerce. Catholics and Protestants, the subjects of monarchs and the citizens of republics, natives of the north and of the south, alike thirsted for the price of blood, alike participated in robbery and murder. In 1774, the British cabinet refused its assent to the imposition, by the colonial legislatures, of duties on the importation of slaves. "We cannot," said the Secretary, Lord Dartmouth, "allow the colonies to check or discourage in *any degree* a traffic so beneficial to the nation!"

The feelings of humanity and the powers of conscience were on this subject almost universally and totally paralyzed. So late as 1783, in the trial of a civil cause in London, it appeared in evidence, that one hundred and thirty-two Africans had been thrown into the sea by the captain of a slaver to defraud the underwriters. Minutes of the evidence were submitted to the government; but the victims were only *negroes*, and their murderer was unmolested.

In 1786, the number of unhappy beings annually torn from Africa was estimated at 100,000. Of these, it was admitted at least 20,000 perished on the voyage; and of those who survived to enter a state of hopeless bondage, 20,000 more, exhausted by suffering and despair, sunk into the grave within two years.

Individuals were occasionally found who protested against the traffic, but their voices were unheeded. For two centuries not a word in reprobation of the trade had been uttered within the walls of the British senate. This long silence was first broken by Mr. David Hartley, who in 1776 moved in the House of Commons, that the slave-trade was "contrary to the laws of God and the rights of man." But the moral sense of Great Britain, and indeed of the world, was then too obtuse to recognize these simple and now obvious truths; and the resolution was promptly rejected. Seven years after, a petition against the trade, the first ever offered, was presented by the Quaker Society to the House of Commons. But that body did not even condescend to consider it — the Premier, Lord North, coolly observing, that the traffic had, in a commercial view, become *necessary* to almost every nation in Europe.

On the 7th of July, 1783, shortly after this official declaration, SIX Quakers* met in London "to consider what steps they should take for

* William Dillwyn, George Harrison, Samuel Hoare, Thomas Knowles, John Lloyd, and Joseph Woods. Their names are registered in heaven, let them not be forgotten on earth.

THE RELIEF AND LIBERATION OF THE NEGRO SLAVES IN THE WEST INDIES, *and* FOR THE DISCOURAGEMENT OF THE SLAVE-TRADE ON THE COAST OF AFRICA."

When we reflect on the peculiar circumstances under which these men assembled, we cannot but regard their meeting as one of the sublimest instances of Christian faith unrecorded in the sacred volume, — a faith which, according to the promise, was effectual in removing mountains. At the moment of their meeting, the maritime powers of Europe were actively engaged in the trade, — a trade against which no petition had ever been presented, except from the very sect to which they belonged, and which had, within a few days, like certain petitions in modern times, been ordered to "*lie on the table.*" They had, moreover, just witnessed the impunity of the wretch who had deliberately drowned one hundred and thirty-two of his fellow-men, — an impunity which warned them of the utter insensibility of the public to the sufferings of the miserable negroes.

And who were these six men who under such circumstances presumed to attempt the abolition of slavery and the slave-trade — who aspired to move the moral world — to arrest the commerce of nations — to proclaim liberty to the captive, and the opening of the prison doors to them that were bound? Did they sway the councils, or lead the armies of empires? — were they possessed of learning to command the attention of the wise and great, or of eloquence to mould at their will the passions of multitudes? They were humble and obscure individuals, belonging to a small and despised sect, and precluded by their religious tenets and social condition from all political influence. But they discovered from the Book of God, what had escaped many wise and good men, that the trade in question was opposed alike to the attributes and the precepts of the Almighty Ruler of nations.

In laboring, therefore, for its suppression, they were assured of his approbation; and without regarding their own weakness, or the obstacles before them, they proceeded steadily in the path of duty, leaving the result to HIM with whom all things are possible.

They determined to hold frequent meetings, of which regular minutes were kept. Their first object was to enlighten and purify the public mind, and for this purpose they entered into negotiations with the proprietors of various newspapers, and secured a space in their columns for such articles respecting the trade as they might choose to insert. They likewise circulated books and pamphlets on the subject. The seeds thus scattered germinated slowly, but ultimately yielded a glorious harvest. Within two years a second petition was presented, and like the first was treated with neglect. The third year, the six associates, with the aid of some friends, engaged the celebrated Clarkson as their agent; and so successful were his labors in exciting the sensibilities of the British public, that it was found expedient to divest the enterprise of its sectarian character, and the committee added six to their number from other denominations. This new committee soon became an important body, receiving and appropriating the pecuniary contributions to the cause, and directing and cheering the labors of its advocates. Gradually, members of Parliament, dignitaries of the church, and political leaders subscribed to the funds of the committee, and avowed their hostility to the trade.

Petitions were multiplied, and the government so far condescended to notice the rising excitement, as to appoint a commission to inquire into the alleged atrocities of this branch of the British commerce. On the 9th of May, 1788, only five years after the first meeting of the committee, the House of Commons voted that they would at the next session take into consideration the complaints against the African slave-trade.

It is unnecessary for our purpose to pursue the details of this instructive history. It has already taught us the possibility of rousing the public attention, however lethargic, by appeals to the conscience and understanding, and the influence which Christian zeal and faith, unaided by wealth and power, are capable of exerting. The few remaining facts we shall notice convey the important lesson, that no cause, however pure, no truth, however obvious, can shield their advocates from obloquy, when prejudice and selfishness find it expedient to assail them; and also, that constancy in maintaining and inculcating the great principles of justice and humanity will finally be crowned with success.

No sooner did a parliamentary inquiry threaten to expose the abominations and endanger the continuance of the traffic, than its advocates, reckless alike of truth and decency, vindicated its policy, and attacked with vindictive fury those who were laboring to destroy it. Abolition was denounced in Parliament as "hypocritical, fanatic, and methodistical." It would lead, it was asserted, to "insurrection, massacre and ruin in the colonies; and in Great Britain, to the reduction of her revenue, the decay of her naval strength, and the bankruptcy of her merchants and manufactures." The trade was justified by the press, and even ministers of religion stepped forth to vindicate it on scriptural authority.* In 1791, a bill was brought in for the suppression of the trade. The opposition to it was malignant and successful. The measure was pronounced fit only for the bigotry of the twelfth century. Lord John Russell termed it "visionary and delusive, a feeble attempt to serve the cause of humanity, as other nations would pursue the trade if abolished by Great Britain." Mr. Stanley insisted that it was the intention of Providence, from the beginning, *that one set of men should be slaves to another;* and he complained that the trade had been condemned from the pulpit!

The friends of abolition were ridiculed by Lord Chancellor Thurlow from the woolsack; and the Duke of Clarence, who afterwards, as WILLIAM THE FOURTH, gave his assent to the bill abolishing slavery throughout his dominions, regardless of parliamentary decorum, declared, in his place in the House of Lords, that the abolitionists were hypocrites and fanatics; and in the application of these epithets included Mr. Wilberforce by name.

Ten times did Mr. Wilberforce, in the House of Commons, endeavor to procure the suppression of the traffic, and ten times was he doomed to defeat. So late as 1807, Lord Castlereagh, in the British senate,

* As illustrative of public opinion at this time, we give the titles of two pamphlets published in London in 1788, viz.: "Slavery no Oppresion," and "Scriptural Researches on the Licitness of the Slave-Trade, and showing its conformity with the principles of natural and revealed religion, delineated in the writings of the word of God." *By the Rev. R. Harris.*

vindicated the trade on scriptural grounds, and avowed that, in his opinion, the advantages resulting from it were so great, that were it not now existing, the trade ought forthwith to be established. But the triumph of justice and the reward of faith and perseverance were nigh at hand. On the 25th of March, 1807, twenty-four years after the formation of the Quaker committee, the slave-trade was abolished by act of Parliament.

Splendid and glorious as was this triumph, it was incomplete while shared by Great Britain alone. The whole of Christendom was yet to be brought to abjure a commerce condemned alike by reason and revelation. A long course of negotiation ensued, and treaty after treaty was made for the abandonment of the traffic, until, in 1830, every Christian nation in Europe and America had prohibited it.

The Quaker committee, as we have seen, proposed, in 1783, not merely the discouragement of the African slave-trade, but also "the liberation of negro slaves in the West Indies." The struggle for this last object was continued after the accomplishment of the former for thirty-one years; when, on the 4th of August, 1838, negro slavery wholly ceased throughout the British West Indies, and every legal disability, founded on color, was utterly abolished.

Thus has been accomplished the most astonishing revolution in opinion and practice the world has ever witnessed, with the exception of the establishment of Christianity. And let it be remembered, that this revolution was effected solely by the exhibition of truth, and by bold and persevering appeals to the conscience and understanding of mankind. No miracles have wrought conviction, no force has subdued opposition. Public opinion was gradually enlightened and converted, and then roused into action, and with resistless energy it smote to the earth a stupendous system of wickedness and cruelty.

Surely we may learn from this history a very different lesson from that which many of our politicians and moralists are fond of inculcating, that because public opinion is against them, *therefore* abolitionists should cease to do well, and learn to do evil — should abandon their opposition to slavery and acquiesce in popular iniquity. Let us take the six Quakers for our example, and resolve to persevere, while life shall be spared, in our assaults upon slavery, not inquiring how many are against us, knowing assuredly that God is for us. But should the advocates of emancipation, in some moment of weakness or of trial, be tempted to cast a desponding and inquiring glance over the field of battle, and to recall to his recollection the events of the campaign, he will see nothing in the array of hostile forces to damp his courage, nor in the review of the past to lower his confidence of victory.

The great object proposed by the friends of human liberty, so far as relates to the Federal Government, is the abolition of slavery within its "exclusive jurisdiction." But we have been given to understand,* that "the immediate abolition of slavery in the District of Columbia is utterly impracticable." That the *present* administration do not *choose* to abolish it, is not more true than that the British Parliament of 1783 did not choose to abolish the slave-trade; and it is equally true that the

* Public letter of John Quincy Adams of 25th May, 1839.

abolition of slavery in the District of Columbia is now far more probable and practicable than was that of the slave-trade and West India slavery at the formation of the Quaker committee. But why is the immediate abolition of slavery in the District utterly impracticable? "Because public opinion throughout the Union is against it." This is a good reason for predicting that the next Congress will not grant abolition, but not why the friends of abolition should cease their efforts to change public opinion, in order that a future Congress may grant what we know the next will refuse.

In many respects the abolitionists of the present day are placed in circumstances similar to those in which their predecessors found themselves in 1783. They, like us, had to contend with the hostility of the Government, with the interests and prejudices of slave-holders in the Legislature,* with clerical defenders of cruelty and oppression, with mercantile cupidity, and with heartless politicians. But in many other respects they were less favored than we are. They were struggling *against* the spirit of the age; we are coöperating with it. They were advancing untried theories; we can point to the West Indies and South America for the practical and successful operation of our doctrines. They were striving to influence a government in a great degree independent of the people; we are petitioning a government that is the mere creature of the popular will. They were few and despised; the hatred and persecution we have experienced attest the importance attributed to us. They were without political influence; where suffrage is universal, 300,000 petitioners will not be overlooked by politicians. They could bring their facts and arguments before the public only by hiring a space in the columns of a few newspapers; we have numerous periodicals, many of them of the largest size, exclusively devoted to the propagation of our opinions, while many religious and political journals are aiding us in exhibiting the evils of slavery and the advantages of emancipation. They were cheered by no official sanction of their efforts; we are encouraged and stimulated, in many instances, by the approving voice of the representatives of the people.

We ask Congress to abolish slavery in the District; is the prayer presumptuous or unconstitutional? If so, it becomes not the House of Representatives to rebuke us; for, on the 9th of January, 1829, that body "Resolved that the Committee on the District of Columbia be instructed to inquire into the expediency of providing *by law* for the gradual abolition of slavery within the District, in such manner that the interests of no individual shall be injured thereby." Here we have the solemn admission of the popular and most numerous branch of the Legislature, that the question of abolition is one of *expediency* alone, and not of constitutional power; and that slavery may be terminated by law, without injury to any individual. And what sentiments on this subject have been uttered by the State Legislatures? In 1828 the Legislature of PENNSYLVANIA instructed their members of Congress "to procure, if practicable, the passage of a law to abolish slavery in

* Many of the Commoners and Lords were deeply interested in West Indian plantations; and a large estate, well stocked with slaves, was held by a chartered Society, of the established Church.

the District of Columbia." In 1829, the Assembly of NEW YORK voted to direct the representatives from that State "to make every proper exertion to effect the passage of a law for the abolition of slavery in the District of Columbia." In 1837, the Senate of MASSACHUSETTS "Resolved that Congress, having exclusive legislation in the District of Columbia, possess the right to abolish slavery and the slave-trade therein, and that the early exercise of such right is demanded by the enlightened sentiment of the civilized world, by the principles of the Revolution, and by humanity." The other House, the same session, "Resolved that Congress, having exclusive legislation in the District of Columbia, possess the right to abolish slavery in said District, and that its exercise should only be restrained by a regard to the public good." The next session both branches of the Legislature resolved "That the rights of justice, the claims of humanity, and the common good alike demand the entire suppression of the slave-trade now carried on in the District of Columbia." In 1838, the House of Representatives of the Legislature of MAINE "Resolved that the continuance of slavery within the sacred enclosure and chosen seat of the National Government is inconsistent with a due regard to the enlightened judgment of mankind, and with all just pretensions on our part to the character of a free people, and is adapted to bring into contempt republican liberty, and render its influence powerless throughout the world." The same year the Legislature of VERMONT, without a dissenting voice, instructed the Representatives in Congress "to use their utmost efforts to procure the abolition of slavery and the slave-trade in the District of Columbia." Yet there are those who would fain paralyze all our efforts by the assurance that public opinion is against us!

But we are urged to desist, not only because our object is impracticable, but also because it is *unlawful*. "When the people," we are told, "are bound by laws emanating from a legislative assembly wherein they have no representatives, *their will* must be ascertained by manifestations from themselves." But why ought Congress to ascertain the will of the people of the District? Because "the Declaration of Independence derives all just powers of the Government from the consent of the governed." But are laws binding only on such as approve of them? No. "When the people are represented in the legislative assembly, the *consent of the whole* must be inferred from the voice of the representative majority." Now it so happens that the whole people of the United States, by the voice of the representative majority, assented to the provision of the Constitution, that a district, ten miles square, should be placed under the absolute and exclusive jurisdiction of Congress. To this arrangement the people inhabiting the present District gave their assent through their representatives. Afterwards, when they themselves were set off, by the Legislatures of Virginia and Maryland, to be the subjects of this exclusive jurisdiction, they, through their representatives in the Legislatures, consented to be thus placed under the authority of Congress. And shall we now be gravely told, after these people have thus consented to be governed, in all cases whatsoever, by the National Legislature, and after the people of the United States have, for this purpose, vested unlimited and exclusive jurisdiction in Congress, that it is contrary to the principles of the Declaration of Independence that this jurisdiction should secure to each inhabitant of the District the "inalienable rights of life, liberty, and the pursuit of happiness?" Again, if the Declaration derives the powers of the government from the consent of the governed, from what representative majority, we would ask, are we to infer the *consent* of six thousand of the people of the District to be reduced to chattels — to be robbed of the rights of humanity — to be converted, with their wives and children, into articles of merchandise?

Surely the friends of emancipation will not, after their past experience, look upon public opinion as an *invincible* enemy — still less will they believe that the Declaration of Independence is the death-warrant of human rights in the national domain. The principles for which they are contending are the principles of the Declaration; the means they are using are those given them by the Constitution — freedom of speech and of the press — petition and the elective franchise; and, by the blessing of God on these principles and means, they will yet convert public opinion into an ally — will yet purge the capital of the Republic of its loathsome plague, and restore the Federal Government to its legitimate functions, of establishing justice and securing the blessings of liberty.

Bedford, September, 1839.

A VIEW OF THE ACTION

OF THE

GENERAL GOVERNMENT.

Our Fathers, in forming the Federal Constitution, entered into a guilty compromise on the subject of slavery, and heavily is their sin now visited upon their children. By that instrument, the continuance of the African slave-trade was guaranteed for twenty years;—a larger proportional representation in Congress, and a larger vote in the election of the Executive, was accorded to the slave-holding, than to the other States:—the power of the nation was pledged to keep the slave in subjection; and should he ever escape from his fetters, his master was authorized to pursue and to seize him, in any and every of the sovereign States composing our wide-spread confederacy.

We are not about to exhibit the corrupting influence of this compact on the religious sympathies and sentiments of our countrymen, in regard to slavery; nor is it our present purpose to trace the retributive justice of Heaven in that recklessness of human life, and in that contempt of human and divine obligations which are hurrying on the slave States to anarchy and barbarism; or in the eagerness so generally exhibited by our northern politicians and merchants, to barter the constitutional rights of themselves and their fellow-citizens, for the votes and the trade of the South.*

We propose simply to take a view of the action of the Federal Government in behalf of slavery,—a subject that has yet been but partially investigated; and we flatter ourselves that in the course of our inquiries we shall develop facts which, with some at least of our readers, will possess the merit of novelty. These facts, for the most part, derive their origin from

THE FEDERAL RATIO OF REPRESENTATION.

The Constitution provides that the members of the Lower House of Congress shall be proportioned to the free inhabitants of the States they represent, *except* that in each State three-fifths of the slave population shall be for this purpose considered as free inhabitants. In other words, every five slaves are to be counted as three white persons. For example, if by law every 60,000 free inhabitants may elect a representative, a district containing 45,000 whites and 25,000 slaves, becomes by the *federal ratio* entitled to a member. This stipulation in the Constitution has from the beginning given the slave-holders an undue weight in the national councils. A few instances will illustrate its practical effect. The whole number of the House of Representatives is at present 242—sent from 26 States. Of these, the following are *slave* States, viz.:—Delaware, Maryland, Virginia, North Carolina, South Carolina, Georgia, Kentucky, Tennessee, Alabama,

* Before this language is condemned as harsh and exaggerated, we beg the reader to recall some of the prominent events of the last few years, connected with this subject,—the Lynch clubs and cruel inflictions of the South—the sacking of the Charleston post-office—the wholesale and unpunished murders at Vicksburg—and the frequent burnings alive of negroes, and in particular of McIntosh, taken by the citizens of St. Louis from the prison, chained to a tree, and consumed by a slow fire—and the advice of Judge Lawless to the Grand Jury, not to notice the diabolical atrocity, because it was, in fact, the act of the community! As to the North, we point in our justification to the innumerable mobs excited by politicians against the friends of emancipation—the various attempts made by the State authorities to propitiate the South by a surrender of the freedom of speech and of the press—to the zeal of the merchants in our seaports in getting up anti-abolition meetings—to the conflagration of Pennsylvania Hall, and to the martyrdom of Lovejoy. In truth, our whole land is strowed with monuments of the wickedness and tyranny of slavery—monuments which declare, in no doubtful language, that our common national sin is not unheeded by HIM to whom vengeance belongeth.

Mississippi, Louisiana, Missouri and Arkansas. These States, with a free population of 3,823,389, have 100 members; while the *free* States, with a free population nearly double, viz., 7,003,-451, have only 142 members. One representative is at present allowed to 47,700 inhabitants. Now were the slaves omitted in the enumeration, the slave States would have only 75 members. Hence it follows, that at the present moment, the slave-holding interest has a representation of TWENTY-FIVE members in *addition* to the fair and equal representation of the free inhabitants. There is certainly no good reason why the owners of human chattels should, by the fundamental law of a *Republic*, have greater privileges awarded to them than to the holders of any other kind of property whatever. But such is the compact; we seek not to change or violate it, but only to explain its operation.

Each State has as many votes for President as it has members of Congress. The rule of representation in the Lower House has already been explained; in the Senate it is different and *each* State, whatever be its population, has two senators, and no more. The free population of the slave States, as already stated, is *half* that of the others; but their *number* being equal, their representation in the Senate is also equal.

If free population were the principle of representation in the Federal Government, as it is with scarcely an exception in all the States, the slave States would have,

	In the Senate,	13 members.
	In the House,	75
Electoral votes for president,		88
They *have*,	In the Senate,	26 members.
	In the House,	100
Electoral votes for President,		126

Here we find the secret of the power of the South, and of the obsequiousness of the North. Ohio, with a population of 947,-000, has 19 members; while Virginia, with a free population of 200,000 LESS, has *two* members MORE. Take another example. Pennsylvania has 30 electoral votes; the States of South Carolina, Georgia, Alabama, Mississippi, Louisiana, and Kentucky, with an *aggregate* free population of 189,791 *less* than Pennsylvania, have 53 electoral votes!

It cannot be supposed that this vast and most unequal representation and consequent political power will be unemployed by its possessors. On the contrary, the slave-holders in Congress have uniformly succeeded in effecting their objects, when united among themselves. In 1836, this slave-power in Congress was adroitly turned to pecuniary profit. The Surplus Revenue remaining in the Treasury on the 1st of January, 1837, was to be distributed, and the rule of distribution became a question. The income, it is true, had been derived chiefly from the industry and enterprise of the North; but the South insisted, and with her usual success, that instead of dividing the money according to population, it should be apportioned among the States according to their *electoral votes*. By this rule, the slave States, notwithstanding their inferiority in population, would share alike with the free, so far as regarded the number of their senators; and with regard to their representatives, they would secure an apportionment of money on account of three-fifths of their two millions of slaves.

The sum allotted by this gross and monstrous rule to the States of South Carolina, Georgia, Alabama, Mississippi, Louisiana, and Kentucky, was $6,754,588; while Pennsylvania, with a free population *larger* than that of all these six States together, was to receive only $3,823,353; so that, in fact, the slave-holders of these States received, man for man, just about twice as many dollars from the national treasury as the hard-working citizens of Pennsylvania!

Notwithstanding this slave representation, the free States have a majority of members; and hence it becomes important to investigate

THE SOURCES OF THE SLAVE-HOLDING INFLUENCE IN CONGRESS.

These may be regarded as threefold: First, their anxiety to protect and perpetuate slavery renders the Southern members united in whatever measures they consider important for this purpose, while the representatives from the North, having no common bond of union, are divided in opinion and effort. Secondly, a slave State, having more votes to bestow on a presidential candidate, and more members in Congress to support or oppose the administration than a free State of equal white population, is of course of greater consequence in the estimation of politicians; and hence arises an influence reaching to every measure, and weighing upon every question. Thirdly, the peculiar temperament of the Southern gentlemen, together with their observation of the servility of the Northern politicians, has induced them to resort, and with great success, to INTIMIDATION as a means of influence.

The practice adopted by the slave-holders of threatening on all occasions to dissolve the Union, unless they are permitted to govern it, has been too long and firmly established to need illustration. We will at present merely give a few recent instances of outrageous menaces; and to justify what we have said of the servility of Northern politicians, it is sufficient to observe, that these menaces were unrebuked.

On the 18th of April, 1836, a petition against the continuance of slavery in the District of Columbia was presented to the House of Representatives, when Mr. SPEIGHT, of North Carolina, declared in his place, that "he had great respect for the chair as an officer of the House, and a great respect for him personally; and *nothing but that respect* prevented him from rushing to the table and *tearing that petition to pieces.*" Of course it was to be understood that the order of the House and the rights of Northern petitioners were respected, not from any constitutional obligations, but solely because the speaker, himself a slave-holder, was acceptable to Southern gentlemen.

Mr. HAMMOND, of South Carolina, the same session, in a speech, used the following language: "I warn the abolitionists, ignorant, infatuated barbarians as they are, that if chance shall throw any of them into *our hands*, he may expect a *felon's death.*"

Mr. LUMPKIN remarked in the Senate, (January, 1838,) "If abolitionists went to Georgia, they would be *caught;*" and Mr. PRESTON declared in the same debate — "Let an abolitionist come within the borders of South Carolina, if we can catch him, we will try him, and notwithstanding all the interference of all the governments on earth, including the Federal Government, we will HANG him." *

It seems probable from these declarations that abolitionists, in their Southern travels, will meet with "barbarians" quite as "ignorant and infatuated" as themselves: and also that the gibbet is to be the fate of any member of Congress, who shall by his votes or speeches dare to identify himself with the abolitionists, and afterwards enter the slave-region.

Such are the sources of the slave-holding influence in Congress. The following pages will exhibit many of the results of this influence, and the first to which the reader's attention is called, is

THE OBSEQUIOUSNESS OF THE PRESIDENTIAL CANDIDATES.

As slave-holders are ready to hang abolitionists when they can "catch" them, it is not to be supposed that they will elect any of the proscribed sect President of the United States. Of course, it becomes important for such gentlemen as aspire to that honor, that their ideas on the subject of human rights should be adapted to the meridian of the slave-region.

Previous to the last presidential canvass, Mr. VAN BUREN, being a candidate, thought it prudent to write a letter for publication, containing the following passage:

"I prefer that not only you, but all the people of the United States, shall now understand, that if the desire of that portion of them which is favorable to my election to the chief magistracy should be gratified, I must go into the presidential chair *the inflexible and uncompromising opponent* of any attempt on the part of Congress to abolish slavery in the District of Columbia, *against the wishes of the slave-holding States.*"

Wr. WHITE was a rival candidate, and deemed it expedient to give his pledge also, which he did in these terms:

"I do not believe Congress has the power to abolish slavery in the District of Columbia; and if that body did possess the power, I think

* Yet this Carolina Senator, who is thus ready to sanction wholesale murder for opinion's sake, in defiance "of all the governments on earth," and the government in heaven, too, has been nominated for the office of Vice President of the United States, by the WHIG party, in the State of Ohio, a party professing great attachment to the cause of *constitutional* liberty!

the exercise of it would be the *very worst policy*. Holding these opinions, I would act on them in any situation in which I could be placed, and for both reasons would, if called on to act, *withhold my assent to any bill having in view such an object*."

General Harrison, a third candidate, also, as we have understood, wrote his letter, but not having it before us we cannot quote it. We presume, however, it was thought sufficient, since an address in his behalf from his political friends in Virginia, assured the public that "*he is sound to the core on the subject of slavery*."

Mr. Webster, the fourth and last candidate, had many years before fully committed himself as to the power of Congress over slavery in the District. He gave no pledge, and received no vote from any slave State.

Another presidential election is approaching, and Mr. Clay is announced as the opposing candidate to the present incumbent. This gentleman's position with regard to human rights, has been deemed at the South equivocal and unsatisfactory. It is true he is a slave-holder, and although for more than twenty years an officer, and now the President of the Colonization Society, he has refrained from availing himself of the opportunities he has possessed of manumitting his slaves, and permitting them to enjoy in Africa the liberty which he insists it would be dangerous to allow them in America. Still his *language* and *professions*, in relation to the "delicate subject," have been indiscreet. In 1827, he maintained in a public speech the right and policy of the Federal Government to aid the Colonization Society, and insisted that the annual increase of the colored population, bond and free, namely 52,000, might be transported to Africa.

"If," said the orator, "I could be instrumental in eradicating this deepest stain (slavery) upon the character of our country, and removing all cause for reproach on account of it by foreign nations — if I could only be instrumental in ridding of this foul blot, that revered State (Virginia) that gave me birth — or that not less beloved State (Kentucky) which kindly adopted me as her son, I would not exchange the proud satisfaction which I should enjoy for all the honor of all the triumphs ever decreed to the most successful conqueror.*

* Speech before the American Colonization Society. 10*th Rep.*, p. 12.

In the same speech he remarked, in reference to such as objected to the agitation of the slavery question, —

"If they would repress all tendencies towards liberty and ultimate emancipation, they must do more than put down the benevolent efforts of this Society. They must go back to the era of our liberty and independence, and muzzle the cannon which thunders its annual joyous return. They must revive the slave-trade, with all its train of atrocities. They must suppress the workings of British philanthropy, seeking to meliorate the condition of the unfortunate West India slaves. They must arrest the career of South American deliverance from thraldom. They must blow out the moral lights around us, and extinguish the greatest torch of all which America presents to a benighted world, pointing the way to their rights, their liberties and their happiness. They must penetrate the human soul, and eradicate the light of reason and the love of liberty. Then, and not till then, *when universal darkness and despair prevail, can you* PERPETUATE SLAVERY, *and repress all sympathies and all humane and benevolent efforts among freemen, in behalf of the unhappy portions of our race who are doomed to bondage.*"

It is not surprising that such sentiments should excite distrust of Mr. Clay at the South; a distrust by no means likely to be dissipated by the following extract from "The Life of the Hon. Henry Clay, by George G. Prentiss," published some years since, — an extract which has been zealously circulated of late by Southern papers, devoted to the support of *Northern men with Southern principles.*

"The commencement of Mr. CLAY'S political career may be dated as far back as the year 1797, — a period at which he had scarcely begun the practice of law. The people of Kentucky were then about to elect a convention to frame a new constitution for the State. And one feature of the plan which had been submitted to them was a provision for the *final emancipation of the slave population.* The strongest prejudices of a majority of the people, in every part of the State, were arraigned against this measure, and MR. CLAY was aware of the fact; his SENTIMENTS and his FEELINGS were on the side of EMANCIPATION; and without taking a moment's heed to his popularity, he entered into the defence of his FAVORITE POLICY, with all the deep and unquenchable ardor of his nature. His vigorous pen was busy in the public journals, and his eloquent voice was raised in almost every assemblage, in favor of the election of men to the convention who would contend for the ERADICATION OF SLAVERY. A conviction of the expediency and necessity of EMANCIPATION has been spreading farther and farther among our countrymen, and taking deeper and deeper root in their minds, and it requires not the spirit of prophecy to foretell the END. This rapid and continued triumph of the PRINCIPLES, of which it was the object of MR. CLAY'S first political labors to establish, may well be a source of pride to him and honest exultation to his friends."

Mr. Clay's course in Congress had, moreover, not been satisfactory to the slave-party. He had not advocated the annexation of Texas — he had not denied the constitutional power of Congress to abolish slavery in the District — he had expressed himself in favor of receiving abolition petitions — and, above all, he had voted against Mr. Calhoun's bill establishing a censorship of the press; a bill which received the sanction of Mr. Van Buren and his partisans, the two New York senators, Messrs. Wright and Tallmadge.

The administration party at the South were making great use of all these circumstances against Mr. Clay, and it became obvious that unless he could conciliate the slave-holders, he had little prospect of success.

The Mobile "Commercial Register" thus announced the demand of the South:

> "We must do by Mr. Clay as the South have done by Mr. Van Buren — leave him not an inch of neutral ground to stand upon between the South and the fanatics. *We must push him as far as Mr. Van Buren was pushed.* The southern safety demands it. *He must measure the whole length*, and walk altogether off the middle neutral ground which he occupies, OR THE SOUTH WILL REJECT AND SPURN HIM."

In this state of things, a petition from some of the inhabitants of the District *against* abolition was put into the hands of Mr. Clay, and he determined to make such a use of it as might save him from being rejected and spurned by the South. Accordingly, a SPEECH in support of the petitions was prepared, *submitted to the consideration of his friends,* and finally delivered in the Senate of the United States on the 7th of February, 1839. In this memorable *document* he vindicates the Senate from all intentional violation of the right of petition in their mode of disposing of the abolition petitions — he declares himself "irresistibly impelled to do whatever is in his power to dissuade the public from continuing to agitate a subject fraught with the most direful consequences." He distinguishes the abolitionists from those who are content to keep their conscientious objections against slavery to themselves, and from those who think the constitutional right of petition has been invaded by Congress; and then draws a false and distorted picture of those whom he pleases to term "the real ultra abolitionists." With these men, he tells us, "the deficiency of the power of the General Government is nothing — the acknowledged and incontestable powers of the States are nothing — civil war, and dissolution of the Union, and the overthrow of a government, in which are concentrated the fondest hopes of the civilized world, are nothing." That it may not be supposed he *now* rejoices in "the working of British philanthropy," he declares, "if the British Parliament treated the West India slaves as freemen, it also treated West India freemen as SLAVES." Daniel O'Connell, on account of his indignant rebukes of American slavery, is denounced by the Kentucky senator, as "the plunderer of his own country, and the libeller of a foreign and kindred people." He then turns to the District of Columbia, and in this focus of the American slave-trade, and slave-ships, and slave-prisons, and slave-coffles, and slave-auctions, he asserts that slavery "exists here in the mildest and most mitigated form," and he argues that Congress cannot rightfully abolish it. On the American slave-trade, he is very explicit and logical: "I deny that the General Government has any authority whatever from the Constitution to abolish what is called the slave-trade, or, in other words, to prohibit the removal of slaves from one slave State to another slave State. The grant in the Constitution" (of power to Congress to regulate commerce between the States) "is of a power of *regulation*, and not prohibition." Mr. Clay's perception of the distinction between regulation and prohibition, was not so clear before he became a candidate for the Presidency. In an address he made to the Kentucky Colonization Society in 1829, after calling the *African* slave-trade "the most abominable traffic that ever disgraced the annals of the human race," he alluded to the act of Congress *prohibiting* it, and remarked, "on the 2d of March, 1807, the act was passed, for which it was my *happy lot to vote.*" "The grant in the Constitution," under which Mr. Clay voted for the act *prohibiting* the trade, was that of power to Congress "to *regulate* foreign commerce."

As if to apologize for having in his youthful days advocated emancipation in Kentucky, he refers in his speech to the inconsiderable number of slaves then in the State: "but," he adds, "if I had been then, or were NOW, a citizen of any of the planting States — the Southern or Southwestern States — I should have opposed, and would continue to oppose, any scheme whatever of emancipation, GRADUAL or IMMEDIATE." In 1797, Mr. Clay was anxious that the Kentucky Convention should take measures "for the eradication of slavery." In 1838, a law was passed submitting to the people the expediency of calling another convention. Mr. Clay avows that, "emancipation had its influence" in procuring the passage of this law; but in regard to the proposed convention, by which his early wishes might have been consummated, he tells us, "*I felt myself constrained to take immediate, bold, and decided ground against it!*" Yet this is the man who, a few years since, would not exchange the satisfaction of being instrumental in eradicating slavery from his country, "for all the honor of all the triumphs ever decreed to the most successful conqueror!" Verily, slavery has achieved a triumph that attests its withering power over exalted genius and high and generous aspirations, — a triumph for which humanity must weep, and patriotism blush.

We are now prepared to investigate the direct action of the Federal Government in behalf of slavery; and commencing with appointments to office, we will proceed to trace this action, first, in laws and measures of a local and private nature, and then in attempts to promote the general interests and perpetuity of the institution.

APPOINTMENTS TO OFFICE.

As the citizens of the free States are nearly double in number to those of the slave States, it might naturally be supposed that the former would furnish the larger share of the great officers of the Union. To such as have indulged this supposition, the following extract from a speech lately delivered in the Senate of the United States, by Mr. Davis of Massachusetts, will no doubt afford very startling information.

"This interest (slavery) has ruled the destinies of the republic. For FORTY out of FORTY-EIGHT years, it has given us a President from its own territory and of its own selection. During all this time, it has not only had a President, sustaining its own peculiar views of public policy, but through him, has held and used in its own way, the whole organization of all the departments, and all the vast and controlling patronage incident to that office, to aid it in carrying on its views and policy, as well as to protect and secure to it every advantage.

"Let us explore a little further and see how the Houses of Congress have been organized. For THIRTY years out of THIRTY-SIX, that interest has placed *its own speaker* in the chair of the other House, thus securing the organization of committees, and the great influence of that station. And, sir, while all other interests have, during part of the time, had the chair (vice presidency) in which you preside assigned to them as *an equivalent* for these great concessions, yet in each year, when a President *pro tem.* is elected, who upon the contingencies mentioned in the Constitution will be the President of the United States, that interest has INVARIABLY given us that office. Look, I beseech you, through all the places of honor, of profit, and privilege; and there you will find the representatives of this interest in numbers that indicate its influence. Does not, then, this interest rule, guide, and adapt public policy to its own views, and fit it to suit the action and products of its own labor?"

Let us see how far the *present* amount of slave interest in the Federal Government justifies the general statement made by Mr. Davis. The presidential chair, it is true, is filled by a northern man; but he is one who pledged himself to this interest before he was elected; who had manifested his devotion to this interest, by giving his vote for a censorship of the press, for the avowed purpose of restraining the circulation of anti-slavery papers; and who was elected to his present station by southern votes! Be it recollected, moreover, that the southern journals have insisted that a *northern* man with *southern* principles, could more effectually subserve this interest as President, than a slave-holder.

In the office of Vice President, we have a slave-holder from Kentucky, presiding over the deliberations of the Senate.

A slave-holder is seated in the chair of the House of Representatives, appointing committees on the District of Columbia, enforcing gag resolutions against such as would repeal or modify the laws of Congress violating the rights of man, and deciding all questions of order in discussions bearing upon the GREAT INTEREST.

A desire is now manifested by the South to bring into the Supreme Court of the United States certain questions touching the rights and duties of the free States, relative to slaves who may come or be brought within their limits. Since the year 1830 there have been FIVE appointments to the bench of this court, and ALL from slave States. The majority of the court, including the Chief Justice, are citizens of those States. But when these questions come before the court, it may be highly important for the slave-holders to have an ATTORNEY GENERAL to argue them, in whom they can confide. Accordingly the office is filled by Mr. GRUNDY, who lately evinced his qualifications for the station, by expressing in his place as Senator from Tennessee, his approbation of LYNCH LAW, as applied to abolitionists. At the head of the department of STATE, whence issue instructions for conventions and treaties, protecting the African slave-trade from British cruisers, and the American slave-trade from the interference of British colonial authorities, and also for conventions for the return of fugitive slaves, is placed a gentleman from GEORGIA.

At the court of Great Britain we are represented by a slave-holder from Virginia, who, under the direction of the gentleman from Georgia, is bargaining about the value of shipwrecked negroes, and threatening the British government with the vengeance of the Republic, if it shall hereafter dare to liberate slaves who may be forced into its colonies.

At the head of the NAVY DEPARTMENT we behold a citizen of the North, enjoying the reward of his labor, in concocting one of the most virulent volumes in vindication of slavery, and vituperation of its opponents, that has ever issued from the press.

A slave-holder from SOUTH CAROLINA, distinguished for his negotiation in Mexico for the surrender of fugitive slaves, presides over the WAR DEPARTMENT.

KENTUCKY furnishes a POSTMASTER-GENERAL whose devotion to the "interest" had led him to authorize every Postmaster to act as censor of the press, and to take from the mails every paper adverse to slavery. Thus have the slave-holders seized upon the Federal Government, and converted, as we shall presently see, what was intended as the palladium of liberty, into the shield of despotism.

THE FEDERAL GOVERNMENT AND THE TERRITORIAL LAWS OF FLORIDA.

By the Constitution, Congress has "power to dispose of and make all needful regulations respecting the territory belonging to the United States." Under this provision the territorial legislatures are permitted to enact laws which are in force till abrogated by Congress, and that body legislates directly for the territories whenever it thinks proper. Hence it is morally responsible for the territorial legislation.

On the 11th of February, 1834, Messrs. J. & M. Garnett and *Maria* Garnett, all of Virginia, presented a petition to Congress, setting forth that they were the owners of certain slaves whom they hired to persons in Florida; and that by a law of the territory a tax of ten dollars was imposed on every slave owned by a non-resident; and they prayed Congress to relieve them from the payment of this tax. It was obvious that this tax tended to discourage slave-holders from sending their slaves into Florida and there hiring them at high rates to the new settlers, who had not capital enough immediately to stock their plantations. Congress, without hesitation, abolished the tax. The law thus annulled was not in itself revolting to justice or humanity. But there was *then*, and still is, a law of Florida of a very different character.

On the 4th of February, 1832, it was enacted that whenever a judgment for debt was recovered in the territory against a free negro or mulatto, and the judgment was not satisfied in *five* days, *the debtor should be* SOLD *at auction to pay the judgment.* Imprisonment for debt is now deemed a relic of barbarism, but here we have an instance of insolvent debtors being SOLD for the benefit of their creditors, virtually by the authority, and directly with the sanction of the Congress of the United States! The practical operation of this law is to convert free negroes into slaves. A recent sale under it will illustrate its character. Within a few months a free negro was sold at Appalachicola for TEN years, to satisfy a debt which, *including legal costs*, amounted to seventy dollars; so that his services were valued at seven dollars a year! The common wages paid in that part of the country for slave-labor, may be learned from the following notice, taken from the Brunswick (Ga.) Advertiser, 25th of January, 1838:

"*Wanted to hire.*—The undersigned wish to hire one thousand negroes, to work on the Brunswick canal, of whom one-third may be WOMEN. Sixteen dollars per month will be paid for steady, prime men, and thirteen dollars for able *women*.

F. & A. PRATT,
P. M. NIGHTENGALE."

It is obvious that a sale under this law, for a *term* of years, is equivalent to a sale for life. The debtor may be sold from hand to hand, and at the expiration of his term may find himself under the lash of a driver in Louisiana or Missouri, without the possibility of proving his title to freedom. Yet, a proposition in Congress to repeal this most inhuman and profligate law would be laid upon the table, and not a representative of the people be permitted to say a word on the subject.

ACTION OF CONGRESS IN BEHALF OF THE SLAVE-HOLDERS OF LOUISIANA.

On the 31st of May, 1830, the House of Representatives adopted a resolution, directing the Secretary of the Treasury to ascertain and report the number of hands (slaves) required per acre in the sugar cultivation. The Secretary accordingly issued a circular, proposing a number of interrogatories respecting the cultivation of sugar, and among others, the following: "The number of hands (slaves) required to cultivate a given quantity of land planted with cane, and to perform all the labor necessary in the manufacture of sugar in the different places where it is made."

This circular was widely distributed, and the answers returned to it were published at public expense; and thus were the sugar growers instructed, by means of the Federal Government, with what number of slaves to stock their plantations; what expense they must incur in feeding and clothing them, and what number of *new* slaves they must annually procure to keep up the "force." From the information thus furnished, it appeared that the destruction of slaves in this culture is so great, that there is a yearly excess of deaths over births of TWO AND A HALF PER CENT.* This waste of life is supplied from the breeding farms of Maryland and Virginia. Turning from this private and local action of the Federal Government, we will now take a view of its enlarged and comprehensive efforts for the general protection and perpetuity of the slave system. The advocates of that system have always looked with distrust and alarm upon the free colored people, and have deemed it good policy to prevent their acquisition of power and influence: hence the

EFFORTS OF THE FEDERAL GOVERNMENT TO OPPRESS AND DEGRADE THE FREE PEOPLE OF COLOR.

The Constitution of the United States acknowledges no right or disqualification founded on complexion; but those who have administered it, have made the tincture of the *skin* of far greater importance than the qualities of either the head or the heart. So early as 1790, Congress passed an act prescribing the mode in which "any alien, being a WHITE person," might be naturalized and admitted to the rights of an American citizen.

Two years after, an act was passed for organizing the militia, which was to consist of "each and every free, able-bodied WHITE male citizen," &c. No other government on earth prohibits any portion of its citizens from participating in the national defence; and this strange and degrading prohibition, utterly

* See Report of Secretary of the Treasury, January 19, 1831.

repugnant to the principles both of the Declaration of Independence and of the Constitution, marks the solicitude of the Federal Government to pursue the policy most agreeable to the slaveholders. But not content with this insult to colored citizens, another, and perhaps a still more wanton and malignant one, was offered by the Government in the act of 1810, organizing the Post Office Department. The 4th Section enacts that "no other than a free WHITE person shall be employed in carrying the mail of the United States, either as post-rider or *driver* of a carriage carrying the mail," under a penalty of fifty dollars.

Any vagabond from Europe, any fugitive from our own prisons, may take charge of the United States mail; but a native born American citizen, of unimpeachable morals, and with property acquired by honest industry, may not, if his *skin* be dark, guide the horses which draw the carriage in which a bag of newspapers is deposited.*

Such are the insults heaped by the Federal Government on the colored citizens throughout the States; let us see what conduct it pursues towards them *on its own territory*, over which it possesses "exclusive jurisdiction."

In 1820, Congress passed a law authorizing the WHITE citizens of the city of Washington to elect WHITE city officers; thus making a *white skin* an indispensable qualification for both suffrage and office. The officers thus elected were specially empowered by the national legislature "to prescribe the terms and conditions on which *free negroes and mulattoes* may reside in the city." In pursuance of this grant of power, the *white* officers passed an ordinance (May 31, 1827) requiring all the free colored persons then in Washington and wishing to remain, to be registered; and enacting, that if any free man with a colored

* The following letter of instruction from the Postmaster General to one of his deputies, written in 1828, is a curious commentary on this law.

"SIR, — The mail may not, in any case whatever, be in the custody of a *colored* person. If a colored person is employed to lift the mail from the stage into the Post Office, it does not pass into his custody, but the labor is performed in the presence and under the immediate direction of the WHITE person who has it in custody: but if a *colored* person takes it from a tavern and carries it himself to the Post Office, it comes into his custody during the time of carrying it; which is contrary to law. I am, &c.,

JOHN MCLEAN.

skin should presume to *play at cards*, or even to be *present* while *another* free colored person was playing, he should be fined not exceeding five dollars; that if he should have a *dance* in his house, without permission from the *white* Mayor, he should be fined not exceeding ten dollars; that should he take the liberty to go out of his own house *after ten o'clock at night*, without a pass from a Justice of the Peace, or "some respectable citizen," (!) he might be compelled to pass the rest of the night "in a lock-up house," and the next morning be fined ten dollars; and should any dark complexioned free man be guilty of drunkenness or profane language, he should be fined not exceeding three dollars. Thus we see with what zeal the Washington Corporation endeavors to prevent the colored citizens from affecting the manners and fashions of their white brethren. But there are still more serious matters. A colored citizen from any of the States, taking up his residence in the Capital of the Republic, is required within a certain time, not only to be registered, but also to find *two freehold sureties* in the penalty of five hundred dollars, for his good behavior; and if he does not, he is to be imprisoned till he consents to leave the seat of the Federal Government; and if he does not *prove* that he is a freeman, he shall be *sold as a slave to pay his jail fees!*

In 1830, a bill to establish the territorial government of IOWA was before Congress. A slave-holder from Alabama moved to exclude colored persons from the right of suffrage; and the obedient Senate consented.*

Such are the abominable and iniquitous means used by and with the sanction of Congress for the degradation and oppression of colored citizens. We are next to take a view of

SLAVERY UNDER THE AUTHORITY OF THE FEDERAL GOVERNMENT.

It is well known that Congress is the local legislature of the District of Columbia, and of all the territories belonging to the Union, and with powers far exceeding those possessed by any

* In 1787, when our fathers established the government of the Northwestern Territory, they prohibited slavery, and disfranchised no man on account of his complexion.

State Legislature, being unfettered with constitutional restrictions. The authority vested in Congress over the District and territories, is virtually despotic, being "an exclusive jurisdiction in all cases whatsoever." Yet we have long had slave-holding territories. The vast domain acquired by the purchase of Louisiana, has, under the authority of Congress, been stocked with slaves, excepting so much as is north of 36½° north latitude, which is, by Act of Congress, specially protected from the pollution. This very law is one of the most decided acts of the Federal Government in behalf of slavery; for by means of it, the immense territory south of this line was deliberately surrendered to all the cruelties and abominations of the system; it was moreover an express acknowledgment by the Government of its power to prohibit slavery throughout the *whole* territory, and that it had made a COMPROMISE, a bargain between humanity and cruelty, religion and wickedness; and had erected, on an arbitrary line, a partition wall between slavery and liberty.

But it is in the District of Columbia, and under the shadow of the proud Capitol, that the action of the Federal Government in behalf of slavery is exhibited in its most odious and disgusting forms. We shall have occasion presently to exhibit the seat of the National Government as the great slave mart of the North American continent, "furnished with all appliances and means to boot." The old slave-laws of Virginia and Maryland, marked by the barbarity of other days, form by Act of Congress the slave-code of the District. Of this code, a single sample will suffice. A slave convicted of setting fire to a building, shall have his head cut off, and his body divided into quarters, and the parts set up in the most public places! But let it not be supposed that Congress has not itself legislated directly on the subject of slavery. An Act of 15th May, 1820, gives the Corporation of Washington power to "punish corporeally any SLAVE for a breach of any of their ordinances." Happy would it have been for the honor of our country, if the sympathies of its rulers in behalf of slavery had been exhibited only on the national domain; but they pervade every portion of the confederacy, as is but too apparent in

THE INTERFERENCE OF THE FEDERAL GOVERNMENT FOR THE RECOVERY OF FUGITIVE SLAVES.

The Federal Constitution contains the following clause: "No person held to service or labor in one State under the laws thereof, escaping into another, shall in consequence of any law or regulation therein be discharged from such service or labor, but shall be delivered up on claim of the party to whom such service or labor may be due."

At the time this constitution was adopted, the cultivation and manufacture of cotton had not so far progressed, as to paralyze, by their profits, the conscience of the nation, or to divest it of the sense of shame; and hence this clause, although relating to slaves, forbears to name them. It was inserted to satisfy the South; and its obvious meaning is, that slaves escaping into States in which slavery is abolished by law, shall not *therefore* be deemed free by the State authorities, but shall be delivered by those authorities to his master. This clause imposes an obligation on the States, but confers no power on Congress; and the Constitution moreover declares, that "the powers not delegated to the United States by the Constitution, nor prohibited by it to the States, are reserved to the States respectively, or to the people." Hence it follows, that as the power of recovering these fugitives is not delegated to Congress, it is reserved to the several States, who are bound to make such laws as may be deemed proper, to authorize the master to recover his slave. Nevertheless, the Federal Government in its zeal for slavery, has not scrupled to assume power never delegated to it, and has exercised that power in contemptuous violation of every principle, which in free countries directs the administration of justice. If a Virginian enters New York, and claims as his property a horse which he finds in the possession of one of our citizens, an impartial jury is selected to pass on his claim, — witnesses are orally and publicly examined, — the claimant is debarred from all private intercourse with the jury; and when the trial is over, the jury retire to deliberate on their verdict, under the charge of an officer who is sworn to keep them apart, and not to suffer any person to speak with them; nor can the horse be at last recovered but with the unanimous consent of the jury. But let the Virginian claim, not the horse, but the CITIZEN HIMSELF, as his beast of burden, and the Federal Government makes all things easy for him. By the Act of 1793, the slave-holder may himself, without oath, or process of any kind, seize his prey where he can find him, and at his leisure, (for no time is specified,) drag him before any Justice of the Peace in the place, whem he may prefer.* This justice is a State officer, and of the lowest judicial grade, and under no legal obligation to execute an act of Congress, and entitled to no fees for his services. He is therefore peculiarly accessible to improper influences. Before this magistrate, who is not authorized to compel the attendance of witnesses in such a case, the slave-holder brings his victim, and if he can satisfy this judge of his own choice, "by oral testimony or *affidavit*," and for aught that appears in the law, by his own oath, that his claim is well founded, the wretched prisoner is surrendered to him as a slave for life, torn from his wife and children, bereft of all the rights of humanity, and converted into a chattel, — an article of merchandise, — a beast of burden!!

The Federal Constitution declares: — "In suits at common law, where the value in controversy shall exceed *twenty dollars*, the right of TRIAL BY JURY shall be preserved;" but the Act of 1793, in suits in which "the value in controversy" exceeds all estimation, dispenses with trial by jury, and indeed with almost every safeguard of justice and personal liberty.

This law, iniquitous as it is, does not require State officers to *anticipate* the pursuit of the slave-holder, and to seize and imprison their fellow-men, on mere suspicion that they *may* be claimed as slaves. What the Federal Government dares not do in the States, it accomplishes on its own exclusive territory, and in a manner which, for atrocious wickedness and tyranny, leaves

* In New York the Legislature has interfered, and forbidden a Justice of the Peace to act, and has therefore virtually declared the Act of Congress to be unconstitutional, — and that the power of prescribing the mode in which fugitives shall be restored, belongs exclusively to the States.

far in the shade the vilest acts of European despotism. This is indeed strong language; but alas! language is too feeble adequately to represent the turpitude of the laws and practices sanctioned by the Federal Government in the District under its "exclusive jurisdiction."

By the Act of 1793, a justice can take no step for the restoration of a fugitive slave, till the fact of his being one is proved before him on oath. But in the Metropolis of the Nation,—in the city called by the name of the Father of his Country, a Justice of the Peace may commit to the UNITED STATES PRISON, and into the costody of the UNITED STATES MARSHAL, any man he may choose to suspect of being a fugitive slave. Notice is then given in the newspapers of the commitment, and the unknown owner is warned to take away his property, or it will be sold according to LAW, to pay JAIL FEES.

After the doors of the dungeon have closed upon the victim, no magistrate, no court, no jury take cognizance of his claims of freedom. The jailer is the only tribunal to which he can appeal, and how *disinterested* a tribunal will presently be seen. If a free man, no master can of course lawfully claim him, and not being claimed, he is sold at auction to raise money to pay an officer of the Federal Government for the trouble and expense of keeping him a few weeks in prison. What civilized government of the old world practises more execrable wickedness? *

The whole depth of this villany is not yet sounded. The disclosures we are now about making should make every ear to tingle, and every heart to quake. No doubt it will occur to many that if a free man, all the prisoner has to do, to obtain his liberation, is to prove his freedom. Prove his freedom while

* Not as an apology for this expression, but as a reason why the writer feels more sensibly than perhaps many others on this subject, he thinks proper to mention that a free colored man belonging to his neighborhood in West Chester County, N. Y., on going to Washington some years since, was there legally kidnapped, and advertised by the Marshal to be sold to pay his jail fees. A Washington paper containing the advertisement providentially fell into the hands of a citizen of the County who knew the man. A public meeting was called, and the Governor of the State, De Witt Clinton, at their request, demanded from the President his immediate release as a citizen of New York.

locked up in his cell! Where is his counsel? — where his process for commanding the attendance of witnesses? where the court sitting in open day to investigate his right to freedom? where the jury to pass upon his case? The marshal, or his deputy the jailer, is the only human being, except his fellow-victims, to whom he can tell his tale. The marshal is the judge, and the sole judge of his prisoner's title to freedom. He is the arbiter of happiness and misery, of liberty and bondage: he opens the door of the dungeon, and at his sovereign will bids his captive go forth to enjoy the rights and fulfil the duties of a rational, accountable, and immortal being, or conducts him to the human shambles erected in the city of Washington, and there sells him under the hammer as a SLAVR FOR LIFE. Compared with this tremendous jurisdiction, the powers vested in the highest judicial officer in our country dwindle into insignificance. And should *such* a judge be disinterested? The very question is shocking to our every idea of justice. Disinterested! Screened from the public eye — accountable only to that Being who seeth in secret — declaring his judgment in the recesses of the prison, he should of all men be most exempt from human passion and infirmity. *Yet to this judge the law offers a high and tempting bribe to sell men he knows to be free, and thus to become a manufacturer of slaves.* Will this statement be credited? It cannot, and ought not to be, without full and unequivocal proof, and to that proof we now appeal; premising for the better understanding of our proof, that the marshal is required to maintain the suspected fugitives while in his custody, and is entitled to fees for receiving them, &c., and if unreclaimed, has no means of procuring payment of his expenses and fees but from the proceeds of the sale of his prisoners; and further, that the *whole* of those proceeds are permitted by law to remain in his pocket, unless *after* the sale the master should be discovered, and should claim the balance.

On the 11th of January, 1827, the committee on the District of Columbia, to whom the subject had been referred by the House of Representatives, reported that "in this District, as in all the slave-holding States in the Union, the legal presumption is, that persons of color going at large without any evidences of their freedom, are absconding slaves, and *primà facie* liable to all the legal provisions applicable to that class of persons." They state that in the part of the District ceded by Virginia, a FREE negro may be arrested and put in jail for three months on *suspicion* of being a fugitive; he is then to be hired out to pay his *jail fees;* and if he does not prove his freedom within twelve months, is to be sold as a SLAVE. This statement is followed by the remark, "the committee do not consider any alteration of the law in the County of Alexandria in relation to this subject, necessary!" In the County of Washington, ceded by Maryland, they inform us, "If a *free* man of color should be apprehended as a runaway, he is subjected to the payment of all *fees and rewards* given by law for apprehending runaways; and upon failure to make such payment, is liable to be sold as a slave." That is, a man *acknowledged to be free*, and unaccused of any offence, is to be sold as a *slave* to pay the "fees and rewards given by law for apprehending *runaways*." If Turkish despotism is disgraced by any enactment of equal atrocity, we are ignorant of the fact. Even the committee thought this law rather hard, and therefore they "recommended such an alteration of it as would make such charges payable by the corporation of Washington."* But the Federal Government, unwavering in its devotion to slavery, made no alteration, and the code of Washington is to this day polluted by unquestionably the most iniquitous statute in Christendom. Laws are sometimes more profligate than those who are called to administer them, and the committee assure us that the marshal has in all cases refrained from selling his prisoners for fees and charges, when their right to freedom has been established; and in consequence of not availing himself of the privilege allowed him by this law, he had incurred, in the last eight years, a personal loss of $500! In other words, the marshal's sense of justice, decency, and humanity, exceeded that of the rulers of our Republic.

On the 29th of January, 1829, the committee on the District of Columbia made a report in obedience to the instructions of

* See Reports of Committee, 2 Sess., 19 Cong., Vol. I, No. 43.

the House of Representatives, "to inquire into the slave-trade as it exists in and is carried on through the District." The report proposes no interference on the part of Congress, but is virtually an apology for this vile traffic, as is apparent from the following heartless sentiments and false assertions.

> "The trade alluded to is presumed to refer more particularly to that which is carried on with the view of transporting slaves to the South, which is one way of gradually diminishing the evil complained of here; while the situation of these persons is considerably *mitigated by being transplanted to a more genial and bountiful clime.* Although violence may sometimes be done to their feelings in the separation of families, it is by the laws of society which operate upon them as property, and cannot be avoided as long as they exist; yet it should be some consolation to those whose feelings are interested in their behalf, to know that *their condition is more frequently bettered, and their minds happier by the exchange.*" *

To this report is appended a letter (January 13, 1829,) from the marshal to the committee, containing most important and heart-rending statements.

It appears from this letter, that from the 1st of January, 1826, to 1st of January, 1828, there were committed to the Washington prison, as runaways, 101.

Proved to be free, and discharged,	15
Unclaimed, and sold for maintenance, and charges, and fees,	5
Proved to be slaves, and delivered to their masters,	81
	101

In 1828, committed as runaways, 78.

Proved to be free,	11
Unclaimed, or sold for jail fees, etc.	1
Delivered to their masters,	66
	78

Here then is proof, official documentary proof, that in three years, 179 human beings were, by the authority of the Federal Government, arrested in *one* county of the District, and committed to prison on no allegation of crime, but merely to aid the slave-holders in trampling upon those great principles of human rights, for the protection of which the National Government was professedly founded. It is also in proof, that of these

* Reports of Committees, 2 Sess., 20 Cong., No. 60.

179 prisoners, 26 were, by the confession of the marshal, *free* men; men whom (as appears from the report we have quoted,) he had a *legal* right to consign to hopeless and awful bondage, merely because they were too poor to pay the expenses of their unjust imprisonment; and who were indebted for their liberty, not to the laws and constitution of their country, but to the beneficence of their jailer—a beneficence too, exercised at his own pecuniary loss. Proof also is here given, that six persons unclaimed as slaves, were, by the judgment of this same jailer, without counsel, witnesses, or trial, sentenced to be sold as slaves for the purpose of raising money, the whole of which, as we shall presently see, was paid over to the judge who pronounced the sentence. The marshal gives in his letter the particulars of the sale of five unclaimed negroes, as follows:

Si—Amount of jail fees, etc.	$84 82
Offered for sale according to law, and no person being willing to give $84.82, he was purchased by Tench Ringgold, the marshal, for that sum, and afterwards sold by him to Robert Bown for $20, by which the marshal lost	64 82
Hannah Green sold for	$61 00
Maintenance, &c.	48 71
Balance remaining in marshal's hands,	$12 29
Lewis Davis sold for	$250 00
Amount of fees, &c.	50 07
Balance remaining in marshal's hands,	$199 93
James Green sold for	$80 00
Fees and maintenance,	49 66
Balance remaining in marshal's hands,	$30 34
Arthur Neal sold for amount of his jail fees and maintenance, to the marshal, being	$46 06
Sold afterwards by private sale to J. G. Hutton for	40 00
Lost by marshal,	$6 06

The letter concludes thus:

"The marshal has always considered it to be his duty, whenever a negro was committed as a runaway by a Justice of the Peace, who in all cases under the law commits them, which negro had not in his possession proof of his freedom, but alleged himself to be a freeman, to write to any part of the United States to persons who the negro affirmed could prove his freedom, urging them to send on their certificates of such negro being free; and in many instances, these letters of the marshal or his jailer have been the means of bringing proof that the negro was free.

"The law of Maryland in force in this District, directs that the balance of sales of negroes (sold as runaways) *shall remain in the marshal's hands* until the runaway was identified as the property of some master; and in conformity thereto, the marshal has uniformly handed over such balance whenever the master proved his property. In a late case, Mr. Sprigg, of Louisiana, lost a valuable slave, who escaped from him, and made his way to this District, and was committed to my custody, advertised and sold, according to law, leaving a balance of *five hundred dollars*, after paying maintenance, &c., in my hand. The negro was carried to Louisiana by the person who purchased him of me, discovered by his former master, Mr. Sprigg, who sent on here and claimed his money. Having ascertained that this negro was the property of Mr. Sprigg, I paid the $500 on demand to his agent here, Mr. Josiah Johnson, Senator of Congress from that State.

TENCH RINGGOLD, *Marshal Dis. Col.*"

Such are the secrets of the prison-house established by the Federal Government. It may be well to contemplate them in detail. It appears from the cases of SI and NEAL, that the Marshal of the United States, after deciding on the liberty or bondage of his prisoners, is allowed to take his *fees* in human flesh, and the condemned becomes the *property* of the very judge who sentenced him to servitude, and who carries him into the market there to make out of him as much money as he can. True it is, Mr. Ringgold's speculations appear not to have been very productive, but other jailer-judges may have less honesty, or more skill in negro flesh. The marshal, it seems, sold his fees in the shape of SI, for only $20. No reason is assigned for this nominal price. Very probably it was a case similar to the one described by Mr. Miner, in his speech on the floor of the House of Representatives, in 1829. "In August, 1821," said Mr. M., "a black man was taken up, and imprisoned as a runaway. He was kept confined until October, 1822, four hundred and five days. In this time, vermin, disease, and misery had deprived him of the use of his limbs. He was rendered a cripple for life, and finanly discharged, *as no one would buy him.*'

The Hannah and James Green sold for fees, were most likely

man and wife, and may remind us that the law we are considering is utterly reckless of the most sacred relations. The proceeds of three of the five sold in 1826–7, after deducting fees, &c., is $242.56; and this sum, according to law, the marshal retains till called for; but if the negroes were free, then, there being no claimant, the money can never be called for, and becomes the perquisite of office; and the income of the judge of course fluctuates according to the number he condemns to slavery. Thus does the law literally press upon the marshal the wages of unrighteousness—thus does it bribe him to the commission of wickedness. In one instance, the receipts of a single condemnation were $500, of which the marshal was deprived only by a most extraordinary accident.

And now let us review the conduct of the Federal Government towards the free colored citizen of any State, who presumes to visit the city of Washington. At the will of a Justice of the Peace he is thrown into prison. His jailer, if he possesses the humanity and disinterestedness of Mr. Ringgold, may, if he pleases, write letters to distant parts of the confederacy, although he knows that a favorable answer may keep some hundred dollars from finding their way into his pocket. If no such answer arrives, without any evidence that the letter of inquiry was ever received, the poor wretch is condemned as a slave, and the price of his bones and muscles is paid to the judge who condemned him.

And by whom is this accursed law kept in force? By *northern* Representatives and Senators in Congress. On the 8th of February, 1836, the House of Representatives resolved, that "Congress ought not to interfere in *any way* with slavery in the District of Columbia," and no less than eighty-two northern men had the hardihood to record their names in favor of the resolution. To place, if possible, in a still stronger light, the conduct of these men, it may be mentioned that the law we have been considering belonged to the code of Maryland at the time the District was ceded, and was continued in force by Act of Congress. In the meantime, the Legislature of Maryland, composed of slave-holders, yielding to the spirit of the age, has erased this foul stain from her statute book, while our northern Democrats, with liberty and equality forever on their lips, in hope of getting a few southern votes for their party, discover that Congress ought not to interfere in any way with slavery in the District, although it is by the authority of Congress that freemen are there converted into slaves.

We will now place side by side two advertisements, one published by authority of Congress, in which northern men have the majority; the other by authority of the slave State of Maryland,—the first relating to a *woman* and *infant* claiming to be FREE, the other to a man confessing himself a SLAVE.

"NOTICE.—Was committed to the jail of Washington County, District of Columbia, as a runaway, a negro WOMAN, by the name of Polly Leiper, and her *infant* child William. * * * * Says she was set free by John Campbell, of Richmond, Va., in 1818 or 1819. The owner of the above-described *woman* and *child*, if any, are requested to come and prove them, and take them away, or *they* will be SOLD FOR THEIR JAIL FEES AND OTHER EXPENSES, AS THE LAW DIRECTS.

TENCH RINGGOLD,
Marshal."

May 19, 1827.

"RAN AWAY.—Was committed to the jail of Washington County, Maryland, on the 24th of December last, a mulatto man who calls himself *John McDaniel*, about 25 years of age. * * *Says he belongs* to William Hill, living at Falmouth, Va., and was sold to John Daily, living somewhere in the South. The owner of the said slave is requested to come and take him away, or *he will be released, according to law.*

CHRISTIAN NEWCOMB, Jun.,
Sheriff."

December 10, 1827.*

The endeavors of the Federal Government to secure the restoration of fugitive slaves to their masters, are not confined either to the District of Columbia, or to the States of this confederacy. Even American diplomacy must be made subservient to the interests of the slave-holders, and republican ambassadors must bear to foreign courts the wailings of our government for the escape of human property.

On the 10th of May, 1828, the House of Representatives requested the President

"To open a negotiation with the British Government, in the view to obtain an arrangement whereby fugitive slaves who have taken refuge

* Both advertisements are taken from the Washington Intelligencer.

in the Canadian provinces of that government, may be surrendered by the functionaries thereof to their masters, upon making satisfactory proof of their ownership of said slaves."

Here was a plain, palpable interference in behalf of slavery by a government which we are often assured by the slave-holders, "has nothing to do with slavery;" and so tame and subservient were the Northern members, that this disgraceful resolution was adopted without even a division of the House! At the next session, the impatience of the slave-holders to know if Great Britain would restore their slaves who had taken refuge in Canada, could brook no longer delay, and the House called on the President to inform them of the result of the negotiation. The President immediately submitted a mass of documents to the House, from which it appeared that the zeal of the Executive, in behalf of "the peculiar institution," had *anticipated* the wishes of the Legislature. Two years *before* the interference of the House, viz., on the 19th of June, 1826, Mr. Clay, Secretary of State, had instructed Mr. Gallatin, American Minister in London, to propose a stipulation for "a mutual surrender of all persons held to service or labor under the laws of either party who escape into the territories of the other." Mr. Clay dwelt on the number of fugitives in Canada, and desired Mr. Gallatin to press on the British Government the consideration that such a stipulation would secure *to the West India planters the recovery of such of their slaves as might take refuge in the American Republic!*

Surely the Federal Government was never intended by its founders to act the part of kidnapper for West India slave-holders.

On the 24th of February, 1827, Mr. Clay again urged Mr. Gallatin to procure this stipulation, and informed him that a treaty had just been concluded with Mexico, *by which that power had engaged to restore our runaway slaves.**

On the 5th of July, 1827, Mr. Gallatin communicated to his government the answer of the British Minister, that "it was

* Such a treaty was negotiated, but the Mexican Congress refused to ratify the base compact.

utterly impossible for them to agree to a stipulation for the surrender of fugitive slaves."

Determined not to take NO for an answer, Mr. Clay desired Mr. Barbour, our then Minister in England, to renew the negotiation, inasmuch as the escape of slaves into Canada is "a growing evil;" but alas, Mr. Barbour replied, that on broaching the subject to the British minister, he had informed him "*the law of Parliament gave freedom to every slave who effected his landing on British ground.*"* To have attempted to march an army into Canada, for the purpose of seizing these fugitives, would have cost rather more than they were worth. There was, however, a territory on our Southern frontier, belonging to a power less able than Great Britain to punish aggressions on her sovereignty, and hence it is that we are called to consider

THE INVASION OF FLORIDA, AND DESTRUCTION OF FUGITIVE SLAVES BY THE FORCES OF THE FEDERAL GOVERNMENT.

On the 15th of March, 1816, Mr. Crawford, Secretary of War, addressed a letter to General Jackson, informing him that there was a fort in Florida, occupied by between two hundred and fifty and three hundred blacks, and that they and the hostile Creek Indians were guilty of secret practices to inveigle negroes from the frontiers of Georgia, and directing him to call the attention of the Commandant at Pensacola to the subject. The Secretary added, that should the Commandant decline interfering, and should it be determined that the destruction of the negro fort does not require the sanction of Congress, means will be promptly taken for its reduction.

General Jackson, however, had *before* the receipt of this despatch, "assumed the responsibility" of sending his orders respecting this very fort to Gen. Gaines.

"If the fort harbors the negroes of our citizens, or of friendly Indians living within our territory, or holds out inducements to the slaves of our citizens to desert from their owners' service, *it must be destroyed.*

* State papers, 2 Sess., 20th Congress, Vol. I.

Notify the governor of Pensacola of your *advance into his territory, and for the express purpose of destroying these lawless banditti.*" The letter concludes with directions to restore the stolen negroes to their rightful owners. *Letter of 8th of April,* 1816.

Owing to some cause not explained, Gen. Gaines did not fulfil his instructions; and a gun boat was sent up the Appalachicola river by order of Commodore Patterson, and on the 27th of July attacked the fort by firing red-hot shot at it. A shot entered the magazine, which exploded. The result is thus stated in the official report:

"Three hundred negroes, *men, women and children,* and about twenty Indians, were in the fort; of these, two hundred and seventy were killed, and the greater part of the rest *mortally* wounded."

Commodore Patterson in his letter to the Secretary of the Navy, observes:

"The service rendered by the destruction of this fort, and the band of negroes who held it and the country in its vicinity, is of great and manifest importance to the United States, and particularly those States bordering on the Creek nation, as it had become a general rendezvous for *runaway slaves* and disaffected Indians — an asylum where they found arms and ammunition to protect themselves against their owners and the government. This hold being destroyed, they have no longer a place to fly to, and will not be so liable to *abscond.* The force of the negroes was daily increasing, and they had commenced several plantations on the banks of the Appalachicola."*

We are not aware that this gallant achievement called forth at the time any testimony of approbation from the government. It was probably regarded as an unnecessary destruction of property. Gen. Jackson's orders were to *restore* the negroes "to their rightful owners," not to kill them. But times have changed; abolition doctrines are spreading, and hereafter our officers, and soldiers, and sailors, may feel some reluctance at being sent on kidnapping expeditions. Hence, after the lapse of twenty-three years, the government has deemed it good policy to evince their estimation of such services, by rewarding the

* State papers, 2 Sess., 15th Congress, No. 65.

heroes of Appalachicola. The following is taken from the Washington Globe:

"NOTICE. — The sum of FIVE THOUSAND FOUR HUNDRED AND SIXTY-FIVE DOLLARS having been appropriated by an Act of Congress, passed at the *last* session, to be distributed as prize money among the officers and crews, their, or either of their heirs or legal representatives, of the gun boats, numbered 149 and 154, who in the month of July, 1816, blew up and destroyed a fort occupied by fugitive negroes and Indians, on the river Appalachicola, all persons having claims upon the sum so appropriated, are notified to present and prove the same without delay at the office of the Fourth Auditor of the Treasury Department, in the City of Washington.

"*Fourth Auditor's Office, May 23d*, 1839."

It is now time to advert to one of the most extraordinary exploits of American diplomacy, viz.:

COMPENSATION FOR FUGITIVE SLAVES OBTAINED BY THE FEDERAL GOVERNMENT.

The presence of British armed vessels in our Southern waters, during the last war, afforded an opportunity to many of the slaves to escape from bondage. In 1814, and while the war was raging in all its fury, commissioners were appointed to treat of peace, and instructions were given to them as to the stipulations to be inserted in the treaty. These instructions contain the following remarkable passage:

"The negroes taken from the Southern States should be returned to their owners, or *paid* for at their full value. If these slaves were considered as non-combatants, they ought to be restored: if as property, they ought to be paid for." Moreover, this stipulation is expressly included "in the conditions on which you are to *insist* in the proposed negotiations." *Letter of Instructions from Mr. Monroe, Secretary of State, 28th January*, 1814.*

Thus we see that not even the calamities of war could divert the attention of the Federal Government from the peculiar interests of the slave-holders. The commissioners were faithful to the charge thus given to them: and in the treaty concluded

* American State papers, Vol. IX, p. 364

at Ghent, adroitly provided for the restoration of *slaves;* and in such obscure terms as ultimately secured a far more extensive concession than the British negotiators had any intention of making.

The 1st article is as follows:

> "All territory, places, and possessions whatever, taken from either party, by the other during the war, or which may be taken after the signing of this treaty, shall be restored without delay; and without causing any destruction or carrying away of the artillery or other public property *originally captured* in said forts or places, and which shall *remain* upon the exchange of the ratifications of this treaty, or any *slaves* or other private property."

The treaty was ratified at Washington on the 17th of February; and *six* days after, three commissioners appointed by the government appeared in the Chesapeake, authorized to demand and receive the slaves on board the British squadron still in our waters.

Captain John Clarelle happened to be at the moment in command of the British forces, and he positively refused to give up a single fugitive; contending that the stipulation in the treaty related only to slaves "originally *captured* in forts or places," and remaining in such forts or places at the exchange of the ratifications, and had no reference to slaves who had voluntarily sought protection on board British vessels.

A few days after, Admiral Cockburn arrived and a similar demand was made upon him. He also refused to surrender any *fugitives*, as such were not included in the treaty, but gave up eighty slaves which were found on Cumberland Island at the time that place was *captured*, and who had not been removed previous to the exchange of ratifications; this being a case directly within the true meaning and intention of the treaty. The Secretary of State then applied to the British Charge d'Affaires at Washington, requesting him to direct the Naval Commanders in the Chesapeake to give up the fugitives on board their vessels; but Mr. Baker declined interfering, taking the same view of the article as the Admiral had done. In the meantime, the squadron had sailed for Bermuda. The Government, tracking the scent of a fugitive with bloodhound keenness, forthwith despatched an agent to Bermuda in pursuit, to demand the negroes of the Governor. The worthy Englishman, nettled at a requisition so derogatory to the honor of his country, replied, "he would rather Bermuda, with every man, woman and child in it, were sunk under the sea, than surrender one slave that had sought protection under the flag of England."

The agent, (Thomas Spalding,) nothing daunted, now assumed the diplomatist, and addressed a long argumentative despatch to Admiral Griffith, commanding on the Bermuda station, demanding the fugitives, and promising to furnish him with a particular list of the slaves claimed, which he expected to receive in a few days from the United States. The Admiral very cavalierly assured Mr. Spalding that it was quite unnecessary for him to wait at Bermuda for the expected document, since there was, neither at Bermuda nor any other British island or settlement, any authority "competent to deliver up persons, who, during the late wars, had placed themselves under the protection of the British flag."*

From British Governors and admirals, our Government now turned to the British Cabinet, and found that there also it was held a point of honor to keep faith, even with runaway slaves. Lord Castlereagh declared that the government never would have assented to a treaty requiring the surrender of persons who had taken refuge under the British standard. Again was the demand made, and again was it unequivocally rejected. But the administration refused to yield, and insisted on a reference of the question to the decision of a friendly power, and named the Emperor of Russia as umpire. After tedious negotiation, this point was carried: and in 1818, a convention was concluded at London, submitting the true construction of the treaty to the Emperor, who decided in favor of the slaveholders. It now became necessary to determine how the number of slaves, and their value, should be ascertained. Another negotiation ensued, which resulted in a second convention, by which it was agreed that each party should appoint a certain

* State papers, 14th Congress, 2d Session. Senate documents, No. 28.

number of Commissioners, who should form a Board to sit at Washington, to receive and liquidate the claims of the masters. But difficulties soon arose. The American Commissioners insisted on *interest*, which the others refused to allow. Negotiations again commenced, till at last the British Cabinet, wearied with the pertinacity of the American Government, and sick of the controversy, entered into a third convention, (13th of Nov., 1826,) by which the enormous sum of ONE MILLION TWO HUNDRED AND FOUR THOUSAND DOLLARS was paid and received in full of all demands.

Thus after a persevering negotiation, conducted for twelve years, at Washington, in the Chesapeake Bay, at Bermuda, at London,and at Petersburg, did our government succeed in obtaining most ample compensation for the fugitives. Commissioners were then appointed to distribute this sum; and after fixing an average value on each slave proved to have been carried away, it was found that a *surplus still remained;* and this surplus was divided among the masters!

Having now seen the success that attended the pursuit of fugitive slaves, let us next witness the

EFFORTS OF THE FEDERAL GOVERNMENT TO RECOVER SHIPWRECKED SLAVES.

Considering the extent of the American slave-trade, it is not surprising that our SLAVERS are occasionally driven out of their course; and are sometimes wrecked upon the dangerous reefs abounding in the neighboring Archipelago.

On the 3d of January, 1831, the brig Comet, a regular slaver from the District of Columbia, on her usual voyage from Alexandria to New Orleans, with a cargo of one hundred and sixty-four slaves, was lost off the island of Abaco. The slaves were saved, and carried into New Providence, where they were set at liberty by the authorities of the island. A portion of the cargo (146 head) was insured at New Orleans for $71,330.

On the 4th of February, 1839, the brig Encomium, from Charleston to New Orleans, with forty-five slaves, was also wrecked near Abaco, and the slaves carried into New Providence, where, like their predecessors, they were declared to be free.

In February, 1835, the Enterprise, another slaver from the National Domain, on her voyage to Charleston, with seventy-eight slaves, was driven into Bermuda in distress. The passengers, instead of being thrown into prison, as Bermudians would have been in Charleston under similar circumstances, were hospitably treated, and permitted to go at large. These successive and unexpected transmutations of slaves into freemen, roused the ready zeal of the Federal Government. Directly on the loss of the Comet, instructions were sent from Washington to our Minister, to demand of the British Government the value of the cargo. In 1832, another despatch was forwarded on the subject. The instructions were again renewed in 1833, the Secretary of State remarking, this case "*must* be brought to a conclusion; the doctrine that would justify the liberation of our slaves, is too dangerous to a large section of our country to be tolerated."

In 1834, fresh instructions were sent, and a demand ordered to be made for the value of the slaves in the Encomium.

In 1835, similar instructions were sent relative to the Enterprise.

In 1836, the instructions were renewed; the Secretary observing to Mr. Stevenson, "In the present state of our diplomatic relations with the Government of His Britannic Majesty, *the most immediately pressing* of the matters with which the United States Legation at London is now charged, is the claim of certain American citizens against Great Britain for a number of slaves, the CARGOES of three vessels wrecked in British islands in the Atlantic."

From a long and labored communication from Mr. Stevenson to Lord Palmerston, we extract the following *morceau.*

"The undersigned feels assured that it will only be necessary to refer Lord Palmerston to the provisions of the Constitution of the United States, and the laws of many of the States, to satisfy him of the *existence* of slavery, and that slaves are there regarded and protected as property; that by these laws, there is in fact *no distinction in principle between property in persons and property in things; and that the Government have more than once, in the most solemn manner, determined that slaves killed in the service of the United States, even in a state of war, were to be regarded as property, and not as persons, and the Government held responsible for their value."*

No answer having been vouchsafed to this letter, and the argument being exhausted, Mr. Stevenson tried the virtue of a diplomatic hint that the United States would go to war for their slaves; expressing his hope in a letter to Lord Palmerston, that the British Government would

"Not longer consent to postpone the decision of a subject which had been for so many years under its consideration; and the effect of which can be none other than to throw not only additional impediments in the way of an adjustment, and increase those feelings of dissatisfaction and irritation which have already been excited; but by possibility tend to *disturb and weaken the kind and amicable relations which now so happily subsist between the two countries, and on the preservation of which, so essentially depend the interests and happiness of both." Letter of* 31*st December*, 1836.

The British Cabinet, after long delays, reluctantly consented to pay for the cargoes of the Comet and Encomium on the ground that at the time the slaves composing them were liberated, slavery still existed in the British West Indies; but inasmuch as the emancipation Act had been passed before the arrival of the Enterprise, *her* passengers could not be recognized by British courts as property, and therefore the government could not and would not pay for them. The letter of Lord Palmerston announcing this determination, concluded as follows:

"Slavery being now abolished throughout the British empire, there can be no well-founded claim for compensation in respect of slaves, who, under *any circumstances*, may come into British colonies, any more than there would be with respect to slaves brought into the United Kingdom."

This announcement was received in high dudgeon at Washington. Mr. Forsyth, the Secretary of State, wrote (27th March, 1837) to Mr. Stevenson, that the principles on which the claim of the owner of the slaves on board the Enterprise had been rejected, "are regarded by the PRESIDENT as inconsistent with the respect due from all foreign powers to the *institutions* of a friendly nation!" Mr. Van Buren it seems is yet to learn that our republican institution of negro slavery, instead of being regarded with respect, is viewed with scorn and detestation by the civilized world. He is not, however, ignorant of the influence which *his* respect for it will have on the next presidential election. Mr. Forsyth proceeded:

"The soundness of the principle is explicitly denied, and the serious consequences with which, in the judgment of the PRESIDENT, it is fraught to the *property and tranquillity* of our citizens, call imperatively upon HIM to announce to his majesty's government, immediately and solemnly, that its application to them *never can be acquiesced in by the government of the United States.*" * * * * "The PRESIDENT has been *particularly affected* by the declaration, that no claim for slaves coming into the British dominions, under any circumstances, will be entertained by his majesty's government. Although the President well knows that such is not the intention of his majesty's government, yet this declaration, if not regarded as an invitation, will be the strongest inducement to the flight or abduction of slaves, by fraud or force, from their masters; and if adhered to, cannot fail to be considered, especially by the sufferers from its influence, as an evidence of a spirit hostile to the repose and security of the United States." * * * * "Irritated by discussion without agreement, DISCUSSION WILL BE ABANDONED FOR RETALIATION OR RETORTION; and sooner or later, the cordial good will, at present so happily existing between the two countries, will be converted into BITTER HOSTILITY—the forerunner of incalculable injuries to both."

Mr. Stevenson was directed to lay this bullying epistle "*in extenso*" before the British Minister. Lord Palmerston, in his reply, did not condescend to notice the threats of Messrs. Van Buren and Forsyth, but calmly *repeated* the assurance, that

"Slavery being now abolished throughout the British empire, there can be no well-founded claim on the part of any foreigner in respect of slaves, who, under *any circumstances whatever*, may come into the British colonies, any more than there would be in respect to slaves who might come into the United Kingdom."

The Federal Government did not deem it expedient, on the receipt of this despatch, to declare war against Great Britain, but preferred making another attempt at negotiation; and a most extraordinary attempt it was. Mr. Stevenson was instructed

(12th March, 1838) to ascertain whether the British government

"Are prepared *at once* to enter upon the negotiation of a convention for regulating the disposition of slaves belonging to the United States that may be carried by force into the colonies lying contiguous to our territories, or driven in by stress of weather, with a view to the prevention of the ill effects to be apprehended from future collisions upon a subject so liable to produce in the people of the respective countries a high degree of excitement and irritation. In the *meantime*, the President, anxious to avoid every thing that might tend in the least degree to disturb the amicable relations subsisting between the two countries, WILL ABSTAIN from taking those steps for the security of the rights and property of our citizens which the recent decision of her majesty's government, in the absence of any agreement upon the subject, would render necessary, *until* opportunity is offered for *receiving the answer* of her majesty's government, to the application which you are hereby directed to make."

It would be doing injustice to Mr. Van Buren to suppose him capable of the weakness of believing that such a proposition would be listened to after the reiterated declarations to the contrary by Lord Palmerston. The correspondence it was known would be published before the next election; and the South would perceive that the President, although a Northern man, had done what he could to sustain "the rights and property" of the slave-holders. A reprieve, it will be seen, was granted to her majesty's government until an opportunity was afforded for receiving its answer. On the 10th of July, 1838, Mr. Stevenson laid before the British minister the terms of the required treaty, which were, —

1st. That Great Britain should "refrain from *forcing* liberty upon such American slaves" as might hereafter be compelled to enter British colonial ports.

2d. That she should prohibit the landing of such slaves in the colonies.

3d. That when unavoidably landed, they should be placed under *military* guard till their owners could re-ship them.

The *answer*, big with the fate of Britain, and which was to terminate Mr. Van Buren's long-suffering and forbearance, was returned on the 10th of July, 1838, — and such an answer! The American minister is assured that "an engagement on the part of Great Britain not to *force* liberty upon American slaves, would appear to assume a *preference* to slavery on the part of such persons, which is scarcely consistent with the known principles of human nature;" and moreover, that such engagement is wholly unnecessary, since the British law forces no slave to leave a master he wishes to serve. But that a law depriving American slaves in the British dominions of the right of habeas corpus, "would be so entirely at variance with every principle of the British Constitution, that *no government would venture to propose it to Parliament, and no Parliament would agree to adopt it.*" And as to placing American slaves under a military guard, that they might be restored to their masters, it would be a duty "*so repugnant to every feeling of the officers and men of the British army,* that her majesty's government would in any case be extremely unwilling to call upon her majesty's troops to perform it; and, in the next place, it is doubtful whether the troops could be so employed consistently with the law now in force for the abolition of the slave-trade, and her majesty's government could not propose to Parliament the *repeal of that law.*"

Such was the answer, — and not only has it been received, but it has been submitted to Congress; and yet Mr. Van Buren still *abstains* "from taking those steps for the security of the rights and property of our citizens" which the decision of her majesty's government renders necessary!

Thus for eight successive years has the cabinet at Washington been sending instructions to their agents in England to procure payment for these cargoes of human flesh: nor has Congress been wanting in zeal on the same subject. *Twice* has the Senate called on the President to report the progress of the negotiation. The first call (7th February, 1837) asked for a copy of the

"Correspondence with the Government of Great Britain in relation to the *outrage* committed on our flag, and the rights of our citizens, by the authorities of Bermuda and New Providence, in *seizing* the slaves on board the brigs 'Encomium' and 'Enterprise,' engaged in the *coasting trade*, but which were forced by shipwreck and stress of weather into the ports of those islands."

The language of this resolution indicates the influence exerted by slavery over the Federal Government. Should a murderer escape from England and land on our shores, we refuse to surrender him to the justice of his country; but when the West India authorities refuse to deliver two hundred and eighty-seven innocent men, women and children, thrown by the tempest under their protection, into hopeless, interminable slavery, the Senate solemnly pronounce the refusal to be an *outrage* on our flag, and the rights of our citizens. Moreover, the liberation of these persons is spoken of as a *seizure* of them, and the *slavers* carrying human cargoes to market, are most audaciously declared to have been engaged in the *coasting trade!* The real trade in which these vessels were engaged, was

THE AMERICAN SLAVE-TRADE UNDER THE PROTECTION AND REGULATION OF THE FEDERAL GOVERNMENT.

We shall first exhibit the character and extent of this trade, and then show that it is in fact carried on under the protection and regulation of the Federal Government.

The competition of free with slave-labor in the bread-stuffs and some other productions of Maryland, Virginia, and North Carolina, has greatly reduced the value of slaves as laborers in those States; and hence the disposition manifested there some years since, to get rid of this unprofitable portion of their population. But the rapid extension of the cotton and sugar cultivation in the extreme South, together with the settlement of the new States of Alabama, Mississippi, Missouri, and Arkansas, occasioned a prodigious demand for slaves; and the agriculturists of Virginia and the neighboring States discovered that their most lucrative occupation was that of raising live stock for the Southern and Western markets. In Georgia and South Carolina it has also been found more advantageous to export their supernumeraries to Mobile, New Orleans, or Natchez, than to employ them on their well-stocked plantations. Hence has grown up an almost incredible transfer of slaves from the North to the South; and recently a new market has been opened in Texas, giving an additional stimulus to the trade. It is impossible to ascertain the exact amount of this trade, as the Secretary of the Treasury in his annual report on the commercial statistics of the United States, has never included any statements respecting this branch of the "coasting trade." But, indeed, the returns from the several Custom Houses of the size and value of the human cargoes cleared for the Southern ports, if given, would afford a very inadequate idea of the extent of the traffic, since it is carried on by land as well as by sea. Whole coffles of chained slaves are driven long and painful journeys in the interior of the Republic, much in the same manner as in the wilds of Africa. The Rev. Mr. Dickey in a published letter thus describes a coffle he met on the road in Kentucky:

"I discovered about forty black men all chained together in the following manner: each of them was handcuffed, and they were arranged in rank and file; a chain perhaps forty feet long was stretched between two ranks, to which short chains were joined, which connected with the handcuffs. Behind them were, I suppose, *thirty women* in double rank, *the couples tied hand to hand.*"

The Presbyterian Synod of Kentucky, in an address, in 1835, to the churches under their care, speaking of this trade, say:

"Brothers and sisters, parents and children, husbands and wives, are torn asunder, and permitted to see each other no more. These acts are *daily* occurring in the midst of us. The shrieks and agony often witnessed on such occasions, proclaim with a trumpet tongue the iniquity of OUR system. There is not a neighborhood where these heart-rending scenes are not displayed. *There is not a village or road* that does not behold the sad procession of *manacled* outcasts, whose mournful countenances tell that they are exiled by force from all that their hearts hold dear."

J. K. PAULDING, the present Secretary of the Navy, gives the following picture of a scene he witnessed in Virginia:

"The sun was shining out very hot, and in turning an angle of the road we encountered the following group: first, a little cart drawn by one horse, in which five or six half naked black children were tumbled like pigs together. The cart had no covering, and they seemed to have been actually broiled to sleep. Behind the cart marched three black women, with head, neck and breasts uncovered, and without shoes or stockings; next came three men, bareheaded, half naked, and *chained together with an ox-chain.* Last of all came a white man—a white man, Frank!—on horseback, carrying pistols in his belt, and who, as we passed him, had the impudence to look us in the face without blushing. I should like to see him hunted by bloodhounds. At a house where we stopped, a little further on, we learned that he had bought these miserable beings in Maryland, and was marching them in this manner to some of the more southern States. Shame on the State of Maryland! I say—and shame on the State of Virginia, and every State through which this wretched cavalcade was permitted to pass. Do they expect that such exhibitions will not dishonor them in the eyes of strangers, however they may be reconciled to them by education and habit?"*

The annexed picture, it will be perceived, is drawn by a *southern* pencil.

"Place yourself in imagination for a moment in their condition—with *heavy galling chains* riveted upon your person, *half-naked*, *half-starved*, your back *lacerated* with the knotted whip, travelling to a region where your condition through time will be second only to the wretched creatures in hell. This depiction is not visionary—would to God that it was!" *Editorial, Maryville (Tennessee) Intelligencer*, 4th *October*, 1835.

* "Letters from the South, written during an excursion in the summer of 1816." New York, 1817. Vol. I, Letter XI, p. 117.

It may be thought by some that the elevation to a seat in the Cabinet, of a gentleman who expresses himself with so much warmth and fearlessness against one of the "peculiar institutions of the South," militates against our idea that the influence of the Federal Government is exerted in behalf of slavery. Singular as it may appear, the appointment of Mr. Paulding is nevertheless strongly corroborative of the opinion we have advanced; and the explanation is at once easy and amusing. The "Letters from the South" were reprinted in 1835, and form the fifth and sixth volumes of an edition of "Paulding's works." The letter from which we have quoted consists of fourteen pages, devoted to the subject of slavery. On turning to the corresponding letter in the *recent* edition we find it shrunk to *three* pages, containing no allusion to the internal trade, nor anything else that could offend the most sensitive Southerner. In the nineteenth letter, as printed in 1817, there is not a word about slavery. In the same letter, as published in 1835, we meet with the following most wonderful *prediction*—a prediction that has lately been cited in the newspapers as a proof of the sagacity and foresight of the Secretary of the Navy:—

"The second cause of disunion will be found in the slave population of the South, *whenever* the misguided, or wilfully malignant zeal of the advocates of emancipation, shall institute, *as it one day doubtless will*, a crusade against the constitutional rights of the slave-owners, by sending among them fanatical agents and fanatical tracts, calculated to render the slaves disaffected, and the situation of the master and his family dangerous; when appeals shall be made under the sanction of religion to the passions of these ignorant and excited blacks, calculated and intended to rouse their worst and most dangerous passions, and to place the very lives of their masters, their wives, and their children in the deepest peril; *when societies are formed* in the sister States for the avowed purpose of virtually destroying the value

As we are about to enter into particulars respecting the American slave-trade, it may not be uninteresting to inquire who are its victims. They are *native born Americans.* But of what color and descent? This will no doubt be deemed by many a very unnecessary question; and no little indignation will probably be excited when we answer that large numbers of these victims are *white* men and women, and the *children of American citizens.*

People at the North are disposed to be incredulous when they hear of *white* slaves at the South: and yet a little reflection would convince them not only that there must be such slaves under the present system, but that in process of time a large proportion of the slaves must be as white as their masters. Were there no other sources of information respecting the complexions of the southern slaves, the newspaper notices of run-

of this principal item in the property of a southern planter; when it becomes a question mooted in the Legislatures of the States, or of the general government, whether the rights of the master over his slave shall be any longer recognized or maintained, and when it is at last evident that nothing will preserve them but secession, then will certain of the stars of our beautiful constellation "start madly from their spheres and jostle the others in their wild career."

In the title of the new edition, the *date* of the "excursion" is modestly omitted, but the reader is not informed that the spirit of prophecy descended upon the writer, not while journeying at the South, but while witnessing in New York the operations of *the predicted* societies, and *after* the city had been convulsed by the abolition riots.

In 1836, Mr. Paulding published his "Slavery in the United States." In this work both the Old and New Testament are made to give their sanction to slavery. Great Britain, in abolishing slavery in the West Indies, is charged with having "committed robbery under cover of humanity."—(p. 51.) "A community of free blacks rising among the ruins of States, lords of the soil, smoking with the habitations and blood of their exterminated masters and families," would, we are assured, be only fulfilling "the wishes" of the abolitionists.—(p. 56.) The advocates of immediate emancipation recommend, it is asserted, "indiscriminate marriages between the whites and blacks,"—(p. 61), and well educated respectable females amongst them are apparently anxious "to become the mothers of mulattoes."—(p. 62.) Slavery, we are told, "is becoming gradually divested of all its harsh features, and is now only the bugbear of the imagination,—(p. 26;) and Mr. Paulding affirms—"In a residence of several years within the District, and a pretty extensive course of travel in some of the southern States, (the excursion in the summer of 1816, we suppose,) we never saw or heard of any such instances of cruelty. We *saw no chains* (!) and heard no stripes."—(p. 168.)

We trust our readers are now fully convinced of this gentleman's qualifications for the office of Secretary of the Navy, and of Mr. Van Buren's consistency in appointing him.

aways would most abundantly confirm our assertion. Of these notices, we give the following as samples.

"$100 *Reward.*—The above reward will be paid for the apprehension of my man William. He is a very bright mulatto—*straight, yellowish hair.* I have no doubt he will change his name, and try to pass himself for a WHITE MAN, which he may be able to do, unless to a close observer.

August 9. T. S. PICHARD."

"$100 *Reward.*—Ran away from James Hyhart, Paris, Kentucky, on the 29th of June last, the mulatto boy Norton, about fifteen years old, a very bright mulatto, and would be taken for a WHITE BOY, if not closely examined. His hair is black and *straight,* &c."—*New Orleans True American,* 11*th August,* 1836.

"$100 *Reward*—Will be given for the apprehension of my negro (!) Edmund Kenney. He has *straight* hair, and complexion so nearly WHITE, that it is believed a stranger would suppose *there was no African blood in him.* He was with my boy Dick a short time since in Norfolk, *and offered him for sale,* and was apprehended, but escaped under pretence of being a WHITE MAN.

ANDERSON BOWLES.

Richmond Whig, 6*th January,* 1836."

"$50 *Reward* will be given for the apprehension and delivery to me of the following slaves: Samuel, and Judy his wife, with their four children, belonging to the estate of Sacker Dubberly, deceased.

I will give $10 for the apprehension of William Dubberly, a slave belonging to the estate. William is about 19 years old, QUITE WHITE, and would not readily be mistaken for a slave.

JOHN T. LANE.

Newbern Spectator, 13*th March,* 1837."

"$100 *Reward.*—Ran away from the subscriber, a bright mulatto man slave, named Sam. *Light sandy hair, blue eyes, ruddy complexion* —is so WHITE as very easily to pass for a free WHITE MAN.

EDWIN PECK.

Mobile, April 22, 1837."

"$50 *Reward.*—I will give the above reward of fifty dollars for the apprehension and securing in any jail, so that I get him again, or delivering to me in Dandridge, E. Tenn., my mulatto boy, named Preston, about twenty years old. It is supposed he will try to pass as a *free* WHITE MAN.

Oct. 12, 1838. JOHN ROPER."

"*Ran away* from the subscriber, working on the plantation of Col. H. Tinker, a bright mulatto boy, named Alfred. Alfred is about eight years of age, pretty well grown, has *blue eyes, light flaxen hair, skin disposed to freckle.* He will try to pass as FREE BORN.

S. G. STEWART.

Green County, Alabama."

In the *New Orleans Bee*, of June 22, 1831, P. BAHI advertises as a runaway, "Maria, with a CLEAR WHITE complexion!"

Mr. Paxton, a Virginia writer, tells us in his work on slavery, that "the best blood in Virginia flows in the veins of the slaves."

Dr. Torrey, in his work on domestic slavery in the United States, p. 14, says:

> "While at a public house in Fredericktown, there came into the bar-room, on Sunday, a decently dressed white man, of quite a light complexion, in company with one who was totally black. After they went away, the landlord observed that the *white man* was a slave. I asked him with some surprise how that could be possible? To which he replied, that he was a descendant, by female ancestry, of an African slave. He also stated, that not far from Fredericktown, there was a slave estate on which there were several *white* females, of as fair and elegant appearance as white ladies in general, held in legal bondage as *slaves!!*"

A Missouri paper, reporting the trial of a *slave boy*, remarks:

> "All the physiological marks of distinction which characterize the African descent, had disappeared. His skin was *fair*, his hair soft, straight, fine and white, his eyes blue, but rather disposed to the hazel-nut color, nose prominent, the lips small and well formed, forehead high and prominent."

In the summer of 1835, a slave-holder from Maryland arrested as his fugitive a young woman in Philadelphia. A trial ensued, when it was most conclusively proved that the alleged slave, Mary Gilmore, was the child of poor *Irish* parents, and had not a drop of African blood in her veins.

A paper printed at Louisville, Ky., the "Emporium," relates a circumstance that occurred in that city, in the following terms.

> "A laudable indignation was universally manifested among our citizens on Saturday last, by the exposure of a woman and two children for sale at public auction, at the front of our principal tavern. The woman and children were as WHITE as any of our citizens: indeed, we scarcely ever saw a child with a fairer or clearer complexion than the younger one." *Niles's Register, June,* 1821.

Mr. Niles tells us, in his Register, that Mr. Calhoun, the late Vice President, had related to him the case of a man "placed on the stand for sale as a slave, whose appearance, in *all respects*, gave him a better claim to the character of a WHITE MAN, than most persons so acknowledged could show." *Register*, 25*th Oct.* 1834.

We will now attempt to give the reader some idea of the *extent* of the trade — a trade in which human beings of every shade, from the purest white to the deepest black, are made articles of merchandise, and treated with cruelty little if any less than that which has made the African slave-trade the execration of the civilized world.

"Dealing in slaves," says the Baltimore Register, "has become a large business; establishments are made in several places in Maryland and Virginia, at which they are sold like cattle: these places of deposit are strongly built, and well supplied with iron thumb-screws and gags, and ornamented with cowskins and other whips, oftentimes bloody."

The advertisements of the Baltimore traders show that the Maryland Colonization Society, in their endeavors to suppress the slave-trade, may find a field for their labors less distant than the coast of Africa. We annex some samples.

"*Austin Woodfolk*, of Baltimore, wishes to inform the slave-holders of Maryland and Virginia, that their friend still lives to give cash and the highest price for negroes," &c.

"*General Slave Agency Office.* — Gentlemen planters from the South, and others who wish to purchase negroes, would do well to give me a call.

LEWIS SCOTT."

"*Cash for two hundred Negroes.* — The highest cash prices will be paid for negroes of both sexes, by application to me or my agent, at Booth's Garden.

HOPE H. SLATER."

"*For New Orleans.* — A coppered, copper-fastened packet-brig, Isaac Franklin, will sail on the 1st of February, for Baltimore. *Those having servants to ship* will do well by making early application to James F. Purvis," &c.

Human flesh is now the great staple of Virginia. In the Legislature of this State, in 1832, THOMAS JEFFERSON RANDOLPH declared that Virginia had been converted into "*one grand menagerie, where men are reared for the market like oxen for the shambles.*" This same gentleman thus compared the foreign with the domestic traffic.

"The trader (African) receives the slave, a stranger in aspect, language, and manner, from the merchant who brought him from the interior. But *here*, sir, individuals whom the master has known from infancy — whom he has seen sporting in the innocent gambols of childhood — who have been accustomed to look to him for protection, *he tears from the mother's arms, and sells into a strange country, among a strange people, subject to cruel taskmasters.* In my opinion it is *much worse.*"

Mr. Gholson, of Virginia, in his speech in the Legislature of that State, January 18, 1831, (see Richmond Whig,) says:

"The legal maxim of *partus sequitur ventrem* is coeval with the existence of the rights of property itself, and is founded in wisdom and justice. It is only on the justice and inviolability of this maxim, that the master foregoes the service of the female slave, has her nursed and attended during the period of her gestation, and raises the helpless and infant offspring. The value of the property justifies the expense; and I do not hesitate to say, that *in its increase consists much of our wealth.*"

Professor Dew, now President of the College of William and Mary, Virginia, in his review of the debate in the Virginia Legislature, 1831–2, speaking of the revenue arising from the trade, says:

"A full equivalent being thus left in the place of the slave, this emigration becomes an advantage to the State, and does not check the black population as much as at first view we might imagine, because it furnishes every inducement to the master to attend to the negroes, to ENCOURAGE BREEDING, and *to cause the greatest number possible to be raised.* * * Virginia is, in fact, a NEGRO-RAISING STATE for other States."

Mr. C. F. Mercer asserted in the Virginia Convention of 1729:

"The tables of the natural growth of the slave population demonstrate, when compared with the increase of its numbers in the Commonwealth for twenty years past, that an annual revenue of not less than a *million and a half of dollars* is derived from the *exportation* of a part of this population." *Debates*, p. 99.

Professor E. A. Andrews gives a conversation he had with a trader on board a steamboat on the Potomac, in 1835.

"In selling his slaves, N——— assures me he never separates families; but that in *purchasing* them he is often compelled to do so, for that his business is to purchase, and he must take such as are in the market. Do you often buy the wife without the husband? Yes, very often; and frequently, too, they sell me the mother, while they keep the children. I have often known them take *away the infant from the mother's breast, and keep it, while they sold her.* Children from one to eighteen months old, are now worth about one hundred dollars." *

The town of Petersburg, in Virginia, seems to enjoy a large share of this commerce, judging from the advertisements of its merchants.

"*Cash for Negroes.*—The subscribers are particularly anxious to make a *shipment* of negroes shortly. All persons who have slaves to part with, will do well to call as soon as possible.

OVERLY & SAUNDERS."

"The subscriber being desirous of making *another shipment* by the Brig Adelaide, to New Orleans, on the first of March, will give a good market price for fifty negroes, from *ten* to thirty years old.

HENRY DAVIS."

"The subscriber wishes to purchase *one hundred slaves*, of both sexes, from the age of *ten* to thirty, for which he is disposed to give much higher prices than have heretofore been given. He will call on those living in the adjacent counties to see any *property*.

ANSLEY DAVIS."

But of all the Virginia merchants, Mr. Collier, of Richmond, seems to be the most enterprising. We give extracts from his Notice:

"*Notice.*—This is to inform my former acquaintances, and the public generally, that I yet continue in the SLAVE-TRADE, *at Richmond, Virginia*, and will at all times buy and give a fair market price for *young negroes.* Persons in this State, Maryland, or North Carolina, wishing to sell lots of negroes, are particularly requested to forward their wishes to me at this place. Persons wishing to purchase lots of negroes, are requested to give me a call, as I keep constantly on hand at this place, *a great many* for sale; and have at this time the use of one hundred young negroes, consisting of boys, young men, and girls. I will sell at all times, at a small advance on cost, to suit purchasers.

* Slavery and the Domestic Slave Trade in the United States, p. 147.

I have comfortable rooms, with a *jail* attached, for the reception of the negroes; and persons coming to this place to sell slaves, can be accommodated, and every attention necessary will be given to have them well attended to; and when it may be desired, the reception of the company of *gentlemen dealing in slaves* will conveniently and attentively be received. My situation is very healthy and suitable for the business. LEWIS A. COLLIER."

Joseph Wood, of Hamburg, South Carolina, a "gentleman dealing in slaves," advertises that he "has on hand a likely parcel of *Virginia* negroes, and receives new supplies *every fifteen days.*"

"120 *Negroes for sale.*—The subscriber has just arrived *from Petersburg, Virginia,* with one hundred and twenty likely young negroes, of both sexes, and every description, which he offers for sale on the most reasonable terms. The lot now on hand consists of plough-boys, several likely and well-qualified house servants, of both sexes, several women with small children, *small girls,* suitable for nurses, and several SMALL BOYS WITHOUT THEIR MOTHERS. BENJAMIN DAVIS.

Hamburg, S. C., Sept. 28, 1838."

And what are the pecuniary results of this commerce? Mr. Mercer, as we have seen, estimated the annual revenue to Virginia from the export of human flesh, at *one million and a half of dollars.* But this was in 1829, before the trade had reached its present palmy state. "The Virginia Times," in 1836, in an article on the importance of increasing the banking capital of the Commonwealth, estimates the number of slaves exported for sale the "last twelve months," at FORTY THOUSAND; each slave averaging six hundred dollars, and thus yielding a capital of TWENTY-FOUR MILLIONS, of which the editor thinks at least thirteen millions might be contributed for banking purposes.*

In 1837, a committee, appointed at a public meeting of the citizens of Mobile, on the subject of the existing pecuniary pressure, in their report stated:

"So large has been the return of slave labor, that purchases by Alabama, of that species of property from other States since 1833, have amounted to TEN MILLIONS OF DOLLARS ANNUALLY."

* Niles's Register.

Let us now visit the "Metropolis of the Nation," the very heart of this mighty commerce in the bodies and souls of men. The District of Columbia, from its relative situation to the breeding States, forms a convenient depot for the negroes, previous to their exportation; and the non-interference of Congress gives the traders "under the exclusive jurisdiction" of the Federal Government, as unlimited power over the treatment and stowage of their human cargoes, as their brethren enjoy on the coast of Guinea.

Hence large establishments have grown up upon the national domain, provided with prisons for the safe-keeping of the negroes till a full cargo is procured; and should at any time the factory prisons be insufficient, the public ones, erected by Congress, are at the service of the dealers, and the United States Marshal becomes the agent of the slave-trader!

It must be admitted that the following pictures of the scenes witnessed in the District of Columbia, are drawn by impartial hands. So long ago as 1802, the Grand Jury of Alexandria, complaining of the trade, remarked:

"These dealers in the persons of our fellow-men collect within this District, from various parts, numbers of these victims of slavery, and lodge them in some place of confinement until they have completed their numbers. They are then turned out into our streets, and exposed to view *loaded with chains*, as though they had committed some heinous offence against our laws. We consider it as a grievance, that citizens from a distant part of the United States should be permitted to come within the District and pursue a traffic fraught with so much misery to a class of beings entitled to our protection by the laws of justice and humanity; and that the interposition of civil authority cannot be had to prevent parents being wrested from their offspring, and children from their parents, without respect to the ties of nature. We consider these grievances demanding Legistative redress"—that is, redress by Congress.

In 1816, Judge Morell, of the Circuit Court of the United States, in his charge to the Grand Jury of Washington, observed, speaking of the slave-trade:

"The frequency with which the streets of the city had been *crowded with manacled captives*, sometimes on the Sabbath, could not fail to shock the feelings of all humane persons."

The same year, John Randolph moved in the House of Representatives for a committee

"To inquire into the existence of an inhuman and illegal traffic of slaves carried on, in, and through the District of Columbia, and report whether any or what measures are necessary for putting a stop to the same."

The motion was adopted; had it been made twenty years later, it would, under the rules of the House, have been laid on the table, "and no further action had thereon."

The Alexandria Gazette of June 22d, 1827, thus describes the scenes sanctioned by our professedly republican and Christian Legislature:

"Scarcely a week passes without some of these wretched creatures being driven through our streets. After having been confined, and sometimes manacled in a loathsome prison, they are turned out in public view to take their departure for the South. The children and some of the women are generally crowded into a cart or wagon, while others follow on foot, not unfrequently *handcuffed and chained together.* Here you may behold fathers and brothers leaving behind them the dearest objects of affection, and moving slowly along in the mute agony of despair—there the young mother sobbing over the infant whose innocent smiles seem but to increase her misery. From some you will hear the burst of bitter lamentation, while from others, the loud hysteric laugh breaks forth, denoting still deeper agony."

In 1828, a petition for the suppression of this trade was presented to Congress, signed by more than *one thousand inhabitants of this District.*

In 1829, the Grand Jury of Washington made a communication to Congress, in which they say:

"Provision ought to be made to prevent purchasers, for the purpose of removal and transportation, from making the cities of the District, depots for the *imprisonment* of the slaves they collect. The manner in which they are brought and confined in these places, *and carried through our streets*, is necessarily such as to excite the most painful feelings. It is believed that the whole community would be gratified by the *interference of Congress* for the suppression of these receptacles, and the exclusion of this *disgusting traffic* from the District."

In 1830, the "Washington Spectator" thus gave vent to its indignation.

"*The slave-trade in the Capital.*—Let it be known to the citizens of America, that at the very time when the procession which contained the President of the United States and his Cabinet was marching in triumph tò the Capitol, another kind of procession was marching another way; and that consisted of colored human beings, *handcuffed in pairs*, and driven along by what had the appearance of a man on horseback! A similar scene was repeated on Saturday last; a drove, consisting of males and females, *chained in couples*, starting from Roly's tavern on foot for Alexandria, where with others they are to embark on board a slave-ship in waiting to convey them to the South. Where is the O'Connell in this Republic that will plead for the emancipation of the District of Columbia?"

The advertisements of the dealers indicate the *extent* of the traffic. The National Intelligencer of the 28th of March, 1836, printed at Washington, contained the following advertisments:

"*Cash for five hundred Negroes*, including both sexes, from *ten* to twenty-five years of age. Persons having likely servants to dispose of, will find it their interest to give us a call, as we will give higher prices in cash than any other purchaser who is now or may hereafter come into the MARKET.

FRANKLIN & AMFIELD, Alexandria."

"*Cash for three hundred Negroes.*—The highest cash price will be given by the subscriber, for negroes of both sexes, from the ages of twelve to twenty-eight.

WILLIAM H. WILLIAMS, Washington."

"*Cash for four hundred Negroes*, including both sexes, from twelve to twenty-five years of age.

JAMES H. BIRCH, Washington City."

"*Cash for Negroes.*—We will at all times give the highest prices in cash for likely young negroes of both sexes, from ten to thirty years of age.

J. W. NEAL & Co., Washington."

Here we find three traders in the District, advertising in one day for *twelve hundred* negroes, and a fourth offering to buy an indefinite number.

In a later number of the Intelligencer, we find the following:

"*Cash for Negroes.*—I will give the highest price for likely negroes from ten to twenty-five years of age.

GEORGE KEPHART."

"*Cash for Negroes.*—I will give cash and liberal prices for ANY number of young and likely negroes, from *eight* to forty years of age.

Persons having negroes to dispose of will find it to their advantage to give me a call at my residence on the corner of Seventh street and Maryland Avenue, and opposite Mr. William's *private jail.*

WILLIAM H. RICHARDS."

"*Cash for Negroes.* — The subscriber wishes to purchase a number of Negroes for the *Louisiana and Mississippi market.* Himself or an agent at all times can be found at *his jail,* on Seventh street.

WM. H. WILLIAMS."

The unhappy beings purchased by these traders in human flesh, men and women, and children of *eight* years old, are sent to the South, either over land in coffles, or by sea, in crowded slavers. Fostered by Congress, these traders lose all sense of shame; and we have in the National Intelligencer the following announcement of the regular departure of *three slavers,* belonging to a single factory.

"*Alexandria and New Orleans Packets.* — Brig *Tribune,* Samuel C. Bush, master, will sail as above on the 1st of January — Brig *Isaac Franklin,* Wm. Smith, master, on the 15th of January — Brig *Uncas,* Nath. Boush, master, on the 1st of February. They will continue to leave this port on the 1st and 15th of each month, throughout the shipping season. *Servants that are intended to be shipped, will at any time be received for safe-keeping at twenty-five cents a day.*

JOHN AMFIELD, Alexandria."

This infamous advertisement of the regular sailing of three slavers, with the offer of the use of the factory prison, appears in one of the principal journals of the United States. Its proprietor has several times been chosen printer to Congress, and there is no reason for believing that he has ever lost the vote of a northern member for this prostitution of his columns.

But the climax of infamy is still untold. This trade in blood; this buying, imprisoning, and exporting of boys and girls eight years old; this tearing asunder of husbands and wives, parents and children, is all legalized *in virtue of authority delegated by Congress!!* The 249th page of the laws of the city of Washington is polluted by the following enactment, bearing date 28th July, 1838:

"For a LICENSE to trade or traffic in slaves for profit, four hundred dollars."

A terrific feature of this trade is the mortality it occasions. A writer in the New Orleans Argus of 1830, in an article on the sugar cultivation, thus coolly estimates one item of expenditure.

"The loss by death in bringing slaves from a northern climate, which our planters are under the necessity of doing, is not less than TWENTY-FIVE PER CENT."

If the change of climate be thus fatal, then those who survive this change must, of course, be deemed more valuable, as the planters will run less hazard in buying them after having become *acclimated.* Now what language do southern advertisements hold on this point? We have of course room for only a few *specimens,* but they attest the superior value attached to acclimated negroes, and of course the loss of life attributed to "bringing slaves from a northern climate."

"I offer my plantation for sale. Also seventy-five *acclimated negroes.* O. B. COBB.
Vicksburg Register, Dec. 27, 1838."

"I will sell my Old River plantation, near Columbia, in Arkansas, also *one hundred and thirty acclimated negroes.* BEN. HUGHES.
Port Gibson, 14*th Jan.*"

"*Probate Sale.*—Will be offered for sale at public auction to the highest hidder *one hundred and thirty acclimated slaves.*
G. W. KEETON,
Judge of the Parish of Concordia, La.
March 22, 1837."

General Felix Houston advertises in the *Natchez Courier,* April 6th, 1838, "Thirty very fine *acclimated* negroes."

But the waste of life in the process of acclimation, is but a portion of the mortality caused by this murderous traffic. If we call to mind the crowded slavers—the chained coffles—the dreary journeys of hundreds of miles—the forced separation of husbands and wives, parents and children—the broken hearts and fevered brains of the helpless victims, we cannot question that the sufferings of multitudes are shortened by a premature death. We could detail various suicides, induced by the horrible anticipation of this loathsome transfer, but one shall suffice, and that related by the present SECRETARY OF THE NAVY. This gentleman, in his southern excursion, fell in company with a coffle-driver, and in the first (not the last) editions of his letters from the South, gives the confessions made by the wretch himself in his presence.

"All along the road, it seems, he made it his business to inquire where lived a man who might be tempted to become a party in this *accursed traffic*; and when he had got some half dozen of these poor creatures, *he tied their hands behind their backs*, and drove them three or four hundred miles or more, bareheaded and half naked, through the burning southern sun. 'I made one bad purchase though,' continued he, 'I bought a young mulatto girl, a lively creature, a great bargain. She had been the favorite of her master, who had lately married. The difficulty was to get her to go, for the poor creature loved her master. However, I swore most bitterly I was only going to take her to her mother's at——, and she went with me, though she seemed to doubt me very much. But when she discovered, at last, that we were out of the State, I thought she would go mad, and, in fact, the next night she drowned herself in the river close by. I lost a good five hundred dollars by this foolish trick.'" *Vol.* I, p. 121.*

We now put it to the consciences of our readers, if the facts developed in the preceding pages do not amply justify the following pregnant remarks of the editor of a late New Orleans Journal:

"The United States law (prohibiting the African slave-trade,) may, and probably does put MILLIONS into the pockets of the people living between the Roanoke and Mason and Dixon's line; still we think it would require some casuistry to show that the present slave-trade from that quarter *is a whit better than the one from Africa*." *New Orleans Courier*, 15*th Feb*. 1839.

Such is the character and extent of the American slave-trade, impudently and wickedly called by the Senate, "the coasting trade,"—a trade protected and regulated by the very government which in the Treaty of Ghent, with wonderful assurance, declared that "the traffic in slaves is irreconcilable with the principles of justice and humanity."

The government may be fairly said to protect the trade, when it refuses to exercise its constitutional power to suppress it.

* It was not, it would seem, till the honorable Secretary turned politician, that he discovered that slavery is now "only the bugbear of the imagination."

The very fact that slave-traders are *licensed in the District*, is a full and complete acknowledgment that there is authority competent to forbid their nefarious business. The continuance of the traffic under the immediate and "exclusive jurisdiction" of the National Government, stamps with sin and disgrace every member of Congress who assents to it; and more especially, and with peculiar infamy, those northern members who, for party purposes, vote that "Congress ought not in *any way* to interfere with slavery in the District of Columbia."

But we are constantly told by the apologists of slavery that the American slave-trade is beyond the constitutional control of the Federal Government; yet that government abolished the *African* slave-trade, and no human being ever questioned its right to do so. But whence was that right derived? Solely from the 8th Section of the 1st Article of the Constitution, viz.:—

> "Congress shall have power to regulate commerce with foreign nations, and among the several States."

In virtue of this delegation of power Congress has made it a capital crime to carry on commerce in *African* slaves. Now this legislative prohibition of the traffic is constitutional, is proved by the highest possible authority, even the Constitution itself; for that instrument, after giving Congress power to regulate commerce with foreign nations, *restricts it* from abolishing the African slave-trade before the expiration of twenty years.* To *regulate*, we are told, does not include the power to destroy; yet it seems the power to regulate commerce with foreign nations does include the power to interdict an odious, cruel, and wicked branch of it. By what logic then will it be shown that the power to regulate the commerce among the several States,

* The phraseology of this restriction shows that it was intended to limit the power to regulate commerce as well "among the several States" as with foreign nations. "The *migration*, or importation of such person as any of the existing States shall think proper to admit, shall not be prohibited by the Congress prior to the year one thousand eight hundred and eight."—*Art.* 1, *Sec.* 9. If any State should think proper to admit slaves *migrating* from another State, it was not to be restrained from doing so till 1808. If it should think proper to *import* slaves from a foreign country, it might do so, notwithstanding the wishes of Congress, till the same period.

does not include the power to interdict a traffic in men, women, and children? Is it more wicked, more base, more cruel, to traffic in African savages than in native born Americans—in WHITE men, and women, and children—in the offspring of our own citizens, and not unfrequently, of very distinguished citizens? Yet it is this abominable commerce that our government fosters and protects. We have seen its watchful guardianship over this trade in its unceasing endeavors to obtain compensation from Great Britain for two hundred and eighty-seven slaves thrown by the winds and waves under her protection. Mr. Van Buren, our Minister in England, in an official note on this subject, (Feb. 25, 1832,) remarked:—

> "The Government of the United States respecting the actual and unavoidable condition of things at home, while it most sedulously and rigorously guards against the further introduction of slaves, *protects* at the same time by reasonable laws the rights of the owners of that species of property in the States where it exists, and *permits* its transfer coastwise from one of these States to another, under suitable restrictions to prevent the fraudulent introduction of foreign slaves."

By the act of Congress of March 2d, 1807, masters of vessels under forty tons burden, are forbidden to transport coastwise from one port to another in the United States any person of color to be sold or held as a slave, under the penalty of $800 for each slave so transported.

By the same act, masters of vessels, over forty tons burden, sailing coastwise from one port to another, and *intending to transport persons of color to be sold or held as slaves*, must first make out duplicate manifests, specifying the names, age, sex, and stature of the persons transported, and the names and residence of their owner or shipper. These manifests are to be delivered to the collector of the port, who is to retain one and return the other to the master, with "*a permit*" endorsed on it, "authorizing him to proceed to the port of destination." If the master presumes to transport a slave without such permit, not only is the vessel forfeited, but the master is to pay a penalty of $1000 for each slave shipped. On the arrival of the vessel at the port of destination, the manifest, with the permit, is to be handed to the collector, who thereupon is to grant a "*permit*" for the landing of the slaves, and if any are landed without such permit, the master forfeits one thousand dollars. So it seems Congress may prohibit the slave-trade in vessels *under* forty tons; but according to northern politicians, it would be unconstitutional to prohibit it in vessels *over* forty tons; and according to the slave-holders, such a prohibition would cause a dissolution of the Union! But alas! the permission, regulation, and protection of this traffic is in perfect keeping with

THE DUPLICITY OF THE FEDERAL GOVERNMENT IN REGARD TO THE SUPPRESSION OF THE AFRICAN SLAVE-TRADE.

The great struggle for the abstract principles of human liberty in which our fathers engaged with so much zeal, had, at the close of the revolutionary war, excited a very general conviction of the injustice of slavery. When the convention appointed to form a Federal Constitution assembled, the northern and many of the southern delegates were disposed to give the new government such unqualified power over the commerce of the nation, as would enable it to abolish a traffic no less at variance with our republican professions than with the precepts of humanity and religion. A portion of the southern delegates, however, insisted on a temporary restriction of this power as the price of their adhesion to the Union; and their threat of marring the beauty, symmetry, and strength of the fair fabric about to be erected, by withdrawing from it the support of the States they represented, unfortunately induced the convention to yield to their wishes, and to insert in the Constitution a clause restraining Congress from abolishing the African slave-trade for twenty years. Mr. Madison has left us the following history of this iniquitous clause.

"The southern States would not have entered into the union of America without the temporary permission of that trade. The gentlemen from South Carolina and Georgia argued in this manner: 'We have now liberty to import this species of property, and much of the property now possessed has been purchased, or otherwise acquired in contemplation of improving it by the assistance of imported slaves.

What would be the consequence of hindering us from it? The slaves of Virginia would rise in value, and we should be obliged to go to your markets.'" *Debates in Virginia Convention.*

We have here the solution of much contradictory action on the part of slave-holders in regard to this trade. It seems to have been early discovered that its abolition would be advantageous to the slave-breeders, but not to the slave-buyers. Owing to climate, soil, and productions, slave-labor is less profitable in Maryland and Virginia than in the more southern States; hence the greater demand for this labor in the latter States has, since the cessation of importation, caused a constant influx of slaves from the former. The breeders in Maryland and Virginia have, for the most part, striven in good faith for the total suppression of the African trade; while those who originally refused to enter the Union unless permitted, for at least twenty years, to import their slaves directly from Africa, hove since evinced very little desire to secure to their neighbors the monopoly of the market.

Whenever the opponents of abolition find it convenient to refer to the action of the Federal Government on the subject of slavery, they laud and magnify its horror of the *African* slave-trade, and exultingly point to the law of Congress, branding it with the penalties of *piracy*. And yet we are inclined to believe that the conduct of our government in relation to this very subject, is one of the foulest stains attached to our national administration. Has the trade been suppressed? Has the Federal Government in good faith endeavored to suppress it? These are important questions, and we shall endeavor to solve them by an appeal to facts and official documents.

In a debate in Congress in 1819, Mr. Middleton, of South Carolina, stated that in his opinion, 13,000 Africans were annually smuggled into the United States. Mr. Wright, of Virginia, estimated the number at 15,000. The same year, Judge Story, of the Supreme Court of the United States, in a charge to a grand jury, thus expresses himself:—

"We have but too many proofs from unquestionable sources, that it (the African trade) is still carried on with all the implacable ferocity and insatiable rapacity of former times. Avarice has grown more subtle in its evasions, and watches and seizes its prey with an appetite quickened rather than suppressed by its guilty vigils. *American citizens* are steeped to their very mouths (I can scarcely use too bold a figure,) in this stream of iniquity."

On the 22d of January, 1811, the Secretary of the Navy wrote to the commanding naval officer at Charleston:

"I hear, not without great concern, that the law prohibiting the importation of slaves has been violated in *frequent instances*, near St. Mary's, since the gun-boats have been withdrawn from that station."

On the 14th of March, 1814, the collector of Darien, Georgia, thus wrote to the Secretary of the Treasury:

"I am in possession of undoubted information, that African and West India negroes are almost daily illicitly introduced into Georgia, for sale or settlement, or passing through it to the territories of the United States, for similar purposes. These facts are notorious, and it is not unusual to see such negroes in the streets of St. Mary's; and such too, recently captured by our vessels of war, and ordered for Savannah, were illegally bartered by *hundreds* in that city, for this bartering (or *bonding*, as it is called, but in reality *selling*,) actually took place efore any decision had passed by the court respecting them. I can-ot but again express to you, sir, that these irregularities and mockings the laws by men who understand them, are such that it requires the nediate interposition of Congress to effect the suppression of this ffic; for as things are, should a faithful officer of the Government rehend such negroes, to avoid the penalties imposed by the laws, *proprietors disclaim them, and some agent of the Executive demands delivery of the same to him, who may employ them as he pleases, or efect a sale of them by way of bond for restoration of the negroes when egally called on so to do, which bond is understood to be forfeited, as the amount of the bond is so much less than the value of the property.* After much fatigue, peril, and expense, *eighty-eight* Africans are seized and brought to the surveyor at Darien; they are demanded by the Governor's agent. Notwithstanding the knowledge which his excellency had that these very Africans were some weeks within six miles of his excellency's residence, there was no effort, no stir made by him, his agents or subordinate state officers, to carry the laws into execution; but no sooner was it understood that a seizure had been effected by an officer of the United States, than a demand is made for them; and it is not difficult to perceive, that the very aggressors may, by a forfeiture of the *mock bond*, be again placed in possession of the smuggled property."

In 1817, General David B. Mitchell, Governor of Georgia, resigned the Executive chair, and accepted the appointment, under the Federal Government, of Indian Agent at the Creek Agency. He was afterwards charged with being concerned, in the winter of 1817 and 1818, in the illegal importation of Africans. The documents in support of the charge, and those also which he offered to disprove it, were placed by the President in the hands of Mr. Wirt, the Attorney-General of the United States, who, on the 21st of January, 1821, made a report on the same. From this report, it appears that no less than ninety-four Africans were smuggled into Georgia, and carried to Mitchell's residence. Mr. Wirt concludes his report with the expression of his conviction,

"That Gen. Mitchell is guilty of having prostituted his power as Agent for Indian Affairs at the Creek Agency, to the purpose of aiding and assisting in a conscious breach of the Act of Congress of 1807, in prohibition of the slave-trade, and this from mercenary motives."*

On the 22d of May, 1817, the Collector at Savannah wrote to the Secretary of the Treasury:

"I have just received information from a source on which I can implicitly rely, that it has already become the practice to introduce into the State of Georgia, across St. Mary's River, from Amelia Island, E. Florida, Africans who have been carried into the port of Ferdinanda. It is further understood that the evil will not be confined altogether to Africans, but will be extended to the worst class of *West India slaves.*"

Captain Morris, of the Navy, informed the Secretary of the Navy, 18th of June, 1817:

"Slaves are smuggled in through the numerous inlets to the westward, where *the people are but too much disposed to render every possible assistance.* Several hundred slaves are now in Galveston, and persons have gone from New Orleans to purchase them."

On the 17th of April, 1818, the Collector at New Orleans wrote to the Secretary of the Treasury:

"No efforts of the officers of the customs alone can be effectual in preventing the introduction of Africans from the westward: to put a stop to that traffic, a naval force suitable to those waters is indispensable; and vessels captured with slaves *ought not to be brought into this port, but to some other in the United States, for adjudication.*"

* Senate Papers, 1st Session, 17th Cong., No. 93.

We may learn the cause of this significant hint, from a communication made the 9th of July, in the same year, to the Secretary, by the Collector at Nova-Iberia.

"Last summer I got out State warrants, and had negroes seized to the number of eighteen, which were part of them *stolen out of the custody of the coroner;* the balance were condemned by the District Judge, and the informers received their part of the net proceeds from the State Treasurer. Five negroes that were seized about the same time, were tried at Opelousa in May last, by the same judge. He decided that some Spaniards that were supposed to have set up a *sham claim*, stating that the negroes had been *stolen from them on the high seas*, (!!) should have the negroes, and that the *persons who seized them should pay half the costs*, and the State of Louisiana the other. This decision had such an effect as to render it almost impossible for me to obtain any assistance in that part of the country."

The Secretary of the Treasury, in a letter to the Speaker of the House of Representatives, 20th January, 1819, remarked:

"It is understood that proceedings have been instituted under the State authorities, which have terminated in the SALE of persons of color illegally imported into the States of Georgia and Louisiana, during the years 1817 and 1818. There is no authentic copy of the acts of the Legislatures of these States upon this subject in this department, but it is understood that in both States, Africans and other persons of color, illegally imported, are directed to be *sold for the benefit of the State*."*

We have now, we think, proved from high authority, that notwithstanding the legal prohibition of the slave-trade, the people, the courts, and the executive authority in the planting

* In 1835, the New York Journal of Commerce asserted that vessels had been recently fitted out in that port for the African slave-trade.

The Boston Express, of 17th December, 1838, thus gives the substance of the statements made by Mr. Elliott Cresson, of the Pennsylvania Colonization Society, in a public address delivered a few days before in Boston:

"Out of 177 slave ships which arrive at Cuba every year, five-sixths are owned and fitted out from ports in the United States, and the enormous profits accruing from their voyages remitted to this country. One house in New York received lately for its share alone the sum of $250,000. Baltimore is largely interested in this accursed traffic as well as New York—and even Boston, with all her religion and morality, does not disdain to increase her wealth by a participation in so damnable a business. A gentleman of the highest respectability lately informed Mr. Cresson that a sailor in this city told him that he had received several hundred dollars of hush money, to make him keep silent, and when he mentioned the names of his employers, the gentleman says he was actually afraid to repeat them, so high do they stand in society. A captain in the merchant service, from New York, was lately offered his own terms by two different houses, provided he would undertake a slave voyage."

Of the truth of these statements we know nothing.

States, have afforded facilities for the importation of Africans. It now becomes important to inquire how far the Federal Government has enforced the penalties imposed by the Act forbidding the trade.

On the 7th of January, 1819, Joseph Nourse, Register of the Treasury, in an official document submitted to Congress, certified that there were no records in the Treasury Department of any forfeitures under the act of 1807, abolishing the slave-trade! So that notwithstanding the thirteen or fifteen thousand slaves, said by Southern members of Congress to be annually smuggled into the United States — notwithanding American citizens were declared by a Judge of the Supreme Court to be "steeped to their very mouths in this stream of iniquity," *not one single forfeiture* had in eleven years reached the Treasury of the United States! Mr. Nourse, however, states that it was *understood* that there had been recently *two* forfeitures, one in South Carolina, and the other in Alabama. Respecting the first, we have no information; of the latter, we are able to present the following extraordinary history.

The Collector at Mobile, writing Nov. 15, 1818, to the Secretary of the Treasury, remarks:

"Should West Florida be given up to the Spanish authorities, both the American and Spanish vessels, it is to be apprehended, will be employed in the importation of slaves, with an ultimate destination to this country; and even in its present situation, the greatest facilities are afforded for obtaining slaves from Havana and elsewhere through West Florida. *Three* vessels, it is true, were taken in the attempt last summer, but this was owing rather to *accident* than any well-timed arrangement to prevent the trade."

These three vessels brought in one hundred and seven slaves. By what mistake they were captured we are not informed, but another letter from the collector shows us how the "accident" was remedied.

"The vessels and cargoes and slaves have been delivered on *bonds;* the former to the owners, and the slaves to three other persons. The Grand Jury found true bills against the owners of the vessels, masters and supercargo, *all of whom have been discharged* — why or wherefore, I cannot say, except that it could *not* be for want of proof against them."

From this letter it is most probable that the forfeiture of which Mr. Nourse had heard, if any in fact occurred, was the collusive forfeiture of the bonds.*

We most freely acknowledge that so far as the statute book is to be received as evidence, there can be no question of the sincerity and zeal with which the Federal Government has labored to suppress the African slave-trade: but laws do not execute themselves, and we shall now appeal to the statute book, and to the minutes of Congress, to convict the government of gross hypocrisy and duplicity.

It is difficult to understand why men who are engaged in breeding slaves for the market, or why men who are employed in buying and working slaves, should have any moral or religious scruples about the African trade; and when we find political leaders professing to be ready to sacrifice the Union to secure the perpetuity of the *American* trade, we may surely be excused for doubting the sincerity of their denunciations against the foreign traffic.

In the year 1817, a new and sudden zeal was excited in Congress for the abolition of the trade, and this zeal, as we shall see, was the offspring of the efforts of Virginia to colonize the free blacks. The Legislature of that State had for years been anxious to get rid, not of the slaves, but of the free negroes. On the 1st of January, 1817, the Colonization Society, the result of Virginia policy, was organized at Washington, and immediately presented a memorial to Congress, praying for national countenance. The committee to whom this memorial was referred, reported (11th Feb.) two resolutions: — 1st, calling on the President to enter into negotiations with foreign powers for the "entire and immediate abolition of the traffic in slaves;" and 2d, asking him to obtain the consent of Great Britain to our colonizing free people of color at Sierra Leone. Thus early was the cause of colonization connected with the agitation in Congress about the slave-trade; a connection from which, as we shall presently see, the Society reaped a very large pecuniary

* The documents we have quoted on this subject, are to be found in Reports of Committees. 1st Sess., 21st Cong., No. 348.

advantage. The resolutions were not acted on, and the next session, Mr. Mercer, regarded in Virginia as the father of the Society, succeeded in getting a vote of the House (Dec. 30th, 1817,) instructing the committee on the memorial from the Society, to report on the expediency of rendering the laws against the slave-trade more effectual. Of this committee Mr. Mercer was himself the chairman; and he recommended in his report, that the President should take measures for procuring *suitable territory in Africa for colonizing free people of color, with their own consent;* and that armed vessels should occasionally be sent to Africa for the purpose of interrupting the trade. The suggestions of the committee were not adopted, but the ensuing session, (March 3, 1819,) a new act against the slave-trade was passed, which gave "a local habitation" to the present colony of Monrovia, and was equivalent to a liberal and national grant to the Society. By this act, the President was authorized to restore to their country, such Africans as might be captured on board of slavers, or illegally introduced into the United States; and he was to appoint agents on the coast to receive them. Mr. Monroe, then President of the United States, was a zealous colonizationist, and was afterwards placed at the head of an auxiliary. Let us see what use he made of the powers entrusted to him by the act of 1819. Many years after, an inquiry was instituted in Congress as to the expenditures under this law, and the Secretary of the Navy (1830,) reported that

"Two hundred and fifty-two persons* of this description (recaptured Africans,) have been removed to the settlement provided by the Colonization Society on the coast of Africa; and that there had been

* We have not been able to ascertain from what sources these Africans were obtained, but that they were not *all* of them trophies of the zeal of our cruisers in the cause of humanity, appears from the following extracts from official documents: "There are now in the charge of the Marshal of Georgia, 248 Africans, taken out of a South American privateer, the 'General Ramirez,' *whose crew mutinied, and brought the vessel into St. Mary's, Georgia.*" *Letter of Secretary of Navy, February 7th,* 1821. "A decision of the Supreme Court, in the case of the 'General Ramirez,' placed under the control of the Government from 125 to 130 Africans, who were brought into Georgia, and arrangements are making *to send them to the Agency.*"—(Liberia.) *Report of Secretary of Navy, Dec. 2d,* 1825.

expended therefor, the sum of *two hundred and sixty-four thousand seven hundred and ten dollars.* * * * The practice has been to furnish these persons with provisions for a period of time after being landed in Africa, varying from six months to one year; to provide them with houses, arms and ammunition; to pay for the erection of fortifications, for the building of vessels for their use, and, in short, to *render all the aid required for the founding and support of a colonial establishment.*"

A report from Amos Kendall, Fourth Auditor of the Treasury, discloses more particularly the manner in which the "*Act in addition to the Acts prohibiting the slave-trade,*" was made subservient to the purposes of the Colonization Society.

"In May, 1822, the Secretary of the Navy directed that *ten* liberated Africans should be delivered to Mr. J. Ashmun for transportation to Africa. The Secretary authorized him to take out, at the *expense of the Government*, 15,000 hard brick, 5,000 feet of assorted timber, 30 barrels of ship bread, eight of tar, four of pitch, four of rosin, and two of turpentine." * * * "In the simple grant of power to an agent to *receive* recaptured negroes, it requires broad construction to find a grant of authority to colonize them, to build houses for them, to furnish them with farming utensils, to pay instructors to teach them, to purchase ships for their commerce, to build forts for their protection, to supply them with arms and munitions, and to employ the army and navy in their defence."*

It cannot be denied that the friends of colonization had great encouragement to proceed in their warfare against the slave-trade. Accordingly, Mr. Mercer, as the chairman of the committee to whom a memorial from the Society had been referred, reported (May 9th, 1820,) a *bill incorporating the Society*, and another *making the slave-trade piracy;* and likewise two resolutions, the first, requesting the President to negotiate with foreign powers, "*on the means of effecting an entire and immediate abolition of the slave-trade;*" and another requesting him to make such use of the public armed vessels as may aid the *efforts of the Colonization Society.* The first resolution was adopted, and the consideration of the other postponed. A few days after, (May 15th,) the Act making the African slave-trade piratical, was passed. But laws do not execute themselves: and if any

* Senate Documents, 2 Sess., 2 Cong.

slave-trader has suffered death in the United States as a pirate, we confess our ignorance of the fact.*

It certainly required some little assurance in the House of Representatives thus to order a negotiation with foreign powers for the suppression of the trade, when the Federal Government had itself been so remiss in its efforts, that both Houses of the British Parliament had, the year *before*, (July, 1819,) addressed the Prince Regent, praying him to renew "his beneficent endeavors, more especially with the Governments of France and *the United States of America*, for the effectual attainment of an object we all profess to have in view:" and a negotiation had already been actually commenced with our Government, proposing to concede "to each other's ships of war, a qualified right of search, with a power of detaining the vessels of either State, *with slaves actually on board;*" † and a positive refusal to this proposal had already been returned. There is no evidence that our Government ever took a single measure in consequence of this resolution; and under all the circumstances of the case, it is not uncharitable to believe that it was intended to save appearances.

We must now beg the reader's attention to a new act in this farce of suppressing the slave-trade.

In 1814, our government concluded a war with Great Britain, and in the treaty of peace, gave its assent to the following article:

> "Whereas the traffic in slaves is irreconcilable with the principles of humanity and justice; and whereas His Majesty and the United

* In 1820, a slave vessel, the Science, fitted out at New York, and commanded by Adolphe Lacoste, of Charleston, South Carolina, was captured on the coast of Africa, by the United States ship Cyane, and Lacoste sent home for trial. The trial took place in the Circuit Court of the United States, before Judge Story. The evidence was full and unequivocal; Lacoste was convicted, and sentenced to five years' imprisonment, and to the payment of a fine of $3,000. Had the crime been committed a few months later, the penalty would have been death, under the new law, declaring the trade piracy. Lacoste received a *full* pardon from the President; and the reader may thence judge, whether, had he been convicted as a pirate, his life would have been much in danger. The reasons assigned for the pardon were youth, previous good character, and an aged mother. *Niles's Register, April* 20, 1822.

† Letter from Lord Castlereagh to Mr. Rush, June 20, 1818.

States are desirous of continuing their efforts to promote its entire abolition, it is hereby agreed, that both the contracting parties shall use their best endeavors to accomplish so desirable an object."

On the 29th of January, 1823, Mr. Stratford Canning, the British Minister at Washington, addressed a letter to the Secretary of State, reminding him of this pledge, and calling on the American Government either to assent to the plan proposed by Great Britain, or to suggest some other efficient one in its place. *After* the reception of this letter, and *before* the return of an answer, the following resolution was passed (28th Feb.) by the House of Representatives, viz.:

"Resolved, That the President of the United States be requested to enter upon and prosecute, from time to time, such negotiations with the several maritime powers of Europe and America, as he may deem expedient, for the effectual abolition of the African slave-trade, *and its ultimate denunciation as piracy, under the laws of nations, by the consent of the civilized world.*"

The British Minister was then informed, in answer to his letter, that the *plan* proposed by the United States was a *mutual* stipulation to annex the penalty of piracy to the offence of participating in the trade, by the citizens and subjects of the two parties. Mr. Canning replied, that

"Great Britain desires no other, than that any of her subjects who so far defy the laws and dishonor the character of their country as to engage in a trade of blood, proscribed not more by the act of the Legislature than by the national feeling, should be detected and brought to justice even by *foreign hands*, and from under the protection of her flag."

He, nevertheless, urged a limited concession of the right of search, as the only *practical* cure of the evil; and he communicated the fact, that so late as January, 1822, it was stated officially by the Governor of Sierra Leone, "that the fine rivers of Nunez and Pongas were entirely under the control of renegade European and *American* slave-traders." He then proposed that a mutual right of search should be conceded, to be confined to a fixed number of cruisers on each side; to be restricted to certain parts of the ocean; and that to prevent abuses, these cruisers should act under regulations prepared by mutual consent; and moreover, that this concession should be made only for a short time, that if found inconvenient in practice, it might be discontinued.*

But the Republic stood on its dignity, and would not condescend to yield a concession which Great Britain, France, Spain, Portugal, the Netherlands, Denmark, Sweden, Tuscany, the Hans Towns, Naples, and Sardinia, have thought it no degradation to make in the cause of humanity.

But still the American Government was *very* anxious that every man of every nation, who engaged in the traffic of slaves on the coast of Africa, (not in the District of Columbia,) should be hung by the neck till he was dead; and forthwith, in obedience to the resolution of February 28, despatches were forwarded to the Cabinets of France, Spain, Portugal, Russia, the Netherlands, Buenos Ayres, and Colombia, announcing the desire of the United States to declare the trade piracy, by the common consent of nations.

It is generally understood that a pirate is an enemy to the human race, and may be put to death by any government in whose hands he may chance to fall. If this was not the purport of the proposition to the House of Representatives, that the trade should be denounced "as PIRACY under the laws of nations, by the *consent of the civilized world*," we may well ask, what did it mean?

On the 24th of June, 1823, instructions were forwarded to our Minister in England, authorizing him to conclude a treaty with Great Britain on the subjcet of the slave-trade, on certain conditions. "The *draft* of a convention," says the Secretary of State, "is herewith enclosed, which, IF the British Government should agree to treat upon this subject, on the basis of a *legislative* prohibition of the slave-trade by both parties under the penalties of PIRACY, you are authorized to propose and conclude."

Now it should be remembered that at this time the trade was not piratical by the British laws, and the English Ministry could not make it so by treaty. We therefore proposed a *condition*

* Letter from Mr. Stratford Canning, to the Secretary of State, April 18, 1823.

with which possibly they might not have it in their power to comply. The ministry, however, when made acquainted with the condition, felt confident of the acquiescence of Parliament. "The British Plenipotentiaries," says Mr. Rush, in his letter to the Secretary of State, "gave their unhesitating consent to the principle of denouncing the traffic as piracy, *provided* we could arrive at a common mind on all the other parts of the plan proposed."

The treaty, nearly verbatim with the draft sent from Washington, was signed at London on the 13th of March, 1824; and a few days afterwards, according to a previous understanding, and in fulfilment of the *condition* exacted by us, Parliament passed an act, declaring that all British subjects found guilty of slave-trading "shall suffer death without benefit of clergy, and loss of lands, goods and chattels, as PIRATES, felons and robbers upon the seas, ought to suffer."

This treaty provided, in substance, that the cruisers of either party on the coast of Africa, *America*, and the West Indies, may seize slaves under the flag of the other, and send them *home* to the country to which they belonged, where they should be proceeded against as pirates. So that in fact, the whole concession made by us to Great Britain amounted to no more than permitting her to arrest *our* pirates, and to deliver them to *our* courts for trial; and in return, she granted us precisely the same right with respect to her pirates.

The treaty was submitted of course to the Senate for ratification, which, under the circumstances of the case, one would think, must have followed as a matter of course. The Senate, however, thought otherwise. The treaty was laid before them on the 30th of April; but as they delayed to act upon it, the British Minister at Washington became uneasy, and on the 16th of May addressed a letter to the Secretary of State, complaining of the postponement of the ratification, especially as the project of the convention had *originated* with the United States, and as Great Britain "had not hesitated an instant to comply with the preliminary act desired by the President," the legislative prohibition of the slave-trade under the penalties of piracy.

The President naturally feeling his own good faith compromitted by the hesitation of the Senate, now sent them a confidential message, urging the ratification of the treaty. He remarked that the rejection of the treaty would subject the Executive, Congress, and the nation,

> "To the charge of *insincerity* respecting the great result of the final suppression of the slave-trade. To invite all nations, with the statute of piracy in our hands, to adopt its principles as the law of nations, and yet to deny to all the common rights of search for the pirate, whom it would be impossible to detect without entering and searching the vessels, would expose us not simply to the charge of inconsistency."

The Senate, after long debates, finally ratified the treaty, in a mutilated form. They struck out the word "America," in the clause authorizing the seizure of slavers on "the coasts of Africa, America, and the West Indies." They also expunged the articles applying the provision of the treaty to vessels *chartered*, as well as owned by the citizens or subjects of either party; and to the citizens or subjects of either party carrying on the trade under *foreign flags;* and they added an article authorizing either party to terminate the treaty at any time, on giving six months' notice.

It will have been observed, from the documents we have quoted, that the slaves imported into the United States, have been chiefly introduced through the Spanish possessions on our southern frontiers, slavers direct from Africa rarely having the hardihood to enter our ports, and discharge the cargoes; while small vessels from the West Indies have occasionally found their way into the southern waters. Of course the treaty as altered by the Senate, would afford but little interruption to this mode of stocking the plantations of Louisiana and the neighboring States.

As *chartered* vessels were excepted, our traders would only have to hire slavers instead of owning them, to be exempted from the hazard of being arrested and sent home for trial, by British officers; or even if on board their own vessels, by running up a *foreign flag*, they would escape the penalties of piracy.

The British Cabinet refused to agree to the treaty thus despoiled of all its efficiency; but with wonderful simplicity, they proposed to restrict the right of search on the coast of America, to the coast of the *southern* States. This proposition was of course promptly rejected by our Minister in England.

The British Government, vainly cherishing the hope that the United States might still consent to some combined effort to destroy a trade they professed to abhor, offered, through their Minister at Washington, to consent to a treaty, word for word the same as the one the Senate had ratified, with the single exception of restoring the word "America." To this, Mr. Clay, then Secretary of State, replied, that

"From the views entertained by the Senate, it would seem unnecessary and inexpedient any longer to continue the negotiation respecting the slave convention, with any hope that it can assume a form satisfactory to both parties. That a similar convention had been formed with Colombia, on the 10th of December, 1824, excepting that the *coast of America was excepted from its operation;* and yet, notwithstanding this conciliatory feature, the Senate *had by a large majority refused to ratify it.*"*

Negotiations have since been renewed on this subject; and France has united with Great Britain, in urging the Cabinet at Washington to coöperate with them in putting an end to the African slave-trade. The correspondence has not been made public, but we learn from the Edinburgh Review, for July, 1836, that the final answer of the American Government is, that

"*Under no condition, in no form, and with no restriction, will the United States enter into any convention, or treaty, or combined efforts of any sort or kind with other nations, for the suppression of this trade.*"

To our readers we leave the task of making their own comments on this history of duplicity and hypocrisy; and proceed to other details.

On the 2d of November, 1825, the Colombian Minister at Washington, in the name of his government, invited the United States to send delegates to a Congress of the South American

* The documents quoted on this subject, may be found in the State Papers, 1st Sess., 19 Cong., vol. 1; and in Reports of Committees, 1st Sess., 21 Cong., vol. 3, No. 348.

Republics, to be held at Panama. In enumerating the topics to be discussed in the proposed Congress, he remarked:

"The consideration of means to be adopted for the entire abolition of the African slave-trade, is a subject sacred to humanity, and interesting to the policy of the American States. To effect it, their energetic, general and uniform coöperation is desirable. *At the proposition of the United States*, Colombia made a convention with them on this subject, which *has not been ratified by the Government of the United States.* Would that America, which does not think politic what is unjust, might contribute in union, and with common consent, to the good of Africa!"

This document was submitted to the Senate, and on the 16th of January, 1826, a committee of the Senate made a report in relation to it, in which they observe:

"The United States have not certainly the right, and ought never to feel the inclination to dictate to others who may differ with them on this subject," (the slave-trade,) "nor do the committee see the expediency of *insulting other States by ascending the moral chair*, and proclaiming from thence mere abstract principles, of the rectitude of which each nation enjoys the perfect right of deciding for itself."

The remarks made on this occasion by Mr. White, a Senator from Tennessee, are worthy of observation.

"In these new States (the South American Republics,) some of them have put it down in their fundamental law, 'that whoever owns a slave shall cease to be a citizen.' Is it then fit that the United States should disturb the quiet of the *southern and western States* upon any subject connected with slavery? I think not. Can it be the desire of any prominent politician in the United States, to divide us into parties upon the subject of slavery? I hope not. Let us then cease to talk about slavery in this House; let us cease to negotiate upon any subject connected with it."

We have seen most abundantly that slave-holders have no objection to talk about slavery in Congress, or to negotiate about it with foreign nations, when the object is to guard their beloved institution from danger. It is only on the abominations of the system, and the means of removing it, that every tongue must be mute, and the Federal Government passive. As that government refuses to enter into any combined efforts for the suppression of this trade, and makes none of its own, we may reasonably suppose that our citizens are *now* largely engaged in it. Let us see if this supposition accords with facts.

PRESENT PARTICIPATION OF CITIZENS OF THE UNITED STATES IN THE AFRICAN SLAVE-TRADE.

In pursuance of a treaty with Spain, certain commissioners are appointed by Great Britain to reside at Havana. On the 25th of October, 1836, these commissioners wrote to their government:

"To our astonishment and regret, we have ascertained that the Anaconda and Viper, the one on the 6th, and the other on the 10th, current, cleared out and sailed from here for the Cape de Verd Islands under the AMERICAN flag. These two vessels *arrived* at the Havana, fitted in every particular for the slave-trade, and took on board a cargo which would alone have condemned as a slaver, any vessel belonging to the nations that are parties to the equipment article."

They remark that the declaration of the American President *not to make the United States a party to any convention on the subject of the slave-trade,*

"Has been the means of inducing American citizens to build and fit in their ports vessels only calculated for piracy, or the slave-trade — to enter this port, and in concert with the Havana slave-traders, to take on board a prohibited cargo, *manacles*, &c., and proceed openly to that notorious depot for this iniquitous traffic, the Cape de Verd Island, *under shelter of the national flag;* and we may add, that while these AMERICAN SLAVERS were making their final arrangements for departure, the Havana was *visited more than once by American ships of war.*"

This statement and others we are are about to present to the reader, explain *the practical results, and probably the secret motives* of the rejection by the Senate of the slave-trade convention with Great Britain. The commissioners proceed:

"Two AMERICAN vessels, the Fanny Butler and Rosanna, have proceeded to the Cape de Verd Islands and the coast of Africa, under the AMERICAN flag, upon the same inhuman speculation. * * * We cannot conceal our deep regret at the NEW and DREADFUL impetus imparted to the slave-trade of this island, by the manner in which some American citizens impunibly violate every law, by embarking *openly* for the coast of Africa under their NATIONAL flag, with the *avowed* purpose of bringing slaves to this market. We are likewise assured that it is intended, by means of this *flag*, to supply slaves for the vast province of TEXAS; agents from there being in constant communication with the Havana slave merchants."*

We are fearful of trespassing upon the patience of the reader while we enter into the details necessary to demonstrate the increased activity given to the trade by the action of the Federal Government; but these details are essential to an exhibition of the horrible duplicity of the government, and the foul disgrace in which the flag of the Republic is steeped, by being made the ægis of the very wretches whom our legislators pretend to regard as pirates.

We learn from Buxton's late work on the present state of the trade, that

"The Venus, said to be sharpest clipper built vessel ever constructed at Baltimore, left that place in July, 1838, and arrived at Havana on the 4th of the August following. She sailed from thence in September for Mozambique; there she took a cargo of slaves, being all this time under *the flag of the United States.* On the 7th of January, 1839, she landed 860 negroes near Havana under Portuguese *colors,*" p. 23.

In certain documents, lately published by the British Parliament we have the *names* of *eleven* vessels, which sailed under the flag of the United States, from Havana to Africa for slaves in 1837, and of *nineteen* more, which sailed in 1838. Major McGregor, special magistrate for the Bahamas, in a letter to Mr. Buxton mentions the wreck of the schooner Invincible, a slaver, on the 28th of October, 1837, and adds:

"The captain's name was Potts, a native of Florida. The vessel was fitted out at Baltimore in America, and three-fourths of the crew were natives of the United States, although they pretended to be only passengers."

The major also mentions another slaver, with a cargo of 160 Africans, being wrecked on one of the islands, and says:

"This pretended Portuguese vessel was fitted out at Baltimore, United States, having been formerly a pilot boat, called the Washington. The supercargo was an American citizen of Baltimore,' pp. 23, 186.

* Buxton's African Slave Trade, p. 21.

Mr. Mitchel Thompson, an officer on board the British ship-of-war Sappho, thus wrote at Jamaica in the spring of 1839, to a gentleman of Philadelphia:

"Almost *half* the vessels employed in this trade and furnished to either the Spaniards or the Portuguese are from America, and seem to have been built at Baltimore, from which place they sail chartered for some port in Cuba with *lumber;* which lumber is converted into slave-decks on their arrival at the destined port. To this is now added copper, casks, and food, with the necessery slave irons; and now also is added the requisite number of Spaniards as part complement of the ship's company; *with American papers and flag, they escape our cruisers, as the concession of the right of mutual search has not been made by America.*"

A recent letter from an officer of the British ship-of-war Pelican, published in the London papers, mentions that this ship had lately captured an AMERICAN schooner, the Octavia of Baltimore, with 220 slaves.

The editor of the Baltimore Chronicle states that Captain McDonald, of the brig North, just arrived from Africa, reported that the Captain of the British brig of war Partaga, told him in conversation, that they had fallen in with several vessels which had the appearance of being slavers, but having *American colors and papers* furnished by the Consul at Havana, he had to let them pass; but afterwards he fell in with them with *slaves on board,* that being proof positive of their true character.

Mr. Buchanan, Governor of Liberia, in a letter written from the colony, and published in the New York Journal of Commerce of July 6, 1839, says:

"Never was the AMERICAN FLAG so extensively used by those pirates upon liberty and humanity as at present. Probably THREE-FOURTHS of the vessels boarded by the English cruisers and found to be slavers are PROTECTED by American PAPERS AND THE AMERICAN FLAG.*

* The American and Russian flag bear very different relations towards the African slave-trade. On the 2d of April, 1836, the Russian Consul in New York, published in the papers, by special instructions from his Government, a "Consular Notice," in which he declared that "no slave-trader, in any circumstances whatever, when seized under the *Russian flag,* or otherwise, can invoke the aid of the Imperial Government to screen him from just and well-merited punishment."

In the spring of 1839, three American slavers were captured by British cruisers, and carried into Sierra Leone. They were the Clara, Wyoming, and Eagle, and all under AMERICAN captains, and furnished with AMERICAN papers. They had no slaves on board, but were fitted up for the trade, having slave-decks, manacles, &c., &c.

At Sierra Leone it was decided that the English courts had no jurisdiction over these vessels, and of course that their capture was unauthorized. But inasmuch as the character of the vessels was obvious, and they were engaged in a trade declared piratical by the American Congress, it was deemed both prudent and friendly to send them home for trial, and they arrived at New York in June last, under the charge of a British ship-of-war. A more unwelcome present could not have been offered to the Federal Government than these three slavers. An acceptance of them would have involved various inconvenient consequences. In the first place the President would have been compelled, by a due regard to the feelings of his southern constituents, to inquire by what authority British officers had presumed to arrest these ships, interrupt their voyages, and transport them across the Atlantic, contrary to the known and recorded will of the Senate of the United States. This would have led to an embarrassing negotiation, and likewise to a very undesirable discussion in the newspapers, and would probably have strengthened the hostility at the North to slavery and the slave-trade. If, on the other hand, the government acquiesced in this treatment of American slavers, then our courts would be occupied in trials in which it would be impossible to avoid touching upon "the delicate subject," and men might be sentenced to the gallows, merely for buying and selling their fellow-men. It would moreover be permitting Great Britain to do without a treaty what she had entreated us to permit her to do by treaty, and which we had refused. An expedient was was adopted which avoided these embarrassments. The Government, it is said, thought proper not to recognize these ships as American property, and therefore declined receiving them. By this course all public judicial investigations and disclosures were prevented; and the whole matter was hushed up as quickly as possible. The avowed reasons for this decision have not been made public.

We will now recall to the recollection of our readers the remark of the British commissioners, that "while the American slavers were making their final arrangements for departure, the Havana was visited more than once by American ships-of-war." In other words our naval officers showed no disposition to arrest such of their countrymen as were engaged in the slave-trade, and to send them home for trial and punishment. It no doubt seems very strange to foreigners that the American navy should be so exceedingly remiss in seconding the zeal of the Federal Government in suppressing the slave-trade — but it is a trite remark that foreigners cannot understand our institutions — the conduct of the navy is perfectly natural, and precisely such as might rationally be expected. We have no knowledge of any slaver having been molested by an American armed vessel for the last fifteen years. It is not necessary for our cruisers to go to Africa to capture slavers. The trade passes our very doors, and slavers are to be found by *those who look for them* off the port of Baltimore, and along the shores of Cuba and Texas.

The New York Journal of Commerce, speaking of the seizure of slavers by *British* cruisers, remarks:

> "The capture of a slaver by an *American* cruiser is a thing unheard of for many years, and wholly unexpected. Scores of slave-vessels are caught every year by British cruisers, and we will not do our national vessels the injustice to suppose that they never could catch any, if they were so *disposed*."

But why should they be "so disposed?" About one-half of our naval officers are the sons of slave-holders, and can we expect that they will voluntarily assist in bringing men to the gibbet for trading in African savages, while their own fathers are engaged in buying and selling their fellow-countrymen?

Again, pecuniary reward, professional promotion, and public applause, are the chief incentives to military enterprise. Our officers have been recently taught that efforts to capture or destroy *fugitive slaves* will be liberally rewarded from the national treasury; but when have they been *paid* for capturing slavers?

It is natural that our young and ardent officers should pant for promotion, and that they should turn their anxious and expectant gaze upon the dispenser of professional favors, the SECRETARY OF THE NAVY. Should they read this gentleman's work, "Slavery in the United States," they will have little hope of getting into his good graces by any exhibition of zeal against the African slave-trade. They will learn from the head of the naval department, that the introduction of negro slaves into our country was in "accordance with the sanction of holy writ, as conveyed in the twenty-fifth chapter of Leviticus," p. 42; and they will be led to infer the benevolent tendency of the traffic from the following authoritative declaration of the innocency and happiness of slavery itself.

> "That slavery is a great moral evil, or that its existence or continuance detracts one tittle, one *atom* from the happiness of the slaves, our own experience and observation directly contradict," p. 126.

We presume Mr. Paulding alludes to the experience and observation acquired in his intercourse with coffle-drivers during his excursion in 1816. Our officers are moreover instructed by the Secretary, that although

> "The white and black races of men are probably the nearest to each other of all these varieties (animals with similar instincts), they are not homogeneous any more than the orang-outang, the ape, the baboon, and the monkey, who possibly may ere long find a new sect of philanthropists to sustain their claim to amalgamation," p. 271.

But should our officers inquire how far public opinion would justify and commend them for breaking up the voyages of American merchants, seizing their vessels, and exposing their commanders and crews to an infamous death, what answer would be returned by *facts*?

The editor of the New York Journal of Commerce declared, in his paper of 20th June, 1835:

> "We pledge ourselves to prove, to the satisfaction of the President or Secretary of War, that slave-ships have, within the past year, been actually fitted out at the port of New York."

Has the Secretary of War, the President, or any grand jury called on the editor to redeem his pledge?

The New Orleans Courier of May 21, 1839, after commenting on the present extent of the African slave-trade, remarks:

"If such have been the results produced by the injudicious efforts of the English philanthropists, we may well doubt the *policy* of the law of Congress which has prohibited the importation of slaves from Africa, — a policy, that by all we can learn, has no other effect than to cause the planter of Louisiana to pay to the Virginia slave-holder one thousand dollars for a negro which *now* in Cuba, and by-and-by in Texas, may be bought for half the money. It is known to those acquainted with the character of the African, that he is more patient and less unruly than the Virginia or Maryland negro — his very ignorance of many things makes him less *dangerous* in a community like ours, and his constitution is better suited to our climate. In transporting him from his own country, his position too in civilization is bettered, not worsted.

"The more we examine and reflect on the policy the TEXANS are likely to pursue in this matter, openly or covertly, the more we are convinced that Texas should be annexed to the Union, or else *Congress should repeal the law prohibiting the importation of slaves from Africa.* Otherwise the culture of sugar and cotton in Louisiana will suffer greatly by the cheaper labor which the planters of Cuba and Texas can and will employ."

Here we find a public and cold-blooded proposal to reöpen the African slave-trade. And was this proposal received with horror by the public? Alas! even the northern press has scarcely condemned it. Multitudes of our papers have not noticed it — others have republished the article without a single remark, and the "New York Express," a leading Whig and commercial journal, introduces the diabolical proposal to its readers as "The following *interesting* comments of the New Orleans Courier." Openly to approve the proposal, might offend some fanatical subscribers — openly to condemn it, might injure the Whig party at the South.

The New York "Courier and Enquirer," another Whig and commercial journal, contained (July 27, 1839,) the following editorial:

"Rio Janeiro papers have reached us to the 31st of May last. The chief information from Brazil, which they contain of *interest here*, is that of the capture of two vessels under Portuguese colors by a British ship-of-war, shortly after leaving Rio, on suspicion that they were fitted out for the slave-trade. We are not astonished that these captures should have excited much indignation to Rio. Whatever may be thought of the trade itself, *the people generally are engaged in it and interested in its success*, and it is asking a little too much of them to remain quiet while foreign vessels enter their harbor, take in provisions, remain there as long as it suits their purpose, and then sally forth, break up their enterprises, and bring back their property to be condemned under their very noses."

This appeared shortly after the three American slavers, captured by British cruisers, had been sent into New York — hence the indignation of the editor — hence the news from Rio was "of interest" in New York. It is excessively impudent in the English to take it for granted that the laws of the United States and Brazil against the trade, were enacted in good faith. It matters not that Brazil had declared the trade piracy, — and that the cruisers only delivered to the Brazilian government their own pirates. The Brazilian people, like our own, are engaged in the trade and interested in its success, and it is a great outrage for foreigners to interfere !

Let the officers of our navy learn from this, not to break up the enterprise of our merchants, and to bring back their property to be condemned under their very noses.

RENEWED ACTION OF THE FEDERAL GOVERNMENT IN BEHALF OF THE COLONIZATION SOCIETY.

We have already seen the character and extent of the aid afforded by the Government to the Colonization Society under pretence of providing for *recaptured* Africans. Some of the southern members of Congress, not fully understanding the true tendency of this Society, and believing its influence hostile to slavery, objected to this aid on constitutional grounds, and it was discontinued, after an expenditure of $264,000. That the Society is now more justly estimated appears from the following recent testimonies in its behalf.

On the 10th of January, 1839, Mr. Henry Wise, a member of Congress from Virginia, delivered an address before the Colonization Society of that State. He remarked that a few years since he became suspicious of the Society, in consequence of the sentiments avowed by some of its members. That he had before that time been "the zealous and active friend and advocate of the great original principles of the design, *to secure and fortify the institution of slavery itself* by colonizing the free people of color;" but he confesses that "the line of demarcation is *now* too strongly drawn between abolition and colonization ever to be crossed. Their principles are diametrically opposed to each other, and their warfare will tend to press each to occupy its appropriate ground and position. The Colonization Society must now maintain that great original principle upon which it was founded, "*friendship to the slave-holder.*"

In the month previous to the delivery of this speech, the Baldwin (Alabama) Colonization Society issued an address recommending colonization,

> "Because it proposes to remove from among us a degraded, useless, and vicious race.
>
> "Because we consider the measure of all others best calculated to preserve good order and proper discipline among *our slaves.*
>
> "Therefore we deem the plan of removing them (free blacks) from the United States, the most effectual method of counteracting the abolitionists. It is known that *they* are the most violent opponents which the scheme of colonization has to encounter. *Their penetration has discovered its tendency*, and they denounce it as a scheme originating among slave-holders for the perpetuation of slavery. . . . .
>
> "Nor should it be forgotten, that it (Africa,) is the natural home of the negro race, and at a safe distance, whence *they can never return to the injury of our slave population.*" *African Repository for March*, 1839.

Thus we see that the Society is now regarded as a friend and ally by both descriptions of slave-holders, the breeders and the planters. It is not to be supposed that Mr. Van Buren is an inattentive observer of the signs of the times. Colonization is just now very popular in Virginia, Georgia, Alabama, Mississippi, and Louisiana. Mr. Clay's speech was delivered on the 7th of February, and was certainly calculated to propitiate the slave-holders. He is, moreover, President of the Colonization Society, and it would be unwise to suffer him to engross the influence of "the most effectual method of counteracting the abolitionists." On the 19th of February, twelve days after Mr.

Clay's speech, the intentions of the government were announced in the following letter, which was widely circulated.

"I ought here to inform you that the government of the United States has came to our aid by furnishing cannon, small arms, both muskets, pistols, swords and rockets, and an abundant supply of ammunition, and two fine boats — also made our governor their agent for *recaptured Africans* (!) at a salary of $1500 a year, which is so much money *bestowed on the Society;* and I confidently believe that a ship-of-war will be sent to *the coast of Africa to suppress the slave-trade.* There never was a time when African colonization had so strong claims on the benevolent public.

Respectfully yours,
SAMUEL WILKINSON,
General Agent of the American Col. Soc."

Thus, while Mr. Clay can only make speeches in behalf of the great antidote to abolition, his rival is lavishing upon it the public funds under the palpably false pretence of providing for recaptured Africans. When it is recollected that our navy *recaptures no Africans,* and that if we had any such Africans to restore to their own country, they might be sent to Liberia in the regular vessels at a trifling expense, it must, we think, be admitted that these appropriations to the Colonization Society, and this addition of $1500 per annum to the salary of their governor, is a fraudulent application of the public money, to promote the interests of slave-holders and the perpetuity of slavery.

There are still many at the North who view the *African* slave-trade with abhorrence, and great pains have been taken to impress them with the belief that the colonization of *American* negroes upon the African coast, is the "ONLY efficient means of suppressing it." Here Mr. Van Buren's bounty to the Society is regarded as his contribution to the destruction of this commerce. The New York Journal of Commerce affirms that the late grants "will have an important influence in checking the slave-trade."

African negroes, we well know, sell every slave exported from that continent; we have the testimony of Mr. Madison, that the *white* citizens of the Southern States would not have entered the American Union, had they not been indulged in the African trade for twenty years; and, even now, many of them are anxious for its restoration. But *American negroes* transported to Africa, will put to the blush the civilization, and Christianity, and chivalry of the South, and will manfully resist the temptation to which multitudes of our own citizens readily yield, of making merchandise of their fellow-men! Do we seek to solve this enigma by a reference to the *moral character* of our free negroes? Mr. Clay, the President of the Society, assures us that they are, "of all descriptions of our population, the most corrupt, depraved and abandoned;" and Mr. Mercer, a vice president, pronounces them "a horde of miserable people — the objects of universal suspicion — subsisting by plunder." So far from the Liberian colony being a restraint on the slave-trade, it will become a rendezvous for slavers, and the colonists themselves will be either their victims or factors. We cannot spare room for all the reasons on which this opinion is founded. Let the following *facts* suffice.

"The Liberia Herald mentions the capture of *three* Spanish slavers, by the British brig Curlew, *while lying within the harbor of Monrovia.*" *African Repository for March*, 1836.

"Boats have been sent from the Spanish slavers into the St. Paul's, *and slaves have been bought in that river.*" *Letter from the Governor of Liberia*, 8*th of January*, 1836. *Afr. Rep.*

The St. Paul's penetrates the heart of the colony, and the settlements of Caldwell and Millsburg are on its banks!

"Within a year, FOUR SLAVE FACTORIES have been established almost within sight of the colony." *Captain Nicholson's report to Secretary of the Navy*, 8*th January*, 1837.

"To-morrow, the schooner sails for New Sestos, to take on board a cargo of slaves which I have ready there. I have been obliged to have *one hundred sets of shackles made at Cape Mesurada*"—(Monrovia.)* *Intercepted letter of* 28*th September*, 1838, *from the captain of a slaver to his owners at Havana, and published by British Parliament.*

"On the 15th of February, 1838, arrived at this port, a vessel under American colors named the MONROVIA, last from Liberia, with a bill of sale and list of crew from the *collector of that colony.* This vessel had neither register nor a sea letter. I have ascertained, without

* This letter is dated at *Little Bassa*, in Liberia, and between Monrovia and Cape Palmas.

doubt, that she is a vessel belonging to Don Pedro Blanco,* of the Gallinas, has put in here, directed to his agent, for a fit-out for the coast, and that a cargo of slaves is ready for her. There is a *black* man on board, for a flag captain — *speaks English well* — learned that he is a complete pilot on board to all the inlets between Sierra Leone and Gambia. He *cannot read or write.*

"Don Pedro Blanco's *agent in Liberia* is J. N. Lewis, commission merchant." *Letter of February 28th,* 1838, *from British Consul for the Cape de Verd Islands, to Lord Palmerston. British Documents.*

INTERCOURSE OF THE GOVERNMENT WITH THE INDIANS MADE SUBSERVIENT TO SLAVERY.

It has been long customary, in every treaty of peace, after an Indian war, to insert an article for the surrender of prisoners, "white or black," or of "all citizens of the United States, white inhabitant or negroes." It is doubtful whether the southern Indians, in their wars, made any slaves *prisoners*, strictly speaking. Servitude with the Indians is so much lighter than with the planters, that the slaves are ever ready to exchange Christian for heathen masters; and many of them have embraced the opportunity, afforded by Indian wars, of escaping from the "quarters," and seeking refuge in the wigwam.

In 1802, Congress passed a law whereby the government assumed the obligation of indemnifying the citizens for all robberies and trespasses they might suffer from the Indians; and the amount of the indemnification was to be deducted from the annuities or other moneys which might be due from the government to the Indians. The treaty stipulation to restore negroes was nugatory in practice, as the Indians felt probably no disposition to execute it. Still the stipulation imposed an obligation, and laid the foundation of a *claim* on the part of the government. These introductory remarks will aid the reader in comprehending the extraordinary and iniquitous transaction we shall now proceed to unfold.

On the 8th of January, 1821, a treaty was concluded at Indian Springs, between the United States and the Creek nation. The federal negotiators were D. M. Forney, of North

* A notorious slave merchant, connected with a house in Havana.

Carolina, and David Meriwether, of Georgia. By this treaty the United States purchased certain lands belonging to the Creeks. The consideration for these lands was two-fold; first a certain sum of money, and secondly, the following stipulation in the words of the treaty:

> "And as *a further consideration* for said cession, the United States do hereby agree to pay the State of *Georgia*, whatever balance may be found due by the Creek nation, to the citizens of that State, whenever the same shall be ascertained in conformity with reference made by the Commissioners of Georgia, and the chiefs, headmen, and warriors of the Creek nation, to be paid in five annual instalments, without interest, *provided* the same shall not exceed the sum of $250,000, the Commissioners of Georgia executing to the Creek nation a full and final relinquishment of all claims of the citizens of Georgia against the Creek nation, for property taken or destroyed PRIOR to the Act of Congress, of one thousand eight hundred and two, regulating the intercourse with the Indian tribes." *See Treaty, Laws of U. S.—6th Vol.* p. 771.

For whatever trespasses the Georgians had suffered from the Creeks *since* 1802, they had been compensated by the Federal Government. An opportunity was now offered for wringing from these poor and ignorant savages, compensation for every alleged injury committed by them from the first settlement of the country up to the year 1802! They were about to sell their lands, and were made to believe that they were answerable for every pig and calf which they or their ancestors had ever stolen from their pale-faced neighbors. The Georgians, however, kindly agreed that they would not demand more than $250,000; and the United States most benevolently stipulated, that if the Georgians would give the Creeks a receipt in full, that then, whatever balance should be found due on these claims, should be paid out of the national treasury; this stipulation being expressly declared to be part of the consideration given for the land, it is therefore obvious, that $250,000 of the consideration or price of the land was withheld by the United States, wherewith to liquidate "whatever balance," not exceeding that sum, might be found due to the Georgians. This is certainly one of the most extraordinary treaties in the annals of diplomacy. The claims to be paid are all undefined, and unlimited as to time, except that no one *can be* of a shorter standing than *twenty years!* And these ancient and undescribed claims, after laying dormant for twenty years, are now to be paid for by a set of poor half-famished Indians, who can neither read nor write — paid for, too, out of the price which the Federal Government is pleased to allow them for their lands; and this compulsory payment and virtual robbery are disguised under the form of a treaty, to which the Indians are required to attach their *marks.* Among *ourselves,* contracts and debts cannot ordinarily be enforced after *six* years; but no statute of limitations is permitted to avail the helpless tenant of the forest. When claims between white men are to be liquidated by a tribunal, each party is heard in his own behalf; but in the present case, a commissioner, appointed by the President, heard the allegations of the Georgians only, and awarded them what sums he thought proper, from funds honestly belonging to the Creeks.

The testimony offered by the Georgians has not been published, but we may readily believe it was of a character according with the whole transaction. The award was communicated to Congress,* and we extract from it the following summary of allowance for SLAVES, alleged to have been killed or stolen by the Creeks, viz.:

In the year	1799,	2 slaves,	$800
	1780,	1 "	300
	1781,	3 "	1,100
	1782,	2 "	750
	1784,	2 "	1,000
	1788,	49 "	17,600
		1 "girl,"	250
		1 "negro woman killed,"	325
	1789,	8 slaves,	2,320
		1 "negro boy,"	400
	1790—1801,	21 slaves,	7,950
Total,		91 slaves,	$32,795

This statement gives rise to various reflections. We observe, in the first place, that through the agency of the Federal Government, a Georgia slave-holder recovers from the Indians

* State papers, 1 Sess., 20 Cong., H. of R., Vol. vii, Doc. 268.

$800, for two slaves who had escaped from him or his ancestors FORTY years before! The enormous valuation of these slaves also deserves notice. It seems, slaves are supposed to have been worth, in 1779, when there was no sugar nor cotton cultivation in Georgia, nor man-market in New Orleans, and at a time when the whole State was overrun with foreign troops, and its cities in possession of the enemy, *four hundred dollars a head*, — double the price they commanded after the peace.

From the *dates* of these several claims, we may form some idea of the nature of the testimony by which they were supported. Of eye-witnesses, it is scarcely possible there could have been one — of family traditions, guesses, and assertions, there was, no doubt, abundance. It must not be supposed the Creeks had to pay for negroes only. In the Indian wars occurring between 1779 and 1802, the Georgians lost various other chattels, for which compensation was allowed on the same liberal scale. How the value of a Georgia calf or pig, forty years before, was ascertained, we are not informed; but probably by the same process by which it was discovered, that in 1789 a "negro boy" was worth $400. But whatever was the road travelled by the United States Commissioners, they arrived at the conclusion that the Creeks owed the Georgians, for property taken or destroyed, negroes included, $101,319. This sum, deducted from the $250,000 retained by the Government, left a balance of $148,681.

Can the reader doubt for a moment to whom this balance justly belonged? A certain value was of course set upon the land purchased of the Creeks; a portion of that value was paid in money, and as a "further consideration," the United States assumed the payment of the Georgia claims to the amount of $250,000. Had there been no claims, the money reserved would of course have belonged to the Creeks. But if the extent of the claims was grossly exaggerated, and the Indians were made to believe they owed more than double the real amount, can there be a question, that on every principle of honor and equity the balance left belonged to the Creeks? Thus thought the Creeks, and they accordingly petitioned Congress for this balance, as due to them in part payment for their lands;* but Congress thought differently, and not one cent was ever restored to them.

The Georgians who had been so lucky as to have ancestors who had lost cows, horses, and negroes in the Indian wars, now cast a wistful eye upon this balance. True it was, their antiquated claims had been settled in a manner agreed to by themselves, and receipts in full had been given, and most extravagant compensation had been awarded to them. But still, here was about $150,000, which most certainly did not belong to the Government — and as to paying it to *Indians*, why that was out of the question; and so they modestly asked for it themselves. Their petition was referred to the Committee on Indian affairs; and on the 7th of January, 1834, its chairman, Mr. Gilmer, a representative from *Georgia*, reported in favor of the petitioners. He contended that the claimants were entitled, not merely to the value of the property taken, but *also* to compensation for being deprived of its use.

"A careful examination," proceeds the report, "of the merits of the claims, founded on the *increase* of the *female* slaves which were taken and carried away by those Indians, would, it is believed, lead to a similar result. Those who are at all conversant with the considerations which form the criterion by which the value of slave property is estimated, know that a much higher value is set on a *female* slave, in consequence of an anticipation of increase. Therefore, as the claimant whose female slave was taken by those Indians, and carried away, had a *property in expectancy* in the issue of such female slave, principles of common sense and common justice would award to the rightful owner a restitution of such increase, or an equivalent in lieu thereof."†

People at the North may sometimes count their chickens before they are hatched; but it would have been a still more occult operation for Congress to have calculated the market value, in 1834, of the children which *might* have been born of the "negro woman killed" in 1788; and Mr. Gilmer himself admitted that the subject was attended with difficulty. It was not, however, necessary to enter into such abstruse inquiries;

* State papers, 2 Sess., 20 Cong., Vol. ii, Doc. 80.

† Reports of Committees, 1 Sess., 23 Cong., Doc. 140.

all that was wanted was the adoption of some rule which would certainly *absorb the whole balance*, and at the same time give to a transfer to the pockets of the Georgians of money belonging to the Creeks, the *appearance* of a payment under the treaty. It was discovered that an allowance of interest at the rate of six per cent. on the several awards, from the *date* of each claim, would answer the purpose. Thus, on the award of $800 for two slaves taken in 1779, *fifty-five* years' interest, or $2,640, would be allowed. In this way the claimants would get the entire balance, and might divide it *pro rata* among them. Mr. Gilmer accordingly reported a bill, allowing the interest: and it is needless to say that it became a law.*

Having witnessed the justice meted by the Federal Government to the Creek Indians, we request the reader's attention to the treatment experienced by the Seminoles, and to

THE ORIGIN OF THE FLORIDA WAR.

It will be recollected that in 1816 the slave-holders complained that their fugitive slaves found refuge in Florida, then be-

* The claim for interest was early made, and was refused by the President, on the report of the Attorney-General, Mr. Wirt, to whom it had been referred. The report, after showing that the demand for interest was not justified by law or practice, proceeded to insist that it was, moreover, *inequitable.* The following extract places in a strong light the injustice of Gilmer's bill, and the servility of the northern members who voted for it.

"If the Commissioner, in assessing these damages, has given to the citizens of Georgia strict and stinted measure, there is nothing offensive to equity in their asking for interest; but if he has already given them *vindictive,* and even *double* damages, the addition of interest to *such* damages is not, I think, a demand for which equity, of her own accord, would cry aloud. . . . . Has the Commissioner been strict in calling on the Georgia claimants for *proof* of the affirmative fact that the property for which they made their claims was *in being, and within* the Creek nation at the date of the respective treaties? On the contrary, he has, in *every instance, presumed this fact in favor of the claimants, without proof.* . . . . As to the standard of value — the epoch, with relation to which the values are to be considered, is from 1783 to 1802; that is, from twenty to forty years ago. The region of country to be regarded with reference to the same subject, is the frontiers of Georgia. In relation to *that country,* and in relation to *that time,* negroes, old and young, men, women and children, are valued at an average of $365.-80; horses of all ages and descriptions are valued at an average of $87.41: and in the same proportion in regard to other articles, which I understand is fixing the property at an average of *double its value* at that time, and in that quarter of the country. If this be so, equity, so far from demanding, would revolt from the proposition of adding interest to such a valuation — it would be usury, not interest — prodigality, not justice." *Rep., No.* 128, 1 *Sess.,* 20 *Cong.*

Yet this usury and prodigality were voted to the Georgia slave-holders by northern members, at the expense of the Indians.

longing to the crown of Spain; and that, regardless of the obligations of neutrality, a naval force had been sent by the Government up the river Appalachicola, to destroy a fort containing about 300 negroes, most of whom were slaughtered. This territory was afterwards ceded to the United States; and for several years past, the Government has been waging a relentless and most disastrous war against its aboriginal inhabitants, with the avowed design of driving them from the Peninsula. It is not our design to write the history of this war, but merely to expose its true origin, and to explain the motives which have led the whites to insist on the expulsion of the Seminoles, and the causes which have induced the latter to offer a resistance unparalleled in savage warfare, for persevering and desperate courage and ferocity.

The sacrifice on our part, of blood, of treasure, and of military honor in this war, is well known to be prodigious. THIRTY MILLIONS of dollars have already, it is said, been expended — our best generals have been baffled, and their laurels withered; and our troops have perished in great numbers, in contests with their savage foe, and by the sickliness of the climate. And yet no rational cause is assigned by the Government for this disastrous war. No reason is given why it is necessary, at all hazards, and at every expense, to drive the Seminoles from Florida. The whites are few in number, have far more land than they can occupy, and certainly do not want the wet and unwholesome everglades possessed by the Indians, and into which, we are told, white men can only penetrate at certain seasons of the year, without exposing their lives to almost certain destruction. But were the Seminoles so *numerous* that it was necessary to remove them, to make room for the whites, or so powerful as to render it unsafe to plant white settlements in Florida? We learn from official reports, that they numbered about 3000! *

* I herewith enclose for your information, a copy of the general plan of operations which I have adopted for the removal of the Seminoles. I have assumed that the round number of *three thousand* embraces all, of every description." *Wiley Thompson, Jr., Agent, Sept.* 3, 1835. "I consider the population, *including negroes*, not to exceed 3000, of which I should say 1600 ARE FEMALES." *Joseph Harris, Disbursing Agent of Florida Indians, Sept.* 29, 1835.

Major-General Jessup, the commanding officer of the army, and well acquainted with the existing condition of the Territory, in a letter to the Secretary of War, Feb. 11, 1837, makes the following candid avowal:

"We have committed the error of attempting to remove them (the Seminoles) when their lands were *not* required for agricultural purposes; when they were *not in the way* of the *white* inhabitants, and when the greater portion of their country was an *unexplored wilderness*, of the interior of which we were as ignorant as of the interior of China. . . . . I do not consider the country south of Chickasa Hatchee *worth the medicines* we shall expend in driving the Indians from it."

Why, then, all this waste of blood and treasure? We answer — TO PREVENT FUGITIVE SLAVES FROM FINDING AN ASYLUM AMOMG THE INDIANS!

We well know how unwillingly this truth will be received by those among us who contend that the North has nothing to do with slavery; but we appeal to *facts* — and to facts about which there is and can be no dispute.

Florida borders upon two slave States, Alabama and Georgia, and is not far distant from two others, Mississippi and Louisiana. It is not, therefore, surprising that slaves from these States, escaping from their masters, should seek refuge in the huts of the Seminoles. We have already seen that the Federal Government have lately awarded upwards of $5000 to the gallant officers and seamen who destroyed 300 fugitive slaves in Florida, in 1816. The terrible example then made, was not, it seems, effectual; for in 1825, the War Department issued an order on the subject of fugitive slaves among the Seminoles, and the Indian Agent at Tallahassee was directed to take measures to enable the claimants to identify their property for its immediate restoration. "Let the chiefs distinctly understand," wrote the Agent, agreeably to his instructions, "*that they are not to harbor runaway negroes;* and that they will be required to give up such negroes as are now residing within their limits." *

* State papers, 1 Sess., 19 Cong., Vol. iv, Doc. 74, p. 82.

An Alabama paper, speaking of the war, makes the following confession:

"It is the power to entice away and instruct in bush-fighting so many of our slaves, that we would wish to annihilate. *These Seminoles cannot remain in the Peninsula of Florida without threatening the internal safety of the South.*"

In 1834, a petition, signed by about one hundred of the inhabitants of Alachua county, Florida, was presented to President Jackson, praying for his interposition against the Seminoles.

"While the lawless and indomitable people (says the petition) continue where they now are, the *owners of* slaves in our territory, and even in the *States contiguous*, cannot for a moment, in any thing like security, enjoy the possession of this *description of property.* Does a negro become tired of the service of his owner, he has only to flee to the Indian country, where he will find ample safety against pursuit. It is a fact which, if not susceptible of proof, is notwithstanding, and upon good ground, firmly believed, that there is at this time living under the protection of the Seminole Indians, a large number, probably more than one hundred slaves, who have absconded from their masters in the neighboring States and in Florida, since the treaty of Camp Moultrie. Within a few weeks several parties are known to have sought and found shelter in the nation, where they continue secure against every effort of their owners to recover them. . . . . There are, as it is believed, more than five hundred negroes residing with the Seminole Indians, four-fifths of whom are runaways, or descendants of runaways. . . . . It is perfectly obvious that during the existence of such a state of things, the interests of this fertile and promising section of Florida cannot flourish; and we are constrained to repeat, that there is no rational prospect for the better, so long as the *Indians are suffered to remain* in their present location."

The petition concludes with recommending "the immediate and efficient action of the government." *

In the spring of 1839, a sort of armistice was concluded with the Seminoles. This gave vast offence to the slave-holders, and at a public meeting held at Tallahassee, it was resolved, "That the peninsula of Florida is the last place in the limits of the United States wherein the Indians should be *permitted to remain.*" For this assertion, the following among other reasons was assigned: "*If located in Florida, all the runaway slaves will find refuge and protection with them.*"

* 1 Sess., 24 Cong., Doc. 271.

The New Orleans Courier of July 27, 1839, in reference to this same subject remarks:

> "Every year's delay in subduing the Seminoles adds to the risk of their being joined by *runaway slaves from the adjacent States*, and increases the danger of *a rising among the serviles.*"

SLAVERY, then, is the key which unlocks the enigma of the Florida war. To break up a refuge for runaway slaves, THIRTY MILLIONS have already been expended; and if necessary, thirty millions more will be expended for the same object.

But it may be said, however satisfactorily the foregoing facts may account for the conduct of the Federal Government, they do not explain the astonishing and peculiar inveteracy manifested by these Seminoles towards the whites. Other tribes have without difficulty been removed to the west of the Mississippi; why then do these Indians alone offer a resistance to a superior power, more determined and more heroic than perhaps any recorded in history? Again does SLAVERY solve the difficulty.

It is very obvious that the Seminoles have been universally *exasperated.* Their extreme hatred to the whites has unquestionably been owing in part to the gross and wicked frauds which they believe (with too much apparent reason) were practised in the treaty of Payne's Landing, under which they were required to remove from Florida. But the great and prevailing cause of their deep-seated hostility, is to be sought for in a long train of frauds and injuries, of which they have been the victims on account of their slaves; and likewise in the dread of *Christian* slavery, entertained by the negroes who belong to, or have joined the Seminoles.

Of the hostile chiefs, the most active, persevering, and daring, was the celebrated OSEOLA. It is said that this man's mother was seized and carried into Georgia as a slave, under pretence that she was the daughter of a fugitive negress. If this story, which has found its way into the public papers, be true, the wrongs of the mother have been terribly avenged by the son.

That the reader may understand the narratives we are about to lay before him, he must bear in mind that the Seminoles, like their more civilized neighbors, are slave-holders, but, unlike them, they exercise their authority in such a manner as to render their slaves unwilling to leave them. The slaves are in fact little more than tenants of kind and familiar landlords, and regarded with horror the very idea of being transferred from their heathen to Christian masters. But there were many of the whites who were exceedingly anxious to make the transfer. The agent, Wiley Thompson, thus wrote to the Secretary of War (October 27, 1834):

"There are many *very likely* negroes in this nation. Some of the whites in the adjacent settlements manifest *a restless desire* to obtain them, and I have no doubt that Indian-raised negroes are now in possession of the whites."

The volume of documents submitted to Congress, June 3, 1836, and entitled "Seminole Hostilities," from which we quote, contains many illustrations of the agent's assertion; we can spare room for only a portion of them.

It appears that Conchattimico, a Florida chief, was the possessor of a number of slaves, the title to whom was disputed by another Indian, who sold his *claim* to a white man. The means taken by the purchaser to obtain the slaves, are thus described by the agent in his letter to the War Department, January 20, 1834:

"I was informed by the sub-agent, that Conchattimico sent a runner for him not long since; that he immediately repaired to the old chief's town, where he arrived in the night, and found the Indians and negroes greatly excited and in arms; and that very soon thereafter Vacca Pechassie, with fifteen or more of his warriors in arms arrived, for the purpose of aiding in resistance of a threatened violent attempt to force the slaves out of Conchattimico's possession. Persons interested in the adverse claim, were frequently seen hovering about the reserve; and the chief was informed that attempts had been made to bribe commanders of steamboats, on the river, to aid in accomplishing the capture of the slaves. . . . Under such circumstances I could not but approve the order given by the sub-agent to Conchattimico, to *defend his property by force*, should a violent attempt be made to wrest it from him."

Shortly after this, Judge Cameron, of the United States District Court, investigated the white man's claim to these slaves, and pronounced it groundless. Notwithstanding this decision, the claim was again *sold* to a company of whites, who resolved to relieve the chief of his property. But as the chief intended to protect it by force of arms, the enterprise was not free from danger. The expedient resorted to by the kidnappers is thus explained in a letter from the late Governor of the Territory to the Secretary of War, May 23, 1836.

"I herewith transmit you a petition from the Indian chief Conchattimico, to be laid before Congress should you consider that necessary. Taking forcibly the slaves of this chief, after those men had created an alarm among the white inhabitants which resulted in *disarming* the Indians, was an outrage well calculated to rouse them to hostility. The alarm was *concerted* by these violators of all law, solely with the view of obtaining, without danger of resistance, the slaves of the chief. I have no expectation the slaves referred to in the petition will ever be obtained, as I take it for granted they have been carried to a great distance and sold."

This Conchattimico was a *friendly* chief, having no intercourse with the hostile Seminoles; but on the report being raised that he was about to join the enemy, *he surrendered his arms* to quiet the apprehensions, real or affected, of his white neighbors. No sooner had he thus rendered himself defenceless, than a party of Georgians carried off his slaves, twenty in number, and valued at $15,000.

We have already seen how profitable it is for a Georgian to lose a slave among the Indians; but Congress has provided no fund to indemnify the Indian master for the slaves of which *he* may be robbed by Georgians.

Another friendly Florida chief, Pechassie, thus complains to the agent (28th July, 1835):

"I am induced to write you in consequence of the depredations making, and attempted to be made on my farm, by a company of men, negro-stealers; some of whom are from Columbus, (Georgia,) and have connected themselves with Brown and Douglas. It is reported, and believed by all the white people around here, that a large number of them will very shortly come down here, and attempt to take off Billy, Jim, Rose and her family, and others (slaves.) . . . I should like to have your advice how I should act. I dislike to make any trouble, or have any difficulty with the white people; but if they will trespass on my premises, and on my rights, I must defend myself the best way I can. . . Please direct me how to act in this matter. Douglas and his company hired a man, who has *two large trained dogs for the pur-*

pose, to come down and take Billy. The man came, but seeing he could do nothing alone, has gone off somewhere, probably to recruit. He is from Mobile, and follows for a livelihood catching runaway negroes with these large dogs."

By a letter from the United States Attorney, we find that Pechassie was subsequently "robbed of all the negroes he had, six in number."

As these robberies were committed on *friendly* chiefs, and *after* the commencement of the Seminole war, they excited the attention and alarm of the officers of government, and hence probably it is that official notice was taken of them. They may give us some idea of the provocations which preceded and caused the war. Indeed, the documents before us incidentally show, that the "likely negroes" of the Seminoles now in arms, were as strongly coveted by the whites, as the slaves of the friendly chiefs. By a treaty made with the Seminoles in 1832, the Federal Government, with its usual solicitude for the interests of slave-holders, assumed the payment of all claims on the Indians for "SLAVES and other property," to the amount of $7,000. A scramble of course ensued for the money, and a voluminous correspondence took place between the agent and the Secretary of War, respecting claims for Indian slaves; and it appears that the Seminoles had been harassed for years by the contrivances of the whites to rob them of their slaves. The following is a sample. It seems that a Mrs. Hanna claimed a negro woman and *her increase*, in possession of the Seminoles. The claim had been made known to the War Department, and so long ago as the 8th of March, 1828, the following mandate had been issued to the Indian agent:

"The Secretary of War directs that you *forthwith* deliver to Mary Hanna, widow, or her agent, the slaves *claimed* by her, and take a bond imposing the obligation on her to abide by such decision as it may be esteemed proper to seek, in testing the right of ownership in the property in question."

We have here a specimen of the justice meted by our government to the Indians. A woman claims a slave in the possession of an Indian. Without the slightest inquiry into the justice of the claim, the property is ordered to be wrested *forthwith* from the possessor and delivered to the claimant, and then, as if in utter mockery, the woman is to give her bond to abide any decision that may hereafter be made as to the legality of her claim. Who is to obtain this decision? Certainly not the woman; and should the poor ignorant Indian go to law, where would he look for Mrs. Hanna or her slaves? From some cause not explained, the wicked and absurd order of the Secretary was not executed; and on the 2d of March, 1835, *seven* years after, a second order from the Secretary of War directed the agent "to afford whatever facilities may be in his power, upon the *claim being established by proper proof before the competent tribunal*, to have the property restored to Mrs. Hanna." Should the reader be struck with the remarkable *moral* difference between these two orders, the explanation is easy,—the office was filled at the time of the first order by a slave-holder; at the time of the second, by a northern gentleman. The agent now investigated the case, and it was discovered that the father of Mrs. Hanna, about the year 1815, had sold the woman in question, then full grown, to a Seminole, for forty steers, and had afterwards, as was alleged, *given* the same woman to his daughter; and on this pretended gift Mrs. Hanna claimed, not merely the woman, who had now lived twenty-five years with the Indians, but also all the children she had borne within that time!

On the 12th of December, 1834, the agent wrote to the Secretary, that a Seminole woman of the name of Nelly, inherited from her father "a considerable number of slaves," that a man named Floyd claims the whole of them by virtue of a bill of sale, and that Nelly insists that "Floyd imposed on her by presenting for her signature a bill of sale for all the negroes, instead of a written authority to him to recover some for her."* The agent adds, he has seen no one who pretends that Floyd paid her for the negroes, and that the universal impression is, that she was grossly imposed upon.

If civilized and Christian slave-holders are ready to murder, or, to use Mr. Preston's phrase, to HANG abolitionists for

*A portion of them were claimed by another Indian.

questioning their moral right to hold property in man, we may judge what must have been the exasperation of the Seminoles at these multiplied attempts to rob them of their slaves.

There is still another mode in which slavery has operated to produce and continue the war in Florida. Although the expulsion of the Seminoles from the peninsula was devoutly desired by the whites, no inclination was felt to send their "likely negroes" to the west of the Mississippi. Of these negroes some were stolen, others claimed under fraudulent pretexts, and others it was proposed to *purchase* of their masters. General R. K. Call addressed a letter to President Jackson, (March 22, 1835,) asking leave "to purchase ONE HUNDRED AND FIFTY" of the Seminole negroes. "These negroes," he affirms, "are violently opposed to leaving the country. If the Indians are permitted to convert them into SPECIE, one great obstacle in the way of removal may be overcome." The applicant was informed that no permission was necessary, there being no legal prohibition to the Indians selling their slaves. Agents were forthwith despatched to the nation, to buy up negroes. Mr. W. Thompson, the agent, however, assumed the responsibility of prohibiting these agents from commencing their negotiations; and assigned his reasons in a very able letter to the Secretary of War (April 27, 1835):

"The intercourse laws," he remarked, "prohibited the purchase of an Indian pony by a member of civilized society, without permission from the agent; and why, but because the Indian is considered in a state of pupilage, and incapable of protecting himself against the arts and wiles of civilized man? If the Indian's interest in a pony is of so much importance in the estimation of the government, as to require such strict guards to be thrown around it, the protection of his interest in his slave should be esteemed more important, by as much as the latter is more valuable than the former species of property. If, in the regulation of the sale of ponies, the United States exercise a rightful power, the obligation on them to guard the interest of the Indian in his slave, is greatly more imposing. The negroes in the nation dread the idea of being transferred from their present state of ease and comparative liberty, to bondage and hard labor, under overseers, on sugar and cotton plantations.

"They have always had a great influence over the Indians. They live in villages separate, and in many instances remote from their owners, and enjoying equal liberty with their owners, with the single exception that the slave supplies his owner annually from the product of his little field, with corn in proportion to the amount of the crop—in no instance that has come to my knowledge, exceeding ten bushels; the residue is considered the property of the slave. Many of these slaves have stocks of horses, cows and hogs, with which the Indian owner never assumes a right to intermeddle. I am thus particular on this point, that you may understand the true cause of the *abhorrence* of the negroes, *of every idea of change.* And the indulgence so extended to the slave, will enable you to credit the assertion, that *an Indian would almost as soon sell his child as his slave*, except when under the influence of intoxicating liquors."

We have here a picture of certainly a very extraordinary system of slavery. Slaves abhorring a change, and masters no more thinking of selling a slave than a child! But then these Indians were heathen, and perhaps it was from not adverting to this fact, that General Call took for granted they would be glad to convert men, women, and children into SPECIE. President Jackson was equally inconsiderate. The agent was answered:

"The President is of opinion that the opportunity to SELL their slaves will be an inducement for the Seminoles to remove. . . . Nor is it considered that the permission to the Indians to sell would be an inhuman act. It is not to be presumed the condition of these slaves *would be worse than that of others in the same section of country.*"

To this presumption of executive philanthropy, the agent forcibly replied, June 17th, 1835:

"The remark in your letter that 'it is not to be presumed the condition of these slaves would be worse than that of others in the same section of country,' is true; yet you will agree with me, that the same remark would be applicable to myself, or to any other individual in the United States, as we should, if subjected to slavery, be in the precise condition of our fellow slaves. . . . Any one at all acquainted with the condition of the negro, as connected with his Indian owner here, could not fail to admit that the change with him would be *oppressively great.*"

Mr. Thompson farther remarked to the Secretary of War:

"If the Department could be satisfied that the undeniable *abhorrence* of the negroes in this nation to the idea of being transferred from the present state of ease and comparative freedom, to sugar and cotton plantations, under the control of *severe task-masters*,* had been made

* Mr. Thompson was not an abolitionist, but had lately been a representative in Congress from the State of Georgia.

to subserve the views of government, by inducing the negroes to exert their known influence over the Indians, through pledges made to them, accompanied by assurances that their removal west would, more than any thing else, serve to secure the existing relations between them and the Indians, then surely the Department, instead of classing them with the Indian skins and furs, would require a punctilious redemption of those pledges. I have not heard of a solitary Indian desiring the privilege to sell."

The President at last yielded, and the agent was authorized to prohibit any person entering the nation to buy slaves. But it was too late: the negroes well knew how anxious the whites were to possess them, and they reasonably feared that if the Indians were expelled, instead of being permitted to accompany their kind masters, they would be consigned to the cruel and detested service of Georgia and Alabama planters. Hence, impelled by the most powerful motives which can stimulate the heart and nerve the arm of man, they resisted to the utmost the emigration of their masters, and in the deadly struggle that ensued, evinced their devotion to the Indians, and their abhorrence of the whites, by a ferocious and successful courage which may well send a thrill of fearful anticipation throughout the slave-region.

We now submit to our readers whether the facts we have exhibited do not prove beyond all doubt that the blood and treasure expended in the Florida war, have been expended for the *sole purpose of breaking up a refuge for fugitive slaves;* and that the Seminoles have been goaded into their extraordinary and desperate resistance, *by the frauds and robberies of slaveholders?*

THE EFFORTS OF THE FEDERAL GOVERNMENT TO PREVENT THE ABOLITION OF SLAVERY IN THE ISLAND OF CUBA.

At the time of the Congress of Panama, Spain was still at war with her late colonies, and of course they were authorized, by every principle of national law, as well as of self-defence, to carry their arms into the dominions of their enemy. Cuba was at a short distance, devoted to the royal cause, and affording a depot for a naval force ever ready to prey upon the commerce of the republics. Under these circumstances, Mexico and Colombia meditated the invasion and conquest of that island. But these republics, on achieving their own freedom, had given freedom to their slaves; and it was probable that they would manifest equal regard for human rights, were they to become masters of Cuba. These remarks will explain the following extract from the instructions given to the ministers appointed to represent the United States at the Congress:

"It is required by the frank and friendly relations which we most anxiously desire ever to cherish with the new republics, that you should, without reserve, explicitly state that the United States have too much at stake, in the fortunes of Cuba, to allow them to see with indifference a war of invasion prosecuted in a desolating manner, or to see employed, in the purposes of such a war, one race of the inhabitants combating against another, upon principles and with motives that must inevitably lead, if not to the extermination of one party or the other, to the most shocking excesses. The humanity of the United States in respect to the weaker, and which in such a terrible struggle would probably be the suffering portion, and the duty to defend themselves against the *contagion* of such near and dangerous examples, would constrain them, even at the hazard of losing the friendship of Mexico and Colombia, to employ all the means necessary to their security."*

The obvious meaning of all this, in plain English, divested of its diplomatic circumlocution, is simply that the Federal Government, in order to protect the slavery of the South from the shock it might receive from emancipation in Cuba, would, if necessary, go to war with our sister republics to prevent the invasion of that island.

But so long as Spain refused to acknowledge the independence of her revolted colonies, the war would be continued, Cuba would be exposed to invasion, and the slave States to the "contagion," of emancipation. Hence the cabinet at Washington became exceedingly anxious to act the part of peace-makers. Our Minister at St. Petersburg was instructed "to endeavor to engage the Russian Government to contribute its best exertions towards terminating the existing contest between Spain and her colonies. From the vicinity of Cuba to the United States, its

*Letter of Instructions from Mr. Clay, Secretary of State, to Messrs. Anderson and Sargent, May 8th, 1826.

valuable commerce, and *the nature of its population*, their government cannot be indifferent to any political change to which that island may be destined."*

Spain also was implored, through the American Minister at Madrid, to be reconciled to her undutiful children.

"*It is not for the new republics*," said Mr. Clay in his letter, (27th April, 1825,) to Mr. Everett, "that the President wishes you to urge upon Spain the expediency of concluding the war. If the war should continue between Spain and the new republics, and those islands (Cuba and Porto Rico) should become the object and theatre of it, their fortunes have such a connection with the people of the United States, that they could not be indifferent spectators; and the possible contingencies of a protracted war *might bring upon the Government of the United States duties and obligations, the performance of which, however painful it should be, they might not be at liberty to decline*."†

The proposed invasion was abandoned; but the fears of our government were not allayed. The war continued, and some contingency arising from it might give liberty to the tens of thousands in Cuba pining in bonds. A new attempt was made to induce Spain to remove the danger by concluding the war. On the 22d of October, 1829, Mr. Van Buren, then Secretary of State, instructed Mr. Van Ness, our Minister in Spain, to press upon that court a reconciliation with the South American republics.

"Considerations," he remarked, "*connected with a certain class of our population, make it the interest of the southern section of the Union*, that no attempt should be made in that island to throw off the yoke of Spanish dependence; the first effect of which would be *the sudden emancipation of a numerous slave population, whose result could not but be very sensibly felt upon the adjacent shores of the United States*."

Fortunate is it for the cause of humanity, that the greatest republic upon earth had not the power to prevent "the sudden emancipation of a numerous slave population" in the British West Indies, on the 1st of August, 1838, "whose result," blessed

* Letter from Mr. Clay to Mr. Middleton, 10th May, 1825.

† Senate Documents, 1st Sess., 19 Cong., Vol. iii.

be God, is and will be "very sensibly felt on the adjacent shores of the United States." *

The subject of the Panama mission was debated at great length in both Houses of Congress, and frequent allusions were made by the speakers to Cuba. Let us hearken to the sentiments expressed by some of our republican legislators.

Mr. Randolph of Virginia:—"Cuba possesses an immense negro population. In case those States (Mexico and Colombia) should invade Cuba at all, it is unquestionable that this invasion will be made with this principle, — this genius of universal emancipation, — this sweeping anathema against the white population in front, — and then sir, *what is the situation of the southern States?*"

Mr. Johnson of Louisiana:—"We know that Colombia and Mexico have long contemplated the independence of that island (Cuba.) The final decision is now to be made, and the combination of forces and plan of attack to be formed. What, then, at such a crisis, becomes the duty of the Government? Send your ministers instantly to this diplomatic assembly, where the measure is maturing. Advise with them — remonstrate — MENACE, if necessary, against a step so dangerous to us, and perhaps fatal to them."

Mr. Berrien of Georgia:—"The question to be determined is this: With a due regard to the safety of the southern States, can you suffer these islands (Cuba and Porto Rico) to pass into the hands of BUCCANEERS, drunk with their new-born liberty? If our interests and our safety shall require us to say to these new republics, Cuba and Porto Rico *must* remain as they are, we are free to say it, and by the blessing of God and the *strength of our arms*, to enforce the declaration; and let me say to gentlemen, these high considerations do require it. The *vital* interests of the South demand it."

These new republics were stigmatized by this honorable gentleman as buccaneers; not that they were robbers, but because they had *ceased* to rob the poor and helpless; and the evidence of their being drunk with liberty, was their *practical* acknowl-

* The following extract from the Raleigh Register (N. C.) proves that the idea of interference by our Government to prevent West India emancipation, was contemplated by some of the slave-holders.

"*Emancipation of West India Slavery.*

"The news brought by the late arrivals of the determination of Great Britain, to emancipate the slaves of her West India Islands, is replete with interest to the people of this Union. If such a measure is in contemplation, and we see no reason to doubt it, *can our Government look quietly on, and see it consummated?*"

edgment of the principles of human rights, *professed* in our declaration of independence.

Mr. FLOYD of Virginia: — "So far as I can see, in all its bearings, it (the Panama Congress) looks to the conquest of Cuba and Porto Rico; or, at all events, of tearing them from the crown of Spain. The interests, if not safety of our own country, would rather require us to interpose to prevent such an event, and I would rather take up arms to prevent than to accelerate such an occurrence." *Congressional Debates*, 2d vol.

The facts and sentiments we have now exhibited, prove beyond cavil, that this mighty republic volunteered to solicit the aid of foreign monarchs to perpetuate slavery in Cuba, and was strongly disposed to incur the hazard and calamities of war in the cause, — not of liberty, but of bondage.

Having noticed our watchful guardianship over Cuba, we will next advert to

THE HOSTILITY OF THE FEDERAL GOVERNMENT TO HAYTI.

To do justice to this part of our subject, we must beg the patience of the reader while we briefly lay before him a few historical facts.

The Island of St. Domingo was one of the most valuable colonies belonging to the crown of France. It is about 450 miles long, and 150 wide. Its population in 1790, was estimated as follows:

White inhabitants,	42,000
Free colored inhabitants,	44,000
Slaves,	600,000
Total,	686,000

Of the free colored inhabitants, numerically equal with the whites, many were men of education and property, landed proprietors, and the holders of slaves. Still they were debarred from all political privileges on account of their complexion. At the commencement of the French Revolution, the National Assembly abolished this discrimination on account of color, and gave the *free* blacks in the colonies, the same civil rights that were possessed by their white brethren. The pride of the latter led them to refuse submission to this humiliating decree of the mother country, and a *civil* war between the whites and the free blacks ensued. No interference whatever with the rights of slave-holders as such, had at this time been attempted, either in France or the colony; and the dissensions which convulsed the island, for a long time related exclusively to the political condition of the free colored population. In August, 1791, a partial insurrection of the slaves occurred, favored by the quarrels of their masters. In some instances the free blacks united with the whites, in their efforts to suppress the insurrection, and in others, they availed themselves of the aid of the revolted slaves, against the planters.

In 1792, the French Government sent over three commissioners, with 6000 troops, to enforce their decree respecting the free blacks, and to restore order. Many of the planters, however, still resisted, while others took sides with the Government; and the distractions of the island were now aggravated by a civil war between the *whites themselves.*

A portion of the planters, abhorring the attempt of the Government to elevate the free blacks to a political equality with themselves, now intrigued with Great Britain to seize upon the island, and thus to save them from the degrading consequences of republican principles. In compliance with their invitation, conveyed through their agent, M. Charmilly, an expedition was fitted out at Jamaica, for the capture of St. Domingo; and on the 19th of September, 1793, arrived at Jeremie. Only a few days before the appearance of the British fleet on the coast, one of the French commissioners, who happened at the moment to be acting alone, in the absence of his colleagues, having received intelligence of the intended invasion, and knowing the disaffection of the planters, issued a hasty proclamation, giving freedom to all the slaves, as the only means of preserving the colony from conquest.*

The free negroes and the manumitted slaves united in defend-

* The ensuing year, 1794, by a decree of the National Assembly, slavery was formally abolished throughout *all* the French colonies.

ing the island against the invaders, while an army of 2000 of the white inhabitants ranged themselves under the British standard. The French commissioners soon after returned to France; great numbers of the planters emigrated; and the island was virtually abandoned to the blacks, except so much of it as was occupied by the British troops. These troops were from time to time reinforced by detachments from Europe and the West Indies — but in vain. The blacks under Toussaint, who was appointed by the government at home, "Governor General of the armies of St. Domingo," continued the contest for about five years, and finally succeeded in driving the English from the island. Britain being in the mean time at war with France, her naval forces prevented all intercourse between the colony and the mother country: and the blacks, thus left to themselves, declared themselves independent on the 1st of July, 1798, and organized the Government of HAYTI.

The peace of Ameins afforded Bonaparte an opportunity to attempt the subjugation of the island, and the reduction of its inhabitants to slavery.

Early in January, 1802, a French army of 20,000 men was landed in St. Domingo, and various reinforcements afterwards followed.

The war was waged with atrocious cruelty on the part of the French, and the blacks, aided by the climate, succeeded in destroying about 40,000 of their enemies in eleven months; and on the 19th of November, 1802, the wrecks of the invading army surrendered to Dessalines, the black chief. Since this time Hayti has continued an independent nation, perfectly inoffensive in all its foreign relations; and its entire sovereignty is at present fully acknowledged by both France and England, and undisputed by any power on earth.

It is now important to inquire, what has been the conduct of the United States towards this heroic republic?

Twelve years after slavery had been abolished by a decree of the French Government; after the expulsion of the armies of England and France; when for three years not a hostile foot had pressed the soil of Hayti; when a regularly organized government was in full operation; and without one solitary cause of complaint against the new State, the American Congress passed an act, (February 28, 1806,) "to suspend the commercial intercourse between the United States and certain parts of the Island of St. Domingo." These certain parts were defined in the act, to be such parts as were *not* "in the possession and under the acknowledgment of France;" and of course included the whole island. As there was at this time no war in *fact*, between Hayti and France, and the latter was prevented by the naval superiority of England, and her own continental wars, from sending a single soldier to Hayti, the sole object of this act was to distress and harass the Haytiens by depriving them of the bread-stuffs and other necessaries they were accustomed to receive from this country. It was a piece of wanton cruelty, unrequired by the obligations of neutrality; and demanded by France in a tone of arrogance, which would have secured its rejection, had not the intended victims been *black*. Bonaparte, irritated by the loss of his army, and the defeat of his designs upon Hayti, resolved to starve, if possible, a people whom he could not conquer; and he found in the Federal Government, a willing instrument of his vengeance. His Minister at Washington, in a letter to the Secretary of State, demanded an immediate cessation of the commerce between the citizens of the United States and "the rebels of St. Domingo — that race of African slaves, the reproach and the refuse of nature;" and he enforced his demand with the information: "The Emperor and King, my master, expects from the dignity and candor of the Government of the Union, that an end be put to it promptly." * The letter was written in January; and in February the act required was passed, and continued in force for two years.

The invitation to the United States to send ministers to the Congress of Panama, has been already mentioned. In the document conveying the invitation, it was remarked:

"On what basis the relations of Hayti, and other parts of our hemisphere that shall hereafter be in like circumstances, are to be placed, is a question simple at first view, but attended with serious difficulties

* American State Papers, Vol. v, p. 154.

when closely examined. These arise from the different manner of regarding Africans, and from their different rights in Hayti, the United States, and in the American States. This question will be determined at the Isthmus." *

The invitation was accepted, and the instructions to our ministers contained the following:

"Under the actual circumstances of Hayti, the President does not think that it would be proper at this time to recognize it as a new State." †

This, be it remembered, was just a quarter of a century since the Haytiens had declared and maintained their independence, and at a moment when they were enjoying the blessings and exercising the prerogatives of an independent State, and at peace with all the world. And what motive prompted the United States thus to exert its influence to prevent the Congress of Panama from recognizing Hayti "as a new State?"—none other than the apprehension that the admission of a palpable truth, the independence of a black republic, would prove dangerous to the perpetuity of American slavery. Is this slander? Let the members of Congress speak for themselves. The following sentiments were elicited in the debate on the Panama mission:

Mr. Berrien of Georgia:—"Consistently with our own safety, can the people of the South *permit* the intercourse which would result from establishing relations of any sort with Hayti? Is the emancipated slave, his hands *yet* reeking" (thirty-two years after slavery had been abolished by the French Government) "in the blood of his murdered master, to be admitted into their ports, to spread the doctrines of insurrection, and to strengthen and invigorate them, by exhibiting in his own person an example of successful revolt? Gentlemen must be sensible, this cannot be. The great principle of self-preservation will be arrayed against it. I have been educated in sentiments of habitual reverence for the Constitution of the United States: I have been taught to consider the union of these States as essential to their safety. The feeling is nowhere more universal or more strong than among the people of the South. But they have a *stronger* feeling: need I name it? Is there any who hears and does not understand me? Let me implore gentlemen not to call that feeling into *action* by this disastrous policy."

* Senate Documents, 1st Sess., 19 Cong., Vol. iii.

† Letter of Mr. Clay, Secretary of State, 8th May, 1826.

In plain English, the slave-holders love slavery more than they do the Union; and would sacrifice the last, rather than acknowledge as free, a people who had once been slaves.

Mr. Benton of Missouri:—"The peace of eleven States in this Union will not permit the fruits of a successful negro insurrection to be exhibited among them; it will not permit the fact to be seen and told, that for the murder of their masters and mistresses, they are to find friends among the white people of the United States."

Mr. Hamilton of South Carolina:—"It is proper that on this occasion I should speak with candor and without reserve: that I should avow what I believe to be the sentiments of the southern people on this question; and this is, that *Haytien independence is not to be tolerated in any form.* * * * * A people will not stop to discuss the nice metaphysics of a *federative* system, when havoc and destruction menace them in their doors."

Mr. Hayne of South Carolina:—"With nothing connected with slavery can we consent to treat with other nations; and least of all ought we to touch the question of the independence of Hayti in conjunction with the revolutionary governments whose own *history* affords an example scarcely less fatal to *our* repose. These governments have proclaimed principles of liberty and equality, and have marched to victory under the banner of universal emancipation. You find men of color at the head of their armies, in the Legislative halls, and in the Executive departments. * * * * Our policy with regard to Hayti is plain; we NEVER can acknowledge her independence. * * * * Let our Government direct all our Ministers in South America and Mexico, to PROTEST against the independence of Hayti."

Gentlemen, when they talk in a passion, rarely talk wisely or consistently. Mr. Hayne insists that we cannot *touch* the question of the independence of Hayti in conjunction with the American revolutionary governments; and yet in the next breath, he is for opening negotiations with *all* these governments on this very subject. Almost every slave-holder assures us that the slaves, if emancipated, could not take care of themselves; and yet Mr. Hayne proclaims the important fact, that the armies of these same governments have "marched to victory," with colored men at their head; and that colored men are found in their Legislative halls and Executive departments!

Mr. Johnson of Louisiana:—"It may be proper to express to the South American States the unalterable opinion entertained here in regard to the intercourse with them. The unadvised recognition of that island, (Hayti) and the public reception of their ministers, will nearly sever our diplomatic intercourse, and bring about a separation and alienation alike injurious to both. I deem it of the highest concern to the political connection of these countries, to *remonstrate* against a measure so justly offensive to us, and to make that remonstrance EFFECTUAL." *Congressional Debates*, Vol. II.

Thus the gentleman from Louisiana looked upon the recognition of Hayti by other and independent States, as a measure so offensive to us, as to afford us ground for quarrelling with them.

We will now advance twelve years in our history, and see if the lapse of time has softened the hatred of our rulers of Hayti. On the 17th of December, 1838, a petition was presented to the House of Representatives, praying for the establishment of the usual international relations with that republic. No sooner was the purport of the petition announced, than vehement objections were made to it, and no less than thirty-two members had the hardihood to vote against even its reception. They were, however, in the minority; and on a motion being made to refer it to the Committee on Foreign Relations, the chairman of that committee, himself a slave-holder, advocated the reference, as the best way of stifling the discussion, observing that "several similar memorials had been sent there the last session, which had never been reported on. This would take a similar course; *it would never be heard of again.*" With this intimation, the petition was referred. A motion was then made to instruct the committee to report on the petition; but, to stop the discussion, the previous question was moved, and the motion denied by a great majority. A few extracts from the speeches delivered on this occasion may be useful, as showing the temper and logic displayed by the southern members.

Mr. LEGARE of South Carolina:—"It (the petition) originates in a design to revolutionize the South and convulse the Union, and ought therefore to be rejected with reprobation. As sure as you live, sir, if this course is permitted to go on, the sun of this Union will go down—it will go down in BLOOD—and go down to rise no more. I will vote unhesitatingly against nefarious designs like these. They are treason; yes, sir, I pronounce the authors of such things traitors—traitors not to their country only, but to the WHOLE HUMAN RACE."

Mr. WISE of Virginia:—"We are called to recognize the insurrectionists who rose on their French masters. A large portion of those now in power in this black republic, are slaves who cut their masters' throats. Christophe himself was an insurrectionist and a revolutionist.

Their government has the stamp of such an origin. And will any gentleman tell me now, that slaves, aided by an English army, (and it is consolatory to think, when we are threatened by abolitionists with having our throats cut at the South, that these slaves in St. Domingo, though ten to one in number, never could have succeeded in insurrection, but for the aid of the British army,) ought to be recognized by this Government, and that their being such is no argument against it? No, it is the abolition spirit alone which would have us say to these men, whose hands are yet red with their masters' blood,—'You shall be recognized as freemen; we wish to establish international relations with you.' Never will I—never will my constituents be forced into this. This is the only body of men who have emancipated themselves by butchering their masters. They have long been free, I admit: yet, if they had been free for *centuries*,—if Time himself should confront me, and shake his hoary locks at my opposition,—I should say to him, I owe more to my constituents—to the quiet of my people—than I owe or can owe to mouldy prescriptions, however ancient."

The consolation enjoyed by this gentleman, from the conviction that the Haytiens are indebted to a British army for their liberty, is not a little ludicrous. There has never been but one British army in Hayti, and that was sent for the purpose, not of emancipation, but of conquest; and instead of aiding the blacks, it was joined by two thousand of the planters, who looked to it as the means by which they were to recover their authority over their former slaves. Yet this army, thus aided, found itself vanquished by the depised blacks; and in May, 1798, under Brigadier General Maitland, capitulated to Toussaint, the black general. The history of St. Domingo affords much and valuable instruction to slave-holders, but certainly very little *consolation.*

It may not be uninteresting to state a few facts relative to the present condition of a republic which so powerfully excites the apprehensions of southern gentlemen, and to the magnitude of the commerce which our northern politicians are willing to sacrifice for southern votes.

The advocates of slavery are fond of representing the Haytiens as a horde of barbarians. We therefore give the following evidence, published by the British Parliament, and taken before one of its committees.

Evidence of Vice Admiral, the Hon. Charles Fleming, Member of Parliament:—"He could not speak positively of the increase of the

Haytien population since 1804, but believed it had *trebled* since that time.* They now feed themselves, and they *export* provisions, which neither the French nor the Spaniards had ever done before. He saw a sugar estate near Cape Haytien, General Boulon's, extremely well cultivated and in beautiful order. A new plantation was forming on the opposite side of the road. Their victuals were very superior to those in Jamaica, consisting chiefly of meat, cattle being very cheap. He saw no marks of destitution anywhere. The country seemed improving, and trade increasing. The estate he visited near the Cape was large; it was calculated to make three hundred hogsheads of sugar. It was as beautifully laid out and as well managed as any estate he had seen in the West Indies. His official correspondence as Admiral with the Haytien Government, made him attribute much efficiency to it, and it bore strong marks of civilization. There was a better policy in Hayti than in the new South American States; the communication was more rapid; the roads were much better. One had been cut from Port-au-Prince to Cape Haytien that would do honor to any country. A regular port was established. The government is one quite worthy of a civilized people."

"In 1831, the imports into France from Hayti exceeded in value the imports from Sweden, Denmark, the Hanseatic Towns, Holland, Austria, Portugal, the French West Indies, or China." *McCulloch's Dictionary of Commerce*, p. 637.

In 1833, the imports from Hayti into the United States exceeded in value our imports from Prussia, Sweden and Norway, Denmark and the Danish West Indies, Ireland and Scotland, Holland, Belgium, Dutch West Indies, British West Indies, Spain, Portugal, all Italy, Turkey and the Levant, or any one of the South American republics. And what protection is afforded to this commerce by the Federal Government — a government willing to negotiate in every court of Europe for compensation for shipwrecked or fugitive negroes?

"Our trade with Hayti is embarrassed; it is subjected to severe discriminating duties. We are probably the least favored of any people in the ports of the republic. Tonnage duties and vexatious port charges discourage and oppress our commerce there. I am assured that, but for these impediments, the trade from this country with that would be greatly extended. The acknowledged cause of all the embarrassments to that trade is founded in the fact, that our Government refuses to recognize the Government of Hayti. We stand aloof, as if they were a lawless tribe of savages. While all other powers have long since acknowledged them as an independent sovereignty, we refuse to recognize them. Others profit by their commerce at our

* By the census of 1824, the population was stated at 935,000. It is unquestionably upwards of a million at the present time.

expense. We have no representative at the island of any grade, nor have they a public officer accredited here. No commercial relation, therefore, exists between the two Governments." *Speech of Mr. Grennell in the House of Representatives, December 18th*, 1838.

If the treatment which Hayti has received from the United States, evinces the hatred of our republic to emancipation, we have a proof no less strong of its attachment to slavery, in

THE CONDUCT OF THE FEDERAL GOVERNMENT TOWARDS TEXAS.

In 1829, the Republic of Mexico having achieved her own independence, gave liberty to every slave within her limits. This State had a vast and fertile, but thinly peopled territory, adjacent to Louisiana. In this territory, within a few years past, a large number of adventurers from the United States had taken up their residence, with the consent, and under the jurisdiction of Mexico. These adventurers sighed for the sweets of slavery, which they had enjoyed in their native land; and as the soil was adapted to the cotton cultivation, they became restless under the requirement of the Government, either to till it themselves, or honestly to pay those who tilled it for them. Hence they conceived the idea of transferring their allegiance from Mexico to another republic less tenacious of human rights. Nor was a large portion of that other republic less anxious to acquire a new market for slaves, and a new territory which would give to the slave-holding interest a preponderance in the national councils. Judge Upshur, in 1829, remarked in the Virginia Convention: "If Texas should be obtained, which he strongly desired, it would raise the price of slaves, and be a great advantage to the slave-holders in that State." Mr. Doddridge, another member, said, "The acquisition of Texas will greatly enhance the value of the property in question." *Debates*, p. 89. And in 1832, Mr. Gholston declared in the Virginia Legislature, that "he believed the acquisition of Texas would raise the price of slaves fifty per cent. at least." Virginia, it will be recollected, is a *breeding* State, and therefore interested in the opening of a new market. The planting States have no wish to raise the *price* of slaves, but are deeply concerned for the perpetuity of the system. One of their distinguished politicians published a series of essays on the policy of annexing Texas to the United States: a territory which, he contended, was large enough to be divided into NINE SLAVE STATES, which would counterbalance the increasing number of free States at the North.

The Federal Government, ever ready to promote the slaveholding interest, commenced a negotiation for the purchase of Texas, and offered *four millions of dollars* for the territory.* The offer was promptly rejected, and other means were resorted to.

Texan land companies were formed at the North, for the sale of extensive tracts of land, said to have been obtained by grants from the Mexican Government. Capitalists, politicians, and demagogues participated in these splendid schemes of speculation, and became vociferous in the cause of Texan liberty. At the same time, crowds of emigrants repaired to the territory, many carrying their slaves with them. At last, these men, feeling themselves strong enough, raised the standard of rebellion in September, 1835, and on the 2d of the succeeding March, issued their declaration of independence. The Mexicans, of course, endeavored to quell the insurrection; but, although nominally fighting with their own subjects, they were in fact contending against *an invasion from the United States.* The truth of this assertion will scarcely be questioned: yet it may be well to support it by a few facts. The following extracts from the journals of the day, will, it is presumed, be sufficient:

"*Who will go to Texas?* — Major J. W. Harvey of Lincolnton has been authorized by me, with the consent of Major-General Hunt, an agent in the western counties of North Carolina, to receive and enroll volunteer emigrants to Texas; and will conduct such as may wish to emigrate to that Republic, about the 1st of October next, at the expense of the Republic of Texas.

J. P. Henderson,
Brig. Gen. of the Texan Army."

North Carolina Paper.

* See instructions from Mr. Van Buren, Secretary of State, to Mr. Poinsett, Minister to Mexico, August 25, 1829.

"*Three Hundred Men for Texas.*—General Dunlap of Tennessee is about to proceed to Texas, with the above number of men. The whole corps are now at Memphis. Every man is completely armed, the corps having been originally raised for the Florida war. This force, we have no doubt, will be able to carry every thing before it." *Vicksburg (Miss.) Register.*

"Since early last winter, a series of transactions has passed before us in open day, the undisguised object of which has been to enlist troops, and procure arms to aid the Texans in their war with Mexico. Troops have been enlisted—arms have been obtained. Their military parades have been exhibited in our streets—they have embarked at our wharf—have proceeded to Texas—united themselves with her troops, and joined with them in war against Mexico. Is it not a fact that every stand of public arms deposited at this place by the State, has been sent to Texas, with the connivance of those who had charge of them?" *Cincinnati Gazette.*

Meetings were held in various places, and speeches made, and resolutions passed in favor of the Texan *patriots.*

At a meeting in Cincinnati, of the friends of Texas, it was resolved:

"That no law, either human or divine, except such as are formed by tyrants for their sole benefit, forbids our assisting the Texans; and such law, if any exists, we do not as Americans choose to obey."

The Federal Government, far from taking any efficient measures to arrest this invasion of a friendly and neighboring State, sent an imposing force under Gen. Gaines, *into the Mexican territory,* under the pretence of protecting the frontiers!—with what result is shown by the following article.

"About the middle of last month, Gen. Gaines sent an officer of the United States army into Texas, to reclaim some deserters. He found them already enlisted in the Texan service to the number of *two hundred.* They still wore the uniform of our army, but refused of course to return. The commander of the Texan army was applied to, to enforce their return, but his only reply was, that the soldiers might go, but that he had no authority to send them back. This is a new view of our *Texan relations.*" *Pensacola Gazette.*

The adventurers in Texas had no sooner set up for themselves, than they adopted a constitution, in which they aimed, first, to secure to themselves and their children for ever, the blessings of slavery; and secondly, to acquire the aid and protection of the United States. The first object was to be attained by a constitutional prohibition of both private and legislative emancipation; and by making it a fundamental law of the Republic, that no free black or mulatto person should reside within its boundaries; and the second object, by giving to the United States in perpetuity, a monopoly of the slave-market in Texas, — the importation of slaves from any other country being absolutely prohibited, thus promising to realize the golden visions of the Virginia breeders.*

A feverish impatience now pervaded the southern States for the acknowledgment of Texan independence; — an impatience in which the northern speculators fully participated. Acknowledgment, it was seen, must precede annexation, since the latter could only be effected by a treaty with Texas as an independent power. Still policy required that this measure should be cautiously managed, lest the North should become alarmed at this scheme for vesting the whole political power of the Union in the hands of the slave-holders, and the northern members of Congress be found for once refractory.

Congress met in December, 1836, and on the 22d of the same month, President Jackson sent them a special message in relation to Texas. He remarked:

"Prudence seems to dictate that we should still stand aloof, and maintain our present attitude, if not till Mexico, or one of the great foreign powers shall recognize the independence of the new Government, at least until *the lapse of time, or the course of events shall have proved beyond all cavil or dispute the ability of that country to maintain their separate sovereignty, and to uphold the Government constituted by them.*"

* To aid the deception intended to be practised on these breeders, the President of Texas issued his proclamation April 3, 1836, declaring that "Whereas the *African* slave-trade is equally revolting to the best feelings of our nature and to the benign principles of the Christian religion; is destructive to national morals and to individual humanity:" therefore, all officers were commanded to be vigilant in suppressing the *African* slave-trade. This precious piece of hypocrisy was worthy of the new Republic. On the 1st of January, 1836, the British Commissioners at Havana informed their Government, "within the last six weeks, considerable sums of money have been deposited by American citizens in certain mercantile houses, for the purpose of making additional purchases of negroes for Texas." Buxton, in his late work, says, "I have been informed on high authority that within the last twelve months, (1837-8,) 15,000 negroes were imported from Africa into Texas," p. 25. The sugar planters of Louisiana, as we have seen, are complaining that while they are compelled to import slaves from Virginia at $1000 a head, the Texan planters are importing them direct from Africa at half price.

This message dissipated all apprehensions on the part of the friends of freedom, of a speedy acknowledgment, and relieved Congress from the remonstrances and petitions with which their tables would otherwise have been loaded.

It was obvious, however, that if we could contrive to become embroiled in a war with Mexico, we might then seize upon Texas, and hold it by right of conquest, without any violation of our neutral obligations: and that by this process, the annexation might be effected with even more facility than by a compact with Texas as an independent power. Accordingly, about two weeks after the late message, the President sent another to Congress on our grievances against Mexico — grievances about which the people at large knew and cared nothing. This message recommended the passage of a law authorizing the President to employ a naval force against Mexico if she refused "to come to an amicable adjustment of the matters in controversy between us, upon another demand thereof, made *from on board one of our vessels of war on the coast of Mexico*." This proposition was coldly received, neither Congress nor the nation seeming to approve of such a novel and summary way of declaring war; and no one having the slightest desire for war, except those who were anxious for the annexation. It being found that a war could not be had, another game was played. The session was to close on the 3d of March. The strongest opposition to Texas was to be apprehended in the Lower House. Four days before the termination of the session, a motion was there made to add a clause to the appropriation bill, making provision for the salary of a diplomatic agent to Texas. There was no time for long speeches, and the motion was adopted with the amendment "to be sent by the President whenever he shall receive satisfactory evidence that Texas is an independent power, and shall see fit to open a diplomatic intercourse with her." The late message proved that the President had not yet received "the satisfactory evidence," and anticipated it only from the action of the great *foreign* powers, or "the lapse of time." Little hesitation, therefore, was felt in leaving the subject under the control of the Executive. The House of Representatives, in which there was a majority of northern members, having been thus managed, and a salary secured for a Minister to Texas, the veil was thrown aside in the Senate, and two days before the end of the session, it was

"Resolved, That the State of Texas having established and maintained an independent government, capable of performing those duties, foreign and domestic, which appertain to independent governments, and it appearing that there is no longer any reasonable prospect of the successful termination of the war by Mexico against said State, it is expedient and proper, and in conformity with the laws of nations and the precedents of this Government in like cases, that the independent political existence of said State be acknowledged by the Government of the United States."

As the whole tenor of this resolution was in direct opposition to the message of the 22d of December, and as nothing had occurred since that date to weaken the positions assumed in the message, one of the senators in opposing the resolution, very naturally alluded to the views entertained by the President. On this, Mr. Walker, a senator from Mississippi, rose in his place and declared, that "*he had it from the President's own lips, that if he were a senator, he would vote for this resolution!!*"

At eleven o'clock of the night of the 3d of March, an hour before his term of office expired, and just as the Senate was about adjourning, the President sent them the nomination of a Minister to Texas!!

The conduct of the Federal Government towards Texas and Hayti, places in a strong light the influence of slavery on our national councils. The latter State has been independent both in name and in fact for thirty-seven years, yet we still refuse to recognize her. Twelve months after Texas declared her independence, she was received by us into the family of nations, and honored by an interchange of diplomatic agents. For thirty-five years, the soil of Hayti has not been trodden by an invader; only *ten* months before the acknowledgment of Texas, a Mexican army was carrying terror and destruction through its territory. That army had indeed been defeated, but another was preparing to renew the contest. Hayti had long been at peace with all the world. Mexico claimed Texas as its own, and solemnly avowed its determination to chastise and suppress the revolt. Hayti achieved her independence after a long and arduous struggle with powerful armies, and has a population of a million to maintain it. Texas, when acknowledged, could appeal only to the fortunate result of a single battle as evidence of her national power, while she had no more than 60,000 inhabitants to contend against the eight millions of Mexico. With Hayti, we had a large and valuable commerce, while our commerce with Texas was only in expectancy. Yet has slavery estranged our Government from the one nation, and led it to welcome to its embrace another, incomparably inferior in political strength and moral worth.

The indecent haste with which Texas was acknowledged, and the trickery by which the acknowledgment was effected, were prompted by the desire of annexation. A southern journal speaks thus frankly on the subject:

> "Does any sober observer contend — can he in the face of facts, — that Texas has substantially, according to the usages of nations, accomplished her independence? Was there not an even chance, to put the matter on the most favorable footing, that the victory of Jacinto might this campaign be reversed? But natural *feeling* has outstripped the prudence of our Government, usually discreet and judicious, *and social sympathy* has done what political precedent, and possibly expediency, might not have sanctioned. The debate in the British Parliament shows how well *State papers* and official ceremonies" (viz., the President's Message,) "may delude, or seem to delude foreign governments. While Lord Palmerston and O'Connell were defending our Government from any improper haste in acknowledging the independence of Texas, the deed is consummated." *The Port Gibson* (*Miss.*) *Southerner.*

The whole slave region, with scarcely an exception, demanded a union with the new State. "The very reasons," said the Charleston Mercury, "so intemperately urged by the North against it, that it will increase the political weight of the southern States, and perpetuate and extend the curse of slavery, *are our best reasons for it.*"

The Legislatures of South Carolina, Mississippi, and Tennessee, all passed resolutions in favor of the annexation. Many individuals at the North had likewise a deep pecuniary interest in the question. They had speculated largely in Texas lands, but their titles would be of but little value, so long as they depended on the faith of the lawless adventurers who possessed the country. Could that country be received into the Union, and subjected to the acts of Congress and the jurisdiction of the Supreme Court, their purchases might ensure to themselves or their families, princely estates. A writer in the Salem Gazette, (Mass.) probably a speculator, in vindicating the annexation, thus appealed to the avarice of New England:

> "It is calculated that the value of one kind of property in the South, slaves, will be enhanced so much, that that portion of our country will realize one or two hundred millions of dollars; and the South cannot be enriched without benefiting the North—*the money will naturally come here at last.*"

The people of Texas were no less desirous of annexation than southern slave-holders, or northern speculators. The plan of union was avowed from almost the very commencement of the rebellion. In August, 1836, S. F. Austin, in an address offering himself as a candidate for the Presidency, told the people:—"I am in favor of the annexation, and will do all in my power to effect it with the least possible delay." W. H. Jack, a candidate for the Legislature, declared: "I am decidedly and unequivocally in favor of annexing Texas to the United States." Gen. Houston, the Commander-in-chief, intimated that "the annexation was essential to the interests of the new country." The Texan Congress resolved, "that the President of the Republic of Texas be empowered and authorized to despatch a commissioner or commissioners to the United States of America, to obtain a negotiation of our independence, and enter into a treaty with that Government for a union on a footing with the original States." The first condition prescribed for this proposed union, was, "THE FREE AND UNMOLESTED AUTHORITY OVER THEIR SLAVE POPULATION!"

On the 4th of August, 1837, the negotiation was opened by the Texan Minister at Washington, by a proposition "to unite the two people under one and the same government." The acceptance of this proposition would of course have been equivalent to a declaration of war against Mexico; a responsibility which Mr. Van Buren did not see fit to assume, especially in the recess of Congress. He declined entering into the negotiation, on the grounds that the United States were at present at peace with Mexico, and that that power had not acknowledged the independence of Texas. As this answer merely *postponed* the annexation on account of an obstacle easily removed, it was entirely satisfactory to the South; and the more so as the President's message to Congress on the 4th of the ensuing December wore a very belligerent aspect towards Mexico.

This formal attempt at annexation roused the fears of the North, and innumerable remonstrances against the measure were presented to Congress. In the meantime Mexico, by proposing a submission of her differences with the United States to arbitration, removed all pretence for immediate war. Under these circumstances, the southern delegation in Congress thought it most prudent not to press the annexation. The Texans, moreover, finding themselves unmolested by Mexico, who had become involved in war with France, and observing the strong hostility manifested towards the measure in the United States, formally withdrew her application for admission into the Union. It is folly, however, to suppose that the project of annexation is abandoned, either by the South or by Texas; nor does it need the gift of prophecy to foresee that the first favorable opportunity of making war upon Mexico, will be readily embraced by the Federal Government. Should such a war be effected, the dominion of the WHIP may perhaps be extended from Maryland to Panama.

It may not be amiss here to compare the conduct of the Federal Government towards the Texan and the Canadian rebels. The first were slave-holders reëstablishing slavery on a soil from which it had been banished; and they enjoyed from the first the sympathy of our government, who took care to interpose no real obstacle to an invasion on their behalf from the United States: while for the purpose of aiding them it labored to excite an immediate war with Mexico. The Canadian rebels were professedly fighting for liberty, and should they succeed, there was no probability that negro slavery would crown their triumph. They, like the Texans, looked to us for aid; but the President, *now* alive to the obligations of neutrality, and finding the existing laws insufficient to enforce them, applied to Congress, and received additional powers. Troops were sent to the frontiers, not to swell by desertion the ranks of the rebels, but in good faith, forcibly to prevent American citizens from aiding the revolt. No attempt was ever made to punish any of the abettors of the Texan rebels; but the *judicial* as well as the military power of the Government was exerted to enforce the duties of neutrality on the Canadian frontier; and indictments and trials and imprisonments have taught the impressive lesson, that American citizens may not with impunity make war upon a friendly nation, except for the purpose of trampling upon the rights of man.

"While Mackenzie and Case are lying in a solitary dungeon, for attempting to liberate Canada, the Texan agent is openly enlisting men at Buffalo, to serve in an expedition against Mexico." *Lewiston Telegraph.*

But hear the confession of the official journal of the administration:

"There is no doubt, we believe, that *vessels of war* of light draught of water—brigs and schooners—are preparing in the United States, for Texas, to be commanded by *young officers of the American Navy.*" *Washington Globe.*

Yet not a finger has been raised to prevent these hostile and illegal armaments. The truth is, a war with Mexico is ardently desired by the slave-holders, and the President was for *negotiating on board an armed vessel.* A war with Great Britain, emphatically an anti-slavery nation, is now viewed with horror and dismay by the whole South,* and the Executive has sedulously endeavored to avoid it.

We have now presented numerous instances of the action of the Federal Government in behalf of slavery; but our task is not completed. We are still to view that Government, which,

* A distinguished southern senator, speaking of the importance of preserving our neutrality on the Canada frontier, declared that in his opinion "a war with England would be the heaviest calamity that could befall the country."

in the language of the Constitution, was established "to secure the blessings of LIBERTY to ourselves and our posterity," assailing the constitutional rights of the citizen, in order to rivet the fetters of the slave; striving to extinguish the freedom of the press, the freedom of debate, and the right of petition, to perpetuate property in human flesh. These, we are sensible, are strong assertions: we solicit attention to the facts on which they are founded, and first to

THE ATTEMPT OF THE FEDERAL GOVERNMENT TO ESTABLISH A CENSORSHIP OF THE PRESS.

In the summer of 1835, the Anti-Slavery Society in New York, directed their publisher to forward a number of their periodical papers, containing facts and disquisitions on the subject of slavery, to various southern gentlemen of distinction, in the hope of exciting by this means, a spirit of inquiry among persons of influence and character. But it was precisely such a spirit of inquiry, that the advocates of perpetual bondage feared might be fatal to their favorite institution. Hence they affected to believe that the papers sent to the *masters*, were intended to excite the slaves to insurrection, and they succeeded in maddening the populace to fury. A mob broke into the Charleston Post Office, and seizing a quantity of anti-slavery papers, burned them in the street. This outrage was virtually approved by the City Council; and at a public meeting, a committee of "gentlemen" was appointed to take charge of the northern mail on its arrival, accompany it to the Post Office, and see that no papers advocating the rights of man should be delivered to their owners. The Postmaster informed the head of the department, that under existing circumstances, he had determined to suppress all anti-slavery publications, and asked for instructions for the future. It should here be recollected, that of all the political advisers of the President, Mr Kendall, at this time acting as Postmaster-General, was the most odious to the opposite party. He had been appointed during the recess of the

Senate, and it was regarded as a matter of course, that on the meeting of that body, in which the opposition had a majority, his nomination would be rejected. The Constitution forbade a censorship of the press, and had the people been disposed to delegate so formidable a power, they certainly would not have vested it in the 10,000 deputies of the Postmaster-General. The law moreover expressly required every postmaster to deliver the papers received by him to the persons to whom they were directed.

Such were the circumstances under which Mr. Kendall returned his famous answer. After stating that not having seen the papers in question, he could not judge of their character, but had been *informed* that they were incendiary, inflammatory and insurrectionary, he added:

> "By no act or direction of mine, official or private, could I be induced to aid knowingly in giving circulation to papers of this description, directly or indirectly. We owe an obligation to the laws, but a higher one to the communities in which we live; and if the former be perverted to destroy the latter, *it is patriotism to disregard them.* Entertaining these views, I cannot sanction and will not condemn the step you have taken."

This letter taught the Senate that the new officer was willing to conduct the Post Office in a manner calculated to protect the "domestic institution" from the assaults of truth and argument, and *his nomination was confirmed.* Mr. Kendall was at the date of his letter, a member of the Cabinet, and it was understood that the novel, extraordinary, and dangerous doctrine of that letter received the sanction of the President.

On the opening of Congress, President Jackson in his message recommended the "passing of such a law as will prohibit under severe penalties, the *circulation* in the southern States through the mails, of incendiary publications *intended* to instigate the slaves to insurrection." The proposed law, it seems, was not to prohibit the printing of certain papers, nor their committal to the mails in the northern States, but only their *circulation* in the slave-region. Of course certain persons, — postmasters, we presume, — were to be required, under "heavy penalties," to stop these papers; and they were necessarily to be judges of the character of the papers, and of the intentions of their writers. From what code of despotism did our very democratic President derive his plan for destroying the efficiency of the PRESS? By a contemptible quibble, this plan was to evade the constitutional guaranty of the freedom of the press. It was not to interfere with the press — not at all — it was merely to prevent the circulation of its productions! The press was still to be free to pour forth its arguments against slavery, only "heavy penalties" were to prevent the people from reading them! The reason moreover assigned for this proposed high-handed act of tyranny, was a most malignant and wilful calumny. It was to prevent the circulation in the southern States of publications *intended* to excite the slaves to insurrection. Such a proposal from the first magistrate of the country to Congress, and following the affair at Charleston, and Mr. Kendall's letter, irresistibly fixes upon the members of the Anti-Slavery Society at New York, the charge of sending papers into the southern States for the purpose and with the desire of effecting the massacre of their fellow-citizens. If the President really believed that such was the object of the New York abolitionists, and such the character of their publications, and if he thought it his official duty to bring the subject before Congress, he owed it to himself, to the country, to truth and to justice, to have submitted to Congress the *facts and documents* on which he founded his proposed invasion of the constitutional rights of his fellow-citizens. But he cautiously avoided specifying a single fact, or quoting a single sentence in support of his tremendous accusation, or in justification of his most unwarrantable proposition; and when written to by the acting committee of the New York Society for proof of his charge against them, he deemed it most prudent not to return an answer! Surely the burden of proof rests upon him who, in a solemn official address to the Legislature, holds up a portion of his fellow-citizens as miscreants engaged in plotting murder and insurrection, and urges the enaction of a law to counteract their execrable machinations.

It is often difficult to prove a negative; but in this instance, the falsehood of the President's charge is amply demonstrated by an official document from the slave-holders themselves. We give this document, not to exculpate the members of the New York Society from a calumny which their own characters abundantly refute, but to show in a strong light the unprincipled means to which the Federal Government is capable of resorting to uphold the "peculiar institution" of the South.

A grand jury in Alabama conceived the bright idea, that the publication of tracts at the North against slavery might be arrested by indicting the publishers as felons, and then demanding them from the Governors of their respective States as *fugitives* from southern justice. It was necessary, however, to specify in the indictment, the precise crime of which they had been guilty; a necessity which the President regarded as not applicable to his message. We may well suppose, therefore, that the grand jury would endeavor to secure the success of this, their first experiment, by selecting from the various publications alluded to by the President and Mr. Kendall, as sent to the South for the purpose of exciting insurrection, the most insurrectionary, cut-throat passages, they could find. Behold the result.

"State of Alabama,
Tuscaloosa county. } Circuit Court, September Term, 1835.

The grand jurors, * * * * upon their oath present, that Robert G. Williams, *late of said county*, being a wicked, malicious, seditious, and ill-disposed person, and being greatly disaffected to the laws and government of said State, and feloniously, wickedly, maliciously, and seditiously contriving, devising, and intending to produce *conspiracy, insurrection and rebellion* among the slave population of said State, and to alienate and withdraw the affection, fidelity, and allegiance of said slaves from their masters and owners, on the tenth day of September, in the year of our Lord one thousand eight hundred and thirty-five, at the county aforesaid, feloniously, wickedly, maliciously, and seditiously did cause to be distributed, circulated and published, a seditious paper, called 'THE EMANCIPATOR,' in which paper is published according to the tenor and effect following, that is to say: '*God commands, and all nature cries out, that* MAN *should not be held as property. The system of making* MEN *property, has plunged* 2,250,000 *of our fellow-countrymen into the deepest physical and moral degradation, and they are every moment sinking deeper.*' In open violation of the Act of the General Assembly in such case made and provided, to the evil and pernicious example of all others in like case offending, and against the peace and dignity of the State of Alabama." *

In the Senate, the recommendation of the President was referred to a committee, who reported a bill prohibiting postmasters from delivering "any pamphlet, newspaper, handbill, or other printed paper, or pictorial representation, *touching the subject of slavery*, in any State in which their circulation is prohibited by law." The object of this bill was, by means of federal legislation, to build around the slave States a rampart against the assaults of light and truth. Its absurdity was equalled only by its wickedness. Not a newspaper containing a debate in Congress, a report from a committee, a message from the President, a letter from the West Indies, "touching the subject of slavery," could be legally delivered from a southern post office; and thousands of postmasters were to be employed in opening envelopes and poring over their contents, to catch a reference to the "domestic institution."

By this bill, the Federal Government virtually surrendered to the States, the freedom of the press, and nullified the guaranty of this inestimable privilege, given by our fathers in the Constitution to every citizen. This bill, moreover, prepared the way for the destruction of civil and religious liberty. If every paper touching the subject of slavery might be suppressed, then the same fate might just as constitutionally be awarded to every paper *touching* the conduct of the administration, or the doctrine of the Trinity. It established a censorship of the press on one subject, which might afterwards be extended to others. Yet this bill, absurd and unconstitutional as it was, went through its regular stages with little opposition, till the important question was taken on its engrossment;—the vote stood eighteen to eighteen. The casting vote was now required from Mr. Van Buren, who, as Vice President, occupied the chair. He gave it for the slave-holders, and received from them, at the ensuing

* Another count was added for distributing "The Emancipator," but without giving any extracts. It is scarcely necessary to add, that Williams had never been in Alabama. Yet on this indictment, he was demanded of the New York Executive as a fugitive felon, by the Governor of Alabama.

election, sixty-one electoral votes, by means of which he became President of the United States.* On the final question, the bill was rejected, and this attempt to trammel the press for the protection of slavery, defeated. A very different result, however, has attended

THE EFFORT OF THE FEDERAL GOVERNMENT TO NULLIFY THE RIGHT OF PETITION AND THE FREEDOM OF DEBATE.

For thirty years past, petitions have been presented to Congress for the abolition of slavery in the District of Columbia, and the national territories; and, until latterly, were received and treated like other petitions. But having within a few years prodigiously increased in number, and some northern members having shown a disposition to advocate their prayer, a most extraordinary course has been pursued in relation to them. The reason of this course is explained by the following passage from a speech by Mr. Strange, a senator from North Carolina.

> "Every agitation of this subject (slavery,) weakens the moral force in our favor, and breaks down the moral barriers which now serve to protect and secure us. *We have everything to lose and nothing to gain by agitation and discussion.*"

The frankness of this confession is as remarkable as its truth is unquestionable; and it shows us why the advocates of slavery, instead of meeting their opponents in argument, have sought to silence them by brute force and penal enactments.

One of the most unequivocal and undoubted of all constitutional rights is that of petition, and it is, moreover, expressly guaranteed by the Constitution. But this right has been most audaciously nullified by both branches of the national legislature. The Senate have not, it is true, avowedly refused to receive anti-slavery petitions, but they have adopted a course which answers the same purpose. The practice for some years past has been to lay the question of reception on the table with-

* The two senators from New York, Messrs. Wright and Tallmadge, political friends of Mr. Van Buren, supported the bill. It is due to justice to mention that the bill was finally lost by the votes of several *southern* senators.

out deciding it, and the question not being in fact received, cannot be discussed, nor any measure respecting it taken. This course is no less at variance with the constitutional rights of the petitioners, than it is with those of the members of the Senate. The rights of petition and freedom of debate are both nullities, if the body to which a prayer is addressed, is prohibited from listening to it, and the individual members are prohibited from noticing it. Would it be no violation of the Constitution were the Senate to order that every petition, "touching the subject of slavery," should be delivered to their doorkeeper, to be committed by him to the flames? And yet in what particular are the rights of the petitioners more respected by the practice we have mentioned? The petitions are not indeed burned, but they are left in the pockets of those to whom they were entrusted; and not being received, the Senate is supposed to be ignorant of their contents, and of course no member is permitted to discuss their merits, or to propose any measure founded upon them. Let us now turn to what is regarded as the *popular branch*,—the House of Representatives,—intended to be the special guardian of the liberties of the PEOPLE, as the Senate is of the rights of the States.

In May, 1836, a committee reported to the House a resolution, prefaced with this extraordinary avowal:

> "Whereas it is extremely important and desirable, that the AGITATION on this subject (slavery) should be finally arrested for the purpose of restoring *tranquillity* to the public mind, your committee respectfully recommend the following resolution."

Here then is an acknowledged, unblushing interference by the Federal Government, in behalf of slavery; an avowed interference to arrest that agitation, which we are assured by Mr. Strange, "breaks down the moral barriers" which serve to protect and secure a system of iniquitious cruelty and oppression. To arrest this agitation, the committee did not scruple to recommend a measure, breaking down the constitutional barriers erected to protect and secure the rights and liberties of the people of the United States. The resolution reported by the committee, was adopted by the House on the 26th of May, 1836, and is in these words:

"Resolved, That all petitions, memorials, and propositions relating *in any way, or to any extent* whatever to the subject of slavery, shall without being either printed or referred, be laid on the table, and that no farther action whatever shall be had thereon." Ayes 117—Nays 68.

It is worthy of remark, that of the ayes, no less than sixty-two were from the free States! The advocates of this resolution, conscious that it could bear discussion as little as slavery itself, caused it to be adopted through the operation of the previous question, by a *silent* vote.

We have exhibited the character of slavery and the slave-trade at the seat of the Federal Government, and have shown that Congress is the local legislature of the District of Columbia, having "exclusive jurisdiction over it in all cases whatever." Now one of the peculiar atrocities of this resolution is, that it wrests from every member of the House, his constitutional right to *propose* such measures for the government of the District as justice and humanity may require. Slaves might be burned alive in the streets of the Capital; the slavers might be crowded to suffocation with human victims; every conceivable cruelty might be practised, and no one member of the local legislature could be permitted to propose even a committee of inquiry, "relating in any way, or to any extent whatever, to the subject of slavery."

The fact that sixty-two northern members on this occasion arrayed themselves on the side of the slave-holders, affords a melancholy and alarming proof of the corrupting influence which slavery is exerting on the morality and patriotism of the free States.

The foolish and wicked expedient to "restore tranquillity" to the people, by trampling on their rights and gagging their representatives, failed of success. The petitioners at this session were 34,000—at the next the number was swelled to ONE HUNDRED AND TEN THOUSAND! and the gag was renewed. During the session of 1837–8, the number rose to THREE HUNDRED THOUSAND. Early in the last mentioned session, a member from Vermont presented a petition for the abolition of slavery in the District of Columbia, and took the liberty to offer some remarks on the subject of slavery. This attempt to break down "the moral barriers," thew the southern members into great trepidation, and the scene which ensued illustrates the system of *intimidation* to which we have already adverted. The member was interrupted by a gentleman from Virginia, calling aloud, and asking his colleagues to retire with him from the hall; — another from Georgia exclaimed, that he hoped the whole southern delegation would do the same; — a third from South Carolina declared, that all the representatives from that State "had already signed an agreement." The House adjourned, and a southern member invited the gentlemen from the slave-holding States to meet immediately in an adjoining room. The meeting was held, but its proceedings were not made public. The result, however, was manifested in the introduction, next morning, of another gag resolution, directing all memorials, petitions and papers touching the abolition of slavery in the national territories, and the American slave-trade, to be laid on the table, without being printed, read, *debated*, or referred, and that no farther action should be had thereon. Through the acquiescence of northern members, it was passed by a *silent vote.*

At the beginning of the next session, a meeting of the administration members was held, at which it was determined to renew the gag: and as a proof of the devotion of the Democratic party at the North to the cause of slavery, it was arranged that now, for the first time, the odious measure should be proposed by a northern man: nay, not merely a northern man, but a native of New England — a representative from New Hampshire. The resolution was accordingly introduced, and was passed on the 12th of December, 1838, and has given notoriety to the name of *Atherton.*

Thus we see a persevering, systematic effort on the part of Congress to protect slavery by suppressing debate, and throwing contempt upon the petitions of hundreds of thousands of American citizens. That this should be done by slave-holders, was perhaps to be expected; but that they should be aided in such a desperate assault upon constitutional liberty by northern men, for the paltry consideration of southern votes and southern trade, is mortifying and alarming. The meeting of extremes is a trite illustration of human inconsistency. If in Doctor Johnson's time the loudest yelps for liberty were heard from the drivers of slaves, the loudest yelps in the northern States against aristocracy, chartered monopolies and oppression of the poor, are now heard from men who are laboring to perpetuate the bondage of millions, by gag laws and restrictions on the freedom of speech and the press. These men are acting from party views, and are rushing to battle under the war-cry of "VAN BUREN AND SLAVERY," in hopes, through southern auxiliaries, of enjoying the spoils of victory. Others again, without the slightest sympathy in the political principles of these men, and with their ears stuffed, and their heart padded with cotton, are coöperating with them in behalf of slavery, from their love of southern trade.* We will here close our protracted investigation with a brief

RECAPITULATION OF THE ACTION OF THE FEDERAL GOVERNMENT IN BEHALF OF SLAVERY.

This action we have found exhibited (omitting constitutional provisions),

1. In its appointments to office.
2. In its legislation for Florida.

* The following are strong and amusing instances of the meeting of extremes. In the spring of 1837, the *Whig* merchants of New York sent a deputation to Washington, to request the President to adopt certain measures to relieve the commercial embarrassments of the country. The request was declined, and a great meeting was convened to receive the report of the deputation. The report, which was adopted by the meeting, recommended efforts to displace Mr. Van Buren, and as one means of effecting this object, exhorted the merchants to "appeal to our brethren of the South for their generous coöperation; and *promise* them that those who believe the possession of property of *any* kind" (not excepting men, women, and children,) "is an evidence of merit, will be the last to interfere with the rights of property of *any* kind; discourage any effort to awaken an excitement, the bare idea of which *should make every husband and father shudder with horror*." In plain English, if the slave-holders would make common cause with the New York merchants against Mr. Van Buren, they in return would make common cause with the slave-holders against the abolitionists. But Democrats know the value of southern votes quite as well as the Whigs. Accordingly we find in the Washington Globe of February 9, 1839, a speech *intended* to have been delivered, but prevented by the gag resolution, by Mr. Eli

3. In its interference in behalf of the slave-holders in Louisiana.

4. In its efforts to degrade the free people of color.

5. In its tolerance of slavery in territories under its exclusive jurisdiction.

6. In its arbitrary, unconstitutional, and wicked laws for the arrest of fugitive slaves.

7. In its negotiation with Great Britain and Mexico for the surrender of fugitive slaves.

8. In its invasion of Florida, in pursuit of fugitive slaves.

9. In its negotiations with Great Britain for compensation for slaves who had taken refuge on board British ships-of-war.

10. In its negotiation with Great Britain for compensation for slaves shipwrecked in the West Indies.

11. In its tolerance, protection, and regulation of the American slave-trade.

12. In its duplicity, with regard to the abolition of the African slave-trade.

Moore, a double-refined Democrat, President of the New York Trades Union, and representative from that city in Congress. This gentleman tells us "the wild, enthusiastic, and impetuous spirit which kindled the fires of Smithfield, and strewed the plains of Palestine with the corses of the crusaders, stands with lighted and uplifted torch hard by the side of abolitionism, ready to spread conflagration and death around the land;" he declares that "so long as the DEMOCRATIC or State Rights party shall maintain the ascendency, the efforts of the abolitionists will be comparatively innoxious;" and he announces what will be no less news to the New York merchants than it is to abolitionists, that "the Federal or NATIONAL BANK PARTY believe the Federal Legislature not only have the power to abolish slavery in this District of Columbia, *but also in the States*."

Almost immediately after the publication of this speech, the Democratic papers contained the following announcement:—"JUST AND MERITED.—The Hon. Eli Moore, of the City of New York, has been appointed surveyor of that port." The reward was paid by the President and Senate.

But the most extraordinary instance of the devotion of northern Democracy to southern despotism, we have yet met with, was lately given in the City of New York. A set of men, calling themselves "delegates of the *Democratic republican party* (*!!*) for the several wards," assembled to make preparations for commemorating the declaration that "all men are born free and equal." They resolved to have an orator for the occasion; but so ardent and sublimated was their love of liberty, that no northern Democrat was worthy, in their opinion, to declaim before them on the "self-evident truths," and the blessing of the Federal Union. So they selected for their Fourth of July orator, JOHN C. CALHOUN, of South Carolina, who had evinced his attachment to the Union by his efforts to excite civil war—to the liberties of his country, by his gag resolutions, and his bill establishing a censorship of the press—and to the rights of man, by his avowed desire for the everlasting bondage of millions of his fellow-men. The presidential election is approaching, the vote of South Carolina is doubtful, and a compliment to Mr. Calhoun may not be useless to Mr. Van Buren.

13. In its present virtual toleration of the trade.
14. In its appropriations to the Colonization Society.
15. In its Indian treaties in behalf of slave-holders.
16. In its attempted expulsion of the Seminoles for harboring fugitive slaves.
17. In its efforts to prevent the abolition of slavery in Cuba.
18. In its conduct towards Hayti.
19. In its conduct towards Texas.
20. In its attempt to establish a censorship of the press.
21. In its invasion of the right of petition, and the freedom of debate.

Such has been the action in behalf of human bondage, of a Government which, in the language of the Constitution, was formed to establish JUSTICE, and secure the blessings of LIBERTY.

And by whom are the men composing the Government, which thus perverts the objects of its institution, invested with their power? They are the agents, the mere instruments of the people of the United States — of the North and the East, as well as of the West and the South. This consideration calls us to consider

THE RESPONSIBILITY OF THE FREE STATES.

The advocates of slavery and the tools of party, are continually telling us that "*the North has nothing to do with slavery.*" A volume might be filled with facts, proving the fallacy of this assertion. There is scarcely a family among us that is not connected, by the ties of friendship, kindred, or pecuniary interest, with the land of slaves. That land is endeared to us by a thousand recollections — with that land we have continual commercial, political, religious, and social intercourse. There, in innumerable instances, are our personal friends, our brothers, our sons and our daughters. How malignant and foolish then is the falsehood, that the thousands and tens of thousands of abolitionists among us, are anxious to see that land reeking in blood! But the more intimate are our connections with that land, the more exposed are we to be contaminated by its pollutions; and the more imperatively are we bound to seek its real welfare.

Let it then sink deep in our hearts — let it rest upon our consciences, that in every wicked and cruel act of the Federal Government in behalf of slavery, the people of the North have participated, — we might almost say that for all this wickedness and cruelty, they are *solely responsible;* since it could not have been perpetrated but with the consent of *their* representatives. Vast and fertile territories, which might now have been inhabited by a free and happy population, have by northern votes been converted, to use the langauge of the poet, into

"A land of tyrants, and a den of slaves."

By northern senators have our African slavers been protected from the search of British cruisers. By northern representatives is the American slave-trade protected, and the abominations enacted in the Capital of the Republic, sanctioned and perpetuated: and northern men are the officiating ministers in the sacrifice of constitutional liberty on the altar of Moloch. But representatives are only the agents of their constituents, speaking their thoughts, and doing their will. THE PEOPLE OF THE NORTH have done "this great wickedness." When *they* repent, when *they* love mercy, and seek after justice, their representatives will no longer rejoice to aid in transforming the image of God into a beast of burden — then will the human shambles be overthrown in the Capital — then will slavers, "freighted with despair," no longer depart from the port of Alexandria, nor chained coffles traverse the streets of Washington. Then will the powers of the Federal Government be exercised in protecting, not in annihilating the rights of man; and then will the slave-holder, deprived of the countenance of the free States, as he is already of nearly all the rest of the civilized world, be led to reflect calmly on the character and tendency of the institution he now so dearly prizes, and seek his own welfare and that of his children in its voluntary and peaceful abolition.

But here we are confronted with direful prophecies. Let us then proceed to inquire into

THE PROBABLE INFLUENCE OF THE ANTI-SLAVERY AGITATION ON THE PERMANENCY OF THE UNION.

Before we can predict what this influence will be, we must first inquire, what will probably be the direction and aim of the agitation? Every State possesses all the powers of independent sovereignty, except such as she has delegated to the Federal Government. All the powers not specified in the Constitution as delegated, are by that instrument reserved. Among the powers specified, that of abrogating the slave codes of the several States is not included; on the contrary, the guaranty of the continuance of the African slave-trade for twenty years, the provision for the arrest of fugitive slaves, and the establishment of the federal ratio of representation, all refer to and acknowledge the existence of slavery under State authority. If, therefore, the abolitionists, unmindful of their solemn and repeated disclaimers of all power in Congress to legislate for the abolition of slavery in the States, should, with unexampled perfidy, attempt to bring about such legislation, and if Congress, regardless of their oaths, should ever be guilty of the consummate folly and wickedness of passing a law emancipating the slaves held under State authority, the Union would most unquestionably be rent in twain. The South would indeed be craven could it submit to such profligate usurpation; it would be compelled to withdraw, not for the preservation of slavery alone, but for the protection of all its rights; and indeed the liberties of every State would be jeoparded under a government, which, spurning all constitutional restraints, should assume the omnipotence of the British Parliament. But it is scarcely worth while to anticipate the consequence of an act which can never be perpetrated so long as the people of the North retain an ordinary share of honesty and intelligence.

We have, under all the circumstances of the case, sufficient reasons for believing that the anti-slavery of the North will carry its action to the very limits of the Constitution, but not beyond them. In despite of the coalitions of parties and the intrigues of politicians, liberty of speech and of the press will be maintained, and the discussion of slavery will be extended by the very efforts made to arrest it. Let us suppose this discussion to be attended with its natural and probable result, the conversion of the great mass of the northern people to the principles and avowed objects of the abolitionists. Of course, those principles and objects will be embraced by their representatives in Congress. In this case, we may expect that slavery will be abolished in the District of Columbia, and that it will be prohibited in the territories hereafter to be formed on the west of the Mississippi. Thus far the constitutional power of Congress cannot be rationally questioned. Independent of the exclusive jurisdiction over the territories granted to Congress, we have the precedent of the ordinance of 1787, prohibiting slavery in the Northwest Territory, and the more recent precedent of the prohibition of it in the Louisiana territory north of $36\frac{1}{2}^{\circ}$ of north latitude. The American slave-trade is now, and has been for upwards of thirty years, prohibited in vessels under forty tons' burden. It would not be easy to show that the Constitution forbids its prohibition in vessels *over* forty tons' burden. We may therefore take it for granted, that the *Senate's coasting trade* will be legally abolished. Should the land traffic not be also destroyed, it would not be for want of disposition, or constitutional power in Congress, but on account of the extreme difficulty which would exist in preventing evasions of the law.

We have now the sum total of national legislation which, on our present supposition, will result from the anti-slavery action at the North. Yet we are positively assured that such legislation would cause a dissolution of the Union. Now admitting the constitutional right and the moral obligation of our national legislators, to pass the laws in question, it would be difficult to decide by what code of morals they could be excused from the discharge of their duty by the apprehension of consequences. If God governs the world, more is to be feared from rebellion, than from obedience to his will. If his wisdom and goodness are both infinite, his will is and must be an infallible standard of expediency. If it be folly to barter a single soul for the whole world, would it be wise to expose a nation to the wrath of

Heaven, for a boon which we now hold, and would continue to hold at the pleasure of men who are daily threatening to deprive us of it?

But we have no fears that Congress will ever find the faithful discharge of their duty conflicting with the welfare and preservation of the Union. How far selfish and influential individuals may succeed in raising up at the South a party for secession, it is impossible to predict; but it is not difficult to show that a separation founded on the legislation we have specified, would be most preposterous and disastrous, and therefore we may reasonably presume it will not occur.

Should the slave States secede, they would do so, we may suppose, for one or more of the following reasons, viz.:

1. To protect their rights from invasion.
2. To guard and perpetuate the institution of slavery.
3. To increase their wealth and power.

The North is the strongest portion of the confederacy; and whenever, unmindful of the federal compact, it wickedly and forcibly usurps power to the prejudice of the South, secession is the only resource left to the latter for the protection of its rights. But a disregard to the *wishes*, does not necessarily imply a violation of the *rights* of the South. Not one of the measures we have contemplated as the probable result of the anti-slavery agitation, encroaches on the constitutional rights of the South; and therefore secession, however it might be professedly justified, would in fact be prompted by other motives than that of self-defence. But so long as the Federal Government confines its action against slavery within the limits of the Constitution, in what way would secession tend to guard and perpetuate the institution?

It is natural that the slave-holders should wish to destroy the influence of the abolitionists, and hence they have very unjustifiably expressed fears respecting them which they do not feel, and circulated calumnies which they do not believe. The following admissions reveal the *true* nature of the apprehensions entertained by the slave-holders.

Mr. CALHOUN, alluding in the Senate to opinions expressed by some of his southern colleagues, exclaimed:

"Do they expect the abolitionists will resort to arms, and commence a crusade to liberate our slaves by force? Is this what they mean when they speak of the attempt to abolish slavery? If so, let me tell our friends of the South who differ from us, that the war which the abolitionists wage against us, is of a very different character, and far more effective — it is waged not against our lives, but our character."

Mr. DUFF GREEN, the editor of the United States Telegraph, and the great champion of slavery, thus expressed himself in his paper:

"We are of those who believe the South has nothing to fear from a servile war. We do not believe that the abolitionists *intend*, nor could they if they would, excite the slaves to insurrection. The danger of this is remote. We believe that we have most to fear from the organized action upon the *consciences* and fears of the slave-holders themselves; from the insinuation of their dangerous heresies into our schools, our pulpits, and our domestic circles. It is only by *alarming the consciences* of the weak and feeble, and diffusing among our people a morbid sensibility on the question of slavery, that the abolitionists can accomplish their object." *

We would now respectfully submit to Mr. Calhoun's consideration, whether a secession would tend in any way to defend the *characters* of slave-holders from the war he contends is waged against them; or fortify their *consciences* against the "dangerous heresies" by which they are assailed.

The new slave-nation would acquire from her separate independence, no new power to darken the understandings, or benumb the consciences of her citizens. The freedom of the press throughout the whole slave-region, is already extinguished.† Not one single newspaper, from Maryland to Florida,

* The New York Whig merchants may learn from this candid avowal, that the "bare idea" of the abolition excitement does *not* make every "husband and father shudder with horror" at the South, whatever it may do in Wall street.

† This assertion will not probably be denied, still it may not be amiss to adduce *southern* proof of its truth. *The Missouri Argus*, published at St Louis, speaking, in April, 1839, of an editor in Ohio, remarked: "Mr. Hammond deems the coöperation of the Eastern fanatics to be all-important to the success of Whiggery, and fears that the timid course of his brother editors on this subject may be productive of mischief. He should recollect, however, that the abolition editors in slave States will not dare to avow their opinions. It would be INSTANT DEATH to them."

dares to raise its voice in favor of immediate emancipation; and a southern publication, for expressing views unfavorable to slavery, notwithstanding its bitter denunciations of abolitionists, was lately taken from a post-office in Virginia, and in pursuance *of the laws of the State*, committed to the flames by order of the public authorities; and when the laws are silent, Lynch clubs are ready to visit with infamous and cruel penalties the man who presumes to advocate the inalienable rights of man. What new ramparts could the southern confederacy build around their beloved institution? What new weapons could they forge against freedom of discussion?

At the North, the discussion of slavery is now greatly restricted by political and mercenary considerations; but such considerations would be dissipated in a moment by secession. The very demagogues who are now fawning upon the slave-holders for their votes, would, when they had no longer votes to bestow, seek popularity in ultra hatred to slavery.

The anti-slavery agitation at the North is at present chiefly confined to the religious portion of the community; it would then extend to all classes, and be embittered by national animosity. Slavery would appear more odious and detestable than ever, after having destroyed the fair fabric of American Union, and severed the ties of kindred and of friendship, to rivet more firmly the fetters of the bondman.

The slave-holders are now our fellow countrymen and citizens; they would then be foreigners who had discarded our friendship and connection, that they might trample with more unrestrained violence upon the rights and liberties of their fellow-men. These considerations show that any expectation of extinguishing or weakening the anti-slavery feeling at the North by separation, must be utterly futile.

A separation would, moreover, deprive the institution of the protection of the Federal Government. Should the slaves attempt to revolt, the masters would be left to struggle with them, unaided by the fleets and armies of the whole Republic.

And by what power would the master recapture his fugitive who had crossed the boundary of the new empire? Now he may hunt him through the whole confederacy, nor is the trembling wretch secure of his liberty, till he beholds the British standard waving above him. *Then* freedom would be the boon of every slave who could swim the Ohio, or reach the frontier line of the free republic. And this frontier line, be it remembered, *would be continually advancing South.* The anti-slavery feelings of the North, aggravated as they would be by the secession, would afford every possible facility to the fugitive, and laws would then be passed, not for the restoration of human property, but for the protection of human rights.

Would the dissolution of the Union afford the southern planters a more unrestricted enjoyment of the foreign or domestic slave-trade? Alas! from the moment of separation, slave-trading becomes PIRACY in fact, as well as in name, and the crews of New Orleans and Alexandria, as well as of African slavers, would swing on northern gibbets.

We confess then our utter inability to perceive in what possible mode a secession of the southern States would tend to guard and perpetuate the institution of slavery.

Would a dissolution of the Union augment the power and wealth of the slave States? The power and wealth of a nation depend on its population, industry and commerce. The increase of the white population at the South is now small, compared with the wonderful tide of life which is rolling over the western plains. And when the southern region shall be insulated from the sympathies of the whole civilized world, and consecrated to a stern and remorseless despotism,—a despotism sooner or later to be engulfed in blood,—by what attraction will it divert the tide of emigration from the fair prairies of the west, to its own sugar and cotton-fields? If, even now, armed patrols must traverse at night the streets and highways that the whites may sleep in safety, and military preparation is essential to domestic security,* what husband or father will take up his residence in the new empire, when withdrawn from the protection of the

* "A state of military preparation must always be with us a state of perfect domestic security. A profound peace, and consequent apathy, may expose us to the danger of domestic insurrection." *Message of Gov. Hayne to the Legislature of South Carolina*, 1833.

Federal Government and the friendship of its neighbors? The slaves are now rapidly gaining on their masters, and will increase in a still greater ratio after the separation, since the prudent and the enterprising will abandon the doomed region, and few or none will enter it from without. Hence it is obvious that the white population of the southern States could gain no accession from their erection into a separate confederacy.

Would secession augment the wealth of the South? Be it remembered that there is now no one restriction on southern industry and enterprise which separation would remove. The slave-holders in Congress, with rare exceptions, have conducted the affairs of the nation to suit themselves. So far as the interests of the northern manufacturer were identified with the tariff, they have been sacrificed at the mandate of the cotton-grower; and so far as national legislation can promote the wealth of the South, the statutes are already enacted.

It will not be denied that the larger portion of the strength of the Union,—population, money, commerce, and shipping,—is to be found at the North. In all these elements of national power, the South participates equally with the North. The foreign invader is kept from her shores, and her property abroad is protected from spoliation at least as much by the power of the North as by her own. Her strength for all purposes of defence, is the strength of the Union. What would it be after secession? True it is, the South would receive Texas into her arms, but she would derive neither honor nor power from the loathsome embrace. Annexation *now* would insure to her the political dominion of the whole Republic, but *after* secession, would cause rather weakness than strength.

As we can discover no possible advantage which the South could derive from secession, we are convinced that the threats of dissolving the Union, which her statesmen are so prodigal in scattering, are the ebullitions of passion, or the devices of policy, rather than the result of mature determination. This conviction is strengthened by still further considerations.

Should the slave States withdraw without any aggression on their rights, but for the sole purpose of enjoying in greater privacy and tranquillity the sweets of slavery, they would leave the whole North in a state of high exasperation. The ligaments which have so long bound us together, cannot be ruthlessly and wantonly torn asunder, without causing deep and festering wounds, the consequences of which the imagination revolts from anticipating. And in what light would the dark and gloomy despotism be viewed by the civilized world? Mankind would behold, and wonder, and despise. The new State would be excluded from the companionship of nations. Her cotton would indeed be still purchased, as we buy the coffee of Hayti; but with the least possible intimacy. Already is our Minister at London treated with contumely, because he is a slave-holder; as the representative only of the men who had shattered the American Republic to secure the permanency of human bondage, he would not be endured at any court in Europe, with the exception of Constantinople. In a few years, the slaves would attain a frightful numerical superiority over their masters. The dread of insurrection within, and of aggression from without, would realize the prediction of holy writ, when men's hearts shall fail them for fear, and for looking after those things which are coming on the earth. At length the fatal period would arrive, when, stung with insults and injuries, the new empire would appeal to arms; and should a hostile army land upon its shores, the standard of emancipation would be reared, and slavery would expire in blood.*

We well know with what indignant feelings these pages will at first be read by many; and fortunate shall we deem ourselves

* "March 29, 1779. The committee appointed to take into consideration the circumstances of the *southern* States, and the ways and means for their safety and defence, report: That the State of South Carolina, as represented by the delegates of the said State, and by Mr. Huger, who has come hither at the request of the governor of said State, on purpose to explain the particular circumstances thereof, *is unable to make any effectual efforts with militia, by reason of the great proportion of citizens necessary to remain at home to prevent insurrection among the negroes, and to prevent the desertion of them to the enemy*. That the state of the country and the *great numbers* of those people among them, expose the inhabitants *to great danger* from the endeavors of the enemy to excite them either to revolt or desert." *Secret Journal of Congress*, Vol. i, p. 105.

Whether the South Carolinians are from their present "particular circumstances," less in danger from a foreign invader than in 1779, may be seen from the following statement: In 1790 there were in that State 107,094 slaves and 140,178 whites; in 1830, the *colored* population was 323,322, the white only 257,863.

should we escape the imputation of writing to promote insurrection and disunion. But we appeal from the decision of angry passion, to that of calm reflection. Do we not speak the words of truth and soberness? Do not the signs of the times warrant our predictions? In what respect do the sentiments we have uttered conflict with the lessons of history, or the character of human nature? Do we love the union of the States? (!) If such a love can descend by inheritance, we should possess it; if it can be founded on the most thorough conviction of the importance of union not merely to the prosperity of our country, but to the happiness of numerous and beloved children and relatives, we should possess it. If the history of the States of Greece, of Italy, of Holland, of Germany, of South America, and of our own land, demonstrates the blessings of union and the calamities of separation, then should the prayer of every American ascend to Heaven for the perpetuity of the American Union. But let it be a union for the preservation, not the destruction of liberty: a union cemented by a sacred observance of the constitutional compact, not enforced by gag laws, a censorship of the press, and the abrogation of the right of petition; a union in conformity with the will of God, not in contempt of his authority; a union that shall be regarded as a common blessing, not held as a boon from the South, ever ready to be withdrawn as a penalty for the discharge of moral and political duties.

May Almighty God in mercy preserve the friends of emancipation from the sin and folly of even hazarding the Union, by the slightest encroachment on the constitutional rights of the South, and may he give them grace to maintain their own rights in defiance of every menace.

APPENDIX.

HAVING mentioned the charge made by President Jackson against the New York abolitionists, in his message to Congress, and alluded to the letter they addressed to him respecting it, we have thought it might be useful to insert here the letter itself, as showing more in detail one of the unwarrantable expedients to which the Federal Government has resorted in behalf of slavery.

"*To the President of the United States:*

"SIR:—In your message to Congress of the 7th instant, are the following passages: 'I must also invite your attention to the painful excitement produced in the South, by attempts to circulate through the mails, inflammatory appeals, *addressed to the passions of the slaves*, in prints and in various sorts of publications, *calculated to stimulate them to insurrection, and produce all the horrors of a servile war*. There is, doubtless, no respectable portion of our countrymen who can be so far misled as to feel any other sentiment than that of indignant regret, at conduct so destructive of the harmony and peace of the country, and *so repugnant to the principles of our national compact, and to the dictates of humanity and religion*.' You remark, that it is fortunate that the people of the North have 'given so strong and impressive a tone to the sentiments entertained against the proceedings of the misguided persons who have engaged in these *unconstitutional and wicked attempts*.' And you proceed to suggest to Congress, 'the propriety of passing such a law as will prohibit, under severe penalties, the circulation in the southern States, through the mails, of incendiary publications, *intended to instigate the slaves to insurrection*.'

"A servile insurrection, as experience has shown, involves the slaughter of the whites, without respect to sex or age. Hence, sir, the purport of the information you have communicated to Congress and to the world, is, that there are American citizens who, in violation of the dictates of humanity and religion, have engaged in unconstitutional and wicked attempts to circulate, through the mails, inflammatory appeals addressed to the passions of the slaves, and which appeals, as is implied in the object of your proposed law, are *intended* to stimulate the slaves to indiscriminate massacre. Recent events irresistibly confine the application of your remarks to the officers and members of the American Anti-Slavery Society and its auxiliaries.

"On the 28th of March, 1834, the Senate of the United States passed the following resolution:

"'Resolved, That the President, in relation to the public revenue, has assumed upon himself authority and power not conferred by the Constitution and laws, but in derogation of both.'

"On the 5th of the ensuing month, you transmitted to that body your 'solemn protest' against their decision. Instructed by your example, we now, sir, in behalf of the Society of which we are the constituted organs, and in behalf of all who are associated with it, present to you this, our 'solemn protest,' against your grievous and unfounded accusations.

"Should it be supposed that in thus addressing you we are wanting in the respect due to your exalted station, we offer, in our vindication, your own acknowledgment to the Senate: 'Subject only to the restraints of truth and justice, the free people of the United States have the undoubted right as individuals, or collectively, orally, or in writing, at such times and in such language and form as they may think proper, to discuss his (the President's) official conduct, and to express and promulgate their opinions concerning it.'

"In the exercise of this 'undoubted right,' we protest against the judgment you have pronounced against the abolitionists.

"*First*, because, in rendering that judgment officially, you assumed a power not belonging to your office.

"You complained that the resolution censuring your conduct, 'though adopted by the Senate in its legislative capacity, is, in its effects and in its characteristics, essentially *judicial*.' And thus, sir, although the charges of which we complain were made by you in your executive capacity, they are, equally with the resolution, essentially *judicial*. The Senate adjudged that your conduct was unconstitutional. You pass the same judgment on our efforts. Nay, sir, you go farther than the Senate. That body forbore to impeach your motives — but you have assumed the prerogatives, not only of a court of law, but of conscience, and pronounce our efforts to be *wicked* as well as unconstitutional.

"*Secondly*, we protest against the *publicity* you have given to your accusations.

"You felt it to be a grievance, that the charge against you was 'spread upon the Journal of the Senate, published to the nation and to the world, made part of our enduring archives, and incorporated in the history of the age. The punishment of removal from office, and future disqualification, does not follow the decision; but the *moral influence* of a solemn declaration by a majority of the Senate, that the accused is guilty of the offence charged upon him, has been as effectually secured as if the like declaration had been made upon an impeachment expressed in the same terms.'

"And is it nothing, sir, that we are officially charged by the President of the United States, with wicked and unconstitutional efforts, and with harboring the most execrable intentions? and this, too, in a document spread upon the Journals of both Houses of Congress, published to the nation and to the world, made part of our enduring archives, and incorporated in the history of the age? It is true, that although you have given judgment against us, you cannot award execution. We are not, indeed, subjected to the penalty of murder; but need we ask you, sir, what must be the *moral influence* of your declaration, that we have intended its perpetration?

"*Thirdly*, we protest against your condemnation of us *unheard*.

"What, sir, was your complaint against the Senate? 'Without notice, *unheard*, and untried, I find myself charged, on the records of the Senate, and in a form unknown in our country, with the high crime of violating the laws and Constitution of my country. No notice of the charge was given to the accused, and no opportunity afforded him to respond to the accusation — to meet his accusers face to face — to cross-examine the witnesses — to procure counteracting testimony, or to be heard in his defence.'

"Had you, sir, done to others as it thus seems you would that others should do to you, no occasion would have been given for this protest. You most truly assert, in relation to the conduct of the Senate, 'It is the policy of our benign system of jurisprudence, to secure in all criminal proceedings, and even in the most trivial litigations, a fair, unprejudiced, and impartial trial.' And by what authority, sir, do you except such of your fellow-citizens as are known as abolitionists from the benefit of this benign system? When has a fair, unprejudiced, and impartial trial been accorded to those who dare to maintain that all men are equally entitled to life, liberty, and the pursuit of happiness? What was the trial, sir, which preceded the judgment you have rendered against them?

"*Fourthly*, we protest against the *vagueness* of your charges.

"We cannot more forcibly describe the injustice you have done us than by adopting your own indignant remonstrance, against what you deemed similar injustice on the part of the Senate: 'Some of the first principles of natural right and enlightened jurisprudence, have been violated in the very form of the resolution. It carefully abstains from averring in *which* of the late proceedings the President has assumed upon himself authority and power not conferred by the Constitution and laws. Why was not the certainty of the offence, the nature and cause of the accusation, set out in the manner required in the Constitution, before even the humblest individual, for the smallest crime, can be exposed to condemnation? Such a specification was due to the accused, that he might direct his defence to the real points of attack. A more striking illustration of the soundness and necessity of the rules which forbid *vague and indefinite generalities*, and require a reasonable certainty in all judicial allegations, and a more glaring instance of the violation of these rules, have seldom been exhibited.'

"It has been reserved for you, sir, to exhibit a still more striking illustration of the importance of these rules, and a still more glaring instance of their violation. You have accused an indefinite number of your fellow-citizens, without designation of name or residence, of making unconstitutional and wicked efforts, and of harboring intentions which could be entertained only by the most depraved and abandoned of mankind; and yet you carefully abstain from averring *which* article of the Constitution they have transgressed; you omit stating when, where, and by whom these wicked attempts were made; you give no specification of the inflammatory appeals which you assert have been addressed to the passions of the slaves. You well know that the '*moral influence*' of your charges will affect thousands of your countrymen, many of them your political friends—some of them heretofore honored with your confidence—most, if not all of them, of irreproachable characters; and yet, by the very vagueness of your charges, you incapacitate each one of this multitude from proving his innocence.

"*Fifthly*, we protest against your charges because they are *untrue*. Surely, sir, the burden of proof rests upon you. If you possess evidence against us, we are, by your own showing, entitled to 'an opportunity to cross-examine witnesses, to procure counteracting testimony, and to be heard in [*our*] defence.' You complained that you had been denied such an opportunity. It was not to have been expected, then, that you would make the conduct of the Senate the model of your own. Conscious of the wrong done to you, and protesting against it, you found yourself compelled to enter on your defence. You have placed us in similar circumstances, and we proceed to follow your example:

"The substance of your various allegations may be embodied in the charge, that *we have attempted to circulate, through the mails, appeals addressed to the passions of the slaves, calculated to stimulate them to insurrection, and with the intention of producing a servile war.*

"It is deserving of notice, that the *attempt* to circulate our papers is alone charged upon us. It is not pretended that we have put our appeals into the hands of a single slave, or that, in any instance, our endeavors to excite a servile war have been crowned with success. And in what way were our most execrable attempts made? By secret agents, traversing the slave country in disguise, stealing by night into the hut of the slave, and there reading to him our inflammatory appeals? You, sir, answer this question by declaring that we attempted the mighty mischief by circulating our appeals 'THROUGH THE MAILS!' And are the southern slaves, sir, accustomed to receive periodicals by mail? Of the thousands of publications mailed from the Anti-Slavery office for the South, did you ever hear, sir, of one solitary paper being addressed to a slave? Would you know to whom they were directed, consult the southern newspapers, and you will find them complaining that they were sent to public officers, clergymen, and other influential citizens. Thus it seems we are incendiaries, who place the torch in the hands of him whose dwellings we would fire! We are conspiring to excite a servile war, and announce our design to the masters, and commit to their care and disposal the very instruments by which we expect to effect our purpose! It has been said that thirty or forty of our papers were received at the South, directed to free people of color. We cannot deny the assertion, because these papers may have been mailed by others for the sinister purpose of charging the act upon us. We are, however, ready to make our several affidavits, that not one paper, with our knowledge, or by our authority, has ever been sent to any such person in a slave State. The free people of color at the South can exert no influence in behalf of the enslaved; and we have no disposition to excite odium against them, by making them the recipients of our publications.

"Your proposal that a law should be passed, punishing the circulation, through the mails, of papers *intended to excite the slaves to insurrection*, necessarily implies that such papers are now circulated; and you expressly and positively assert, that we have attempted to circulate appeals addressed to the passions of the slaves, and *calculated to produce all the horrors of a servile war*. We trust, sir, your proposed law, so portentous to the freedom of the press, will not be enacted, till you have furnished Congress with stronger evidence of its necessity than unsupported assertions. We hope you will lay before that body, for its information, the papers to which you refer. This is the more necessary, as the various public journals and meetings which have denounced us for entertaining insurrectionary and murderous designs, have in no instance been able to quote from our publications, a single exhortation to the slaves to break their fetters, or the expression of a solitary wish for a servile war.

"How far our writings are '*calculated*' to produce insurrection, is a question which will be variously decided according to the latitude in which it is discussed. When we recollect that the humble school-book, the tale of fiction, and the costly annual have been placed under the ban of southern editors for trivial allusions to slavery—and that a southern divine has warned his fellow-citizens of the danger of permitting slaves to be present at the celebration of our national festival, where they might listen to the Declaration of Independence, and to eulogiums on liberty,—we have little hope that our disquisitions on human rights will be generally deemed safe and innocent, where those rights are habitually violated. Certain writings of one of your predecessors, President Jefferson, would undoubtedly be regarded, in some places, so insurrectionary as to expose to popular violence whoever should presume to circulate them.

"As therefore, sir, there is no common standard by which the criminality of opinions respecting slavery can be tested, we acknowledge the foresight which prompted you to recommend that the 'severe penalties' of your proposed law should be awarded, not according to the character of the publication, but the *intention* of the writer. Still, sir, we apprehend that no trivial difficulties will be experienced in the application of your law. The writer may be anonymous, or beyond the reach of prosecution, while the porter who deposits the papers in the post-office, and the mail-carrier who transports them, having no evil intentions, cannot be visited with the 'severe penalties;' and thus will your law fail in securing to the South that entire exemption from all discussion on the subject of slavery, which it so vehemently desires. The success of the attempt already made to establish a censorship of the press, is not such as to invite farther encroachment on the rights of the people to publish their sentiments.

"In your protest, you remarked to the Senate: 'The whole Executive power being vested in the President, who is *responsible* for its exercise, it is a necessary consequence that he should have a right to employ agents of his *own choice*, to aid him in the performance of his duties, and to *discharge* them when he is no longer *willing* to be RESPONSIBLE for their acts. He is equally bound to take care that the laws be faithfully executed, whether they impose duties on the highest officer of State, or the *lowest subordinates* in any of the departments.'

"It may not be uninteresting to you, sir, to be informed in what manner your 'Subordinate' in New York, who, on your 'responsibility,' is exercising the functions of censor of the American press, discharges the arduous duties of this untried, and until now, unheard-of office. We beg leave to assure you, that his task is executed with a simplicity of principle, and celerity of despatch, unknown to any censor of the press in France or Austria. Your subordinate decides upon the incendiary character of the publications committed to the post-office, by a glance at the wrappers or bags in which they are contained. No packages sent to be mailed from our office, and directed to a slave State, can escape the vigilance of this inspector of canvas and brown paper. Even your own protest, sir, if in an anti-slavery envelope, would be arrested on its progress to the South, as 'inflammatory, incendiary, and insurrectionary in the highest degree.'

"No veto, however, is *as yet* imposed on the circulation of publications from any printing-office but our own. Hence, when we desire to send 'appeals' to the South, all that is necessary is, to insert them in some newspaper that espouses our principles, pay for as many thousand copies as we think proper, and order them to be mailed according to our instructions.

"Such, sir, is the worthless protection purchased for the South, by the most unblushing and dangerous usurpation of which any public officer has been guilty since the organization of our Federal Government. Were the Senate, in reference to your acknowledged responsibility for the conduct of your subordinates, to resolve 'that the President, in relation to the suppression of certain papers in the New York Post Office, has assumed upon himself authority and power not conferred by the Constitution and laws, but in derogation of both,' instead of protesting against the charge, you would be compelled to acknowledge its truth, and you would plead the *necessity* of the case in your vindication. The weight to be attached to such a plea, may be learned from the absurdity and inefficacy of the New York censorship. Be assured, sir, your proposed law to punish the *intentions* of an author, will, in its practical operations, prove equally impotent.

"And now, sir, permit us respectfully to suggest to you the propriety of ascertaining the *real* designs of abolitionists, before your apprehensions of them lead you to sanction any more trifling with the LIBERTY OF THE PRESS. You assume it as a fact, that abolitionists are miscreants, who are laboring to effect the massacre of their southern brethren. Are you aware of the extent of the reproach which such an assumption casts upon the character of your countrymen? In August last, the number of Anti-Slavery Societies known to us was 263; we have *now* the names of more than 350 societies, and accessions are daily made to the multitude who embrace our principles. And can you think it possible, sir, that these citizens are deliberately plotting murder, and furnishing us with funds to send publications to the South 'intended to instigate the slaves to insurrection?' Is there any thing in the character and manners of the free States, to warrant the imputation on their citizens of such enormous wickedness? Have you ever heard, sir, of whole communities in these States subjecting obnoxious individuals to a mock trial, and then, in contempt of law, humanity, and religion, deliberately murdering them? You have seen, in the public journals, great rewards offered for the perpetration of horrible crimes. We appeal to your candor, and ask, were these rewards offered by abolitionists, or by men whose charges against abolitionists you have condescended to sanction and disseminate?

"And what, sir, is the character of those whom you have in your message held up to the execration of the civilized world? Their enemies being judges, they are *religious* fanatics. And what are the haunts of these plotters of murder? The pulpit, the bench, the bar, the professor's chair, the hall of legislation, the meeting for prayer, the temple of the Most High. But strange and monstrous as is this conspiracy, still you believe in its existence, and call on Congress to counteract it. Be persuaded, sir, the moral sense of the community is abundantly sufficient to render this conspiracy utterly impotent the moment its machinations are exposed. Only PROVE the assertions and insinuations in your message, and you dissolve in an instant every Anti-Slavery Society in our land. Think not, sir, that we shall interpose any obstacle to an inquiry into our conduct. We invite, nay, sir, we entreat the appointment by Congress of a Committee of Investigation to visit the Anti-Slavery office in New York. They shall be put in possession of copies of all the publications that have been issued from our press. Our whole correspondence shall be submitted to their inspection; our accounts of receipts and expenditures shall be spread before them, and we ourselves will cheerfully answer under oath whatever interrogatories they may put to us relating to the charges you have advanced.

"Should such a committee be denied, and should the law you propose, stigmatizing us as felons, be passed without inquiry into the truth of your accusation, and without allowing us a hearing, then shall we make the language of your protest our own, and declare that, 'If such proceedings shall be approved and sustained by an intelligent people, then will the great contest with arbitrary power which had established in statutes, in bills of rights, in sacred charters, and in constitutions of government, the right of every citizen to a notice before trial, to a hearing before condemnation, and to an impartial tribunal for deciding on the charge, have been made in VAIN.'

"Before we conclude, permit us, sir, to offer you the following assurances.

"Our principles, our objects, and our measures, are wholly uncontaminated by considerations of party policy. Whatever may be our respective opinions as citizens, of men and measures, as abolitionists we have expressed no political preferences, and are pursuing no party ends. From neither of the gentlemen nominated to succeed you, have we any thing to hope or fear; and to neither of them do we intend, as abolitionists, to afford any aid or influence. This declaration will, it is hoped, satisfy the partisans of the rival candidates that it is not necessary for them to assail our rights by way of convincing the South that they do not possess our favor.

"We have addressed you, sir, on this occasion, with republican plainness and Christian sincerity; but with no desire to derogate from the respect that is due to you, or wantonly to give you pain. To repel your charges, and to disabuse the public, was a duty we owed to ourselves, to our children, and above all to the great and holy cause in which we are engaged. That cause we believe is approved by our Maker; and while we retain this belief, it is our intention, trusting to His direction and protection, to persevere in our endeavors to impress upon the minds and hearts of our countrymen, the sinfulness of claiming property in human beings, and the duty and wisdom of immediately relinquishing it.

"When convinced that our endeavors are wrong, we shall abandon them; but such conviction must be produced by other arguments than vituperation, popular violence, or penal enactments.

ARTHUR TAPPAN,
WILLIAM JAY,
JOHN RANKIN,
ABRAHAM L. COX,
JOSHUA LEAVITT,
SIMEON S. JOSELYN,
LEWIS TAPPAN,
THEODORE S. WRIGHT,
SAMUEL E. CORNISH,
ELIZUR WRIGHT, JR.

Executive Committee."

NEW YORK, Dec. 26, 1835.

ON THE

CONDITION OF THE FREE PEOPLE OF COLOR

IN THE UNITED STATES.

It appears from the census of 1830, that there were then 319,467 free colored persons in the United States. At the present time the number cannot be less than 360,000. Fifteen States of the Federal Union have each a smaller population than this aggregate. Hence if the whole mass of human beings inhabiting Connecticut, or New Jersey, or any other of these fifteen States, were subjected to the ignorance and degradation and persecution and terror we are about to describe as the lot of this much-injured people, the amount of suffering would still be numerically less than that inflicted by a professedly Christian and republican community upon the free negroes. Candor, however, compels us to admit that, deplorable as is their condition, it is still not so wretched as colonizationists and slave-holders, for obvious reasons, are fond of representing it. It is not true that free negroes are "more vicious and miserable than slaves *can* be,"* nor that "it would be as humane to throw slaves from the decks of the middle passage, as to set them free in this coun-

* Rev. Mr. Bacon, of New Haven, 7 Rep., Am. Col. Soc., p. 99.

try,"* nor that "a sudden and universal emancipation without colonization, would be a greater CURSE to the slaves themselves, than the bondage in which they are held."

It is a little singular, that in utter despite of these rash assertions slave-holders and colonizationists unite in assuring us, that the slaves are rendered *discontented* by *witnessing* the freedom of their colored brethren; and hence we are urged to assist in banishing to Africa these sable and dangerous mementoes of liberty.

We all know that the wife and children of the free negro are not ordinarily sold in the market, that he himself does not toil under the lash, and that in certain parts of our country he is permitted to acquire some intelligence, and to enjoy some comforts, utterly and universally denied to the slave. Still it is most unquestionable, that these people grievously suffer from a cruel and wicked prejudice — cruel in its consequences, wicked in its voluntary adoption and its malignant character.

Colonizationists have taken great pains to inculcate the opinion that prejudice against color is implanted in our nature by the Author of our being; and whence they infer the futility of every effort to elevate the colored man in this country, and consequently the duty and benevolence of sending him to Africa, beyond the reach of our cruelty.† The theory is as false in fact

* African Repository, Vol. IV, p. 226.

† "Prejudices, which neither refinement, nor argument, nor education, NOR RELIGION ITSELF can subdue, mark the people of color, whether bond or free, as the subjects of a degradation *inevitable and incurable.*" *Address of the Connecticut Col. Society.* "The managers consider it clear that causes exist, and are now operating, to prevent their improvement and elevation to any considerable extent as a class in this country, which are fixed, not only beyond the control of the friends of humanity, but of *any human power:* CHRISTIANITY cannot do for them here, what it will do for them in Africa. This is not the *fault* of the colored man, *nor of the white man,* but an ORDINATION OF PROVIDENCE, *and no more to be changed than the laws of nature.*" *15th Rep., Am. Col. Soc.,* p. 47.

"The people of color must, in this country, remain for ages, probably for ever, a separate and distinct caste, weighed down by causes powerful, universal, invincible, which neither legislation nor CHRISTIANITY can remove." *African Repository,* Vol. VIII, p. 196.

"Do they (the abolitionists) not perceive that in thus confounding all the distinctions which GOD himself has made, they arraign the wisdom and goodness of Providence itself? It has been his divine pleasure, to make the black man black, and the white man white, and to distinguish them by other *repulsive* constitutional differences." *Speech in Senate of the United States, February* 7, 1839, *by Henry Clay, President of the Am. Col. Soc.*

as it is derogatory to the character of that God whom we are told is LOVE. With what astonishment and disgust should we behold an earthly parent exciting feuds and animosities among his own children; yet we are assured, and that too by professing Christians, that our heavenly Father has implanted a principle of hatred, repulsion and alienation between certain portions of his family on earth, and then commanded them, as if in mockery, to "love one another."

In vain do we seek in nature for the origin of this prejudice. Young children never betray it, and on the continent of Europe it is unknown. We are not speaking of matters of taste, or of opinions of personal beauty, but of a prejudice against complexion, leading to insult, degradation and oppression. In no country in Europe is any man excluded from refined society, or deprived of literary, religious, or political privileges on account of the tincture of his skin. If this prejudice is the fiat of the Almighty, most wonderful is it, that of all the kindreds of the earth, none have been found submissive to the heavenly impulse, excepting the white inhabitants of North America; and of these, it is no less strange than true, that this divine principle of repulsion is most energetic in such persons as, in other respects, are the least observant of their Maker's will. This prejudice is sometimes erroneously regarded as the *cause* of slavery; and some zealous advocates of emancipation have flattered themselves that, could the prejudice be destroyed, negro slavery would fall with it. Such persons have very inadequate ideas of the malignity of slavery. They forget that the slaves in Greece and Rome were of the same hue as their masters; and that at the South, the value of a slave, especially of a female, rises, as the complexion recedes from the African standard.

Were we to inquire into the geography of this prejudice, we should find that the localities in which it attains its rankest luxuriance, are not the rice-swamps of Georgia, nor the sugar-fields of Louisiana, but the hills and valleys of New England, and the prairies of Ohio! It is a fact of acknowledged notoriety, that however severe may be the laws against the colored people at the South, the prejudice against their *persons* is far weaker than among ourselves.

It is not necessary, for our present purpose, to enter into a particular investigation of the condition of the free negroes in the slave States. We all know that they suffer every form of oppression which the laws can inflict upon persons not actually slaves. That unjust and cruel enactments should proceed from a people who keep two millions of their fellow-men in abject bondage, and who believe such enactments essential to the maintenance of their despotism, certainly affords no cause for surprise.

We turn to the free States, where slavery has not directly steeled our hearts against human suffering, and where no supposed danger of insurrection affords a pretext for keeping the free blacks in ignorance and degradation; and we ask, What is the character of the prejudice against color *here?* Let the Rev. Mr. Bacon, of Connecticut, answer the question. This gentleman, in a vindication of the Colonization Society, assures us, "The *Soodra* is not farther separated from the *Brahim* in regard to all his privileges, civil, intellectual, and moral, than the negro from the white man by the prejudices which result from the difference made between them by the GOD OF NATURE." *Rep. Am. Col. Soc.*, p. 87.

We may here notice the very opposite effect produced on abolitionists and colonizationists, by the consideration that this difference *is* made by the GOD OF NATURE; leading the one to discard the prejudice, and the other to banish its victims.

With these preliminary remarks we will now proceed to take a view of the condition of the free people of color in the non-slave-holding States; and will consider in order, the various disabilities and oppressions to which they are subjected, either by law or the customs of society.

1. GENERAL EXCLUSION FROM THE ELECTIVE FRANCHISE.

Were this exclusion founded on the want of property, or any other qualification deemed essential to the judicious exercise of the franchise, it would afford no just cause of complaint; but it is founded solely on the color of the skin, and is therefore irrational and unjust. That taxation and representation should be inseparable, was one of the axioms of the fathers of our Revolution, and one of the reasons they assigned for their revolt from the crown of Britain. But *now*, it is deemed a mark of fanaticism to complain of the disfranchisement of a whole race, while they remain subject to the burden of taxation. It is worthy of remark, that of the thirteen original States, only *two* were so recreant to the principles of the Revolution, as to make a *white skin* a qualification for suffrage. But the prejudice has grown with our growth, and strengthened with our strength; and it is believed that in *every* State constitution subsequently formed or revised, (excepting Vermont and Maine, and the revised constitution of Massachusetts,) the crime of a dark complexion has been punished, by debarring its possessor from all approach to the ballot-box.* The necessary effect of this proscription in aggravating the oppression and degradation of the colored inhabitants, must be obvious to all who call to mind the solicitude manifested by demagogues, and office-seekers, and law-makers, to propitiate the good will of all who have votes to bestow.

2. DENIAL OF THE RIGHT OF LOCOMOTION.

It is in vain that the Constitution of the United States expressly guarantees to "the citizens of each State, all the privileges and immunities of citizens in the several States:" — It is in vain that the Supreme Court of the United States has solemnly decided that this clause confers on every citizen of one State the right to "pass through, or reside in any other State for the purposes of trade, agriculture, professional pursuits, or *otherwise*." It is in vain that "the members of the several State Legislatures" are required to "be bound by oath or affirmation to support" the Constitution conferring this very guaranty. Constitutions and judicial decisions and religious obligations are alike outraged by our State enactments against people of color. There is

* "From this remark the revised constitution of New York is *nominally* an exception, colored citizens, possessing a *freehold* worth two hundred and fifty dollars, being allowed to vote; while suffrage is extended to *white* citizens without any property qualification.

scarcely a slave State in which a citizen of New York, with a dark skin, may visit a dying child without subjecting himself to legal penalties. But in the slave States we look for cruelty; we expect the rights of humanity and the laws of the land to be sacrificed on the altar of slavery. In the free States, we had reason to hope for a greater deference to decency and morality. Yet even in these States we behold the effects of a miasma wafted from the South. The Connecticut Black Act, prohibiting, under heavy penalties, the instruction of any colored person from another State, is well known. It is one of the encouraging signs of the times, that public opinion has recently compelled the repeal of this detestable law. But among all the free States, OHIO stands preëminent for the wickedness of her statutes against this class of our population. These statutes are not merely infamous outrages on every principle of justice and humanity, but are gross and palpable violations of the State constitution, and manifest an absence of moral sentiment in the Ohio Legislature, as deplorable as it is alarming. We speak the language, not of passion, but of sober conviction; and for the truth of this language we appeal, first, to the statutes themselves, and then to the consciences of our readers. We shall have occasion to notice these laws under the several divisions of our subject to which they belong; at present we ask attention to the one intended to prevent the colored citizens of other States from removing into Ohio. By the constitution of New York, the colored inhabitants are expressly recognized as "citizens." Let us suppose, then, a New York freeholder and voter of this class, confiding in the guaranty given by the Federal constitution, removes into Ohio. No matter how much property he takes with him; no matter what attestations he produces to the purity of his character, he is required by the Act of 1807, to find, within twenty days, two freehold sureties in the sum of five hundred dollars for his *good behavior;* and likewise for his *maintenance,* should he at any future period, from any cause whatever, be unable to maintain himself, and in default of procuring such sureties, he is to be removed by the overseers of the poor The Legislature well knew that it would generally be utterly impossible for a stranger, and especially a *black* stranger, to find such sureties. It was the *design* of the Act, by imposing impracticable conditions, to prevent colored emigrants from remaining within the State; and in order more certainly to effect this object, it imposes a pecuniary penalty on every inhabitant who shall venture to "harbor," that is, receive under his roof, or who shall even "employ" an emigrant who has not given the required sureties; and it moreover renders such inhabitant so harboring or employing him legally liable for his future maintenance!

We are frequently told that the efforts of the abolitionists have in fact aggravated the condition of the colored people, bond and free. The *date* of this law, as well as the date of most of the laws composing the several slave-codes, shows what credit is to be given to the assertion. If a barbarous enactment is *recent*, its odium is thrown upon the friends of the blacks; if *ancient*, we are assured that it is *obsolete*. The Ohio law was enacted only four years after the State was admitted into the Union. In 1800 there were only three hundred and thirty-seven free blacks in the territory, and in 1830, the number in the State was nine thousand five hundred. Of course a very large proportion of the present colored population of the State must have entered it in ignorance of this iniquitous law, or in defiance of it. That the law has not been universally enforced, proves only that the people of Ohio are less profligate than their legislators; that it has remained on the statute book for thirty-two years, proves the depraved state of public opinion and the horrible persecution to which the colored people are legally exposed. But let it not be supposed that this vile law is in fact obselete, and its very existence forgotten.

In 1829, a very general effort was made to enforce this law, and about *one thousand free blacks* were in consequence of it driven out of the State, and sought a refuge in the more free and Christian country of Canada. Previous to their departure, they sent a deputation to the Governor of the Upper Province, to know if they would be admitted, and received from Sir James Colebrook this reply:—"Tell the *republicans* on your side of the line, that we royalists do not know men by their color. Should you come to us, you will be entitled to all the privileges of the rest of his majesty's subjects." This was the origin of the Wilberforce colony in Upper Canada.

We have now before us an Ohio paper containing a proclamation by John S. Wiles, overseer of the poor in the town of Fairfield, dated 12th March, 1838. In this instrument notice is given to all "black or mulatto persons" residing in Fairfield, to comply with the requisitions of the Act of 1807 within twenty days, or the law would be enforced against them. The proclamation also addresses the white inhabitants of Fairfield in the following terms: "Whites, look out! If any person or persons *employing* any black or mulatto person, contrary to the third section of the above law, you may look out for the breakers." The extreme vulgarity and malignity of this notice indicates the spirit which gave birth to this detestable law, and continues it in being.

Now what says the constitution of Ohio? "ALL are born free and independent, and have certain natural, inherent, inalienable rights; among which are the enjoying, and defending life and liberty, *acquiring, possessing and protecting property*, and pursuing and attaining happiness and safety." Yet men who had called their Maker to witness that they would obey this very constitution, require impracticable conditions, and then impose a pecuniary penalty and grievous liabilities on every man who shall give to an innocent fellow-countryman a night's lodging, or even a meal of victuals in exchange for his honest labor!

3. DENIAL OF THE RIGHT OF PETITION.

We explicitly disclaim all intention to imply that the several disabilities and cruelties we are specifying are of universal application. The laws of some States in relation to people of color are more wicked than others; and the spirit of persecution is not in every place equally active and malignant. In none of the free States have these people so many grievances to complain of as in Ohio, and for the honor of our country we rejoice to add, that in no other State in the Union has their right to petition for a redress of their grievances been denied.

On the 14th of January, 1839, a petition for relief from certain legal disabilities, from colored inhabitants of Ohio, was presented to the *popular* branch of the Legislature, and its rejection was moved by George H. Flood.* This rejection was not a denial of the prayer, but an *expulsion of the petition itself*, as an intruder into the House. "The question presented for our decision," said one of the members, "is simply this — Shall human beings, who are bound by every enactment upon our statute book, be *permitted* to *request* the Legislature to modify or soften the laws under which they live?" To the Grand Sultan, crowded with petitions as he traverses the streets of Constantinople, such a question would seem most strange; but American Democrats can exert a tyranny over *men who have no votes*, utterly unknown to Turkish despotism. Mr. Flood's motion was lost by a majority of only *four* votes; but this triumph of humanity and republicanism was as transient as it was meagre. The *next* day, the House, by a large majority, resolved

"That the blacks and mulattoes who may be residents within this State, have no constitutional right to present their petitions to the General Assembly for any purpose whatsoever, and that any reception of such petitions on the part of the General Assembly is a mere act of privilege or policy, and not imposed by any expressed or implied power of the Constitution."

The phraseology of this resolution is as clumsy as its assertions are base and sophistical. The meaning intended to be expressed is simply, that the constitution of Ohio, neither in terms nor by implication, confers on such residents as are negroes or mulattoes, any right to offer a petition to the Legislature for any object whatever; nor imposes on that body any obligation to notice such a petition; and whatever attention it may please to bestow upon it, ought to be regarded as an act not of duty, but merely of favor or expediency. Hence it is obvious, that the *principle* on which the resolution is founded is, that the reciprocal right and duty of offering and hearing petitions *rests solely on consti-*

* It is sometimes interesting to preserve the names of individuals who have perpetrated bold and unusual enormities.

tutional enactment, and not on moral obligation. The *reception* of negro petitions is declared to be a mere act of *privilege or policy*. Now it is difficult to imagine a principle more utterly subversive of all the duties of rulers, the rights of citizens, and the charities of private life. The victim of oppression or fraud has no *right* to appeal to the constituted authorities for redress, nor are those authorities under any obligation to consider the appeal; the needy and unfortunate have no right to implore the assistance of their more fortunate neighbors; and all are at liberty to turn a deaf ear to the cry of distress. The eternal and immutable principles of justice and humanity, proclaimed by Jehovah, and impressed by him on the conscience of man, have no binding force on the Legislature of Ohio, unless expressly adopted and enforced by the State constitution!

But as the Legislature has thought proper thus to set at defiance the moral sense of mankind, and to take refuge behind the enactments of the constitution, let us try the strength of their entrenchments. The words of the constitution, which it is pretended sanction the resolution we are considering, are the following, viz.:—"The *people* have a right to assemble together in a peaceable manner to consult for their common good, to *instruct their representatives*, and to apply to the Legislature for a redress of grievances." It is obvious that this clause confers no rights, but is merely declaratory of existing rights. Still, as the right of the people to apply for a redress of grievances is coupled with the right of *instructing their representatives*, and as negroes are not electors, and consequently are without representatives, it is inferred that they are not part of *the people*. That Ohio legislators are not Christians would be a more rational conclusion. One of the members avowed his opinion that "none but voters had a right to petition." If, then, according to the principle of the resolution, the constitution of Ohio denies the right of petition to all but electors, let us consider the practical results of such a denial. In the first place, every female in the State is placed under the same disability with "blacks and mulattoes. No wife has a right to ask for a divorce — no daughter may plead for a father's life. Next, no man under twenty-one years — no citizen of any age, who from want of sufficient residence, or other qualification, is not entitled to vote — no individual among the tens of thousands of aliens in the State, however oppressed and wronged by official tyranny or corruption, has a right to seek redress from the representatives of the people, and should he presume to do so, may be told, that, like "blacks and mulattoes," he "has no constitutional right to present his petition to the General Assembly for any purpose whatever." Again, the State of Ohio is deeply indebted to the citizens of other States, and also to the subjects of Great Britain, for money borrowed to construct her canals. Should any of these creditors lose their certificates of debt, and ask for their renewal; or should their interest be withheld, or paid in depreciated currency, and were they to ask for justice at the hands of the Legislature, they might be told, that any attention paid to their request must be regarded as a "mere act of privilege or policy, and not imposed by any expressed or implied power of the Constitution," for, not being voters, they stood on the same ground as "blacks and mulattoes." Such is the folly and wickedness in which prejudice against color has involved the legislators of a republican and professedly Christian State in the nineteenth century.

4. EXCLUSION FROM THE ARMY AND MILITIA.

The Federal Government is probably the only one in the world that forbids a portion of its subjects to participate in the national defence, not from any doubts of their courage, loyalty, or physical strength, but merely on account of the tincture of their skin! To such an absurd extent is this prejudice against color carried, that some of our militia companies have occasionally refused to march to the sound of a drum when beaten by a black man. To declare a certain class of the community unworthy to bear arms in defence of their native country, is necessarily to consign that class to general contempt.

5. EXCLUSION FROM ALL PARTICIPATION IN THE ADMINISTRATION OF JUSTICE.

No colored man can be a judge, juror, or constable. Were the talents and acquirements of a Mansfield or a Marshall veiled in a sable skin, they would be excluded from the bench of the humblest court in the American republic. In the slave States generally, no black man can enter a court of justice as a witness against a white one. Of course a white man may, with perfect impunity, defraud or abuse a negro to any extent, provided he is careful to avoid the presence of any of his own caste, at the execution of his contract, or the indulgence of his malice. We are not aware that an outrage so flagrant is sanctioned by the laws of any *free* State, with one exception. That exception the reader will readily believe can be none other than OHIO. A statute of this State enacts, "that no black or mulatto *person* or *persons* shall hereafter be permitted to be sworn, or give evidence in any court of record or elsewhere, in this State, in any cause depending, or matter of controversy, when either party to the same is a WHITE person; or in any prosecution of the State against any WHITE person."

We have seen that on the subject of petition the Legislature regards itself as independent of all obligation except such as is imposed by the constitution. How mindful they are of the requirements even of that instrument, when obedience to them would check the indulgence of their malignity to the blacks, appears from the 7th Section of the 8th Article, viz.—"All courts shall be open, and every *person*, for any injury done him in his lands, goods, person or reputation, shall have remedy by due course of law, and right and justice administered without denial or delay."

Ohio legislators may deny that negroes and mulattoes are citizens, or people; but they are estopped by the very words of the statute just quoted, from denying that they are "*persons*." Now, by the constitution every *person*, black as well as white, is to have justice administered to him without denial or delay. But by the law, while any unknown *white* vagrant may be a witness in any case whatever, no black suitor is permitted to offer a witness of his own color, however well established may be his character for intelligence and veracity, to prove his rights or his wrongs; and hence in a multitude of cases, justice is denied in despite of the constitution; and why denied? Solely from a foolish and wicked prejudice against color.

6. IMPEDIMENTS TO EDUCATION.

No people have ever professed so deep a conviction of the importance of popular education as ourselves, and no people have ever resorted to such cruel expedients to perpetuate abject ignorance. More than one third of the whole population of the slave States are prohibited from learning even to read, and in some of them, free men, if with dark complexions, are subject to stripes for teaching their own children. If we turn to the free States, we find that in all of them, without exception, the prejudices and customs of society oppose almost insuperable obstacles to the acquisition of a liberal education by colored youth. Our academies and colleges are barred against them. We know there are instances of young men with dark skins having been received, under peculiar circumstances, into northern colleges; but we neither know nor believe, that there have been a dozen such instances within the last thirty years.

Colored children are very generally excluded from our common schools, in consequence of the prejudices of teachers and parents. In some of our cities there are schools *exclusively* for their use, but in the country the colored population is too sparse to justify such schools; and white and black children are rarely seen studying under the same roof; although such cases do sometimes occur, and then they are confined to elementary schools. Some colored young men, who could bear the expense, have obtained in European seminaries the education denied them in their native land.

It may not be useless to cite an instance of the malignity with which the education of the blacks is opposed. The efforts made in Connecticut to prevent the establishment of schools of a higher order than usual for colored pupils, are too well known to need a recital here; and her BLACK ACT, prohibiting the instruction of colored children from other States, although now expunged from her statute book through the influence of abolitionists, will long be remembered to the opprobrium of her citizens. We ask attention to the following illustration of public opinion in another New England State.

In 1834 an academy was built by subscription in CANAAN, New Hampshire, and a charter granted by the Legislature; and at a meeting of the proprietors it was determined to receive all applicants having "suitable moral and intellectual recommendations, without other distinctions;" in other words, without reference to *complexion*. When this determination was made known, a town meeting was forthwith convened, and the following resolutions adopted, viz.:

"Resolved, that we view with *abhorrence* the attempt of the abolitionists to establish in this town a school for the instruction of the sable sons and daughters of Africa, in common with our sons and daughters.

"Resolved, that we will not associate with, nor in any way countenance, any man or woman who shall hereafter persist in attempting to establish a school in this town for the *exclusive* education of blacks, *or* for their education in conjunction with the whites."

The frankness of this last resolve is commendable. The inhabitants of Canaan, assembled in legal town meeting, determined, it seems, that the blacks among them should in future have no education whatever; they should not be instructed in company with the whites, neither should they have schools exclusively for themselves.

The proprietors of the academy supposing, in the simplicity of their hearts, that in a free country they might use their property in any manner not forbidden by law, proceeded to open their school, and in the ensuing spring, had twenty-eight white, and fourteen colored scholars. The crisis had now arrived when the cause of prejudice demanded the sacrifice of constitutional liberty and of private property. Another town meeting was convoked, at which, without a shadow of authority, and in utter contempt of law and decency, it was ordered, that the academy should be forcibly removed, and a committee was appointed to execute the abominable mandate. Due preparations were made for the occasion, and on the 10th of August, three hundred men with about two hundred oxen, assembled at the place, and taking the edifice from off its foundation, dragged it to a distance, and left it a ruin. No one of the actors in this high-handed outrage was ever brought before a court of justice to answer for this criminal and riotous destruction of the property of others.

The transaction we have narrated expresses in emphatic terms the deep and settled hostility felt in the free States, to the education of the blacks. The prejudices of the community render that hostility generally effective without the aid of legal enactments. Indeed, some remaining regard to decency and the opinion of the world, has restrained the Legislatures of the free States, with *one exception*, from consigning these unhappy people to ignorance by "decreeing unrighteous decrees," and "framing mischief by a law." Our readers, no doubt, feel that the exception must of course be OHIO.

We have seen with what deference Ohio legislators profess to regard their *constitutional* obligations; and we are now to contemplate another instance of their shameless violation of them. The constitution which these men have sworn to obey declares,

> "NO LAWS SHALL BE PASSED to prevent the poor of the several townships and counties in this State from an *equal* participation in the schools, academies, colleges, and universities in this State, which are endowed in whole, or *in part*, from the revenue arising from *donations* made by the United States, for the support of *colleges and schools* — and the door of said schools, academies, and universities shall be open for the reception of scholars, students, and teachers of every *grade*, without ANY DISTINCTION OR PREFERENCE WHATEVER."

Can language be more explicit or unequivocal? But have any donations been made by the United States for the support of colleges and schools in Ohio? Yes; by an Act of Congress, the sixteenth section of land in *each* originally surveyed township in the State was set apart as a donation for the express purpose of endowing and supporting common schools. And now, how have the scrupulous legislators of Ohio, who refuse to acknowledge any other than constitutional obligations to give ear to the cry of distress — how have they obeyed this injunction of the constitution respecting the freedom of their schools? They enacted a law in 1831, declaring that, "when any appropriation shall be made by the directors of any school district, from the treasury thereof, for the payment of a teacher, the school in such district shall be open" — to whom? — "*to scholars, students, and teachers of every grade, without distinction or preference, whatever*," as commanded by the constitution? Oh no! — "shall be open to all the WHITE children residing therein!" Such is the impotency of written constitutions, where a sense of moral obligation is wanting to enforce them.

We have now taken a review of the Ohio laws against free people of color. Some of them are of old, and others of recent date. The opinion entertained of all these laws, new and old, by the *present* legislators of Ohio, may be learned by a resolution adopted in January last, (1839) by both houses of the Legislature.

"Resolved, that in the opinion of this General Assembly it is unwise, impolitic, and inexpedient to repeal *any* law now in force imposing disabilities upon black or mulatto persons, thus placing them upon an equality with the whites, so far as this Legislature can do, and indirectly inviting the black population of other States to emigrate to this, to the manifest injury of the public interest."

The best comment on the *spirit* which dictated this resolve is an enactment by the *same* Legislature, abrogating the supreme law which requires us to "do unto others as we would they should do unto us," and prohibiting every citizen of Ohio from *harboring or concealing* a fugitive slave, under the penalty of fine or imprisonment. General obedience to this vile statute is alone wanting to fill to the brim the cup of Ohio's iniquity and degradation. She hath done what she could to oppress and crush the free negroes within her borders. She is now seeking to rechain the slave who has escaped from his fetters.

7. IMPEDIMENTS TO RELIGIOUS INSTRUCTION.

It is unnecessary to dwell here on the laws of the slave States prohibiting the free people of color from learning to read the Bible, and, in many instances, from assembling at discretion to worship their Creator. These laws, we are assured, are indispensable to the perpetuity of that "peculiar institution," which many masters in Israel are now teaching, enjoys the sanction of

HIM who "will have all men to be saved, and to come to the knowledge of the truth," and who has left to his disciples the injunction "search the Scriptures." We turn to the free States, in which no institution requires that the light of the glorious gospel of Christ should be prevented from shining on any portion of the population, and inquire how far prejudice here supplies the place of southern statutes.

The impediments to education already mentioned, necessarily render the acquisition of religious knowledge difficult, and in many instances impracticable. In the northern cities, the blacks have frequently churches of their own, but in the country they are too few and too poor to build churches and maintain ministers. Of course they must remain destitute of public worship and religious instruction, unless they can enjoy these blessings in company with the whites. Now there is hardly a church in the United States, not exclusively appropriated to the blacks, in which one of their number owns a pew, or has a voice in the choice of a minister. There are usually, indeed, a few seats in a remote part of the church, set apart for their use, and in which no white person is ever seen. It is surely not surprising, under all the circumstances of the case, that these seats are rarely crowded.

Colored ministers are occasionally ordained in the different denominations, but they are kept at a distance by their white brethren in the ministry, and are very rarely permitted to enter their pulpits; and still more rarely, to sit at their tables, although acknowledged to be ambassadors of Christ. The distinction of *caste* is not forgotten, even in the celebration of the Lord's Supper, and seldom are colored disciples permitted to eat and drink of the memorials of the Redeemer's passion till after every white communicant has been served.

8. IMPEDIMENTS TO HONEST INDUSTRY.

In this country ignorance and poverty are almost inseparable companions; and it is surely not strange that those should be poor whom we compel to be ignorant. The liberal professions are virtually sealed against the blacks, if we except the church, and even in that, admission is rendered difficult by the obstacles placed in their way in acquiring the requisite literary qualifications;* and when once admitted, their administrations are confined to their own color. Many of our most wealthy and influential citizens have commenced life as ignorant and as penniless as any negro who loiters in our streets. Had their complexion been dark, notwithstanding their talents, industry, enterprise and probity, they would have continued ignorant and penniless, because the paths to learning and to wealth would then have been closed against them. There is a conspiracy, embracing all the departments of society, to keep the black man ignorant and poor. As a general rule, admitting few if any exceptions, the schools of literature and of science reject him—the counting house refuses to receive him as a bookkeeper, much more as a partner — no store admits him as a clerk — no shop as an apprentice. Here and there a black man may be found keeping a few trifles on a shelf for sale; and a few acquire, as if by stealth, the knowledge of some handicraft; but almost universally these people, both in town and country, are prevented by the customs of society from maintaining themselves and their families by any other than menial occupations.

In 1836, a black man of irreproachable character, and who by his industry and frugality had accumulated several thousand dollars, made application in the City of New York for a carman's license, and was refused solely and avowedly on account of his

* Of the truth of this remark, the trustees of the Episcopal Theological Seminary at New York, lately (June, 1839) afforded a striking illustration. A young man, regularly acknowledged by the bishop as a candidate for orders, and in consequence of such acknowledgment entitled, by an *express statute* of the seminary, to admission to its privileges, presented himself as a pupil. But God had given him a dark complexion, and *therefore* the trustees, regardless of the statute, barred the doors against him, by a formal and deliberate vote. As a compromise between conscience and prejudice, the professors offered to give him *private* instruction—to do in secret what they were ashamed to do openly—to confer as a favor what he was entitled to demand as a right. The offer was rejected.

It is worthy of remark, that of the trustees who took an *active* part against the *colored* candidate, one is the PRESIDENT *of the New York Colonization Society;* another a MANAGER, and a third, one of its public champions; and that the bishop of the diocese, who wished to exclude his candidate from the theological school of which he is both a trustee and a professor, lately headed a recommendation in the newspapers for the purchase of a packet ship for Liberia, as likely to "render far more efficient than heretofore, the enterprise of colonization."

complexion! We have already seen the effort of the Ohio Legislature to consign the negroes to starvation by deterring others from employing them. Ignorance, idleness, and vice, are at once the punishments we inflict upon these unfortunate people for their complexion; and the crimes with which we are constantly reproaching them.

9. LIABILITY TO BE SEIZED, AND TREATED AS SLAVES.

An able-bodied colored man sells in the southern market for from eight hundred to a thousand dollars; of course he is worth stealing. Colonizationists and slave-holders, and many northern divines, solemnly affirm, that the situation of a slave is far preferable to that of a free negro; hence it would seem an act of humanity to convert the latter into the former. Kidnapping being both a lucrative and a benevolent business, it is not strange it should be extensively practised. In many of the States this business is regulated by law, and there are various ways in which the transmutation is legally effected. Thus, in South Carolina, if a free negro "entertains" a runaway slave, it may be his own wife or child, he himself is turned into a slave. In 1827, *a free woman and her three children* underwent this benevolent process, for *entertaining* two fugitive children of six and nine years old. In Virginia all emancipated slaves remaining twelve months in the State, are kindly restored to their former condition. In Maryland a free negro who marries a white woman, thereby acquires all the privileges of a slave—and generally, throughout the slave region, including the District of Columbia, every negro not known to be free, is mercifully considered as a slave, and if his master cannot be ascertained, he is thrown into a dungeon, and there kept, till by a public sale a master can be provided for him. But often the law grants to colored men, *known to be free*, all the advantages of slavery. Thus, in Georgia, every *free* colored man coming into the State, and unable to pay a fine of one hundred dollars, become a slave for life; in Florida, insolvent debtors, *if black*, are SOLD for the benefit of their creditors; and in the District of Columbia a free colored man, thrown into jail on suspicion of being a slave and proving his freedom, is required by law to be sold as a slave, if too poor to pay his jail fees. Let it not be supposed that these laws are all obsolete and inoperative. They catch many a northern negro, who, in pursuit of his own business, or on being decoyed by others, ventures to enter the slave region; and who, of course, helps to augment the wealth of our southern brethren. On the 6th of March, 1839, a report by a Committee was made to the House of Representatives of the Massachusetts Legislature, in which are given the *names* of seventeen free colored men who had been enslaved at the South. It also states an instance in which twenty-five colored citizens, belonging to Massachusetts, were confined at one time in a southern jail, and another instance in which seventy-five free colored persons from different free States were confined, all preparatory to their sale as slaves according to law.

The facts disclosed in this report induced the Massachusetts Legislature to pass a resolution protesting against the kidnapping laws of the slave States, "as invading the sacred rights of citizens of this commonwealth, as contrary to the Constitution of the United States, and in utter derogation of that great principle of the common law which presumes every person to be innocent until proved to be guilty;" and ordered the protest to be forwarded to the Governors of the several States.

But it is not at the South alone that freemen may be converted into slaves "according to law." The Act of Congress respecting the recovery of fugitive slaves, affords most extraordinary facilities for this process, through official corruption and individual perjury. By this Act, the claimant is permitted to *select* a justice of the peace, before whom he may bring or send his alleged slave, and even to prove his property by *affidavit.* Indeed, in almost every State in the Union, a slave-holder may recover at law a human being as his beast of burden, with far less ceremony than he could his pig from the possession of his neighbor. In only three States is a man, claimed as a slave, entitled to a trial by jury. At the last session of the New York Legislature a bill allowing a jury trial in such cases was passed by the lower House, but rejected by a *democratic* vote in the Senate, democracy in that State being avowedly only *skin* deep, all its principles of liberty, equality, and human rights depending on complexion.

Considering the wonderful ease and expedition with which fugitives may be recovered by law, it would be very strange if mistakes did not sometimes occur. *How* often they occur cannot, of course, be known, and it is only when a claim is *defeated*, that we are made sensible of the exceedingly precarious tenure by which a poor friendless negro at the North holds his personal liberty. A few years since, a girl of the name of Mary Gilmore was arrested in Philadelphia, as a fugitive slave from Maryland. Testimony was not wanting in support of the claim; yet it was most conclusively proved that she was the daughter of poor *Irish* parents—having not a drop of negro blood in her veins; that the father had absconded, and that the mother had died a drunkard in the Philadelphia hospital, and that the infant had been kindly received and *brought up in a colored family*. Hence the attempt to make a slave of her. In the spring of 1839, a colored man was arrested in Philadelphia, on a charge of having absconded from his owner *twenty-three* years before. This man had a wife and family depending upon him, and a home where he enjoyed their society; and yet, unless he could find witnesses who could prove his freedom for more than this number of years, he was to be torn from his wife, his children, his home, and doomed for the remainder of his days to toil under the lash. *Four* witnesses for the claimant swore to his identity, although they had not seen him before for twenty-three years! By a most extraordinary coincidence, a New England captain, with whom this negro had sailed *twenty-nine* years before, in a sloop from Nantucket, happened at this very time to be confined for debt in the same prison with the alleged slave, and the captain's testimony, together with that of some other witnesses, who had known the man previous to his pretended elopement, so fully established his freedom, that the court discharged him.

Another mode of legal kidnapping still remains to be described. By the Federal Constitution, fugitives from *justice* are to be delivered up, and under this constitutional provision, a free negro may be converted into a slave without troubling even a justice of the peace to hear the evidence of the captor's claim. A fugitive slave is of course a felon; he not only steals himself, but also the rags on his back which belong to his master. It is understood he has taken refuge in New York, and his master naturally wishes to recover him with as little noise, trouble, and delay as possible. The way is simple and easy. Let the Grand Jury indict A. B. for stealing wearing apparel, and let the indictment, with an affidavit of the criminal's flight, be forwarded by the Governor of the State to his Excellency of New York, with a requisition for the delivery of A. B. to the agent appointed to receive him. A warrant is, of course, issued to "any constable of the State of New York," to arrest A. B. For what purpose? — to bring him before a magistrate where his identity may be established? — no, but to deliver him up to the foreign agent. Hence, the constable may pick up the first likely negro he finds in the street, and ship him to the South; and should it be found, on his arrival on the plantation, that the wrong man has come, it will also probably be found that the mistake is of no consequence to the planter. A few years since, the Governor of New York signed a warrant for the apprehension of seventeen Virginia negroes, as fugitives from justice.* Under this warrant, a man who had lived in the neighborhood for three years, and had a wife and children, and who claimed to be free, was seized, on a Sunday evening, in the public highway, in West Chester County, N. Y., and without being permitted to take leave of his family, was instantly handcuffed, thrown into a carriage, and hurried to New York, and the next morning was on his voyage to Virginia.

Free colored men are converted into slaves not only by law, but also contrary to law. It is, of course, difficult to estimate the extent to which illegal kidnapping is carried, since a large num-

* There is no evidence that he knew they were negroes, or that he acted otherwise than in perfect good faith. The alleged crime was stealing a boat. The *real* crime, it is said, was stealing themselves and escaping in a boat. The most horrible abuses of these warrants can only be prevented by requiring proof of identity before delivery.

ber of cases must escape detection. In a work published by Judge Stroud, of Philadelphia, in 1827, he states, that it had been *ascertained* that more than *thirty* free colored persons, mostly children, had been kidnapped in that city within the last two years.*

10. SUBJECTION TO INSULT AND OUTRAGE.

The feeling of the community towards these people, and the contempt with which they are treated, are indicated by the following notice, lately published by the proprietors of a menagerie, in New York. "The proprietors wish it to be understood, that people of color are not permitted to enter, *except when in attendance upon children and families.*" For two shillings, any white scavenger would be freely admitted, and so would negroes, provided they came in a capacity that marked their dependence; their presence is offensive, *only* when they come as independent spectators, gratifying a laudable curiosity.

Even death, the great leveller, is not permitted to obliterate, among Christians, the distinction of caste, or to rescue the lifeless form of the colored man from the insults of his white brethren. In the porch of a Presbyterian Church, in Philadelphia, in 1837, was suspended a card, containing the form of a deed, to be given to purchasers of lots in a certain burial ground, and to enhance the value of the property, and to entice buyers, the following clause was inserted: "No person of *color*, nor any one who has been the subject of *execution*, shall be interred in said lot."

Our colored fellow-citizens, like others, are occasionally called to pass from one place to another; and in doing so are compelled to submit to innumerable hardships and indignities. They are frequently denied seats in our stage coaches; and although admitted upon the *decks* of our steamboats, are almost universally excluded from the cabins. Even women have been forced, in cold weather, to pass the night upon deck, and in one instance

* Stroud's Sketch of the Slave Laws, p. 94.

the wife of a colored clergyman lost her life in consequence of such an exposure.

The contempt poured upon these people by our laws, our churches, our seminaries, our professions, naturally invokes upon their heads the fierce wrath of vulgar malignity. In order to exhibit the actual condition of this portion of our population, we will here insert some *samples* of the outrages to which they are subjected, taken from the ordinary public journals.

In an account of the New York riots of 1834, the *Commercial Advertiser* says:

"About twenty poor African (native American) families, have had their all destroyed, and have neither bed, clothing, nor food remaining. Their houses are completely eviscerated, their furniture a wreck, and the ruined and disconsolate tenants of the devoted houses are reduced to the necessity of applying to the corporation for bread."

The example set in New York was zealously followed in Philadelphia.

"Some arrangement, it appears, existed between the mob and the white inhabitants, as the dwelling-houses of the latter, contiguous to the residences of the blacks, were illuminated and left undisturbed, while the huts of the negroes were singled out with unerring certainty. The furniture found in these houses was generally broken up and destroyed—beds ripped open and their contents scattered in the streets. . . . . The number of houses assailed was not less than twenty. In one house there was a *corpse, which was thrown from the coffin, and in another a dead infant was taken out of the bed, and cast on the floor, the mother being at the same time barbarously treated.*" *Philadelphia Gazette.*

"No case is reported of an attack having been *invited* or *provoked* by the residents of the dwellings assailed or destroyed. The extent of the depredations committed on the *three* evenings of riot and outrage can only be judged of by the number of houses damaged or destroyed. So far as ascertained, this amounts to FORTY-FIVE. One of the houses assaulted was occupied by an unfortunate cripple, who, unable to fly from the fury of the mob, was so beaten by some of the ruffians, that he has since died in consequence of the bruises and wounds inflicted. . . . . For the last two days the Jersey steamboats have been loaded with numbers of the colored population, who, fearful their lives were not safe in this, determined to seek refuge in another State. On the Jersey side, tents were erected, and the negroes have taken up a temporary residence, until a prospect shall be offered for their perpetual location in some place of security and liberty." *National Gazette.*

The facts we have now exhibited, abundantly prove the extreme cruelty and sinfulness of that prejudice against color which we are impiously told is an ORDINATION OF PROVIDENCE. Colonizationists, assuming the prejudice to be natural and invincible, propose to remove its victims beyond its influence. Abolitionists, on the contrary, remembering with the Psalmist, that "It is HE that hath made us, and not we ourselves," believe that the benevolent Father of us all requires us to treat with justice and kindness every portion of the human family, notwithstanding any particular organization he has been pleased to impress upon them. Instead, therefore, of gratifying and fostering this prejudice, by continually banishing from our country those against whom it is directed, abolitionists are anxious to destroy the prejudice itself; feeling, to use the language of another, that "It is time to recognize in the humblest portions of society, partakers of our nature with all its high prerogatives and awful destinies — time to remember that our distinctions are *exterior* and evanescent, our resemblance real and permanent — that all is transient but what is moral and spiritual — that the only graces we can carry with us into another world, are graces of divine implantation, and that amid the rude incrustations of poverty and ignorance there lurks an imperishable jewel — a SOUL, susceptible of the highest spiritual beauty, destined, perhaps, to adorn the celestial abodes, and to shine forever in the mediatorial diadem of the Son of God. *Take heed that ye despise not one of these little ones.*"

ADDRESS

TO THE FRIENDS OF CONSTITUTIONAL LIBERTY, ON THE VIOLATION BY THE UNITED STATES HOUSE OF REPRESENTATIVES OF THE RIGHT OF PETITION.

1840.

To the Friends of Constitutional Liberty:—

There was a time, fellow citizens, when the above address would have included the People of the United States. But, alas! the freedom of the press, freedom of speech, and the right of petition, are now hated and dreaded by our Southern citizens, as hostile to the perpetuity of human bondage; while, by their political influence in the Federal Government, they have induced members at the North to unite with them in their sacrilegious crusade against these inestimable privileges.

On the 28th of January last, the House of Representatives, on motion of Mr. Johnson, from Maryland, made it a standing rule of the House that "no petition, memorial, resolution, or other paper, praying the abolition of slavery in the District of Columbia, or any State or Territory of the United States, in which it now exists, shall be received by the House, or entertained in any way whatever."

Thus has the right of petition been immolated in the very Temple of Liberty, and offered up, a propitiatory sacrifice to the demon of slavery. Never before has an outrage so unblushingly profligate been perpetrated upon the Federal Constitution. Yet, while we mourn the degeneracy which this transaction evinces, we behold, in its attending circumstances, joyful omens of the triumph which awaits our struggle with the hateful power that now perverts the General Government into an engine of cruelty and loathsome oppression.

Before we congratulate you on these omens, let us recall to your recollection the steps by which the enemies of human rights have advanced to their present rash and insolent defiance of moral and constitutional obligation.

In 1831, a newspaper was established in Boston, for the purpose of disseminating facts and arguments in favor of the duty and policy of immediate emancipation. The Legislature of Georgia, with all the recklessness of despotism, passed a law, offering a reward of $5000, for the abduction of the editor, and his delivery in Georgia. As there was no law by which a citizen of Massachusetts could be tried in Georgia, for expressing his opinions in the capital of his own State, this reward was intended as the price of BLOOD. Do you start at the suggestion? Remember the several sums of $25,000, of $50,000, and of $100,000, offered in Southern papers for kidnapping certain abolitionists. Remember the horrible inflictions by Southern Lynch clubs. Remember the declaration, in the United States Senate, by the brazen-fronted Preston, that, should an abolitionist be caught in Carolina, he would be HANGED. But, as the slave-holders could not destroy the lives of the abolitionists, they determined to murder their characters. Hence, the President of the United States was induced, in his Message of 1835, to Congress, to charge them with plotting the massacre of the Southern planters; and even to stultify himself, by affirming that, for this purpose, they were engaged in sending, by *mail*, inflammatory appeals to the *slaves* — sending papers to men who could not read them, and by a conveyance through which they could not receive them! He well knew that the papers alluded to were appeals on the immorality of converting men, women, and children, into beasts of burden, and were sent to the masters for *their* consideration. The masters in Charleston, dreading the moral influence of these appeals on the conscience of the slave-holding community, forced the Post Office, and made a bonfire of the papers. The Postmaster-General, with the sanction of the President, also hastened to their relief, and, in violation of oaths, and laws, and the Constitution, established ten thousand censors of the press, each one of whom was authorized to abstract from the mail every paper which *he* might think too favorable to the rights of man.

For more than twenty years, petitions have been presented to Congress, for the abolition of slavery in the District of Columbia. The right to present them, and the power of Congress to grant their prayer, were, until recently, unquestioned. But the rapid multiplication of these petitions alarmed the slaveholders, and, knowing that they tended to keep alive at the North, an interest in the slave, they deemed it good policy to discourage and, if possible, suppress all such applications. Hence Mr. Pinckney's famous resolution, in 1836, declaring, "that all petitions, or papers, relating *in any way, or to any extent* whatever to the *subject of slavery*, shall, without being printed or referred, be laid on the table; and no further action whatever shall be had thereon!"

The peculiar atrocity of this resolution was, that it not merely trampled upon the rights of the petitioners, but took from each member of the House his undoubted privilege, as a legislator of the District, to introduce any proposition he might think proper, for the protection of the slaves. In every slave State there are laws affording, at least, some nominal protection to these unhappy beings; but, according to this resolution, slaves might be flayed alive in the streets of Washington, and no representative of the people could offer even a resolution for inquiry. And this vile outrage upon constitutional liberty was avowedly perpetrated "to repress agitation, to allay excitement, and reëstablish harmony and tranquillity among the various sections of the Union!!"

But this strange opiate did not produce the stupefying effects anticipated from it. In 1836, the petitioners were only 37,000 — the next session they numbered 110,000. Mr. Hawes, of Kentucky, now essayed to restore tranquillity by gagging the uneasy multitude; but, alas! at the next Congress, more than

300,000 petitioners carried new terror to the hearts of the slave-holders. The next anodyne was prescribed by Mr. Patten, of Virginia, but its effect was to rouse from their stupor some of the northern Legislatures, and to induce them to denounce his remedy as "a usurpation of power, a violation of the Constitution, subversive of the fundamental principles of the government, and at war with the prerogatives of the people." * It was now supposed that the people must be drugged by a *northern* man, and *Atherton* was found a fit instrument for this vile purpose; but the dose proved only the more nauseous and exciting from the foul hands by which it was administered.

In these various outrages, although all action on the petitions was prohibited, the papers themselves were received and laid on the table, and *therefore* it was contended, that the right of petition had been preserved inviolate. But the slave-holders, maddened by the failure of all their devices, and fearing the influence which the mere sight of thousands and tens of thousands of petitions in behalf of liberty, would exert, and taking advantage of the approaching presidential election to operate upon the selfishness of some northern members, have succeeded in crushing the right of petition itself.

That you may be the more sensible, fellow citizens, of the exceeding profligacy of the late RULE, and of its palable violation of both the spirit and the letter of the Constitution, which those who voted for it had sworn to support, suffer us to recall to your recollection a few historical facts.

The framers of the Federal Constitution supposed the right of petition too firmly established in the habits and affections of the people, to need a constitutional guaranty. Their omission to notice it aroused the jealousy of some of the State conventions, called to pass upon the constitution. The *Virginia* convention proposed, as an amendment, "that every *freeman* has a right to petition, or apply to the Legislature, for a redress of grievances." And this amendment, with others, was ordered to be forwarded to the different States, for their consideration. The conventions of North Carolina, New York, and Rhode Island, were held

* Resolutions of Massachusetts and Connecticut, April and May, 1838.

subsequently, and, of course, had before them the Virginia amendment. The North Carolina convention adopted a declaration of rights, embracing the very words of the proposed amendment; and this declaration was ordered to be submitted to Congress, before that State would enter the Union. The conventions of New York and of Rhode Island incorporated in their *certificates of ratification*, the assertion that "Every *person* has a right to petition or apply to the Legislature for a redress of grievances"—using the Virginia phraseology, merely substituting the word *person* for *freeman*, thus claiming the right of petition even for slaves; while Virginia and North Carolina confined it to freemen.

The first Congress, assembled under the Constitution, gave effect to the wishes thus emphatically expressed, by proposing, as an amendment, that "Congress shall make no law respecting an establishment of religion, or prohibiting the free exercise thereof, or *abridging* the freedom of the press, or the right of the people peaceably to assemble, and *to petition Government* for a redress of grievances." This amendment was duly ratified by the States, and when members of Congress swear to support the Constitution of the United States, they are as much bound by their oath to refrain from abridging the right of petition, as they are to fulfil any other constitutional obligation. And will the slave-holders and their abettors dare to maintain that they have not foresworn themselves, because they have abridged the right of the people to petition for a redress of grievances by a RULE of the House, and not by a *law?* If so, they may by a RULE require every member, on taking his seat, to subscribe to the creed of a particular church, and then call their Maker to witness that they are guiltless of making a *law* "respecting an establishment of religion, or prohibiting the free exercise thereof."

The right to petition is one thing, and the disposition of a petition after it is received, is another. But the new rule makes no disposition of the petitions; it PROHIBITS THEIR RECEPTION; they may not be brought into the legislative chamber. Hundreds of thousands of the people are debarred all access to their representatives, for the purpose of offering them a prayer.

It is said that the manifold abominations perpetrated in the District are no grievances to the petitioners, and *therefore* they have no right to ask for their removal. But the right guaranteed by the Constitution, is a right to ask for the redress of *grievances*, whether personal, social, or moral. And who, except a slave-holder, will dare to contend that it is no grievance that our agents, our representatives, our servants, in our name and by our authority, enact laws erecting and licensing markets in the Capital of the Republic, for the sale of human beings, and converting free men into slaves for no other crime than that of being too poor to pay United States officers the JAIL FEES accruing from an iniquitous imprisonment?

Again, it is pretended that the objects prayed for are palpably unconstitutional, and that *therefore* the petitions ought not to be received. And by what authority are the people deprived of their right to petition for any object which a majority of either House of Congress, for the time being, may please to regard as unconstitutional? If this usurpation be submitted to, it will not be confined to abolition petitions. It is well known that most of the slave-holders *now* insist, that all protecting duties are unconstitutional, and that on account of the tariff the Union was nearly rent by the very men who are now horrified by the danger to which it is exposed by these *petitions!* Should our northern manufacturers again presume to ask Congress to protect them from foreign competition, the southern members will find a precedent, sanctioned by northern votes, for a rule that "no petition, memorial, resolution, or other paper, praying for the IMPOSITION OF DUTIES FOR THE ENCOURAGEMENT OF MANUFACTURES, shall be received by the House, or entertained in any way whatever."

It does indeed require southern arrogance to maintain that, although Congress is invested by the Constitution with "exclusive jurisdiction, in all cases whatsoever," over the District of Columbia, yet that it would be so palpably unconstitutional to abolish the slave-trade, and to emancipate the slaves in the District, that petitions for these objects ought not to be received. Yet this is asserted in that very House, on whose minutes is recorded a resolution, in 1816, appointing a committee, with power to send for persons and papers, "to inquire into the existence of an inhuman and illegal traffic in slaves, carried on, in and through the District of Columbia, and report whether any, and what means are necessary for putting a stop to the same:" and another, in 1829, instructing the Committee on the District of Columbia to inquire into the expediency of providing by law, "for the gradual abolition of slavery in the District."

In the very first Congress assembled under the Federal Constitution, petitions were presented, asking its interposition for the mitigation of the evils, and final abolition of the African slave-trade, and also praying it, as far as it possessed the power, to take measures for the abolition of slavery. These petitions excited the wrath and indignation of many of the slave-holding members, yet no one thought of refusing to receive them. They were referred to a select committee, at the instance of Mr. Madison himself, who "entered into a critical review of the circumstances respecting the adoption of the Constitution, and the ideas upon the limitation of the powers of Congress, to interfere in the regulation of the commerce of slaves, and showed that they undoubtedly were not precluded from interposing in their importation; and generally to regulate the mode in which every species of business shall be transacted. He adverted to the western country, and the cession of Georgia, in which Congress have certainly the power to *regulate the subject of slavery;* which shows that gentlemen are mistaken in supposing that Congress cannot constitutionally interfere in the business in any degree whatever. He was in favor of committing the petition, and justified the measure by repeated precedents in the proceedings of the House." *U. S. Gazette*, 17*th Feb.*, 1790.

Here we find one of the earliest and ablest expounders of the Constitution, maintaining the power of Congress to "regulate the subject of slavery" in the national territories, and urging the reference of abolition petitions to a special committee.

The committee made a report, for which, after a long debate, was substituted a declaration, by the House, that Congress could not abolish the slave-trade prior to the year 1808, but had a right so to regulate it as to provide for the humane treatment of the slaves on the passage; and that Congress could not interfere in the emancipation or treatment of slaves in the *States*.

This declaration gave entire satisfaction, and no farther abolition petitions were presented, till after the District of Columbia had been placed under the "exclusive jurisdiction" of the General Government.

You all remember, fellow citizens, the wide-spread excitement which a few years since prevailed on the subject of SUNDAY MAILS. Instead of attempting to quiet the agitation, by outraging the rights of the petitioners, Congress referred the petitions to a committee, and made no attempt to stifle discussion.

Why, then, we ask, with such authorities and precedents before them, do the slave-holders in Congress, regardless of their oaths, strive to gag the friends of freedom, under *pretence* of allaying agitation? Because conscience does make cowards of them all—because they know the accursed system they are upholding will not bear the light—because they fear, if these petitions are discussed, the abominations of the American slave-trade, the secrets of the prison-houses in Washington and Alexandria, and the horrors of the human shambles licensed by the authority of Congress, will be exposed to the scorn and indignation of the civilized world.

Unquestionably the late RULE surpasses, in its profligate contempt of constitutional obligation, any act in the annals of the Federal Government. As such it might well strike every patriot with dismay, were it not that attending circumstances teach us that it is the expiring effort of desperation. When we reflect on the past subserviency of our northern representatives to the mandates of the slave-holders, we may well raise on the present occasion, the shout of triumph, and hail the vote on the recent RULE as the pledge of a glorious victory. Suffer us to recall to your recollection the majorities by which the successive attempts to crush the right of petition and the freedom of debate have been carried.

Pinckney's	Gag was passed	May, 1836,	by a majority of 51
Hawes's	"	Jan. 1837,	58
Patton's	"	Dec. 1837,	48
Atherton's	"	Dec. 1838,	48
Johnson's	"	Jan. 1840,	6

Surely, when we find the majority against us reduced from 58 to 6, we need no new incentive to perseverance.

Another circumstance which marks the progress of constitutional liberty, is the gradual diminution in the number of our northern *serviles*. The votes from the free States in favor of the several gags were as follows:

For Pinckney's,	62
For Hawes's,	70
For Patton's,	52
For Atherton's,	49
For Johnson's,	28

There is also another cheering fact connected with the passage of the RULE which deserves to be noticed. Heretofore the slave-holders have uniformly, by enforcing the previous question, imposed their several gags by a silent vote. On the present occasion they were twice baffled in their efforts to stifle debate, and were, for days together, compelled to listen to speeches on a subject which they have so often declared should not be discussed.

A base strife for southern votes has hitherto, to no small extent, enlisted both the political parties at the North in the service of the slave-holders. The late unwonted independence of northern politicians, and the deference paid by them to the wishes of their own constituents, in preference to those of their southern colleagues, indicate the advance of public opinion. No less than forty-nine northern members of the administration party voted for the Atherton gag, while only twenty-seven dared to record their names in favor of Johnson's; and of the representation of SIX States, *every vote* was given *against* the rule, without distinction of party. The tone in which opposite political journals denounce the late outrage may warn the slave-holders that they will not much longer hold the North in bonds. The leading administration paper in the city of New York regards the RULE with "utter abhorrence;" while the official paper of the opposition, edited by the State printer, trusts that the names of the recreant northerners who voted for it may be "handed down to eternal infamy and execration."

The advocates of abolition are no longer consigned to unmitigated contempt and obloquy. Passing by the various living illustrations of our remark, we appeal for our proofs to the dead. The late WILLIAM LEGGETT, the editor of a Democratic Journal in the city of New York, was denounced, in 1835, by the "Democratic Republican General Committee," for his abolition doctrines. Far from faltering in his course, on account of the censure of his own party, he exclaimed, with a presentiment almost amounting to prophecy, "The stream of public opinion now sets against us, but it is about to turn, and the regurgitation will be tremendous. Proud in that day may well be the man who can float in triumph on the first refluent wave, swept onward by the deluge which he himself, in advance of his fellows, had largely shared in occasioning. Such be my fate; and, living or dying, it will in some measure be mine. I have written my name in ineffaceable letters on the abolition record." And he did live to behold the first swelling of the refluent wave. The denounced abolitionist was honored by a Democratic President with a diplomatic mission; and since his death, the resolution condemning him has been EXPUNGED from the minutes of the Democratic committee.

Of the many victims of the recent awful calamity in our waters, what name has been most frequently uttered by the pulpit and the press in the accents of lamentation and panegyric? On whose tomb have freedom, philanthropy, and letters been invoked to strew their funeral wreaths? All who have heard of the loss of the Lexington are familiar with the name of CHARLES FOLLEN. And who was he? One of the men officially denounced by President Jackson as a gang of miscreants, plotting insurrection and murder—and recently a member of the Executive Committee of the American Anti-Slavery Society.

Let us then, fellow-citizens, in view of all these things, thank God and take courage. We are now contending, not merely for the emancipation of our unhappy fellow-men, kept in bondage under the authority of our own representatives — not merely for the overthrow of the human shambles erected by Congress on the national domain — but also for the preservation of those great constitutional rights which were acquired by our fathers, and are now assailed by the slave-holders and their northern auxiliaries. That you may remember these auxiliaries and avoid giving them new opportunities of betraying your rights, we annex a list of their dishonored names.

The following twenty-eight members from the free States voted in the affirmative on the recent GAG RULE.

MAINE.

Virgil D. Parris,	Albert Smith.

NEW HAMPSHIRE.

Charles G. Atherton,	Ira A. Eastman,
Edmund Burke,	Tristram Shaw.

NEW YORK.

Nehemiah H. Earle,	James de la Montayne,
John Fine,	John H. Prentiss,
Nathaniel Jones,	Theron R. Strong.
Governeur Kemble,	

PENNSYLVANIA.

John Davis,	George M'Cullough,
Joseph Fornance,	David Petriken,
James Gerry,	William S. Ramsay.

OHIO.

D. P. Leadbetter,	George Sweeney,
William Medill,	Jonathan Taylor,
Isaac Parrish,	John B. Weller.

INDIANA.

John Davis,	George H. Proffit.

ILLINOIS.

John Reynolds.

Let us turn to our more immediate representatives, and, we trust, more faithful servants. Our State Legislatures will not refuse to hear our prayers. Let us petition them immediately to rebuke the treason by which the Constitution has been surrendered into the hands of the slave-holders; let us implore them to demand from Congress, in the name of the free States, that they shall neither destroy nor abridge the right of petition, — a right without which our government would be converted into a despotism.

We call on you, fellow-citizens of every religious faith and party name, to unite with us in guarding the citadel of our country's freedom. If there are any who will not coöperate with us in laboring for the emancipation of the slave, surely there are none who will stand aloof from us while contending for the liberty of themselves, their children, and their children's children.

To the rescue, then, fellow citizens! and, trusting in HIM without whom all human effort is weakness, let us not doubt that our faithful endeavors to preserve the rights HE has given us, will, through HIS blessing, be crowned with success.

NEW YORK, FEBRUARY 13, 1840.

INTRODUCTORY REMARKS

TO THE REPROOF OF THE AMERICAN CHURCH CONTAINED IN THE RECENT "HISTORY OF THE PROTESTANT EPISCOPAL CHURCH IN AMERICA," BY THE BISHOP OF OXFORD.

1846.

It is not probable that the reader has ever seen the History mentioned in our title. That a history of the American Church, from its earliest date down to the death of Bishop White, written by a dignitary of the mother Church, distinguished alike by his honored name and elevated rank, should be almost unknown in this country, is a singular and very peculiar fact. No people are more sensitive than ourselves to the opinions of foreigners; and American Episcopalians naturally feel much interest in the views entertained of them by their English brethren. Indeed, the interest is not confined to such views, but extends to whatever affects the English Church. The parties which agitate the establishment are reflected in our controversies; and the tracts and volumes issued by the theological combatants on the other side of the water, are republished and eagerly perused on this. Yet here is a history of ourselves, in no small degree eulogistic, and on various accounts claiming our attention, which has been virtually suppressed.

It is indeed true, that as soon as the book reached our shores, one or two of our "enterprising publishers" announced their intention of reprinting it, and one of the proposed editions was to have been introduced to the notice of the Church under the auspices of a RIGHT REVEREND editor. But these announcements have been followed by "expressive silence." More than twelve months have elapsed, and the Church is still without an American copy of the History. This concealment of Dr. Wilberforce's work is obviously intentional, and not accidental. The very title of the book and the name of the author would have secured a rapid sale for the reprint. Some weighty motive must have induced our publishers to abandon their original intention, at the sacrifice of pecuniary interest. The motive is obvious, and probably one or more southern bishops have exerted their influence. The author of the History, in the course of his work, advances certain doctrines on the subject of SLAVERY, and of CASTE IN THE CHURCH, which it is thought inconvenient to discuss, and which cannot be admitted in this Republic without sealing the condemnation of almost every Christian sect among us, and overwhelming our own Church with shame and confusion. There are, it is to be feared, but few among our twelve hundred clergymen, who, on reading the History, would not find their consciences whispering, "Thou art the man," and who would not be anxious to conceal the volume from their parishioners. Hence its suppression.

It is common to personify the Church, and to speak of her as of some spotless celestial being; and yet she, in fact, consists of her clerical and lay members, each one of whom must personally answer at the bar of Christ for his participation in every sin committed by the Church. Surely, it would be more becoming Christian men to inquire how far they are individually guilty of the offences charged upon them by Bishop Wilberforce, than to endeavor to stifle investigation, by burying in oblivion the faithful and Christain rebuke of their English brother.

Religious establishments tend to render the clergy obsequious to the civil ruler, and our voluntary system tempts them to do homage to the most capricious and irresponsible of all tyrants, the will of the multitude. Let us see what true and faithful allegiance our "Primitive and Apostolic Church" has borne to this American despot.

On the 21st of August, 1831, occurred the negro insurrection and massacre at Southampton, Virginia. This disastrous event necessarily directed public attention, both at the North and the South, to the subject of slavery. In one portion of the Union, stronger fetters were forged for the bondman, and greater efforts made to banish to Africa the free colored man, whose presence it was supposed quickened the aspirations of the slave for freedom. In the other portion, this insurrection impressed on a few pious and reflecting minds a conviction both of the moral and political evils of slavery, and of the duty of combined action for its total abolition. In 1832 the New England Anti-Slavery Society was formed, and the succeeding year witnessed the organization of the American Anti-Slavery Society. Auxiliary associations sprang rapidly into being, funds were liberally bestowed, presses were established, and publications portraying the abominations of the system were abundantly scattered throughout the land.

This agitation both alarmed and irritated the slave-holders; and while on the one hand they endeavored to intimidate the abolitionists by their murderous violence, they appealed to the selfish passions of the northern community, by promising their votes and their trade to such only as would aid in suppressing the discussion of slavery. Immediately, our contending factions and our commercial cities rivalled each other in demonstrations of sympathy for their "southern brethren," and of abhorrence for abolitionists. The clergy, yielding to the blast, generally observed a prudent silence, while a few, to prove their freedom from fanaticism, assailed the abolitionists for their violence and rashness, protesting, however, against being considered the advocates of slavery "in the abstract."

On the clergy of the South, however, a more onerous task was imposed. The northern movement was a *religious* one, impelled by a belief of the sinfulness of slavery. Hence it became important that southern consciences should be encased in mail, impenetrable to anti-slavery missiles. The fabrication of such a panoply was consigned to the ministers of Christ, and significant hints were given them that they must not shrink from the work.

A meeting of slave-holders in Mississippi, after resolving that any individual who should circulate anti-slavery papers in the State "is justly worthy, in the sight of God and man, of IMMEDIATE DEATH," voted, "that the CLERGY of the State of Mississippi be hereby recommended at once to take a stand upon this subject, and that their further silence in relation to this subject (slavery) will, in our opinion, be subject to *serious censure*."

This pastoral admonition from the Lynchers was received with due reverence by those to whom it was directed. Presently two Mississippi Presbyteries passed resolutions in favor of the Christian character of slavery. A Mississippi divine published an elaborate vindication of the system, and a Methodist periodical in the State announced that it would "recognize the right of man to hold property in man."

In other slave States the clergy were suddenly aroused to a new energy in vindicating the *divine* institution of human bondage. Presbyteries, Methodist conferences, Baptist associations, individual ministers, were busily at work descanting on the sin of Ham, and the curse pronounced on Canaan, discussing Hebrew servitude, and proving that negro slavery was not forbidden in the New Testament. As a specimen of the fulminations launched by some of these servants of the Most High against abolitionists, we may cite the peroration of an address to a meeting of slave-holders in South Carolina by the Rev. Mr. Postell, of the Methodist Church. "Shun abolition as you would the DEVIL. Do your duty as citizens and Christians, and in heaven you will be rewarded, and delivered from abolitionism."

In this mighty rivalry in preaching smooth things to the slave-holders, "the sects" were not permitted to gain a triumph. On the 27th of November, 1836, the Rev. George W. Freeman, after morning service, ascended the pulpit of Christ Church, Raleigh, North Carolina, and announced to his delighted hearers the good news that the slavery of white men and of black men, of the wise and of the simple, of the learned and of the ignorant, was sanctioned by God, and approved by Jesus Christ and his holy apostles. This commissioned ambassador of the Redeemer proclaimed, "THAT NO MAN NOR SET OF MEN IN OUR

DAY, UNLESS THEY CAN PRODUCE A NEW REVELATION FROM HEAVEN, ARE ENTITLED TO PRONOUNCE SLAVERY WRONG; and that SLAVERY AS IT EXISTS AT THE PRESENT DAY IS AGREEABLE TO THE ORDER OF DIVINE PROVIDENCE."

The fact that any institution involves *duties*, proves its lawfulness, since no duty can attach to a sinful practice. Hence our preacher, after employing the morning of the Lord's day in expounding the *divine rights* of the slave-holders, devoted the afternoon of the same holy time in proclaiming their *duties*. The slave-holder was reminded that he was under a moral obligation to punish his slaves when they deserved punishment; but he must not be too severe, nor chastise when in a passion; nor ought he to overwork them. He is bound, moreover, to have the slave children baptized, and *orally* taught to say the Creed, the Lord's Prayer, and the Ten Commandments. "It is not necessary," said the man of God, "that they should be taught to read;" but, nevertheless, the master was declared to be as responsible for the souls of his slaves as for those of his own children! Such are the duties which spring from this Scriptural institution; duties which, fortunately for the master's convenience, involve no regard for the marriage of his slaves, no respect for their conjugal or parental rights, and impose no restrictions on the sale of men, women, and children in the market; at least, no obligations of this sort were adverted to by the preacher.

These two sermons certainly formed the most acceptable offering which any clergyman had yet laid on the altar of slavery. The hints about the bondage of *white* men, the necessity of a *new revelation*, before slavery could be pronounced *wrong*, and the connection of *religious duties* with the institution, could not fail of convincing the slave-holder, that in the EPISCOPAL CHURCH he would find an asylum from the taunts and reproaches of the civilized world; that from her altars he could gather balm for his wounded conscience, and that in her courts, he could, without distraction, form his schemes of traffic in human beings, and forge the chains by which they were to be held in subjection. It was, of course, important that slave-holders generally should participate in the joyful intelligence imparted to the congregation of Christ Church. The news might be spread by the press, but what assurance could be given that the gratifying declarations made by Mr. Freeman, a private and obscure Presbyter, were authorized by competent ecclesiastical authority? The sermons were published under the imposing title of "THE RIGHTS AND DUTIES OF SLAVE-HOLDERS," and bore the following *imprimatur* from the Bishop of the Diocese:

"RALEIGH, Nov. 30, 1836.

"Rev. and Dear Brother,—I listened with *most unfeigned pleasure* to the discourses delivered last Sunday, on the character of slavery and the duties of masters. And as I learn a publication of them is solicited, I beg, from a conviction of their being urgently called for at the present time, that you will not withhold your consent.

"With high regard, your affectionate friend,
and Brother in the Lord,
"L. S. IVES.

"To the Rev. GEORGE W. FREEMAN."

This letter was obviously written, not for its professed purpose of overcoming Mr. Freeman's reluctance to appear in print, but to let the slave-holders of North Carolina know, that although their bishop was a northern man, his conscience was thoroughly acclimated; and that bold and startling as were the doctrines of the Raleigh preacher, they would be maintained in all their length and breadth by Episcopal authority. The CHURCH in North Carolina, by this authoritative publication, far exceeded all the "sects," in the slave region, in her fearless championship of slavery in the "abstract," and "as it exists at the present day." But the diocese was not permitted long to enjoy this proud preëminence. Her sister of South Carolina quickly shared it with her. The Society for "the Advancement of Christianity," (!) consisting of clergymen and laymen, with the Bishop at their head, seized upon Freeman's pamphlet, and reprinted it, *imprimatur* and all, as a *religious tract for gratuitous distribution.*

But there was still one circumstance, which, in times of alarm and despondency, was calculated to weaken the confidence of the slave-holder in the strength and permanency of the fortress which had thus kindly opened its gates to receive him. Most of the religious denominations of the South were connected with their northern brethren by general ecclesiastical judicatories. Already had alarming discussions occurred in the Presbyterian Assembly, and the Methodist Conference, and the Baptist Mission Board, and it was painfully apparent that in these bodies "the rights and duties of slave-holders" were viewed in very different colors from the glowing tints in which Freeman had painted them. The Episcopal Church at the South was subject to the jurisdiction of the GENERAL CONVENTION, and what security could be given that a body embracing northern as well as southern delegates, would not repudiate the doctrines of the Raleigh sermons? Lynch law could indeed control the southern pulpit as well as the southern press; but the consciences and the characters of the slave-holders were assailed from the North. *There* the *Dissenters* were gradually abandoning the cause of human bondage. Under the strong pressure of public opinion, and in utter contempt of the well-known sentiments of the Church of England, and indeed of the moral sense of Christendom, could it be hoped that the northern section of the Episcopal Church would, in General Convention, tolerate, much less approve of the extreme, ultra pro-slavery views of the Rev. George W. Freeman?

All questions of this sort were most explicitly answered by the last Convention, as appears by an extract from the minutes of the House of Clerical and Lay Delegates:

> "The following message was received: 'House of Bishops, Oct. 22, 1844. The House of Bishops inform the House of Clerical and Lay Deputies, that they have nominated the REV. GEORGE W. FREEMAN, D. D., rector of Immanuel Church, Delaware, a missionary BISHOP, to exercise Episcopal functions in the State of Arkansas, and in the Indian Territory, south of 36 1-2 degrees of parallel of latitude, and to exercise Episcopal supervision over the Missions of the Church in the REPUBLIC OF TEXAS. Attest, Jonathan M. Wainwright, Sec'y.'
>
> "On motion of Rev. Dr. Tyng, the nomination of the Bishop of Arkansas and Texas (as above) was UNANIMOUSLY assented to."

It was not enough thus to elevate the reckless defender of slavery to the high and holy office of a Bishop in the Church of God, but he must be selected as an apostle to Texas! There was, indeed, a peculiar significance in this selection. The odium in which the people of Texas were held by the Christian community at large, arose not merely from their general profligacy, but also, and chiefly, from their conduct in relation to slavery. Taking possession of lands belonging to Mexico, they reëstablished slavery upon the very soil from which it had been recently banished by that Roman Catholic government. To secure to themselves the unmolested enjoyment of their human chattels, they raised the standard of rebellion, and with the aid of southern slave-holders erected themselves into an independent Republic. Having thus, as they professed, achieved their own liberty, they adopted a constitution rendering the bondage of others hopeless and perpetual; and outraging alike the dictates of nature and of justice, ordained that no free mulatto should ever live in Texas, thus dooming their own colored offspring, for all time to come, to slavery or to exile!

The southern slave-holders were exceedingly anxious that Texas should be admitted into the Union, for the double purpose of strengthening the slave interest, and opening a new market for the benefit of the breeding States. For the same reasons, in addition to the odious character of the Texans, the proposed annexation was resisted by the almost united moral feeling of the whole North. The question of annexation was agitating the nation when the Convention assembled, and the selection of Freeman as Bishop of Texas was virtually, whether so intended or not, a repudiation by the Protestant Episcopal Church in General Convention assembled, of the *moral objections* urged against the admission of that Republic into our confederacy. The Church sent to the Texans a man who, she knew, would confirm and strengthen them by apostolic instruction and benediction in those great principles of their constitution, which had excited the execration of the Christian world.

Let us now take a view of that institution, which, the Texan Bishop assures us, enjoys the approval of Christ and his Apostles. He tells us,

"There was in general no distinction of *color*, no prevailing difference in the conformation of the features and limbs, no striking dissimilarity in the intellectual powers, to mark the line of separation between the masters and their bondmen, and stamp them as different races of men. No peculiarity of this kind existed which would have prevented those who were slaves, had they been placed in other circumstances, from taking rank in society, and looking forward to the highest distinctions in the community. Had they not been slaves, they would have become magistrates, nobles, or rulers; respected by multitudes as equals, or venerated as superiors."

Here, it will be observed, we have none of the usual nonsense about the curse of Canaan, nor of the usual blasphemy about negroes being created by God for slaves. Jesus Christ and his apostles approved of the bondage of *white* men as intelligent as their masters: and of course the whole of our present bench of Bishops, including Bishop Freeman himself, might, under certain circumstances, be lawfully reduced to slavery, and righteously held as chattels by Christian men.

We are expressly referred in the sermons, to Roman slavery, as that which enjoyed the sanction of the great Head of the Church. And what was ROMAN SLAVERY? Our answer to this question is taken from a very learned work, whose statements are all verified by references to Roman authorities.*

"The slave had no protection against the avarice, rage, or lust of the master, whose authority was founded in absolute property; and the bondman was viewed less as a human being subject to arbitrary dominion, than as an inferior animal, dependent wholly on the will of his owner. At first, the master possessed the uncontrolled power of life and death. He might kill, mutilate or torture his slaves, for any or no offence; he might force them to become gladiators or prostitutes. The temporary unions of male with female slaves were formed and dissolved at his command; families and friends were separated when he pleased. The laws recognized no obligation upon the owners of slaves, to furnish them with food and clothing, or to take care of them in sickness. Slaves could have no property but by the sufferance of their master, for whom they acquired everything, and with whom they could form no engagements which would be binding on him. The master might transfer his rights by either sale or gift, or might bequeathe them by will. A master selling, giving or bequeathing a slave, sometimes made it a provision that he should never be carried abroad, or that he should be manumitted on a fixed day; or that, on the other hand, he should never be emancipated, or that he should be *kept in chains for life*. While slaves turned the handmill, they were generally chained, and had a broad wooden collar, to prevent them from eating

*"Blair's Inquiry into the State of Slavery among the Romans, from the earliest period, to the establishment of the Lombards in Italy."

the grain. The *furca*, which in later language means a gibbet, was, in older dialect, used to denote a wooden fork or collar, which was made to bear upon their shoulders or around their necks, as a mark of disgrace as much as an uneasy burden. Fetters and chains were much used for punishment or restraint, and were, in some instances, worn by slaves during life, through the sole authority of the master. Porters of the gates of the rich were generally chained. Field laborers worked for the most part in irons posterior to the first ages of the Republic. Some persons made it their business to catch runaway slaves.* The runaway, when taken, was severely punished by authority of the master, or by the judge at his desire; sometimes with crucifixion, amputation of a foot, or by being sent to fight as a gladiator with wild beasts; but most frequently by being branded on the brow with letters indicative of his crime. Cruel masters sometimes hired torturers by profession, or had such persons in their establishments, to assist them in punishing their slaves. The noses, and ears, and teeth of slaves were often in danger from an enraged owner; and sometimes the eyes of a great offender were put out. Crucifixion was very frequently made the fate of a wretched slave for trifling misconduct, or from mere caprice. By a decree passed by the Senate, if a master was murdered, when his slaves might possibly have aided him, all his household within reach were held as implicated and deserving of death; and Tacitus relates an instance in which a family of four hundred were all executed."

Such was the slavery which the Bishop of Texas tells us was found "extensively established in the Roman Empire, embracing nearly all the civilized world, by our Saviour, when he appeared on earth; and that neither he, nor his inspired apostles after him, ever expressed any disapprobation of it, or left on record a single precept directing its discontinuance; and what then is the conclusion? Why, surely this much, if nothing farther, that no man nor set of men in our day, unless they can produce A NEW REVELATION FROM HEAVEN ARE ENTITLED TO PRONOUNCE IT WRONG"!

Let us next endeavor to acquire some idea of the *number* of the bondmen, whose prison-house, if we believe the Right Rev.

* This profession is not unknown among ourselves, as appears from the following notice in the *Sumner County* (Alabama) *Whig*.

"NEGRO DOGS.

"THE undersigned having bought the entire pack of Negro Dogs, (of the Hay and Allen stock,) he now proposes to catch runaway negroes. His charges will be Three Dollars per day for hunting, and Fifteen Dollars for catching a runaway. He resides three and one-half miles north of Livingston, near the lower Jones' Bluff road. WILLIAM GAMBEL.

"Nov. 6, 1845—6m."

Texan Father in God, was barred and bolted by Him who gave his life a ransom for many. Gibbon estimates the whole slave population of the Roman Empire in the reign of the Emperor Claudius at SIXTY MILLIONS (I, 53), and Blair regards this estimate as much too *small.*

It is important to ascertain *how* this prodigious multitude were reduced to bondage; because as our spiritual champions of slavery invariably omit to explain the scriptural process of converting free men into slaves, we are left to seek instruction in this branch of our duty from the Romans; since, as in no one instance were they rebuked by Christ and his apostles, for any of their various contrivances for manufacturing slaves, the conclusion is, surely, "this much, if nothing further, that no man nor set of men in our day, unless they can produce a new revelation from Heaven, are entitled" to pronounce any of the Roman methods of making slaves, "wrong."

The most prolific source of slavery was WAR. Livy informs us that after the fall of the Samnites at Aquilone, about 36,000 prisoners were sold; and Plutarch, that 150,000 of the people of Epirus were sold for the benefit of the army under Paulus Æmilius; and we learn from Cicero, that when Pindenissus was taken, the inhabitants were made slaves. Hence, should a Mexican force hereafter make an incursion into Texas, and carry off the Bishop, his wife and children, and sell them to different masters, under whom they should be compelled to spend their days in unceasing toil — condemned to all the misery and degradation of Roman bondmen, — the Bishop would have the consolation of knowing that the treatment he experienced was in perfect consistency with that Gospel which he had himself preached.

COMMERCE was another mode of acquiring slaves. A prodigious slave-trade was carried on in the countries bordering on the Euxine, with various Provinces in Asia, with Thrace, and even with Spain and Great Britain. Here we learn how presumptuous it is to denounce the African slave-trade as sinful.

THE PROFESSION OF CHRISTIANITY was occasionally visited

by the Romans with slavery. At the present day, it affords no security against American slavery, nor deliverance from it.

There were still four other modes of acquiring slaves, which are particularly interesting to us; because, having been copied by us from the Roman law, *we* can have no scruples about their lawfulness: for had they been wrong, Christ and his apostles, according to Bishop Freeman, would have condemned them.

1. The sale of children by their fathers. With us the privilege is confined to the sale of children by a slave mother. In the Bishop's Diocese, this privilege was nearly converted into a necessity, by the constitutional provision which required the bondage or expulsion of every mulatto child.

2. Selling persons convicted of crimes. Among the Romans, persons convicted of certain offences were sold as slaves, and their posterity after them were doomed to bondage. Similar laws for converting free negroes and mulattoes into slaves are in force in several of our States. Thus, in South Carolina, if a free negro "entertains a runaway slave," he forfeits ten pounds; and if, as must generally be the case, he cannot pay the fine, he is sold. In 1827, a free woman and her two children were converted into slaves under this law, for sheltering two fugitive slave children!

3. Debtors sold by their creditors. By a law of the late territory of Florida, approved by Congress, (!) when a judgment obtained against a free colored person, shall remain unsatisfied for *five* days, such person shall be sold to raise money to pay the judgment. The sale was nominally for a term of years, but practically for life.

4. Suspected fugitives were sold as slaves. This Roman device for procuring slaves is now in operation in the District of Columbia, under the immediate sanction of Congress, and in almost every slave State. The process is simple: A man who it is deemed *ought* to be a slave, is arrested on suspicion of being a runaway, and thrown into prison; notice is then given in a newspaper to his supposed master, to come and claim him. If claimed, well; if not, the prisoner is sold as a slave for life, to raise money to pay the expense of his imprisonment.

Having obtained some insight into Roman slavery, as it existed in the time of Christ and his apostles, and with their acquiescence, let us next look at "slavery as it exists at the present day," and which the Bishop of Texas, with the concurrence of the Bishops of North and South Carolina, assures us, "IS AGREEABLE TO THE ORDER OF DIVINE PROVIDENCE."

What is American slavery? Its advocates are fond of hiding its vileness under false definitions. It is not servitude — it is not compulsory labor — it is not arbitrary authority — it is not cruelty — it is not injustice — it is not oppression. These are, indeed, the usual accidents of slavery; but they do not constitute it, and are daily, one and all, found in total separation from it. Slavery is the conversion of a rational, accountable, immortal being, made in the image of God and a little lower than the angels, and for whom Christ died, into a CHATTEL, an article of property, a vendible commodity.* It is not the violation of certain rights, but the annihilation of ALL.† It is the degradation of a man to the level of a brute.‡ Slavery involves the denial of all domestic relations, and consequently the refusal to afford them legal protection.§ The infant slave may be sold or given away long before he sees the light, so that, at the instant of his birth, he belongs to one master and his mother to another.‖ A

* "Slaves shall be deemed sold, taken, reputed and adjudged in law to be *chattels personal* in the hands of their owners, and possessors, and their executors and administrators, to all intents, constructions and purposes whatever." *Law of South Carolina.*

† "A slave is one who is in the power of his master to whom he belongs. The master may sell him, dispose of his person, his industry and his labor. He can do nothing, possess nothing, nor acquire anything but what belongs to his master." *Civil Code of Louisiana.*

‡ "In case the personal property of a ward shall consist of specific articles, such as slaves, working beasts, animals of any kind, the court, if it deem it advantageous for the ward, may at any time pass an order for the sale thereof." *Law of Maryland.*

§ "With the consent of their masters, slaves may marry, and their moral power to agree to such a contract or connection as that of marriage, cannot be doubted; but whilst in a state of slavery it cannot produce *any civil effect*, because slaves are *deprived of all civil rights.*" *Judge Matthews, of Louisiana; Martin's Rep.* VI, 550.

"A slave is never prosecuted for bigamy, or petty treason for killing a husband being a slave, any more than admitted to an appeal for murder." *D. Dulamy, Attorney General of Maryland.* 1 *Md. Rep.*, 561.

‖ "The testator left his negro wench, Pen, to one daughter, and her future increase to another. The court decided the bequest to be good, and that all slave can possess no property; * nor is any promise to him, or agreement with him, binding in law.† Being under the control of his master, he can have no legal right to attend the worship of his Maker. ‡ Like other chattels, he can obtain no legal redress for any injury, however grievous. § The master may indeed recover compensation from any one who damages or kills either his horse or his slave; ‖ but the law refuses to notice

the children born of Pen, after the death of the testator, belonged to the sister of her mistress. *Per Cur.* He who is the absolute owner of a THING, owns all its faculties for profits or increase, as well as the thing itself. This is every day's practice; and it is held that a man may grant the wool of a flock of sheep for years." *Little's Rep.*, III, 275. *Kentucky*, 1823.

* A master made a devise to trustees, for the benefit of his slave Betsey and her children. Devise held to be void. *Per Cur.* "The condition of slaves in this country is analogous to that of the ancient Greeks and Romans, and not that of the feudal times. They are generally considered not as persons, but as THINGS. They can be sold or transferred as *goods* or personal estate; they are held to be *pro nullis, pro mortuis.* By the civil law, slaves could not take property by descent or purchase; and I apprehend this to be the law of this country." *Dess. Rep.* IV, 266. *South Carolina.*

† Application to enforce a contract between master and slave. "*Per Cur.* In the case of Sawney *vs.* Carter, the court refused, on great consideration, to enforce a promise by a master to emancipate his slave, where the conditions of the promise had been partly complied with by the slave. The court proceeded on the principle, that it is not competent to a Court of Chancery to enforce a contract between master and slave, even although the contract should be fully complied with on the part of the slave." *Leigh's Rep.*, I, 72. *Vig.*, 1829.

‡ "150 free negroes and *slaves*, belonging to the African Church, were taken up on Sunday afternoon by the city guard, and lodged in the guard-house. The City Council yesterday morning sentenced five of them, consisting of a Bishop and four ministers, to one month's imprisonment, or to give security to leave the State. Eight other ministers were also sentenced separately to receive ten lashes, or pay a fine each of five dollars." *Charleston Patriot*, 1818.

Those whose punishment is here recorded were *free* negroes; and from their fate, we may judge of the religious privileges of the slaves.

§ "It would be an idle form and ceremony to make a slave a party to a suit, by the instrumentality of which he could recover nothing; or if a recovery could be had, the instant it was recovered, it would belong to the master. The slave can possess nothing, he can hold nothing. He is, therefore, not a competent party to a suit." *Wheeler's Treatise on the Law of Slavery*, p. 197.

‖ "Trespass for killing plaintiff's slave. It appeared the slave was stealing potatoes from a bank near defendant's house. The defendant fired upon him with a gun loaded with *buck-shot*, and killed him. The jury found a verdict for plaintiff for *one dollar.* Motion for new trial. The court hold there must be a new trial; that the jury ought to have given the plaintiff the value of the slave. That if the jury were of opinion the slave was of bad character, some deduction from the usual price ought to be made; but the plaintiff was certainly entitled to his actual damage for killing his slave. Where *property* is in question, the value of the *article*, as nearly as can be ascertained, furnishes a rule from which they are not at liberty to depart." *M'Cord's Rep.*, IV, 156. *South Carolina*, 1827.

any insult or outrage offered to male or female slaves, which does not lesson their price in the market.* The whole life of a slave is appropriated by the master, and no portion of it belongs to himself, to be occupied in promoting his own happiness, or that of his offspring.†

* "There must be a loss of service, or at least a diminution of the faculty of the slave for bodily labor, to warrant an action by the master." *Harris and Johnson's Rep.*, I, 4. *Maryland.*

† "The defendant was indicted for an assault and battery upon Lydia, the slave of one Elizabeth Jones. On the trial, it appeared that the defendant had hired the slave for a year; that during the term, the slave had committed some *small* offence, for which the defendant undertook to chastise her; that while in the act of so doing, the slave ran off, whereupon the defendant called upon her to stop, which being refused, he shot at and wounded her. The defendant was found guilty, and appealed. *Per Cur. Ruffin, J.* The inquiry here is, whether a cruel and unreasonable battery on a slave by the *hirer* is indictable. . . . In criminal proceedings, and indeed in reference to all other persons but the general owner, the hirer and possessor of a slave, in relation to both rights and duties, is, for the time being, the owner. . . . . Upon the general question whether the owner is answerable *criminaliter* for a battery upon his own slave, or other exercise of authority or force not forbidden by *statute,* the court entertains but little doubt. That he is so liable *has never been decided,* nor, as far as is known, been hitherto contended. The established habits and uniform practice of the country, in this respect, are the best evidence of the portion of power deemed by the whole community requisite to the preservation of the master's dominion. This has, indeed, been assimilated at the bar to the other domestic relations, and arguments drawn from the well-established principles which confer and restrain the authority of the parent over the child, the tutor over the pupil, the master over the apprentice, have been pressed on us. The court does not recognize their application. There is no likeness between the cases. They are in opposition to each other, and there is an impassable gulf between them The difference is that which exists between freedom and slavery; and a greater cannot be imagined. In the one, the end in view is the happiness of the youth, born to equal rights with the governor on whom devolves the duty of training the young to usefulness, in a station which he is hereafter to assume among freemen. To such an end, and with such a subject, moral and intellectual instruction seems the natural means, and for the most part, it is found to suffice; moderate force is only superadded to make the others effectual. If that fail, it is better to leave the party to his own headstrong passions and the ultimate correction of the law, than to allow it to be immoderately inflicted by a private person. With slavery it is far otherwise. *The end is the profit of the master,* his security and the public peace. The *subject* is one doomed in his *own person and in his posterity, to live without knowledge, and without capacity to make anything his own, and to toil that others may reap the fruits.*

"What moral considerations shall be addressed to such a being to convince him, what it is impossible but that the most stupid must feel and know can never be true, that he is thus to labor upon a principle of natural duty, or for the sake of his own personal happiness? Such services can only be expected from one who has no will of his own, who surrenders his will in explicit obedience to that of another. Such obedience is the consequence only of *uncontrolled* authority over the body. There is nothing else which can operate to produce the effect. The power of the master must be absolute, to render the submission of the slave perfect. I most freely confess my sense of the harshness of this proposition. I feel it as deeply as any man can. And as a principle of *moral right, every person in his retirement must repudiate it.*

Such is American slavery, not as abused by the cruel and the lawless, but as established by legislative enactments and maintained by judicial decisions. Such is the slavery which George W. Freeman, as minister of the Most High God, declares to be "agreeable to the order of Divine Providence."

Such is the slavery, to the defence of which in God's house on his holy day, the Right Rev. Father in God, LEVI S. IVES, listened with "most unfeigned pleasure." Such is the slavery, whose vindication the churchmen of South Carolina spread on the wings of the wind, for "the advancement of Christianity." And shall there not be a woe now, as in ancient times, "unto them that call evil good, and good evil; that put darkness for light, and light for darkness; that put bitter for sweet, and sweet for bitter?" The guilt of such clerical champions of slavery as Bishops Ives and Freeman, is tremendously aggravated by their personal knowledge of its unutterable abominations. The decision of Judge Ruffin, quoted in the notes, was delivered in Bishop Ives's Diocese, and in which Freeman delivered his notorious sermons. Only *five* days after the latter had declared from the pulpit of Raleigh, that "slavery as it exists at the present day is agreeable to the order of Divine Providence," the following comment appeared in the Newbern (N. C.) Spectator:

"$200 REWARD.—Ran away from the subscriber about three years ago, a certain negro man named Ben, commonly known by the name of Ben Fox. He had but one eye. Also, one other negro by the name of Rigdon, who ran away on the 8th of this month. I will give the reward of one hundred dollars for each of the above negroes, to be delivered to me, or confined in the jail of Lenoir or Jones County, or for THE KILLING OF THEM, SO THAT I CAN SEE THEM.

W. D. COBB."

And now does the reader imagine Mr. Cobb some horrible wretch, who thus publicly offers money for the blood of the *in-*

But in the actual condition of things, it must be so. There is no remedy. THIS DISCIPLINE BELONGS TO SLAVERY." *The State, vs. Mann, Dev. Rep.;* p. 263. *North Carolina*, 1829.

And so it was decided, that a master or his *locum tenens* may, with legal impunity, SHOOT A WOMAN if she will not stand still to be flogged! It is pleasing to see that this judge, while upholding the essential discipline of slavery, is too honest to wait for a new revelation from Heaven to pronounce it *wrong;* and they who profess to believe it right, insult the moral sense of mankind, and lie to their own consciences.

nocent, for even Judge Ruffin admits that no principle of natural duty requires the slave to toil for his master? Mr. Cobb may be a very reputable churchwarden, vestryman, or communicant of the Church in Newbern. He is a law-abiding citizen, and has acted in strict accordance with "slavery as it exists at the present day," and of course "agreeably with the order of Divine Providence." Before he thus compassed the death of two of his fellow-men, he obtained, and published in the same paper with his advertisement, the following proclamation, viz.:

"We do hereby, by virtue of an Act of the Assembly of this State, concerning servants and slaves, intimate and declare if the said slaves (Ben and Rigdon) do not surrender themselves, and return home immediately after the publication of these presents, that any person may KILL and destroy said slaves, by *such means as he or they may think fit*, without accusation or impeachment of any crime for so doing, or without incurring any penalty or forfeiture thereby.

"Given under our hands and seals, this 12th November, 1836.

B. COLEMAN, J. P.
JAS. JONES, J. P."

It may, indeed, be said that this proclamation of the two justices of the peace is an idle mockery, first, because the slaves are by law incapacitated from reading it, and secondly, because it assigns no time for their return, and of course, that they might legally be *flayed alive* an hour after the proclamation was issued. But what is all this to Mr. Cobb? He has strictly pursued the course pointed out by law for murdering slaves in Bishop Ives's Diocese.

Again, the Wilmington (same diocese) Advertiser of July 13, 1838, has the following:

"RUN AWAY, my negro man Richard. A reward of $25 will be paid for his apprehension, DEAD or alive. Satisfactory proof will only be required of his being KILLED. DURANT H. RHODES."

Mr. Rhodes, it must be admitted, is more confiding in human nature than Mr. Cobb. The latter would only pay his money, after beholding with his own eyes the dead bodies of his slaves; whereas, Mr. Rhodes is contented with satisfactory proof that his man Richard has been slaughtered.

We will give one more instance of the taste, feelings, and

morality, springing from slavery in the Bishop's Diocese, extracted from the North Carolina Standard of July 18, 1838, published at Raleigh, the residence of the Bishop, and very probably honored by his constant perusal.

"TWENTY DOLLARS REWARD.—Ran away from the subscriber, a negro woman and two children. The woman is tall and black, and a few days before she went off, *I burnt her with a hot iron on the left side of her face.* I tried to make the letter M, and she kept a cloth over head and face, and a fly bonnet on her head, so as to cover the burn. Her children, &c. MICAJAH RICKS."

It is utterly impossible that the southern clergy, in pleading for the continuance of slavery, should not be conscious that they are pleading for the continued ignorance, wretchedness, and heathenism of millions of their fellow-men.*

Of the necessary heathenism of slavery, little need be said. There may indeed be slaves who are Christians, but they are extraordinary exceptions from the system. Can Christianity take root and flourish where every religious privilege depends on the will of an arbitrary and often Godless master?—where the conjugal and paternal relations are unacknowledged, and in practice unrespected?—where the avenues to knowledge are closed, and ignorance enforced, and where the very ministers of Christ are justly regarded by the slaves as in league with their oppressors? It is, moreover, utterly impossible that competent religious instruction can be afforded to the slaves, without at the same time imparting to them sufficient intelligence to endanger the whole system. Give to the slaves the means of becoming Christians, and you render them both useless and formidable to their masters. What! shall a slave be enabled to contemplate the mysteries of redemption, and yet not understand the iniquity of his own bondage? Shall his heart glow with love for his Saviour, and yet shall he be made to believe that that Saviour approves the cruelty and injustice of which he is daily the victim? Shall

* De Tocqueville describes the slave code as "legislation stained by unparalleled atrocities; a despotism directed against the human mind. Legislation which forbids the slaves to be taught to read or write; and which aims to sink them as nearly as possible to the level of the brutes." But De Tocqueville is a French *Philosophe*. We are not aware that any minister of the CHURCH, in the slave States, has declared this legislation to be sinful.

he be taught, as Bishop Freeman advises, to say the ten commandments, and not perceive that nearly the whole decalogue is violated in his own person? The Bishop says he must also learn his catechism. If he understands it, with what bitter scorn will he repeat, that it is his duty "not to covet or desire other men's goods, but to learn and labor truly to get his own living," recollecting that he is himself robbed, and with the consent and approbation of his spiritual teacher, of every product of his own labor, and that the only possible means whereby he can get his *own* living, is by escaping from the house of bondage! *

One of the "duties of slave-holders" is to have slave children baptized. It is to be hoped, for the sake of decency, that the address to sponsors will on such occasions be omitted, as it would be trifling with sacred things to tell the chattel parents or friends, that they must call upon the child as he grows up to hear sermons, and take care that he be brought to the Bishop for confirmation; since if either the sponsors or the child attempt to leave the plantation without their master's permission, they may legally be shot, and will certainly be scourged. It is, moreover, scarcely reverent to assure these sponsors, to whom the Word of God is a sealed book, and who have, and can have nothing of their own, that is their *duty* to provide that the little article of merchandise be taught "all which a Christian ought to know and believe to his soul's health."

Bishop Freeman is prudently silent on the subject of slave marriages. Surely a minister of the Church must have a front of bronze to use "the form of matrimony" in connecting two slaves. To make persons who are vendible commodities, and

* For these or other reasons, Bishop Ives has himself constructed a catechism, whose admirable qualities he thus describes: "The plainness of its directions enables any person to *apply* it. If our planters, therefore, under a sense of their solemn responsibility to God for the Christian instruction of their slaves, would adopt it, and see to its faithful inculcation, the next generation of *blacks* in our State, at a very small expense, would sufficiently understand the truth as it is in Jesus, WITHOUT KNOWING A LETTER OF THE ALPHABET.". *Spirit of Missions, Nov.* 1842.

There are in the Bishop's diocese, as appears by the last census, 209,783 free white persons over twenty years of age. Of these, 56,609, or nearly one-third, cannot read or write. Hence, the next generation of *whites* in North Carolina may be equally indebted with the blacks, to this catechism, for their knowledge of the truth as it is in Jesus. And yet there may be doubts of the efficiency of this labor-saving machine, seeing it is to be applied by slaveholders, so many of whom do not themselves know a letter of the alphabet.

who can never spend an hour together without the permission of one, and often of two masters, vow, in the presence of Almighty God, to cleave to each other in *riches* and in poverty, in sickness and in health, till parted by death, is but solemn mockery. The priestly prohibition, "Those whom God has joined together, let not man put asunder," is, moreover, not merely in utter contempt of the laws of the land, but at war with the very existence of slavery. If the husband and wife may not be separated at the will of their owners, and according to the state of the market, what becomes of property in man?

As the House of Bishops, in their selection of Dr. Freeman, gave their implied sanction to American slavery, it might be well for them in their next pastoral letter to determine how far, and under what circumstances, the CHURCH allows a slave a plurality of wives. This is the more necessary, as the "sects" are beginning to legislate upon the subject, since the civil power in this particular gives him unbounded liberty. A reverend Professor of the Methodist Church has decided that it is perfectly lawful for an owner to separate husband and wife, and that if there be any sin in the case, it rests upon the shoulders of the slaves, who ought not to have taken vows which their condition disqualifies them from keeping. A Baptist association in Virginia have granted permission to a slave member to take a second wife, his first having been sold into another part of the country; and another association in Georgia is reported to have voted, that a separation of man and wife, by sale or *hire*, to such a distance as precludes personal intercourse, is considered by God as equivalent to death.*

One of the blessed objects for which God instituted marriage, was the care and instruction of the young; and hence the injunction, "Parents, bring up your children in the nurture and admonition of the Lord." But slave children, as we have seen, may be sold or given away before their birth, and are the subjects of traffic at an early age. For this and other reasons, the

* Professor E. A. Andrews, in his letter on "Slavery and the Domestic Slave-Trade," relates that a slave, complaining to him that his wife's master was about selling her, remarked, "This is my *third* wife; both the others were sold to the speculators."

religious education of slaves is, with rare exceptions, wholly out of the question. On the whole, slavery and heathenism are, in the general, indissolubly connected; and Jesus Christ, in approving of the one, consented that millions for whom he died should become the victims of the other!

Of the rights of property, none are more obvious and indisputable than that of buying and selling. Hence the advocates of the African slave-trade in the British Parliament most consistently rested the justification of the commerce on the righteousness of slavery itself. Not a clerical champion of "slavery as it exists at present," questions the moral right

> "To gauge and span,
> And buy the muscles and the bones of man."

And now we call upon our Bishops, either to disabuse the public mind as to the alleged iniquity of the African slave-trade, or else to show from Scripture, that while it is very wicked to buy a savage in Africa and sell him in Cuba, it is a lawful act to buy a fellow-countryman, and possibly a fellow-Christian in North Carolina, and sell him in New Orleans.*

* Bishop Ives's diocese is one of the great breeding districts in which human cattle are raised for the Southern market. As a specimen of the style in which the correspondence of gentlemen engaged in this commerce is conducted, we give a letter from a North Carolina merchant to his consignee, at New Orleans:

"HALIFAX, N. C., Nov. 16, 1839.

Dear Sir — I have shipped in the brig Addison — prices are below —

No. 1.	Caroline Ennis,	$650
" 2.	Silvy Holland,	625
" 3.	Silvy Booth,	487.50
" 4.	Maria Pollock,	475
" 5.	Emeline Pollock,	475
" 6.	Delia Averit,	475

The two girls that cost $650 and $625, were bought before I shipped my first. I have a great many negroes offered to me, but I will not pay the prices they ask, for I know they will come down. I have no opposition in market. I will wait until I hear from you before I buy, and then I can judge what I must pay. Goodwin will send you the bill of lading for my negroes, as he shipped them with his own. Write often, as the times are critical, and it depends on the prices you get, to govern me in buying. Yours, &c.

Mr. Theophilus Freeman, New Orleans. G. W. BARNES."

The above was a small but choice invoice of wives and mothers. Nine days before, viz., Nov. 7, Mr. Barnes advised Mr. Freeman of having

Again, as God approved of the bondage of *white* men, would it not be a laudable enterprise to enlarge the assortments in our slave-markets, by the importation of Russian serfs? If the reduction of millions of the human race to the condition of mere chattels be consistent with the will of God, then, inasmuch as the greater includes the less, who shall say that every minor form of oppression is not equally agreeable to the common Father of mankind?

"Slavery," says Wilberforce, is "a system of the grossest injustice, of the most heathenish irreligion and immorality, of the most unprecedented degradation and unrelenting cruelty." Yet of this system the Episcopal Church is a mighty buttress, and certain of her bishops its reckless and unblushing champions. But could the united logic and eloquence of the whole House of Bishops persuade the mother, as she bends with delight over the infant cherub in the cradle, that the compassionate Redeemer, who took little children into his arms and blessed them, has given his consent that the child of her love, the object of her hopes and prayers, should be torn from her embraces, and sold in the market to the highest bidder, to put money in

shipped a lot of forty-three men and women. Mr. Freeman, informing one of his correspondents of the state of the market, writes (*Sunday*, Sept. 21, 1839), "I bought a boy yesterday 16 years old, and likely, *weighing* 110 pounds, at $700. I sold a likely girl, 12 years old, at $500. I bought a man yesterday, 20 years old, six feet high, at $820; one *to-day*, 24 years old, at $850, black and sleek as a mole."

And are these brokers in human flesh, these butchers of human hearts, bad men? For aught that appears, they are as sound Churchmen, and as heavenly-minded Christians, except in trading in negroes on *Sunday*, as Bishops Ives and Freeman themselves; they are but reducing to practice the doctrines taught by these Right Reverend Fathers. If slavery be right, we must indeed wait for a new revelation before we pronounce the slave-trade wrong. No doubt the trade occasions painful separations, but the rights of property are paramount to the feelings of nature. The Presbyterian Synod of Kentucky, some time since, published an address, in which they thus noticed the domestic slave-trade: "The members of a slave family may (by law) be forcibly separated, so that they shall never more meet again till the final judgment. And cupidity often induces the masters to practise what the law allows. Brothers and sisters, parents and children, husbands and wives, are torn asunder, and permitted to see each other no more. *These acts are daily occurring in the midst of us.* There is not a neighborhood where these heart-rending scenes are not displayed. There is not a village or road that does not behold the sad procession of manacled outcasts, where chains and mournful countenances tell that they are exiled by force from all that their hearts hold dear." And the Synod speak of the *iniquity* of the system! But why is it more iniquitous to fetter slaves than any other animals that we send to market? Why more cruel to separate a child than a calf from its mother?

the pocket of another?* Let the experiment be made, and if that mother be a Christian, she will thank God that she knows and loves her Saviour too well to believe such a blasphemy.

And by what process do our masters in Israel justify American slavery? Do they show its accordance with the divine attributes — with the spirit of the Gospel — with the cultivation of holiness — with the glory of God — with individual happiness and national prosperity? Oh, no — they appeal to Hebrew servitude, and to a few insulated texts in the New Testament.

There is something appalling in the passionate eagerness with which certain ministers of Christ rush forward to lay the blessed Scriptures upon the altar of the southern Moloch. We wish to do these men no injustice, and therefore frankly admit, that some persons may honestly find themselves embarrassed in their endeavors to reconcile certain texts with the obvious cruelty and injustice of human bondage; and we as frankly confess that we shudder at the very idea of one who professes himself called by the Holy Ghost as a preacher of righteousness, teaching his people that American slavery, slavery as it exists in North Carolina, is *not* "WRONG."

The moral sense of every man, when not perverted by pecuniary interest, education, or authority, is itself sufficient to convince him of the iniquity of slavery. The Christian student, therefore, who commences the Scriptural examination of this subject with an unclouded judgment, will come to his work with a firm conviction, that every attribute of slavery is opposed to the *spirit* of the Gospel. Hence, he would be restrained from promptly pronouncing slavery unscriptural only by a painful suspicion that certain passages in the Bible lent it their sanction. He would, however, call to mind that there were some things in Scripture confessedly "hard to be understood," and he would cherish the hope that he did not rightly understand those which apparently contradicted the character of God and the general precepts of his Word. He would, therefore, search the Scriptures, not to find a warrant for slavery, but to reconcile certain

* Benjamin Davis, a slave-trader in Hamburg, S. C., advertised in the Charleston papers, for sale, "SMALL BOYS WITHOUT THEIR MOTHERS."

obscure texts with the love and holiness which beam from every page.

If the patriarchs did, indeed, as is said, hold slaves, he would recollect that they also indulged in polygamy, and were, in several instances, guilty of falsehood.*

* It is not our purpose to enter at large into the Bible argument, but merely to suggest some reasons why they who think American slavery "wrong," are not necessarily impugners of "Revelation." It might be inferred from the confidence and evident delight with which the example of Abraham is urged in vindication of our "domestic institution," that the father of the faithful was also the father of all who traffic in human flesh. If he was, indeed, a slave-holder, he was still very far from being the type of a Southern planter. While childless, he designated one of his slaves as his future heir. He was afterwards prevented, only by Divine appointment, from making the son of the bondwoman heir *with* the son by promise, and was consoled by the assurance that the *former* should become the father of princes, and the founder of a great nation. He moreover entrusted to one of his slaves, the selection of a wife for his favorite son. The three hundred and eighteen servants "born in his house," the Bishop of Texas asserts were "slaves." Still they were men whom he armed and led to battle. They, with their parents, brothers, sisters, wives and children, must have formed a "gang" of about two thousand in number. Yet we find the master of this multitude of slaves leaving his guests to catch a calf to provide dinner for them, while the mistress of this goodly household occupied herself in kneading and baking cakes for her company! A pro-slavery theory can alone blind us to the evidence afforded by these facts; that Abraham was the chief of a clan or tribe, and that the expression, "born in his own house," only indicates that the three hundred and eighteen were not strangers whom he employed on the occasion, but members of the community acknowledging him as its head.

That there was a species of servitude in the East at an early period, as at present, is true; it is also true that it was of a very different character from that which prevailed in the West. *Our* slavery belongs to the Western system. In a late work on Egypt, by Clot Bey, the distinction between the two systems is thus noticed: "There is a prodigious difference between American slavery, and servitude among the Orientals. With them, the institution is neither cruel or disgraceful. It does not regard the slave as a *thing*, a material object, as did the Roman law. It does not make him a mere article of import or export, a matter of speculation, a simple machine, in fact, whose efficiency is estimated as horse power. The West Indian regards in the negro only his corporeal value, and forgets in him the intellectual man; he robs him of his nature. The Mussulman, on the contrary, always beholds a MAN in his slave, and treats him in such a manner, that we may say of Oriental slavery, that it is often a real adoption, and always an admission into an extended family circle.

"Oriental servitude honorably contrasts with our slavery, and above all by its respect for the dignity of human nature. The slave, in Turkey, is not humiliated by his condition: he often proudly boasts that he is of the family of such a Bey, or such a Pasha, and gives his master the title of father. He knows, moreover, that he is not bound for ever to his station by a chain of iron. He has before him examples sufficient to raise his ambition, and to swell his soul with the hope of more brilliant destinies." The author then gives various instances of slaves who had risen to high dignities; and mentions two sons-in-law of the present Sultan, who had both been slaves, and adds, "In Egypt, the superior officers are, for the most part, manumitted slaves." See *Apercu general sur L'Egypte, par A. B. Clot Bey*, 1840. Tom. i, p. 269.

If the Jews were, indeed, allowed to buy slaves of the heathens around them, we must recollect that they were also allowed, nay, even commanded to destroy the inhabitants of Canaan, men, women and children; and slavery was but a commutation of the punishment of death to which God had sentenced them for their sins. Such examples are not precedents for us under the Gospel dispensation without a special warrant. But is it certain that the "bondmen" (so called by our translators, but not distinguished in the original from servants*) were *slaves?* If so, they were the *property* of their masters. Now, how was their property acquired? The heathen around, even their very infants, might be slaughtered, but "He that stealeth a man and selleth him, *or if he be found in his hand,* he shall surely be put to death." Hence the Jewish slaves were to be purchased, but of whom? If the slave-trade constituted part of the Jewish commerce, strange it is that we hear nothing of the slave market in Israel. We know that the Jews *sold themselves.* "If a sojourner or stranger wax rich by thee, and thy brother that dwelleth by him wax poor, *and sell himself* unto the stranger or sojourner by thee," &c. Hence it is possible that as poor Jews sold themselves to rich strangers, poor strangers might sell themselves to rich Jews. There is no evidence that the heathen in Palestine had *slaves* to sell, but many among them might find it convenient to enter into Jewish families as domestics. The servitude of both Jewish and heathen servants seems to have been limited to the year of Jubilee. That this servitude was not founded on the idea of *property* appears from the prohibition, "Thou shalt not deliver unto his master, the servant which is escaped from his master to thee" (Deut. xxiii, 15). This law, whether the fugitive was a Jew or a heathen, is utterly irreconcilable with common honesty, supposing the servant to have

* "The word in the original, sometimes rendered bondman, and sometimes servant, is *Obed.* It is applied to Christ, "Behold my servant whom I uphold," Isaiah, xxiv, 1. It is applied to King Rehoboam, 1 Kings, xii, 7. Ziba, Saul's *Obed,* had himself twenty *Obeds,* 2 Samuel, ix, 10. There is no word in Hebrew for slave, as distinct from servant. We find, 1 Chron. ii, 34, that Sheshan, the head of one of the families of the tribe of Judah, gave his daughter to wife, to his *servant,* an Egyptian; and so far was any disgrace attached in consequence to their children, that the son of this very daughter was enrolled among "the valiant men" of David's army, 1 Chron. ii, 41.

been a mere chattel; and certainly belonged to a very different code of morals from that which enjoins, "If thou meet thy enemy's ox or his ass going astray, thou shalt surely bring it back to him again."

On turning to the New Testament, our inquirer would recollect, that it was written at a time, when, among the Romans, slavery and the exhibitions of the amphitheatre were systems of extraordinary cruelty and of human butchery, and that, although both are alluded to, neither is expressly condemned. True it is, that St. Paul induced a servant to return to his master. If the servant was a freeman, the case proves nothing. If he was a slave, the apostle required his instant manumission, by commanding the master to receive him, "Not now as a servant, but above a servant, a brother beloved ; *receive him as myself*." *

There are instances in which persons, who perhaps held slaves, are spoken of with commendation, but not on that account. None of the churches or individuals commended in the apostolic epistles were faultless, and it would be most monstrous to infer from a general commendation, an apostolic sanction of every error or sin of which they might be guilty.

Were it possible to imagine a kind of slavery divested of all sinful attributes, and consistent alike with the glory of God and the good of man, Bishops Freeman and Ives well know that such is not the character of American slavery. If "slavery as it exists at present," in the Dioceses of these two Bishops, is indeed acceptable to Him who proclaims himself, "The Lord, the Lord God, merciful and gracious, long-suffering and abundant in goodness and truth," then, indeed, is the Bible a riddle, and its morality a paradox. Be it so; a title to negro slaves must at all hazards be found in the Bible. The very character of the Southern priesthood for honesty depends on its production.† What is wanting in proof, must be supplied by bold assertion,

* St. Paul wrote by Onesimus to the Church at Colosse, and in his Epistle speaks of him as "a faithful and beloved brother, who is one of you," Col. iv, 9.

† The clergy of the South, of all denominations, are generally slave-holders. A member of the House of Bishops is said, in a late western newspaper, to own one hundred and seventy slaves.

and all Christendom beyond the slave-region shall be accused of presumption, for not waiting for a *new revelation*, before they dare to pronounce such slavery as exists in North Carolina *wrong!*

And shall we be any longer insulted with the assertion, that the preached Gospel is the divinely appointed means of abolishing slavery? Most certain it is, *that the spirit of the Gospel*, carried into universal practice, would relieve the human family from every moral evil with which it is afflicted; but it is utterly false that the ministrations of our own, or any other Church, will correct a single vice, independent of the character of its ministers, the examples they set, and the doctrines they preach. Would the teachings of a thousand Dr. Freemans loosen the fetters of a single slave? No less than forty missionaries are supported by our Board of Missions in the slave regions. Dare we hope they have induced one master to let his bondmen go free? While the southern clergy vindicate slavery as a Christian institution, they are in danger of producing a result which they as little expect as desire. "Should the priesthood," says a southern writer, once himself a slave-holder, "should the priesthood succeed in convincing the world that slavery is the doctrine of the New Testament, then will INFIDELITY become the true religion of mankind — and not till then." Says another southern writer, and apparently a pious Christian, "I distinctly avow, than when I can be brought to believe that American slavery, taken as a system, is sustained by the teachings of Holy Writ, I must cease to be a believer in the Bible."

But, blessed be God! his priesthood has, in all ages of the Church, afforded the most glorious illustrations of fearless devotion to duty, and of self-denying benevolence, that the world has ever witnessed. While some have claimed to hold their slaves as monarchs their crowns, "by the grace of God," many have witnessed a good confession against human bondage. In the Church of England at the present day, there is not probably a bishop, priest, or deacon, who would endorse the theology of our Texan bishop. But then we are told by the slave-holders, and their tools, the northern demagogues, that England is anti-slavery through envy of our prosperity! Let us, then, hear the English bishops, when such a motive could have no existence.

BISHOP WARBURTON, in a sermon preached in 1776 against slavery and the slave-trade, exclaims,

> "Gracious God! to talk, as in herds of cattle, of property in rational creatures — creatures endowed with all our faculties, possessing all our qualities but that of color — our brethren both by nature and grace, shocks all the feelings of humanity and the dictates of common sense. *Nature created man free, and grace invites him to assert his freedom.*"

BISHOP BURGESS, in a pamphlet against the slave-trade, 1789, says:

> "Such oppression (West India slavery) and such traffic must be swept away at *one blow.* Such horrid offences against God and nature can admit of no medium. If no British subject is exempt from the duty of doing everything in his place towards preventing the continuance of so great a political as well as moral evil, more especially are not those subjects, whose business it is to teach what is every man's concern to know, the *interpreters of God's Word*, which is so frequently violated by West India slavery and its consequences."

BISHOP PORTEUS declared in the House of Lords, 1806, in answering certain *Scriptural* arguments in behalf of slavery, "There was no such thing as perpetual slavery under the Old or New Testament;" and he showed that all Hebrew servants were set at liberty every seventh year, and all others at the Jubilee.

THE BISHOP OF ST. ASAPH, the same year, asserted in the House of Lords, that

> "The principle of perpetual slavery is totally inconsistent with the Jewish law. When we come down to Christianity, we find dealers in slaves are held among the worst of the human race. St. Paul, in his Epistle to Timothy, tells us what the dealers in slaves are, and who are their companions. The slave-dealers are called 'stealers of men,' and their companions are liars, perjurers, murderers, and parricides."

BISHOP HORSELY, in 1799, with Christian boldness, rebuked the nobles of Britain for their wicked toleration of the slave-trade; and vindicated the Gospel of Christ from the aspersions of those who represented it as a shield for cruelty and injustice. After showing that the "men-stealers" classed in the Bible with murderers of fathers and of mothers, were in fact, according to the true meaning of the Greek word, "slave-traders," he proceeded:

"We have reason to conclude, from the mention of 'slave-traders,' by St. Paul, that if any of them should ever find their way to heaven, they must go thither in company with murderers and parricides. My lords, I do certainly admit that there is no prohibition of slavery in the Bible, in explicit terms, such as these words, 'thou shalt not have a slave,' or 'thou shalt not hold any one in slavery.' There is no explicit reprobation of slavery by name. My lords, if I were to say there was no occasion for any such prohibition, because slavery is condemned by something anterior to either the Christian or the Mosaic dispensation, I could support the assertion by grave authorities. Beware, my lords, how you are persuaded to bring under the opprobrious name of *fanaticism* the regard you owe to the great duties of justice and mercy, for the neglect of which, if you should neglect them, you will be answerable to that tribunal, where no prevarication of witnesses can misinform the Judge, where no subtility of an advocate, miscalling the names of things, and putting evil for good, and good for evil, can mislead the judgment."

"Slavery," said LORD MANSFIELD, "is so odious that nothing but positive law can sustain it." His lordship little suspected that a time was approaching when the CHURCH would afford it more efficient support than even positive law, and would herself look to it for support in return. One of our church periodicals has announced that "the Bishop of Georgia, in his Montpelier Institution, is testing the sufficiency of slave-labor to support it. It is not unusual to see in the southern papers, notices of slaves to be sold on account of ecclesiastical corporations. Bishop Wilberforce, in his History, refers to a proposal by the editor of the "Spirit of Missions" to establish a mission school to be supported by slaves, who shall be induced, by the promise of prospective emancipation, to perform so much extra labor in the course of SIXTEEN years as to yield a profit of one hundred per cent. on the capital invested, over and above the ordinary profits extorted by common taskmasters. This revolting scheme, in which it was intended that the slaves would work two hours before sunrise, and two hours after sunset, in all *sixteen* hours out of the four and twenty, and this for sixteen successive years, was pressed upon the Church in an official magazine, published in New York under the supervision of the Missionary Committee, and by an editor holding his appointment from the Board of Missions, including the bishops, and other representatives of the Church elected by the General Convention. In about three months after this publication, the Board assembled, and written remonstrances were presented to them, beseeching them, for the honor of the Church, and the cause of religion and humanity, to disavow the conduct of their editor. These remonstrances excited warm debates, not unmingled with southern arrogance. It was impossible for the Board to express disapprobation of the plan without indirectly censuring Bishops Ives and Elliott. If slaves be indeed property, what objection can there be to converting their bones and muscles into money for the Church? To condemn the editor, would offend the pro-slavery Bishops and clergy; expressly to approve his conduct, would raise a tempest at the North. So, policy was substituted for godly sincerity, and cunning for wisdom. The Board expunged from their minutes the proceedings had on the memorials, and avoiding all intelligible allusion to the scheme which had led to them, ordered the following words to be printed on the future numbers of their *own magazine:*

"It is to be understood by the readers of this periodical, that the Board of Missions are not responsible for the expression of editorial opinions, but simply for the accuracy of facts connected with their operations."

But lest even this extraordinary disclaimer should be supposed to involve a concealed censure on the late "editorial opinions," the resolution recommending it, and which was introduced by a Bishop from a slave State, as chairman of a committee, was preceded by another, declaring, "That, in the opinion of this Board, the Spirit of Missions has been conducted, during the *year past*, with commendable diligence and ability;" and the report of the committee accompanying these resolutions is careful to state that the periodical in question is "gaining reputation and influence, and that if it continues to be conducted with the same ability which it has *of late exhibited*, it will become a powerful auxiliary to the cause."

The subject of slavery had been brought directly and prominently before the Church, by her own appropriate officers. Money, entrusted to the Board for missionary purposes, had been employed through the official magazine, to advocate the cause of human bondage, to condemn emancipation as "ruinous, and forbidden by common sense and *Christian* prudence," and to put in motion a machinery by which money was to be extorted for the coffers of the Church, from the cruel and extraordinary toil of miserable slaves. The memorialists had virtually asked the reverend and right reverend fathers of the Church, in council assembled, Do, or do you not, approve of this conduct of your agent? To this interrogatory, the reverend gentlemen thought it expedient to answer neither yes nor no; but in the notice they ordered to be in future printed on their magazine, they did return a most disingenuous and unworthy reply. No human being ever supposed that the members of the Board, scattered throughout the Union, were responsible for the publication or "expression" in New York, of opinions of which they could have no previous knowledge, and of course no power to prevent. Did the Board intend to enunciate so bold a truism as this? As well might they have given notice that they were not responsible for any heresy or immorality of which their officers might hereafter be guilty. When examined with a critical microscope, the disclaimer has reference to the "expression" — the *printing* of opinions in New York. But in the plain, obvious, popular import of the notice, the disclaimer has reference to the opinions, *after* they are expressed and printed. In this sense alone, had the disclaimer any reference to the subject which induced it. Nay, the Board intended it to be so understood; for they thought proper to order a resolution to be sent to the memorialists, who had "complained of the tendency of an editorial article in the March number of the Spirit of Missions" (carefully avoiding mentioning in the minutes, the *subject* of the article), declaring that the Board had never "held itself responsible for the opinions expressed by the editors of the Spirit of Missions," and had directed "this assertion of irresponsibility to be distinctly placed upon the cover of the future numbers of this periodical."

On this assertion of "irresponsibility" we take issue, and affirm that the Board is responsible to the community, to the Church, and to God, for the opinions of an editor appointed by themselves, under their control, paid out of funds entrusted to their care, published in an official magazine, and printed at the expense of missionary contributions. What! will the Board tell us that *their* editor may make *their* magazine a vehicle for the dissemination of obscenity and infidelity, and that it is no concern of theirs? That he may disparage the Church, insult her bishops, and deny her doctrines, and that they are not responsible? But should he misdate a letter, or omit half a dollar in the acknowledgment of a donation, then, then indeed, they will not shrink from responsibility.

Surely the bishops who concurred in this "assertion of irresponsibility," forgot for the moment their consecration vow, "to be ready with all faithful vigilance to drive away from the Church all strange and erroneous doctrines contrary to God's word."

This disclaimer, like most cunning measures, was a sacrifice of duty to present expediency; a sacrifice which, however common with politicians, we had no right to expect from such a body of men. The truth is, the Board were worried by the memorials. To take no notice of them would probably increase "agitation"—to approve the course of the editor, would disgust many at the North—to condemn it, would offend all at the South. Instead of manfully breaking down this triple hedge, within which they found themselves enclosed, they determined to crawl through it, and for this purpose, disincumbered themselves of a responsibility which God and the Church had commanded them to bear.

Let us now turn to another, but a kindred subject. Whatever may be the struggles of the slave-holder to wring from the Bible a title to his slaves, no reader of the volume of inspiration, whether Christian or infidel, has professed to discover in it a warrant for the establishment of CASTE in the Church of God. However much we may be inclined to appeal to the Scriptures for a license to despise, insult, and oppress our fellow-Christians, on account of their race or natural features, we are effectually deterred by the declarations that one God hath created us—that we have all one Father—that in Christ Jesus there is neither Jew nor Gentile, Greek nor barbarian, bond nor free; and by the commands to do good unto all men, and to *honor all men.* Hence the institution of CASTE in the Church, and the obloquy, injustice, and cruelty connected with it, are not rested, like slavery, on the alleged consent of Christ and his apostles; but simply and frankly on pecuniary interest, personal antipathy, and popular prejudice.

So accustomed have we been from childhood to the distinction of caste, arising from color — so universally is this distinction maintained not merely in the Church, but in all the departments of society, that we have, for the most part, become callous to its iniquity; and our understandings can with difficulty be brought to believe that the merciful precepts of Christ's Gospel were intended to govern our intercourse with men of *dark*, as well as of white complexions. But although we may be insensible to the cruelty of caste, it is otherwise with its victims.

The Rev. T. S. Wright, a liberally educated *colored* clergy man, thus briefly enumerates *some* of the consequences of that system, which our Church has been so active and zealous in maintaining.

"No man can really understand this prejudice unless he feels it crushing him to dust, because it is matter of feeling. It has bolts, screws, and bars, wherever the colored man goes. It has bolts in all the schools and colleges. The colored parent, with the same soul as the white parent, sends his child to the seats of learning, and he finds the door bolted, and sits down to weep beside his boy. Prejudice stands at the door and bars him out. Does the child of the colored man show a talent for mechanics? The heart of the parent beats with hope. He sees the children of the white man engaged in employment, and he trusts there is a door open for his boy to get an honest living, and become a useful member of society. But when he comes to the workshop with his child, he finds a bolt there. But even suppose he can get this first bolt removed, he finds other bars. Let him be ever so skilled as a mechanic, up starts prejudice and says, 'I wont work in the shop, if you do.' Here he is scourged by prejudice, and has to go back and sink down to some of the employments which white men leave for the most degraded. He hears of the death of a child from home, and he goes in a stage or steamboat. His money is received, but he is scourged by prejudice. If he is sick, he can have no bed; he is driven on deck. Money will not buy for him the comforts it gets for all who have not his complexion. He turns to some white friend, and he says, 'Submit, it is an ordinance of God, you must be humble.' I have felt this. As a minister, I have been called to pass often up and down the North River in steamboats. Many a night have I walked the deck, and not been able to lie down in a bed.* Prejudice would, indeed, turn money to dross, where it was offered for these comforts by a colored man. Thus prejudice scourges us from the table, it scourges us from the cabin, from the stage-coach, and from the bed. Wherever we go, it has for us bolts, bars, and rods. Even at the communion table, the colored man can only partake of the crumbs after the others have been served. This prejudice drives the colored man from religion. I have often heard my brethren say, they would have nothing to do with such a religion. They are driven away, and go to infidelity; for even the infidels at Tammany Hall make no distinction on account of color."

That this prejudice may drive some of the sufferers into infidelity is probable; since it has been a common mistake in all ages, to judge of Christianity, not by its own inspired records, but by the conduct of a portion of its fallible ministers. And he who is led to believe that American slavery, and its detestable offspring, American caste, is approved of by Jesus Christ, may well be excused for questioning the divinity of his mission.

Although caste had long existed among us in practice, the exclusion of Mr. Crummell from the General Theological Seminary was the first instance of its recognition, as a part of the ecclesiastical polity of the American Church. Mr. Degrass, the young man whose affecting journal is given by Bishop Wilberforce, was kept out of the Seminary by the personal influence and authority of Bishop Benjamin Onderdonk. But in Mr. Crummell, the bishop found a more impracticable subject, and a petition for admission was presented to the assembled Trustees. The statutes of the institution rendered it imperative on the Trustees to admit all applicants possessing certain qualifications, and these qualifications the bishop honestly informed the Board, *were possessed* by the present applicant. The Board, under these circumstances, found themselves in a dilemma. To reject the young man *on account of his complexion* would not only be illegal, but would excite remark, invite ridicule, and encourage

* The writer has been informed, that the wife of Mr. Wright lost her life in consequence of exposure on the deck of a steamboat, being denied a berth in the cabin, on account of her complexion.

"agitation;" and on the other hand, to admit him, would irritate a prejudice which Bishop Onderdonk had admitted to Degrass was "unrighteous;" and might also hazard the loss of southern contributions to the Seminary. A committee, with Bishop Henry Onderdonk, of Pennsylvania, as chairman, was appointed to consider the application; and their report was more distinguished for brevity than for wisdom. Without assigning a single reason, and without an allusion to the complexion of the applicant, they merely recommended "that the prayer of the petitioner be not granted." The report was adopted, whereupon, Bishop Doane, of New Jersey, asked permission, which was *refused*, to enter his objections on the minutes. Hence the minutes merely record the fact, that a Mr. Crummell had applied for admission into the Seminary and was denied. They afforded no intimation that the Trustees had violated the statutes, no hint that the rejected candidate was not colored like themselves. Should any one wonder why the application was rejected, the natural presumption would be, that the young man was deficient in his literary attainments or moral character, and that the committee who reported against him had benevolently refrained from putting his delinquencies upon record. But Mr. Crummell was a poor, obscure colored man; there was no probability that his case would excite inquiry, or ever be known. Certainly the management of the Trustees was exceedingly adroit. Alas for the wisdom of the wise, and the understanding of the prudent. In a short time the proceedings of the Board were exposed and condemned in the newspapers, not only of New York, but of London, and now form a conspicuous and indelible portion of the "History of the Protestant Episcopal Church in America." The Bishop of New York thought it expedient to vindicate himself in a newspaper publication, in which he condescends to propitiate the "unrighteous prejudice" by a gratuitous sneer at *amalgamation. (!)*

Mr. Crummell sought and obtained ordination in another diocese, and then resolved to embrace an opportunity that offered, of organizing a colored church in Philadelphia. He accordingly repaired to that city, with the usual letter dismissory from his late diocese, and in compliance with the canon, presented it to the bishop. We can readily believe that this last gentleman was not gratified at finding that the young man, who on his recommendation had been excluded from the Seminary, now claimed a canonical residence in his own diocese, as a brother minister of the Church. The canons allowed the bishop no discretion. Mr. Crummell's letter was unexceptionable, and by the laws of the Church, he became entitled, on its delivery, to all the rights and privileges of a clergyman of the Diocese of Pennsylvania. But the bishop was as independent of legal restraints in Philadelphia, as he had been in New York. He informed Mr. Crummell that he would receive his letter, only on the condition that he would pledge himself, in his own behalf, and in behalf of his Church, should he succeed in raising one, *never to apply for a seat in Convention;* and immediately proposed to *write* the pledge. He was told it was unnecessary, as the pledge could not be given. He then positively declared he would not receive him, on which the young minister intimated his intention to return to the diocese he had just left. Here again was an embarrassing dilemma. To disregard a dismissory letter from another diocese, and to send back the bearer, without the slightest objection being made to his character or conduct, might lead to very inconvenient results, and would unquestionably cause much "agitation;" and, on the other hand, to admit a negro to a canonical residence, was to open the door of the Convention to him, the consequence of which would be, that a minister of Christ, with a dark complexion, might sit in the Council of the Church! The bishop, to escape from this dilemma, proposed that he should inform the Convention in his address at its next meeting, that he had been admitted with the *understanding* that he was to have no seat in it. Mr. Crummell, with the same high moral courage which had hitherto marked his course, replied that he could have no agency in the matter. Thwarted in his attempts to make Mr. Crummell surrender his rights as a clergyman, the bishop determined that others should wrest them from him; and consented to receive the dismissory letter, telling him that he would get the Convention to take some order on the subject.

About three weeks after this strange conference, the Convention of the Diocese assembled, and the bishop's address contained the following passage:

"In the Convention of 1795, it was declared that the African Church of St. Thomas, in this city, was 'not entitled to send a clergyman or deputies to the Convention, or to interfere with the general government of the Church.' This law is still retained in our 8th Revised Regulations. The peculiar circumstances which required this restriction may occur, and probably will, in other cases; and I submit for your consideration whether it will not be proper to enact a similar restriction applicable to all clergymen and congregations in this diocese under like circumstances."

It does really seem as if a consciousness of shame and guilt drives our ecclesiastical rulers, when perpetrating oppression and injustice upon *colored* Christians, to hide their meaning in unintelligible and deceptive phraseology.

We here learn that in 1795, the Convention made a certain *declaration*, which to all appearance was *judicial* and not legislative, that a particular Church was *not entitled* to a representation in the Convention. The *reasons* for such a judgment are not given — they may have been good or bad, but the judgment itself was within the jurisdiction of the Convention, since every legislative body must judge of the qualifications of its members, although it cannot prescribe them. It does not appear that the Convention invaded any right, or did more than refuse to acknowledge an unlawful claim.

And yet from the fact that the Church thus excluded was an *African* one, and from the omission of the *reasons* on which the judgment was founded, we have no question that the pretended declaration was a high-handed unconstitutional enactment, disfranchising a rector and his congregation, solely on account of the tincture of their skins; and that the Convention were ashamed to place upon their minutes the unchristian motives by which they were tempted to trample under foot the constitutional rights of a minister of Christ, and the people under his charge.

Bishop Onderdonk, we have seen, called on the Convention to enact a similar restriction, "applicable to all clergymen and congregations," which should hereafter be in "*like circum-*

stances." What circumstances? A state of schism, insubordination, or irregular or illegal incorporation? Oh no; he meant having black skins, but was ashamed to say so.

It will be observed that the legislation recommended is to be prospective, not *ex post facto*. No clergyman or congregation, *now* in the diocese, is to be affected by it. No case *now* calls for this restriction, but cases "*may occur, and probably will*," and it is best to be prepared for contingencies. All this is painful. The bishop, while uttering the words we have quoted, had in his possession the letter dismissory of the very clergyman against whom the proposed restriction was aimed; and who, by his advice, had been shut out of the Theological Seminary, and from whom he had vainly endeavored to obtain a disgraceful surrender of his rights as a minister of the Church. Again, in his address, he tells the Convention, "Letters dismissory have been received and accepted by me as follows," and then gives a list of clergymen received from other dioceses; but Mr. Crummell's name is not among them!

The powers of our Conventions, like those of our State Legislatures, are limited by written constitutions. The Fourth Article of the Constitution of the Pennsylvania Diocese declares that "every clergyman of the Church, of whatever order, being a settled minister of some parish in this State, *shall be entitled to a seat and vote in the Convention*," provided he has had a canonical residence of a certain time, &c. The Tenth Article prescribes the mode of altering the Constitution, by the joint action of *two* successive Conventions, and thus takes away the power of doing it by a simple resolution.

Ruffian mobs had on several occasions, within the past few years, assailed the unoffending blacks in Philadelphia, sacked their dwellings, and torn down their houses of worship, and all on account of the complexion their Maker had given them. And how was this wicked, cruel prejudice against color, rebuked by the Episcopal Church in Pennsylvania? Why, the Convention, at the instigation of the bishop,

"*Resolved*, That the following clause be added to the 8th Revised Regulation adopted in 1829, and hereafter to be taken as part thereof:

'No Church in this diocese, in like peculiar circumstances with the African Church of St. Thomas, shall be entitled to send a clergyman or deputies to the Convention, or to interfere with the general government of the Church.''

Thus were colored clergymen and colored Christians driven, in contempt and utter violation of canonical law, from the enclosure of the Church, as they had been, by abandoned wretches, from the sanctuary of their own homes. The bishop, clergy, and lay deputies of the Pennsylvania Church, make common cause with the rioters in the streets, in a general crusade against negroes and mulattoes! This act of the Convention brands for all future time every minister of Christ, and every member of his mystical body, who may trace his descent from the land of Cyprian and Tertullian, as belonging to a distinct and degraded caste, and debars them from all participation in the government of the Redeemer's Church. This act forcibly thrusts a portion of the Church into schism, and repudiates one of the fundimental conditions on which the Diocese of Pennsylvania consented, in 1784, to acknowledge a general ecclesiastical government in the United States, viz., "That to make canons and laws, there be no other authority than that of a representative body of the clergy and laity conjointly." The great truth, "HE HATH MADE US, AND NOT WE OURSELVES," is set at naught by the Pennsylvania Convention; and in the indulgence of an "unrighteous prejudice," or in a cowardly submission to it, they have sacrificed both the independence and the unity of the Church, the dignity of the ministerial office, and that love which Christ made the badge and test of discipleship. And this lawless and profane excision of their brethren, these men attempted to veil under the strange and indefinite phraseology of "all in like peculiar circumstances with the African Church of St. Thomas!" If anything can possibly add to the shame of this transaction, it is that the vote was taken without discussion; not one single member of that large body, clergyman or layman, having the independence to rise in his place and protest against an act, at variance alike with the principles of the Church, and the precepts of its Divine Head. And what is the apology, the only apology which the Churchmen of Pennsylvania can offer for this wanton insult and oppression of their colored brethren? an apology that aggravates, instead of excusing their conduct. Popular prejudice required that colored clergymen and delegates should be excluded from the Convention! It is disheartening to the patriot, to see our public men, those to whom high and important trusts are confided, so often governing themselves, not by the immutable principles of justice and rectitude, but by the ever varying opinions of the multitude. But oh! it is sickening to the soul, to witness the Church of Christ sacrificing to popular clamor, her own holy and glorious attribute of being a light and a guide to a benighted and a sinful world.

Bishop Onderdonk of New York, in his charge of 1843, to the Convention, remarked:

> "Taking the Gospel for our guide, we must see in the Church and the world, essentially antagonistic bodies. The Church was formed *not to coöperate with the world, but to oppose it*—to attack the wicked principles and practices to which it is in bondage, and to come to no terms with it on any other principles than its entire surrender of its opposition to the pure and holy spirit of the Gospel, and its entire submission to the rule which Christ, through his Church, would establish over it for good. . . . . Let us ever, by the grace of God, be careful that in our intercourse with it, we adorn the doctrine of God our Saviour in all things; and then go forward in our Master's work, indifferent save for its own sake, *whether the world be pleased or offended;* and, indeed, looking for the ill will and opposition from it, which that Master and his divine Word have prepared us to expect."

Glorious truths! Godly counsels! worthy of an age of martyrs and confessors. Alas, that they should have been in the lips of him who uttered them, *Vox et preterea nihil!* Let the diary of the young candidate for orders, given in the "History," tell how this bold-spoken bishop crouched before a prejudice which his own tongue confessed to be "unrighteous;" and sacrificed duty and independence, lest the Seminary should lose the support of "the South!"

Rank and caste are essentially different; and while the former is sanctioned by the Bible, which requires us to render honor to those to whom honor is due, the latter is heathenish in its origin and character. Rank is founded on condition, and is usually connected with personal distinctions and acquirements. It unavoidably springs from the organization of society; and while it may confer privileges, is not necessarily inconsistent with the claims of justice and humanity. Caste, on the contrary, regards *races*, irrespective of the individuals composing them. In Hindostan, it both elevates and depresses—with us, its only effects are degradation, cruelty, and wretchedness. In the former country, the two extremes of caste are the Brahmins and Soodras,* and the gulf between them is wider and more impassable than that which in our own separates the whites and the blacks. And yet the American Church may learn an edifying lesson from the temporary cessation of caste in the presence of a Hindoo idol.

"I was surprised," says Dr. Claudius Buchanan, in the journal of his tour to the Temple of Juggernaut, in Orissa, in 1806, "to see the Brahmins, with their heads uncovered, in the open plain, and falling down in the midst of the Soodras, before the horrid shape, and mingling so complacently with that 'polluted caste;" but this proved what I had before heard, *that so great a god is this, that the dignity of high caste disappears before him.* This great king recognizes no distinction of rank among his subjects. All men are equal *in his presence.*"

We have long gloried in the conviction, not only that we are a true Church, but that, besides ourselves, there is none other. Too many among us are disposed to look down upon Christians of other names, with much the same feeling with which the pharisee beheld the publican who came to the temple to pray. It seems to be not unfrequently forgotten, that the glory of the Church consists, not in her organization, nor in her rites and ceremonies, but in her *holiness*, which, like the Shechinah of the ancient temple, proclaims the presence of the Divine Lord.

The Church is, unquestionably, spiritually diseased, so far as

* "Soodras may be frequently seen carrying water in a cup, and entreating the first Brahmin they meet, to put his toe into it; after which they drink the water, and bow or prostrate themselves before the Brahmin, who bestows his blessing upon them. Others preserve some of this holy water in their houses. Not only is the body of a Soodra laid prostrate before the Brahmin, to lick the dust of his feet, but his soul is also sacrificed to his honor. If a Soodra dare to listen to the salvation-giving Vedu, he is to be punished for his sacrilege. If a Brahmin happen to be repeating any part of the Vedu aloud, a Soodra, if near, shuts his ears and runs away. If a Soodra enter the cook-room of a Brahmin, the latter throws away all his earthen vessels as defiled; nay, the very touch of a Soodra makes a Brahmin unclean, and compels him to bathe in order to wash away the stain." *Ward's View of the Hindoos*, pp. 79, 107.

she ceases to be, in the language of Bishop Onderdonk, "antagonistic to the world, and to attack its wicked principles and practices." Tried by this test, what is the comparative health and vitality of the Pennsylvania Episcopal Convention, and the Pennsylvania Presbyterian Synod? The latter body, like the first, is composed of clerical and lay deputies; and although named from the State in which most of its members reside, embraces various churches in Maryland. On the 30th of September, 1839, the Synod held its session at Elkton, in the latter State; and of course in the midst of slave-holders. Two colored members took their seats, and assisted in organizing the body. Their presence excited the indignation of some of the rabble in Elkton; and a letter was addressed to a member, recommending the retirement of the two delegates. The letter was shown to them, and they immediately left the town. The Synod was uninformed of what had occurred, until after their departure, whereupon the following resolution was adopted:

"Whereas, this Synod have learned that two of their number, the Rev. Jacob Rhodes, and Mr. Stephen H. Gloucester, colored brethren, have withdrawn, and returned to their homes, in consequence of representations that their presence occasioned some unusual excitement in a portion of the community; therefore,

"*Resolved*, That the Synod regret the existence of a prejudice so unreasonable; and, especially, regret that their brethren, whose right to a seat in this body stands on the same basis as that of any of its members, should have felt themselves called upon to relinquish privileges to which they were justly entitled, and in the enjoyment of which they should have been sacredly protected."

The Rev. Mr. Kip, in his recent work,* describing a visit he made to the Propaganda College in Rome, says:

"The students, about eighty in number, were ranged on the two sides of the chapel, and presented a strange mixture of all nations and colors. I counted among them five Chinese, and two *Africans*. Yet here they all sat side by side, without any distinction, singing together the praises of their common Lord. Surely it must be acknowledged that, in this respect, Rome carries out her own catholic principles, and declares not only in words but by her actions, that "God hath made of one blood all nations of men, to dwell on the face of the earth." She recognizes no distinction of climate or country in the house of God.

* Christmas Holidays in Rome. 1846.

We had just before, as we entered the door of the chapel, witnessed a similar evidence of this catholic spirit. An old man, *black as possible*, in an ecclesiastical dress, was just getting into a carriage. He was assisted by two priests, who, with many bows and demonstrations of respect, were taking leave of him."

We trust Mr. Kip remembered with pain the exclusion of colored candidates for orders from the "Propaganda" of his own Church, and the obloquy heaped on his colored brethren in the ministry, by the Pennsylvania Convention, and that he will joyfully aid in infusing into the Episcopal Church "the catholic principles" so honorably manifested by Papists at Rome and Presbyterians at Elkton.

In the course of these remarks we have expressed ourselves strongly, because we felt deeply; and on reviewing our language we see no cause to modify it. But while we cannot doubt that the acts we have censured were morally wrong, we are too painfully sensible of the frailty of our common nature, to intimate that a Christian profession, to be sincere, must be without offence. Nor are we forgetful of the power of pecuniary interest, parochial dependence, and habitual prejudice, in warping the judgment, beguiling the conscience, and hardening the heart, in relation to slavery and caste. Much, also, of what has been wrong in our ecclesiastical proceedings, has unquestionably arisen, not from reflection, but from the want of it. Nevertheless, the responsibilities of the Church are of awful magnitude, extending to the life that now is, and to that which is to come; and they are shared by all her members, however humble.

The Church militant will find her strength and safety only in unceasing conflict with the world, however dire may be the strife. The blood of martyrs has ever proved the seed of the Church. But when she grows faint-hearted, and distrusting the "armor of righteousness" provided by the Captain of her salvation, seeks for weapons of earthly mould, and calls to her aid the selfish passions and sinful prejudices of society, she is treacherous to her Lord, and forms a truce with his enemies fatal to herself. Henceforth her energies, no longer directed against the strongholds of sin, are wasted in "doubtful disputations," and on unprofitable rites and ceremonies. The world is satisfied, and applauds her discretion and moderation, because, although she may retain the form of Godliness, she has parted with its power.

Had the American Church from the first fought a good fight against slavery and caste, these abominations, which now so much impair her usefulness, and so widely extend the dominion of the great enemy of souls, would have been swept from our land; a new proof would have been given of the divine character of our holy religion, and the Christian priesthood would have acquired new claims to the gratitude and reverence of mankind. Our Church has hitherto erred in no small measure from ignorance and inadvertence. Such a plea can no longer avail her. A voice from abroad — a voice she can neither stifle nor deride — calls her to repentance and reformation. The reproof of Bishop Wilberforce must and will be heard. The sensibilities of Christians in our land are awakening to the momentous questions to which we have referred. The various denominations around us are daily breaking the ties which have hitherto bound them to the cause of the oppressor. Numerous Churchmen among ourselves are complaining of the league which their clergy and representative bodies have formed with human bondage; and the Church of England is marking and lamenting the delinquencies of her daughter. If the Church values the approbation of her Divine Master; if she appreciates the character and objects of her own holy mission; if she desires to avoid agitation in her councils, she must be more than the promulgator and advocate of an abstract theology, however pure and truthful in itself. She must *practically* exhibit the blessed Gospel as at once the antagonist and corrective of every form of wickedness that mars the happiness of man in this world, as well as the next; she must, in short, manifest FAITH WHICH WORKETH BY LOVE, PURIFIETH THE HEART, AND OVERCOMETH THE WORLD.

A LETTER

TO THE RIGHT REV. L. SILLIMAN IVES,

BISHOP OF THE PROTESTANT EPISCOPAL CHURCH IN THE STATE OF NORTH CAROLINA.

RIGHT REVEREND SIR:

History tells us of a certain bishop who was taken prisoner in battle, while fighting against the king of France. The Pope, indignant that a prelate of the church should be held as a captive, demanded his instant liberation. To this mandate the king replied by sending his Holiness the bishop's blood-stained armor, with the words of Scripture, "This have we found: know now, whether it be thy son's coat or no."

And surely the ambassador of HIM who came to preach deliverance to the captive, and liberty to them that are bruised, as effectually disguises and denies holy office, when he chants the praises of slavery, with all its inseparable and unutterable abominations, as when he arrays himself in the garment of the warrior, and participates in the work of human butchery. Of all the bishops of the church, you alone aspire to the championship of human bondage. Your brother of Texas reposes on the laurels he has won in the service of the slave-holders. Others of your reverend and right reverend brethren are content to enjoy the unrequited toils of their bondmen, without provoking the attention of the public to the discrepancy between their religion and their practice. You alone throw down the gauntlet to the whole of Christendom beyond the slave region. It was not enough that you had already endorsed with the whole weight of your Episcopal influence the frantic assertions, that "NO MEN NOR SET OF MEN IN OUR DAY, UNLESS THEY CAN PRODUCE A NEW REVELATION FROM HEAVEN, ARE ENTITLED TO PRONOUNCE SLAVERY WRONG," and that "SLAVERY, AS IT EXISTS AT THE PRESENT DAY, IS AGREEABLE TO THE ORDER OF DIVINE PROVIDENCE;" you must introduce the subject into the council of your church, and entertain your convention with a picture of the blessedness of North Carolina slaves, and with sneers at the wailing of your fellow Christians over their "imaginary" suffering. Should we seek for the cause of your peculiar ultraism in behalf of human chattelism, we should probably find it in the tendency of human nature, under a change of position, to vibrate from one extreme to the other; and which is exemplified in the proverbial cruelty and arrogance of the slave, when elevated to the post of DRIVER. Had you, when preparing for the ministry among your native hills of New York, been told that the day would come when you would claim to hold your fellow-men as bondmen by the grace of God, and would scoff at the sufferings of southern slaves, the answer of Hazael to the prophet would have trembled on your lips.

Your late address to the convention of your diocese contained the following extraordinary passages:

"From this place I went, by the request of my friend, Josiah Collins, Esq., directly to the estates on Lake Scuppernong, which had been without stated ministerial services for the greater part of the year. Here, and in the neighboring parish at Pettigrew's chapel, I passed the remainder part of the season of Lent, holding daily services, delivering lectures, and commencing a new course of oral catechetical instructions to the servants. This course is to embrace the prominent events and truths of the Old and New Testaments, as connected with man's fall and redemption, and is designed to follow the oral catechism I have already published. The services here were of the most gratifying character, fully justifying all that has been said and anticipated of the system of religious training heretofore pursued on these plantations. When I saw master and servants standing side by side in the holy services of Passion week — when I saw all secular labor on these plantations suspended on Good Friday, and the cleanly clad multitude thronging the house of prayer, to pay their homage to a crucified Saviour —

and when I saw on the blessed Easter morn, the master with his goodly number of servants kneeling with reverent hearts and devout thanksgivings to take the bread of life at the same altar — I could not but indulge the hope that ere long my spirit may be refreshed by such scenes in every part of my diocese; while I could not help believing that, had some of our brethren of other lands been present, they would have been induced to change the note of their wailing over imaginary suffering, into the heartfelt exclamation, 'Happy are the people that are in such a case; yea, blessed are the people *who have the Lord for their God.*'

"Often, at such times, have I wished for the presence of my friend, the good Bishop of Oxford, as I have felt assured that, could he but once witness what it is my happiness to witness, though in a too imperfect state, his manly heart would prompt him to ask instant pardon of the American church, for having spoken so harshly upon a subject which he so imperfectly understood; and that he would perceive that his Christian sympathy might find a much more natural vent in efforts to remove the cruel oppressions of the factory system in his own country, and his Christian indignation a much more legitimate object of rebuke in the English churchmen who have helped to rivet that system upon their land."

If ever TRUTH is peculiarly obligatory, it is when a bishop, acting in his high and holy office, addresses a council of the church of God. We are here informed that our brethren of other lands have raised a "note of wailing over IMAGINARY suffering;" and the context forbids us to understand the expres sion in any other sense than a solemn official declaration that southern slavery is unattended with real actual suffering! The assurance is also avowed, that had the Bishop of Oxford witnessed the scenes at Scuppernong, he would have been prompted to ask instant pardon of the American church, for having spoken so harshly upon a subject which he so imperfectly understood. Such an assurance is no less wonderful than unwarranted. The subject on which the bishop is accused of having spoken harshly and without understanding it, is American slavery, and the support afforded it by the American church.

Your address, sir, is the first response made to the Bishop of Oxford's reproof of the American church. So long as it was hoped the reproof would be *suppressed* in this country, a most profound silence was observed respecting it. Scarcely an Episcopalian in the country seemed to know that the history of his church had been written by an eminent English divine. But no sooner is an extract from his history published, bearing upon the horrors of southern slavery, and the delinquencies of our bishops and clergy respecting it, than you think proper to represent him as imperfectly acquainted with the subject, and profess to believe that, if better informed, he would ask instant pardon of the church for what he had written.* It is to be regretted, sir, that you found it inexpedient to specify the alleged suffering which you pronounce *imaginary*, or to point out a single mistake into which your good brother of Oxford has fallen, and which would tend in any degree to verify your charge against him of *imperfectly* understanding his subject. But sir, there are writers against whom *you*, a northern man, will not think it decorous to bring a similar charge. The following witnesses, you will perceive, differ from you as to the blessedness of southern slavery, and dare to call it *wrong*, without waiting for a new revelation from Heaven.

WAHINGTON:—"Your late purchase of an estate in the colony of Cayenne, with a view of emancipating the slaves on it, is a generous and noble proof of your humanity. Would to God a like spirit might diffuse itself generally into the minds of the people of this country." *Letter to Lafayette*, 10*th May*, 1786.

JEFFERSON:—"Can the liberties of a nation be thought secure, when we have removed the only firm basis—a conviction in the minds of the people that these liberties are the gift of God—that they are not to be violated but with his wrath? Indeed I tremble for my country when I reflect that God is just; that his justice cannot sleep for ever; that, considering numbers, nature, and natural means only, a revolution of the wheel of fortune, an exchange of situation is among possible events; that it may become possible by supernatural interference. The Almighty has no attribute which can take side with us in such a contest." *Notes on Virginia.*

* "No doubt, the whole church of England might with equal propriety be called to ask pardon of her American daughter, as it is to be hoped every one of her bishops, priests and deacons, most cordially concurs in the propriety and justice of the Bishop of Oxford's reproof. The Bishop of Norwich, in a letter of 19th October, 1840, to an American gentleman who had furnished him with certain papers, including portions of Freeman's Sermon, and Bishop Ives's endorsement of it, remarks: "I have always considered it as an anomaly, that any State professing Christianity could for a moment tolerate a tyranny so utterly at variance with every feeling of justice and humanity, but I never could have believed that any individuals existed, *calling themselves ministers of the gospel*, whose minds were so darkened by prejudice and self-interest as to avow an approval of slavery and its evil consequences, had I not found them so unequivocally confirmed in the documents above mentioned."

MADISON: — "Many circumstances at the present moment seem to concur in brightening the prospects of the Society, and cherishing the hope that the time will come when the *dreadful calamity* which has so long afflicted our country, and filled so many with despair, will be gradually removed." *Letter to American Colonization Society*, 29*th December*, 1831.

MONROE: — "We have found that this evil (slavery) has preyed upon the very vitals of the community, and has been prejudicial to *all the States* in which it has existed." *Speech in Virginia Convention.*

WILLIAM PINKNEY: — "It is really matter of astonishment to me, that the people of Maryland do not blush at the very name of freedom. Not content with exposing to the world, for near a century, a speaking picture of *abominable oppression*, they are still ingenious to prevent the hand of generosity from robbing it of half its horrors." *Speech on Slavery in Maryland House of Delegates*, 1789.

PATRICK HENRY: — "It is a debt we owe the purity of our religion, to show that *it is at variance* with that law which warrants slavery." *Letter to A. Benezet.*

MANUMISSION SOCIETY OF NORTH CAROLINA: — "In the eastern parts of the State, the slaves considerably outnumber the free population. Their situation there *is wretched beyond description.* Impoverished by the mismanagement which we have already attempted to describe, the master, unable to supply his own grandeur and maintain his slaves, puts the unfortunate wretches upon short allowance, scarcely sufficient for their sustenance, so that a great part go half naked and half starved much of the time. . . . Generally, throughout the State, the African is an abused, a monstrously outraged creature.' *Report*, 1826.

JOHN RANDOLPH: — "Sir, I envy neither the head nor the heart of that man, *from the North*, who rises here to defend slavery on principle." *Speech in Congress*, 1829.

MR. MOORE: — "Slavery as it exists in Virginia, may be regarded as the *heaviest calamity* which has ever fallen to this portion of the human race. One of the evils which arises from it, is the irresistible tendency which it has to undermine and destroy everything like *virtue and morality* in the community." *Speech in Virginia Legislature*, 1832.

THOMAS M. RANDOLPH: — "It is a practice, and an increasing practice, in parts of Virginia, TO REAR SLAVES FOR MARKET. How can an honorable mind, a patriot and a lover of his country, bear to see this Ancient Dominion converted into one vast menagerie, where *men are reared for market like oxen for the shambles?*" *Speech in Virginia Legislature*, 1832.

REV. R. J. BRECKENRIDGE, of Baltimore: — "What is slavery as it exists among us? We reply, it is that condition, enforced by the laws of one half of the States of this confederacy, in which one portion of the community, called masters, is allowed such power over another portion, called slaves, as —

"1. To deprive them of the entire earnings of their own labor, except only so much as is necessary to continue labor itself, by continuing healthy existence — thus committing *clear robbery*.

"2. To reduce them to the necessity of universal concubinage, by denying to them the civil rights of marriage — thus breaking up the dearest relations of life, and encouraging *universal prostitution*.

"3. To deprive them of the means and opportunities of moral and intellectual culture; in many States making it a high penal offence to teach them to read — thus *perpetuating* whatever evil there is that proceeds from ignorance.

"4. To set up between parents and their children an authority higher than the impulse of nature and the *laws of God*, which breaks up the authority of the father over his own offspring, and at pleasure separates the mother at a returnless distance from her child — thus abrogating the clear laws of nature, thus outraging all decency and justice, and degrading and oppressing thousands upon thousands of beings created like themselves in the image of the Most High God. THIS IS SLAVERY, as it is daily exhibited in every slave State." *African Repository*, 1834.

SYNOD OF KENTUCKY: — "Brutal stripes, and all the various kinds of personal indignities are not the only species of cruelty which slavery licenses. The law does not recognize the family relations of a slave, and extends to him no protection in the enjoyment of domestic endearments. The members of a slave family may be forcibly separated, so that they shall never more meet till the final judgment; and cupidity often induces the masters to practise what the law allows. Brothers and sisters, parents and children, husbands and wives are torn asunder, and permitted to see each other no more. These acts are daily occurring in the midst of us. The shrieks and the agony often witnessed on such occasions proclaim with a trumpet tongue, the INIQUITY AND CRUELTY OF OUR SYSTEM." *Address*, 1835.

HENRY CLAY: — "I consider slavery as a curse — a curse to the master — a wrong, a grievous wrong to the slave. In the *abstract*, it is all wrong, and no possible contingency can make it right." *Colonization Speech*, 1836.

T. MARSHALL, of Fauquier county, Virginia: — "Slavery is ruinous to the whites. The master has no capital but what is vested in HUMAN FLESH. The father, instead of being richer for his sons, is at a loss to provide for them. There is no diversity of occupations, no incentive to enterprise. *Labor of every species is disreputable*, because performed mostly by slaves. Our towns are stationary, our villages almost everywhere declining, and the general aspect of the country marks the curse of a wasteful, idle, reckless population, who have no interest in the soil, and care not how much it is impoverished." *Speech in Virginia Legislature*, 1845.

And now, sir, what will you do with this host of witnesses, which might be indefinitely enlarged? Will *you*, a northern man, charge *these* witnesses with an imperfect knowledge of slavery? By no means; but you may say of them, quite as truly as of the Bishop of Oxford, that, had they only been at Scuppernong last Good Friday and Easter Sunday, they would have "been prompted to ask instant pardon" of the American church, for having spoken so harshly of an institution which she enjoys, defends, and blesses.

Warburton, in his Divine Legation (vol. II, p. 92,) informs us that the ancient sages held it lawful and expedient to teach one doctrine to the people at large, and an opposite one to a select number. Hence the *double doctrine* of these philosophers — the one external, intended for the public, and known as the *exoteric;* the other internal, common to friends and disciples, and denominated the *esoteric.* The slave-holders of the present day have their *double doctrine* also; and to distinguish between the *exoteric* and the *esoteric,* it is only necessary to ascertain whether the language used is intended for effect on the north or the south side of Mason and Dixon's line. For the purpose of illustrating this double doctrine, which in the sequel will be found very useful in explaining the spiritual phenomena witnessed at Scuppernong, I will call your attention to the *exoteric* teachings of those distinguished sages, Governors Hayne and Hammond, both within a few years chief magistrates of South Carolina. The former, in his message to the Legislature, in 1833, thus speaks to the South Carolina lawgivers, but only for the purpose of being overheard by the people of the North:

> "It is a remarkable fact, that even during the revolutionary war, when the State was overrun by a barbarous enemy, marching openly under the banner of emancipation, *our domestics could not be seduced from their masters,* but proved a source of STRENGTH, and not of weakness, to the country."

Governor Hayne, no doubt, adopted the maxim of the Grecian philosophers, that truth and utility do not always coincide; for he was, of course, too well informed in the history of his native State not to have been conscious that the "remarkable fact" thus officially announced was an impudent invention of his own. Let us listen to the testimony borne by history to the *fidelity* of South Carolina domestics, and the *strength* they yielded to the country during the revolutionary war:

> "*March* 29, 1799.—The committee appointed to take into consideration the *circumstances of the Southern States,* and the ways and means

for *their* safety and defence, report: That the State of SOUTH CAROLINA (as represented by the delegates of said State, and by Mr. Huger, who has come hither, at the request of the Governor of said State, on purpose to explain the peculiar circumstances thereof) is UNABLE to make any effectual efforts with the militia, by reason of the great proportion of citizens *necessary to remain at home to prevent insurrection among the negroes, and prevent their desertion to the enemy.*" *Secret Journal of Congress*, Vol. II, p. 105.

"The negroes *seduced* and taken from the inhabitants of SOUTH CAROLINA in the course of the war, remained subject to the disposal of the enemy. They were successively shipped to the West Indies; and it is asserted, on the authority of the best informed citizens of South Carolina, that more than TWENTY THOUSAND slaves were lost to the State in consequence of the war." *Col. H. Lee's Memoirs of the Revolutionary War in the Southern Department*, Vol. II, p. 456.

Dr. Ramsay was a native of South Carolina, and in 1809, published his History of the State, in the city of Charleston. Is it to be believed that the governor had never heard of the following facts recorded by the historian? Speaking of the campaign of 1779, Ramsay tells us:

"The forces under the command of General Provost marched through the richest settlements of the State, where are the fewest white inhabitants in proportion to the number of slaves. The hapless Africans, allured with the hopes of freedom, *forsook their owners*, and repaired in great numbers to the royal army. They endeavored to recommend themselves to their new masters by discovering where their owners had concealed their property, and were assisting in carrying it off." Vol. I, p. 312.

Describing the invasion the next year, he says:

"The slaves a *second* time *flocked* to the British army." Vol. I, p. 336.

Again: "Immediately after the surrender (of Charleston,) five hundred negroes were ordered to be put on board the ships for *pioneers* to the royal forces in New York." Vol. I, p. 35.

Finally: "It has been computed by good judges, that between the years 1775 and 1783 the State of South Carolina lost TWENTY-FIVE THOUSAND negroes!!" Vol. I, p. 475.

The census of 1790 found the whole number of slaves, men, women, and children, in South Carolina, to be only 107,000. Now if a few years before, of those physically capable of seeking refuge in the British camp and fleet, no less than twenty-five thousand availed themselves of the presence of the enemy to escape from their masters, we may form some idea of the *truth* of Governor Hayne's eulogium on the *fidelity of South Carolina slaves.*

The object of the Governor's mendacious FACT was to lead the people of the North to believe that their sympathy for the slaves was misplaced, that their suffering was "imaginary;" since, if they retained their allegiance to their masters, in the presence of a British emancipating army, they must certainly be very well contented with their condition.

In 1822, there was in Charleston a rumor of an intended servile insurrection; and this very gentleman, then Colonel Hayne, patrolled the streets one whole night, at the head of five companies of soldiers, to prevent the faithful domestics from cutting their masters' throats. No less than thirty-five "domestics" were soon after tried, convicted, and *hung*, for their *intended* insurrection; and in this judicial butchery, this same Colonel Hayne played his part as one of the judges!

The Governor did not see fit to refer to the fidelity of southern slaves during the *more recent* war of 1812. Let us supply his omission. A memorial presented to Congress by certain Virginia and Maryland slave-holders, and to be found in the documents of the 2d Sess., 20th Cong., sets forth, that "in July and August, 1814, the enemy made several landings on the northern neck of Virginia. All the militia in this peninsula were called into service, and the *property* (slaves) was pretty well protected. On a sudden, an order came, that all the troops should be marched to the defence of Washington; and this neck of eighteen miles wide was emptied of all its efficient force for nearly six weeks. During the absence of the forces there was nothing to restrain our slaves, and they FLOCKED IN HUNDREDS TO THE ENEMY."

Governor Hammond, another South Carolina sage, addressing the North from the floor of Congress, 1st of February, 1836, taught the following *exoteric* doctrine:

> "Sir, our slaves are a peaceful, kind-hearted, and affectionate race, *satisfied with their lot, happy in their comforts, and devoted to their masters.*" It will not be an easy thing to seduce them from their fidelity."

And now, sir, for a little *esoteric* doctrine relative to the "devotion" of slaves to their masters. Soon after the hanging of domestics by dozens in Charleston, a pamphlet appeared there, entitled "Reflections occasioned by the Late Disturbances in Charleston," attributed to Gen. T. Pinkney. It was an essay on the dangers to be apprehended from the slave population, and the means of averting them. Of the "*house servants*" it is said:

"They are the *most dangerous;* their intimate acquaintance with all the circumstances relating to the interior of the dwellings, the confidence reposed in them, and the information they unavoidably obtain from hearing the conversation and observing the habitual transactions of their owners, afford them the most ample means for TREACHEROUS BLOODSHED AND DEVASTATION. The success, therefore, of servile conspiracies mainly depends on this class for taking off by *midnight murder* their unsuspecting owners; and the late trials, by exhibiting so large a portion of this description among the ringleaders of the conspiracy, afford a melancholy proof of their promptitude to become actors in such scenes," p. 14.

Another pamphlet came out the same year at Charleston, said to be from the pen of Edwin C. Holland, Esq., and called "A Rufutation of the Calumnies circulated against the Southern and Western States." It concluded with the following *esoteric* advice:

"Let it never be forgotten, that our negroes are truly the *Jacobins* of the country; that they are the *anarchists and the domestic enemy;* the *common enemy* of civilized society; and the *barbarians* who would, if they could, become the DESTROYERS OF OUR RACE."

"We of the South," says the Maysville (Tennessee) Intelligencer, "are emphatically surrounded by a dangerous class of beings — *degraded, stupid savages* — who, if they could but once entertain the idea that immediate and unconditional death would not be their portion, would reënact the St. Domingo tragedy."

Says the Southern Religious Telegraph:

"Hatred to the whites, with the exception in some cases of attachment to the person and family of the master, is nearly universal among the black population. We have, then, a foe cherished in our own bosoms — a foe willing to draw our LIFE BLOOD whenever the opportunity is offered."

The slave-holders, when thus cautioning each other against

the intense hatred felt for them by the slaves, seem never to ask themselves, "Is there not a cause?"

The double doctrine is not confined to the laity; even the CLERGY occasionally condescend to use it. One of the most astonishing specimens of the clerical *exoteric* to be met with in the writings of southern divines, is furnished by the Rev. J. C. THORNTON, President of the Centenary College, Clinton, Mississippi. This gentleman, in a volume entitled an "Inquiry into the History of Slavery, 1841," but in reality, a philippic against abolitionists, scoffing at the alleged ignorance of the slaves, thus exclaims:

"They are *so* 'ignorant' that they are chiefly all in the South members of three or four denominations, Protestant Episcopalians, Presbyterians, Baptists, Methodists; among all of whom are colored ministers of exalted standing, who would honor any pulpit in America. When those who are not church members are added to the above, it will make *at least* TWO MILLIONS of slaves in regular attendance on divine worship," pp. 108—110.

To these specimens of the reverend gentleman's veracity, we add one of his refinement. Addressing, in his book, by *name*, two anti-slavery writers at the North, he tells them—

"Bring forward your son, out with your daughter, and either shall have an Angola negro before night," p. 140.

As the whole number of slaves, including children, at the last census, was rather *less* than three millions, and at the least TWO millions of these are in regular attendance on divine worship, it must be confessed that the slaves are the greatest church-going people in the world. "Happy are the people that are in such a case." But before indulging in our pious gratulations, let us attend to the *esoteric* teaching on the subject of slave religion. In a sermon preached before an association of planters in Georgia, by the Rev. C. C. Jones, and published at Savannah, 1831, we have the following confessions:

"The description which the Apostle Paul, in his Epistle to the Romans, gives of the heathen world, will apply, with very little abatement, to our negroes. They lie, blaspheme, are slothful, envious, malicious, inventors of evil things, deceivers, covenant breakers, implacable, unmerciful. Numbers of the negroes do not go to church, and cannot tell who Jesus Christ is, nor have they ever heard so much as the ten commandments read and explained. . . . . Generally speaking, they appear to be without hope, and without God in the world—A NATION OF HEATHEN IN OUR VERY MIDST."

The report of the Synod of South Carolina and Georgia, made 5th of December, 1833, and published at Charleston, makes the following revelations:

"Who would credit it, that in these years of revival and benevolent effort, in this Christian republic, there are OVER TWO MILLIONS of human beings in the condition of *heathen*, and in some respects in a worse condition? From long-continued and close observation, we believe that their moral and religious condition is such that they may justly be considered the HEATHEN of this Christian country, and will bear a comparison with heathen in any part of the world. . . . It is universally the fact throughout the slave-holding States, that either custom or law prohibits them the acquisition of letters, and consequently they can have no access to the Scriptures. . . . . In the vast field, extending from an entire State beyond the Potomac to the Sabine river, and from the Atlantic to the Ohio, there are, to the best of our knowledge, not *twelve* men exclusively devoted to the religious instruction of the negroes. As to *ministers of their own color*, they are destitute, infinitely, both in point of numbers and qualifications, to say nothing of the fact that such a ministry is looked upon with distrust, and discountenanced. But do not the negroes have access to the Gospel through the stated ministry of the whites? No. . . . . We venture the assertion, that if we take the whole number of ministers in the slave-holding States, *but a very small portion pay any attention to them*. . . . . The negroes have no regular and efficient ministry; as a matter of course, NO CHURCHES; neither is there sufficient room in the white churches for their accommodation. We know of but *five* churches in the slave-holding States built expressly for their use. . . . We may now inquire if they enjoy the privileges of the Gospel in private, in their own houses, or on their own plantations. Again we return a negative answer. They have NO BIBLES to read at their own fireside, they have no family altars; and when in affliction and sickness, or death, they have no minister to address to them the consolations of the Gospel, nor to bury them with solemn and appropriate services."

Certainly the reverend President of "Centenary College, Clinton, Mississippi," and the Synod of South Carolina and Georgia, differ somewhat as to the religious character of *two millions of slaves*. According to the one, they are regular attendants on divine worship; according to the other, they are "in the condition of HEATHEN." According to the one, among the Episcopalian, Presbyterian, Baptist, and Methodist slaves there are "*colored* ministers of exalted standing, who would honor any pulpit in America." According to the other — "As to ministers of their own color, they are destitute *infinitely*, both in point of number and qualifications."

A writer in the Charleston Courier tells us, "There are upwards of 20,000 colored persons in Charleston and on the Neck, and there are but inadequate accommodations and opportunities for their attendance on the preaching of the Word of God, by admission to *galleries* in *some* of our churches; there being *many* which do not even vochsafe them that privilege." A late writer in the Charleston Mercury, opposing a proposition to form colored congregations, remarks:

> "It has been the policy of this State, not to admit the teaching to the slaves, either of reading or writing; we all know why this is so. No matter from what combination of causes, the result has been produced, in this part of the country, 'for weal or for wo,' our lives and fortunes are indissolubly connected with the preservation of that institition. It needed no great scope of argument to satisfy those who framed our laws, that *the expansion of intellect*, the hundred influences which education generates, would be very inconsistent with habits of *obedience*, which was the corner-stone of the institution.'"

Let us now apply this double doctrine to the case of the slave Christians of Scuppernong, and see whether we cannot find some *esoteric* revelations which might cause the Bishop of Oxford to pause a little before he asks pardon for his reproof of the American church.

It seems that, during Lent, you visited certain plantations "which had been without stated ministerial services for the greater part of the year." In the midst of this destitution of the means of grace, you appeared on the ground, and "commenced," — for it appears you had no time to finish, — "a new course of *oral* catechetical instruction to the servants." How far the *servants* were permitted to listen to your daily lectures and services, and whether they enjoyed the *oral* instruction on other days than the Sabbath, is uncertain, since no mention is made of the suspension of labor on the plantations, except on Good Friday. However this may be, certain results are recorded. You saw masters and servants *standing side by side* in the holy services of Passion week. Probably the church in which you officiated had no *galleries*, and hence when the services required the congregation to stand, you saw the masters and slaves standing on the *same floor*. Had you seen them *sitting together* in the same pews, we could better have understood their position, and should have shared your surprise. On Good Friday, all secular labor was suspended. This, of course, was not the effect of the *oral* instruction to the servants, but an act of civility on the part of the masters to the bishop, who had made the visit by particular request. On this day, you saw the "cleanly clad multitude thronging the house of prayer, *to pay homage to a crucified Saviour*." It was far easier to see a large gang of slaves standing in the church, than to see the motive which brought them there. It is not to be supposed that, during the bishop's visit, the slaves were told to throw down their hoes, and put on clean chothes, merely to spend Good Friday in dancing, or roaming over the plantations. Whatever may have been the piety of the "multitude," they were most unquestionably *ordered* to go to church, and a sound flogging would have been the fate of every truant. On the blessed Easter morn you behold "the master with his *goodly* number of servants kneeling with reverent hearts and devout thanksgivings, to take the bread of life at the *same* altar." As no Protestant Episcopal church has as yet more than *one* altar or communion table, the communicants, as a matter of course, knelt at the same. As the service was performed by you, it was of course performed with rubrical correctness; and, not being interrupted with narratives of personal experiences and feelings, it is not very obvious how you made the discovery that the *goodly number of servants* knelt with reverent hearts and devout thanksgivings.

You flatter yourself, sir, that if these sights had been witnessed by some of "our brethren from other lands" (probably Northern and English abolitionists,) they would have changed their note of wailing over *imaginary* suffering into the jubilant chant, "Happy are the people that are in such a case; yea, blessed are the people who have the Lord for their God!!" Be assured, sir, that unless they very *imperfectly understood* the subject, no such exclamations would be prompted by their hearts, nor escape from their lips. They would not regard as happy the masters who compelled a goodly number of their fellow Christians to toil for them without wages; and the more easily to keep them in subjection, prevented the *expansion of their intellect*, and denied them the common rights of humanity, and particularly that of searching the Scriptures. They would not regard the *multitude* of slaves happy, because excused from labor on Good Friday, while toiling under the lash every other week day in the year; nor, finally, would they pronounce masters and slaves happy, merely because they were seen to receive the communion on Easter Sunday.

Most true it is, that he who has the Lord for his God is blessed, whether he bleeds under the lash of the slave-driver, or expires a martyr at the stake; and equally true is it, that his blessedness affords no justification to his brother for treating him as a beast of burden, or offering his life a sacrifice to religious intolerance. No Christian will deny the power of the Holy Spirit to penetrate the gloomy prison house of southern bondage, and to enlighten, sanctify, and save its miserable inmates. But the blessings of grace, as of providence, are ordinarily bestowed in return for the use of appointed means; and where those means are withheld, or partially applied, or grossly perverted, other evidence may justly be required, that the slave has made the Lord his God, than the simple fact that he is seen to receive the communion in his master's church, and in his company. It is somewhat questionable whether your spirit would have been equally refreshed at the sight of a multitude of Presbyterian, Baptist, or Methodist slaves, receiving the communion from the hands of a minister destitute of Episcopal ordination; or whether you would have been equally assured of *their* blessedness. Yet you well know, sir, that in the choice of their church and creed the slaves are for the most part passive; and that, had the Scuppernong communicants been sent to auction on Easter Monday, they would each thenceforth have worshipped in the place and manner directed by "the highest bidder."

The Southern churches number their slave communicants by

thousands; but profession is not principle; and in all ages and countries, there has ever been a ready conformity to the religion of the ruling despot. Where the slave makes no religious profession, the cause is for the most part to be found in the indifference of the master.

The *esoteric* teaching on this subject is not calculated to inspire very strong confidence in slave piety. In an account of the "Intended Insurrection," published by the authorities of Charleston, 1822, it is stated, that of those executed several had been "class-leaders." "Jack Green was a preacher; Billy Palmer exceedingly pious, and a communicant of the church of his master; Jack Purcell, no less devout." The ensuing year, the Rev. Dr. Dalcho, assistant minister of St. Michael's church, Charleston, published a pamphlet in vindication of slavery, but had the decency to omit his name on the title-page.* Alluding to the late conspirators, he says:

"I write, with feelings of the deepest regret, that some of the conspirators were preachers, class-leaders, and communicants; thus *verifying* the truth of a remark which teachers have too often occasion to make, that THERE IT LITTLE CONFIDENCE TO BE PLACED IN THE RELIGIOUS PROFESSIONS OF NEGROES. I speak generally. Much animal excitement may be, and oftentimes is, produced, where but little real devotion is felt in the heart. I sympathize most sincerely with the very respectable and pious clergyman, whose heart must still bleed at the recollection that his confidential class-leader, but a week or two before his just conviction, had received the communion of the Lord's Supper from his hand. This *wretch* had been brought up in his pastor's family, and was treated with the same Christian attention as was shown to their children."†

Says the venerable and Rev. Dr. Nelson, a native of Tennessee, and formerly President of Marion College, Missouri:

"The concentrated recollection of *thirty years* furnishes me with *three* instances only, where I could say I have reason, from the known walk of that slave, to believe him or her a sincere Christian."

The Rev. C. C. Jones, probably better acquainted with the

* Practical Considerations, founded on the Scriptures, relative to the Slave Population of South Carolina. By a South Carolinian.

† But the wretch was the *slave* of his pastor.

religious character of the slaves than any other southern minister, says, in his sermon already quoted:

> "Of THE PROFESSORS OF RELIGION among them, there are many of questionable piety, who occasion the different churches great trouble in discipline, for they are extremely ignorant, and frequently are guilty of *the grossest vices*."

After such facts and confessions, you cannot, sir, be surprised, should your brethren from other lands be a little sceptical about the "reverent hearts and devout thanksgivings" of the goodly number of the Scuppernong negroes. But, alas! sir, there are indeed far weightier reasons than these facts and confessions, to justify such scepticism.

The *very peculiar character* of that Christianity which is offered to the slaves is well calculated to insure its rejection by them. LOVE is the great motive, argument, and command of the Gospel. God is love. God so loved the world, that he gave his only begotten Son. We love God, because he first loved us. Love one another, so shall all men know that ye are my disciples. One is your Father, which is in heaven; all ye are brethren. When *we* are cruelly and unjustly treated, we know that we suffer in violation of the precepts of our religion, and we are taught to pray for the offender, that his sin may be forgiven. Far different is the religion offered to the slave. He is instructed that the common Father of all has authorized a portion of his children to convert the others into articles of merchandise. The favored children, moreover, are permitted to withhold from their brethren the revelation made by their Heavenly Father, and which he has declared is able to make them wise unto salvation. The slave also learns, by experience, that to him is denied the marriage and the parental relations — blessed boons, expressly conferred by God upon others. While this religion calls on some to be diligent in business, that they may provide for their families, he is informed that this same religion requires from him unceasing and unrepining toil, for the sole benefit of his happier brethren. A future life is indeed revealed to him, and he is promised happiness in *another* world, on certain conditions; among which are, always, *obedience* to his master, and refusal to *escape* from bondage. The slave is taught that those privations and sufferings which he endures, and which outrage his moral sense, are in perfect accordance with the precepts of his religion; and that to pray for the *forgiveness* of his oppressor would be but to insult that Divine Majesty which clothed the oppressor with power, and authorized him to use it in crushing his weaker brother.

Such is the Christianity presented to the slave — a religion which his own consciousness must tell him is partial, severe, and unjust, nullifying in the case of the *black* man the holy and benevolent precepts it gives to his *white* brother, and sanctifying a system of cruelty and oppression, which every faculty of his soul tells him is wrong.

And by whom is this species of Christianity received, beyond the slave-region? Almost the whole of Christendom rejects it as spurious. The wise and good of all countries abhor it. The bishops of the Church of England denounce it. Not a bishop at home, in a free State, dare give it his sanction. And yet it is supposed that the poor *slave*, who of all others has the most reason to reject a religion which sinks him below humanity, will cordially embrace it.

Not only is this religion necessarily repugnant to the natural moral sense of the slaves, but the very persons who preach it must be objects of their distrust and aversion. No minister addresses the slaves on a plantation, but by *permission* of the master; nor is any slave ordinarily admitted to Christian ordinances, but by the same permission, expressed or implied. Hence the minister virtually addresses the slave as the agent of his master, and, instead of letting the slave perceive that he sympathizes in his sufferings, and laments and condemns his oppression, he labors to impress him with the belief that God Almighty sanctions the servitude beneath which he groans, and requires from him a ready submission to it. Is it in human nature that *such* shepherds should be loved by the flock?

No clergyman at the South has probably labored more zealously in behalf of the spiritual interests of the slaves than the Rev. C. C. Jones; but, unhappily, he has labored as the agent of the masters, and the supporter of human bondage; and what has been his success? Listen to his story, as related in the Tenth Report of the Association for the Religious Instruction of the Negroes in Liberty county, Georgia:

> "I was preaching," says he, "to a large congregation, on the Epistle to Philemon; and when I insisted on *fidelity and obedience* as Christian virtues in servants, and upon the authority of Paul, CONDEMNED THE PRACTICE OF RUNNING AWAY, *one-half of my audience deliberately rose up and walked off with themselves;* and those who remained looked anything but satisfied with the preacher or his doctrine. After dismission, there was no small stir among them; some solemnly declared that there was no such Epistle in the Bible; others, that it was not the Gospel; others, that *I preached to please the masters;* others, that they did not care if they never heard me preach again," p. 24.

Had Mr. Jones been untrammelled by the theory of slavery and the interests of the masters, he would have preached a very different sermon, and experienced very different treatment. After reading the Epistle, he would have told his audience that the text left it wholly uncertain whether Onesimus was a slave or a hired servant; that, in either case, the apostle had no power to compel him to return to his master; and that, of course, his return was wholly voluntary; that, so far from being in disgrace, or liable to arrest on his journey, he was sent by the apostle as "a faithful and beloved brother," a messenger to a Christian church (Col. iv, 9); that, if he was in fact a slave, then the apostle demanded his immediate emancipation, by requiring his master to receive him, "not now *as a slave,* but above a slave, a brother beloved." The preacher might then have pressed upon his hearers, from the injunctions of the apostle, the duties of forgiveness and kindness. Such a sermon would have recommended Christianity to the slaves, and exposed the preacher to be lynched by the masters.

In 1792–'93, a number of American citizens were held as slaves in Algiers, and by as valid and sacred a title as that by which any slave is held in North Carolina. Indeed, these American slaves were held by precisely the same title, the fortune of war, as were a great portion of the Roman slaves, whose bondage you and Bishop Freeman insist was approved by Christ and his apostles. These slaves, one hundred and five in number, in a petition to Congress, declared: "We are employed daily at the most laborious work, without respect of persons, and shut up at night in two *slave-prisons*." What would have been the feelings of these slaves towards an English clergyman, in the pay of the Dey, who, with his permission, should have preached to them from the Epistle to Philemon, urging upon them fidelity and obedience to their Algerine masters as Christian duties, and assuring them, on the authority of St. Paul, of the great sin they would commit in attempting to escape from their "slave-prisons?"

Mr. Jones has prepared a catechism for the slaves. In this manual of religious instruction, they are asked, "Is it right for the servant to run away? or is it right to harbor a runaway?" To this question, the slaves are required to respond an emphatic "No."

Is there a slave, is there a white man, who believes that the Rev. C. C. Jones, if, through some misfortune or violence, he should be reduced to bondage in Russia or Turkey, would not, in spite of his catechism, embrace the first favorable opportunity "to run away?" or, if he could not run away himself, that he would be restrained by scruples of conscience from *harboring* a fellow-countryman, who had partially succeeded in making his escape? Yet the wretched slaves are required by their religious teachers to believe that God requires them to remain voluntarily in a state of ignorance and degradation, and even to refuse their aid to their wives, children and friends, who are endeavoring to recover their liberty! Such a doctrine is alone sufficient to give the negroes a disgust to the religion of which they are assured it forms a part. And now let me ask, Who believes or acknowledges this doctrine, beyond the slave-region? Is there a minister of Christ, except among the slave-holders, who would so far expose his sacred character to public abhorrence, as to betray a fugitive slave to the kidnappers? Who thinks it a sin at the North or in Europe to harbor a runaway? Who, at the North, except here and there a needy attorney, policeman, or a merchant ready to barter his character for southern custom, is vile enough to carry into practice the doctrine of Mr. Jones's negro catechism, and bewray him that wandereth, or refuse to hide the outcasts, or to be a covert to them from the face of the spoiler?

Not only is Christianity presented to the slaves by its ministers in an odious and disgusting form, but these very ministers are perceived by the slaves to be the agents of the masters, and to preach to "*please them*," and are themselves almost universally *owners of human beings*, buying and selling men, women, and children. Is it possible that such men can be honored, and trusted, and beloved, by the slaves, as their spiritual teachers, friends, and guides?

But, alas! Christianity is rendered still more repulsive to the slave by the fact that not only do its teachers make merchandise of their brethren in Christ, but that organized churches are not unfrequently

"Christian brokers in the trade of blood,"

appropriating the profits of the traffic to the support of the priest and the temple!

A fugitive slave told his friends at the North that he had ceased receiving the Lord's Supper in the church to which he had been attached, because the CHURCH had sold his brother to pay for their communion plate; and "I could not bear," said he, "to go forward and receive the communion from vessels which were the purchase of my brother's blood."

We have no *proof* of the truth of this anecdote, but we have most abundant evidence of its credibility. Says the Rev. J. Cable, in a printed letter of the 20th March, 1846:

"I have lived eight years in a slave State (Virginia), and received theological education at the Union Theological Seminary near Hampden Sydney College. Those who know anything about slavery, know the worst kind is *jobbing slavery*—that is, hiring out slaves from year to year, while the master is not present to protect them. It is the interest of the one who hires them to get the worth of his money out of them, and the loss is the master's, if they die. What shocked me more than anything else, was the CHURCH engaging in this jobbing of slaves. The college church which I attended, held slaves enough to pay the pastor, Mr. Stanton, one thousand dollars a year; of which the church members, as I understood, did not pay a cent. The slaves, who had been *left to the church* by some pious mother in Israel, had increased so as to be a large and increasing fund. These were hired out on Christmas day of each year—the day on which they celebrate the birth of our Saviour—to the highest bidder. These worked hard the whole year to pay the pastor $1,000, and it was left to the caprice of the employers whether they ever heard one sermon. Since the abolitionists have made so much noise about the connection of the church with slavery, the Rev. Elisha Balenter informed me the church has sold this property, and put the money into other stock. There were *four* churches near the college that supported the pastor, in whole or in part, in the same way, viz.: Cumberland church, John Kirk, pastor; Briney church, Wm. Plummer, pastor (since Dr. P., of Richmond); Buffalo church, Mr. Cochran, pastor; Pisgah church, near the Peaks of Otter, J. Mitchell, pastor."

The Rev. Mr. Paxton, a Virginian, and once a slave-holder, states, in his "Letters on Slavery," that the church in Virginia, of which he was pastor, owned SEVENTY SLAVES, and that his salary was chiefly derived from the hire of their labor.

In 1832, Mrs. Ann Pray, of Georgia, left a legacy of certain slaves to the American Missionary Board of Commissioners—a legacy very properly declined by the Board.

"A prime gang of ten negroes, accustomed to the culture of cotton and provisions, belonging to *the Independent Church*, in Christ Church parish," was advertised for sale in the Charleston Courier of 12th February, 1835.

In the Savannah Republican, 23d March, 1845, C. O'Neal, sheriff, advertised eight slaves for sale for cash, to satisfy a mortgage in favor of "*The Board of Directors of the Theological Seminary of the Synod of South Carolina and Georgia.*"

So it seems the Seminary loans its money on the security of a certain amount of human flesh, and this under the direction of the very Synod whose report "on the religious instruction of the colored population" we have already quoted. Deeply are these pious Christians exercised in their minds about the *heathenism* of their brethren whom they are selling for *cash*, to educate young gentlemen for the ministry!

The "Spirit of Missions" some time since informed its readers, that "the Bishop of Georgia, in his Montpelier Institution, is testing the sufficiency of SLAVE-LABOR to support it." It is to be hoped Bishop Elliott will before long favor the public with the result of his interesting and very Christian experiment.

In the southern church, moreover, the desire for the salvation of the negroes is in entire subserviency to the supposed interests of the masters. The New Orleans Picayune of 16th August, 1841, has the following:

"Chauncey B. Black was brought before Recorder Baldwin, charged with tampering with slaves. It was proved that he was seen conversing with a number of them in the street; that he asked them if they could read and write, and if they would like a Bible. This was the amount of the testimony against him. *In palliation of his conduct*, it was shown that he was a regularly appointed agent of the Bible Society in New Orleans, to distribute the Bible to such as would accept of it. The Society, however, disclaimed *having the most distant intention of giving the Scriptures to slaves;* and it was said Black had exceeded his commission in offering it. But as it appeared to be a misunderstanding on his part, and not intentional interference with the peculiar institution, he was discharged with a *caution not to repeat his offence.*"

Now hear the New Orleans Presbytery, in their Report of 1846:

"There are within the bounds of the presbytery at least 100,000 colored persons, most of whom are slaves. It is a lamentable fact, that by far the greater part are *famishing and perishing for the bread of life.*"

With what ineffable scorn must the slaves regard such lamentations over their famine for the bread of life, from the lips of men who have not the most distant intention of giving the Scriptures to slaves!

The Southern Religious Telegraph had opened its columns to a series of papers in behalf of Christianizing the slaves. Some of the Virginians became alarmed, and forthwith the obsequious editor announces:

"At the suggestion of some of our fellow-citizens, who regard the discussion of the religious instruction of slaves *inexpedient* at this time, we *cheerfully* comply with their wishes, and will discontinue for the present the publication of articles on the subject."

Says the Georgia Conference Missionary Society, in its Report for 1838:

"Our missions among the *whites* have shared in this season of refreshing from the presence of the Lord. The missions to the slaves have not been distinguished by so great a multiplication of church members, chiefly because the mode of operation *is essentially* different. It is deemed *imprudent* to foster among the colored people those great excitements which minister so powerfully to the building up of our societies among the whites."

Here we have an avowal, that, from prudential reasons—that is, from regard to the security of slave property—the slaves have been deprived by these Methodist missionaries of certain auxiliaries supposed to be highly conducive to salvation.

In 1835, the slave-holders of Charleston, having sacked the Post Office, and riotously destroyed some anti-slavery papers found in it, called a public meeting, for the avowed purpose of controlling the freedom of the mail. The Charleston Courier, giving the particulars of the meeting, announced that

"The CLERGY of all denominations attended in a body, lending *their sanction* to the proceedings, and adding by their presence to the impressive character of the scene."

The sacrifice of decency in attending this lawless meeting, was not the only one which the Charleston clergy offered on the altar of slavery. The slave-holders resolved:

"That the thanks of this meeting are due to the reverend gentlemen of the clergy in this city who have so *promptly* and so *effectually* responded to the public sentiment, by suspending their schools, in which the *free colored population* were taught; and that this meeting deem it a patriotic action, worthy of all praise, and proper to be imitated by the teachers of similar schools throughout the State."

It is quite in character, that the Charleston slave-holders should deem it a *patriotic* act in the ministers of the Lord Jesus Christ to drive *black* children from their Sunday schools; but what judgment will be formed of these pusillanimous clergymen by HIM who has commanded his servants not to fear what *man* can do unto them? Most truly says the Bishop of Oxford:

"It is a time for martyrdom, and the American church has scarcely produced a single confessor."

There is still another to be added to the formidable obstacles already enumerated, to the conversion of the slaves. Their very position compels them to live in constant violation of many of the imperative obligations of Christianity.

The slave is a participator of that humanity with which the Saviour clothed himself at his incarnation. As a MAN, therefore, he is placed by God in various relations, imposing corresponding duties; as a son, he is bound to honor his parents; as a brother, to love his kindred, and relieve their distresses; as a husband, to cleave to his wife till parted by death; as a father, to provide for the sustenance and education of his offspring. But the law of the land has nullified that of God, and insulates the slave from all the relations of humanity, and abrogates the obligations resulting from them. Yet the southern priesthood, in the name of the Lord Jesus Christ, give their sanction to this law, reducing to CHATTELS the very beings for whom HE died. Well, indeed, has a foreign author remarked:

> "Whatever may have been the unutterable wickedness of slavery in the West India Islands, there it never was baptized in the Redeemer's hallowed name, and its corruptions were not concealed in the garb of religion. That acme of piratical turpitude was reserved for the professed disciples of Jesus in America."

You flatter yourself, sir, that, could the Bishop of Oxford have witnessed the services at Scuppernong which you have described, his views of American slavery would have undergone such a total change, that he would have asked instant pardon of the American church, for rebuking her subserviency to this terrific institution. Having said nothing of the church that was not literally true, and substantiated by most abundant proof, the bishop could have had no motive or excuse for asking pardon. So far from having his abhorrence of slavery *diminished* by the scenes on which you dwell with so much complacency, he would have found in them new proofs of the degeneracy of the church, and of the corrupting influence of human bondage.

With what indignation would your good brother have witnessed the masters bringing their fellow-men to the house of prayer, kneeling with them at the Lord's table, partaking with them of the emblems of the Saviour's body and blood, the next day driving them to the field as the ox to the furrow, and perhaps the day after tearing them from their wives and children, and selling them to the dealer in human flesh, to be conveyed to distant markets!

Think you, sir, the bishop would have felt very penitent for his condemnation of slavery, had he, on leaving Scuppernong, repaired to Wilmington, still in your *diocese,* and there recognized some of the Easter Sunday communicants among the *manacled passengers* described in the following letter?

"As I went on board the steamboat at Wilmington, I noticed eight colored men, *handcuffed and chained together in pairs,* four women, and eight or ten children — all standing together in the bow of the boat, in charge of a man standing near them. Coming near them, I perceived that they were all greatly agitated, and, on inquiring, I found that they were all slaves who had been born and raised in *North Carolina,* and had just been sold to a speculator, who was now taking them to the *Charleston market.* Upon the shore was a number of colored persons, women and children, waiting the departure of the boat. My attention was particularly arrested by two colored females, who stood together a little distance from the crowd, and upon whose countenances was depicted the keenest sorrow. As the last bell was tolling, I saw the tears gushing from their eyes — *they were the wives of two of the men in chains.* There, too, were mothers and sisters, weeping at the departure of their sons and brothers; and there, too, were fathers, *taking the last look of their wives and children.* My eye now turned to those in the boat, and, although I had tried to control my feelings amidst my sympathy for those on shore, I could conceal them no more, and found myself literally weeping with those that wept. I stood near them, when one of the husbands saw his wife on the shore wave her hand for the last time; his manly efforts to restrain his feelings gave way, and, fixing his watery eyes upon her, he exclaimed, 'This is the most distressing thing of all — my dear wife and children, farewell!' Of the poor women on board, *three of them had husbands whom they left behind.* Sailing down Cape Fear River twenty-five miles we touched at the little village of Smithport, on the south side of the river. It was at this place that one of the slaves lived, and here were his *wife and five children.* While at work on Monday last, his purchaser took him away from his family, carried him *in chains* to Wilmington, where he remained *in jail.* As we approached the wharf, a flood of tears burst from his eyes. The boat stopped but a moment, and, as she left, he espied his wife on the stoop of a house some rods from the shore, and with one hand, which was not in the handcuff, he pulled off his old hat, and, waving it towards her, he exclaimed, 'Farewell!' After a few moments' silence, conflicting passions seemed to tear open his breast, and he exclaimed, 'What have I done, that I should suffer this? Oh! my wife and children — I want to live no longer!'" *Christian Advocate and Journal.*

And is this most accursed traffic in the sheep of *your* flock an "imaginary suffering?"

Not contented with lauding the blessedness of southern slavery, you proceed to taunt Great Britain with her factory system, and to sneer at your brethren of the mother church for riveting such a system on their land. A vast amount of sympathy is constantly expended by the dealers in human flesh on the English poor; and he who, without compunction, sends a mother to market, or ploughs her back with the lash, finds his bowels of compassion yearning over the "cruel oppressions" of a factory child on the other side of the Atlantic!

It was the declaration of the Almighty, in reference to his own peculiar people, "the poor shall never cease out of the land" — a prediction virtually repeated by our Saviour, and as literally fulfilled in regard to every other land as it was in Palestine. No system of government, no form of religion, has ever caused the poor to cease out of the land. Much poverty, no doubt, springs from bad government and wicked wars; but a far larger portion from the vice, improvidence, indolence, and misfortune, incident to humanity. Owing to the corruption of our nature, poverty often invites oppression; which no government, however paternal, can prevent. In our own land, we have armies of paupers, exclusive of nearly three millions of our fellow-countrymen, who are reduced by law to absolute penury. Yet this is the country, above all others, in which extent of territory, cheapness of land, and demand for labor, should secure, if possible, a competency for all. Is it, then, sir, a matter of surprise, that poverty should abound in England, where a population, nearly equal to that of the whole United States, is crowded into a space less than your own diocese? Owing to British industry and enterprise, the wages of labor are *higher in England* than in any other part of Europe; and, owing to the freedom of the press and of the government, the *English* poor are probably the least oppressed of any in the Eastern World. And yet, of all the paupers of Europe, Asia, and Africa, it is only over those of England that the slave-holders raise "the note of wailing."

As you thought proper to taunt the Bishop of Oxford with "the cruel oppressions of the factory system," it might have been expected that you would *specify* the oppressions to which you refer, that it might be seen whether, like the abominations of North Carolina slavery, they were authorized *by law*, and sanctioned by bishops, or proceeded solely from the cupidity and cruelty of individuals.

It is also to be wished, that you had condescended to contrast the English and American factory systems, that we might know wherein we differ. Such a comparison would not probably result as much to our credit as you suppose. The two systems differ — first, in the rate of wages, arising from the difference in the demand and supply of labor in the two countries; and, secondly, in the paternal solicitude of the British Parliament to protect juvenile operatives from the avarice of their employers, and in the utter indifference of our republican legislatures on the subject. You speak of English churchmen helping to rivet the factory system on their land. It is to be regretted, sir, that you deal so largely in generalities, and are so averse to particular statements. How and when have English churchmen riveted the factory system on their land? Has any presbyter of the Established Church lauded it as a divine institution, and received a mitre in return, through the influence of the cotton spinners? Has any bishop, in a charge to his clergy, attempted to vindicate the system against the reproaches of the Americans, by pronouncing the sufferings of the operatives "imaginary?" or has he represented a cotton mill as a little heaven upon earth, because labor was suspended in it on Good Friday, and because some of the hands partook of the sacrament on Easter Sunday?

It is true the English bishops, as members of the House of Lords, have participated in the enactment of laws relating to factories. How far *such* laws authorize the "cruel oppressions" to which you refer, you do not tell us; but something of their character may be learned from the following official notice:

"All the clauses of the Factories Regulation Act being now in full operation, the inspectors of factories deem it expedient, in order to remove any doubts as to the employment of children subject to restricted hours of labor, to issue the following NOTICE:

"1. No child under nine years of age can be employed in any cotton, flax, or wool factory.

"2. No child between nine and thirteen years of age can be employed or even allowed to remain in such factory, without the certificate of a physician or surgeon, countersigned by a magistrate or an inspector of factories, certifying in the form set forth in the 13th section, the strength and appearance of such child.

"3. No child between nine and thirteen years of age can be employed in such factory, without producing weekly a schoolmaster's certificate, that the child has, for two hours at least, for six out of seven days of the week next preceding, attended his school, excepting in cases of sickness, to be certified in such manner as such inspector may appoint; and in case of any holiday, and in case of absence from any other cause allowed by such inspector, or by any justice of the peace in the absence of the inspector.

"4. No child between nine and thirteen years of age can be employed or even allowed to remain in such factory longer than forty-eight hours in any one week, and not more than nine hours in any one day.

"5. No child under thirteen years of age can be employed in any silk mill more than ten hours in one day.

"The above, and all other provisions of the Factories Regulation Act, together with all orders and regulations issued by the inspectors, in their several districts, under the authority of this act, must be strictly observed, in the mills and factories subject to the said act.

LEONARD HORNER,
THOMAS JONES HOWARD,
ROBERT S. SAUNDERS,
Inspectors of Factories.

"WHITEHALL, JUNE 22, 1836."

It was, sir, exceedingly imprudent to provoke a comparison between the oppressions of the slave and the factory systems. The oppressions *of a system* are of course such as the system *authorizes*. What is the power, sir, which the slave system authorizes *you* to exert over *your* slaves? Chief Justice Henderson, of your own diocese, thus summarily answers the question: "The master has an almost absolute control over the *body* and *mind* of his slave. The master's *will* is the slave's will." * This, surely, sir, is pretty ample authority to be confided, even to a Christian bishop. But let us descend to particulars, and pursue the comparison which you have so rashly introduced — let us contrast the powers vested in *you*, by the laws of North Carolina, over your slave, with the powers over his operative vested by act of Parliament in the English manufacturer.

1. *You* may with legal impunity offer your unoffending slave,

* 2 Devereaux's North Carolina Reports, 543.

whether male or female, any insult or outrage, however gross, not extending to life or limb.

The manufacturer is as responsible in law for an outrage committed on his operative, as on any other person.

2. *You* are restricted by law, under a penalty of two hundred dollars, from teaching your slave to read. *Statutes of North Carolina*, 1830.

The manufacturer is allowed by law to give his operatives any instruction they may please to receive; but he can employ no child under thirteen years of age who has not at least two hours schooling a day for six days in the week.

3. *You* may flog your slave at pleasure, with or without cause; and if, instead of standing still under your lash, when ordered to do so, he retreats from you, *you* are authorized, by a solemn judicial decision, made in your diocese, to take up your gun and SHOOT HIM.*

The manufacturer, for shooting his operative under similar circumstances, would be convicted of murder, and undoubtedly hung.

4. *You* are permitted by law (Haywood's Manual, 525), to keep your slave on *one quart of corn per day.*

The manufacturer feeds his operative by contract, or the latter provides his own food.

5. *You* are authorized to prevent your slave from receiving any religious instruction, and you may also compel him to receive just such as you please.

The manufacturer can exercise no legal authority over the conscience of his operative.

6. *You* may forbid your slave from seeing his wife and children, and may send him to market where and when you think proper.

The manufacturer has no similar privileges.

7. *You* may, at your own will and pleasure, torment your slave by scourging, by imprisonment, by clipping his ears, by branding him with a hot iron, by fastening an iron collar about his neck, and by the various modes which malignity may devise.

* Case of the State *vs.* Man, 1 Dev. Rep., p. 263, N. Carolina, 1829.

The manufacturer is responsible to his operative, as well as to public justice, for any personal injury he may inflict on him.

8. *You* are at liberty, if your slave runs away, to pursue him with bloodhounds; and should he be torn by the brutes, you would be guiltless — under the slave code.

The manufacturer, by similar conduct, would subject himself to severe punishment.

9. *You* are authorized by law, if your slave absconds, and you do not know where to find him, to gratify your vengeance against him by offering, in the public papers, a reward for his MURDER.

The manufacturer, for such an offer in regard to his operative, would be regarded and punished as a villain.

10. *You* may compel your slave to toil for you from youth till old age, without other compensation than such food and raiment and shelter as may be requisite to enable him to labor.

The manufacturer can obtain the services of no operative except by contract; and the wages, whether more or less, are such as the latter consents to accept.

11. *You* are the legal proprietor of every shred of property acquired by your slave, by his own industry, by gift, by devise, or by accident. If he picks up a sixpence in the street, it is YOURS.

The manufacturer has no claim on his operative, except for the labor he has agreed to render for a certain compensation.

12. The children of *your* female slave are your property, and you may work, flog, or sell them, at will.

The manufacturer has no authority over the children of his operative, except by contract with the parent, and in accordance with the requirements of an act of Parliament.

13. *You* may compel your slave to toil as many hours in the four and twenty, as his physical strength may enable him.*

The manufacturer is restrained by act of Parliament, from exacting more than *ten* hours labor, for a day's work.

* The law of South Carolina is more considerate: it allows the master to compel his slave to work *only* FIFTEEN hours a day in the summer, and FOURTEEN in winter. 2 *Brevard's Digest*, 243.

Verily, sir, the North Carolina Bishop's little finger is thicker than the Englishman's loins.* But of course you only vindicate slavery in the abstract, not its *abuses*. Please to recollect, sir, that you have given your Episcopal sanction to "SLAVERY AS IT EXISTS AT THE PRESENT DAY." This, in its most limited sense, means slavery as at present *established by law*. And now, sir, will you please to tell us what *are* the *abuses* of a legal system which takes away an innocent man's liberty, renders him a piece of animated merchandise, deprives him of all volition, places him entirely at your will, denies him all the fruits of his labor, divests him of the character of a son, a husband, and a father, and utterly debars him from the pursuit of his own happiness? If in all this there is none other than "imaginary suffering," do let us know what you consider the "cruel oppressions of the factory system."

Most dangerous, odious, and corrupting would be your power over your slave, even were it intrusted to none other but a RIGHT REVEREND FATHER IN GOD; but, alas! the power you

* Whole sheets, nay, a volume might be filled with illustrations of the bishop's legal prerogatives. But it is unnecessary to cumber the page with proofs of what he will not deny. He will not be rash enough to challenge the writer for proofs of the alleged atrocities of the slave laws. To prevent, however, a captious objection, it may be well to state, that, *strictly*, a North Carolina slave-holder has not a legal right to offer a reward for the murder of his slave, unless he is previously outlawed, which he may be by two justices, if he runs away, conceals himself, and, to maintain life, kills a hog, or any animal of the cattle kind. *Haywood's Manual*, p. 521.

In point of *fact*, it is believed these rewards are generally offered without an outlawry; nor is there the least reason to believe that the omission of this formality, in killing a slave, would, in North Carolina, attract any legal animadversion. We give a few advertisements, from a great mass selected from southern papers, for the purpose of showing the putrid state of public opinion in the slave States. These advertisements are revelations of unconscious villany; and their voluntary publication in the journals of the day indicates that the atrocities they disclose are regarded by the community as in accordance with common usage and conventional propriety.

J. P. Ashford, in the Natchez Courier of 21st August, 1838.—"Run away, a negro girl, called Mary; has a small scar over her eye; a good many teeth missing. The letter A is branded on her *cheek* and *forehead*."

M. Ricks, in the Raleigh Standard (N. C.), 18th July, 1838.—"Ran away, a negro woman, and two children. A few days before she went off, I *burnt* her with a hot iron, on the left side of her face. *I tried to make the letter M.*"

A. Ross, in "Charleston (S. C.) Courier," of 1825.—"Ran away, a negro girl, sixteen or seventeen years of age. Lately branded on the left cheek thus—R, and a piece taken out of her ear on the same side. The same letter *on the inside of her legs*."

T. Engry, in the New Orleans Bee, of 27th October, 1837.—"Ran away, negress Caroline; had on a collar with *one prong turned down*."

possess is, in your diocese, a vendible commodity; and any vile, brutal infidel, may, for a little money, or by virtue of a gift or devise, acquire the same tremendous legal prerogatives over his slave, as are enjoyed by yourself.

If slavery be indeed an institution so evidently enjoying the divine sanction, that it is presumption to pronounce it *wrong*, it must be a good institution, and Christian benevolence must require us to labor for its extension. This duty is indeed zealously discharged at present by our southern brethren, but under the *exoteric* plea of "extending the area of human freedom." But why mask with a lie a work of love and mercy, which God approves?

There are considerations connected with the efforts of the southern clergy to sustain slavery, which they would do well to ponder: If the condition of the slave be, as most of them confess it is, generally unfavorable to religious faith and personal holiness, then there is danger that, at the great day of account, the blood of souls will be found on the skirts of those who have striven to justify and to perpetuate that condition.

J. Henderson, in the Grand Gulf (Miss.) Advertiser, of 20th of August, 1838.—"Ran away, a black woman, Betsey; *had an iron bar* on her right leg."

J. Macoin, in the New Orleans Bee, 11th August, 1838.—"Ran away, the negress Fanny; *had on an iron band about her neck.*"

T. J. De Tampert, in the Mobile Chronicle, June 15, 1838.—"Ran away, a negro boy, about twelve years old; had *round his neck a chain dog collar*, with De Tampert engraven on it.

Peter Campbell, in the Charleston Courier, February 26, 1836, after describing two runaways, adds, "Two hundred dollars will be given for Billy, and one hundred dollars for Pompey, if lodged in jail; or fifty dollars for BILLY'S HEAD."

W. D. Cobb, in the Newbern (N. C.) Spectator, 2d December, 1836.—"I will give the reward of one hundred dollars for the above negroes, to be delivered to me, or confined in the jail of Lenoir or Jones county, *or for killing them so that I can see them.*"

Durant H. Rhodes, in the Wilmington (N. C.) Advertiser, 13th July, 1838. "Ran away, my negro man, Richard. A reward of twenty-five dollars will be given for his apprehension, dead or alive. Satisfactory proof will only be required of his being KILLED."

Enoch Foy, in the Newbern (N. C.) Spectator, 5th January, 1838.—"Ran away, a negro man, Sampson. Should he resist in being taken, so that violence is necessary to arrest him, I will not hold any person *liable for damages should the slave be killed.*"

J. McDonald, in the Appalachicola Gazette, 9th May, 1841, advertises three runaway slaves, and offers one hundred and fifty dollars "to any one who will KILL THE THREE, or fifty for either one,"

Every man, without exception, when he makes the case *his own*, and examines it solely by the light of nature, pronounces slavery a sin and a curse. Now, it is very possible that many who may be convinced, by the labors of yourself and others, that slavery is sanctioned by the Gospel, may also arrive at the conclusion that a religion, thus outraging the moral sense implanted in the human heart by the Creator, cannot proceed from Him.*

A portentous infidel philanthropy is rife in the land, false and delusive in its professions, and tending in its consequences to anarchy and misery. Fonnded not on the love of God, and obedience to his commands, but on wild abstract political theories, it pretends to seek the happiness of mankind by means which can have no influence in purifying the heart, and checking the progress of vice. Those who watch the signs of the times, not from the retirement of their studies, but amid the busy haunts of men, KNOW that the conduct of *many* of the clergy has given to this spurious philanthropy a mighty and most disastrous impulse.† They are constantly seen tithing mint, and anise, and cummin, and all manner of herbs, while mercy and justice, so far as regards the colored population, are apparently utterly disregarded by them. The public has witnessed a reverend assembly of divines discussing day after day the sinfulness of marrying the sister of a deceased wife, and at

* Said Mr. Fries, on the floor of Congress, in reference to a southern member who had attempted a biblical vindication of slavery: "I wish it to be distinctly understood by my constituents and the country, IF it (American slavery) is proved to be a divine institution, sanctioned by the word of God, I AM AN INFIDEL; but gentlemen must pardon me, if I do not adopt their construction of the Bible on this point."

† This truth is admitted and deplored in a late publication by the Rev. Mr. Patton, of Hartford, Conn., entitled, "Pro-Slavery Interpretations of the Bible productive of Infidelity." Says the reverend author, "Infidels profess to go for a reformation in morals, and they boldly contend that Christianity is the chief obstacle in the way of success. They declare that the church and the Bible are corrupt on the score of morals, and that so far from an argument being derived from that quarter in favor of Christianity, the very reverse is true;" and he quotes the following avowal made by an infidel at a recent convention of free-thinkers in New York: "I have done with the old arguments against Christianity, and have adopted a more efficient plan. Now, I work altogether through the moral reformations of the day, and through them attack religion, and find I can accomplish more than by any other means."

last deposing from the ministry a brother who had committed the offence. Yet had this same brother bought another man's wife, used her as his beast of burden, tore from her her children as they became fit for market, and finally disposed of her to some trafficker in human flesh, no ecclesiastical censure would have fallen upon him, and he would have been freely welcomed to the pulpits of the very men who deposed him. We have had pastoral admonitions *against* dancing, and sermons in abundance *in favor* of human bondage; nay, right reverend fathers in God proclaim, that "no man nor set of men in our day, unless they can produce a new revelation from Heaven, are entitled to pronounce slavery *wrong*," and that "slavery as it exists at the present day is agreeable to the order of Divine Providence." We have Bible Societies for supplying the destitute, and our churches and halls resound with eulogiums on the sacred volume, but scarcely a solitary minister at the South is known to suggest, that possibly the laws which virtually forbid one-half of the population to read the Bible, may not be acceptable to its Divine Author, while the Bible society of the largest city in the South disclaims all intention of giving Bibles to *slaves*. Great discussions as well as heats are excited by the question whether the word *baptize* or *immerse* shall be inserted in Bibles intended for heathen in Asia, but the most profound apathy is evinced on the question whether any Bible at all shall be given to the "nation of heathen in our very midst." Missionaries are sent to the ends of the earth, but to three millions of our own countrymen groaning in bondage, and sunk in ignorance, is given only a little "oral instruction," and of that little, no small portion is confined to the duty of obedience, and the sin of running away.

Much is said of the importance of a learned ministry, and contributions are solicited from the pious, to found and maintain theological seminaries. Yet no sooner does a candidate for holy orders apply for the instruction thus provided, than reverend and right reverend trustees proceed to inspect the *tincture of his skin*, and unless it rises to the othodox standard, the door of the seminary is shut in his face. We have in certain quarters, line upon line, and precept upon precept, on the necessity, the importance, the dignity of apostolic succession. But when this "heavenly gift of ministerial commission," is borne by an ambassador of Christ not colored like themselves, bishops and presbyters are seen treating the "heavenly gift" with contumely, rarely if ever admitting the possessor into their pulpits, and scornfully and lawlessly refusing him a seat in the council of the church.

We have among us, a poor, ignorant, persecuted, but unoffending people. They are the least of Christ's brethren, and as such, are specially commissioned by HIM to receive in his behalf the tokens of our love and gratitude. Are we taught by our pastors thus to regard them? Does the noisy demagogue, prating about equal rights and universal suffrage, find no apology for giving the lie to his professions, and trampling upon his colored fellow citizens, in the conduct of the Church herself? Will those who drive from the schools of the prophets, youths anxious to qualify themselves for the service of our common Lord, venture to rebuke the inhumanity of the proprietors of our stage-coaches, our packets, and our railroads, for excluding from their conveyances, these unhappy people, however decent their deportment, and however urgent their business? The Jews despised the Samaritans, and were too proud to receive at their hands even a cup of water. But the Saviour, disregarding an unholy although popular prejudice, ate and drank and lodged with them; declared to them his divine mission, and in his inimitable parable, selected one of them as an illustration of the great law of love, to the condemnation of the proud and heartless but orthodox Priest and Levite.

Surely it is not surprising that the efforts of so large a portion of the Christian ministry to sanctify SLAVERY and CASTE, should give great occasion to the enemies of the Lord to blaspheme, and to His *friends* for grief and perplexity. No small number of those friends, failing to make due allowance for the frailty of our fallen nature, and forgetting the trials arising from the dependence of the clergy on popular support, have rashly and weakly imagined, that the influence of the church is *neces-*

sarily adverse to an enlarged and practical application of the benevolent precepts of the Gospel. Hence they have unhappily indulged the vain expectation that they could cherish more freely the benign impulses of Christianity when released from the restraints of ecclesiastical organizations. Such men, by gradually neglecting the appointed means of grace, have made shipwreck of their faith, and listening to the voice of the charmer, and deluding themselves with the belief that they were doing God service, have united with demagogues, scoffers, and infidels in unholy and chimerical schemes of expansive benevolence.

It may well be questioned, how far those who by the most solemn vows have dedicated themselves to the service of the sanctuary, can lawfully *confine* their time and labor to the removal of any one moral or political evil. They are to declare the *whole* counsel of God, and to watch over and feed the flocks entrusted to their charge. But the ministers of Christ are faithless to their high and holy mission, when in the name of their Master, they give their assent to injustice and cruelty and oppression; and *by their own example*, teach their people to despise the poor and helpless. The great Head of the Church has warned us against that fear of man which bringeth a snare, and demands that his ambassadors shall deliver his message of mercy and love, regardless alike of the displeasure of such as are in high places, and of the scoffs and clamor of the Godless multitude. The tree is known by its fruits, and that is not the religion of the Gospel which fails to inculcate glory to God, *and* peace and good will to men.

DECEMBER, 1846.

ADDRESS

TO THE INHABITANTS OF NEW MEXICO AND CALIFORNIA, ON THE OMISSION BY CONGRESS TO PROVIDE THEM WITH TERRITORIAL GOVERNMENTS, AND ON THE SOCIAL AND POLITICAL EVILS OF SLAVERY.

FRIENDS AND FELOW COUNTRYMEN:

A NUMBER of citizens interested in your welfare, and anxious to promote your prosperity, have deputed us to address you in the present crisis of your affairs. It may be in our power to communicate to you facts with which you are not familiar, and to offer you considerations deserving your reflection. We therefore solicit your patient and dispassionate attention.

You complain that since your annexation to the United States, you have been denied the protection and advantages of civil government. Your complaint is well-founded, and the solemn promises made to you in the name of the Federal Government have been most flagrantly violated. Pains have been and will be taken to deceive you as to the persons who have, in denying you a government, been regardless alike of your rights and your interests. Permit us first to remind you of the solemn and official pledges made to you, and then to show you by whom, and from what motives, those pledges have been broken.

On the 7th July, 1846, Commodore Sloat landed at Monterey,

and taking possession of California by right of conquest, declared in his proclamation addressed to the inhabitants:

"Henceforth California will be a portion of the United States, and its peaceable inhabitants will enjoy the same rights and privileges as the citizens of any other portion of that territory, with all the rights and privileges they now enjoy, *together with the privilege of choosing their own magistrates and other officers*, for the administration of justice among themselves."

On the 17th August of the same year, R. F. Stockton, "Governor of the territory of California," by proclamation thus confirmed the promise given by Commodore Sloat:

"The territory of California now belongs to the United States, and will be governed as soon as circumstances may permit *by officers and laws similar to those by which the other territories of the United States are regulated and protected.*"

General Kearney succeeded Stockton as Governor, and on the 1st of March, 1847, addressed a proclamation to the inhabitants, in which, avowedly under instructions from the President, he declared:

"It is the wish and intention of the United States to procure for California, as speedily as possible, *a free government like that of their own territories*, and they will very soon invite the inhabitants to exercise the rights of free citizens, *with the choice of their own representatives*, who may enact such laws as they may deem best adapted to their own interests and well-being."

The people of New Mexico were in like manner assured by Gen. Kearney on the 18th August, 1846, in a proclamation issued by him at Sante Fe:

"It is the wish and intention of the United States to provide for New Mexico a *free government* with the least possible delay, similar to those in the United States, and the people of New Mexico will then be called to exercise the *rights of freemen* in electing their own representatives to the territorial government."

Such were the full and explicit pledges given to the people of both provinces. They were to have territorial legislatures, and elect their own representatives. But perhaps these pledges were unauthorized by the Cabinet at Washington. Unhappily for the faith and honor of the Federal Government, such a supposition is refuted by the instructions given to Gen. Kearney, dated at Washington, 3d June, 1846:

> "Should you conquer and take possession of New Mexico and California, you may assure the people of those provinces that it is the wish and design of the United States to provide for them a *free government* with the least possible delay, similar to that which exists in our Territories. They will then be called *to exercise the rights of freemen in elect ing their own representatives to the territorial legislature.*"

How have these solemn and repeated pledges been redeemed?

In December, 1847, the President recommended Congress to provide for the adjoining territory of Oregon a territorial government, adding that the people "should have the *right of suffrage*, be represented in a territorial legislature, and by a delegate in Congress." This then by his own pledges was the model of the government to be provided for you; yet no such recommendation was ever made by him in regard to *you*. Slave-holders intended to move into your territory with their slaves, and slave-breeders were anxious to open for their stock new markets on your soil. But it was known that you were averse to human bondage, and if intrusted with the promised powers of self-government, those powers would be exercised in behalf of human rights. Hence it was determined, in utter contempt of all the pledges made to you, to keep you in a state of vassalage, until slavery had been irrevocably fastened upon you. Three territories, Oregon, New Mexico, and California, were to be organized. In the first of these, the people had already formed a provisional government, and had had the wisdom and virtue to prohibit slavery. Of this territory, the slave-holders had no hope of gaining possession; their designs were centered on the other two. To facilitate those designs, the Senate, consisting one-half of slave-holders, by the aid and treachery of a few northern members passed a bill (July 22, 1848) for the organization of the three territories. By this bill, such a government was given to Oregon as had been promised to *you*. The people were invested with the right of suffrage, and a territorial legislature was established, consisting of representatives chosen by the inhabitants. To New Mexico and California were assigned despotic governments, exercised by officers named by the President, while the people of the two territories were as totally excluded from all participation in the choice of rulers and the enactment of laws, as the negro slaves of South Carolina. Not a ballot-box was to be seen throughout the whole extent of the new territories. Thus did the President and his partisans redeem the pledges made to you through Sloat, Stockton, and Kearney. Your northern friends in the House of Representatives refused to sanction this base perfidy, and rejected the bill. Do you complain that you were thus deprived of a government to be administered by the President's delegates, a government in which you had no part or lot, a government which falsified the pledges given you, which insulted and degraded you by treating you as a conquered and servile race, while all the privileges of American citizens promised to you were given in full measure to your neighbors? No, you feel and acknowledge the protecting care of your friends, and will see in their rejection of this base attempt to cheat and humble you, an earnest of their future devotion to your best interests. But justice to Oregon required that she should not be left without a government merely because the slave-holders wished to wrong you. The House of Representatives therefore passed a separate bill, establishing a territorial government for that territory, and in compliance with the wish of the inhabitants inserted in it a clause securing them forever from the curse of slavery. This bill became a law at the end of the session, but the President, on affixing his signature to it, made a declaration in writing that he would have vetoed a similar bill for *you!* Regardless of this insulting announcement, the House of Representatives early the next session prepared two separate bills, giving a territorial government to New Mexico and California, in conformity with the previous pledges, and similar in its provisions to that given to Oregon, and protecting the two territories from slavery. For want of time, only the bill for California was passed. It was sent to the Senate, and that body by a formal vote refused even to take it into consideration! On the

13th of December, the petition from the people of New Mexico, praying for a territorial government, and to be protected from slavery, was presented to the Senate. Mr. Calhoun, the leader of the slave-holders, instantly denounced it as "disrespectful and MOST INSOLENT," and the petitioners were spoken of as "a conquered people."

At the close of the session the usual appropriation bill providing for the expenses of the Federal Government was passed by the House of Representatives. The slave-holders now thought they had an opportunity of coercing your friends into a sacrifice of your interests. A clause was added to the bill extending the Constitution and laws of the United States over the two territories, and vesting in the President unlimited powers of government, and the appointment of officers at *his* discretion. It mattered not that all this was in contemptuous violation of the pledges given you. A purpose was to be served. By the acknowledged laws of nations, a conquered people retain their own laws till altered by the new sovereign. Your laws prohibiting slavery had not been repealed by the conquest. It was contended that the extension of the Constitution and laws *of the United States* over the two territories would virtually repeal the existing laws, and thus open the door for the establishment of negro slavery among you. The loss of the appropriation bill would throw the whole fiscal affairs of the government into confusion. The debts due to individuals would be suspended. Salaries would remain unpaid, &c., &c. It was hoped your friends would shrink from the responsibility of causing such wide-spread disorder by rejecting the bill on account of the obnoxious clause outraging your rights. Yet your interests required that some government should be established for you, and almost any temporary government was better than none. The House had in vain attempted to give you a proper one, and to preserve you from anarchy, they accepted the miserable substitute provided by the slave-holders, but defeated the object for which that substitute had been contrived, by adding a clause recognizing and continuing in force your *existing laws.* On this the Senate abandoned their plan, passed the appropriation bill securing their own pay, and adjourned, leaving you a prey to anarchy.

Soon after the adjournment, Mr. Foote, one of the senators devoted to the extension of slavery, published an article declaring that he was "*authorized to say*" that if the amendment recognizing your existing laws had been agreed to, "it would inevitably have defeated the civil and diplomatic appropriation bill, *as President Polk had already in part prepared his veto to the bill!*"

The slave power has resolved that you shall have no government but such as shall establish the dominion of the WHIP. From a dominion so loathsome and blighting, your northern friends have hitherto rescued you; and to explain their motives, and to invite your earnest coöperation, we now proceed to lay before you a statement of some of the moral and political evils experienced in the United States from the same accursed institution with which *you* are threatened. Never have the comparative influences of free and slave labor on public prosperity and happiness been more fairly tested, or more certainly decided than in this country. Of the thirty States composing our Union, fifteen maintain and enforce, and fifteen reject and abhor the principle of property in men, women and children. By pondering the facts we are about to present, you will be enabled to judge whether your northern friends in the course they have pursued have consulted or sacrificed your true interests.

Slavery is an institution exclusively for the rich. We might as well talk of *poor* men owning herds of cattle and studs of horses, as gangs of negroes. When an infant will bring a hundred, a woman four or five hundred, and a man from eight hundred to a thousand dollars, slaves are not commodities to be found in the cabins of the poor. There is also a peculiarity in slave labor that necessarily confines it to the wealthy. The women and children, being *property*, must be owned together with the male laborers. Hence it is almost impossible to find a master who is the possessor of only a single slave. Our last census shows that the two sexes among the slaves are about equal in number, and that there are *two* children under ten years of age for every male above that age. Hence if a planter owns three men, we may take it for granted that his slave family consists of at least *twelve* persons, viz., three men, three women, and six children. It has been ascertained by various statistics that the whole number of slave-holders in the United States is probably less than 248,000, not *one-third* of the adult white male population of the United States. Yet this small body of men engross the greater portion of the land and wealth of the slave region, forming in fact a powerful feudal aristocracy, possessing nearly three millions of serfs, and governing and oppressing at pleasure the rest of the population. They are always banded together for the preservation and extension of their own power, and always, for obvious reasons, endeavoring to identify their private interests with the public welfare. In what manner that welfare is promoted by their guardianship, we will now show you.

1. INCREASE OF POPULATION.

The ratio of increase of population, especially in this country, is one of the surest tests of public prosperity. Let us then here examine the impartial testimony of the late census. From this we learn that the increase of population in the free States from 1830 to 1840, was at the rate of thirty-eight per cent., while the increase of the *free* population in the slave States was only twenty-three per cent. Why this difference of fifteen in the two ratios? No other cause can be assigned than slavery, which drives from their borders many of the virtuous and enterprising, and at the same time deters emigrants from other States and from foreign countries from settling among them.

The influence of slavery on population is strikingly illustrated by a comparison between Kentucky and Ohio. These two States are of nearly equal areas, Kentucky, however, having about 3000 square miles more than the other.* They are separated only by a river, and are both remarkable for the fertility of their soil; but one has, from the beginning, been cursed with

* American Almanac for 1843, p. 206.

slavery, and the other blessed with freedom. Now mark their respective careers.

In 1792, Kentucky was erected into a State, and Ohio in 1802.

	Free population of Kentucky.	Free population of Ohio.
1790,	61,227,	A wilderness.
1800,	180,612,	45,365
1810,	325,950,	230,760
1820,	437,585,	581,434
1830,	522,704,	937,903
1840,	597,570,	1,519,467

The representation of the two States in Congress, has been as follows:

	Kentucky.	Ohio.
1802,	6,	1
1812,	9,	6
1822,	12,	14
1832,	13,	19
1842,	10,	21

The value of land, other things being equal, is in proportion to the density of the population. Now the population of Ohio is 38.8 to a square mile, while the free population of Kentucky is but 14.2 to a square mile — and probably the price of land in the two States is much in the same proportion. We are told, much of the wealth is invested in negroes — yet it obviously is a wealth that impoverishes; and no stronger evidence of the truth of this assertion is needed, than the comparative price of land in the free and slave States. The two principal cities of Kentucky and Ohio are Louisville and Cincinnati; the former with a population of 21,210, the latter with a population of 46,338. Why this difference? The question is answered by the *Louisville Journal.* The editor, speaking of the two rivial cities, remarks:

"The most potent cause of the more rapid advancement of Cincinnati than Louisville is the ABSENCE OF SLAVERY. The same influences which made Ohio the young giant of the West, and is advancing Indiana to a grade higher than Kentucky, have operated in the *Queen* City. They have no *dead weight to carry*, and consequently have the advantage in the race."

In 1840, Mr. C. M. Clay, a member of the Kentucky Legislature, published a pamphlet against the repeal of the law prohibiting the importation of slaves from the other States. We extract the following:

"The world is teaming with improved machinery, the combined development of science and art. *To us it is all lost; we are comparatively living in centuries that are gone; we cannot make it, we cannot use it when made.* Ohio is many years younger, and possessed of fewer advantages than our State. Cincinnati has manufactories to sustain her; last year she put up one thousand houses. Louisville, with superior natural advantages, as all the world knows, wrote 'to rent,' upon many of her houses. OHIO IS A FREE STATE, KENTUCKY A SLAVE STATE."

Mr. Thomas F. Marshall, of Kentucky, in a pamphlet published the same year, and on the same subject, draws the following comparison between Virginia and New York:

"In 1790, Virginia, with 70,000 square miles of territory, contained a population of 749,308. New York, upon a surface of 45,658 square miles, contained a population of 344,120. This statement exhibits in favor of Virginia a difference of 24,342 square miles of territory, and 405,188 in population, which is the *double* of New York, and 68,600 more. In 1830, after a race of forty years, Virginia is found to contain 1,211,405 souls, and New York 1,918,608, which exhibits a difference in favor of New York of 707,203. The increase on the part of Virginia will be perceived to be 462,097, starting from a basis more than twice as large as that of New York. The increase of New York, upon a basis of 344,120, has been 1,574,488 human beings. Virginia has increased in a ratio of 61 per cent., and New York in that of 566 per cent.

"The total amount of property in Virginia under the assessment of 1838, was $211,930,508. The aggregate value of real and personal property in New York, in 1839, was $654,000,000, exhibiting an excess in New York over Virginia of capital of $442,069,492.

"Statesmen may differ about policy, or the means to be employed in the promotion of the public good, but surely they ought to be agreed as to what prosperity means. I think there can be no dispute that New York is a greater, richer, a more prosperous and powerful State than Virginia. What has occasioned the difference? . . . . . There is but one explanation of the facts I have shown. The clog that has stayed the march of her people, the incubus that has weighed down her enterprise, strangled her commerce, kept sealed her exhaustless fountains of mineral wealth, and paralyzed her arts, manufactures and improvement, is NEGRO SLAVERY."

These statements were made before the results of the last census were known. By the census of 1840, it appears that in the ten preceding years,

The population of Virginia has increased 28,392
In the same time the population of N. Y. increased 710,413
The rate of increase in Virginia was .... 2.3 per cent.
" " New York, ... 33.7 "
Virginia has 12 5 free inhabitants to a square mile.
New York 52.7 " " " "

In 1790, Massachusetts, with Maine, had but 378,717 inhabitants.
" Maryland, ... 319,728 "
In 1840, Massachusetts alone, ... 737,699 "
" Maryland, ... 469,232 "

Now let it be recollected that Maryland is nearly *double* the size of Massachusetts. In the last there are 98.3 free inhabitants to the square mile; in the former only 27.2.

If we turn to the new States, we find that slavery and freedom have the same influence on population as in the old. Take, for instance, Michigan and Arkansas. They came into the Union about the same time.

In 1830, the population of Arkansas was 30,388
In 1840, " " 97,574
In 1830, " Michigan, ... 31,639
In 1840, " " 212,267

The ratio of increase of white inhabitants, for the last ten years, has been in Arkansas as 200 per cent.; in Michigan, 574 per cent. In both instances the increase has been chiefly owing to emigration; but the ratio shows the influence of slavery in retarding emigration. Compare also Alabama and Illinois.

In 1830, the free population of Alabama, was 191,975
" " " Illinois, ... 157,455

Excess in favor of Alabama, ... 34,520

In 1840, free population of Illinois, ... 476,183
" " " Alabama, ... 337,224

Excess in favor of Illinois, ... 138,959

We surely need not detain you with further details on this head, to convince you what an enormous sacrifice of happiness and prosperity is now offered on the altar of slavery. But of the character and extent of this sacrifice you have as yet had only a partial glimpse. Let us proceed to examine,

2. THE STATE OF EDUCATION IN THE SLAVE STATES.

The maxim that "knowledge is power," has ever more or less influenced the conduct of aristocracies. Education elevates the inferior classes of society, teaches them their rights, and points out the means of enforcing them. Of course, it tends to diminish the influence of wealth, birth, and rank. In 1671, Sir William Berkley, then Governor of Virginia, in his answer to the inquiries of the Committee of the Colonies, remarked, "I thank God that there are no free schools nor printing presses, and I hope we shall not have them these hundred years." The spirit of Sir William seems still to preside in the councils of his own Virginia, and to actuate those of the other slave States.

The power of the slave-holders, as we have already shown you, depends on the acquiescence of the major part of the white inhabitants in their domination. It cannot be, therefore, the interest or the inclination of the sagacious and reflecting among them, to promote the intellectual improvement of the inferior class.

In the free States, on the contrary, where there is no caste answering to your slave-holders — where the *people* literally partake in the government, mighty efforts are made for general education; and in most instances, elementary instruction is, through the public liberality, brought within the reach of the children of the poor. Lamentable experience proves that such is not the case where slave-holders bear rule.

The last census gives us the number of white persons over twenty years of age in each State, who cannot read *and* write. It appears that these persons are to the *whole* white population in the several States as follows, viz.:

Connecticut, ····· 1	to every 568		Louisiana, ····· 1	to every	38 1-2
Vermont, ······· 1	"	472	Maryland, ···· 1	"	27
New Hampshire, · 1	"	310	Mississippi, ···· 1	"	20
Massachusetts, ··· 1	"	166	Delaware, ····· 1	"	18
Maine, ·········· 1	"	108	S. Carolina, ··· 1	"	17
Michigan, ······· 1	"	97	Missouri, ····· 1	"	16
Rhode Island, ···· 1	"	67	Alabama, ····· 1	"	15
New Jersey, ····· 1	"	58	Kentucky, ···· 1	"	13 1-2
New York, ······ 1	"	56	Georgia, ······ 1	"	13
Pennsylvania, ···· 1	"	50	Virginia, ······ 1	"	12 1-2
Ohio, ··········· 1	"	43	Arkansas, ····· 1	"	11 1-2
Indiana, ········ 1	"	18	Tennessee, ···· 1	"	11
Illinois, ········· 1	"	17	N. Carolina, ··· 1	"	7*

It will be observed by looking at this table, that Indiana and Illinois are the *only* free States, which in point of education are surpassed by *any* of the slave States: for this disgraceful circumstance three causes may be assigned, viz., their recent settlement, the influx of foreigners, and emigration from the slave States. The returns from New York, Rhode Island, New Jersey and Pennsylvania, are greatly affected by the vast number of foreigners congregated in their cities, and employed in their manufactories and on their public works. In Ohio, also, there is a large foreign population; and it is well known that comparatively few emigrants from Europe seek a residence in the slave States, where there is little or no employment to invite them. But what a commentary on slavery and slave-holders is afforded by the gross ignorance prevailing in the old States of South Carolina, Virginia, and North Carolina! But let us proceed. The census gives a return of "scholars at public charge."

Of these, there are in the free States, ················· 432,173
" " slave States, ················· 35,580

Ohio alone has 51,812 such scholars, — more than are to be found in the 13 slave States! Her neighbor Kentucky has 429!! Let us compare in this particular the *largest* and the *smallest* State in the Union.

Virginia has scholars at public charge ··················· 9,791
Rhode Island ······································ 10,912†

* This summary from the return of the census, is copied from the Richmond (Va.) Compiler.

† See American Almanac for 1842, page 226.

But we have some *official* confessions, which give a still more deplorable account of southern ignorance. In 1837, Governor Clarke, in his message to the Kentucky Legislature, remarked, "By the computation of those most familiar with the subject, ONE THIRD OF THE ADULT POPULATION OF THE STATE ARE UNABLE TO WRITE THEIR NAMES."

Governor Campbell reported to the Virginia Legislature, that from the returns of 98 clerks, it appeared that of 4,614 *applications for marriage licenses in* 1837, *no less than* 1,047 *were made by men unable to write.*

These details will enable you to estimate the impudence of the following plea in behalf of slavery:

> "It is by the existence of slavery, exempting so large a portion of our citizens from the necessity of bodily labor, that we have leisure for *intellectual pursuits*, and the means of attaining a liberal education." *Chancellor Harper, of South Carolina, on Slavery. Southern Literary Messenger, Oct.* 1838.

Whatever may be the leisure enjoyed by the slave-holders, they are careful not to afford the means of literary improvement to their fellow-citizens who are too poor to possess slaves, and who are, by their very ignorance, rendered more fit instruments for doing the will, and guarding the human property of the wealthier class.

3. INDUSTRY AND ENTERPRISE.

In a community so unenlightened as that of the slave States, it is a matter of course that the arts and sciences must languish, and the industry and enterprise of the country be oppressed by a general torpor. Hence multitudes will be without regular and profitable employment, and be condemned to poverty and numberless privations. The very advertisements in the newspapers show that, for a vast proportion of the comforts and conveniences of life, they are dependent on northern manufactures and mechanics. Slavery has rendered labor disgraceful; and where this is the case, industry is necessarily discouraged. The great staple of the South is cotton; and we have no desire to undervalue its importance. It is, however, worthy of remark, that its cultivation affords a livelihood to only a small proportion of the free inhabitants; and scarcely to any of those we are now addressing. Cotton is the product of slave labor, and its profits at home are confined almost exclusively to the slave-holders. Yet on account of this article, we hear frequent vaunts of the agricultural riches of the South. With the exception of cotton, it is difficult to distinguish your agricultural products arising from slave, and from free labor. But admitting, what we know is not the fact, that *all* the other productions of the soil are raised *exclusively* by free labor, we learn from the census, that the agricultural products of the North exceed those of the South, cotton excepted, $226,219,714. Here then we have an appalling proof of the paralyzing influence of slavery on the industry of the whites.

In every community a large portion of the inhabitants are debarred from drawing their maintenance directly from the cultivation of the earth. Other and lucrative employments are reserved for them. If the slave-holders chiefly engross the soil, let us see how you are compensated by the encouragement afforded to mechanical skill and industry.

In 1839, the Secretary of the Treasury reported to Congress, that the tonnage of vessels built in the United States was 120,988; built in the slave States and Territories, 23,600, or less than one-fifth of the whole! But the difference is still more striking, when we take into consideration the comparative *value* of the shipping built in the two regions:

In the free States the value is $6,311,805
In the slave States, ...704,291*

It would be tedious and unprofitable to compare the results of the different branches of manufacture carried on at the North and at the South. It is sufficient to state that, according to the census, the value of the manufactures

In the free States is $334,139,690
In the slave States..................................83,935,742

* See American Almanac for 1843, page 153.

Having already compared Ohio and Kentucky in reference to population and education, we will pursue the comparison as to agricultural and mechanical industry. On account of contiguity, and similarity of extent, soil and climate, no two States can perhaps be so aptly contrasted for the purpose of illustrating the influence of slavery. It should also be borne in mind that Kentucky can scarcely be called a cotton State, having in 1840 raised only 607,456 pounds of that article. Hence the deficiency of agriculture and other products in Kentucky arises, not from a peculiar species of cultivation, but solely from the withering effects of slavery.

	Ohio.	Kentucky.
Wool,	3,685,315 lbs.	1,786,842
Wheat,	16,571,661 bushels	5,803,152
Hay,	1,022,037 tons	88,306
Fulling Mills,	205	5
Printing-offices,	159	34
Tanneries,	862	387
Commercial houses in foreign trade,	53	5
Value of machinery manufactured,	$875,731	$46,074

In one species of manufacture the South apparently excels the North, but unquestionably it is in appearance only. Of 9,657 distilleries in the United States, no less than 7,665 were found in the slave States and Territories; but for want of skill and capital, these yield 1,992 gallons less than the other.

Where there is so much ignorance and idleness, we may well suppose that the inventive faculties will be but little exercised; and accordingly we find that of the 545 patents granted for new inventions in 1846, only 80 were received by the citizens of the slave States. We have thus offered to our readers the testimony of figures, as to the different state of society under freedom and slavery; suffer us now to present you pictures of the two regions, drawn not by abolitionists, but by southern artists, in unguarded hours. Mr. Clowney, of South Carolina, thus portrayed his native State, in the ardor of debate on the floor of Congress:

"Look at South Carolina now, with her houses deserted and falling to decay; her once fruitful fields worn out and abandoned for want of timely improvement or skilful cultivation; and her thousands of acres of inexhaustible lands, still promising an abundant harvest to the *industrious* husbandman, lying idle and neglected. In the interior of the State where I was born, and where I now live, although a country possessing all the advantages of soil, climate, and health, abounding in arable land, unreclaimed from the first rude state of nature, there can now be found many neighborhoods where the population is too sparse to support a common elementary school for children. Such is the deplorable condition of one of the oldest members of this Union, that dates back its settlement more than a century and a half, while other States, born as it were but yesterday, already surpass what Carolina is or ever has been, in the happiest and proudest day of her prosperity."

This gentleman chose to attribute the decline of South Carolina to the tariff, rather than to the obvious cause, that one-half of the PEOPLE of South Carolina are poor, ignorant, degraded SLAVES, and the other half suffering in all their faculties and energies, from a moral pestilence which they insanely regard as a blessing and not a curse. Surely it is not owing to the tariff, that this ancient member of the Union has 20,615 white citizens over twenty years of age who do not know their letters; while Maine, with double her population, has only 3,241.

Now look upon a very different picture. Mr. Preston, of South Carolina, not long since delivered a speech at Columbia in reference to a proposed railroad. In this speech, in order to stimulate the efforts of the friends of the road, he indulged in the following strain:

"No southern man can journey (as he had lately done) through the Northern States, and witness the prosperity, the industry, the public spirit which they exhibit — the sedulous cultivation of all those arts by which life is rendered comfortable and respectable — without feelings of deep sadness and shame as he remembers *his own neglected and desolate home*. There, no dwelling is to be seen abandoned — not a farm uncultivated. Every person and every thing performs a part towards the grand result; and the whole land is covered with fertile fields, with manufactories, and canals, and railroads, and edifices, and towns, and cities. We of the South are mistaken in the character of these people, when we think of them only as peddlers in horn flints and bark nutmegs. Their energy and enterprise are directed to all objects great and small within their reach. The number of railroads and other modes of expeditious intercommunication knit the whole country into a closely compacted mass, through which the productions of commerce and of the press, the comforts of life, and the means of knowledge, are universally diffused; while the close intercourse of travel and of business makes all neighbors, and promotes a common interest and a common sympathy. How different the condition of these things at the South! *Here* the face of the country wears the aspect of premature old age and decay. NO IMPROVEMENT IS SEEN GOING ON, nothing is done for posterity. No man thinks of anything beyond the present moment."

Yet this same Mr. Preston, thus sensitively alive to the superior happiness and prosperity of the free States, declared in the United States Senate,

"Let an abolitionist come within the borders of South Carolina, if we can catch we will try him, and notwithstanding all the interference of all the governments of the earth, including the Federal Government, we will HANG him."*

In other words, the slave-holders, rather than part with their slaves, are ready to murder, with all the formalities of law, the very men who are laboring to confer on them the envied blessings of the North.

4. FEELINGS OF THE SLAVE-HOLDERS TOWARDS THE LABORING CLASSES.

Whenever the great mass of the laboring population of a country are reduced to beasts of burden, and toil under the lash, "bodily labor," as Chancellor Harper expresses it, must be disreputable, from the mere influence of association. Hence it is that *white* laborers at the South are styled "mean whites." At the North, on the contrary, labor is regarded as the proper and commendable means of acquiring wealth; and our most influential men would in no degree suffer in public estimation, for holding the plough, or even repairing the highways. Hence no poor man is deterred from seeking a livelihood by honest labor from a dread of personal degradation. The different light in which labor is viewed at the North and the South is one cause of the depression of industry in the latter.

* We are well aware that Mr. Preston has denied, what no one asserted, that he had said an abolitionist, if he came into South Carolina, would be executed by Lynch law. He used the words we have quoted. (See "New York Journal of Commerce," Jan. 6th, 1838.)

Another cause is the ever-wakeful jealousy of the aristocracy. They fear the PEOPLE; they are alarmed at the very idea of power and influence being possessed by any portion of the community not directly interested in slave property. Visions of emancipation, of agrarianism, and of popular resistance to their authority, are ever floating in their distempered and excited imaginations. They know their own weakness, and are afraid you should know it also. Henee it is their policy to keep down the "mean whites." Hence their philippics against the lower classes. Hence their constant comparison of the laborers of the North, with their own slaves; and hence, in no small degree, the absence among them of those institutions which confer upon the poor that knowledge which is *power.* Do you deem these assertions uncharitable? Listen to their own declarations:

"We believe the servitude which prevails in the South far preferable to that of the *North*, or in Europe. Slavery will exist in all communities. There is a class which may be nominally free, but they will be virtually *slaves.*" *Mississippian, July 6th*, 1838.

"Those who depend on their daily labor for their daily subsistence can never enter into political affairs; they never do, never will, never can." *B. W. Leigh in Virginia Convention*, 1829.

"All society settles down into a classification of capitalists and laborers. The former will *own* the latter, either collectively through the government, or individually in a state of domestic servitude, as exists in the Southern States of this confederacy. If LABORERS ever obtain the political power of a country, it is in fact in a state of REVOLUTION. The capitalists north of Mason and Dixon's line, have precisely the same interest in the labor of the country, that the capitalists of England have in their labor. Hence it is that they must have a strong federal government (!) *to control* the labor of the nation. But is precisely the reverse with us. We have already not only a right to the proceeds of our laborers, but we OWN a *class of laborers* themselves. But let me say to gentlemen who represent the great class of capitalists in the North — beware that you do not drive us into a separate system; for if you do, as certain as the decrees of Heaven, you will be compelled to *appeal to the sword to maintain yourselves at home.* It may not come in your day; but your children's children will be covered with the blood of domestic factions, and will see *a plundering mob contending for power and conquest.*" *Mr. Pickens, of South Carolina, in Congress, 21st Jan.*, 1836.

So the way to prevent *plundering* mobs, is to enslave the poor! We shall see presently, how far this expedient has been successful in preventing *murdering* mobs.

"In the very nature of things there must be classes of persons to discharge all the different offices of society, from the highest to the lowest. Some of these offices are regarded as *degrading*, although they must and will be performed. Hence those manifest forms of dependent servitude which produce a sense of superiority in the masters or employers, and of inferiority on the part of the servants. Where these offices are performed by *members of the political community*, a DANGEROUS ELEMENT is obviously introduced into the body politic. Hence the alarming tendency to violate the rights of property by agrarian legislation, which is beginning to be manifest in the older States, where UNIVERSAL SUFFRAGE *prevails without* DOMESTIC SLAVERY.

"In a word, the institution of domestic slavery supersedes the *necessity* of AN ORDER OF NOBILITY, AND ALL THE OTHER APPENDAGES OF A HEREDITARY SYSTEM OF GOVERNMENT." *Governor M'Duffie's Message to the South Carolina Legislature*, 1836.

"We regard SLAVERY *as the most safe and stable basis for free institutions in the world.* It is impossible with us, that the conflict can take place between labor and capital, which makes it so difficult to establish and maintain free institutions in all wealthy and highly civilized nations where such institutions do not exist. Every plantation is a little community, with the master at its head, who concentrates in himself the united interests of capital and labor, *of which he is the common representative.*" *Mr. Calhoun, of South Carolina, in the U. S. Senate, Jan. 10th*, 1840.

"We of the South have cause now, and shall soon have greater, to congratulate ourselves on the existence of a population among us, which excludes the POPULACE which in effect rules some of our northern neighbors, and is rapidly gaining strength wherever slavery does not exist — a populace made up of the dregs of Europe, and the most worthless portion of the native population." *Richmond Whig*, 1837.

"Would you do a benefit to the horse or the ox by giving him a cultivated understanding, a fine feeling? So far as the MERE LABORER has the pride, the knowledge, or the aspiration of a freeman, he is unfitted for his situation. If there are sordid, servile, *laborious* offices to be performed, is it not better that there should be sordid, servile, laborious beings to perform them?

"Odium has been cast upon our legislation, on account of its forbidding the elements of education being communicated to slaves. But in truth what injury is done them by this? *He who works during the day with his hands*, does not read in the intervals of leisure for his amusement, or the improvement of his mind, or the exception is so very rare as scarcely to need the being provided for." *Chancellor Harper of South Carolina. Southern Literary Messenger.*

This same gentleman delivered an oration on the 4th of July, 1840, reviewing the principles of the two great political parties, and although he supported Mr. Van Buren's administration, in consideration of its devotion to the slave interest, he frankly inquires:

"Is there anything in the principles and opinions of the great DEMOCRATIC RABBLE, as it has been justly called, which should induce *us* to identify ourselves with that? Here you may find every possible grade and hue of opinion which has ever existed in the country. Here you may find loafer, and loco-foco, and agrarian, and all the rabble of the city of New York, the most corrupt and depraved of rabbles, and which controls, in a great degree, the city itself, and through that, as being the commercial metropolis, exercises much influence over the State at large.

"What are the essential principles of democracy as distinguished from republicanism? The first consists in the dogma, so portentous to us, of the natural equality and unalienable right to liberty of every human being. Our allies, (!) no doubt, are willing at *present* to modify the doctrine in *our favor*. But the spirit of democracy at large makes no such exceptions, nor will these (our allies, the northern democrats) continue to make it, longer than necessity or *interest* may require. The second consists in the doctrine of the divine right of majorities; a doctrine not less false and slavish and absurd, than the ancient doctrine of the divine right of kings."

Mr. Robert Wickliffe, of Kentucky, in a speech published in the *Louisville Advertiser*, in opposition to those who were adverse to the importation of slaves from the States, thus discourseth:

"Gentlemen wanted to drive out the black population, that they may obtain WHITE NEGROES in their place. WHITE NEGROES have this advantage over black negroes, they can be converted into voters; and the men who live upon the sweat of their brow, and pay them but a dependent and scanty subsistence, can, if able to keep ten thousand of them in employment, come up to the polls, and change the destiny of the country.

"How improved will be our condition when we have such white negroes as perform the servile labors of Europe, of Old England, and he would add now of *New England;* when our body servants and our cart drivers and our street sweepers are *white negroes* instead of black. Where will be the independence, the proud spirit, and the chivalry of Kentuckians then?"

Had the gentleman looked across the river, he might have found an answer to his question, in the wealth, power, intelligence and happiness of Ohio.

In reading the foregoing extracts, it is amusing to observe how adroitly the slave-holders avoid all recognition of any other classes among them than masters and slaves. Who would suspect from their language, that they were themselves a small minority of the white inhabitants, and that their own "white negroes" could, if united and so disposed, outvote them at the polls? It is worthy of remark that in their denunciations of the *populace*, the *rabble, those who work with their hands*, they refer not to complexion, but to condition; not to slaves, but to the poor and laborious of their own color.

Slavery, although considered by Mr. Calhoun "the most stable basis of free institutions in the world," has, as we shall presently show you, in fact, led to grosser outrages in the social compact, to more alarming violations of constitutional liberty, to more bold and reckless assaults upon "free institutions" than have ever been even attempted by the much-dreaded agrarianism of the North.

5. STATE OF RELIGION.

The deplorable ignorance and want of industry at the South, together with the disrepute in which honest industry is held, cannot but exercise, in connection with other causes, a most unhappy influence on the morals of the inhabitants. There are between two and three millions of slaves, who are kept by law in brutal ignorance, and who, with few exceptions, are virtually heathens.*

There are also among them more than 200,000 free negroes, thus described by Mr. Clay: — "Contaminated themselves, they extend their vices to all around them." †

If evil communications corrupt good manners, the intimate intercourse of the whites with these people must be depraving: nor can the exercise of despotic power by the masters, their wives and children, be otherwise than unfavorable to the benevolent affections.

* "From long-continued and close observation, we believe that their (the slaves') moral and religious condition is such that they may justly be considered the HEATHEN of this Christian country, and will bear comparison with heathen in any country in the world. The negroes are destitute of the Gospel, and ever will be under the present state of things." *Report published by the Synod of South Carolina and Georgia, Dec.* 3, 1833.

† Speech before the American Colonization Society.

It is with pain we are compelled to add, that the conduct and avowed sentiments of the southern clergy in relation to slavery, necessarily exert an unhappy influence. Most of the clergy are themselves slave-holders, and are thus personally interested in the system, and are consequently bold and active in justifying it from Scripture, representing it as an institution enjoying the divine sanction. An English author, in reference to these efforts of your clergy forcibly remarks :

> "Whatever may have been the unutterable wickedness of slavery in the West Indies, *there* it never was baptized in the Redeemer's hallowed name, and its corruptions were not concealed in the garb of religion. That acme of piratical turpitude was reserved for the professed disciples of Jesus in America."

And well has John Quincy Adams said,

> "The spirit of slavery has acquired not only an overruling ascendency, but it has become at once intolerant, proscriptive, and sophistical. It has crept into the philosophical chairs of the schools. Its cloven hoof has ascended the pulpits of the churches — professors of colleges teach it as a lesson of morals — ministers of the Gospel seek and profess to find sanctions for it in the word of God."

The ministers live in the midst of slavery, and they *know* that the system on which they bestow their benedictions, is, in the language of Wilberforce, "a system of the grossest injustice, of the most heathenish irreligion and immorality; of the most unprecedented degradation and unrelenting cruelty." Surely, we have reason to fear that the denunciation of Scripture against false prophets of old, will be accomplished against the southern clergy, "Because they ministered unto them before their idols, and caused the House of Israel to fall into iniquity, therefore have I lifted mine hand against them, saith the Lord God, and they shall bear their iniquity." *Ezek.* 44: 12.

Under such ministrations it cannot be expected that Christian zeal and benevolence will take deep root and bear very abundant fruit. This is a subject on which few statistics can be obtained. We have no means of ascertaining the number of churches and ministers throughout the United States of the various denominations. Some opinion, however, may be formed of the religious character of a people, by their efforts for the moral improvement of the community. In the United States there are numerous voluntary associations for religious and benevolent purposes, receiving large contributions and exercising a wide moral influence. Now, of all the large benevolent societies professing to promote the welfare of the whole country, and asking and receiving contributions from all parts of it, we recollect but one that had its origin in the slave-region, and the business of which is transacted in it, and that is the AMERICAN COLONIZATION SOCIETY. Of the real object and practical tendency of this Society it is unnecessary to speak — you understand them.

In the Tenth Report of the American Sunday School Union (p. 50) is a table showing the number of Sunday School scholars in each State for the year 1834. From this table we learn that

There were in the free States,	504,835	scholars.
" " slave "	82,532	"
The single State of New York had	161,768	"

About twice as many as in the thirteen slave States.

And is it possible that this literary and religious destitution, together with the vicious habits of the colored population, should have no effect on the moral character of the whites?

We entreat your patient and dispassionate attention to the remarks and facts we are about to submit to you on the next subject of inquiry.

6. STATE OF MORALS.

Christianity, by controlling the malignant passions of our nature, and exciting its benevolent affections, gives a sacredness to the rights of others, and especially does it guard human life. But where her blessed influence is withdrawn, or greatly impaired, the passions resume their sway, and violence and cruelty become the characteristics of every community in which the civil authority is too feeble to afford protection.

No society is free from vices and crime, and we well know that human depravity springs from another source than slavery.

It will not, however, be denied that circumstances and institutions may check those evil propensities to which we are all prone; and it will, we presume, be admitted that in forming an opinion of the moral condition and advancement of any community, we are to be guided in our judgment, not by insulated facts, but by the *tone of public opinion*. Atrocities occur in the best-regulated and most virtuous States, but in such they excite indignation and are visited with punishment; while in vicious communities they are treated with levity and impunity.

In a country where suffrage is universal, the representatives will but reflect the general character of their constituents. If we are permitted to apply this rule in testing the moral condition of the South, the result will not be favorable.

In noticing the public conduct of public men, we are not sensible of violating any principle of courtesy or delicacy; we touch not their private character or their private acts; we refer to their language and sentiments, merely as one indication of the standard of morals among their constituents, not as conclusive proof apart from other evidence.

On the 15th of February, 1837, R. M. Whitney was arraigned before the House of Representatives for contempt in refusing to attend when required before a committee. His apology was that he was afraid of his life, and he called, as a witness in his behalf, one of the committee, Mr. Fairfield, since Governor of the State of Maine. It appeared that in the committee, Mr. Peyton, of Virginia, had put some interrogatory to Whitney, who had returned a written answer which was deemed offensive. On this, as Mr. Fairfield testified, Peyton addressed the Chairman in these terms: "Mr. Chairman, I wish you to inform this witness, that he is not to insult me in his answers: if he does, God damn him! I will take his life on the spot!" Whitney rose and said he claimed the protection of the committee, on which Peyton exclaimed, "God damn you, you shan't speak, you shan't say one word while you are in this room; if you do I will put you to death!" Soon after, Peyton, observing that Whitney was looking at him, cried out, "Damn him, his eyes are on me — God damn him, he is looking at me — he shan't do it — damn him, he shan't look at me!"

The newspaper reports of the proceedings of Congress, a few years since, informed us that Mr. Dawson, a member from Louisiana, went up to Mr. Arnold, another member, and said to him, "If you attempt to speak, or rise from your seat, sir, by God I'll cut your throat!"

In a debate on the Florida war, Mr Cooper having taken offence at Mr. Giddings, of Ohio, for some remarks relative to slavery, said in his reply, "If the gentleman from Ohio will come among my constituents and promulgate his doctrines there, he will find that Lynch law will be inflicted, and that the gentleman will reach an elevation which he little dreams of."

In the session of 1841, Mr. Payne, of Alabama, in debate, alluding to the abolitionists, among whom he insisted the Postmaster-General ought to be included, declared that he would proscribe all abolitionists, he "would put the brand of Cain upon them — yes, the mark of HELL, and if they came to the South he would HANG THEM LIKE DOGS!"

Mr. Hammond, of South Carolina, at an earlier period thus expressed himself in the House: "I warn the abolitionists, ignorant, infatuated barbarians as they are, that if chance shall throw any of them into our hands, they may expect a FELON'S DEATH!"

In 1848, Mr. Hale, a senator from New Hampshire, introduced a bill for the protection of property in the District of Columbia, attempts having been made to destroy an Anti-Slavery press. Mr. Foote, a senator from Mississippi, thus expressed himself in reply: "I invite him (Mr. H.) to the State of Mississippi, and will tell him beforehand, in all honesty, that he could not go ten miles into the interior, before he would grace one of the tallest trees of the forest, with a rope around his neck, with the approbation of every virtuous and patriotic citizen, and that, if necessary, I SHOULD MYSELF ASSIST IN THE OPERATION."

And now, do these honorable gentleman, with all their profanity and vulgarity, breathing out threatenings and slaughter, represent the feelings, and manners, and morals of the slave-holding community? We have seen no evidence that they have lost a particle of popular favor in consequence of their ferocious violence. Alas! their language has been reëchoed again and again by public meetings in the slave States; and we proceed to lay before you overwhelming proof that in the expression of their murderous feelings towards the abolitionists, they have faithfully represented the sentiments of their constituents.

7. DISREGARD FOR HUMAN LIFE.

We have already seen that one of the blessings which the slave-holders attribute to their favorite institution, is exemption from popular tumults, and from encroachments by the democracy upon the rights of property. Their argument is, that political power in the hands of the poor and laboring classes is always attended with danger, and that this danger is averted when these classes are kept in bondage. With these gentlemen, life and liberty seem to be accounted as the small dust of the balance, when weighed against slavery and plantations; hence, to preserve the latter they are ever ready to sacrifice the former, in utter defiance of laws and constitutions.

We have already noticed the murderous proposition in relation to the abolitionists, made by Governor McDuffie to the South Carolina Legislature in 1835: "It is my deliberate opinion that the *laws* of every community should punish this species of interference, by DEATH without benefit of clergy." In an address to a legislative assembly, Governor McDuffie refrained from the indecency of recommending *illegal* murder; but we will soon find that the public sentiment of the South by no means requires that abolitionists shall be put to death with legal formalities; but on the contrary, the slave-holders are ready, in the language of Mr. Payne, to "hang them like dogs."

We hazard little in the assertion, that in no civilized Christian community on earth is human life less protected by law, or more frequently taken with impunity, than in the slave States of the Federal Union. We wish to impress upon you the danger and corruption to which you and your children are exposed from the institution, which, as we have shown you, exists by your sufferance. But you have been taught to respect this institution; and hence it becomes necessary to enter into details, however painful, and to present you with authorities which you cannot reject. What we have just said of the insecurity of human life, will probably be deemed by you and others as abolition slander. Listen, then, to slave-holders themselves:

"We long to see the day," said the Governor of Kentucky in his message to the Legislature, 1837, "when the law will assert its majesty, and stop the wanton destruction of life which almost *daily* occurs within the jurisdiction of this commonwealth. MEN SLAUGHTER EACH OTHER WITH ALMOST PERFECT IMPUNITY. A species of common law has grown up in Kentucky, which, were it written down, would, in all civilized countries, cause her to be re-christened, in derision, THE LAND OF BLOOD."

The present Bishop of the Episcopal Church in Kentucky,* a few years since, published an article on the murders in that State. He states that some with whom he had conversed estimated them at eighty per annum; but that he had rated them at about thirty; and that he had ascertained that for the last three years, there had not been "an instance of capital punishment in any *white* offender."

"It is believed," says he, "there are more homicides on an average of two years in *any* of our more populous *counties*, than in the whole of several of our *States* of equal, or nearly equal, population to Kentucky'

Governor McVay, of Alabama, in his message to the Legislature, November 15, 1837, thus speaks:

"We hear of homicides in different parts of the State continually, and yet have few convictions, and still fewer executions! Why do we hear of stabbings and shootings almost *daily* in some part or other of our State?"

"DEATH BY VIOLENCE.—The moral atmosphere in our State appears to be in a deleterious and sanguinary condition. Almost every exchange paper which reaches us, contains some inhuman and revolting case of murder, or death by violence. *Not less than* FIFTEEN deaths by violence have occurred, to our certain knowledge, within the past three months." *Grand Gulf Miss. Advertiser, 27th June*, 1837.

"CONTEMPT OF HUMAN LIFE.—In view of the crimes which are daily committed, we are led to inquire whether it is owing to the

* It is believed this gentleman is *not* a slave-holder.

inefficiency of our laws, or to the manner in which these laws are administered, that this FRIGHTFUL DELUGE OF HUMAN BLOOD FLOWS THROUGH OUR STREETS AND OUR PLACES OF PUBLIC RESORT." *New Orleans Bee*, 23d *May*, 1838.

At the opening of the Criminal Court in New Orleans, November 4th, 1837, Judge Lansuque delivered an address, in which, speaking of the prevalence of violence, he used the following language:

"As a Louisiana parent, I reflect with terror, that our beloved children, reared to become one day honorable and useful citizens, may be the victims of these votaries of vice and licentiousness. Without some powerful and certain remedy, our streets will become BUTCHERIES, OVERFLOWING WITH THE BLOOD OF OUR CITIZENS!"

While the slave-holders are terrified at the idea of the "great democratic rabble," and rejoice in human bondage as superseding the necessity of "an order of nobility, and all the appendages of a hereditary government," they have established a reign of terror, as insurrectionary and as sanguinary in principle, as that created by the sans culottes of the French Revolution. We indulge in no idle declamation, but speak the words of truth and soberness.

A public meeting, convened in the *church (!!)* in the town of Clinton, Mississippi, 5th of September, 1835—

"Resolved, that it is our decided opinion, that any individual who dares to circulate, with a view to effectuate the designs of the abolitionists, any of the incendiary tracts or newspapers now in the course of transmission to this country, is justly worthy, in the sight of God and man, of immediate death; and we doubt not that such would be the punishment of any such offender, in any part of the State of Mississippi where he may be found."

It would be tedious to copy the numerous resolutions of similar import, passed by public meetings in almost every slave State. It is well known that the promoters of those lawless and sanguinary proceedings, did not belong to the "rabble"—they were not "mean whites," but rich, influential slave-holders. A meeting was held in 1835 at Williamsburgh, Virginia, which was harangued by no less a personage than JOHN TYLER, once Governor of the State, and since *President of the United*

States: under this gentleman's auspices, and after his address, the meeting resolved—

> "That we regard the printing and circulating within our limits, of incendiary publications, tending to excite our slaves to insurrection and rebellion, as treasonable acts of the most alarming character, and that when we detect offenders in the act, we will inflict upon them condign punishment, without resorting to any other tribunal."

The profligacy of this resolution needs no comment. Mr. Tyler well knew that the laws of Virginia, and every other State, were abundantly sufficient to punish crime: but he and his fellow-lynchers wished to deter the people from receiving and reading anything adverse to slavery; and hence, with their usual audacity, they determined to usurp the prerogative of courts and juries, and throw down all the bulwarks which the law has erected for the protection of innocence.

Newspapers are regarded as the mirrors of public opinion. Let us see what opinions are reflected in those of the South.

The *Charleston Courier*, 11th August, 1835, declared that "the *gallows and the stake*" awaited the abolitionists who should dare to "appear in person among us."

> "The cry of the whole South should be death, instant death to the abolitionist, wherever he is caught." *Augusta (Geo.) Chronicle.*

> "Let us declare through the public journals of our country, that the question of slavery is not and shall not be open to discussion; that the system is too deep-rooted among us, and must remain forever; that the very moment any private individual attempts to lecture us upon its evils and immorality, and the necessity of putting means in operation to secure us from them, in the same moment his tongue shall be cut out and cast upon the dunghill." *Columbia (S. C.) Telescope.*

This, it will be noticed, is a threat addressed, not to the northern abolitionists, but to the great majority of the white inhabitants of the South; and they are warned not to express *an opinion* offensive to the aristocracy.

> "Awful but Just Punishment.—We learn, by the arrival of the steamboat Kentucky last evening from Richmond, that Robinson, the Englishman mentioned in the *Beacon* of Saturday, as being in the vicinity of Lynchburg, was taken about fifteen miles from that town, and HANGED on the spot, for exciting the slaves to insurrection." *Norfolk (Va.) Beacon, 10th August,* 1835.

"We can assure the Bostonians, one and all, who have embarked in the nefarious scheme of abolishing slavery at the South, that lashes will hereafter be spared the backs of their emissaries. Let them send out their men to Louisiana; they will never return to tell their sufferings, but they shall expiate the crime of interfering with our domestic institutions, by being BURNED AT THE STAKE." *New Orleans True American.*

"Abolition editors in slave States will not dare to avow their opinions. It would be instant DEATH to them." *Missouri Argus.*

Here, again, is a threat directed against any person, who may happen to have the command of types and printer's ink.

Now, we ask what must be the state of society, where the public journals thus justify and stimulate the public thirst for blood? The very idea of *trial* is scouted, and the mob, or rather the slave-holders themselves, are acknowledged to be the arbiters of life and death. The question we put to you as to the *state of society*, has been already answered by the official declarations of the Governors of Kentucky and Alabama, and of Judge Lansuque, of New Orleans; as well as by the extracts we have given you from some of the southern journals, relative to the frequency of murders among them. We could farther answer it, by filling sheets with accounts of fearful atrocities. But we purposely refrain from referring to assassinations and private crimes; for such, as already remarked, occur in a greater or less degree in every community, and do not necessarily form a test of the standard of morals. But we ask your attention to a test which cannot be questioned. We will present for your consideration a series of atrocities, perpetrated, not by individuals in secret, but in open day by the *slave-holding populace.*

We have seen that two of the southern papers we have quoted, threaten abolitionists with THE STAKE. This awful and horrible punishment has been banished, by the progress of civilization, from the whole of Christendom, with the single exception of the American slave States. It is scarcely necessary to say, that even in them, it is unknown to the laws, although familiar to the people. It is also deserving of remark, that the two journals which have made this atrocious threat were published, not among the rude borderers of our frontier settlements, but in the populous cities of Charleston and New Orleans, the very centres of southern refinement.

"TUSCALOOSA (Ala.), June 20, 1827.—The negro [one who had killed a Mr. M'Neilly] was taken before a justice of the peace, who *waived his authority*, perhaps through fear, as a crowd of persons had collected, to the number of seventy or eighty, near Mr. People's [the justice's] house. He acted as president of the mob, and put the vote, when it was decided that he should be immediately executed by being *burned to death.* The sable culprit was led to a tree, and tied to it, and a large quantity of pine knots collected and placed around him, and the fatal torch applied to the pile, even against the remonstrances of several gentlemen who were present, and the miserable being was in a short time burned to ashes. This is the *second* negro who has been *thus* put to death, without judge or jury, in this country."

On the 28th of April, 1836, a free negro was arrested in St. Louis (Missouri) and committed to jail on a charge of murder. A mob assembled and demanded him of the jailer, who surrendered him. The negro was then chained to a tree *a short distance from the Court House*, and burned to death.

"After the flames had surrounded their prey, and when his clothes where in a blaze all over him, his eyes burnt out of his head, and his mouth seemingly parched to a cinder, some one in the *crowd*, more compassionate than the rest, proposed to put an end to his misery by shooting him, when it was replied that it would be of no use, since he was already out of his pain. 'No,' said the wretch, 'I am not, I am suffering as much as ever; shoot me, shoot me.' 'No, no,' said one of the fiends who was standing about the sacrifice they were roasting, 'he shall not be shot, I would sooner slacken the fire, if that would increase his misery;' and the man who said this was, we understand, an *officer of justice*." *Alton Telegraph.*

"We have been informed that the slave William, who murdered his master (Huskey) some weeks since, was taken by a party a few days since *from the sheriff* of Hot Spring, and *burned alive!* yes, tied up to the limb of a tree and a fire built under him, and consumed in a slow lingering torture." *Arkansas Gazette, Oct.* 29, 1836.

The *Natchez Free Trader*, 16*th June*, 1842, gives a horrible account of the execution of the negro, Joseph, on the 5th of that month for murder.

"The body," says that paper, "was taken and chained to a tree immediately on the bank of the Mississippi, on what is called Union Point. The torches were lighted and placed in the pile. He watched unmoved the curling flame as it grew, until it began to entwine itself around and feed upon his body; then he sent forth cries of agony painful to the ear, begging some one to blow his brains out; at the same time surging with almost superhuman strength, until the staple with which the chain was fastened to the tree, not being well secured, drew out, and he leaped from the burning pile. At that moment the sharp ring of several rifles was heard, and the body of the negro fell a corpse to the ground. He was picked up by two or three, and again thrown into the fire and consumed."

"ANOTHER NEGRO BURNED.—We learn from the clerk of the Highlander, that while wooding a short distance below the mouth of the Red River, they were *invited to stop a short time and see another negro burned.*" *N. O. Bulletin.*

Thus we see that burning negroes alive is treated as a spectacle, and strangers are invited to witness it. The victim of this exhibition was the negro Enoch, said to have been an accomplice of Joseph, and was burned a few days after the other.

We have thus given you no less than *six* instances of human beings publicly burned alive in four slave States, and in each case with entire impunity to the miscreants engaged in the horrible murder. But these were cases which *happened* to be reported in the newspapers, and with which we *happened* to become acquainted. There is reason to believe that these executions are not of rare occurrence, and that many of them, either through indifference or policy, are not noticed in the southern papers.

A recent traveller remarks:

"Just before I reached Mobile, two men were *burned alive* there in a slow fire in the open air, in the presence of the *gentlemen* of the city. No word was breathed of the transaction in the newspapers." *Martineau's Society in America*, Vol. I, p. 373.

But the murderous spirit deplored by the Governors of Kentucky and Alabama, and the "frightful deluge of human blood" complained of by the New Orleans editor, had no reference to the murder of *negroes.* Men who can enjoy the sight of negroes writhing in flames, and are permitted by the civil authorities to indulge in such exhibitions, will not be very scrupulous in taking the lives of each other. It is well known how incessantly the work of human slaughter is going on among them; and no reader of their public journals can be ignorant of the frequent occurrence of their deadly street fights. But, for the reason already given, we meddle not with these. We charge the slave-holding community, as such, with *sanctioning* murder, and protecting the perpetrators, and setting the laws at defiance. This we know is a grievous charge, and most grievous the proof of it. But mistake not our meaning. God forbid we should deny that many of the community to which we refer, utterly abhor the atrocities we are about to detail. We speak of the murderous feelings of the slave-holding community, just as we speak of the politics, the manners, and the morals of any other community, freely acknowledging that there are numerous and honorable exceptions. For the general truth of our assertion, we appeal to the authorities and the facts we have already laid before you, and to those we are about to offer.

You have already seen that the pro-slavery press has recommended the murder of such northern abolitionists as may be caught in the South; we now ask your attention to the efforts made by the slave-holders to get prominent abolitionists into their power.

In 1831, a citizen of Massachusetts established a newspaper at Boston, called the Liberator, and devoted to the cause of negro emancipation. The undertaking was perfectly legal, and he himself, having never been in Georgia, had of course violated none of her laws. The Legislature, however, forthwith passed a law, offering a bribe of $5000 to any person who would arrest and bring to trial and conviction, in Georgia, the editor and publisher of the Boston paper. This most atrocious law was "approved" on the 26th of December, 1831, by WILLIAM LUMPKIN, the Governor. The object of the bribe could have been no other than the abduction and murder of the conductor of the paper—his *trial* and *conviction* under Georgia laws being a mere pretence: the Georgia courts have as much jurisdiction over the press in Paris as in Boston. A Lynch court was the only one that could have taken cognizance of the offence, and its proceedings would undoubtedly have been both summary and sanguinary.

The horrible example thus set by the Georgia Legislature was not without its followers.

At a meeting of slave-holders at Sterling, Sept. 4, 1835, it was formally recommended to the Governor to issue a proclamation, offering the $5000 appropriated by the Act of 1831, as a reward for the apprehension of *either* of *ten* persons named in the resolution, citizens of New York and Massachusetts, and one a subject of Great Britain; not one of whom it was even pretended had ever set his foot on the soil of Georgia.

The *Milledgeville (Ga.) Federal Union*, of Feb. 1, 1836, contained an offer of $10,000 for kidnapping A. A. Phelps, a clergyman residing in the city of New York.

The Committee of Vigilance of the Parish of East Feliciana offered in the Louisiana Journal of 15th of Oct. 1835, $50,000 to any person who would deliver *into their hands* Arthur Tappan, a New York merchant.

At a public meeting of the citizens of Mount Meigs, Alabama, 13th of August, 1836, the Honorable (!) Bedford Ginress in the chair, a reward of $50,000 was offered for the apprehension of Arthur Tappan, or La Roy Sunderland, a clergyman of the Methodist Church residing in New York.

Let us now witness the practical operation of that murderous spirit which dictated the foregoing villanous bribes. We have already seen the conduct of the slave-holding community to *negro* offenders; we are now to notice its tender mercies to men of its own color.

In 1835, there was a real or affected apprehension of a servile insurrection in the State of Mississippi. The slave-holders, as usual on such occasions, were exceedingly frightened, and were exceedingly cruel. A pamphlet was afterwards published, entitled "*Proceedings of the Citizens of Madison County, Miss., at Livingston, in July*, 1835, *in relation to the trial and punishment of several individuals implicated in a contemplated insurrection in this State. Prepared by Thomas Shuckelford, Esquire. Printed at Jackson, Miss.*" This pamphlet, then, is the *southern* account of the affair; and while it is more minute in its details than the narratives published in the newspapers at the time, we are not aware that it contradicts them. It may be regarded as a sort of semi-official report, put forth by the slave-holders, and published under their implied sanction. It appears, from this account, that in consequence of "rumors" that the slaves meditated an insurrection — that a colored girl had been heard to say that "she was tired of waiting on the white folks — wanted to be her own mistress for the balance of her days, and clean up her own house, &c.," a meeting was held at which resolutions were signed, organizing a committee, and authorizing them "*to bring before them any person or persons, either white or black, and try in a summary manner any person brought before them, with power to hang or whip, being always governed by the laws of the land, so far only as they shall be applicable to the case in question; otherwise to act as in their discretion shall seem best for the benefit of the country and the protection of its citizens.*"

This was certainly a most novel mode of erecting and commissioning a court of judicature, with the power of life and death, expressly authorized to act independently of "the laws of the land."

The constitution of the State of Mississippi, which no doubt many of the honorable judges of the court had on other occasions taken an oath to support, contains the following clause:—

"No person shall be accused, arrested or detained, except in cases ascertained by law, and according to the forms which the same has prescribed; and no person shall be punished, but in virtue of a law established and promulgated prior to the offence, and legally applied."

Previous to the organization of this court, FIVE slaves had already been HUNG by the people. The court, or rather, as it was modestly called by the meeting who erected it, "the committee," proceeded to try Dr. Joshua Cotton, of New England. It was proved to the satisfaction of the committee that he had been detected in many low tricks — that he was deficient in feeling and affection for his second wife — that he had traded with negroes — that he had asked a negro boy whether the slaves were whipped much, how he would like to be free, &c. It is *stated* that Cotton made a confession that he had been aiming to bring about a conspiracy. The committee condemned him to BE HANGED IN AN HOUR AFTER SENTENCE.

William Saunders, a native of Tennessee, was next tried. He was convicted "of being often out at night, and giving no satisfactory explanation for so doing"—of equivocal conduct—of being intimate with Cotton, &c. Whereupon, by a unanimous vote, he was found guilty and sentenced to be HUNG. He was executed with Cotton on the 4th of July.

Albe Dean, of Connecticut, was next tried. He was convicted of being a lazy, indolent man, having very little *pretensions* to honesty—of "pretending to make a living by constructing washing machines"—of "often coming to the owners of runaways, to intercede with the masters to save them from a whipping." He was sentenced to be HUNG, and was executed.

A. L. Donavan, of Kentucky, was then put on his trial. He was suspected of having traded with the negroes—of being found in their cabins, and enjoying himself in their society. It was proved that "at one time he actually undertook to release a negro who was tied, which negro afterwards implicated him," and that he once told an overseer "it was cruel work to be whipping the poor negroes as he was obliged to do." The committee were satisfied, from the evidence before them, that Donavan was an emissary of those deluded fanatics of the North, the abolitionists. He was condemned to be HUNG, and suffered accordingly.

Ruel Blake was next tried, condemned and HUNG. "He protested his innocence to the last, and said his life was sworn away."

Here we have a record of no less than TEN men, five black and five white, probably all innocent of the crime alleged against them, deliberately and publicly put to death by the slave-holders, without the shadow of legal authority.

The *Maysville (Ken.) Gazette*, in announcing Donavan's murder, says, "He formerly belonged to Maysville, and was a much respected citizen."

A letter from Donavan to his wife, written just before his execution, and published in the Maysville paper, says:

"I am doomed to die to-morrow at twelve o'clock, on a charge of having been concerned in a negro insurrection, in this State, among many other whites. We are not tried by a regular jury, but by a committee of PLANTERS appointed for the purpose, who have not time to wait on a person for evidence. . . . . . Now I must close by saying, before my Maker and Judge, that I go into his presence as innocent of this charge as when I was born. . . . . I must bid you a final farewell, hoping that the God of the widow and the fatherless will give you grace to bear this most awful sentence."

And now, did these butcheries by the Mississippi PLANTERS excite the indignation of the slave-holding communities? Receive the answer from an editor of the *Ancient Dominion*, replying to the comments of a northern newspaper.

"The Journal may depend upon it that the Cottons and the Saunderses, men confessing themselves guilty of inciting and plotting insurrection, will be HANGED UP wherever caught, and that *without the formality of a legal trial*. Northern or southern, such will be their inevitable doom. For our part, WE APPLAUD the transaction, and none in our opinion can condemn it, who have not a secret sympathy with the Garrison sect. If northern sympathy and effort are to be cooled and extinguished by such cases, it proves but this, that the South ought to feel little confidence in the professions it receives from that quarter." *Richmond Whig.*

About the time of the massacre in Clinton county, another awful tragedy was performed at Vicksburg in the same State. FIVE men, said to be *gamblers*, were HANGED by the mob on the 5th July, in open day.

The *Louisiana Advertiser*, of 13th July, says:

"These unfortunate men claimed to the last, the privilege of American citizens, the *trial by jury*, and professed themselves willing to submit to anything their country would legally inflict upon them; but we are sorry to say, their petition was in vain. The black musicians were ordered to strike up, and the voices of the supplicants were drowned by the fife and drum. *Mr. Riddle, the Cashier of the Planters' Bank*, ordered them to play Yankee Doodle. The unhappy sufferers frequently implored a drink of water, *but they were refused*."

The sympathy of the Louisiana editor, so different from his brother of Richmond, was probably owing to the fact, that the murdered men were accused of being gamblers, and not abolitionists.

When we said these five men were hung by the *mob*, we did not mean what Chancellor Harper calls the "democratic rabble."

It seems the cashier of a bank, a man to whom the slave-holders entrust the custody of their money, officiated on the occasion as Master of Ceremonies.

A few days after the murders at Vicksburg, a negro named Vincent was sentenced by a Lynch club at Clinton, Miss., to receive three hundred lashes, for an alleged participation in an intended insurrection. We copy from the *Clinton Gazette:*

"On Wednesday evening Vincent was carried out to receive his stripes, but the ASSEMBLED MULTITUDE were in favor of *hanging* him. A vote was accordingly *fairly* taken, and the hanging party had it by an overwhelming majority, as the politicians say. He was remanded to *prison*. On the day of execution a *still larger crowd was assembled*, and fearing that the public sentiment might have changed in regard to his fate, after everything favorable to the culprit was alleged which could be said, the vote was taken, and his *death was demanded by the people*. In pursuance of this sentiment, so unequivocally expressed, he was led to a black jack, and suspended to one of its branches. WE APPROVE ENTIRELY OF THE PROCEEDINGS; THE PEOPLE HAVE ACTED PROPERLY."

Thus SIXTEEN human beings were deliberately and publicly murdered, by assembled crowds, in different parts of the State of Mississippi, within little more than ONE WEEK, in open defiance of the laws and constitution of the State.

And now, we ask, what notice did the chief magistrate of Mississippi, sworn to support her constitution, sworn to execute her laws — what notice, we ask, did he take of these horrible massacres? Why, at the next session of the Legislature, Governor Lynch, addressing them in reference to abolition, remarked:

"Mississippi has given a *practical* demonstration of feeling on this exciting subject, that may serve as an impressive admonition to offenders; and however we may regret the occasion, we are constrained to admit that necessity will sometimes prompt a summary mode of trial and punishment unknown to the law."

The iniquity and utter falsehood of this declaration, as applied to the transactions alluded to, are palpable. If the victims were innocent, no necessity required their murder. If guilty, no necessity required their execution contrary to law. There was no difficulty in securing their persons and bringing them to trial.

In 1841, an *unsuccessful* attempt was made in Kentucky to murder a man. The assailants were arrested and lodged in jail for trial. Their fate is thus related in a letter by an eye-witness, published in the Cincinnati Gazette:

"*Williamstown, Ky., July* 11, 1841.

"The unfortunate men, Lyman Couch and Smith Maythe, were taken out of jail on Saturday about 12 o'clock, and taken to the ground where they committed the horrid deed on Utterback, and at 4 o'clock were HUNG on the tree where Utterback lay when his throat was cut. The jail was opened by force. I suppose there were from FOUR TO SEVEN HUNDRED people engaged in it. Resistance was all in vain. There were three speeches made to the mob, but all in vain. They allowed the prisoners the privilege of clergy for about five hours, and then observed that they had made their peace with God, and they deserved to die. The mob was conducted with coolness and order, more so than I ever heard of on such occasions. But such a day was never witnessed in our little village, and I hope never will be again."

The fact that this atrocity was perpetrated in "our little village," and by a rural population, affords an emphatic and horrible indication of the state of morals in one of the oldest and best of our slave States.

Would that we could here close these fearful narratives; but another and more recent instance of that ferocious lawlessness which slavery has engendered, must still be added. The following facts are gathered from the *Norfolk (Va.) Beacon*, of 19th Nov., 1842.

George W. Lore was, in April, 1842, convicted in Alabama, on circumstantial evidence, of the crime of murder. The Supreme Court granted a new trial, remarking, as is stated in another paper, that the testimony on which he was convicted was "unfit to be received by any court of justice recognized among civilized nations." In the mean time, Lore escaped from jail, and was afterwards arrested. He was seized by a mob, who put it to vote, whether he should be surrendered to the civil authority or be *hung*. Of 132 votes, 130 were for immediate death; and he was accordingly HUNG at Spring Hill, Bourbon County, on the 4th of November.

And now, what think you of Mr. Calhoun's "most safe and stable basis for free institutions?" Do you number TRIAL BY

JURY among free institutions? You see on what basis it rests — the will of the slave-holders. "In New York," we are told by high southern authority, "you may find loafer, and loco-foco, and agrarian, and the most corrupt and depraved of rabbles." But we ask you, where would your life be most secure if charged with crime,—amid the rabble of New York, or that of Clinton, Vicksburg, and Williamstown? We think we have fully proved our assertion respecting the disregard of human life felt by the slave-holding community; and of course their contempt for those legal barriers which are erected for its protection. Let us now inquire more particularly how far slavery is indeed a stable basis on which free institutions may securely rest.

8. DISREGARD FOR CONSTITUTIONAL OBLIGATIONS.

Governor McDuffie, in his speech of 1834 to the South Carolina Legislature, characterized the Federal Constitution as "that miserable mockery of blurred, and obliterated, and tattered parchment." Judging from their conduct, the slave-holders, while fully concurring with the Governor in his contempt for the national parchment, have quite as little respect for their own State constitution and laws.

The "tattered parchment" of which Mr. McDuffie speaks, declares that "the citizens of each State shall be entitled to all the privileges and immunities of citizens of the several States."—Art. IV, Sec. 2. Notwithstanding this express provision, there are in almost every slave State, if not in all, laws for seizing, imprisoning, and then selling as slaves for life, citizens having black or yellow complexions, entering within their borders. This is done under pretence that the individuals are supposed to be fugitives from bondage. When circumstances forbid such a supposition, other devices are adopted for nullifying the provision we have quoted. By a law of Louisiana, every free negro or mulatto, arriving on board any vessel as a *mariner* or passenger, shall be immediately imprisoned till the departure of the vessel, when he is to be compelled to depart in her. If such free negro or mulatto returns to the State, he is to be imprisoned for FIVE years.

The jailer of Savannah some time since reported TEN STEWARDS as being in his custody. These were free citizens of other States, deprived of their liberty solely on account of the complexion their Maker had given them, and in direct violation of the express language of the Federal Constitution. If any free negro or mulatto enters the State of Mississippi, for any cause, however urgent, any white citizen may cause him to be punished by the sheriff with thirty-nine lashes, and if he does not immediately thereafter leave the State, he is SOLD AS A SLAVE.

In Maryland, a free negro or mulatto, coming into the State, is fined $20, and if he returns he is fined $500, and on default of payment, is sold AS A SLAVE. Truly indeed have the slaveholders rendered the Constitution a blurred, obliterated, and tattered parchment. But whenever this same Constitution can, by the grossest perversion, be made instrumental in upholding and perpetuating human bondage, then it acquires, for the time, a marvellous sanctity in their eyes, and they are seized with a holy indignation at the very suspicion of its profanation.

The readiness with which southern Governors prefer the most false and audacious claims, under color of constitutional authority, exhibits a state of society in which truth and honor are but little respected.

In 1833, seventeen slaves effected their escape from Virginia in a boat, and finally reached New York. To recover these slaves *as such*, a judicial investigation in New York would be necessary, and the various claimants would be required to prove their property. A more convenient mode presented itself. The Governor of Virginia made a requisition on the Executive of New York for them as fugitive *felons*, and on this requisition, a warrant was issued for their arrest and surrender. The pretended felony was stealing the *boat* in which they had escaped.

In 1839, a slave escaped from Virginia on board of a vessel bound to New York. It was *suspected*, but without a particle of proof, that some of the crew had favored his escape; and immediately the master made oath that *three* of the sailors, naming them, had feloniously STOLEN the slave; and the Governor, well knowing there was no slave-market in New York, and that no man could there be held in slavery, had the hardihood to demand the surrender of the mariners on the charge of grand larceny; and, in his correspondence with the Governor of New York, declared the slave was worth six or seven hundred dollars, and remarked that *stealing* was "recognized as a CRIME by all laws, human and divine."

In 1841, a female slave, belonging to a man named Flournoy, in Georgia, was discovered on board a vessel about to sail for New York, and was recovered by her master. It was afterwards supposed from the woman's story, that she had been induced by one of the passengers to attempt her escape. Whereupon Flournoy made oath that John Greenman did feloniously STEAL his slave. But the Governor of New York had already refused to surrender citizens of his State on a charge so palpably false and absurd. It was therefore deemed necessary to trump up a very different charge against the accused; and hence Flournoy made a second affidavit, that John Greenman did *feloniously steal and take away three blankets, two shawls, three frocks, one pair of ear-rings, and two finger-rings, the property of deponent.* Armed with these affidavits, the Governor demanded the surrender of Greenman under the Constitution. Not an intimation was given by His Excellency, when he made the demand, of the *real facts* of the case, which, in a subsequent correspondence, he was compelled to admit. It turned out that the woman, instead of being stolen, went voluntarily, and no doubt joyfully, on board the vessel; and that the wearing apparel, &c., were the clothes and ornaments worn by her; nor was there a pretence that Greenman had ever touched them, or ever had them in his possession.

We have said that the slave-holders hold their *own* laws and constitutions in the same contempt as those of the Federal Government, whenever they conflict with the security and permanency of slavery. One of the most inestimable of constitutional privileges is TRIAL BY JURY; and this, as we have seen, is trampled under foot with impunity, at the mandate of the slave-holders. Even John Tyler, as it appears, is for inflicting summary punishment on abolitionists, by a Lynch club, "without resorting to any other tribunal."

We now proceed to inquire how far they respect the liberty of speech and of the press.

9. LIBERTY OF SPEECH.

The whole nation witnessed the long successful efforts of the slave-holders in Congress, by their various gag resolutions, and through the aid of recreant northern politicians, to destroy all freedom of debate adverse to "the peculiar institution." They were themselves ready to dwell, in debate, on the charms of human bondage; but when a member took the other side of the question, then, indeed, he was out of order, the Constitution was outraged, and the Union endangered. We all know the violent threats which have been used, to intimidate the friends of human rights from expressing their sentiments in the national legislature.

"As long," says Governor McDuffie to the South Carolina Legislature, "as long as the halls of Congress shall be *open* to the *discussion* of this question, we can have neither peace nor security."

The *Charleston Mercury* is, on this subject, very high authority; and in 1837 its editor announced that

"Public opinion in the South would now, we are sure, justify an *immediate resort to* FORCE *by the southern delegation, even on the* FLOOR OF CONGRESS, were they forthwith to SEIZE AND DRAG FROM THE HALL any man who dared to insult them, as that eccentric old showman, John Quincy Adams, has dared to do."

When so much malignity is manifested against the freedom of speech, in the very sanctuary of American liberty, it is not to be supposed that it will be tolerated in the house of bondage. We have already quoted a southern paper, which declares that the moment "any private individual attempts to lecture us on the evils and immorality of slavery, that very moment his tongue shall be cut out and cast upon the dunghill."

In Marion College, Missouri, there appeared some symptoms of anti-slavery feeling among the students. A Lynch club assembled, and the Rev. Dr. Ely, one of the professors, appeared before them, and denounced abolition, and submitted a series of resolutions passed by the faculty, and among them the following:

"We do hereby forbid all discussions and public meetings among the students upon the subject of domestic slavery." The Lynchers were pacified, and neither tore down the college nor hung up the professors; but before separating they resolved that they would oppose the elevation to office of any man entertaining abolition sentiments, and would withhold their countenance and support from every such member of the community. Indeed, it is obvious to any person attentive to the movements of the South, that the slave-holders dread *domestic* far more than foreign interference with their darling system.

10. LIBERTY OF THE PRESS.

The constitutions of all the slave States guarantee, in the most solemn and explicit terms, the liberty of the press; but it is well understood that there is one exception to its otherwise unbounded license: property in human flesh is too sacred to be assailed by the press. The attributes of the Deity may be discussed, but not the rights of the master. The characters of public, and even of private men, may be vilified at pleasure, provided no reproach is flung upon the *slave-holder*. Every abuse in Church or State may be ferreted out and exposed, except the cruelties practised upon the slaves, unless when they happen to exceed the ordinary standard of cruelty established by general usage. Every measure of policy may be advocated, except that of free labor; every question of right may be examined, except that of a man to himself; every dogma in theology may be propagated, except that of the sinfulness of the slave-code. The very instant the press ventures beyond its prescribed limits, the constitutional barriers erected for its protection sink into the dust, and a censorship, the more stern and vindictive from being illegal, crushes it into submission. The midnight burglary perpetrated upon the Charleston Post Office and the conflagration of the anti-slavery papers found in it, are well known. These papers had been sent to distinguished citizens, but it was deemed inexpedient to *permit* them to read facts and arguments against slavery. Vast pains have been taken to keep slave-holders as well as others ignorant of every fact and argument that militates against the system. Hence Mr. Calhoun's famous bill, authorizing every southern postmaster to abstract from the mails every paper relating to slavery. Hence the insane efforts constantly made to expurgate the literature of the world of all recognition of the rights of *black* men. Novels, annuals, poems, and histories, containing sentiments hostile to human bondage, are proscribed at the South, and northern publishers have had the extreme baseness to publish mutilated editions for the southern market.*

In some of the slave States laws have been passed establishing a censorship of the press, for the exclusive and special benefit of the slaveholders. Some time since an anti-slavery pamphlet was mailed at New York, directed to a gentleman in Virginia. Presently a letter was received from William Wilson, postmaster at Lexington, Va., saying:

> "I have to advise you that a law, passed at the last session of the Legislature of this State, which took effect on the first day of this month, makes it the duty of the postmasters or their assistants to report to some magistrate (under penalty of from $50 to $200), the receipt of all *such* publications at his office; and if, on examination, the magistrate is of opinion they come under the provision of the law, it is his duty to have them BURNT in his presence — *which operation was performed on the above mentioned pamphlet this morning.*"

The Rev. Robert J. Breckenridge, a well-known zealous opponent of abolition, edited, in 1835, "The Baltimore Religious Magazine." A number of this magazine contained an article from a correspondent, entitled "Bible-Slavery." The tone of this article not suiting the slave-breeders of Petersburg, (Va.,) the subscribers were deprived of the numbers forwarded to them through the post-office of that town. The magazines were taken from the office, and on the 8th of May, 1838, were burnt in the street, before the door of the public reading-room, in the *presence and by the direction of the mayor and recorder!*

* The Harpers, of New York, in reply to a letter from the South, complaining of the anti-slavery sentiments in a book they had recently published, stated: "Since the receipt of your letter we have published an edition of the 'Woods and Fields,' *in which the offensive matter has been omitted.*"

It is surely unnecessary to remark, that this Virginia law is in contemptuous violation of the constitution of Virginia, and of the authority of the Federal Government. The act of Congress requires each postmaster to deliver the papers which come to his office to the persons to whom they are directed, and they require him to take an oath to fulfil his duty. The Virginia law imposes duties on an officer over whom they have no control, utterly at variance with his oath, and the obligations under which he assumed the office. If the postmaster must select, under a heavy penalty, for a public bonfire, all papers bearing on slavery, why may he not be hereafter required to select, for the same fate, all papers hostile to Popery? Yet similar laws are now in force in various slave States.

Not only is this espionage exercised over the mail, but measures are taken to keep the community in ignorance of what is passing abroad in relation to slavery, and what opinions are elsewhere held respecting it.

On the first of August, 1842, an interesting address was delivered in Massachusetts, by the late Dr. Channing, in relation to West India emancipation, embracing, as was natural and proper, reflections on American slavery. This address was copied into a New York weekly paper, and the number containing it was offered for sale, as usual, by the agent of the periodical at Charleston. Instantly the agent was prosecuted by the South Carolina Association, and was held to bail in the sum of one thousand dollars, to answer for his CRIME. Presently after, this same agent received for sale a supply of "Dickens' Notes on the United States," but having before his eyes the fear of the slave-holders, he gave notice in the newspapers, that the book would "be submitted to highly intelligent members of the South Carolina Association for *inspection*, and IF the sale is approved by them, it will be for sale — if not, not." And so the population of one of the largest cities of the slave-region were not permitted to read a book they were all burning with impatience to see, till the volume had been first *inspected* by a self-constituted board of censors! The slave-holders, however, were in this instance afraid to put their power to the test; the people might have rebelled if forbidden to read the "Notes," and hence one of the most powerful, effective anti-slavery tracts yet issued from the press was permitted to be circulated, because people *would* read what Dickens had written. Surely, you will not accuse us of slander, when we say that the slave-holders have abolished the liberty of the press. Remember the assertion of the editor of the *Missouri Argus:* "Abolition editors in the slave States will not dare to avow their opinions: it would be INSTANT DEATH to them."

11. MILITARY WEAKNESS.

A distinguished foreigner, after travelling in the Southern States, remarked that the very aspect of the country bore testimony that, defenceless and exposed as they are, it would be madness to hazard a civil war; and surely no people in the world have more cause to shrink from an appeal to arms. We find at the South no one element of military strength. Slavery, as we have seen, checks the progress of population, of the arts, of enterprise, and of industry. But above all, the laboring class, which in other countries affords the materials of which armies are composed, is regarded at the South as a most deadly foe; and the sight of a thousand negroes with arms in their hands, would send a thrill of terror through the stoutest hearts, and excite a panic which no number of the veteran troops of Europe could produce. Even now, laws are in force to keep arms out of the hands of a population which ought to be a reliance in danger, but which is dreaded by day and night, in peace and war.

During our revolutionary war, when the idea of negro emancipation had scarcely entered the imagination of any of our citizens —when there were no "fanatic abolitionists," no "incendiary publications," no "treasonable" anti-slavery associations; in those palmy days of slavery, no small portion of the southern militia were withdrawn from the defence of the country to protect the slave-holders from the vengeance of their own bondmen! This you would be assured was abolition slander, were not the fact recorded in the national archives. *The Secret Journal of Congress* (Vol. I, p. 105) contains the following remarkable and instructive record:

"*March 29th*, 1779.—The committee appointed to take into consideration the *circumstances of the Southern States*, and the ways and means for *their* safety and defence, report, That the State of South Carolina (as represented by the delegates of the said State, and by Mr. Huger, who has come hither at the request of the Governor of said State, on purpose to explain the particular circumstances thereof,) is UNABLE to make any effectual efforts with militia, by reason of the great proportion of citizens *necessary to remain at home, to prevent insurrection among the negroes*, and to prevent the desertion of them to the enemy. That the state of the country, and the great number of these people among them, expose the inhabitants to *great danger*, from the endeavors of the enemy to excite them to revolt or desert."

At the first census, in 1790, eleven years after this report, and when the slaves had unquestionably greatly increased their numbers, they were only 107,094 *fewer* than the whites. If, then, these slaves exposed their masters "to great danger," and the militia of South Carolina were obliged to *stay at home* to protect their families, not from the foreign invaders, but the domestic enemies, what would be the condition of the little blustering nullifying State, with a foreign army on her shores, and 335,000 slaves ready to aid it, while her own white population, *militia* and all, is but as two whites to three blacks?

Slave-holders, in answer to the abolitionists, are wont to boast of the fidelity and attachment of their slaves; among themselves they freely avow their dread of these same faithful and attached slaves, and are fertile in expedients to guard against their vengeance.

It is natural that we should fear those whom we are conscious of having deeply injured, and all history and experience testify that fear is a cruel passion. Hence the shocking severity with which, in all slave countries, attempts to shake off an unrighteous yoke are punished. So late even as 1822, certain slaves in Charleston were *suspected* of an *intention* to rise and assert their freedom. No overt act was committed, but certain blacks were found who professed to testify against their fellows, and some, it is said, confessed their intentions.

On this ensued one of the most horrible judicial butcheries on record. It is not deemed necessary, in the chivalrous Palmetto State, to give grand and petit juries the trouble of indicting and trying slaves, even when their lives are at stake. A court, consisting of two justices of the peace and five freeholders, was convened for the trial of the accused, and the following were the results of their labors:—

July 2	6	hanged,
" 12	2	"
" 26	22	"
" 30	4	"
August 9	1	"
Total	35	"

Now let it be remembered that this sacrifice of human life was made by one of the lowest tribunals in the State; a tribunal consisting of two petty magistrates and five freeholders, appointed for the occasion, not possessing a judicial rank, nor professing to be learned in the law; in short, a tribunal which would not be trusted to decide the title to an acre of ground — we refer not to individuals composing the court, but to the court itself;— a court which has not power to take away the land of a white man, hangs black men by dozens!

Listen to the confessions of the slave-holders with regard to their happy dependents; the men who are so contented under the patriarchal system, and whose condition might well excite the envy of northern laborers, "the great democratic rabble."

Governor Hayne, in his message of 1833, warned the South Carolina Legislature, that "a state of *military preparation* must always be with us a state of perfect *domestic* security. A profound peace, and consequent apathy, may expose us to the danger of *domestic insurrection.*" So it seems the happy slaves are to be kept from insurrection by a state of military preparation. We have seen that, during the revolutionary *war*, the Carolina militia were kept at home watching the slaves, instead of meeting the British in the field; but now it seems the same task awaits the militia in a season of profound peace. Another South Carolian* admonishes his countrymen thus:

"Let it never be forgotten that our negroes are truly the Jacobins of the country; that they are the anarchists, and the domestic enemy, THE COMMON ENEMY OF CIVILIZED SOCIETY, AND THE BARBARIANS WHO WOULD, IF THEY COULD, BECOME THE DESTROYERS OF OUR RACE."

Again, "Hatred to the whites, with the exception, in some cases, of attachment to the person and family of the master, is nearly universal among the black population. We have then a FOE, cherished in our very bosoms—a foe WILLING TO DRAW OUR LIFE-BLOOD whenever the opportunity is offered; in the mean time intent on doing us all the mischief in his power." *Southern Religious Telegraph.*

In a debate in the Kentucky Legislature, in 1841, Mr. Harding, opposing the repeal of the law prohibiting the importation of slaves from other States, and looking forward to the time when the blacks would greatly out-number the whites, exclaimed:

"In such a state of things, suppose an insurrection of the slaves to take place. The master has become timid and fearful, the slave bold and daring—the white men, overpowered with a sense of superior numbers on the part of the slaves, cannot be embodied together; *every man must guard his own hearth and fireside.* No man would even dare for an hour to leave his own habitation; if he did, he would expect on his return to find his wife and children massacred. But the slaves, with but little more than the shadow of opposition before them, armed with the consciousness of superior force and superior numbers on their side, animated with the hope of liberty, and maddened with the spirit of revenge, embody themselves in every neighborhood, and furiously march over the country, visiting every neighborhood with all the horrors of civil war and bloodshed. And thus the yoke would be transferred from the black to the white man, and the master fall a bleeding victim to his own slave."

Such are the terrific visions which are constantly presenting themselves to the affrighted imaginations of the slave-holders; such the character which, *among themselves,* they attribute to their own domestics.

Attend to one more, and that one an extraordinary confession:

"We of the South are emphatically surrounded by a dangerous class of beings—degraded and stupid savages, who, if they could but

* The author of "A Refutation of the Calumnies inculcated against the Southern and Western States."

once entertain the idea that immediate and unconditional death would not be their portion, would re-act the St. Domingo tragedy. But a consciousness, with all their stupidity, that a ten-fold force, superior in discipline, *if not in barbarity*, would gather from the *four corners of the United States*, and slaughter them, keeps them in subjection. But to the *non-slaveholding States* particularly, are we indebted for a permanent safeguard against insurrection. Without their assistance, the white population of the South would be *too weak* to quiet the innate desire for liberty, which is ever ready to act itself out with every rational creature." *Maysville Intelligencer.*

And now we ask you, if all these declarations and confessions be true,— and who can doubt it? — what must be their inevitable condition, should their soil be invaded by a foreign foe, bearing the standard of EMANCIPATION?

In perfect accordance with the above confession, that to the non-slaveholding States the South is indebted for a permanent safeguard against insurrection, Mr. Underwood, of Kentucky, uttered these pregnant words in a debate, in 1842, in Congress: "THE DISSOLUTION OF THE UNION WILL BE THE DISSOLUTION OF SLAVERY."

The action of the Federal Government is, we know, controlled by the slave interest; and what testimony does that action bear to the military weakness of the South? Let the reports of its high functionaries answer.

The Secretary of War, in his report for 1842, remarked:

"The works intended for the more remote southern portion of our territory, particularly require attention. Indications are already made of designs of the worst character against that region, in the event of hostilities from a *certain quarter*, to which we cannot be insensible."

The Secretary's fears had been evidently excited by the organization of *black* regiments in the British West Indies, and the threats of certain English writers, that a war between the two countries would result in the liberation of the slaves. The report from the Quarter-Master, General Jessup, a southern man, betrays the same anxiety, and in less ambiguous terms:

"In the event of a war," says he, "with either of the great European powers possessing colonies in the West Indies, there will be danger of the peninsula of Florida being occupied by BLACKS from the Islands. A proper regard for the security of our *Southern States* requires that prompt and efficient measures be adopted to prevent such a state of things."

The Secretary of the Navy, a slave-holder, *hints* his fears in cautious circumlocution. Speaking of the event of a war with any considerable maritime power, he says:

"It would be a war of incursions aimed at *revolution.* The first blow would be struck at us through our *institutions;*" he means, of course, "the peculiar institution." He then proceeds to show that the enemy would seek success "in arraying what are supposed to be the hostile elements of our *social system* against each other;" and he admits, that "even in the best event, war on our soil would be the more expensive, the more embarrassing, and the more HORRIBLE in its effects, by compelling us at the same time to oppose an enemy in the field, and *to guard* against all attempts to *subvert our social system.*"

In plain language, an invading enemy would strike the first blow at the slave system, and thus aim at revolution, — a revolution that would give liberty to two and a half millions of human beings; and such a war would be very embarrassing to the slave-holders, and the more horrible, because, as formerly in South Carolina, a large share of their military force would necessarily be employed, not in fighting the enemy, but in guarding the SOCIAL, that is, the "patriarchal system."

No persons are more sensible of their hazardous situation than the slave-holders themselves, and hence, as is common with people who are secretly conscious of their own weakness, they attempt to supply the want of strength by a bullying insolence, hoping to effect by intimidation what they well know can be effected in no other way. This game has long been played, and with great success, in Congress. It has been attempted in our negotiations with Great Britain, and has signally failed.

The slave-holders, whatever may be their vaunts, are conscious of their military weakness, and shrink from any contest which may cause a foreign army to plant the standard of emancipation upon their soil. The very idea of an armed negro startles their fearful imaginations. This is disclosed on innumerable occasions, but was conspicuously manifested in a debate in the Senate. In July, 1842, a bill to regulate enlistments in the naval service being under consideration, Mr. CALHOUN proposed an amendment, that negroes should be enlisted only as *cooks* and *stewards.* He thought it a matter of *great consequence* not to admit blacks into our vessels of national defence. Mr.

BENTON thought *all arms*, whether on land or sea, ought to be borne by the white race.

Mr. BAGBY:—"In the southern portion of the Union, the great object was to *keep arms and a knowledge of arms* out of the hands of the blacks. The subject addressed itself to every southern heart. Self-preservation was the first law of nature, and the South must look to that."

On the motion of Mr. PRESTON, the bill was so amended as to include the army.

And think you that men, thus in awe of their own dependents, shuddering at a musket in the hands of a black, and with a population of two millions and a half of these dreaded slaves, will expose themselves to the tremendous consequences of a union between their domestic and foreign enemies? Of the four who voted against the British treaty, probably not one would have given the vote he did, had he not known to a certainty that the treaty would be ratified.

Think not we are disposed to ridicule the fears of the slaveholders, or to question their personal courage. God knows their perils are real, and not imaginary; and who can question, that with a hostile *British* army in the heart of Virginia or Alabama, the whole slave-region would presently become one vast scene of horror and desolation? Heretofore the invaders of our soil were themselves interested in slave property; *now* they would be zealous emancipationists, and they would be accompanied by the most terrific vision which could meet the eye of a slaveholder, regiments of *black troops*, fully equipped and disciplined. Surely such a state of things might well appall the bravest heart, and palsy the stoutest arm.

We have called your attention to the practical influence of slavery on various points deeply affecting the public prosperity and happiness. These are:

1. Increase of population.
2. State of education.
3. Industry and enterprise.
4. Feeling towards the laboring classes.
5. State of religion.
6. State of morals.
7. Disregard for human life.
8. Disregard for constitutional obligations.
9. Liberty of speech.
10. Liberty of the press.
11. Military weakness.

You will surely agree with us, that in many of these particulars, the southern States are sunk far below the ordinary condition of civilized nations.

Let us inquire whether the inferior and unhappy condition of the slave States can be ascribed to any natural disadvantage, or to any partial or unjust legislation by the Federal Government.

In the first place, the slave States cannot pretend that they have not received their full share of the national domain, and that the narrowness of their territorial limits has retarded the development of their enterprise and resources. The area of the slave States is nearly *double* that of the free. New York has acquired the title of the *Empire* State; yet she is inferior in size to Virginia, Missouri, Georgia, Louisiana, or North Carolina.

Nor can it be maintained that the free States are in advance of the slave States, because from an earlier settlement they had the start in the race of improvement. Virginia is not only the largest, but the *oldest* settled State in the confederacy. She, together with Delaware, Maryland, North Carolina and South Carolina, were all settled before Pennsylvania.

Nor will any slave-holder admit, that Providence has scattered his gifts with a more sparing hand at the South than at the North. The richness of their soil, the salubrity of their climate, the number and magnitude of their rivers, are themes on which they delight to dwell. Hence the moral difference between the two sections of our republic must arise from other than natural causes. It appears also that this difference is becoming wider and wider. Of this fact we could give various proofs; but let one suffice.

At the first census in 1790, the free population of the present free States and Territories was	1,930,125
Of the slave States and Territories,	1,394,847
Difference,	535,278
By the last census, 1840, the same population in the free States and Territories was	9,782,415
In the slave States and Territories,	4,793,738
Difference,	4,988,677

Thus it appears that in 1790 the free population of the South was seventy-two per cent. of that of the North, and that in 1840 it was only forty-nine per cent.; while the difference in 1840 is more than *nine* times as great as it was in 1790.

Fifty years have given the North an increased preponderance of about four and a half millions of free citizens. Another fifty years will increase this preponderance in a vastly augmented ratio. And now we ask you, why this downward course? Is it because the interests of the slave-holders are not represented in the national councils? Let us see. We have already shown you that the *free* population is only forty-nine per cent. of that of the northern States; that is, the inhabitants of the free States are more than *double* the free inhabitants of the slave States. Now, what is the proportion of members of Congress from the two sections?

In the Senate, the slave States have precisely as many as the free; and in the lower House, their members are sixty-five per cent. of those from the free States.*

The Senate has a veto on every law; and as one half of that body are slave-holders, it follows, of course, that no law can be passed without their consent. Nor has any bill passed the Senate since the organization of the government, but by the votes of slave-holders. It is idle, therefore, for them to impute their depressed condition to unjust and partial legislation, since they have from the very first controlled the action of Congress. Not a law has been passed, not a treaty ratified, but by their votes.

Nor is this all. Appointments under the Federal Government are made by the President, with the consent of the Senate, and of course the slave-holders have, and always have had, a veto on every appointment. There is not an officer of the Federal Government to whose appointment slave-holding members of the Senate have not consented. Yet all this gives but an inadequate idea of the political influence exercised by the *people* of the slave States in the election of President, and consequently over the policy of his administration. In consequence of the

* 135 from the free and 88 members from the slave States. According to *free* population, the South would have only 66 members.

peculiar apportionment of Presidential electors among the States, and the operation of the rule of *federal numbers* — whereby, for the purpose of estimating the representative population, five slaves are counted as three white men — most extraordinary results are exhibited at every election of President. In the election of 1848, the electors chosen were 290; of these 169 were from the free, and 121 from the slave States.

The popular vote in the free States was 2,029,551, or one elector to 12,007 voters.

The popular vote in the slave States was 845,050, or one elector to 7,545 voters.*

Even this disproportion, enormous as it is, is greatly aggravated in regard to particular States.

New York	gave 455,761	votes, and	had	36	electors.
Virginia, Maryland, N. Carolina	gave 242,547	"	"	36	"
Ohio	gave 328,489	"	"	28	"
Delaware, Georgia, Louisiana, Alabama, Arkansas, Florida, Texas	gave 237,811	"	"	38	"

These facts address themselves to the understanding of all, and prove, beyond cavil, that the slave States have a most unfair and unreasonable representation in Congress, and a very disproportionate share in the election of President.

Nor can these States complain that they are stinted in the distribution of the *patronage* of the national government. The rule of *federal numbers,* confined by the Constitution to the apportionment of representatives, has been extended, by the influence of the slave-holders, to other and very different subjects. Thus, the distribution among the States of the surplus revenue, and of the proceeds of the public lands, was made according to this same iniquitous rule.

* South Carolina had nine electors, chosen by the Legislature. These are deducted in the calculation.

It is not to be supposed that the slave-holders have failed to avail themselves of their influence in the Federal Government. A very brief statement will convince you, that if they are now feeble and emaciated, it is not because they have been deprived of their share of the loaves and fishes.

By law, midshipmen and cadets, at West Point, are appointed according to the federal ratio; thus have the slave-holders secured to themselves an additional number of officers in the army and navy, on account of their slaves.

Reflect for a moment on the vast patronage wielded by the President of the United States, and then recollect, that should the present incumbent (General Taylor) serve his full term, the office will have been filled no less than *fifty-two* years out of sixty-four by slave-holders! *

Of twenty-one Secretaries of State, appointed up to 5th of March, 1849, only six have been taken from the free States.

For thirty-seven years out of sixty the chair of the House of Representatives has been filled, and its committees appointed by slave-holders.

Of the Judges of the Supreme Court, eighteen have been taken from the slave, and but fourteen from the free States.

In 1842, the United States were represented at foreign courts by nineteen Ministers and Charges d'Affaires. Of these fat offices, no less than thirteen were assigned to slave-holders!

Surely, surely, if the South be wanting in every element of prosperity — if ignorance, barbarity and poverty be her characteristics, it is not because she has not exercised her due influence in the general government, or received her share of its honors and emoluments.

PROSPECTS FOR THE FUTURE.

If, then, with all the natural and political advantages we have enumerated, the progress of the slave States is still downward, and has been so, compared with the other sections of the country, since the first organization of the Government, what are the

* Except one month by General Harrison

anticipations of the distant future, which sober reflection authorizes us to form? The causes which now retard the increase of their population must continue to operate, so long as slavery lasts. Emigrants from the North, and from foreign countries, will, as at present, avoid their borders, within which no attractions will be found for virtue and industry. On the other hand, many of the young and enterprising will flee from the lassitude, the anarchy, the wretchedness engendered by slavery, and seek their fortunes in lands where law affords protection, and where labor is honored and rewarded.

In the meantime, especially in the cotton States, the slaves will continue to increase in a ratio far beyond the whites, and will at length acquire a fearful preponderance.

At the first census, in every slave State there was a very large majority of whites; now, the slaves out-number the whites in South Carolina, Mississippi, and Louisiana, and the next census will unquestionably add Florida and Alabama, and probably Georgia, to the number of negro States.

And think you that this is the conntry, and this the age, in which the republican maxim that the MAJORITY must govern, can be long and barbarously reversed? Think you that the majority of the PEOPLE in the cotton States, cheered and encouraged as they will be by the sympathy of the world, and the example of the West Indies, will forever tamely submit to be beasts of burden for a few lordly planters? And remember, we pray you, that the number and physical strength of the negroes will increase in a much greater ratio than that of their masters.

In 1700 the whites were to the slaves in

N. Carolina as	2.80 to 1,	now as 1.97 to 1
S. Carolina,	1.31 to 1,	" .79 to 1
Georgia,	1.76 to 1,	" 1.44 to 1
Tennessee,	13.35 to 1,	" 3.49 to 1
Kentucky,	5.16 to 1,	" 3.23 to 1

Maryland and Virginia, the great breeding States, have reduced their stock within the last few years, having been tempted, by high prices, to ship off thousands and tens of thousands to the markets of Louisiana, Alabama, and Mississippi.

But these markets are already glutted, and human flesh has fallen in value from fifty to seventy-five per cent. Nor is it probable that the great staple of Virginia and Maryland will hereafter afford a bounty on its production. In these States slave-labor is unprofitable, and the bondman is of but little value, save as an article of exportation. The cotton cultivation in the East Indies, by cheapening the article, will close the markets in the South, and thus it guarantees the abolition of slavery in the breeding States. When it shall be found no longer profitable to raise slaves for the market, the stock on hand will be driven South and sold for what it may fetch, and free labor substituted in its place. This process will be attended with results disastrous to the cotton States. To Virginia and Maryland, it will open a new era of industry, prosperity and wealth; and the industrious poor, the "mean whites" of the South, will remove within their borders, thus leaving the slave-holders more defenceless than ever.

And what will be the condition of such of the poor whites as shall then remain in the slave States? The change to which we have referred will necessarily aggravate every present evil. Ignorance, vice, idleness, lawless violence, dread of insurrection, anarchy, and a haughty and vindictive aristocracy will all combine with augmented energy in crushing them to the earth. And from what quarter can they look for redemption? Think you the planting nobility will ever grant freedom to their serfs, from sentiments of piety or patriotism? Remember that the clergy of all sects and ranks, many of them "Christian brokers in the trade of blood," unite in bestowing their benedicton on the system as a *Christian* institution, and in teaching the slave-holders that they wield the whip as European monarchs the sceptre, "by the grace of God." Remember that the beautiful and affecting contrast between the prosperity of the North and the desolation of the South, already presented to you, was drawn by W. C. Preston, of *hanging* notoriety. The great slave-holders have no idea of surrendering the personal importance and the political influence they derive from their slaves. The Calhouns, Footes, and Prestons, all go for everlasting slavery.

Unquestionably there are many of the smaller slave-holders who would embrace abolition sentiments, were they permitted to examine the subject; but at present they are kept in ignorance. If, then, the fetters of the slave are not to be broken by the master, by whom is he to be liberated? In the course of time, a hostile army, invited by the weakness or the arrogance of the South, may land on her shores. Then, indeed, emancipation will be given, but the gift may be bathed in the blood of the whites and of their children. Or the people — for they will be THE PEOPLE — may resolve to be free, and the dearest interests of thousands may be sacrificed in the contest.

Such, inhabitants of New Mexico and California, is the detestable institution which a few haughty and selfish men are endeavoring to force upon you in order to augment their own political power, and to open new markets for their human cattle; and such are the calamities which their success will entail upon you and your posterity for ages to come. Every dictate of patriotism and of Christian benevolence impels us to resist to the uttermost the extension of this abomination of desolation over the new, fair, and vast addition recently made to our Federal Union. Much as we may prize this splendid acquisition, may it be forever lost to us rather than it should be converted by the American people into a region of ignorance, vice, misery, and degradation by the establishment of human bondage. We wish you to be a free and happy portion of our great Republic, but if the condition of your union with us be your submission to the mandates of the slave-holders, we counsel you, we implore you, by all your obligations to your God, yourselves, your children, and to the opinions of the world, to spurn the loathsome, the sinful condition. You have all the elements essential to the creation of a great, prosperous, and independent empire. If you cannot be free, happy, and virtuous in union with us, be free, happy, and virtuous under a government of your own. But you are not reduced to such an alternative. The slave-holders have refused you a territorial government — form one for yourselves, and declare that no slave shall taint the air you breathe. Let no feudal lord with his hosts of serfs come among you to rob you of your equal share of the rich deposits of your soil — tolerate no servile caste, kept in ignorance and degradation to minister to the power and wealth of an oppressive aristocracy. Be firm and resolute in declaring for independence, unless exempted from the curse of slavery, and the whole North will rally in your behalf. The slave-holders are losing their influence, and are divided among themselves, while their northern allies, withering under the scorn of public opinion, are daily deserting their standard. Be true to yourselves, and your northern friends will be true to you, and ere long you will be received into the Union on the same liberal, safe, and honorable terms on which your neighbors of Oregon have already been admitted. A glorious future of power, opulence, and happiness opens before you. Up, quit yourselves like men, and may the favor of God and the blessings of generations to come rest upon you.

New York, August, 1849.

LETTER

TO HON. WILLIAM NELSON, M. C.,

ON MR. CLAY'S COMPROMISE.

New York, February 11, 1850.

My Dear Sir: — As one of your immediate constituents, permit me to express to you my views on the resolutions lately submitted to the Senate by Mr. Clay. They are skilfully drawn, and their true import seems to me to be generally misunderstood, and in many instances intentionally misrepresented. Various considerations combine to render these resolutions acceptable to that class of our northern politicians, who are anxious to be popular at home, without forfeiting their share of the patronage which is dispensed at Washington, by the slave power. The resolutions are eight in number, and I will examine them in their order.

1. This proposes the admission of California as a State, without the imposition by Congress of any restriction on the subject of slavery, and "*with suitable boundaries.*" These words imply that the present boundaries are unsuitable, and must be altered. Let me now call your attention to the *true reason* for this reservation about boundaries, and respecting which the resolution is

silent. During the war, and before the cession of any territory, the House of Representatives passed the Wilmot Proviso, prohibiting slavery in *all* the territory that might be acquired. On this, the South, with one voice, declared that they would not submit to the exclusion of slavery *south* of 36° 30′. The Legislature of Alabama resolved that they would not recognize "any enactment of the Federal Government which has for its object the prohibition of slavery in any territory to be acquired by conquest or treaty SOUTH of the line of the Missouri compromise." At a public meeting in Charleston, and at which I believe Mr. Calhoun was present, it was resolved that it would be debasing and dishonorable to submit to the prohibition of slavery "beyond what is already yielded by the Missouri compromise;" and innumerable have been the offers and efforts of southern politicians to extend the compromise line to the Pacific. Hence it is not the exclusion of slavery in California to the north of that line, that offends the South; and to admit this anti-slavery State, bounded on the south by 36° 30′, is doing no more than what the South has consented should be done, and is in no sense a compromise. But the free State of California extends *south* of this line, and hence her southern boundary is *unsuitable*, and hence Mr. Clay's resolution makes a tacit provision for depriving the State of so much of her territory as his southern friends have resolved shall not be consecrated to freedom. Mr. Foote, of Mississippi, observed in relation to this very resolution, "I see *no objection* to admitting all California *above* the line of 36° 30′ into the Union, provided another new slave State be laid off within the present limits of Texas." To this laying off another new slave State, Mr. Clay's compromise opposes no obstacle! Had Mr. Clay proposed the admission of California with its "present boundaries," his offer would so far have been a compromise, as to concede something to freedom as a consideration for the surrender of the Wilmot Proviso.

2. The next resolution declares, that "*as slavery does not exist by law, and is not likely to be introduced*" into any of the conquered territories, they should be organized under territorial

governments, without any restriction on the subject of slavery. The proposed assertion by Congress that slavery does not exist *by law* in the territories, is hailed as an all-sufficient balm to the consciences of those who recoil with horror at the idea of being in any degree responsible for the extension of human bondage. And what, let me ask, is this declaration, but the enunciation of a bald truism? We all know there is no law, Mexican or American, recognizing slavery in the territories. Mr. Clay adroitly avoids drawing any inference from this acknowledged fact, but expects the good people of the North will draw for themselves the inference, that because slavery does not exist by law, *therefore* it is prohibited by law. Property in elephants does not exist *by law*, in New York, but still it exists, because it is not prohibited by law. Mr. Clay well knows that Mr. Calhoun and the great mass of the slave-holders contend that *in the absence of a prohibitory law*, men, women and children, as well as horses and sheep, may be held as property in any territory in the United States; and this doctrine Mr. Clay himself nowhere denies. Nay, further, Mr. Calhoun insists, and I believe truly, that slavery *never has been established by law* in any country — that *after* property in man has been acquired, *then*, and not before, laws are passed to protect it. The slave-holders ask for no act of Congress authorizing them to carry their property into the territories. All they ask is that no *prohibitory law* shall be passed, and then they will carry their slaves where they please, and keep them by their own strong hand without law, till in their territorial legislatures they shall pass such laws on the subject as they shall find needful. Not a word in Mr. Clay's compromise contravenes this legal theory, or prevents its reduction to practice. Slavery did once exist by law in these territories; why does it not now? Mr. Clay answers the question by telling us that Mexican law abolished it. Now he perfectly well knows that the Mexican law not only abolished but *prohibited* slavery. If that law was repealed by the conquest, then the old law was revived, and slavery *does now exist by law*. If the law was not repealed by the conquest, then the law is still in force, and slavery is *now prohibited by law*. Why, then, does not Mr. Clay fairly and honestly declare that slavery is now *prohibited* by law? Because this would indeed be a compromise, and would render the Proviso nugatory, and would secure the territories from the curse of slavery. The very omission of such a declaration implies a denial of an existing prohibition, and in such denial he well knows the whole South concurs. So far, then, is Mr. Clay's inconsequential truism from being a compromise, that it surrenders to the South even more than she has demanded, and throws open to the slave-holders the whole territory north as well as south of the Missouri line. But to reconcile the North to this total surrender, they are to be favored by Congress with the *opinion* that IT IS NOT LIKELY that slavery will be introduced into any part of the conquered territory. What is only improbable, is at least *possible*, and hence this legislative *opinion* would, in fact, be a solemn and official declaration, that there is no *legal* prohibition to the introduction of slavery. It is not pretended that this *opinion* which Congress is to volunteer, is to have any legal force whatsoever. But what if time shall prove the opinion to have been erroneous; will it be any consolation to the North for having by their act blighted regions with human bondage, that they had been fooled by an *opinion?*

Mr. Downs, of Louisiana, in reply to Mr. Clay, asserted that there were already in the territories "some four or five hundred slaves;" and another member declared that there would now have been plenty of slaves there had not their masters been apprehensive of the Proviso. If Mr. Clay is correct in his opinion, the slave-holders have been strangely mistaken. It was openly avowed during the war, that the territory to be conquered south of 36° 30′ would be a slave region. Before our army entered the city of Mexico, we were offered all Texas proper, and the whole of New Mexico and California *north* of thirty-seven degrees, an extent of territory equal to nine States of the size of New York. The offer was rejected, and thousands were slaughtered to obtain territory *south* of 36° 30′, to be peopled with slaves. From the first mention of the Proviso, our northern editors and politicians in the slave interest opposed it as unnecessary, because, as they assured us, the soil and climate of these territories were unsuitable to slave labor. The slave-holders knew better, and never endorsed the falsehood of their allies. Mr. Waddy Thompson, of South Carolina, Minister to Mexico, announced to his brethren, writing of California, "Sugar, rice and cotton find there their own congenial clime." *Recollections of Mexico*, p. 234.

Did the South make war upon Mexico only to acquire free territory? Is she now threatening disunion and civil war for a privilege she "is not likely" to exercise?

Upon what does Mr. Clay rest his strange, unnatural opinion? Almost exclusively on the exclusion of slavery from the California constitution. He does not pretend that this exclusion was owing to the unfitness of the soil and climate for slave labor. We all know that the unexpected discovery of gold suddenly collected in California a large *northern population*, naturally averse to slavery, and jealous of the competition of slave labor in digging gold. But does gold exist in Deseret or New Mexico? or is there a large northern population in California, south of 30° 30′? Is it logical to infer that slavery is not likely to be introduced into these territories, even with the sanction of Congress, because under totally different circumstances it has been excluded from California? New Mexico is separated by an imaginary line from Texas, and about half of it is claimed by that slave State. Is it likely that Texan slave-holders will not cross the line with their property, or occupy territory they claim as their own?

The settlers in Deseret have formed a constitution virtually allowing slavery, by not prohibiting it. The gold diggers in California are concentrated far north of 36° 30′; the city of San Francisco is also north of that line, while south of it is a large area, where there is little to obstruct the introduction of slavery. Under these circumstances, there are probably very few men in Congress who would dare on their oaths, to affirm the *opinion* expressed by Mr. Clay. That opinion is at best a calculation of *chances;* a calculation on which no man would hazard a thousand dollars; yet this miserable calculation is offered to the North as a compensation for the surrender of all the political and moral blessings which the Proviso would SECURE.

Mr. Clay utterly demolishes Gen. Cass's argument against the constitutionality of the Proviso, and affirms most positively the right of Congress to prohibit slavery in the territories. But how stands the question of duty and moral consistency between these two gentlemen? Undeniably in favor of the General. He has not, indeed, undertaken to solve the nice and difficult question, whether human bondage is a curse or a blessing. He is sensibly alive to the atrocity of flogging two or three Hungarian women, but makes no comment on laws which subject thousands and tens of thousands of American women to the lash. He calls upon the nation to express its indignation at the execution of a few Hungarian insurgents taken with arms in their hands, but gives no opinion how far it would be right or wrong to shoot certain of his own countrymen, if taken in revolt against worse than Austrian oppression. But he contends that whatever may be the moral character of slavery, Congress has no constitutional right to prohibit it, and *therefore* ought not to prohibit it. On the other hand, Mr. Clay frankly declares that slavery is wrong, "a grievous wrong," that to propagate slavery is to propagate WRONG. He affirms the constitutional power of Congress to prohibit this propagation of wrong, and then calls upon Congress to permit slave-holders to propagate this wrong when and where they please over the whole wide extent of our conquered territory, with the single exception of what may be included within the State of California. Before God and man, Gen. Cass's conclusion from his *premises* is justified, while the conclusion drawn by Mr. Clay from his premises is condemned as hostile to morality and humanity.

3. This resolution merely gives to Texas more territory than she is entitled to, and less than she demands, and is so far a compromise of territorial claims; but in no degree a compromise between the friends and enemies of human rights, since what is to be taken from Texas is to be immediately thrown open to the slave-holders.

4. Texas had, before annexation, pledged her duties on foreign commerce as security to certain creditors. These duties, by annexation were surrendered to the United States. Mr. Clay proposes that the United States shall assume the debts due to these creditors if Texas will relinquish her claims on New Mexico. If justice requires the nation to assume these debts, their assumption ought not to depend on the cession of territory by Texas. If in justice we do not owe these debts, their payment by us will in fact be a gratuity to Texas for the relinquishment of one of the most impudent and fraudulent claims ever made. We have official information, communicated by General Jackson to Congress, that the Texans, when defining the boundaries of their new-born republic, at first determined to include *California;* and beyond all question they had then as much right to San Francisco as they now have to Santa Fé. The proposition of Mr. Clay is therefore to pay Texas for territory to which he admits she has no title, and then to throw open the territory so purchased to the slave-holders. In this, I can see no concession to the North.

5. Congress is to declare it inexpedient to abolish slavery in the District of Columbia, except with the assent of Maryland and the people of the District, and making compensation to the slave-holders. The unlimited power of Congress to abolish slavery in the district is fully conceded, yet he calls on Congress not to do, what many of its members and vast multitudes of their constituents believe it their moral duty to do. In this proposal I can find no other compromise but that of conscience.

6. The next proposal is to prohibit the importation of slaves into the District *for sale.* In other words, the inhabitants are to have a monopoly of the trade in human beings. These good people are not to be deprived of the privilege of importing as many slaves as they may want for their own use, nor of selling husbands, and wives, and children, to be transported to the extremities of the Union; but foreign traders shall no longer be permitted to glut the Washington market with their wares. The moment the resolution passes, human chattels will rise in value

in the capital of our Republic. I object not to the abolition of the trade, since it will remove one of the many abominations with which slavery has disgraced the seat of our national government; but I deny that the proposition involves the slightest concession on the part of the slave-holders. Says Mr. Clay himself, "Almost every slave-holding State in the Union has exercised its power to prohibit the introduction of slaves as merchandise." The power is exercised or not, according to convenience, and as it is thought most profitable to breed or to import slaves.

7. We now come to a grand specific for giving ease to northern consciences, for allaying all irritation, and for restoring a general healthful action throughout the present morbid system of the confederacy! I will give the recipe in full: "*Resolved*, That *more effectual provision* ought to be made by law for the restitution and delivery of persons bound to service or labor in any State, who may escape into any other State or territory of this Union." That I may not be accused of injustice to Mr. Clay in my subsequent remarks, I will quote from his speech on this point: "I do not say, sir, that a *private individual* is obliged to make the tour of his whole State, in order to assist the owner of a slave to recover his property; but I do say, *if he is present* when the owner of a slave is about to assert his rights and regain possession of his property, *that he and every one present*, whether officer or agent of the State government, or private individual, is *bound* to assist in the execution of the laws of their country." "I will go with the farthest senator from the South in this body to make *penal* laws to impose the *heaviest sanctions* upon the recovery of fugitive slaves, and the restoration of them to their owners."

Such is the panacea, and such is the manner in which our medical adviser proposes to administer it. He must not be surprised should some difficulty be experienced in compelling the patient to swallow the draught.

Mr. Clay has long been a favorer of those field sports in which the prey is MAN, and he has the merit, it is believed, of being the first to conceive the grand idea of securing a national intercommunity in these sports, by means of international treaties. So early as the 19th June, 1826, as Secretary of State, he proposed to the British government to throw the Canadas open for this sport, and in return, to British sportsmen should be accorded the privilege of hunting West India negroes throughout the whole extent of the American Republic. But John Bull rejected the tendered reciprocity, and churlishly replied, "The law of Parliament gave freedom to every slave who effected his landing on British ground."

About the same time we requested from Mexico the boon of hunting negroes over her wide area. The desired favor was denied, but we have since forcibly added almost half her territory to our own hunting grounds. Of all the game laws in existence, that of 1793, which regulates the chase of negroes, is the most horrible; yet Mr. Clay is dissatisfied with it, and calls upon Congress to make it "more effectual," and of course more horrible. Should a Virginian come to New York in search of his horse, and find him in possession of another, who claims him as his property, how is he to recover the *animal?* Only by process of law, and that process requires that a jury of twelve impartial men, drawn by lot, shall pass upon the conflicting claims. Neither party has any choice in selecting the jury, nor can either establish his claim by his own evidence. But if the Virginian is hunting a MAN, and sees one that will serve his purpose, and who will fetch a thousand dollars in the southern market, but who claims to belong to himself, how is he to secure him? Why, he may catch his MAN as well as he can, and without warrant may carry him before any justice of the peace whom for sufficient reasons he may think proper to select, and swear that the MAN he has caught is his, and the justice may surrender the MAN to perpetual bondage, degradation, and misery. Various officers besides justices are authorized to act, so that the Virginian has a wide choice. Surely this is hunting made easy by law; but it is not found so easy in practice. Latterly, various States have prohibited their *own officers* from assisting in the chase of human beings, and citizens rarely lend any *unpaid* assistance. Hence a new game law is deemed needful, and Mr. Clay, as we have seen, is pledged to go with "the farthest southern senator," the most devoted lover of the sport, to make it effectual. The Judiciary Committee have accordingly reported a bill now before the Senate. "I agree," said Mr. Mason, one of the farthest southern senators, in his speech on this bill (28th January,) "I agree that the Federal Government *has no power to impose duties of any kind upon officers of State governments as such.*" Of course, the obligation imposed by the law of 1793, upon justices of the peace and other State officers, to catch slaves, are void, and our northern Legislatures, it is admitted, have a right to prohibit them from participating in slave hunts. To obviate this difficulty, it becomes necessary to select other than *State* officers to adjudicate upon questions of higher import than any, with the single exception of life and death, that ever exercise the talents, learning, virtue, and independence of the most august tribunals of any civilized country. And who are the grave and reverend judges appointed by this bill to sit in judgment on the liberty or bondage of native-born Americans? Among these judges are TWENTY THOUSAND POSTMASTERS! Each one of these new judges is authorized to adjudge any man, woman, or child, black or white, to be a vendible chattel; and this judgment is to be founded on any proof that may be satisfactory to said postmaster, in the words of the bill "either by oral testimony or by affidavit," nor is the testimony either oral or by affidavit of the interested claimant excluded; and from this judgment there is no appeal! Slavery is no longer confined to *one* color. The southern papers abound with advertisements offering rewards for fugitive slaves, containing the caution, that the fugitive will probably attempt to pass for a *white* person. A few years since a Maryland slave-holder caught in Philadelphia a white girl (Mary Gilmore), whom he claimed as his *slave.* The case was brought before a Pennsylvania judge, and occupied two days, and it was proved by most abundant, overwhelming evidence, that the alleged slave was the orphan daughter of POOR IRISH PARENTS. The mother had died in the Philadelphia hospital, and the daughter had never been in Maryland. By a pending amendment to this bill, every man and woman who, prompted by the holiest impulses of our nature, shall "harbor or conceal" the prey from the hunter, is to be visited with fine and imprisonment. A few days after Mr. Clay introduced his resolutions, Bruin and Hill, slave-traders in Alexandria, wrote a letter, since published in the newspapers, stating for the information of a free MOTHER in New York who wished to redeem her DAUGHTER from bondage, that they cannot afford to sell "the girl Emily for less than EIGHTEEN HUNDRED DOLLARS." Why this prodigious price? They add, "We have two or three offers for Emily from *gentlemen* from the South. She is said to be the finest looking woman in this country."

Should this devoted victim escape from her keepers, and be afterwards found concealed in her mother's house, not only is she to be carried back and subjected to the fate intended for her, but the MOTHER is liable by the present bill to be sentenced to pay a fine of five hundred dollars to the United States, to pay Messrs. Bruin and Hill one thousand dollars for damages, and be imprisoned six months. We hope, for Mr. Clay's reputation, no "farthest senator from the south" will ask for heavier penalties, for if he does, Mr. Clay is pledged to vote for "the heaviest sanctions" that may be proposed. But suppose this poor girl should find her way to Peekskill, instead of New York, and in your absence, with bursting heart, ask to be sheltered in your house from her pursuers. Can you for a single moment admit the possibility, that your wife, the mother of your children, could, through fear of the law, so unsex herself, as to turn the trembling fugitive into the street, to be caught by the hunters? A thousand times rather would you see the partner of your bosom enduring Mr. Clay's "heaviest sanctions," than bringing ignominy upon herself, and covering her husband and children with shame and confusion of face, by committing a crime so foul and damnable. Mr. Mason, in his speech, insists upon the right of the hunter, "to enter peaceably any inclosure or DWELLING where such slave may be found, for the purpose of taking him." Should this asserted right be incorporated into the *compromise* bill, then may southern ruffians and northern doughfaces ere long be roaming through our bed-rooms and ransacking our closets in search of prey. Should an attempt be made to *enforce* "the heaviest sanctions" for which Mr. Clay is ready to vote, he may be assured the prisons in New York and New England are too few to hold the vast multitudes of men and women who would willingly tenant them, rather than peril their souls by betraying the fugitive or assisting in his capture. Mr. Clay very kindly declines requiring "a private individual *to make the tour of his whole State*" in search of a slave, but he insists that *all who are present* when the game is started, ought to follow the hounds. Could he but enforce this obligation, we should have some grand turnouts in New York and New England, some like the one fancied by the poet:

"Gay luck to our hunters! how nobly they ride,
In the glow of their zeal and the strength of their pride! —
The priest with his cassock flung back on the wind,
Just screening the politic statesman behind —
The saint and the sinner, with cursing and prayer —
The drunk and the sober ride merrily there.
Oh! goodly and grand is our hunting to see,
In this 'land of the brave and this home of the free!'
Right merrily hunting the black man, whose sin
Is the curl of his hair and the hue of his skin!
So speed to their hunting o'er mountain and glen,
Through canebreak and forest — the hunting of men!"

But the Constitution! This instrument declares in substance, that the fugitive slave shall be delivered up; but Mr. Clay, I believe, is the first lawyer who has contended that the obligation of delivery rests upon "private individuals." Even Mr. Mason, in his speech, insists that the mandate to deliver up is "addressed to the *jurisdiction of the State* into which the fugitive may escape." Of course, individual citizens, as such, are under no constitutional obligation to volunteer to catch slaves. But suppose a positive law should enjoin each individual to betray or aid in capturing the fugitive — the question put by the apostles, when legally forbidden to teach in the name of Jesus, would then recur: "Whether it be right in the sight of God to hearken unto you more than unto God, judge ye." It is not merely the right, but the duty of a Christian to refuse an *active* obedience to any and every law of man, which he believes contravenes the commands of his Maker; and then, like the apostles, to offer no forcible resistance to the penalties attached to his disobedience.

Mr. Clay may be assured, that the bill of pains and penalties promised in his seventh resolution, will not have the composing influence he anticipates. Filling our prisons with pious, benevolent, kind-hearted men and woman, will have little effect in suppressing agitation. In his compromising anodyne, Mr. Clay has omitted an important iugredient. Ample provision is to be made for the recovery of southern slaves, but none for the recovery of NORTHERN CITIZENS. If the Constitution gives the southern planter a right to seize his slave in New York or Massachusetts, equally explicit is the grant to citizens of those States to enjoy all the rights of citizenship in South Carolina. Yet, if certain of our citizens, freeholders and electors at home, think proper to visit that State, a prison is the only dwelling they are permitted to occupy; and should the State to which they belong send an agent to inquire why they are immured in a jail, and to bring their case before the Supreme Court of the United States, he is compelled to flee at the hazard of his life!

8. The last item of this grand compromise is virtually a guaranty that the American slave-trade, vile and loathsome as it is, shall be held sacred from prohibition or obstruction by the Federal Government for all time to come. The stars and stripes shall forever protect each coasting vessel that shall be freighted with human misery and despair, and manacled coffles shall, without molestation, be driven across the continent from the Atlantic to the Pacific. The slave-trade in the District, that is, in one single market, Mr. Clay pronounces "detestable," and talks with horror of "the *cortèges* which pass along our avenues of manacled human beings." But why this sudden outburst of indignation against a lawful commerce? Is it dishonorable to sell merchandise? Has not Mr. Clay himself proclaimed, "that is property

which the law makes property?" Why does he dishonor the Washington man-merchants? Is it base to buy and sell human beings? Mr. Clay forgets that this "detestable trade" is, in fact, supported by the gentlemen breeders who sell, and the gentlemen planters who buy. But this trade which is so "detestable," and these *cortèges* which are so horrible on a very little scale, are now to assume a *national* importance, protected and sanctioned by the government of the whole Republic!

Such, sir, is the magnanimous compromise which so many of our Whig and Democratic politicians, now that the *elections are over*, and the solemn pledges made in favor of the Wilmot Proviso *supposed* to be forgotten, are willing to accept as a mighty boon to human rights, and a mighty barrier against the further encroachments of the slave power. In my ears the only language addressed by these eight resolutions, to the North, is the cry of the horseleech — GIVE, GIVE. No test can detect in them, no microscope can make visible the most minute concession to human liberty. Not one single inch of territory does the proposed compromise secure from slavery that is not already rescued from its power. Not one single human being will it save from bondage.

The extension of the Missouri line to the Pacific would at least have rendered all on the north of it free soil; but, says Mr. Clay, most truly, although with a frankness almost insulting to the North, "I say, sir, in my place here, that it is much better for the SOUTH *that the whole subject should be open on both sides an imaginary line of* 36° 30′, *than that slavery should be interdicted positively north of* 36° 30′ *with freedom to admit or exclude it south of* 36° 30′, *at the will of the people!*"

But, Mr. Clay exclaimed, "No earthly power could induce me to vote for the *positive* introduction of slavery south or north of that line," and at this heroic avowal the galleries applauded. But the galleries are not deeply versed in southern tactics. Mr. Clay need apprehend no coercion to extort his reluctant vote for a purpose no one desires or demands. The South have, with one voice, denied the power of Congress either to prohibit or establish slavery in the territories. Said Mr. King, of

Alabama, in reply, "We ask no act of Congress to carry slavery anywhere. I believe we (Congress) have just as much right to prohibit slavery in the territories as to carry it there. We have no right to do one or the other." Other southern senators avowed their concurrence in the doctrine advanced by Mr. King. Hence Mr Clay's defiance of any power on earth to make him do what nobody wants him to do, was, at least, a rhetorical flourish.

But if this pretended compromise is, as I contend, a full and unqualified surrender of all the demands of the North, why did certain ultra senators object to it? A show of resistance might have been deemed politic, as tending to make northern men suppose there must be something granted to them, although they could not tell what. It may also suit the party purposes of some to prolong the present agitation, that they may manufacture more patriotism for the southern market; and, lastly, if any really wish to form a separate republic, in which they expect to have more power than they now enjoy, they will of course reject all concessions, however great. But it is incredible that the mere slave-holders, the men who are only anxious to open new markets for the sale of their stock, and to acquire more votes in Congress, should be averse to a proposition that offers them all they have ever asked, and all that Congress can give them, with the exception of the suppression of the right of petition, and the censorship of the post-office, and these are not now in issue.

But we are told that unless we yield to the demands of the slave-holders, they will dissolve the Union. And what are these demands, which Mr. Clay admits we have full right to refuse? Why, that a small body of men, not probably exceeding 100,000,* shall be at liberty, for their own aggrandizement, to blight with the curse of slavery our vast possessions south of 36° 30′, and whatever portion of Mexico it shall hereafter be found convenient to seize. Thus, at a time when cruelty and

* A late census in Kentucky reveals the fact, that the slave-holders in that State own on an average twenty-two slaves. Should this average be applied to the whole slave region, the number of masters, according to the census of 1840, cannot exceed 117,000!

oppression are elsewhere giving way before the increasing intelligence and morality of the age, we, the Model Republic, are to be the instrument of extending over illimitable regions now free, a despotism more accursed than any other known throughout the civilized world,—a despotism that not only enslaves the body, but crushes the intellect through which man is enabled to distinguish good from evil,—a despotism that annihilates all rights, sets at naught all the affections of the heart, and converts a being made in the image of God into a soulless machine. Tell me not of *exceptions*,—of some lucky chattel, like Mr. Clay's negro, referred to in his speech, who in his master's well-stored kitchen hugs his chain, laughs, and grows fat. He is but a vendible commodity, and to-morrow's sun may behold him toiling under the lash, his wife given to another, and his children with pigs and mules sold at auction to the highest bidder. Tell me not of exceptions,—"the kind owner" may at any moment be exchanged by death or debts, for the hardened, remorseless taskmaster, and the law sanctions every atrocity perpetrated upon the slave.* No, my dear sir, I cannot give my consent, and I hope it will not be given for me by my representative, to curse a vast empire with such an institution, and to doom unborn millions to its unutterable abominations, even to save our southern brethren from the sin and folly of founding a new Republic (!) upon the denial of human rights, and of rendering themselves a byword, a proverb, and a reproach among all the nations of the earth. I value the favor of my God and the salvation of my soul too much to take

*Our doughfaces are always complaining that their employers are slandered at the North. Let the employers speak for themselves. In *Dev. Reports*, (North Carolina,) p. 263, 1829, we find the case of *The State* vs. *Mann*. The defendant attempted to flog a woman slave whom he had hired; she retreated; he ordered her to come to him, but she continuing to retreat, he seized his gun, fired at and wounded her. For this he was indicted. The Court held that he who hires a slave is, for the time being, invested with all the powers of the owner himself to enforce obedience, and that the indictment could not be sustained. Said Judge Ruffin, "The power of the master must be absolute, to render the submission of the slave perfect. I most sincerely confess my sense of the harshness of this proposition. I feel it as deeply as any man can; *and as a principle of moral right, every man in his retirement must repudiate it.* But in the actual state of things it must be so—there is no remedy. THIS DISCIPLINE BELONGS TO SLAVERY." Verily, we are the people to lecture Austria!

part or lot in such great wickedness. Most fully do I agree with Mr. Clay, that Congress has no more constitutional authority over slavery in the States, than in the Island of Cuba; and most fully do I agree with the admission in his speech, but *not to be found in his resolutions*, of the right of Congress to exclude slavery from the conquered territories. Hence, in my opinion, the refusal to exercise this right, even to preserve the Union, would be a CRIME in the sight of God and man. I entertain no apprehension of the severance of the Union for this cause, but should the few slave-holders and the vast multitude of southern people who have no interest in slavery, in their madness separate from us, upon them will rest the sin, and upon them and their children will fall its punishment. Let us do what God commands, and leave to HIM the consequences.

Yours truly,

WILLIAM JAY.

A LETTER

TO THE HON. SAMUEL A. ELIOT, REPRESENTATIVE IN CONGRESS FROM THE CITY OF BOSTON, IN REPLY TO HIS APOLOGY FOR VOTING FOR THE FUGITIVE SLAVE BILL.

1851.

SIR: —

AN English courtier procured a colonial judgeship, for a young dependant wholly ignorant of law. The new functionary, on parting with his patron, received from him the following sage advice, — "Be careful never to assign reasons, for whether your judgments be right or wrong, your reasons will certainly be bad." You have cause to regret that some friend had not been equally provident of your reputation, and intimated that it was only expected of you to vote for Mr. Webster's measures, but by no means to assist him in vindicating them. You did, indeed, vote precisely as those who procured your nomination intended you should; yet, on your return home, you found your name had become a byword and a reproach in your native State. Another election approached, but you declined submitting your recent course to the judgment of the electors, and withdrew from the canvass. But although the people were thus prevented from voting against you, they persisted in speaking and writing against you. Anxious to relieve yourself from the load of obloquy by which you were oppressed, in an evil hour you rashly appealed to the public through the columns of a newspaper, and gave the "reasons" of your vote for the Fugitive Slave Law. You had a high and recent example of the kind of logic suited to your case. You might have indulged in transcendental nonsense, and talked about the climate, soil, and scenery of New England and the wonders of physical geography, and, assuming that negroes were created free, you might have contended that, in voting for a law to catch and enslave them, you had avoided the folly of reënacting the law of God. Reasons of this sort, you and others had declared, "had convinced the understanding and touched the conscience of the nation." Instead of following an example so illustrious and successful, you assign "reasons" so very commonplace, that the most ordinary capacity can understand them, and so feeble, that the slightest strength can overthrow them.

Your first "reason" is, that the delivery of fugitives is a constitutional obligation. By this you mean, that, by virtue of the construction of a certain clause in the Constitution by the Supreme Court, Congress has the power to pass *a* law for the recovery of fugitive slaves. Well, sir, does this constitutional obligation authorize Congress to pass *any* law whatsoever on the subject, however atrocious and wicked? Had you voted for a law to prevent smuggling, in which you had authorized every tide-waiter to shoot any person suspected of having contraband goods in his possession, would it have been a good "reason" for such an atrocity, that the collection of duties was "a constitutional obligation?" You are condemned for voting for an arbitrary, detestable, diabolical law, — one that tramples upon the rights of conscience, outrages the feelings of humanity, discards the rules of evidence, levels all the barriers erected by the common law for the protection of personal liberty, and, in defiance of the Constitution, and against its express provisions, gives to the courts the appointment of legions of slave-catching judges. And your "reason" for all this is, that the delivery of fugitives is "a constitutional obligation!" The "obligation" is not in issue. Please to understand, sir, that it is not denied. It is for the *manner* in which you profess to have discharged the obligation, that you are censured; and be it remembered, that not one of the obnoxious provisions of your law is required by the Constitution. You go on and attempt to enlighten your constituents as to the history of this constitutional obligation. As the obligation affords you no apology for the iniquitous features of your law, its history is, of course, mere surplusage, and serves no other purpose than to divert the attention of your readers from yourself. About two thirds of your apology is occupied with a historical disquisition, which has as much to do with your vindication as the question respecting the existence of a lunar atmosphere. I will not, however, withhold from you whatever benefit you may derive from either your logic or your history, but will give each a fair and honest examination. You inform the public that, at the time the Constitution was formed,

> "Slavery had been abolished in some of the States, and still existed in others. Here seemed an insurmountable incompatibility of interests, and nothing perplexed the wise men of that day—and they were *very* wise men—so much as this topic. At last they agreed that the new Constitution should have nothing to do with it; that the word *slavery* should not be mentioned in it, and that it should be left to the States themselves to establish, retain, or abolish it, just as much after the adoption of the Constitution as before. But in order to secure the existence of the institution to those States who preferred it, it was agreed that the persons escaping from labor to which they were bound, in one commonwealth, and found in another, should be returned to the State from which they had fled. The provision was necessary for the preservation of this interest *in statu quo*. It did not extend slavery. It kept it where it already was, and where it could not have continued if every slave who escaped North was at once free and irreclaimable. The members of the confederacy from the South saw this distinctly, and *deliberately declared* that they could not and would not enter a union with States who would tempt away their slaves with the prospect of immediate and permanent freedom. . . . . . The Constitution was adopted with this provision, and it could not have been adopted without it."

Thus we learn from you, sir, that when the Constitution was formed, "slavery had been abolished in some of the States." It is a pity you did not vouchsafe to tell us which of the States had thus early and honorably distinguished themselves. Of the thirteen American States in 1787, how many, sir, had *by law* abolished slavery? NOT ONE. Your "some States' consisted of Massachusetts alone. And how was slavery abolished there? Not by any express prohibition in her constitution, nor by any act of her Legislature. Fortunately, her constitution, like that of most other States, contained a general declaration of human rights, somewhat similar to the "rhetorical abstraction" in the Declaration of Independence. Two or three years before the Federal Convention assembled, a young lawyer, perceiving that the declaration in the constitution had inadvertently made no exclusion of the rights of men with dark complexions, brought an action for a slave against his master for work done and performed. An upright and independent court, not having the fear of our southern brethren before their eyes, decided that the slave was a MAN, and therefore entitled to the rights which the constitution declared belonged to *all* men, and gave judgment for the plaintiff. In this way, sir, was slavery abolished in Massachusetts, and hence the delegates from Massachusetts in the convention were the only ones who represented a *free* State. And now, sir, what becomes of your "insurmountable incompatibility of interests" arising from the fact that "slavery had been abolished in some States and still existed in others," which you tell us so much perplexed the wise men of that day? We shall see, sir, that on questions touching human bondage the Massachusetts delegation seem to have been slave-holders in heart, and did not partake of the perplexity which troubled the wise men. With the exception of that delegation, there were not probably half a dozen members of the convention who were not slave-holders.

It would seem from your historical review, that the clause in the Constitution respecting fugitive slaves was the grand compromise between the North and the South, without which "the Constitution could not have been adopted;" and that to this clause we owe our glorious slave-catching Union. You fortify this wonderful historical discovery by appealing to the "deliberate declarations" of southern members, that they "would not enter a union with States who would tempt away their slaves," &c. It is to be regretted that you have not deemed it expedient to refer to the records of these declarations, as other students of our constitutional history are wholly ignorant of them. Suffer me, sir, to enter into a few historical details, for the purpose of vindicating the liberty I take to differ with you as to the accuracy of your statements.

The Convention met in Philadelphia, May, 25, 1787. On the 29th of the same month, Mr. Randolph, of Virginia, submitted a plan of government. It contained no allusion to fugitive slaves. On the same day, Mr. Charles Pinckney, of South Carolina, submitted another plan. This last provided for the surrender of fugitive criminals, but was silent about fugitives slaves. On the 15th of June, Mr. Patterson, of New Jersey, submitted a third plan. This also provided for the surrender of fugitives from justice, but not from bondage. On the 18th, Mr. Hamilton announced his plan, but the fugitive slave found no place in it. On the 26th of June, the Convention, having agreed on the general features of the proposed Constitution in the form of resolutions, referred them to "a committee of detail," for the purpose of reducing them to the form of a Constitution. In this resolutions, there was not the most distant allusion to fugitive slaves. On the 6th of August, the committee reported the draft of a Constitution, and yet, strange as you may deem it, the provision without which, you tell us, the Constitution could not have been adopted, was not in it, although there was in it a provision for the surrender of fugitive criminals. For three months had the Convention been in session, and not one syllable had been uttered about fugitive slaves. At last, on the 29th of August, as we learn from the minutes,

> "It was moved and seconded to agree to the following proposition, to be inserted after the 15th article: 'If any person, bound to service or labor in any of the United States, shall escape into another State, he or she shall not be discharged from such service or labor in consequence of any regulation subsisting in the State to which they escape, but shall be delivered up to the person justly claiming their service or labor,' *which passed unanimously.*"

Really, sir, I find in this record but little evidence of the perplexity which distressed our wise men, or of the great compromise between the North and South, on which you dwell.

The 15th article, referred to above, was the article providing for the surrender of fugitives from justice, and this suggested the idea, that it would be well to provide, also, for the surrender of fugitive slaves. In an assembly consisting almost exclusively of slave-holders, the idea was exceedingly relished; and without a word of opposition, the suggestion was unanimously adopted. From Mr. Madison's report we learn that, the day before, Messrs. Butler and Pinckney had informally proposed that fugitive slaves and servants should be delivered up "like criminals."

Mr. Wilson of Penn.:—"This would oblige the Executive of the State to do it at the public expense. Mr. Sherman, of Conn., saw no more propriety in the public seizing and surrendering a slave or servant than a horse." *Madison Papers*, p. 1447.

The subject was here dropped. The next day the motion was made in form, and as Mr. Madison says, "agreed to, *nem. con.*" From the phraseology of the motion, and the objections of Messrs. Wilson and Sherman, it was perfectly understood that the obligation of delivery was imposed on the States, and that no power was intended to be conferred on Congress to legislate on the subject. Messrs. Wilson and Sherman's objections arose from no moral repugnance to slave-catching, but from the inconvenience they apprehended the *State* authorities would be subjected to; and Mr. Wilson perhaps spoke from experience, as his own State had at that very time a law for catching and returning fugitive slaves from other States. The idea, therefore, that this agreement was a *compromise* between the North and South is wholly imaginary, and you, sir, must have mistaken some recent fulminations from the southern chivalry for the 'deliberate declarations" which you suppose were made in the Convention. Believe me, sir, no members of the Convention ever declared they would not enter into the Union, unless it was agreed to surrender fugitive slaves, for the obvious reason, that the northern slave-holders required no threats from their southern brethren to consent to a compact convenient to both. It is very true, sir, that there were compromises, and that there were "deliberate declarations," but they had no reference to the surrender of runaway slaves. I have pointed out your historical mistake, not because it has the remotest bearing on your justification, but because you seem to think that it has.

The first great compromise was between, not the North and the South, but the small and the large States. The one claimed, and the other refused, an equality of suffrage in the national legislature. It was at last agreed, that the suffrage should be equal in one house, and according to population in the other. This was the first compromise. Then came the question, What should constitute the representative population? The Southern States had more slaves than the Northern, and the former insisted that slaves should be included in the representative population. This would have given the Southern States an unfair preponderance in Congress. Moreover, a portion of the Southern States were engaged in the African slave-trade, and, of course, every slave landed on their shores would increase their political power in Congress. To reconcile the North to slave representation, it was offered that *direct taxation* should be proportioned to representation. But the North was reluctant, and, as usual, was bullied into a compromise. Mr. Davie, of North Carolina, made a "deliberate declaration:"

> "He was sure that North Carolina would never confederate on any terms that did not rate them (the slaves) at least as three-fifths. If the Eastern States meant, therefore, to exclude them (the slaves) altogether, the business was at an end." *Madison Papers*, p. 1081.

This threat, and others like it, settled the matter. The compromise, of three-fifths of the slaves to be included in the representative population, was accepted on the motion of *a New England member;* and the consequence is, that the slave States have now twenty-one members in the lower house of Congress more than they are entitled to by their free population. This was the second compromise. There was still a third, far more wicked and detestable, and effected by the "deliberate declarations" of southern members. The "committee of detail" has been already mentioned. It consisted of Messrs. Rutledge of South Carolina, Randolph of Virginia, Wilson of Pennsylvania, Ellsworth of Connecticut, and Gorham of Massachusetts. This committee, it will be recollected, were to reduce to the *form* of a Constitution the resolutions agreed on by the Convention. Neither in the resolutions themselves, nor in the discussions which preceded their adoption, had any reference been made to a guaranty for the continuance of the African slave-trade. Nevertheless, this committee, of their own will and pleasure, inserted in their draft the following clause:

"No tax or duty shall be laid by the legislature on articles exported from any State, *nor on the migration or importation of such persons as the several States shall think proper to admit, nor shall such migration or importation be prohibited.*"

To understand the cunning wickedness of this clause, it must be recollected that Congress was to have power to regulate foreign commerce, and commerce between the States; and hence it might, at a future time, suppress both the foreign and domestic commerce in human flesh, or it might burden this commerce with duties. Hence this artfully expressed perpetual restriction on the power of Congress to interfere with the traffic in human beings. As this grand scheme was concocted in the committee, and not in the Convention, it may be interesting to inquire into its paternity.

In the debates which ensued on this clause, Mr. Ellsworth, one of the committee who reported it,

"Was for leaving the clause as it now stands. *Let every State import what it pleases.* The morality, the wisdom of slavery, are considerations belonging to the States themselves. *What enriches a part enriches the whole*, and the States are the best judges of their particular interests. The old Confederation had not *meddled* with this point, and he did not see any greater necessity for bringing it within the policy of the new one." "As slaves multiply so fast in Virginia and Maryland that it is *cheaper* to raise than to import them, whilst in the *sickly* rice-swamps foreign supplies are *necessary*, if we go farther than is urged [a proposal to permit the trade for a limited time,] we shall be unjust towards South Carolina and Georgia. Let us not intermeddle." *Madison Papers, pp.* 1389, 1391.

This gentleman was one of your "very wise men;" and his mantle has recently fallen upon other wise men from the East. Mr. Wilson, another member of the committee, objected. "All articles imported," said he, "are to be taxed; slaves alone are exempt. This is, in fact, a bounty on that article." The clause was referred to another committee, who modified it by limiting the restriction to 1800. It was moved to guarantee the slave-trade for twenty years, by postponing the restriction to 1808. This motion was *seconded* by Mr. Gorham, another member of the committee. Mr. Randolph, also of the committee, was against the slave-trade, and opposed to any restriction on the power of Congress to suppress it. Two of the committee, then, we find, were against the trade, and three, Messrs. Rutledge, Ellsworth, and Gorham, for perpetuating it. And now, sir, what were the inducements which prevailed on the two wise men from the East to yield their consent to a proposition so wicked and abominable? We are, of course, not informed what passed in the committee, but we can well imagine, from the language used by the chairman and others in the Convention. Said Mr. Rutledge,

> "If the Convention thinks North Carolina, South Carolina, and Georgia will ever agree to this plan (the Federal Constitution) unless their right to import slaves be untouched, the expectation is VAIN. The people of those States will never be such fools as to give up so important an interest."

In other words, "Gentlemen of the North, no Union without the African slave-trade." Said Mr. Charles Pinckney:

> "South Carolina can never receive the plan (of the Constitution) if it prohibits the slave-trade. In every proposed extension of the powers of Congress, that State has expressly and watchfully excepted that of meddling with the importation of negroes." *Madison Papers*, p. 1389.

Mr. Charles C. Pinckney "thought himself bound to declare candidly, that he did not think South Carolina would stop her importations of slaves in any short time." Thus you see, sir, that the "deliberate declarations" to which you allude were made in reference to the continuance of the African slave-trade, and not, as you suppose, to the catching of fugitive slaves. Two New England gentlemen of the committee yielded to these declarations, and sacrificed conscience and humanity for the sake of the Union, and the consideration that what enriched a part enriched the whole. Happily, in this case, southern bluster was met by southern bluster, and it is owing to Virginia, and not to the virtue and independence of New England, that the Constitution was rescued from the infamy of granting a solemn and perpetual guaranty to an accursed commerce.

In Virginia, the slaves, as Mr. Ellsworth remarked, multiplied so fast, that it was *cheaper* to raise than import them. She was then, as now, a breeding State for the southern markets. Hence, her delegates were as ready to bluster for protection, as the South Carolina delegates were for a free trade in men and women. Of course the *motives* assigned were patriotic, not selfish. Mr. Randolph "could never agree to the clause as it stands. He would sooner RISK THE CONSTITUTION." *Madison Papers*, p. 1396. Mr. Madison would not consent to the continuance of the traffic till 1808.

"Twenty years will produce all the mischief that can be apprehended from the liberty to import slaves. So long a term will be more dishonorable to the American character, than to say nothing about it in the Constitution." *Madison Papers*, p. 1427.

Mr. Mason from Virginia denounced the traffic as "infernal." *Madison Papers*, p. 1390. The result of all these threats on each side was, as usual, a compromise, by which Congress was prohibited from suppressing the foreign and internal commerce in slaves for twenty years, and was left at liberty to do as it might see fit, after that period. After twenty years the foreign trade was suppressed, and North and South Carolina and Georgia remained in the Union! Virginia, as well as the other slave States, is greatly interested in the home slave-trade, and that has *not* been suppressed, although Congress has full power over it.

It does not appear from Mr. Madison's report what reply was made in the Convention to the Virginia objections, but in his speech in the Convention of his own State, he tells us:

"The gentlemen from South Carolina and Georgia argued in this manner: We have now liberty to import this species of property, and much of the property now possessed had been purchased or otherwise acquired in contemplation of improving it by the assistance of imported slaves. What would be the consequence of hindering us in this point? The *slaves* of Virginia would rise in value, and we should be obliged to go to your markets." *Elliott's Debates*, III, p. 454.

Certainly, sir, these South Carolina and Georgia delegates were "very wise men," and their predictions are now history, and the planters of Georgia, South Carolina, Mississippi, and Louisiana buy slaves of the Virginia breeders. But what shall I say of the wise men from the East? This horrible compromise, this guaranty of the African slave-trade for twenty years, was carried by the votes of the Massachusetts and Connecticut delegates, and would have been defeated, had they had the courage and virtue to vote against it.

I have indulged in this long digression, to show that the clause in the Constitution respecting fugitive slaves was not, as you represent it, the great compromise of the Constitution, the key-stone of the Union, and that our slave-holding fathers were not, as you suppose, greatly perplexed, nor their consciences deeply wounded, by the existence of slavery in all the States of the confederacy, with one exception. Having disposed of your history, I return to your logic.

Whether the constitutional injunction to surrender fugitive slaves was a compromise or not, is of no practical importance. The clause speaks for itself, and prescribes no mode by which the title of the claimant shall be ascertained, while it expressly implies that the title shall be established before the surrender is made. Hence, the fair presumption is, that the title to a MAN shall be proved, with at least as much certainty and formality as the title to a horse. Had you, sir, in your law, provided that a Virginian shall not come to Boston, and there seize and carry off a husband, wife, or child, but by the same process, and on as strong evidence, as he may now seize and carry off a horse which you claim as your own, instead of finding your name a byword and a reproach, you would have been honored and applauded by your fellow-citizens, and returned to Congress by a triumphant vote; nor is there a syllable in the Constitution which prohibits or discountenances such a mode of deciding the title to a human being. It is in vain, then, sir, that you plead your "constitutional obligation" in justification of your most detestable law. But, as if one wrong could justify another, you plead in your excuse the law of 1793, and you ask in your simplicity of those who condemn your law, if they do not perceive that they are "denouncing their fathers." Well, sir, were our fathers infallible? Pity it is, sir, that you were not on the floor of Congress when that body declared the African slave-trade to be PIRACY. You might then, sir, have risen in your place, and inquired, "Do you not perceive that you are denouncing your fathers, who were very wise men, and who guaranteed for twenty years the very traffic which you now proclaim to be piracy?" Pity it is, sir, that you did not stand by the side of your patron on Plymouth Rock, and whisper in his ear, "Do you not perceive that you are denouncing our fathers?" when he declared, "In the sight of our law the African slave-trader is a PIRATE and a FELON, and in the sight of Heaven an offender beyond the ordinary depth of human guilt." Mr. Webster is better versed in constitutional history than you are, and he well knew that some of our fathers "deliberately declared they would not enter a Union" in which they were to be debarred from pursuing this piratical, felonious, guilty traffic. Our fathers were mostly slaveholders, and yet you, sir, unconsciously denounce both their morality and intelligence, when you affirm the institution of slavery to be "wrong and unwise." And yet all who presume to find fault with your cruel, unjust, wicked law, are guilty, forsooth, of denouncing their fathers!

You tell us that the Convention of 1787 "*agreed that the new Constitution should have nothing to do with slavery.*" I have not been so fortunate as to find the record of this agreement, but if such a compact was indeed made, then seldom, if ever, has a solemn covenant been more grossly and wickedly violated. Is it, sir, in virtue of this agreement, that you voted to fine and imprison every conscientious, humane citizen who may refuse, at the command of a minion of a commissioner, to join in a slave hunt? Did this agreement confer on the holders of slaves an enlarged representation in Congress? Was it in pursuance of this agreement that the importation of slaves was guaranteed for twenty years? Did this agreement authorize the Federal Government to enter into negotiations with Great Britain and Mexico for a mutual surrender of runaway slaves? Was it in pursuance of this same agreement, that our government negotiated with Russia and Spain to prevent emancipation in Cuba, —a traitorous conspiracy with despots against the rights of man? How, sir, was this agreement illustrated, when Daniel Webster, as Secretary of State under John Tyler of glorious memory, made a demand on Great Britain for the surrender of the slaves of the Creole, who had gallantly achieved their liberty, and taken refuge in the West Indies? How comes it, sir, that under this agreement an act of Congress secures to the slave States officers in the navy in proportion to the number of their slaves? How is it, that under this agreement colored men are seized in the District of Columbia, under "the exclusive jurisdiction" of the Federal Government, on the *suspicion* of being slaves, and when that suspicion is rebutted by the non-appearance of any claimant, are sold as slaves for life, to pay their jail fees? Perhaps it would be denouncing our fathers, to say that Messrs. Webster and Cass may search the archives of Austria in vain for any act so utterly diabolical as this, perpetrated by a government which it was agreed "should have nothing to do with slavery." Was it to carry out this famous agreement that the Federal Government officially declared through its Secretary, Mr. Calhoun, that Texas was annexed to preserve the institution of slavery from the perils that threatened it?

Once more, sir. We all know that the slave-holders regard the free blacks as dangerous to the subordination of their slaves, and are contemplating their forcible removal. Think you, sir, Mr. Webster was mindful of the agreement you have discovered, when, on the 7th of last March, in his place in the Senate, he proposed his magnificent scheme of taxing the whole nation untold millions to give additional security to property in human beings?

"If," said the Massachusetts Senator, "any gentleman from the *South* shall propose a scheme of colonization to be carried on by *this government* upon a large scale, for the transportation of free colored people to any colony or *any place in the world*, I should be quite disposed to incur almost any degree of expense to accomplish the object."

The magnitude of the scheme, and the cost at which it is to be accomplished, are thus hinted:

"There have been received into the treasury of the United States EIGHTY MILLIONS of dollars, the proceeds of the sales of the public lands ceded by Virginia. If the residue should be sold at the same rate, the whole aggregate will exceed TWO HUNDRED MILLIONS of dollars. If *Virginia and the South* see fit to adopt any proposition to *relieve* themselves from the free people of color among them, they have my free consent that the *government* shall pay *them* any sum of money out of the proceeds which may be adequate for the purpose."

Will you, sir, please to point out the article of the agreement of 1787, which, while it restricts Congress from having any thing to do with slavery, sanctions an appropriation not exceeding two hundred millions of dollars, for the purpose of strengthening the institution of slavery, by *relieving* the slave-holders from the presence of free people of color, and forcibly transporting to any place in the world hundreds of thousands of native-born Americans, who have as good a constitutional right to the pursuit of life, liberty, and happiness on their native soil, as Mr. Webster himself? Mr. Webster, it seems, now views the subject of negro colonization in precisely the same light that he did thirty years since, although his *intentions* on this, as on various other points, have undergone marvellous changes. We learn from a Massachusetts paper (*Congregationalist*, July 6, 1849,) that this gentleman was in 1822 appointed by a public meeting to draft a constitution for the State Colonization Society. After considerable discussion in the committee he rose and said, "I must leave. I understand the whole project. It is a scheme of the slave-holders to get rid of their free negroes. I will have nothing to do with it."

And how, sir, as a member of Congress, have *you* fulfilled this agreement to have nothing to do with slavery? Not only have you required "good citizens," when commanded, to hunt and catch slaves, but you have even fixed a money value on every slave. If a master fails to recover his fugitive slave through the agency, "direct or indirect," of any citizen, you give him an action for damages. In all other cases of trespass, the damages sustained by the plaintiff are assessed by a jury according to the evidence. You kindly save the master the trouble of proving the value of his lost property, and give him out of the pockets of the defendant $1000, no matter whether the slave was sick or well, young or old. If a woman escapes with a child at the breast, the master is to have $2000! Recollect, sir, this is for *damages* to the slave-holder; the trespasser is to pay to the government, which was to have nothing to do with slavery, another thousand dollars, and to be incarcerated six months. Either, sir, you have wholly mistaken the nature of the "agreement," or the slave-holders, through the aid of their northern auxiliaries, have, in defiance of the agreement, rendered the Federal Government a mighty engine in protecting, extending, and perpetuating the stupendous iniquity of human bondage.

Your first excuse for voting for the recent slave-catching law, after relying on your "constitutional obligation," is, that it is "*practically more favorable to the fugitive than the law of* 1793!!!" The southern lawyers, then, who drafted the bill, were a set of blunderers, and your constituents are blockheads for blaming you for legislating against human rights, when, in fact, you were loosening the bonds of the oppressed, and facilitating escape from the prison-house. Your assertion may well excite astonishment at the South as well as the North, till your *proof* is known, and then, indeed, astonishment will be exchanged for ridicule. You tell us,

> "The *evidence* of such an assertion may be found in the fact, that by the old law every magistrate in Massachusetts, amounting to several hundreds, and so in the other States, were authorized and required to cause the arrest of any fugitive, examine into his case, and deliver him to the claimant, if he was proved to be a slave; while under the new law that power is *limited* to the justices of the United States courts, and to the commissioners appointed by them, not exceeding, perhaps, on an average, six or eight persons in each State."

So it seems the slave-catchers had formerly no difficulty in finding a magistrate among hundreds to aid them, but that now, before they hunt a slave, they must hunt and catch a United States judge, or a commissioner of six or eight in a whole State. Truly a hard case, and yet the slave-holders themselves set the very trap in which they have been caught, and thus it is that, through their folly, and your generosity in not pointing out to them the blunder they were committing, the new law is more favorable to the fugitive than the old one. Surely, sir, it could not have been more perilous to the young West Indian judge to meddle with "reasons," than it is for you. Either, sir, you voted for the law without reading it, or you have forgotten its provision. Be assured, the southern lawyers were as well acquainted as yourself with the fact, that a few individuals, termed "commissioners," had been appointed by the United States courts to perform certain ministerial acts; and that, as these men were now to be promoted to the office of slave-catching judges, they would be wholly inadequate in number to lend efficient aid to the hunters of men. Hence, they inserted in the third section of the bill, the following enactment, which has strangely escaped your recollection, viz.:

> "And it is further enacted, that the Circuit Courts of the United States, and the Superior Courts of *each* organized Territory of the United States, SHALL from time to time ENLARGE THE NUMBER OF COMMISSIONERS with a view to afford reasonable facilities to reclaim fugitives from labor, and to the prompt discharge of the duties imposed by this act."

So that, instead of six or eight commissioners in a State, we are to have as many hundreds, if needed. Nor is this all. By the second section, the power possessed by the Circuit Courts to appoint commissioners is for the first time conferred on the *Territorial* courts, so that there shall be no lack of slave-catching judges in Oregon, Utah, and New Mexico. Instead of your six or eight commissioners in a State, your law contemplates that there shall be one or more in *each county;* for the fifth section provides, that "the better to enable the said commissioners to execute their duties faithfully and efficiently, ... they are hereby authorized and empowered, within their *counties respectively,*" to appoint one or more persons to execute their warrants. So it seems we are to have an unlimited number of judges and executioners. These executioners, expressly appointed to catch slaves, and of course among the most worthless and degraded of the community, are one and all invested with the power of a high sheriff to call out the *posse comitatus*, not merely in his own county, but in every hamlet in the State, and require "good citizens," under pain of fine and imprisonment, to join him in his execrable hunt. Really, sir, your "evidence" that the new law is more favorable to the fugitive than the old one falls short of demonstration.

You thus apologize for not giving the alleged fugitive a trial by jury:

> "There was no more trial by jury provided for under the old law than under the new law. The claim of a jury trial is entirely *new;* never thought of till modern discussions of the subject begun. For fifty-seven years our fathers and we have been living under the laws which provided no such thing, and now one which makes no such provision is denounced in unmeasured terms as cruel and inhuman. Where have we all been living for half a century?"

Surely, sir, it is a most logical reason for not changing a wicked law, that it has been in force for fifty-seven years. Strange that the legislators of Massachusetts did not perceive the force of this reasoning when they abolished the laws for hanging witches and whipping Quakers. Permit me, sir, to ask, Where had *you* been living when *you* declared it to be the *duty* of Congress to give the fugitive a trial by jury, although for fifty-seven years such a trial had been denied him? You probably forgot, sir, when giving the above "reason," that, not long before you took your seat in Congress, you had, as a member of the Massachusetts Legislature, voted for the following resolution, viz.:

> "We hold it to be the duty of that body (Congress) to pass such laws only in regard thereto as will be maintained by the public sentiment of the free States, where such laws are to be enforced, and which shall especially secure all persons, whose surrender may be claimed as having escaped from labor and service in other States, the right of having the validity of such claim determined by a jury in the State where such claim is made."

So it seems that, while in Boston, you esteemed it the *especial duty* of Congress to grant the fugitive a trial by jury, but that in the atmosphere of Washington you acquired new views of moral philosophy.

Suffer me, sir, also to inquire, Where had Mr. Webster been "living for half a century," when, on the 3d of last June, he introduced into the Senate a bill amendatory of the act of 1793, granting the alleged fugitive a trial by jury whenever he shall make oath that he is not the slave of the claimant?

Another of your "reasons" is, that your law does *not* suspend the *habeas corpus*, and in proof of its innocence in this respect, you refer to the opinion of "legal authority of the highest kind," viz., Mr. Crittenden, of Kentucky. It is very true that the words *habeas corpus* are omitted in your law, as the word *slave* is in the Constitution, but in neither case is the omission of any practical importance. You must be aware, sir, that whenever a person is in the custody of another, if sufficient ground be shown to render it probable that the custody is illegal, the writ is granted as a matter of right. But why is it granted? That the court may at its discretion, according to circumstances, remand or discharge the prisoner. Take away from the court the discretionary power to discharge, and the writ is rendered an idle form. Your law, you say, does not suspend the *habeas corpus;* it is guiltless of such an enormity. A man who is carrying off one of our citizens in chains, may indeed be served with the writ, and he brings his prisoner before the court, and he produces a paper for which he paid ten dollars, and reads from your law, that this paper, called a certificate, "shall be conclusive," and "shall prevent all molestation of said person or persons by any *process* issued by any court, judge, or magistrate, or other person whomsoever." It is because the word *process*, instead of *habeas corpus*, is used, that your law does not suspend the writ of freedom! In vain may the prisoner plead that he is not the person mentioned in the certificate; in vain may he offer to show that the certificate is a forgery; in vain may he urge that the man who signed the certificate was not a commissioner. The little piece of paper costing ten dollars is to save the slave-catcher from "all molestation," not because the writ of *habeas corpus* is suspended, — O, no! but in consequence of the words "any process!"

You refer to two objections, which you say are made to your

law, and endeavor to refute them; viz., the onerous obligations imposed upon the marshal, and the penalties attached to an attempt "to assist in the rescue of the slave after he has been proved to be such." You have evinced your discretion in confining yourself to only four objections made to your law; viz., the denial of a jury trial, the suspension of the *habeas corpus*, the duties of the marshal, and the penalties imposed on an attempt to rescue the slave *after* judgment. With what success, and with what "reasons," you have combated the first two has already been seen. As to the last two, they scarcely merit an answer, and hence you have selected them. If the obligations of the marshal are onerous, he has voluntarily assumed them by accepting the office. If, in a civilized country, a man attempts forcibly to rescue a prisoner in the custody of the law, he must expect to be punished. There are many weighty objections to your law which you have not thought it expedient to notice. Permit me to supply your omission, and to tell you why your law is so intensely odious. And here let me again remind you of the true issue between you and the people. It is not now the constitutional power of Congress under the decision of the Supreme Court to pass a law for the recovery of fugitive slaves, — this is conceded. The odium you have experienced, and against which you have appealed to the public, is caused by your having voted for a law which, in its details, violates the Constitution, and outrages justice and humanity. Throughout your long and labored apology, you avoid grappling with these charges. You vindicate the denial of a jury trial only on the ground that it has been denied for fifty-seven years, and on the authority of Mr. Crittenden affirm that the *habeas corpus* is not suspended; but you avoid the constitutional and moral objections urged against your law.

By the Constitution, fugitive slaves are to be restored to those, and those only, who are legally entitled to their services. The means of ascertaining whether a man is a slave, whether he has fled from his master, and whether the claimant is legally entitled to him, are not defined by the Constitution. It is now intrusted to the discretion of Congress to specify these means, but of course that discretion ought to be exercised in accordance with the Constitution, with justice, and with humanity. The complaint against you is, that you have voted for a law which outrages them all, and against this complaint you have failed to offer the shadow of a vindication.

A Virginian comes to Boston, and there seizes one of the inhabitants as his slave. The man claimed declares the claim to be false and fraudulent. Here, then, is an issue both of law and of fact between two men equally entitled to the protection of law; for the man claimed is on every presumption of law and justice to be regarded as free, till the contrary is proved. The issue between these two men is, I have said, one of fact and of law. Is the person seized the man he is said to be? This is a question of fact. Admitting his identity, is he a slave, and, if so, does he belong to the claimant? These are both questions of law, resting upon facts to be proved. Those familiar with the reports of southern courts know that the title to slaves is a frequent matter of litigation, involving intricate questions respecting the validity of wills, the construction of deeds, the partition of estates, and the claims of creditors. By carrying a slave into a free State, the owner forfeits his title to him while there, and cannot reclaim him; and hence the acts of the claimant himself may be involved in the issue. And now, sir, I ask, have you ever known, or can you conceive of, any issue at law respecting the title to property so awfully momentous to a defendant as the one we are considering? Were your son or daughter the defendant in such an issue, would you not rejoice to purchase a favorable judgment by the contribution of the last cent of your great wealth? Let us, then, proceed to inquire what provision *you*, in the fear of God and the love of justice and humanity, have made for the trial of this tremendous issue, — an issue on the result of which all the hopes of a fellow-man for the life that is, and for that which is to come, are suspended.

In the first place, what is the pecuniary value of the plaintiff's claim to *himself?* — for it would be an insult to humanity to estimate in dollars and cents the blessings of liberty and of the conjugal and parental relations to the unhappy defendant.

You have yourself fixed the value of the plaintiff's claim at *one thousand dollars.* So far, then, the issue is, by your own showing, within the constitutional guaranty of trial by jury in all suits at common law where the matter in controversy is of the value of *twenty* dollars. But is the claim made by the plaintiff "a suit at common law?" What is a *suit?* The Supreme Court thus answers the question :

"We understand it (a suit) to be the prosecution or pursuit of some *claim*, demand, or request. In law language, it is the prosecution of some demand in a court of justice." 6 *Wheaton*, 407.

It seems, then, that the Virginian, in claiming an inhabitant of Boston as his slave, in fact brings *a suit* against him for services due worth one thousand dollars. Now remember, sir, the fugitive is not to be delivered up, as a mass of flesh, or inanimate matter, belonging to the claimant, but as a debtor, in the phraseology of your own law, "*owing* service or labor." The suit is brought for service or labor *due*, and the Constitution provides that the person so owing service or labor shall be delivered to him to whom the same is "*due*." And now, is this suit for service due "a suit at *common law?*" Again let the Supreme Court answer.

"The phrase *common law*, found in this clause (the clause guaranteeing a jury trial,) is used in contradistinction to equity and admiralty and maritime jurisdiction. It is well known, that, in civil causes in courts of equity and admiralty, juries do not intervene, and that courts of equity use the trial by jury only in extraordinary cases, to inform the conscience of the court. When, therefore, we find that the amendment requires that the right of trial by jury shall be preserved in suits at common law, the natural conclusion is, that this distinction was present to the minds of the framers of the amendment. By *common law*, they meant what the Constitution denominated, in the third article, 'law;' not merely suits which the common law recognized among its old and settled proceedings, but suits in which legal rights were to be ascertained and determined, in contradistinction to those where equitable rights alone were recognized, and equitable remedies were administered. . . . . . In a just sense, the amendment, then, may be construed to embrace *all suits* which are not of equity and admiralty jurisdiction, *whatever may be the peculiar form* which they may assume to settle legal rights." 3 *Peters*, 446.

If there be meaning in words, these authorities settle the case, and your law is in palpable violation of the amendment to the

Constitution securing a trial by jury in suits at common law where the matter in controversy exceeds twenty dollars in value. Think not, sir, that I am misrepresenting the Supreme Court. I know well that the *dicta* I have quoted have reference to *white* men, and that they have been virtually set aside in decisions respecting black men. I well know, that in our model republic, law and justice and morality are all cutaneous. But admitting that the Supreme Court have stultified themselves, and virtually denied, that, where a suit was brought for the services of a *black* man, the Constitution required a jury trial, recollect, sir, that not in one single instance has the court decided that the Constitution *prohibited* such a trial. But if not prohibited, then Congress are permitted to accord such a trial, and *both you and Mr. Webster have declared that Congress had a right to grant such a trial, and ought to grant it.* In voting, therefore, for a law denying such a trial, you made a voluntary surrender to the slave-holder of the security which such a trial would have afforded to multitudes of your poor, ignorant, oppressed fellow-men. For this act of cruelty and injustice, committed against your own late conviction of duty, what is your justification? Why, that the blacks had been already deprived of the right of trial by jury fifty-seven years!

Let us now see what tribunal you have substituted for a jury in the trial of one of the most momentous issues that can engage the attention of a court of justice. You have provided for the appointment of an indefinite number of judges, each of whom is to have exclusive jurisdiction of these issues, and from whose judgment there is to be no appeal. The Constitution declares, "The judges, both of the supreme and inferior courts, shall hold their offices during good behavior, and shall, at stated times, receive for their services a compensation, which shall not be diminished during their continuance in office." These judges are appointed by the Senate, on the nomination of the President. Your herd of judges, called commissioners, are appointed by the courts, and hold office during pleasure, and instead of receiving a salary, are rewarded by a rule, the infamy of which, it is believed, belongs to your law exclusively,— a rule which doubles their compensation whenever they decide in favor of the rich plaintiff, and *against* the poor and friendless defendant. But perhaps you will deny that these men are judges; for, if judges, their appointment is palpably unconstitutional. Let us hear the Supreme Court, at a time when it was deemed expedient to maintain that the persons who executed the law of 1793 were *judges*.

"It is plain, that, where a claim is made by the owner out of possession for the delivery of a slave, it must be made, if made at all, *against some other person;* and inasmuch as the right is a right of property, capable of being recognized and asserted by proceedings *before a court of justice between parties adverse to each other*, it constitutes, in the strictest sense, a *controversy* between parties, and a case arising under the Constitution of the United States, within the express delegation of judicial power given by that instrument." 16 *Peters*, 616.

Hence your commissioners are, in the *strictest sense*, judges, exercising "judicial power" delegated by the Constitution.

You pronounce Mr. Crittenden "legal authority of the highest kind." This legal authority understands the sixth section of your law as providing that each commissioner "shall have judicial power and jurisdiction to hear, examine, and decide the case in a summary manner." Now, if a man, having judicial power and jurisdiction to decide controversies between parties adverse to each other, in controversies arising under the Constitution and within the express delegation of judicial power given by that instrument, is not a judge, do tell us who is one. Once more, sir, Mr. Crittenden says, "The legal authority of every tribunal of exclusive jurisdiction, where no appeal lies, is of necessity conclusive upon every tribunal; and therefore the judgment of the tribunal created by this act is conclusive upon all other tribunals." So your commissioner is not only a judge, but he constitutes a tribunal of exclusive jurisdiction, and his judgment is binding even upon the Supreme Court of the United States. And yet, sir, you must deny that this omnipotent commissioner is a judge, or you must admit, that, in the mode of his appointment, you have flagrantly violated the Constitution of your country.

It has been most wickedly asserted by our pro-slavery presses and our pro-slavery politicians, that the surrender of fugitives from labor and fugitives from justice are similar proceedings. The surrender of a fugitive slave involves two questions, that of identity and that of property; and the law makes the decision of the commissioner on both points final and conclusive upon every State and Federal court in the land. The surrender of a fugitive criminal involves only the question of personal identity. The Governor of the State issues his warrant for the apprehension and delivery of a certain person proved to him to be charged with felony. If the officer arrests the wrong person, he does it at his peril, and a writ of *habeas corpus* would immediately release the person wrongfully arrested. Again, it is most fraudulently maintained, that, if the wrong person is by the commissioner adjudged a slave, he may sue for his freedom in a southern court! Should he do so, the exhibition of the commissioner's certificate is by law declared to be conclusive *upon all tribunals*. But even supposing that a southern court, in defiance of law, should go behind the certificate, how is a free colored person from the North, working under the lash on a Mississippi plantation, to prove his freedom? How is he to fee a lawyer? How is he to get into court? If once there, where are his witnesses? They are his friends and acquaintances of his own color residing in the North. How are they to be summoned to Mississippi? Should they venture to enter the State, they would be imprisoned, and perhaps sold into slavery; or even if permitted to enter the court-room, their testimony would by law be excluded, against the claims of a white man. How despicably profligate, then, is the assumption of the advocates of your law, that any injustice committed under it would be repaired by southern courts!

It was not enough, it seems, that the wretched defendant in this momentous issue should be subjected to the jurisdiction of a judge unknown to the Constitution, holding his office by a prohibited tenure, incapable of being impeached, and bribed to decide in favor of the plaintiff by the promise of double fees, but the very trial allowed him must be a burlesque on all the forms and principles of juridical justice. The plaintiff, without notice to the defendant, prepares himself for trial, and when his affidavits or witnesses are all ready, he seizes the unsuspecting victim in the street, and puts him *instanter* on his defence. Had the wretched man been accused of some atrocious crime, he might have demanded bail, and would have been permitted to go at large to seek for counsel, to look for witnesses, and to prepare for trial at some future day, of which he would have due notice. But no such privilege is allowed a man who is accused of *owing service*. One of your commissioners has already decided that the law does not permit him to bail the prisoner. The slave power rides in triumph over all the barriers erected by the wisdom of ages for the protection of human rights. The defendant is brought, generally in irons, before your commissioner judge, who is required "to hear and determine the case of *the claimant* in a summary manner." The law seems not even to imagine the possibility of any defence being made on the part of the defendant. It makes no provision for such a defence, — no assignment of counsel, no summons for witnesses. We shall see presently that if the plaintiff makes out a *primâ facie* title, satisfactory to the commission, it is all the law requires. Let me now call your attention to the practical working of your diabolical law. A man named Rose was lately seized at Detroit, and brought before a commissioner as a fugitive slave. I copy from the newspaper report.

> "Mr. Joy (counsel for defendant) moved a postponement of the trial to a future day, to enable Rose to produce his papers to establish his right to freedom, which papers he had *sworn* were in Cincinnati. The counsel for the claimant denied that the commissioner had any authority under the law to grant a postponement. The commissioner agreed with the counsel for the plaintiff, that *he had no authority to postpone the trial;* and he further declared, that, *even were the papers by which Rose was manumitted present, he could not under the law receive them in evidence.*"

Utterly devilish as was this decision, it was sound law. The plaintiff had proved his title satisfactorily, and this being done, the commissioner was bound by the express words of the law to grant the certificate. He had no right to admit rebutting evidence. It was sufficient to prove that the prisoner had been the slave of the claimant's father, and that the claimant was the heir-at-law of his father. This of itself was satisfactory, and therefore the commissioner had no right to admit in evidence the very deed of manumission granted by the father to the slave. The framers of the law had been as explicit as they dared to be. "Upon satisfactory proof being made by deposition or *affidavit*, to be taken and certified, &c., or by other satisfactory testimony [of course, in writing, and *ex parte*], and with proof, also by affidavit, of the *identity* of the person," &c., the defendant is to be surrendered. Not a hint is given that any testimony may be received to rebut the *satisfactory* proof given by the plaintiff. You have, moreover, sir, provided a species of evidence never before heard of in the trial of an issue. By the tenth section, the claimant may go before a judge or court in Texas, and there make proof by affidavit that *his* slave has escaped. Whereupon, the court or judge is to certify that the proof is satisfactory. A record of this satisfactory proof, together with a description of the fugitive, is to be made, and a certified transcript of this record, "being exhibited to any judge, commissioner, or other officer authorized," &c., "*shall* be held and taken to be full and conclusive evidence of the fact of escape, and that the service or labor of the person escaping is *due* to the party in such record mentioned." Here all defence is taken from the defendant. Should he summon a host of witnesses to prove his freedom, not one could be heard; should he offer a bill of sale from the claimant to another, it could not be received; should he produce a deed of manumission, acknowledged and certified in a southern court, it would be waste paper. And thus a man's freedom is to be sacrificed on an affidavit made a thousand miles off. What, sir, would you think of a law that would authorize the seizure and sale of your property to satisfy a debt which any man in California might think proper to swear, before a Californian judge, was *due* from you to him?

Such, sir, is the *trial* which you, the representative of Boston, a descendant of the Pilgrims, and "a gentleman of property and standing," have accorded to the poor and oppressed. Did the

Constitution require such a prostitution of justice, such an outrage of humanity, at your hands? I need not be told that some of your commissioners have not construed your law as strictly as did the Detroit functionary. Thanks to the force of public opinion, and to the zeal of some benevolent lawyers, whose hearts were not padded with cotton, in some instances defendants have been permitted to call witnesses in their behalf; and some regard has been paid to the ordinary principles of justice. But in all such instances, the spirit of the law and the intentions of its framers have been frustrated.

And now let us listen to your "reason" for justifying all the atrocities and abominations of your law. You gravely tell us, "The entire population of the North has acquiesced in the law of 1793, without thinking itself exposed to the charge of barbarity, and I have only to say, that I do not think the charge any more just now." Certainly, sir, the young colonial judge could not have given a reason less logical or satisfactory. You must be an inattentive observer of passing events, if you are ignorant that the law of 1793 has again and again been denounced as iniquitous, that some of the States have prohibited their officers from assisting in its execution, that numberless petitions have been presented to Congress for its repeal, and that you yourself, instead of acquiescing in it, solemnly declared it to be the duty of Congress so far to alter the law, as to grant the alleged fugitive a trial by jury. Yet the law of 1793, wicked as it was, was justice and mercy compared with yours. The trials under that were almost invariably before judges of the State courts, not appointed like your commissioners for the vile and only purpose of reducing their fellow-men to bondage. These judges were not confined to *ex parte* evidence, were not compelled to receive "as full and conclusive" affidavits made in distant States, and by unknown persons. For the most part, they honestly endeavored, by a patient investigation according to the ordinary rules of evidence, and by holding the plaintiff to strict legal proof, to supply the want of a jury.

David Paul Brown, Esq., of Philadelphia, in a letter of last November, affirms that for the last thirty years he has been engaged as counsel in almost every important fugitive case brought before the judges and courts of Philadelphia, and he tells us, "thanks to those upright and impartial and independent judges by whom the rights of the parties were finally determined," he knows of no instance in which a colored person was, in his opinion, wrongfully surrendered. But he adds, "I have known HUNDREDS who have been illegally and unjustly claimed." This experienced lawyer, commenting on your law, justly says it allows "*ex parte* testimony to be received against the alleged fugitive, which upon no principle known to the common law could be received upon the claim to a horse or a dog." About four weeks after the date of this letter, Mr. Brown was called to defend an alleged fugitive "illegally and unjustly claimed," not before one of the "upright and impartial and independent" Pennsylvania judges, but before one of your ten-dollar slave-catching judges. I beg you to mark the result.

On the 21st of December, a colored man was arrested in the street in Philadelphia, without warrant, and accused of stealing chickens. He was thrust into a carriage, driven to the State House, carried into an upper room, and handcuffed. In this state he was detained till a commissioner arrived. The name of this executor of your law is worthy of remembrance. EDWARD D. INGRAHAM ought to be as much endeared to slave-catchers, as Judge Jeffries was to James the Second.

By some means, the arrest became known, and counsel appeared for the prisoner. Your commissioner was informed that the prisoner had only been seized an hour and a half before, and had not heard the charge against him; that his counsel had had no time to learn the plaintiff's case, nor to prepare for the defence; that there were persons residing at a distance, some in New Jersey and some in Wilmington, who would be important witnesses in his behalf. On these grounds, a motion was made for a continuance. And what, sir, do you suppose was the reply made by the slave-catching judge to this motion? "THE HEARING IS TO BE A SUMMARY ONE: LET IT PROCEED." No doubt you fully participate in Mr. Webster's indignation against Austrian barbarity; but see no barbarity in this accursed proceeding against a *colored* American. The hearing did proceed, and James S. Price, on behalf of the plaintiff, swore that the prisoner was Emery Rice, the man claimed, but knew nothing further about his being a slave, except that he had seen him riding the claimant's horse; had *heard it said* the prisoner was a slave. This was the amount of the testimony on behalf of the claimant. Any honest jury, nay, any honest judge, would instantly have decided in favor of the prisoner. Not so Mr. Edward D. Ingraham. The counsel for the defendant asked again for a postponement, and founded the motion on the *oath* of the defendant, that he could procure six persons, naming them, to testify to his freedom. A delay of ONE HOUR was asked for. This was refused, and the judge (!) sent for a certificate to sign. During the delay thus occasioned, one of the six persons named by the defendant appeared, and swore that he had known the prisoner all his life. That he was not Emery Rice, but Adam Gibson; that he was a free man, having been manumitted by the will of his late master. Mr. Brown produced a copy of the will of the late master, and it so far confirmed the testimony of the witness. Another person in the crowd now came forward, and swore that he also knew the prisoner, and that he was a free person, and that he was Adam Gibson. But all was in vain. The commissioner signed the certificate, and, with an obtuseness of intellect which marked him as a fit subject for a commission of lunacy, declared, "He had no doubt of the identity of the prisoner with the slave Emery Rice, and that *all other proceedings must be before the courts of Maryland*, whither he would send him." * And so the prisoner, without seeing his wife and children, whom he had that morning parted from unsuspicious of danger and unconscious of crime, was hurried off at the expense of our glorious model republic, under an escort of officers, who delivered him, not to the courts of Maryland, but to Mr. William S. Knight, the reputed owner. But Mr. Knight told the officers, "You have brought me a wrong man; this is not Emery Rice; this man is no slave of

* See report in the *New York Tribune*, 25th December, 1850.

mine." And so Adam Gibson returned to Philadelphia, and is now a living illustration of the abominable iniquity of one of the most accursed laws to be found in the statute-book of any civilized nation.

You do not think your law more barbarous than that of 1793. Let me further enlighten you. Judge McLean of the Supreme Court, in his opinion delivered last May in the case of *Norris* vs. *Newton et al.*, remarks, "In regard to the arrest of fugitives from labor, the law [act of 1793] *does not impose any active duties on our citizens generally;*" and he argues in defence of the law, that "it gives no one a just right to complain; he has only to refrain from an express violation of the law." In other words, the law only required individuals to be passive spectators of a horrible outrage, and did not compel them to be active participators in other men's villany. Now, what says your law? Why, that every commissioner may appoint as many official slave-catchers as he pleases, and that each of these menials may "summon and call to their aid the *by-standers* or *posse comitatus* of the proper county, when necessary to insure a faithful observance of the clause of the Constitution referred to in conformity with the provisions of this act, AND ALL GOOD CITIZENS ARE HEREBY COMMANDED TO AID AND ASSIST in the prompt and efficient execution of this law, whenever their services may be required." And what is the fate you have provided for the "good citizen," who, believing slavery to be sinful, cannot, in the fear of God, "aid and assist" in making a fellow-man a slave? Any person "who shall aid, abet, or assist" the fugitive, "directly or indirectly," (cunning words) to escape from such claimant, as, for instance, refusing to join in a slave-hunt when required, shall be fined not exceeding $1000, be imprisoned six months, and pay the claimant $1000. I hope, sir, you are now able to perceive that your law has a preëminence in barbarity over its predecessor. And now, sir, please to recollect, that party discipline, aided by the influence of Messrs. Webster and Clay, and the factory and cotton interests of Boston and New York, could not procure for this atrocious law the votes of *one-half* the members of the House of Representatives. Of two hundred and thirty-two members, only one hundred and nine dared to place their names on an enduriug and shameful record, while many basely deserted their seats, fearing alike to vote either for or against it. You, sir, following Mr. Webster's advice, "conquered your prejudices," and in company with *two* more northern Whigs, one of them a native of Virginia, cast your vote for this bill of abominations. But, although you voted for the law, you do not wish your constituents to suppose you approved of it. "It will not, I trust, be inferred from any thing I have said, that I consider the law which has passed unexceptionable. There are amendments which I strongly desire to be introduced into it." What are the exceptionable features of the law, what are the amendments you desire, you refrain from specifying. But you tell us that you would have labored for those amendments "had it been possible, but every body knows that it was *impracticable*." You allude to the *previous question*, which prevented both discussion and amendments. But why, then, did you vote for an objectionable bill which could not be amended? Here, again, we have one of your unfortunate reasons. "I deem conformity to the design of the Constitution more important than the objectionable details of the bill." So, by your own confession, had there been no previous question, you would have swallowed the bill, with all its objectionable details, out of reverence for the *design* of the Constitution, although that design neither embraced nor required a single one of those details. Did you, sir, vote *against* the previous question? On this point you are silent, and the minutes afford no information; but *if* you did, your vote was a most remarkable aberration from your pro-slavery course in Congress. *After* the previous question had been seconded, it was moved to lay the bill on the table. Had this motion been carried, you might have introduced another bill, omitting the "objectionable details," but you voted with the slave-holders. The slave-holders then moved that the bill be read a third time. Had this been lost, there would have been a chance of correcting the "objectionable details." Again you voted with the slave-holders, and a third time, also, on the main question.

I will now, sir, call your attention to the disastrous influence which your law has exerted on the *moral sense* of the community. Says Coleridge, "To dogmatize a crime, that is, to teach it as a doctrine, is itself a crime." Of this crime of dogmatizing crime, Mr. Webster, and most of our cotton politicians, and, alas! many of our fashionable, genteel divines, are guilty; nor are you innocent, sir, who in your law require "GOOD citizens" to aid in hunting and enslaving their fellow-men.

In former years, and before Mr. Webster had undergone his metamorphosis, he thus, in a speech at New York, expressed himself in regard to the anti-slavery agitation at the North:

> "It (slavery) has arrested the *religious feeling* of the country; it has taken strong hold of the consciences of men. He is a rash man indeed, little conversant with human nature, and especially has he a very erroneous estimate of the character of the people of this country, who supposes that a feeling of this kind is *to be trifled with or despised.*"

This gentleman has become the rash man shadowed forth in his speech, and is trifling with and despising the religious feeling of the North. In his street speech in Boston, in favor of slave-hunting, he avowed that he was well aware that the return of fugitives "is a topic that must excite prejudices," and that the question for Massachusetts to decide was, "whether she will conquer her own prejudice." In his letter to the citizens of Newburyport, he sneeringly alludes to the "cry that there is a rule for the government of public men and private men which is superior to the Constitution," and he scornfully intimates that Mr. Horace Mann, who had objected to your law as wicked, would do well "to appeal at once, as others do, to that high authority which sits enthroned above the Constitution and the laws;" and he gives an extract from a nameless English correspondent, in which the writer remarks, "Religion is an excellent thing except in politics," a maxim exceedingly palatable to very many of our politicians. Aware that the impiety of this sentiment was not exactly suited to the meridian of Massachusetts, he says his friend undoubtedly meant "a fantastical notion of religion." Of course, he regards the religious prejudice against hunting and enslaving men as springing from a fantastic notion of religion. Yet, with a strange fatuity, he confesses that "the teaching of Christ and his apostles is a sure guide to duty in *politics*, as in any other concern of life," utterly oblivious of the fact, that the "higher law," which he ridicules, was proclaimed in that very teaching. Christ taught, "Fear not them (magistrates) who kill the body, but are not able to kill the soul, but rather fear HIM who is able to destroy both soul and body in hell." What taught the apostles? "We must obey God, rather than man." Such teaching it was, that gave birth to "the noble army of martyrs," and this very teaching will induce multitudes of Christians at the present day to hazard fines and imprisonment rather than obey the wicked injunctions of your law. It was this same teaching which, on the publication of your law, induced numerous ministers of Jesus Christ, and various ecclesiastical assemblies, to denounce it as wicked, and obedience to it as rebellion against God. This expression of religious sentiment alarmed both our politicians and our merchants. How could the one expect southern votes, or the other southern trade, if the religious people at the North refused to catch slaves? Hence arose a mighty outcry against the blending of religion with politics, and most fearful were the anathemas against the parsons who desecrated the pulpit by preaching politics, that is, preaching that people ought to obey God rather than the Fugitive Slave Act. Such men were, in the language of one of the New York commercial journals, "clerical preachers of rebellion," and their congregations were exhorted to "leave them to naked walls." But the leaven was at work, and an antidote was greatly wanted. Supply of course follows demand, and forthwith there was a sudden advent of cotton clergymen, preaching against rebellion, and cunningly confounding a conscientious, passive disobedience with forcible resistance. Their sermons, in which virtually

"The image of God was accounted as base,
And the image of Cæsar set up in its place,"

were received with mighty applause by the very men who had been striving to save the pulpit from all contaminating contact with politics, and the reverend preachers of cotton politics were elevated into patriots, and their disquisitions against the "higher law" were scattered on the wings of the commercial press broadcast over the land.* The theology which holds that the

* In one of the most celebrated of these sermons, we find the following broad assertion: — "If God *has* left to men the choice of the *kind* of government they will have, he has *not* left it to their choice whether they will obey human government or not. He has *commanded* that obedience." Our rulers command us, when required by a commissioner's agent, to aid in hunting and seizing our innocent fellow-men, and delivering them into the hands of their task-masters. That the reverend preacher would render a cheerful obedience to such a mandate, there is little doubt. We read that the Jewish rulers, "The chief priests and Pharisees, had given a *commandment*, that, if any one knew where he (Jesus) was, he should show it, that they might take him." Strange is it, that of the college of apostles there was but one "good citizen," who rendered obedience to the powers ordained by God; all the others suffered death for their wilful, deliberate defiance of the laws and the magistrates of the land. As a specimen of the teaching of these cotton divines, I quote from this same admired sermon the following precious piece of information, viz.: — "Nor is it true that the *fugitive slave* is made an *outlaw*, and on that ground justifiable for bloody and murderous resistance of law. He is under *the protection of law*; and if any man injures him, or kills him, the law will avenge him, just *as soon as it would you or me*." To deny the truth of this solemn declaration, made in the house of God, would be, in the reverend gentlemen's estimation, but a portion of "that perpetual abuse of our southern brethren" of which he complains. He must, however, permit us to call his attention to the following advertisements respecting a FUGITIVE SLAVE, published in the Wilmington Journal of the 18th of October last, in pursuance of a law of the State of North Carolina.

"'*State of North Carolina, New Hanover County*. — Whereas complaint upon oath hath this day has been made to us, two of the justices of the peace for the State and County aforesaid, by Guilford Horn, of Edgecombe County, that a certain male slave belonging to him, named HARRY, — a carpenter by trade, about 40 years old, 5 feet 5 inches high, or thereabouts, yellow complexion, stout built, with a scar on his left leg (from the cut of an axe,) has very thick lips, eyes deep sunk in his head, forehead very square, tolerably loud voice, has lost one or two of his upper teeth, and has a very dark spot on his jaw, supposed to be a mark, — hath *absented* himself from his master's service, and is *supposed* to be lurking about in this county, committing acts of felony or other misdeeds: These are, therefore, in the name of the State aforesaid, to command said slave forthwith to surrender himself, and return home to his master; and we do hereby, by virtue of the act of Assembly in such case made and provided, intimate and declare that if the said slave Harry doth not surrender himself and return home immediately after the publication of these presents, that any person or persons may KILL and DESTROY the said slave by such means as he may think fit, without accusation or impeachment of any crime or offence for so doing, and without incurring any penalty or forfeiture thereby.

"Given under our hands and seals, this 29th day of June, 1850.

JAMES T. MILLER, J. P.
W. C. BENTTENCOURT, J. P."

"ONE HUNDRED AND TWENTY-FIVE DOLLARS REWARD will be paid for the delivery of said HARRY to me at Tonsott Depot, Edgecombe County, or for his confinement in any jail in the State, so that I can get him; or one hundred and fifty dollars will be given for his HEAD. He was lately heard from in Newbern, where he called himself Henry Barnes (or Burns) and will be likely to continue the name or assume that of Coppage or Farmer. He has a free mulatto woman for a wife, by the name of Sally Bozeman, who has lately removed to Wilmington, and lives in that part of the town called Texas, where he will likely be lurking.

"GUILFORD HORN.

"*June* 29, 1850."

allegiance we owe to civil government binds the conscience to obedience to its mandates, is the same with which Shakspeare's assassin quieted his scruples when acting under the royal command,—"If a king bid a man be a villain, he is bound by the indenture of his oath to be one."

It is amusing to observe with what awful reverence our merchants and brokers regard the sanctity of human law, when it commands them to catch slaves; a reverence not always felt by them for the statute of usury when the money market is tight.

A vast deal of nonsense and impiety has been recently thrown upon the public in relation to the "higher law," by men who had political and pecuniary interests depending on the good-will of the slave-holders. The whole subject is perfectly simple and intelligible, and has been intentionally misrepresented and mystified.

Human government is indispensable to the happiness and progress of human society. Hence God, in his wisdom and benevolence, wills its existence; and in this sense, and this alone, the powers that be are ordained by him. But civil government cannot exist, if each individual may, at his pleasure, forcibly resist its injunctions. Therefore, Christians are required to *submit* to the powers that be, whether a Nero or a slave-catching Congress. But obedience to the civil ruler often necessarily involves rebellion to God. Hence we are warned by Christ and his apostles, and by the example of saints in all ages, in such cases, not to obey, but to submit and suffer. We are to hold fast our allegiance to Jehovah, but at the same time not take up arms to defend ourselves against the penalties imposed by the magistrate for our disobedience. Thus the Divine sovereignty and the authority of human government are both maintained. Revolution is not the abolition of human government, but a change in its form, and its lawfulness depends on circumstances. What was the "den" in which John Bunyan had his glorious vision of the Pilgrim's Progress? A prison to which he was confined for years for refusing obedience to human laws. And what excuse did this holy man make for conduct now denounced as wicked and rebellious? "I cannot obey, but I can suffer." The Quakers have from the first refused to obey the law requiring them to bear arms; yet have they never been vilified by our politicians and cotton clergymen, as rebels against the powers that be, nor sneered at for their acknowledgment of a "higher" than human law. The Lord Jesus Christ, after requiring us to love God and our neighbor, added, "There is none other commandment greater than these;" no, not even a slave-catching act of Congress, which requires us to hunt our neighbor, that he may be reduced to the condition of a beast of burden. Rarely has the religious faith of the community received so rude a shock as that which has been given it by your horrible law, and the principles advanced by its political and clerical supporters. Cruelty, oppression, and injustice are elevated into virtues, while justice, mercy and compassion are ridiculed and vilified.

But lately, the business of catching slaves was regarded as one of the lowest grades of scoundrelism. Now, great pains are taken by our gentlemen of property and standing to ennoble it; and men of eminence in the legal profession are stooping to take the wages of iniquity, and lending themselves to consign to the horrors of American slavery, men whom they know to be innocent of crime. Nay, we have seen in New York a committee of gentlemen actually *raising money by voluntary contributions* to furnish a slave-catcher with professional services gratis; — a free gift, not to mitigate human misery, but to aggravate the hardships of the poor and friendless a thousandfold. Can men of standing in the community thus openly espouse the cause of cruelty and oppression, and, from commercial and political views, trample upon every principle of Christian benevolence, without corrupting the moral sense of the people to the extent of their influence? When gentlemen club together to hire a lawyer to assist a slave-catcher, no wonder that the commercial press should teem with the vilest abuse of all who feel sympathy for the fugitive. One of the most malignant pro-slavery journals in New York is edited by your colleague and fellow Whig, the Honorable Mr. Brooks, and his brother. I copy, sir, for your consideration, the following article from the *New*

York Evening Express, published during the late trial in that city of Henry Long, an alleged fugitive:

"Two fugitive cases are now before our courts; one that of the negro Henry Long, and the other that of three white Frenchmen, under the extradition treaty with France. The negro's case makes a great deal of noise, because he is black; the three white Frenchmen are hardly heard of. The three white French people pay their own counsel; they may have committed a robbery in Paris, or may not; are perhaps innocent, though possibly guilty; but here they are on trial, with no chance of a trial before a jury! If they are sent back, and are convicted, they go to the galleys, and are slaves for life. The negro, Henry Long, lucky fellow for being black! lives in clover here, and has one of the best speakers in the city, on the best fee, interests all the abolitionists in all quarters, who contribute money freely for his defence, and if he is returned, leaves here canonized as a martyr, and goes back to the condition he was born in, to fatten on hog and hominy, better fed and better clothed than nine tenths of the farm laborers in Great Britain. Another consideration strikes us, and that is, the cost of defending Long will buy his freedom three times over. The very fee of his counsel would purchase his freedom. But to buy him and pay for him, *not steal* him, would leave no room for agitation. And where does this money come from, that cares for Long and neglects the three Frenchmen? From England, in the main, we believe. The abolitionists here do not *contribute it.*"

It would be difficult to find in the Satanic press a more clumsy piece of malignant falsehood. We have here, from the same pen and in the same article, the assertions, that the abolitionists in all quarters, we are assured, "contribute money freely for his defence;" and then the money, it is believed, comes mainly from England. "The abolitionists here do not contribute it." To contribute money for the legal defence of a fugitive is *stealing him.* The cost of defending Long amounted to three times the price that would be asked for him. Long, after his return, sold in Richmond for $750; of course his defence cost $2,250. To whom, and for what was this money paid? Long could not be bought in New York, all advances for the purpose being peremptorily repulsed. His counsel's fee was $300, being all contributed in New York, and about $100 of it being raised by the free colored people. While $300 were thus raised to give Long the chance of a legal defence, gentlemen of the New York Union Safety Committee, of which your colleague has the honor of being a member, contributed $500 to aid the slave-catcher in reducing to bondage a man unaccused of crime!

I am inclined to believe, sir, that you have little cause to congratulate yourself, that, in voting for the Fugitive Slave Law, you have advanced the cause of truth, justice, humanity, or religion.

A refusal to *obey* your wicked law has been artfully represented as a determination to *resist* its execution. Very few of our white population have intimated the most distant intention of resorting to illegal violence. Very many ecclesiastical bodies have denounced your law as so iniquitous, that they could not in conscience obey it; but I challenge you to point to a *single instance* in which such a body has recommended forcible resistance. To the vast accumulation of impiety uttered in support of your law has been added a fiendish ridicule of the benevolent and Christian feeling arrayed against it. It is true, that some of our free blacks and fugitives have declared, that they would, at the hazard of their lives, defend themselves against the kidnapper. Whatever may be thought of the wisdom of such a determination, be assured it will tax your logical powers to the utmost to prove that God has conferred the right of self-defence exclusively upon white men. The slave is a prisoner of war, and instead of being protected by law, he is subjected by it to every conceivable outrage. When murdered, his owner seeks in the courts *damages* at the hands of the murderer, as he would for the death of his horse. For no possible injury committed on his person, either by his owner or others, can he receive compensation, although the law may profess to punish cruelty to him as to other animals. Now it has never been regarded as immoral, by those who admit the right of self-defence, for a prisoner of war to effect his escape by slaying his guard. All this, I know, will horrify a certain class of our divines and politicians. But let them be patient. I am not laying down a doctrine, but stating *facts*, which they may disprove if they can. Let them remember that all the slavery which they delight to find in the Bible was the slavery of *white* men, and that the Roman slaves in the time of Christ, whose bondage, we are told, he and his apostles approved, were held by the *right of war*. White Americans have been held as slaves by the same holy and Scriptural tenure. Let us, then, inquire how the escape and resistance of *white* slaves have heretofore been regarded. In 1535, the white slaves in Tunis alone amounted to twenty thousand. Cervantes, who had himself been a slave in Algiers, says in his writings, "For liberty we ought to risk life itself; slavery being the greatest evil that can fall to the lot of man." Acting upon this precept, he himself, while a slave, planned a general insurrection of the slaves. Yet Cervantes was recognized as a faithful son of the Church, and the license prefixed to his works declares they contain nothing contrary to the Christian religion. The Annual Register for 1763 announces, that, "last month, the Christian slaves at Algiers, to the number of four thousand, rose and killed their guards, and massacred all who came in their way." The insurrection was suppressed, but no one in Europe denounced the insurgents as bloodthirsty wretches, nor regarded their effort as an impious and anti-Christian rebellion against the powers ordained of God. In the reign of Elizabeth, one John Fox, a slave on the Barbary coast, slew his master, and, effecting his escape with a number of his fellow-slaves, arrived in England. The queen, instead of looking upon him as a murderer, testified her admiration of his exploit by allowing him a pension.*

Washington Madison performed a similar exploit on board an American coast slaver, and arrived, with a large number of his fellow-slaves, in the British West Indies. Mr. Webster, then Secretary of State, officially demanded of the British government the surrender of this heroic man as a MURDERER.

In 1793, there were one hundred and fifteen American slaves in Algiers, held by as perfect and Scriptural a tenure as any slave is now held in any part of our wide republic. Had one of these slaves made his escape by killing his Algerine master, would any of our patriotic divines, would any gentleman of the "New York Union Committee of Safety," would even Mr. Webster himself, have pronounced him a murderer? Had the captain of a British ship favored his escape, and given him a passage to

* For the facts on this subject, see the admirable work by Charles Sumner, entitled "White Slavery in the Barbary States."

Boston, would your colleague, the Honorable Mr. Brooks, have accused him of slave stealing? Is it not possible, sir, that, with very many of our casuists and moralists, questions of conscience are decided according to the tincture of a skin?

I will now ask your attention to some of the political consequences resulting from the late measures in which you rejoice, and for which you voted. No sooner had Congress made the required concessions to the slave power, than the advocates of those measures claimed the glory of having given peace to the country, and perpetuity to the Union. Mr. Webster, as one of the chief agents in this blessed consummation, received the congratulations of a crowd in Washington. In his reply he observed:

> "Truly, gentlemen, the last two days have been great days. A work has been accomplished which dissipates doubts and alarms, puts an end to angry controversies, fortifies the Constitution of the country, and strengthens the bond of the Union.
>
> "'Now is the winter of our discontent
> Made glorious summer; . . . . .
> And all the clouds that lowered upon our house
> In the deep bosom of the ocean buried.'"

The glorious summer anticipated by the orator proved cold and brief, and if the lowering clouds were indeed buried in the ocean, the sea has given up its dead. Never before, since the organization of the government, has such a tempest of indignation swept over the land. Never before, in a single instance, has there been manifested throughout the religious portion of the community, of all creeds and names, such a settled determination in the fear of God to withhold obedience to a law of the land. The sentiments of the great mass of the people of the free States, exclusive of the commercial cities, are briefly but emphatically embodied in a resolution of the Common Council of Chicago, viz.:

> "The Fugitive Slave Act recently passed by Congress is revolting to our moral sense, and an outrage on our feelings of justice and humanity, because it disregards all the securities which the Constitution and laws have thrown around personal liberty, and its direct tendency is to alienate the people from their love and reverence for the government and institutions of our country."

How far the clouds which hovered over our house have been dissipated, let the recent rout of Mr. Webster's party in Massachusetts testify. Let his own declaration, a month after the *peace* measures were adopted, that the Union was passing through a *fiery trial*, testify.* How far the work of the two days has fortified the Constitution, let the recent law of Vermont, denounced as an utter nullification of the Constitution, because it rescues the alleged fugitive from the hands of the commissioner, and gives him a jury trial before a State court, testify. When rumors were rife that Mr. Webster intended to repudiate his own thunder, the Wilmot Proviso, the *New York Herald*, the chief northern organ of the slave-holders, promised that, if the senator would indeed pursue a course so patriotic, a grateful country would, at the next election, place him in the presidential chair. But scarcely had the acts advocated by Mr. Webster been consummated, than the *Herald*, with sardonic malice, announces,—

"The predictions of Mr. Clay, that the Compromise Bill would speedily conciliate all parties, and restore the era of good feeling, were exactly the reverse of the actual consequences. Mr. Webster has been cast overboard in Massachusetts. General Cass has been virtually condemned in Michigan. Mr. Dickinson, the President, and his cabinet, have been routed in New York. Mr. Phelps has been superseded in Vermont. Whilst in Ohio, Illinois, Iowa, and Wisconsin, the Free Soilers have carried off the booty." And he winds up with declaring, that the next President "can't be Fillmore nor Webster."

If the "peace measures" have strengthened the bond of the Union, what mean all the meetings lately held to *save the Union?* Why is the tocsin now sounded by the very authors and friends of the measures? How comes it that, in Boston itself, the chairman of a Union meeting contradicts the exulting and jubilant shout of triumph uttered by the Secretary of State, and makes the following doleful announcement?

"The Union, and consequently the existence of this nation, is menaced, and unless there is a great and general effort in their support, we may soon behold the mighty fabric of our government trembling over our heads, and threatening by its fall to crush the prosperity which we have so long and happily enjoyed."

* Letter to Union Meeting in New York, 28th Oct., 1850.

So relaxed has become the bond of our Union, that one hundred gentlemen of property and standing in New York have, under the style and title of "The New York Union Committee of Safety," assumed the onerous task of taking it into their safe keeping. "Committees of safety" are associated with times of peril and anarchy, and are never wanted when alarms have ceased, angry discussions ended, the Constitution fortified, and the bond of Union strengthened.

In this universal panic, in this dread entertained, especially in Boston, by Mr. Webster's friends, of soon seeing the mighty fabric of our government trembling over their heads, it may, sir, be consolatory to you and others to know how so dire a calamity may be averted. The chivalric senator from Mississippi — the gentleman who threatens to hang one senator if he dare place his foot on the soil of Mississippi, who draws a loaded pistol on another, and for a third bears a challenge to mortal combat — was lately in the city of New York. The Committee of Safety found him out, and lauded him for his fearless discharge of duty, and his fervor and devotion to the Union, and welcomed him to the commercial emporium in the name of all who appreciate the blessings we enjoy, and are willing to transmit them to their children. The worthy and conciliatory gentleman very appropriately communicated to the committee having the Union in charge the conditions on which alone it could be saved, notwithstanding its bond had so recently been strengthened. These conditions are, we learn, four in number.

1. "The Fugitive Slave Bill passed by Congress shall remain the law of the land, and be faithfully executed."

Both you and Mr. Webster admit that the Constitution permits a jury trial to the fugitive. Should Congress, in its wisdom, and in obedience to the wishes of the great mass of the northern population, and in the exercise of its constitutional power, elevate property in a human being to the same level with that in a horse, and permit a jury to pass upon the title to it, — *the Union must be dissolved.*

2. "The Wilmot Proviso, that monstrous thing, shall not be revived." It was not courteous, certainly, in Mr. Foote thus to

characterize Mr. Webster's thunder. The claim to this thunder was made in his speech, September, 1847, at the Springfield Convention, which nominated him for President; and the Convention, in his presence, thus declared their devotion to his missile:

"The Whigs of Massachusetts now declare, and put this declaration of their purpose *on record*, that Massachusetts will never consent that Mexican territories, however acquired, shall become a part of the American Union, unless on the *unalterable* condition that there shall be neither slavery nor involuntary servitude, otherwise than in punishment for crime."

The next year Mr. Webster launched his thunder over the Territory of Oregon, and thus in his speech (10th August, 1848) vindicated it from the character now given to it by Mr. Foote:

"Gentlemen from the South declare that we invade their rights when we deprive them of a participation in the enjoyment of territories acquired by the common services and common exertions of all. Is this true? Of what do we deprive them? Why, they say that we deprive them of the privilege of carrying their slaves as slaves into the new territories. Well, sir, what is the amount of that? They say, that in this way we deprive them of going into this acquired territory with their property. Their property! What do they mean by this 'property?' We certainly do not deprive them of the privilege of going into those newly acquired territories with all that, in the general estimate of human society and common and universal understanding of mankind, is esteemed property. Not at all. The truth is just this. They have in their own States peculiar laws which create property in persons. . . . . . The real meaning, then, of southern gentlemen, in making this complaint, is, that they cannot go into the territories of the United States carrying with them their own peculiar law, a law which creates property in persons."

So the Wilmot Proviso was no monstrous thing at all, as applied to Oregon. When the question came up of applying this same Proviso to New Mexico and California, Mr. Webster discovered in these Territories a certain peculiarity of physical geography and Asiatic scenery which he had not discovered in Oregon, and which, he found, rendered it a physical impossibility for southern gentlemen to carry there "a law which creates property in persons," and he therefore gave them full liberty to carry their law into those vast regions, if they could. But at the very moment of giving this liberty to southern gentlemen, he courageously warned them that his thunder was good constitutional thunder, and would be used whenever necessary.

> "Wherever there is an *inch of land* to be stayed back from becoming slave territory, I am ready to insert the principle of the exclusion of slavery. I am pledged to that from 1837, — pledged to it again and again, and I will perform those pledges."

So, should we get another slice of Mexico, or annex Cuba or St. Domingo, Mr. Webster would revive the Wilmot Proviso, and then *he* will be the means, if he succeeds, of dissolving the Union!

3. The next condition announced to the Safety Committee is, — "No attempt shall be made in Congress to prohibit slavery in the District of Columbia."

Now it is the opinion of Mr. Webster, that Congress has the constitutional right, not merely to attempt, but actually to effect, the exclusion of slavery in *all* the Territories of the United States. The District of Columbia being placed by the Constitution expressly under "the exclusive jurisdiction" of Congress, the *constitutional* right to abolish slavery there has rarely been questioned; but it has been contended that good faith to the States which ceded the District forbids such an act of constitutional power. Hence, in 1838, a resolution was introduced into the Senate declaring that the abolition of slavery in the District would be "a violation of good faith," &c. What said Mr. Webster?

> "I do not know any matter of fact, or any ground of argument, on which this affirmation of plighted faith can stand. I see nothing in the act of cession, and nothing in the Constitution, and nothing in the transaction, implying any limitation on the authority of Congress." *

* On the 10th of January, 1838, Mr. Clay moved in the Senate the following resolution, viz.:— "Resolved, that the interference by the citizens of any of the States, with a view to the abolition of slavery in this District, is endangering the rights and security of the people of this District; and that any act or measure of Congress designed to abolish slavery in this District would be a violation of the faith implied in the cession by the States of Virginia and Maryland, a just cause of alarm to the people of the slave-holding States, and have a direct and inevitable tendency to disturb and endanger the Union." Passed, 38 to 8, Mr. Webster voting in the negative. *Senate Journal, 2 Sess. 25 Cong.*, p. 127.

4. The last condition on which the Union can be preserved is, — "No State shall be prevented from coming into the Union on the ground of having slavery." This is an unkind cut at Mr. Webster, since he has again and again pledged himself against the admission of slave States. Even so early as 1819, he advocated, in a public meeting at Boston, a resolution declaring that Congress

"Possessed the constitutional power, upon the admission of any new State created beyond the limits of the original territory of the United States, to make the prohibition of the further extension of slavery or involuntary servitude in such new State a condition of admission. That, in the opinion of this meeting, it is just and expedient that this power should be exercised by Congress upon the admission of all new States created beyond the original limits of the United States."

In his New York speech, in 1837, he averred,

"When it is proposed to bring new members into the political partnership, the old members have a right to say on what terms such new partners are to come in, and *what they are to bring along with them.*"

In his Springfield speech, he insisted,

"There is no one (he forgot Mr. Foote and his other southern friends) who can complain of the North for resisting the increase of *slave representation*, because it gives power to the minority in a manner inconsistent with the principles of our government."

So late as 1848, he proclaimed on the floor of the Senate,

"I shall oppose all such extension (slave representation) at all times and under all circumstances, even against all inducements, against all combinations, against all compromises."

The State of Georgia, in her convention of December last, added a *fifth* condition to those stated by Mr. Foote as indispensable to the preservation of the Union, viz.: — "No act suppressing the slave-trade between the slave-holding States." Unfortunately for Mr. Webster, he is here, for the fifth time, virtually held up as a disorganizer, and an enemy of the Union; for in his speech in the Senate (February 6, 1837) he remarked:

"As to the point, the right of regulating the transfer of slaves from one State to another, he did not know that he entertained any doubt, because the Constitution gave Congress the right to regulate trade and commerce between the States. Trade in what? In whatever was the subject of commerce and ownership. If slaves were the subjects of ownership, then trade in them between the States was subject to the regulation of Congress."

Mr. Webster declared, that the work of the two days in which he rejoiced had fortified the Constitution, and strengthened the bond of the Union; and yet we are now solemnly warned, by the very men and party with whom he is acting, that the bond is to be severed, should Congress pass any one of five laws, all and each of which he, the great expounder, declares the Constitution authorizes Congress to pass. So it seems the great peril to which we are exposed, the course which is to make the fabric of our government to tremble over the heads of the people of Boston, is, not the violation of the Constitution, nor the breach of its compromises, nor the invasion of the rights of the South, but the exercise by Congress of powers which Mr. Webster declares to be undoubtedly constitutional. The abolitionists supposed they were following a safe guide when they confined themselves, in their petitions to Congress for legislative action against slavery, exclusively to such measures as they were assured, by the eminent expounder, were strictly constitutional. The abolitionists have sympathized with this gentleman in the obloquy he incurred, in common with themselves, for holding opinions unpalatable to the slave-holders, and for maintaining the constitutional rights of Congress. Because he insisted, in the Senate, on the power of Congress over slavery and the slave-trade in the District of Columbia, Mr. Rives, of Virginia, was so unkind as to say, that the gentleman from Massachusetts, "if it so pleased his fancy, might disport himself in tossing squibs and firebrands about this hall; but those who are sitting upon a barrel of gunpowder, liable to be blown up by his dangerous missiles, could hardly be expected to be quite as calm and philosophic." Because he presented anti-slavery petitions, and insisted on the duty of Congress to consider them, Mr. King, of Alabama, affirmed that the course which the senator from Massachusetts had taken had "placed him at the head of those men who are inundating Congress with their petitions." Strange as it may now seem, Mr. Cuthbert, of

Georgia, told Mr. Webster to his face in the Senate, "The gentleman had uniformly been opposed to all those measures which tended to quiet the country and heal those sectional dissensions which distract the Union." * Surely, when the abolitionists have so long made Mr. Webster their polar star in all constitutional questions, and have incurred with him the accusation of tossing squibs and firebrands, and of opposing measures which tended to quiet the country and settle sectional dissensions, they had a right to expect from his friends a larger share of compassion and forbearance than they have experienced.

It would seem, sir, that, in the late treaty of peace between the North and the South, it has been agreed and understood, that every power granted by the Constitution whereby slavery can be protected, extended, and perpetuated, is to be actively enforced; and that every power which might be used for curtailing human bondage, however unquestionable may be its grant, shall forever remain dormant, under the penalty of an immediate dissolution of the Union. This, sir, is the treaty which our commercial cities are glorifying; this is the treaty which has turned our "winter of discontent" into "glorious summer." And think you, sir, that the slave-holders, having eyes, see not, and having understandings, perceive not, the haberdashery patriotism which rejoices in such a treaty, and denounces as "fanatics," "vipers," and "woolly-headed philanthropists," all who do not confess it to be a glorious consummation? The southern papers tell us that our Union meetings are got up to "sell a little more tape and flannel," and they remark, "It is very queer that Union meetings are held only in places which trade with the South." Out of regard to their southern brethren, a member of the British House of Commons was insulted in Faneuil Hall by a portion of the Boston people, and forthwith the *New Orleans Delta*, instead of gratefully acknowledging the compliment, remarks, that their "good Union-loving friends in Boston are now solacing the South, with sugar-plums in the shape of resolutions and speeches, and spice in the form of a row, got up on the occasion of the first appearance of

* Speech, June 8, 1836.

George Thompson, an imported incendiary and hireling agitator. Such manifestation possesses an advantage which doubtless constitutes no small recommendation with our good brethren of Boston, — it is very cheap. The *cottoncratical* clerks and warehousemen may raise a hubbub in Faneuil Hall, but the fanatics can slay them at the *polls*."

It is some consolation to those who are now suffering all the contempt and opprobrium which can be thrown both upon their heads and their hearts, because they have refused to follow Mr. Webster in the devious paths in which it has lately been his pleasure to walk, that they have by their constancy and firmness extorted from their southern antagonists a tribute which is not paid to their revilers. Said Mr. Stanley, of Virginia, in his speech in the House of Representatives last March, speaking of a certain class of northern politicians, — "I would say, with a slight alteration of one of Canning's verses, —

> "'Give me the avowed, erect, and manly foe,
> Open I can meet, perhaps may turn, his blow;
> But of all the plagues, great Heaven, thy wrath can send,
> Save, O save me from *a dough-face friend!*'"

In closing this long letter, permit me to advert to the opinion expressed abroad of your Fugitive Law. Mr. Webster thought it convenient to quote the sentiment of a nameless correspondent, as to the mischievous mixture of religion with politics. Possibly the opinion of Dr. Lushington, one of the Lords of the Privy Council, Judge of the Vice-Admiralty Court, and the negotiator, on the part of Great Britain, of a recent treaty with France, may be entitled to at least equal weight. This gentleman, in a private letter to an English friend, and not intended for publication, thus speaks of your law:

"No one can feel more sincerely than myself, abhorrence of the Fugitive Slave Bill, — a measure as cruel and unchristian as ever disgraced any country."

An Irish liberal, writing from Dublin, says:

"I long looked to your country as the ark of the world's liberties. I confess I hope for this no longer. The Fugitive Slave Bill is a shocking sample of the depravity of public sentiment in the United States. So atrocious a measure could not have passed into a law, if the majority of the people had not actively assented, or passively consented. Here, by the preponderating influence of our aristocracy, a small, but compact body, measures are often carried into laws that are very distasteful to multitudes; but such a mean, vile law as the Fugitive Slave Bill could not pass in England."

The English press, Whig, Tory, and Radical, is indignant at the atrocities of your law. The taunt of our slave-holders, that the English had better reform abuses at home, is thus met by a radical journal, *The People:*

"The Americans laugh at us when we speak of American slavery, so long as so many of our fellow-subjects in England and Ireland are perishing from starvation through monarchial and aristocratical tyranny. We answer, that the Americans *know* that the men and women who lift up their voices against American slavery are the enemies of British tyranny and oppression."

Your law, sir, degrades the national character abroad; its excessive servility to southern dictation excites the contempt of the slave-holders for the easy, selfish virtue of their northern auxiliaries, while its outrages upon religion, justice, humanity, and the dearest principles of personal freedom, under pretence of preserving the Union, weaken the attachment of conscientious men for a confederacy which requires such horrible sacrifices for its continuance. All these evils might have been easily avoided by a law satisfying every requirement of the Constitution, and yet treating the alleged fugitive as a MAN, and granting him the same protection as is accorded to an alleged murderer. God gave you, sir, an opportunity for which you ought to have been grateful, of illustrating your Puritan descent by standing forth before the nation as an advocate of justice and freedom, and of the rights of the poor and oppressed. Through a blind devotion to a political leader, you rejected the palm which Providence tendered to your acceptance, and have indelibly associated your name with cruelty and injustice. Had you retired from the notice of the public, as you did from the suffrages of the electors, you had acted wisely. In an evil hour for yourself, you stood forth as the champion of the Fugitive Slave Law. Its enemies rejoice in your rashness, for your feeble apology has rendered its deformities more prominent, and, by failing to vindicate, you have virtually confessed its abominations. May you live, sir, to deplore the grievous error you have committed, and, by your future efforts in behalf of human freedom and happiness, atone for the wound they have received at your hand.

FEBRUARY, 1851

AN ADDRESS

TO THE ANTI-SLAVERY CHRISTIANS OF THE UNITED STATES. SIGNED BY A NUMBER OF CLERGYMEN AND OTHERS.

JUNE, 1852.

FRIENDS AND BRETHREN:—We address you in behalf of the American and Foreign Anti-Slavery Society. Approving of the principles avowed and the measures pursued by that association, we beg leave to submit to you the considerations which peculiarly entitle it at the present juncture to the active sympathy and effectual aid of the friends of the anti-slavery cause.

While the advocates of constitutional government in Europe are lamenting a wide-spread reäction in behalf of despotic authority, the friends of the inalienable rights of man behold with grief and mortification a similar reäction in our own Republic, in behalf of a despotism more inexorable, and more hostile to human progress and happiness, than any which afflicts the eastern continent. In both instances, the reäction is more apparent than real. Opinions in favor of human liberty remain the same, but the expression of them has, to a greater or less degree, been stifled by a sudden, mighty, and combined effort of capitalists and politicians, aided to a great extent by ecclesiastical influence, and in each case accompanied with violated pledges and revolting perfidy.

In our own community, the cause of Christian morals has been deeply wounded, and a new impulse given to infidelity, by the various modes adopted by merchants, politicians, and divines to conciliate the slave-holding interest. Doctrines have been advanced on high authority respecting the supremacy of human laws, which, if true, convict the "noble army of martyrs," including the blessed apostles themselves, of being but felons and traitors. Public men, and even public meetings, have professed in unqualified terms their ignorance of a higher law than the Federal Constitution. Rich men among us have given of their abundance to reduce to slavery the fugitive from bondage; and lawyers, heretofore regarded as reputable, have not shrunk from taking reward against the innocent, and prostituting a noble profession to the service of the slave-catcher. The sympathy heretofore felt for the victim of oppression who had escaped from his prison-house, and the repugnance manifested to aid in his arrest, have been denounced as "prejudices to be conquered;" and lips which once uttered noble words in behalf of human rights, have been busily employed in proclaiming to republicans the duty and the glory of catching slaves. Nay, some professed ambassadors of the merciful Jesus have announced from their pulpits that HE has sanctioned the conversion into articles of merchandise of beings charged with no crime, made a little lower than the angels, and redeemed by his own blood! A law has been passed for the recovery of fugitive slaves, which, for its cool violation of all the received and acknowledged principles of judicial justice, for its outrages on humanity, and for its arbitrary requirement of every citizen to assist in a slave-hunt when commanded by an official menial, is unexampled in the legislation of any Christian country. Yet an active agency in the execution of this most detestable law has been made, even by professed ministers of the gospel, a test of Christian obedience.

The success which has thus far attended the combined effort to which we have referred, has been in a great measure owing to the fancied security of the North and the simulated violence of the South.

The war against Mexico was waged for the acquisition of

slave territory, and great was the fear felt by the North that human bondage would be extended to the shores of the Pacific. No less than fourteen States protested, through their Legislatures, against any enlargement of the area of slavery. The voice of Daniel Webster was raised to warn his countrymen of the impending calamity, and to approve and enforce the great principles announced by the Free Soil Convention at Buffalo. The innate love of liberty was awakened throughout the North, and its representatives in Congress bowed to the will of their constituents; and all the devices of the slave-holders to procure territorial governments for the conquered territories, allowing the slavery of a portion of the inhabitants, were defeated. Soon, the Wilmot proviso, applied, with the assistance of Daniel Webster, to Oregon, secured that important territory to freedom. This was followed by the joyful intelligence that New Mexico and California had both adopted State Constitutions prohibiting slavery. A shout of victory ascended from the North, and the greatness of the triumph was supposed to be attested by the wailings of desperation uttered by the slave-holders. It was at this moment of fancied security that the capitalists and politicians contrived a panic about the Union, and traders in southern votes and merchandise devised the patriotic work of saving the Union, by surrendering the territories of New Mexico and Utah to the slave-holders, and making slave-hunting a national sport, under regulations of extraordinary cruelty. The work was hastened on by the most astounding treachery, supported by the audacious assumption that the law of physical geography and Asiatic scenery rendered it physically impossible that any portion of the vast region conquered from Mexico could ever be trodden by slaves.

A dissolution of the Union could have no other effect on the slave-holding interest than to break down those bulwarks which the Federal Government, from its beginning, has been busy in raising around it, and to rouse all beyond the slave territory into active hostility. But although the Union was in little danger, the work of saving it was no less profitable than patriotic, as it tended to prevent the political and commercial non-intercourse threatened by the South; and the proceedings of Union-saving committees were found a convenient mode of advertising for the trade and the votes of the slave-holders. In this manner an influence was exerted which, aided by the supposed security of the North, led to the so-called Compromise, in which the fruits of the recent victory were all thrown away, with the single exception of the anti-slavery Constitution of California. Something was indeed gained to the *character* of the national capital, by prohibiting the importation of slaves for sale, but nothing to the cause of humanity, since the traffic was only transferred from Washington to Alexandria. In return for the California Constitution, which Congress could not have prevented and did not dare to annul, we have had the prodigious enlargement of the slave State of Texas, the abandonment of New Mexico and Utah to slavery, and the enactment of the fugitive bill, as drafted by the slave-holders themselves, forced through the House of Representatives without discussion, and so intensely odious and wicked, that not even personal interest nor party discipline could induce one half of the members of the Lower House to incur the infamy of giving it their votes.

The political parties, having thus conciliated the slave-holders, entered upon a new race between themselves for power and office, and mutually agreed to prevent, as far as possible, all interference in the race by the avowed friends of human rights. The anti-slavery agitation was to be suppressed at all hazards; and every man who expressed sympathy for the oppressed, or indignation against slave-hunts, was to be driven from either party. By virtue of this compact, similar in its spirit to that which in Europe is smothering every aspiration for freedom, all who protest against the oppression of millions of native-born Americans, are to be deemed disturbers of the public peace, while the powers of slave-holders, like those of kings, are to be regarded as held by the grace of God, and too sacred to be discussed or questioned.

It is under these circumstances, painful, mortifying, and unexpected, that we address ourselves to the anti-slavery Christians of the United States. The whole question of the duty of opposition to slavery rests on the sinfulness of reducing innocent men and women, and their children after them, to articles of merchandise. If human beings may be held as chattels, they are, of course, legitimate subjects of traffic, and the African, no less than the American slave-trade, is a commendable and a Christian commerce. The lawfulness of slavery in no degree depends on the complexion of its victims, since the slavery alleged to be recognized in the Scriptures was unquestionably that of Asiatics and Europeans. None of our clerical champions of the institution ever venture to dwell on its accordance with the attributes of the Deity, or the precepts of the gospel. On what ground, then, is the moral vindication of American slavery rested? On the alleged fact that God permitted the Jews to hold certain heathen as slaves, and that, consequently, it cannot be morally wrong in Americans to hold their own countrymen, and even their fellow-Christians, and often their own children, brothers and sisters, as slaves. Without admitting the premises, we utterly deny the conclusion drawn from them. The Creator and Judge of all men, infinite in wisdom, goodness, justice, and power, selects his own modes of maintaining his moral government, and of inflicting deserved punishment; and none may say unto him, "What doest thou?" To him belongeth vengeance, and none may execute it in his name, except by his appointment. He saw fit to destroy by water a guilty world; but will it be inferred from this act of divine sovereignty that saints have a moral right to drown sinners? For their extreme wickedness, the seven nations of Palestine were doomed to extermination, and the Jews were ordered to take possession of their land, and to put all the inhabitants, men, women, and children, to the sword; to make no covenant with them, nor show mercy unto them. Does this commission to the Jews confer upon us similar rights in other lands? The nations adjoining Palestine were idolatrous and otherwise excessively depraved; and we are assured by pro-slavery divines that God, by an *express revelation*, gave the Jews the privilege of buying and holding their inhabitants as slaves; and hence we are taught that, without any similar revelation to ourselves, we are authorized to keep our own brethren in bonds, and to reduce them to the condition of beasts of burden, in defiance of the express commands of God to do justice and to love mercy, and to do to others as we would they should do unto us. We utterly deny the authorized existence of hereditary chattel slavery in the Jewish commonwealth, such slavery being absolutely forbidden by the universal emancipation proclaimed on each returning Jubilee. But so far as relates to the lawfulness of *American* slavery, it is wholly immaterial whether the Jews held slaves or not, since it is admitted by all that if they did, they acted by virtue of a special and express permission from God, while it is equally admitted that no such permission has been given to us. If American slavery be sanctioned by the religion of Jesus Christ, then, indeed, is that religion an inextricable riddle, both tolerating and forbidding every species of cruelty, injustice, and oppression.

Friends and brethren, we believe before God that American slavery is hateful in his sight, and utterly irreconcilable with the holy and merciful precepts of the gospel of his Son. Hence, we believe it morally wrong to render any voluntary aid in upholding an iniquitous system, or in reducing a fellow-man to bondage.

We are continually told that the Federal Government has nothing to do with slavery, and yet from a very early period its powers have been exerted to protect, to extend, and to perpetuate the institution. It is the object of the American and Foreign Anti-Slavery Society to effect, as far as possible, an entire divorce of the Federal Government from the subject of slavery. In relation to the constitutional powers of the Federal Government, we indulge in no opinions more ultra than such as have been avowed by Daniel Webster himself. With him we hold that Congress is fully authorized to abolish and to forbid slavery in its own territories, to suppress the commerce in slaves between the States, and to refuse admission into the Union of new slave States. We also cordially concur in his "judgment," expressed in his speech in the Senate, on the 7th of March, 1850, that the Constitution does not confer on Congress the right to legislate respecting fugitive slaves. In accordance with these views, the

American and Foreign Anti-Slavery Society aims at delivering the General Government from all entangling alliance with slavery, and they desire to effect this much desired deliverance by inducing the people to select for their representatives in Congress such men only as will resolutely refuse to legislate in behalf of slavery.

But as anti-slavery Christians, our duties in regard to this horrible and sinful system extend beyond the jurisdiction of the Federal Government, and reach even to the slave-holders themselves. True Christianity is an aggressive religion. "Go ye into all the world," was the command of its divine founder. Can it be our duty to send missionaries into China and Hindostan, to rebuke the sins of their inhabitants, and to prostrate in the dust their altars and their gods, and yet to observe the silence of the grave in regard to a sin which, in our own country, reduces millions to ignorance, degradation, and wretchedness, and, by denying them the lamp of life, keeps them in virtual heathenism? Convinced that slavery is a sin, we have not only the right, but are bound by the obligations of Christianity, to oppose it, and to use all lawful means for its abolition, whether in our own or other countries. If slavery be not sinful, then we know not what degree of cruelty and injustice amounts to a violation of the law of God.

A combination of circumstances has led many of our clergy at the North, and nearly all at the South, to regard slavery, with all its inseparable abominations, an exception from the Christian code. We must love all men as ourselves, with the exception of such as are black. With the same exception, we must do good unto all men, and exercise justice and mercy to all. We must give Bibles to men of all lands and all races, except to about three millions of blacks in our midst. The laws must protect the marriage tie, except in the case of these same millions. Supplications must be made for all men, except those among us who are of all men the most miserable. In short, as Christians, we must rebuke every sin except that giant sin of our nation which involves the perpetration of almost every other. But it is affirmed, by way of apology, that we at the North are free from this sin, and have therefore no concern with it. Were the assertion true, the apology would be equally valid for not attempting to overthrow the idolatry of the Hindoos, or the delusions of the false prophet, and for recalling all our missionaries to the heathen. But unfortunately the assertion is utterly destitute of truth. Probably not a sermon is preached in our large city churches which is not listened to by slave-holders; probably not a congregation is assembled in the free States which does not include persons directly or indirectly interested in slavery. How many of our sons are constantly removing to the South, and becoming slave-holders! What numbers of our daughters are mistresses on slave plantations! How many northern clergymen now descant from southern pulpits on the divine rights of slave-holders! And shall we be told that northern Christians have no cause to raise their voices against a sin which is daily corrupting their sons, their daughters, their politicians, and their clergy? Alas! there is a mighty conspiracy, prompted by selfish considerations, to suppress all discussion of this sin, all exhibition of its withering influence on human virtue and happiness. We have great national societies for disseminating Christian truth; but no reader of their tracts and Sunday school books learns from their pages that it is sinful to rob black men of all their rights; to compel them to labor without wages; to deny them the Holy Scriptures; and to send fathers, mothers, and children to market, like cattle and bales of cotton. All other sins are in these publications faithfully and freely rebuked; but every allusion to this great and all-pervading sin of our nation is carefully excluded. Occasionally, a tract or religious biography from the other side of the water is deemed worthy of republication; but it is first submitted to a process significantly termed "cottonizing," and which consists in carefully expunging every expression condemnatory of human bondage. The American and Foreign Anti-Slavery Society, utterly repudiating such a time-serving view of Christian duty, aims at convincing the hearts and understandings of all, both at the North and at the South, of the sinfulness of American slavery.

It must, however, be understood, that this Society directs its labors to the abolition of CASTE as well as of slavery. We have among ourselves a population, each individual of which is a swift witness of our cruelty and unchristian conduct. While protesting against the injustice and oppression practised by our southern brethren, let us not forget the deep guilt of our northern community in their treatment of the free people of color. No casuistry can reconcile the scorn and contumely poured upon these people with the precepts of the gospel of Christ; of that gospel which makes love for each other the badge of the Redeemer's disciples. It is unnecessary to dwell on the privations and disabilities to which our colored citizens are subjected. When the professed ministers of Christ refuse to sit in the councils of the church with their reverend brethren not colored like themselves, and when colored candidates for the ministry are excluded from theological seminaries solely on account of the tincture of their skin, it is not surprising that others should be as regardless of the temporal, as certain of the clergy are of the spiritual welfare of men to whom God has been pleased to give a dark complexion. When the pious colored youth is denied the usual facilities for qualifying him to minister to the diseases of the souls of his people, who shall rigidly condemn the professors of the healing art for denying similar facilities for ministering to the diseases of the body, by excluding colored students from their lecture-rooms? Surely, the ruffians who insult and abuse the colored man, and the demagogues who, availing themselves of a popular prejudice, deny him equality before the law, have high examples to extenuate, if not to justify their pride and cruelty. In striving to secure to our colored people the rights freely accorded to all others, and thus giving them the means of maintaining themselves by honest industry, of developing and improving their talents, and of studying the things which belong to their peace, the Society is pursuing an object in perfect accordance with Christian benevolence, and one that must commend itself to every unprejudiced mind.

In our opposition to slavery and caste, we desire to use no instruments of unsanctified temper; nor have we any wish to conceal those we do use. Believing it sinful to compel an innocent man to serve as a slave, we must refuse to be partakers of other men's sins; and hence, under no circumstances, can we aid in catching or securing fugitive slaves, whatever may be the penalties of our disobedience to a sinful act of Congress. It will be the endeavor of the American and Foreign Anti-Slavery Society to dissuade all from joining in slave-hunts, as a palpable violation of Christian duty. Setting aside the moral turpitude of slavery, the fugitive slave act comprises a mass of iniquity in no degree required by the provisions of the Constitution. The act points out the mode of seizing and surrendering, not slaves, but *persons owing service or labor*, and is therefore applicable to white apprentices, and to persons under contract to labor for a limited time. Apprentices have already been surrendered under it, and there is no reason why others, who are alleged to have hired themselves out for a month or a year, may not be. To illustrate the intense injustice of this act, let us suppose a young man to leave his father's home, in Boston or New York, for California. After the lapse of a year or two, he returns. While pursuing an honest calling, he is arrested in the street, on the charge of stealing — the stereotype charge in such cases, to prevent resistance — and hurried before a commissioner. An affidavit made in California, and there certified by a judge, is read, setting forth that the prisoner is the apprentice of the deponent. Immediately, without being permitted to produce any testimony to rebut a document which the law declares SHALL BE CONCLUSIVE, he is put in irons, and sent on board a vessel departing for the Pacific, without being permitted to take leave of his parents, wife, or children. Do we revolt at the mere supposition of such barbarity? But does the barbarity and injustice depend on the complexion of the victim? That the Constitution requires the perpetration of such horrible outrages on justice and humanity, is denied even by Daniel Webster, the great champion of the law, since he proposed giving the accused the benefit of a trial by jury. We should be faithless to the cause not only of Christianity, but of civil liberty, did we not oppose an enactment so detestably atrocious; one which establishes a title to property in an intelligent, accountable, immortal being, on testimony which in no civilized country would support the claim to a dog.

The cruelty and heartlessness attending the execution of this law, the extraordinary zeal which our rich men and politicians manifest in its behalf, the sanction given to it by popular divines, and the infidel sneers which many of our party presses have deemed it expedient to cast on the advocates of a "higher law" than an act of Congress, have unitedly exerted a most disastrous influence on the tone of public morals. One of the most striking instances of this influence is the vile attempt made in Pennsylvania, under the especial countenance of the Federal Administration, to convert resistance to the execution of the Fugitive Act into the capital crime of high treason. A fugitive, who had been arrested at Boston, was liberated by some of his colored friends, who, finding the door of his room in the court-house open, hustled the officer, and secured the escape of the intended victim. Not a weapon had been provided, not a wound was given; yet the rescue was boldly proclaimed by Mr. Webster, Secretary of State, to be an act of treason, a levying of war against the United States!

On the 11th of September, 1851, a more serious affair occurred. An armed party, headed by a deputy-marshal, attempted to arrest some fugitive slaves in Pennsylvania. The fugitives, aided by some others, stood on their defence. The claimant, a Maryland slave-holder, was shot in the affray, and the fugitives escaped. Five days after, the Governor of Maryland was officially informed, from the "Department of State," that "the District Attorney was especially instructed to ascertain whether the facts would make out the crime of TREASON against the United States, and, if so, to take prompt measures to secure all concerned for trial for that OFFENCE." Faithfully and zealously were the orders from Washington obeyed. Incredible as it may seem, a grand jury was found with consciences sufficiently pliant to present no less than seventy-eight indictments against thirty-nine persons, alleged to have been concerned in the riot. All were indicted for TREASON, as well as for various crimes of inferior grade.

Let it be recollected that the Constitution, to prevent tyrannical prosecutions for constructive treason, declares: "Treason against the United States shall consist ONLY in levying war against them, or in adhering to their enemies, giving them aid and comfort." It may well be supposed that the Government selected for the commencement of the prosecutions the strongest case of the thirty-nine. On the 25th of November, Castner Hanway, a white man of irreproachable character, was placed at the bar, charged, on the oaths of the grand jury, that on the 11th of September, 1851, "HE DID WICKEDLY AND TRAITOROUSLY LEVY WAR AGAINST THE UNITED STATES." The only offence proved against him was, that he was near the scene of action, unarmed, and on horseback, and that, when ordered by the deputy-marshal to aid him in capturing the fugitives, like an honest man, he declined rendering the required assistance. The presiding judge charged the jury that "The Court feel bound to say, that they do not think the *transaction* with which the prisoner is charged with being connected, rises to the dignity of treason or of levying war;" and a verdict of not guilty was returned without hesitation. This verdict led the Government to abandon all the indictments for treason, among which was one against Samuel Williams, a colored man, for levying war against the United States, by *giving notice to the fugitives that a warrant had been issued for their arrest!* But still an effort was made to punish him for this act of benevolence, and he was tried on an indictment for misdemeanor, under the Fugitive Act, for obstructing the arrest by his notice, and for which, if convicted, he was liable to a fine not exceeding one thousand dollars, and imprisonment not exceeding six months. The trial by jury was again vindicated by a verdict of acquital. All the prosecutions were then abandoned in despair; and if the gallows and the prisons were denied their intended victims, the Government could at least beseech the slave-holders to accept the will for the deed, especially as it is said no less than seventy thousand dollars were expended on these prosecutions from the public treasury.

In connection with the Fugitive Act, we ask your attention to the renewed efforts to transport the free people of color to Africa. We freely acknowledge not only the right of these people to seek a more favorable home than this country affords, but also the right and duty of others to afford them, according to circumstances, the aid they may desire for this purpose. But the American Colonization Society proffers them *undesired aid*, and recommends their removal to Africa, as rendering slavery more secure and more profitable, and relieving the country of a population which it represents as a "nuisance." To induce them to accept the proffered aid, the oppressions they here suffer are excused and often justified, while attempts to render their condition here more tolerable, by promoting their intellectual improvement and enlarging the field of their industry, are discountenanced. In short, the whole tendency of the Society is, by rendering their condition here intolerable, to extort their consent to go to Africa. We all know the extreme anxiety of the slaveholders to expel the free blacks from within their borders. Says a late South Carolina paper,* recommending the State "to ship her free negroes to another land," "The very condition and the circumstances that surround the free negro *are in direct hostility and diametrically opposed to the institution of slavery.*" Mr. Webster, in his memorable speech of 7th March, 1850, adroitly recommended himself to his new patrons by declaring that EIGHTY MILLIONS had been received from the sale of lands ceded by Virginia; and that, "If Virginia and the South see fit to adopt any proposition to RELIEVE themselves from the free people of color among them, they have my free consent that the Government shall pay them *any* sum of money out of the proceeds which may be adequate for the purpose." And again: "If any gentleman from the SOUTH shall propose a scheme of colonization to be carried on by this Government upon a large scale, for the transportation of her colored people to any colony *or any place in the world*, I should be quite disposed to incur almost any degree of expense to accomplish the object." Of course, the Secretary of State is willing to tax the whole republic to any amount not exceeding eighty millions, not to benefit the free people of color, not to civilize and Christianize Africa, but to banish to any part of the world hundreds of thousands of

* Greenfield Mountaineer.

his own countrymen, solely and avowedly to *relieve* the slaveholders, and give additional security and permanence to the system of human bondage; and this gentleman is now the public champion of the American Colonization Society. Hence a sense of Christian duty will forbid the American and Foreign Anti-Slavery Society from holding any relation to that Society other than that of uncompromising hostility.

We have in our country a population, free and bond, of between three and four millions, who, merely on account of their complexion, are treated with an almost total disregard of that justice and humanity enjoined by the religion we profess. The American and Foreign Anti-Slavery Society are laboring to secure to them that Christian treatment to which the gospel of Christ entitles them. In this work of mercy, they invoke, and have a right to invoke, the countenance and aid of the Church. We are not unconscious that the Church has, in past ages, been frequently faithless to her high mission of cultivating peace and good-will among men; and he is but little acquainted with passing events who is ignorant that the American Church is at this moment one of the strongest buttresses of American caste and slavery. Would we, then, if we could, destroy the Church? God forbid. If the world is so full of sin and wretchedness notwithstanding the Church, what would it be without a Church? The answer may be found in the cruelties and abominations of paganism. But the ministers of Christ are men of like passions with others, and liable, like others, to be swayed by popular opinion and motives of self-interest. It is possible many of the clergy have not reflected that, in supporting and vindicating slavery, they are lending their countenance to an institution which outrages every moral precept they inculcate from the pulpit. What answer will the northern clerical slave-catcher, or the southern reverend slave-breeder and slave-trader return to the inspired question, "He that loveth not his brother whom he hath seen, how can he love God, whom he hath not seen?" Surely it is worthy of remembrance that, at the day of final account, the Judge will consider as done to himself both the kindness and the cruelty shown to the least of his brethren.

We are constantly reminded that the Church is the great instrument of moral reform. Most gratefully do we allow that the precepts of the gospel are sufficient for all the moral necessities of man. "Do to others as you would they should do unto you, is a law which if obeyed, would of itself banish slavery and oppression from the face of the earth. But unhappily the Church, or at least a portion of her ministers, have not always applied the precepts of the gospel to existing and popular sins. It is certainly no exaggerated statement, that not one sermon in a thousand delivered at the North contains the slightest allusion to the duties of Christians towards the colored population; while at the South multitudes of the clergy are as deeply involved in the iniquities of slavery as their hearers. It is no libel on the great body of our northern clergy to say that, in regard to the wrongs of the colored people, instead of performing the part of the good Samaritan, their highest merit consists in following the example of the priest and Levite, and passing by on the other side, without inflicting new injuries on their wounded brother. But we rejoice to know that there are ministers of Christ among us, and not a few, to whom these remarks are wholly inapplicable; men who pray and preach and labor against slavery and caste, and thus adorn the doctrine of God their Saviour. We rejoice also to know that such ministers are appreciated and honored by Christians abroad of every name. The clergy of England, Scotland, and Ireland decline admitting into their pulpits clergymen from this country holding what they deem heretical doctrines; but can they exclude any for a fouler heresy than that which abrogates all the Christian precepts of justice and mercy in their application to colored men? We trust our friends in Great Britain will not weaken our hands, and strengthen the pro-slavery influence of our churches, by overlooking, in their reception of American clergymen, the course they have pursued at home on the subject of slavery. They may be perfectly assured that the American clergyman, who, abroad, is too dignified to be questioned as to his opinions on human bondage, is at home too patriotic to offer any vigorous opposition to the "peculiar institution" of his country.

We have thus frankly stated the objects of the American and Foreign Anti-Slavery Society, and confidently ask if they are not objects worthy to be pursued by rational, accountable Christian men? Nay, we go farther, and ask, has not a Society pursuing such objects valid claims on the countenance and generous aid of every philanthropist and every Christian in our country?

Hostility to slavery has frequently been associated with various objects of political and moral reform. It is natural it should be so, since the same love for our neighbor which revolts at his oppression seeks to advance his general welfare. But experience has fully proved that associated action cannot be efficiently maintained in behalf of various plans, respecting which the individuals associated entertain diverse opinions. Hence the American and Foreign Anti-Slavery Society, without passing any judgment on other proposed reforms, confine their efforts in their associated capacity to the abolition of caste and slavery, leaving to their members individually the full and entire liberty of advocating and promoting, in such way as they may think proper, any other reforms, moral or political. We believe every man is bound to exercise the elective franchise in the fear of God; but while we shall ever rejoice in the election of virtuous rulers who will do justice and love mercy, it is not the province of the Society to recommend particular individuals for the suffrages of their fellow-citizens.

It is consoling to us to know that, in the sentiments we have expressed, we enjoy the sympathy of almost all without the limits of our own country who bear the Christian name. A vast multitude on our own soil hold the same sentiments, and, did they act with one heart and one voice, would soon triumph over the prejudice which supports caste, would array the Church on the side of mercy, and rescue the Federal Government from its unholy and unconstitutional alliance with slavery. But unfortunately, the sympathies of this multitude, not being concentrated in action and counsel, are in no small degree powerless for good. The anti-slavery host has been divided, and of course enfeebled, by conflicting opinions on topics not immediately affecting the colored man. For the sake of the slave, for the prosperity of the country, for the good of the Church herself, we earnestly desire the union of all abolitionists, and their harmonious action in behalf of their colored brethren. We ask all who approve the opinions we have expressed to give vitality and energy to those opinions, by aiding the American and Foreign Anti-Slavery Society in disseminating and enforcing them.

Public opinion is in this country the controller of legislation. Hence, at one period a traffic in African savages was encouraged by law, as an enlightened and legitimate commerce. At a later period, all but two States were desirous to abandon it, and, as a compromise, Congress was restricted from abolishing it until after twenty years. At a still later period, a commerce which had been guaranteed by the Federal Constitution was, by an act of Congress, denounced as PIRACY. Public opinion now, acting through the legislature, holds him a felon who brings to our shores for sale a native African, while we have just seen a citizen tried for his life because he declined to assist a slave-catcher in reducing to slavery a native American. To buy and sell Africans is wicked, base, and detestable; to buy and sell colored Americans is in perfect accordance with the most exalted position in both State and Church. In the city of New York, we have seen "men of great stakes," merchant princes, and others, lavishing courtesies on the most reckless and violent champions of slavery when they honored them with their presence; and we have seen these same gentlemen giving aid and comfort to the slave-catcher, without losing their place in polite society.

Most certainly public opinion on these subjects is unsound, and ought to be reformed. Very many of our clergy, and their hearers, need to be reminded that the commands of God have no reference to the color of a man's skin, but that all are equally entitled to receive, and are equally bound to render, the justice and benevolence enjoined by HIM who is the common Father of us all. Christians generally are to be warned not to be partakers of other men's sins towards the colored race. The cruelty of State and Federal legislation is to be exposed; the influence of the colonization scheme in exasperating the prejudice against our colored brethren is to be demonstrated, and the public is to be fully instructed in the moral, social, and political evils resulting from slavery and caste.

But how are these great ends to be accomplished? Individual effort can do but little. In the present age, the press is the great lever by which the world is moved, but it can be employed to a great extent only through the united pecuniary contributions of many. The influence of a private abolitionist can rarely reach beyond a contracted neighborhood; but as a member of the American and Foreign Anti-Slavery Society, and a donor to its funds, he may address thousands. The *National Era* was established at Washington with funds supplied by the Society, and since repaid; and it now weekly addresses anti-slavery truth to seventeen thousand subscribers. The Society greatly needs a periodical of its own, but its present funds are insufficient for the establishment of one. Treatises on various branches of this great subject are constantly offered to the Society, but it lacks the means of giving them to the public through the press. Intelligent, well-informed lecturers are wanted to awaken public attention, to collect popular assemblies, and to enlist the sympathies of those whose avocations deny them the opportunity of reading anti-slavery publications. Agents are desired to aid in the formation of auxiliary societies. Editors and authors are to be enlisted in the cause; and frequently information and statistics, to be collected at much expense of time and labor, are needed for the use of members of Congress and other public men. The instrumentalities for influencing public opinion and correcting prejudices and erroneous statements are manifold, but they can be wielded only by associated funds and labors.

A crisis has arrived in which the friends of the anti-slavery cause should reörganize and act together. Unless they do this, their efforts to circumscribe the area of slavery, to break the fetters of the slave, and to rescue the free colored man from his present degradation, will be fruitless. Should the present mighty combination of capitalists, merchants, and politicians, aided by a number of popular divines enlisted in their service, succeed in suppressing all manifestation of sympathy for the slave, all discussion of the abominations of slavery, all compassion for the fugitive, the North will undoubtedly be prepared to sanction the designs now entertained for the erection of New Mexico, Utah, and Southern California into slave States, together with the annexation of Cuba, Hayti, and the Sandwich Islands, all to be added to the domain of the slave-holder. Let us never forget that duties are ours, although events are not, and that whatever may be the form in which it may please Divine Providence to punish our guilty land, he requires us not only to love mercy, but to do justice; a command we fail to obey, so long as we refuse to use lawful means to secure mercy and justice to others. Very many have no other opportunity of obeying this command, in regard to the colored race, than by their pecuniary contributions to the anti-slavery cause. The efforts of the American and Foreign Anti-Slavery Society are now enfeebled by the exhausted state of their treasury.

Friends and brethren, we appeal to you in behalf of the Society. In the language of Scripture, we exhort you to show your faith by your works. So fully aware are our enemies of the importance of influencing public opinion by the press, that a paper has been established at the capital of our Republic for the single and avowed purpose of vindicating and upholding human bondage. A large portion of the newspaper press in our commercial cities is enlisted in the same unholy cause. Public rumor tells us, that a committee in the city of New York, comprising many of its wealthiest citizens, raised a fund of one hundred thousand dollars; and knowing that opposition to slavery has its strongest fortress in the religious sentiment, this committee has spread broadcast through the land multitudes of copies of pro-slavery sermons. While the votaries of Mammon and the aspirants to political power and emolument are thus active and zealous in supporting and extending a horrible and degrading despotism, to further their own selfish and ambitious views, will not the friends of righteousness, justice, and mercy, be up and doing? We beseech you to reply by enrolling your names among the members of the American and Foreign Anti-Slavery Society, and by speedy and liberal contributions to its treasury.

LETTER

TO REV. R. S. COOK, CORRESPONDING SECRETARY OF

THE AMERICAN TRACT SOCIETY.

New York, Monday, Feb. 14, 1853.

Reverend Sir: I have been favored with your letter of the last month, setting forth the pecuniary exigencies of the American Tract Society, and suggesting to my "charitable consideration" a donation to its funds. Few persons hailed with more satisfaction than myself the establishment of your Society, or more cordially approved the truly catholic principles on which it was founded. I long since became one of its 'Life Directors,' and have frequently contributed to its funds. The professed object of the Society was to inculcate Christian faith and practice, and to a very great extent it has been faithful to its profession, and I doubt not that it has been largely instrumental in promoting the spiritual welfare of multitudes.

But the good effected by human agency is seldom without alloy, and for some years, painful doubts have intruded themselves on my mind as to the propriety of the course pursued by the Society in regard to a most momentous subject. Against these doubts I have long struggled, and at times with success. But they have again and again returned with increased force, and they have been so entirely confirmed by some recent developments, that I am constrained to return a most reluctant denial to the application in your letter. I am well aware of the deep responsibility I assume in placing any obstacle, however slight, in the way of the Society. Of this responsibility, the pain I may give valued friends, and the obloquy I may draw upon myself from a very minor portion — I feel the infinitely greater weight of my responsibility to my Maker, for withholding my aid from an agency that has effected so much for his glory and the good of man. This responsibility I have anxiously pondered, and have come to the conviction that I may not avoid it. The facts and reasons which have produced this conviction I will proceed to state. Should they be found insufficient to justify me, they will tend to save others from the error into which I have fallen; and should they, on the other hand, be found valid, they may lead to salutary results.

The classification of sins into those of commission and omission is trite. All Scripture testifies that mere inaction has often incurred the divine wrath. The Jewish priests, although sedulous in the routine of ceremonial duties, were denounced, in the indignant language of inspiration, as "dumb dogs," because they omitted to rebuke popular sins. In the account of the last judgment, those who are to "go away into everlasting punishment" are not condemned as heretics, nor as the perpetrators of crime, but as guilty of having *omitted* to administer to the necessities of Christ's afflicted and oppressed brethren.

You have by this time, sir, anticipated that my charge against the Society is one of OMISSION. There is a giant, and in its influence an all-pervading sin, in our land — a sin which is destroying the peace and happiness of millions, both for the life that is, and for that which is to come; and which is hardening the hearts and paralyzing the consciences of many more by its reflective consequences. Yet the American Tract Society has publicly and officially announced through you, as its organ, that it does not intend to recognize even the existence of this sin!

About a year since the ministers and delegates of the Congregational Union of Fox River, Illinois, addressed a very Christian letter to the Society. In this letter they very forcibly remark:

"We feel sure that the time has come when the continued absence from the publications of your Society of all that relates to slavery, will be significant; that silence can no longer be neutrality or indifference; and that a tract literature which speaks less plainly of slavery than of other specific evils, will conduce to a defective, partial and unsound morality."

In your official reply of 27th February, 1852, without letting a word escape your pen, acknowledging the sinfulness of American slavery, you urge various reasons for not breaking the silence so long observed by the Society respecting human bondage.

"It would seem a sacrifice of a greater to a lesser good, to engage in the discussion of a topic already exhausted, with the likelihood of satisfying none, and with the certainty of alienating multitudes of our best friends," &c.

Your publications, we are informed, must be of a character "calculated to meet the approbation *of all evangelical Christians;*" and you seem to think that, amid the anti-slavery agitation, it is desirable "that *at least one* institution should move forward on the simple errand that brought the Saviour into the world — proclaiming Christ and him crucified," &c.; and you aver "that on no subject, probably, are evangelical Christians more at variance" than on slavery; and you conclude with declaring that "the course of duty seems plain before us to *adhere* as a society to the simple gospel in its essential saving truths." The Union were not convinced by your arguments; on the contrary, they resolved that ere long no catholic society of publication can well refuse to express anti-slavery truth in some of its various forms of moral or Biblical argument, fact or sentiment; and to hasten this desired consummation, they ordered the correspondence to be made public.

I am unable to reconcile the position assumed in your letter with the past action of the Society, or with the usually received ideas of Christian obligation. It seems your tracts must meet the approbation of *all evangelical* Christians. If we ask who these are, we shall be told, such as agree in maintaining the Scriptural authority of certain abstract doctrines. But we all know, that these same Christians differ widely on various questions of moral practice. You are not ignorant that evangelical wine and rumsellers, and drinkers, abound both in town and country; and yet your Society is lavish of its censures on them. It condemns the theatre and race-course, although not a few believers in the evangelical creed frequent both. You issue publications against dancing, and yet how many sons and daughters mingle in the waltz, in the presence and with the consent of their evangelical parents. You condemn travelling on the Sabbath, yet our Sunday steamboats and rail-cars are not without their evangelical passengers. You do not hesitate to rebuke gambling, yet evangelicals may be found at the card and the billiard-table. As far as I can judge, the publications of your Society have been in accordance with the rule you announce on few subjects, except that of human bondage and its attendant atrocities. I know not that in the twenty-seven years of its existence the Society has published a line intended to touch the conscience of an American slave-breeder or trader. On the contrary, especial care has been taken to EXPUNGE from your reprints every expression that could even imply a censure on our stupendous national iniquity. The Society has no hesitation in condemning cruelty, oppression, and injustice, but it shrinks with affright at the very idea of acknowledging that it is cruel, oppressive and unjust to reduce a *black* man to the condition of a beast of burden, to deny him legal marriage, and to sell him and his children to the highest bidder, in company with the beasts of the field. This extreme sensitiveness is shown in the alteration of a passage in your reprint of Gurney's essay on the habitual exercise of love to God. Gurney says:

"If this love had always prevailed among professing Christians, where would have been the sword of the crusader? Where the African slave-trade? Where the odious system which permits to man a property in his fellow-men, and converts rational beings into marketable chattels?" Page 142.

This was meat too strong for the digestion of the Society, and hence it was carefully diluted, so that it might be swallowed without producing the slightest nausea, as follows:

"If this love had always prevailed among professing Christians, where would have been the sword of the crusader? *Where the tortures of the Inquisition?* Where every system of oppression and wrong by which he who has the power revels in luxury and ease at the expense of his fellow-men?" Page 199.

It was an ingenious thought to turn upon the *Inquisition* Gurney's application of his subject to slave-traders and holders, and to lose sight of *property in man*, in indefinite generalities.

Your last report, in announcing the reprint of the memoir of Mary Lundie Duncan, tells us:

"A few pages, which the Committee deemed of less interest to the general reader, or which alluded to *points of disagreement among evangelical Christians*, have been dropped."

The *pages* dropped are indeed few and unimportant, and seemed to have been dropped for the purpose of justifying the word "abridged" on the title-page. But the *passages* dropped are very significant. In her diary for March 22, 1833, the following passage is *expunged* in the Society's edition, while every other word on the page is retained.

"We have been lately much interested in the emancipation of slaves. I never heard eloquence more overpowering than that of George Thompson. I am most thankful that he has been raised up. O that the measure soon to be proposed in Parliament may be effectual."

Poor Mary! The American Tract Society will not allow you to breathe a wish for West India emancipation by act of Parliament, nor to admire the eloquence of an anti-slavery lecturer. The biographer of this lovely and highly gifted saint remarks:

"When George Thompson, the eloquent pleader for the abolition of slavery, was called to visit the United States in the hope that his remarkable power of influencing the public mind might be beneficial there, we find the youthful philanthropist, whose ardent mind glowed with exalted sympathies, and felt an interest in loftier occupations than usually kindle the enthusiasm of girls of her age, embodying her desires for his success, in the following verses."

This paragraph and the lines they introduced are both EXPUNGED from your edition. A Broadway bookseller had already published an *unmutilated* copy of the book, but this religious society, more sensitive than even *New York* traffic to the good will of the slave-holders, suppressed not merely the anti-slavery poetry, but the testimony of a mother to the philanthropic sentiments of her departed daughter! But the work of expurgation did not stop here. In Mary's diary is the following entry:

> "August 1. Freedom has dawned this morning on the British Colonies. *(No more degraded lower than the brutes—no more bowed down with suffering from which there is no redress)* the sons of Africa have obtained the rights of fellow-subjects—the rights of man, the immortal creation of God. (*Now they may seek the sanctuary fearless of the lash—they may call their children their own.*) Hope will animate their hearts and give vigor to their efforts. Oh, for more holy men to show them the way of salvation! The Lord keep them from riot and idleness. They have been so little taught that He only can avert confusion and tumult as the result of their joy. Some Christians there are among their number, who will influence others. My poor fellow travellers through life's short wilderness, may I meet with many of you in heaven, where even I can hope to dwell through the love of my risen Lord! There none will despise the negro whom Jesus Christ hath pitied and redeemed."

The passages in italics and in parentheses are *expunged* in the Society's edition. Mary is permitted to announce that the negroes have become British subjects, to express her apprehensions of riot and idleness, confusion and tumult, as consequences of emancipation, and to indulge the hope of meeting negroes in heaven, where they will not be despised. But she is not permitted to allude to the cruelties and abominations to which these same negroes had been subjected. The expunged passages involve no doctrinal "points of disagreement among evangelical Christians." Why then were they stricken out? Because the same cruelties and enormities to which she alluded, are perpetrated at home by evangelical Christians who belong to and support the American Tract Society.

The Society will not venture the denial of the *truth* of the expunged assertions. It would surely not aver that American slave children *do* belong to their parents. It would be put to confusion by the solemn judicial affirmance of the validity of a bequest of a mother to one person, and of her *unborn* children to another. It would be confuted by the sale of children at auction, and in particular of a sale reported within the few last days, of a child three years old bringing three hundred dollars under the hammer, while a southern paper adverts with pride to the price of human flesh, as evidence of "our agricultural prosperity." Your Society, sir, expunged Mary's assertions, not because they were untrue, but because they are now as true here as they were in the West Indies, and it is the policy of the Society to cover up and conceal whatever reflects odium on the "peculiar institution."

Your Committee tell us in their last Report that they "have never lost sight of their responsibilities to those of tender years;" and it seems they issue *The Child's Paper*, of which great numbers are circulated. Yet the responsibilities to children resting on the Committee permit them to expunge an expression likely to remind us that there are hundreds of thousands of children in our land who are mere articles of merchandise. These very responsibilities are, it seems, perfectly compatible with entire silence respecting the ignorance and degradation of this great multitude "of tender years." The Committee know that in some of our States even a free mother, if her complexion be dark, is, by law, liable to be scourged on her bare back should she be taught teaching her little ones to read your *Child's Paper*, yet not a word of remonstrance escapes the American Tract Society! In the very last number of *The Child's Paper* I read that

> "There are between 10,000 and 12,000 children in the City of New York who never enter a church or school, and who cannot read the Bible. . . . . Here are heathen at home; what is doing for them? . . . . These children must be cared for."

Indeed! And is it nothing to your Society that there are in our country about HALF A MILLION of little black heathen who are prevented by law from reading the Bible? These little heathen have souls as imperishable, destinies as momentous, as the white heathen in New York. Must this half million be cared for? Ah! that is a "point of disagreement among evangelical Christians," and hence the Society must not even recognize the existence of children who do not belong to their parents.

Permit me now to ask your attention to the very different course pursued by the Society in regard to the traffic in the bones and sinews, the mind and soul of immortal MAN, and the traffic in intoxicating drinks. Between twenty and thirty of your tracts are devoted to the subject of intemperance in all its relations. It is curious to observe the desire of your writers to avail themselves of the arguments and illustrations furnished by slavery, and at the same time their extreme caution in avoiding all reference to *American* slavery. Where even by implication, censure is cast on human bondage, it is human bondage in *other* countries than our own. In Tract No. 300, to the excuse of the distiller, that he cannot sacrifice his property, conscience is made to answer:

> "Suppose you were now in *Brazil* and the owner of a large establishment to fit out slave-traders with handcuffs for the coast of *Africa*, and could not change your business without considerable pecuniary sacrifice, would you make the sacrifice, or would you keep your fires and hammers going?"

In remonstrating against the cruelty of the traffic in rum, it is remarked:

> "If a man lives only to make a descent on the peaceful abodes of *Africa*, and to tear away parents from their weeping children, and husbands from their wives and homes, where is the man that will deem this a moral business?" "Other men will prey on unoffending *Africa* and bear human sinews across the ocean to be sold. Have you a right to do it?" No. 305.

Once more, speaking of the duty of rescuing the drunkard, it is asked:

> "What would you not do to pull a neighbor out of the water, or out of the fire, or to deliver him from *Algerine* captivity?" No. 422.

So it seems the Society is at liberty to hold up as cruel and immoral the traffic in human flesh in Africa, Brazil, and Algiers, but not in *our own land* — that being a "point of disagreement among evangelical Christians."

And now, sir, I ask you, on what evangelical principle does the Society condemn the *foreign* slave-trade? Is it because an act of Congress forbids it? The Society has not yet, I believe, like some of its patrons, elevated the lower above the higher law, and made the national statute book the standard of right and wrong. Nor, indeed, can the advocates of the supremacy of the lower law maintain, that an act of Congress can render immoral the conduct of Africans, Algerines and Brazilians, when that conduct is in conformity with the laws of their respective countries. Is it then, in reference to the higher law, the will of God revealed in his blessed gospel, that the *foreign* traffic is condemned? If so, then I ask to what divine precept is it opposed? Buying and selling and the exchange of commodities are essential to human society, and are nowhere condemned in God's word. Why then, sir, I ask in all seriousness is it more immoral for an African to sell, or a Brazilian to buy men and women, than apes and parrots? Is it because men and women are not by the higher law subjects of commerce? Before you reply in the affirmative, remember that our laws, framed for the most part by evangelical Christians, expressly declare vast multitudes of men and women to be mere chattels, vendible articles. Said Henry Clay, on the floor of the Senate, vindicating property in man, "that is property which the law makes property." Now, every slave sold in Africa to a Brazilian merchant, is property by the African law, and is granted, bargained, sold, and delivered by a title as valid as that ever received by Mr. Clay to one of his slaves. Again, then, I ask, why is the sale and purchase of a man in Africa, most undoubtedly a heinous crime, while the immorality of the sale and purchase in Virginia of a fellow countryman and perhaps a fellow Christian, is such an abstruse question, that the American Tract Society will not venture to approach its discussion? Can it be that your Society is silent on this traffic, because it is sanctioned by human law? This can hardly be, since the Society is unsparing in its denunciations of the traffic in rum, notwithstanding the powers that be, ordained as they are of God, have taken the traffic under their peculiar guardianship. Very irreverently does your tract speak of

> "Stale debauch forth issuing from the sties
> That LAW has licensed." No. 240.

You are silent on slavery because, as you say, on no other subject probably "are evangelical Christians more at variance." I think, sir, you greatly overrate the evangelical patrons and advocates of slavery. I doubt whether you can find one hundred evangelical Christians out of the slave States, unconnected in any way with slavery, slave-holders, and cotton, who will publicly avow that American slavery is a righteous institution, and the slave code in accordance with the spirit and precepts of the gospel of Christ. Surely, surely, sir, I should make a most extravagant and reckless estimate were I to compute the evangelical champions of slave-breeding, slave-trading, and slave-catching, at a tythe of the evangelicals who in their practice repudiate total abstinence from intoxicating drinks. Nevertheless, on this last "point of evangelical disagreement," the Society expresses itself without fear and without reserve.

But some of our friends, you may say, insist that the Bible sanctions slavery, and what can we do? And some of your friends also insist that the Bible sanctions moderate drinking, and the *sale* of intoxicating drinks, and what *do* you do? Why, you tell us

> "The great laws of morals are indeed unchanged, but the degrees of light and knowledge which men possess may be very different. We should not deem it right to apply our laws and knowledge in judging of the laws of Sparta which authorized theft — nor our views of the marriage relation, to condemn the conduct of Abraham, David and Jacob. Man's conduct is to be estimated by the light he has."

To the plea that the Bible does not prohibit the traffic it is answered:

> "Where is there a formal prohibition of piracy, or bigamy, or kidnapping, or suicide, or duelling, or the sale of obscene books and paintings? . . . The truth is, that the Bible has laid down great principles of conduct, which on all these subjects could be easily applied, which are applied, and which under the guidance of equal honesty may be as easily applied to the subject of which I am speaking." No. 305.

To assail slavery is to assail its supporters, and you think that the Society, by discussing the subject, would alienate multitudes of its best friends. Similar delicacy, or, if you please, prudence has not been observed towards the advocates of moderate drinking.

"Our next opposition is from a band clothed in *white* — professors of our holy religion — enlisted soldiers of the CHURCH, engaged to every good work of benevolence: they come to intercede for the MONSTER, (moderate drinking,) and oppose our enterprise. What can be the meaning of this? O, where lies this astonishing witchery? What has put the CHURCH TO SLEEP? What has made her *angry* at the call to come forth from the embrace of her deadliest foe?" No. 240.

Were the inquiry made, what witchery has made the CHURCH blind, and deaf and dumb, in regard to the groans and sufferings of millions on our soil denied the word of God, and forcibly kept in ignorance and degradation? — the true answer would be, I am persuaded, "The neutrality of the American Tract Society, and the vast number of the clergy, to whom the fear of man has proved a snare."

Very strange is it that while the Society will not even hint dislike to slavery, it brings against the traffic in rum an array of arguments equally effective and valid against the traffic in men, women and children. Thus you urge the duty of doing as you would be done by, and the remorse we shall feel at death for the suffering we have inflicted, and the great command to love our neighbor (No. 242) — our responsibility to God for the results of our own selfishness (No. 300) — the waste of human happiness (No. 240) — that the traffic "tears asunder the strongest bonds of society, it severs the tenderest ties of nature" (No. 249). To the plea of the rumseller that his trade is his livelihood, it is answered, "beg, dig, do anything, but this. It would be a glorious martyrdom to *starve*, contrasted with obtaining a livelihood by such an employment" (No. 305). "Where have you derived authority to procure a living at a sacrifice of conscience, cheracter and the dearest interests of others?" (No. 239.)

The Society shrinks from the opposition it would encounter

from slave-holders. In your letter already quoted, you vindicate "the *peaceful* course pursued by the Society," and you say

> "When there shall be *unity of sentiment*, and a treatise of standard value shall be written, such as the Committee can approve, *then* there will be propriety in claiming that a Tract press shall engage in this branch of moral discussion."

Unless I mistake your meaning, there is here an implied promise, that when all evangelical Christians are united in condemning slavery, both in theory and practice, and when of course the monster is at his last gasp, and there is no use in striking another blow, *then* the Society will attack him, provided the Committee shall cordially agree as to the weapon to be used. In the meantime, while the monster is in full vigor and extending his ravages, you think it best, "that at least *one* institution should move forward on the simple errand that brought the Saviour into the world — proclaiming Christ and him crucified," &c. Happy is it, sir, that this desire for peace, this longing to proclaim Christ and him crucified, without heeding popular and prevailing sins, was not felt by the Society till *after* it had done battle against gamblers, dancers, theatre-goers, Sabbath-breakers, moderate drinkers, and rumsellers. Your tracts against intemperance display anything but a non-resistant spirit. For example —

> "The demon will daunt the timid. It is noisy and fiery; attack it, and it will roll its eyes and snap its teeth, and threaten vengeance. Attempt to starve it, and it will rage like the famished tiger. Thousands have fed it against their consciences rather than meet its fury. *But fear not.* Be firm—be decided—be courageous, connect your cause with Heaven. It is the cause of God, the cause for which Immanuel died. *Let the demon no longer hide in the sanctuary.* Expel forever the accursed enemy, that the Lord may bless us with life and peace." No. 240.

Possibly the Society has deemed it its duty to coöperate with Union Saving Committees and Baltimore politicians, and cotton merchants, in their patriotic efforts to suppress all discussion of the "delicate subject," a discussion having such disturbing influences on northern trade and politics. Yet such a supposition cannot be allowed, after the noble testimony borne by the Society to the right and benefit of free discussion.

> "There are some great principles in regard to our country which are settled, and which are never to be violated so long as our liberties are safe. Among them are these: that every subject may be subjected to candid and *most free discussion;* that public opinion, enlightened and correct, may be turned against any course of evil conduct; that public opinion is, under God, the prime source of security to our laws and morals, and that men may be induced by *ample discussion*, and by the voice of conscience and of reason, to abandon any course that is erroneous." No. 305.

Such are the rights and benefits of discussion when directed against the *seller of rum;* do they lose all their virtue when directed against the seller of human flesh?

Perhaps your Society revolts at the idea of descending into the arena of politics, but if so, how are we to understand the following exhortation? "Let all who regard the virtue, the honor, and the patriotism of the country, *withhold their suffrages* from those candidates who offer *ardent spirits* as a bribe to secure their elevation to office." But suppose they offer as a bribe to secure their elevation to office, not a glass of brandy and water, but a fresh discovered law of physical geography, precluding all legal restraints on the extension of human bondage — Baltimore platforms, to destroy the liberty of speech, of the press, and the pulpit — indictments for high treason, offering to the Southern Moloch the blood of Christians, who, in the fear of God, refuse when summoned to join in slave-hunts — shall we withhold our suffrages?

On the whole, sir, I cannot but think that your Society has greatly mistaken its duty to God and man, in shrinking from pronouncing slavery, as well as gambling and horse-racing, a moral evil. Unquestionably, the Society has acted in perfect accordance with the *general* policy of the northern church, both Popish and Protestant. That policy is more easily understood than vindicated. So intimate are our commercial relations with the South, and so dependent are our politicians for the most trifling office upon the support of their party by southern votes, that to ask them and our merchants to participate in measures and opinions offensive to their southern patrons, is like asking the favor of them to pluck out a right eye, or cut off a right hand. Of course, the pecuniary and party interests of these men react on the church and religious societies with which they are connected. Hence has grown up a secular and ecclesiastical alliance, offensive and defensive, with slavery. But this alliance, although undoubtedly embracing many worthy men, is nevertheless in direct antagonism with the gospel of Christ, and has consequently led, and is daily leading to most disastrous results. It has caused the avowal by men of high position in both church and state, of principles utterly subversive of that regard for justice and mercy, which is not only one of the peculiar and beautiful features of our holy religion, but also, and especially in a Democracy, one of the strongest safeguards of person and property. Some slave-holders in Congress propose a law, the provisions of which may well have been inspired by that evil and malignant spirit that goeth about seeking whom he may devour — a law openly setting at defiance the established rules of evidence, and levelling in the dust all the barriers erected by the common law around the personal liberty of the citizen — a law requiring every man, at the summons of a miscreant slave-catcher, to assist him in his damnable work — a law seeking by fine and imprisonment to suppress the impulses of humanity and the gushings of Christian sympathy. No sooner is this accursed law proposed, than rival politicians contend for the honor of giving it their support; and no sooner is it enacted, than the two great rival parties strive to gain votes for their presidential candidates by pledging their best endeavors to carry it into execution. Many individuals, however, affirm that a law thus requiring them to participate in deeds of cruelty and injustice, is at variance with the divine commands. Forthwith we have our public men and our party press sneering at the "higher law," and insulting all who acknowledge its paramount authority to an act of Congress; worse than all, we have our ministers of the Lord Jesus Christ descanting from their pulpits on the reverence due to the "powers that be," as ordained of God, and actually urging the duty of obedience to one of the most ungodly and execrable enactments of modern legislation. Occasionally it was indeed admitted, that under peculiar circumstances, and multiplied conditions, we ought to obey God rather than man, but at the same time it was distinctly taught, not merely that we should not *forcibly resist* the Fugitive Law, but that the "higher law" did not dispense with our obligation to catch slaves.

In the zeal, the rivalry and the cruelty displayed in seizing the hapless and innocent fugitive, and hurrying him back to the house of bondage, of mental darkness and bodily suffering, lessons of cruelty and injustice have been set by the rich and moral, which will not be lost on the needy and profligate. Many of our wealthy and influential gentlemen are sowing seeds which may yet yield to them and their children most bitter fruit.

The shocking insensibility of our churches, religious societies and religious men, to the iniquities of slavery, of course involves them in gross inconsistencies, degrades the character of the gospel of Christ, and gives a mighty impulse to infidelity. Never before, in my opinion, has the American Church been in such peril as at present, and from almost every portion of it comes up a cry of distress. There is no failure of *money*. The country is rich, and our wealthy men are liberal, and pride and ostentation and competition secure the erection of gorgeous and expensive churches. But there is a failure of *increase* of ministers and members. The population is outgrowing the church, and the love of many is waxing cold. From men like Tom Paine and most of his followers the church has little to fear. They hate the gospel because their deeds are evil. Their *lives* are a sufficient antidote to their doctrines. But a new class of converts to infidelity is springing up, men whose fearless and disinterested fidelity to truth, mercy and justice, extort unwilling respect. These men reject the gospel, not because it rebukes their vices, but because they are taught by certain of its clergy, and the conduct of a multitude of its professors, that it sanctions the most horrible cruelty and oppression, allowing the rich and powerful forcibly to reduce the poor and helpless to the condition of working animals, articles of commerce, and to keep their posterity in ignorance and degradation to the end of time.

Every argument wrested from the Bible in behalf of slavery applies to the bondage of *white* men. Hence the modern pro-slavery divinity justifies the ancient villanage and the modern serfdom, and would justify their indefinite extension. If it be right to hold three millions of human beings as chattels, it is equally right to hold hundreds of millions. Hence Christianity, if it indeed authorizes this unlimited despotism of the strong over the weak — this vast indefinite annihilation of the conjugal and parental relations — this total abrogation of the rights of conscience, of property, of personal happiness, has surely little claim to our reverence, for its tendency to mitigate the sorrows and troubles of the present life. Certainly it is not wonderful that benevolent, well-meaning men should question divine authority of a religion sanctioning such tremendous enormities, and whose professors recommend the catching of slaves, as a service acceptable to the Deity, when required by act of Congress.

Most orthodox, sir, is the faith professed by the Society? I thank my God and Heavenly Father that he has given me grace to embrace with my whole heart and understanding the doctrines you denominate evangelical. But it behoves us all to remember that a workless faith is a worthless faith. Can we refuse obedience to the second of the two great commandments on which hang all the law and the prophets, and yet hope to be saved for our orthodoxy? Very properly your Society has not confined itself to the simple proclamation of Christ and him crucified, but has added practice to faith by assailing sin in its various forms, laboring to convince the sinner of his guilt, and striving to excite him to repentance and reformation. But the sin most rampant in our land — a sin which counts its victims by millions, and its perpetrators, abettors and apologists by millions more — a sin which taints our holy things, enfeebles our churches, corrupts our statesmen, sways our judges, hardens the hearts of our people, blunts their sense of mercy and justice, and which is crowding the ranks of infidelity — this sin may not be mentioned in our fashionable pulpits to "ears polite," nor even alluded to in the multifarious publications of the American Tract Society.

And now, sir, what is to be done? Your response of course is, NOTHING. You will be at no loss for arguments to show that any anti-slavery action on your part will not merely diminish your receipts, and thus lessen your ability to do good, but will also prevent your tracts and volumes from conveying religious truth to the inhabitants of the slave States. The question of *duty* is not to be decided by an estimate of probable receipts. Nor is it by any means certain that your policy is the wisest in a pecuniary sense, or that one or two tracts condemning American slavery as a moral evil would prove injurious to your treasury. The persistence of the American Board in countenancing slavery in its mission churches, in deference to the contributions of its southern patrons, called into existence the present flourishing and efficient "American Missionary Association," daily growing in strength and public favor. This new institution is almost wholly supported by *former* subscribers to the Board. In the last report of the Board, I find the total amount of donations received the preceding year stated at $299,703.90. Of this sum, $10,267.25 came from the slave States and the District of Columbia. Now the *last* report of the Association announces the receipt of $31,134.60 for the past year. Nearly every cent of this sum is virtually *a premium paid by the Board on its southern subscriptions!* The American Tract Society, if I am not much mistaken, is destined to pay a premium of the like kind.

You will perhaps say that it is better our southern brethren should be saved as slave-holders, breeders, and traders, than not at all, and therefore you will not touch the subject of slavery, because if you do, you cannot reach them with your tracts, which under God might lead to their conversion and salvation. If this principle be correct, it is of wide application. The Territory of Utah is acquiring a large population, and will soon claim admission into the Union. The people are polygamists, but it is better they should be saved as such than not at all. Hence it becomes the duty of the Society, for fear of offending them, to avoid all allusion to the Christian doctrine of marriage, and to "move forward on the simple errand that brought the Saviour into the world, proclaiming Christ and him crucified," and thus rendering the tracts acceptable and useful to our Mormon brethren. So, also, as the usefulness of the minister of Christ depends on his message being heard, he ought to preach smooth things, lest by offending his people, by telling them unwelcome truth, he drive them beyond the sound of the gospel.

I believe, sir, not only that this reasoning is unsound, but that the apprehension on which it is founded is groundless. It is not desired by any that your institution should be converted into an anti-slavery, any more than into an anti-gambling tract society. All that is asked is, that this great and influential Christian association should publicly dissent from the impious claim made by the advocates of American slavery, that this vast mass of accumulated sin and misery is sanctioned by the God of mercy and justice, and allowed by the crucified Redeemer — in other words, that American slavery should share in the condemnation you bestow on "the theatre, the circus and the horse-race."

Were you to issue one or two tracts against American slavery as a moral evil, will it be seriously contended that thenceforth none of your thousands of publications on other subjects would be allowed to cross the frontiers of the slave region? Recollect, sir, that when a human chattel of three years will bring $300 at auction, and its two parents from $1,500 to $2,000, slaves are and must be the possession only of the *rich*. By the census of 1840 (I have not the last at hand) there were in the slave States, 1,016,307 white males over twenty years of age, and of these, — various data assure me it is a *very liberal* estimate, — 200,000 were the holders of slaves. And is it possible, sir, that of this prodigious majority of non-slaveholders, none will read any of your biographies and religious treatises, because they may have heard that you have published one or two little tracts against a sin of which they are themselves guiltless? When "Uncle Tom's Cabin" is sold and read at the South, is it credible that a few slave-holders can exclude all your millions of pages from the vast southern region? Can your agents and colporteurs be excluded from fifteen States of this Union, because of the mighty mass of your publications, twenty or thirty pages are directed against the conduct of a few rich men? The apprehension that should the Society be faithful to the calls of duty its efficiency for good would be impaired, is not, in my opinion, consistent with that Chistian faith so forcibly inculcated in many of your tracts. For myself, I firmly believe that before long the Society will find its present policy productive not of strength, but of weakness. That policy has given birth to the "American Reform Tract and Book Society." In a late acknowledgment of receipts by this infant institution I observe contributions from no less than eight States.

To me it seems obvious that Christians entertaining such contradictory views of the divine attributes of the spirit of the gospel and of Christian obligation as are involved in the justification and condemnation of American slavery, cannot much longer act together in sending missionaries to preach, or employing the press to inculcate a religion respecting the fundamental moral principles of which the two parties entertain such antagonistic opinions.

It is one of the incidents of our imperfect state, that sincere Christians often think they are doing God service, while pursuing opposite paths, and when of course one or the other must tend in a wrong direction. May we accord to others the charity we ask for ourselves, and I pray God that those who condemn in others the sin of oppressing their brethren, may feel their own unworthiness, and remember that they themselves, no less than the wretched slave-catcher, need to be washed in that blood which alone cleanseth from all sin.

I am, reverend sir,

Your obedient servant,

WILLIAM JAY.

LETTER

TO LEWIS TAPPAN, ESQ., TREASURER OF THE AMERICAN MISSIONARY ASSOCIATION.

Dear Sir:—I have read with great pain the exposure, in a late number of the *American Missionary,* of the conduct of the American Board in relation to the Choctaw and Cherokee Indians. This powerful Society has established missions in these two tribes of our Aborigines, who have so far advanced in civilization and the adoption of "our institutions" as to hold and use certain of their fellow-men as beasts of burden. The missionaries sent among these people, instead of teaching them the Christian duties of justice and mercy, have virtually instructed them that they might be good Christians without loving their neighbors, or doing to others as they would others should do unto them. Says a Secretary of the Board, who had visited the missions, "It does not seem to have been the aim of the brethren (missionaries) to exert any direct influence, either by their public or private teachings, upon the system of slavery."

In the last Report we find the Board extolling their converts as saints, and eulogizing the governments established by these slave-holding Indians, although tolerating and perpetrating atrocities unknown to the despotisms of Europe.

We are told, p. 29, "The Choctaws have a GOOD GOVERNMENT. They have a written constitution, with a declaration of rights, which embodies the liberty of the press, trial by jury, the rights of conscience, proper safeguards of person and property, the equality of Christian denominations, and almost every great principle of civil and religious freedom."

Certainly the Board are by no means ultra in their ideas of civil and religious freedom, and the rights of conscience. What is the religious freedom of their own missionaries? "If any citizen of the United States," says a law of this good government, "acting as A MISSIONARY OR PREACHER, or whatever his occupation may be, is found to take an active part in favoring the principles and notions of the most fatal and destructive doctrines of the abolitionists, he shall be compelled to leave the nation, and for ever stay out of it." Of course, men of God like Wesley, Hopkins, and Edwards, are disqualified from preaching the gospel among the Choctaws; for such men would not, like the missionaries of the Board, consent to be gagged on the obligation to do justice and love mercy. Not only must these missionaries be dumb on the iniquities of slavery, but they can remain at their posts only on condition of not violating the law of CASTE, since the statute declares that allowing slaves "to sit at table with them shall be ground to *convict* persons of favoring the principles and notions of abolitionism." So, if a missionary presumes to eat with a slave, perhaps his spiritual son in the gospel, he is to be expelled the nation, and ever stay out of it! and so he is, if he dares to teach a slave to read the Bible without the consent of his master! This good government provides "*proper safeguards of persons and property,*" by enacting that a slave shall possess *no property*, and that his *person* shall be a vendible article. "Civil *freedom*" is secured by a law which declares that if any *free* negroes shall return into the nation, "*they shall be seized and sold to the highest bidder for life.*" By another law, any free negro presuming to enter and remain in the nation is to *receive one hundred lashes on his bare back*, and to forfeit all the property he may possess!

We are officially assured, p. 32, that "The Cherokees have

AN EXCELLENT GOVERNMENT: the usual safeguards for person, property, the rights of conscience, &c., are provided." This same excellent government deprives of all the rights of citizenship every child of a *red* man by a black or yellow wife, declares *void* every marriage of the kind, and subjects the parties to *scourging!* Whoever teaches a slave, or any *free negro*, not of Cherokee blood, to read or write, is to be fined from $100 to $500. This exception in favor of negroes of their own blood is a natural prejudice which our more civilized slave-holders have most effectually conquered. In our Christian slave codes we find no favor whatever shown to negroes of Anglo-Saxon blood. Free negroes are to be expelled from the nation.

And now I ask, what is the inference to be drawn from this strange, false, blundering, but official eulogy of these Indian slave-holding governments? Why, that the slave codes of our Southern States, with all their execrable wickedness, crushing in the dust THREE MILLIONS of immortal beings, are perfectly compatible with *good and excellent* government! Even the government of South Carolina, under which *more than one half* of the whole population, men, women, and children, are articles of merchandise, and robbed of every civil and religious right, is a proper subject of Christian eulogy! What amount of tyranny, cruelty, and wickedness constitutes a *bad* government, we are not informed. Certainly the Board has relieved itself from all suspicion of anti-slavery fanaticism, and has proved itself deserving the pecuniary patronage of our "southern brethren." A few years since, in consequence of pressure from without, it announced to the public that "it can sustain no relation to slavery which implies approbation of the system, and as a Board can have no connection or sympathy with it." But, like many others, the Board has since "conquered its prejudices."

It may be asked, Would you abandon these Indians to heathenism because they are slave-holders? I answer, I would not present the gospel to these or any other people in such a form as to lead them to believe that Christianity authorized *them* to abandon to heathenism the poor and oppressed among them, by subjecting them to enforced ignorance and degradation; and this is what the Board is virtually doing. But why prefer preaching the gospel under a gag, to preaching it with perfect freedom to other Indians who hold no slaves? Had the missionaries, with Christian firmness and fidelity, pointed out to these Indians the wickedness of their laws, and the inconsistency of their slave-holding with the precepts of Christianity, they would no doubt have done great good; and had they been expelled for their fidelity, they would have honored Christ by suffering in his cause, instead of bringing a reproach on his religion by their time-serving policy. In such a case, the Board would have lost some, perhaps all, their southern subscribers; but what amount of subscriptions will compensate for the virtual although silent abrogation among these Indian converts of the second of the two great commandments on which hang all the law and the prophets, so far as it affects their obligations to men not colored like themselves?

I cannot persuade myself that we are justified in the sight of God in concealing any divine command or prohibition, for the purpose of rendering the gospel more palatable to those to whom we present it. I have heretofore occasionally contributed to the funds of the American Board, but can do so no more; and I rejoice that in sending you the enclosed check* I have the full assurance that I am in no degree strengthening influences adverse to the rights, happiness, and religious improvement of an afflicted portion of the human family.

Yours faithfully,

WILLIAM JAY.

For one hundred dollars.

INDEX.